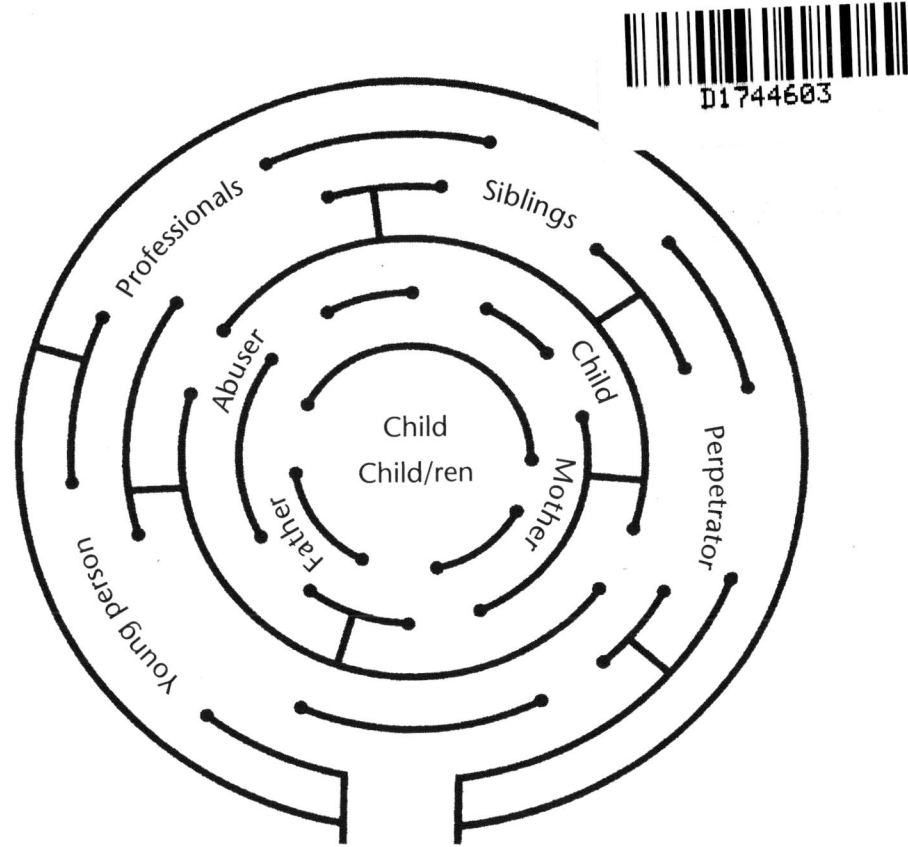

The Complete Guide to Sexual Abuse Assessments

Martin C. Calder

with

Simon Goulding, Helga Hanks, Lynda Regan
Kate Rose, John Skinner and Jane Wynne

Russell House Publishing

First published in 2000 by:
Russell House Publishing Ltd.
4 St. George's House
Uplyme Road
Lyme Regis
Dorset DT7 3LS
England

Tel: 01297-443948
Fax: 01297-442722
e-mail: help@russellhouse.co.uk

British Library Cataloguing-in-publication Data:
A catalogue record for this book is available from the British Library.

ISBN: 1-898924-76-7

Typeset by The Hallamshire Press Limited, Sheffield.
Printed by Redwood Books, Trowbridge

Russell House Publishing

Is a group of social work, probation, education and youth and community work practitioners and academics working in collaboration with a professional publishing team. Our aim is to work closely with the field to produce innovative and valuable materials to help managers, trainers, practitioners and students. We are keen to receive feedback on publications and new ideas for future projects.

*To my wife, Janet, for her continued love, support and encouragement.
She continues to sacrifice many things to facilitate my writing.*

To our daughter, Stacey Laura, who makes life worth living,

and to Charles and May (mum and dad no. 2).

The Complete Guide to Sexual Abuse Assessments

Contents

List of Figures

List of tables

Acknowledgements

To Leigh Library staff for their ability to decipher my handwriting and provide me with the most obscure and seemingly inaccessible materials.

To Russell House Publishing for their continued encouragement and investment in me.

To all the contributors for the quality of their input.

The Contributors

Martin C. Calder MA, CQSW is a child protection co-ordinator with the City of Salford Community and Social Services Directorate. He is currently seconded to implement the new Department of Health assessment framework and parallel documentation. He has interests in making materials accessible to fieldwork staff, and has published widely on a range of child protection matters. His interests include children, juveniles and adults who sexually abuse; mothers in sexually abusing families; all forms of assessment; child protection post-registration practice; and child protection theory. Together with Simon Hackett, he is currently putting together a sister text that will provide workers with guidance on how to apply the assessment framework to a range of presenting child care circumstances other than sexual abuse.

Simon Goulding BA, CQSW is a senior practitioner with Lancashire County Council. He is a founder member of LASOP (Lancashire Adolescent Sex Offender Programme) and he is currently chair of NOTA North-West and co-organiser of Chorley child care training. He undertakes training throughout Lancashire and the North-West on all child protection matters, especially working with adolescent sex offenders. He has authored Lancashire County Council's draft procedures and practice guidance for working with adolescent sex offenders and children. He extends thanks to Bobbie Print for the use of her material.

Helga G.I. Hanks BSc, MSc, DipPsych, AFBPsS Chartered and UKCP registered Consultant Clinical Psychologist, St James's University Hospital, Leeds, Honorary Senior Lecturer, School of Psychology, University of Leeds and Clinical Director of Leeds Family Therapy and Research Centre. Helga has been trained in Psychotherapy and Family Therapy and was a founder member of the Leeds Family Therapy and Research Centre at the University in Leeds.

Her special interests are in child abuse and neglect and in family therapy. She has researched and written extensively both in the UK and abroad.

Lynda Regan is a Project Worker at the Cornerstone Project in Salford. The project is a partnership between Barnardo's and Salford Social Services which delivers a therapeutic service to children and families where there has been an experience of sexual abuse. The views incorporated in this chapter are the author's own and do not necessarily reflect either agency's views. Prior to her current position Lynda worked for ten years as a child care social worker and has experience of working creatively with children on a range of other settings.

Kate Rose is a Child Protection Co-ordinator with the City of Salford Community and Social Services Directorate. She has worked extensively with victims and carers of sexually abused children and has written about issues of living with perpetrator risk and safe care.

John Skinner is a Practice Manager with the North Manchester NSPCC and has worked extensively with adult and adolescent perpetrators of sexual abuse, both in an individual and group work capacity.

Jane M. Wynne MB, ChB, FRCP, FRCPCH, D(Univ.) is a Consultant Community Paediatrician, Leeds General Infirmary and a Senior Lecturer at Leeds University. Jane specialises in developmental paediatrics and is a leading figure both in this country and internationally for her work in child abuse and neglect. She has played a major role in the recognition and treatment of all forms of child maltreatment. Throughout her career she has been highly productive in writing, teaching and conducting research.

Also available from Russell House Publishing by the same author:

Assessing Risk in Adult Males who Sexually Abuse Children:
A Practitioners Guide *(1999)*

Juveniles and Children who Sexually Abuse:
A Guide to Risk Assessment *(1997)*

Working with Young People who Sexually Abuse:
New Pieces of the Jigsaw Puzzle *(1999)*

Mothers of Sexually Abused Children: A Framework for
Understanding, Assessment and Support *(forthcoming 2000)*

Please note

*Martin C. Calder is available for independent training in all areas of sexual abuse assessment. To contact him about rates and availability please e-mail him on **mc@calder31.freeserve.co.uk***

Chapter One

Introduction

Martin C. Calder

There is no accessible, 'one-stop' text to guide practitioners through the unique complexities of conducting assessments in families where sexual abuse of a child has taken place. The time is right to try and remedy this omission, particularly since the effects on victims, mothers and siblings is so varied, yet inevitably profound. Although there will be some adaptations required across cultures and countries if the material is to achieve a broad appeal, there is no doubt that the frameworks on offer have the potential to allow this goal to be achieved.

In the UK, this book is exceptionally timely since the latest central government guidance from London fails to embrace the concept of sexual abuse in any meaningful way. Whilst some attention will be spent on this gap in this chapter, the text itself does not continue with the debate. It allows practitioners to explore issues of relevance and then select the components to use in each particular case they wish to apply it to. The book is thus adaptable to different legislative and procedural contexts and across time.

The Legal and Practice Framework in the UK

The English government is set to introduce a new assessment framework for compulsory adoption by those agencies under the umbrella of the Department of Health, the Department for Education and Employment, and the Home Office. The date for implementation is no later than 31st March 2001. This has been driven by several different forces, and the training pack accompanying the new assessment framework and published in 2000 identifies the following:

- A central policy context that sees the government committed to ending child poverty, tackling social exclusion, and promoting the welfare of all children: so that children can thrive and fulfil their potential as citizens throughout their lives. There is also a drive to improving the quality and management of services responsible for supporting children and families through modernising social services, promoting co-operation between all statutory agencies, and building partnerships with the voluntary and private sector.

- Government objectives for children's social services that include ensuring that children are protected from emotional, physical and sexual abuse and neglect (significant harm); ensuring that children in need gain maximum life chance benefits from educational opportunities, health care and social care; and to ensure that referral and assessment processes discriminate effectively between different types and levels of need and produce a timely response.

- The findings from *Messages from Research* (DoH, 1995) that pointed to a need to refocus as all the energies and time were going into the child protection system at the expense of other children found to be 'in need', but not in need of protection. This had created a system whereby professionals framed cases in such a way as to try and access resources through the child protection system, but these failed when allegations were unsubstantiated and the case was closed without assessing or attending to other needs or problems.

- The current legal framework as set out in the Children Act (1989) which states that every local authority has a general duty to:

  - Safeguard and promote the welfare of children within their area who are in need.

  - So far as is consistent with that duty, to promote the upbringing of such children by their families.

(Section 17(1)).

There is also a clear definition of children in need as follows:

- They are unlikely to achieve or maintain, or to have the opportunity of achieving or maintaining a reasonable standard of health or development without the provision of services by local authority.
- Their health or development is likely to be significantly impaired, or further impaired, without the provision of such services.
- They are disabled.

(Section 17(10))

Under Section 47 of the Children Act the local authority has a statutory duty to investigate wherever it has reasonable cause to suspect that a child who lives, or is found, in their area is suffering, or is likely to suffer, significant harm or where a child is subject of an emergency protection order or is in police protection. The authority is required to make such enquiries as it considers necessary to enable it to decide whether it should take any action to safeguard or promote the child's welfare, either by applying for a court order or by providing services or other help for the child and their family. If access to the child is denied or information withheld the authority must take reasonable steps to obtain access or information unless it is satisfied it already has sufficient information. The investigating authority may call upon other local authorities, health authorities, education authorities and other specified agencies for assistance and these authorities have a duty to assist unless it would be unreasonable in the circumstances.

- The previous central assessment guidance *Protecting Children* (DoH, 1988) predated the Children Act (1989) and the accompanying child protection guidance *Working Together* (DoH, 1991; 1999); was restricted to comprehensive assessments that followed child protection registration; and was structured in such a way that it was used mechanistically by practitioners.
- Inspections of social work practice had identified variable performance in assessments that were often of poor quality; the assessment process was often unclear and unco-ordinated; families were given inadequate early responses when asking for help; there was a lack of systematic approaches to information gathering; a failure to obtain children's views and wishes; a variability of time scales for assessment; and an absence of inter-agency protocols or frameworks for assessing children in need.

About this Book

The new assessment framework (DoH, 2000) is to be seen as a skeleton that needs the flesh adding to it in the many different situations in which practitioners work with children. This should, in my opinion, lead to the emergence of texts that aim to provide up-to-date, evidence-based guidance and materials to frontline practitioners. This book is one such response to help guide staff through a maze of diverse and often conflicting material in the sexual abuse arena. It will be joined by other texts that address non-sexual abuse circumstances (see Calder and Hackett, forthcoming). This book is designed to help workers begin to operationalise the assessment framework, but it is also written to be of much broader appeal and has a broader foundation. It has been written with a number of different audiences in mind, ranging from specialist workers to practitioners, academics and lay people with an interest in the area. Several such people have read sections of the text and have helped me strive to ensure that it can meet their needs.

This book is slightly different than the others I have put together because it looks at the key components that may be involved in a commissioned sexual abuse assessment, and locates them in one place. The advantage of this is that there is now a 'one-stop' text for workers that they can take around and use on a daily basis. Because there are nine chapters on different potential presenting scenarios and a chapter that attempts to provide us with a way forward, there is no space to:

- Provide any context to the problem, such as exploring the size or evolution of the problem.
- Explore theory or definitions in any depth.
- Provide the reader with the battery of appendices that have been reproduced in

the books focusing on one particular component.

In this sense, workers need to use this text as a starting point for their enquiries and cross-reference with my other books as and when they have to undertake a detailed piece of focused work. There is a detailed reference list available for workers to pursue their own enquiries as and when space or interest permits. Given that there is some degree of overlap between the different chapters, rather than repeating the material in several places, the reader is referred to a particular chapter and section for ease of access.

Aims of this chapter

This introductory chapter will attempt to provide:

1. An understanding of the emergence of sexual abuse and the limitations of the central response.

2. The aims of the new Department of Health Assessment Framework (NAF) and its partner document, *Working Together to Safeguard Children*.

3. The advantages and disadvantages of these when managing a sexual abuse case.

4. A summary of the ecological perspective on child maltreatment that is being advocated and a framework for its application in sexual abuse cases.

5. Suggestions on which models of sexual abuse may be superimposed on the new assessment framework to influence thinking and practice.

6. A framework for understanding and managing initial and comprehensive risk assessments.

The Emergence of Sexual Abuse and the Limitations of the Central Response

The English government has failed to embrace the very individual needs of sexual abuse when constructing their latest guidance on assessments (see DoH, 2000). This is not a new omission as their previous guidance (see DoH, 1988) suffered from the same fundamental

limitations. This void has left agencies and individual workers to forge their own individual path, leaving the same wheels to be unnecessarily reinvented (Calder and Horwath, 1999). This is unfortunate when we know that the demands of this work are immense (see Calder, 1999a and Erooga, 1994 for further details). The growth of publications in books and journals around the ever expanding definition of sexual abuse has not assisted many frontline workers as there has been no standardised research, making comparisons very difficult; the books may be expensive and often not easily accessible to staff; and the pace of change in some areas, such as young people who sexually abuse, has made it impossible to apply the latest wisdom at the point, and to the cases, that it is most needed. In many ways, practice is leading research and informing the development of our knowledge base.

Since 1997, I have been involved in trying to synthesise the massive growth of information in this area and make it available to staff in an accessible format with the primary emphasis on operational use. The blend has been on integrating theory, research and practice wisdom across the many disciplines involved and providing adaptable frameworks for use in the field (see Calder, 1997; 1999a, b, and c; forthcoming a and b; Calder and Horwath, 1999; Carich and Calder, forthcoming). They have been well received and have influenced the development of policy and procedures as well as practice.

Child sexual abuse was only formally acknowledged as being criteria for entry into the child protection system in 1980 in the UK. Even when the government accepted sexual abuse as a category needing to be addressed, it failed to provide frontline workers with any materials to guide them in their task. We know that the Department of Health guidance *Protecting Children* (DoH, 1988) neglected the issue of sexual abuse, with the outcome being the emergence of differing approaches to the task. This omission is significant when we know from Faller (1990) that sexual abuse assessments differ from other child protection assessments in a number of critical ways that do not always allow a transfer of skills:

- The likelihood of recidivism is exceptionally high in such cases.
- It is the most likely form of abuse to

prompt workers to remove the abuser from the home rather than the child.

● It is perceived to inflict more harm on its victims.   (pp147–8).

Calder (1999a) has explored theories of evolution in some detail. What is essential for individuals to grasp is the complexity of the problem of child sexual abuse and the lack of detailed central guidance to date. The government has commissioned a large number of research projects to review the child protection system under the initial umbrella of *Messages from Research* (DoH, 1995) and more recently to inform the new assessment framework (DoH, 2000), but sexual abuse has not been singled out for special attention. There has been the research of Farmer and Pollock, 1998; Jones and Ramchandani, 1999;

Monck and New, 1996; Skuse *et al.*, 1998; and there are two chapters of 3000 words each in the training pack reader on sexual abuse from Erooga and Print (2000). These represent advances in our understanding of some aspects of the problem, but they do not collate fragmented and often conflicting information and guide workers through the maze. This is a very sad and worrying omission that needs urgent remedial action, and this book goes some way towards plugging this gap. Calder (1999b) has provided us with a framework that highlights the obstacles to working together: generally, in relation to sexual abuse, and then in relation to young people who sexually abuse. Figure 1 visually portrays the mountains that workers need to climb once they have been provided with a user-friendly and accessible framework.

Figure 1: Obstacles to working together (adapted from Calder, 1999b).

Working together generally	Working together in sexual abuse work	Working together with young people who sexually abuse
● Differences in background and training. ● Varied attitudes to family life. ● Stereotypes and prejudices. ● Role identification and socialisation. ● Differences within and between professionals. ● Status and power. ● Professional and organisational priorities. ● Structure, systems and administration. ● Different roles and responsibilities. ● Lines of authority and decision-making. ● Different perspectives. ● Complexity and co-ordination. ● Communication. ● Underpinning service provision	● Anxiety and child sexual abuse. ● Lack of agency ownership. ● Clashes of philosophy. ● Absence of professional guidance or standards. ● Inadequate supervision. ● Alienation from colleagues. ● Abstraction from other crime. ● Inter-agency factors. ● Socialisation. ● Goal incompatibility. ● Interdependence. ● Performance expectations. ● Resource limitations. ● Punishment versus therapy. ● Interests of child versus offender. ● Role of agencies with statutory responsibilities and those without.	● The battle for lead responsibility (child protection versus criminal justice). ● Diversion or intervention? ● Lack of clarity over legal mandate. ● No uniform response by ACPCs. ● Lack of procedure and practice guidance. ● Poor knowledge base. ● Professional anxieties. ● Lack of societal mandate. ● Lack of clear mandate (particularly the changes in management in *Working Together*). ● Tag onto already stretched child protection system. ● No resources. ● Lack of supervision. ● Professional denial.

Figure 1: cont.

Working together generally	Working together in sexual abuse work	Working together with young people who sexually abuse
• Changes in philosophy. • Organisational restructuring. • Anxiety and child protection.	• Agency as servant and surveyor of the community. • 'Criminality' factor. • Personality factor. • The media contribution. • Complexity. • Societal attitudes. • Legislation. • The role of the courts. • The pace of change. • Resources.	• Territorialism of emerging private sector providers. • Inability to transfer information from similar fields (e.g. adult sex offenders). • Tensions within and between agencies regarding placement of abusers with other children. • Lack of options. • Lack of treatment resources. • Lack of accessible assessment materials. • Lack of a national task force. • Lack of cross-boundary working agreements. • Professional fear of looking foolish. • Difficulties differentiating between 'normal' and 'abusive' sexual behaviour. • Victim-victimiser confusion. • Consequences of intervention and labelling of the young person. • Lack of any agreed definition. • Breadth of the problem: Differences between causal explanations of children and young people who sexually abuse. • Rule of optimism. • Debates over meanings of essential research materials, such as Abel *et al.*

The Aims of the New *Department of Health Assessment Framework* and *Working Together to Safeguard Children*

Both these documents have been heavily influenced by the battery of research studies commissioned by the Department of Health, some of which appeared in their *Messages from Research* (DoH, 1995). Both these documents have been significantly delayed, partly to ensure they are compatible with one another, but probably also to reflect the level of disagreement on content from the consultation process.

The purpose of the new assessment framework is to replace the old 'orange book' (DoH, 1988) at a time when the focus of child protection work is being re-framed to sit more comfortably with a family support approach. The assessment framework indicates clearly that comprehensive ('core') assessments will be undertaken in those cases where a child is deemed to be 'in need' (Section 17) and not simply 'in need of protection' (Section 47). This should, in theory, lessen the potential to squeeze cases through the child protection system to guarantee a service is provided, although it has monumental resource implications for social services who will, as usual, retain lead (and often exclusive) responsibility for the work. As Calder (1999d) has pointed out, in essence, whilst the government are directing social services to assess all children in need under Section 17 to ensure there is a broader identification and delivery of services, this has not been accompanied by resources. The inevitable local response is one of narrowing the threshold for a social work service as Section 47 as this is the one that social services cannot delegate.

We should not 'throw the baby out with the bath water' when responding to the challenge to refocus our services. We need to build and reinforce the best elements of the existing child protection system in order to build on what we know works well. The overarching aim is to ensure a more holistic view is taken of the needs of vulnerable children, to ensure that their health and development are not impaired. What we do not need is a re-framing of 'risk' as 'need' in order to achieve this, although the absence of the concept of risk in the two documents is worrying, short-sighted and potentially dangerous (Calder, in press).

The following section details briefly the main components of the assessment framework:

- Assessment is one of six key areas in the *Quality Protects* programme.
- The new framework will provide a *systematic* way of assessing children and families.
- The assessment will address *three domains*: the child's developmental needs; parental capacity, family and environmental factors.
- The assessment framework has been *integrated* into the revised *Working Together to Safeguard Children*.
- The guidance will be accompanied by *tools* to assist assessment and by *schedules* designed to systematically collect and collate material from individual child and family assessments. The schedules will be the subject of *further development* over a two-year period.

The key principles are that:
- It is *child centred*.
- It is rooted in *child development* (which includes recognition of the significance of timing in a child's life).
- It takes an *ecological approach* of locating the child within the family and the wider community.
- It is based on ensuring *equality of opportunity* for all children and their families.
- It is based on *working in partnership* with families and young people.
- It *builds on the strengths* in each of the three domains.
- It is a *multi-agency approach* model in which it is not just social services departments who are the assessors and providers of service.
- Assessment is seen as a *process* not just a single event.
- *Action and services* should be provided in parallel with assessment, according to the needs of the child and family: not to await 'completion of assessment'.
- It is *grounded in knowledge* derived from theory, research, policy and practice.

The assessment framework is presented visually below (see Figure 2) and is followed by a description of the key components of each strand.

Figure 2: The new assessment framework (DoH, 2000).

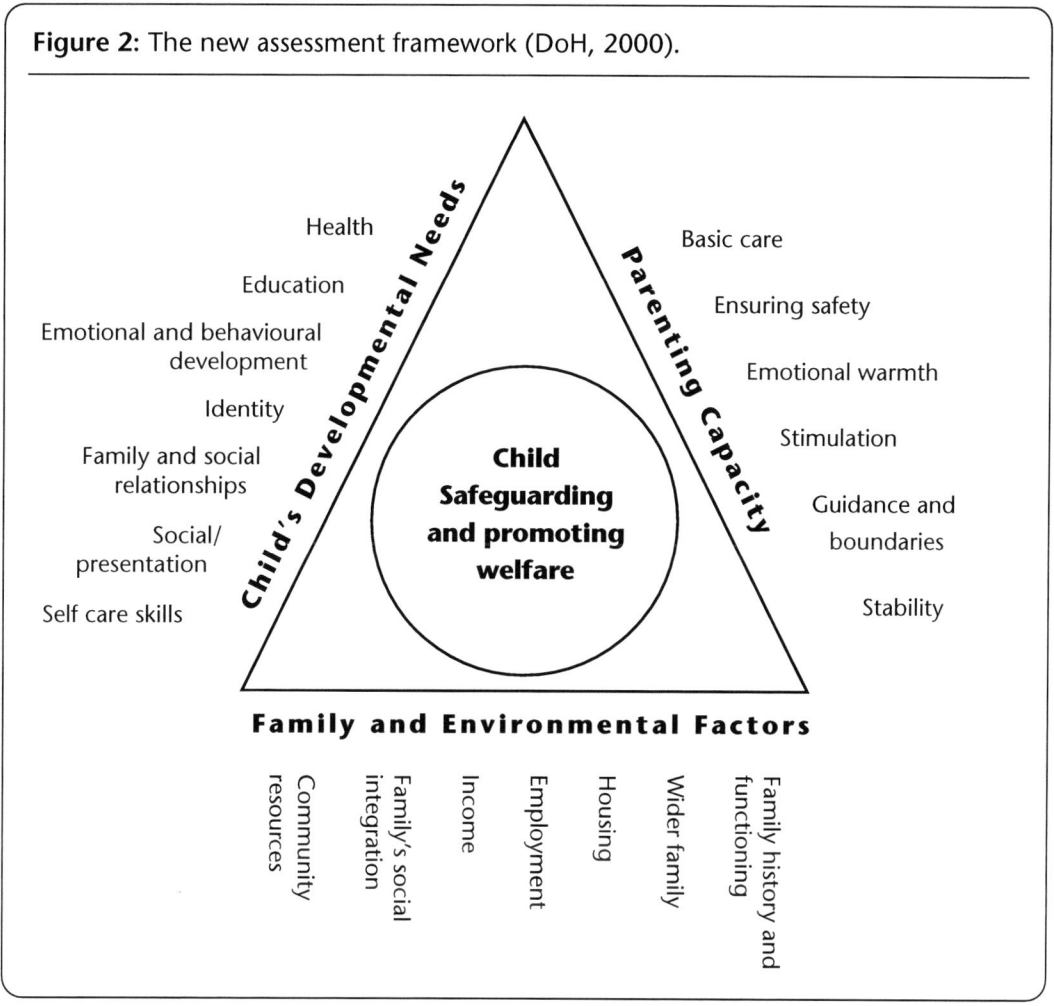

Dimensions of child's developmental needs

1. Health

Includes growth and development as well as physical and mental well being. Involves receiving appropriate health care when ill, an adequate and nutritious diet, exercise, immunisations and developmental checks, dental and optical care and for older children appropriate advice and information on issues that have an impact on health.

2. Education

Covers all areas of a child's cognitive development which begins from birth. Includes opportunities for play and interaction with other children and adults, access to books, an adult interest in school work, progress and achievements and acquiring a range of skills and interests. Appropriate developmental progress involves taking account of a child's starting point and any special educational needs.

3. Emotional and behavioural development

Concerns the appropriateness of response in feelings and actions by a child, initially to parents and caregivers and increasingly to others beyond the family. Includes nature and quality of early attachments, characteristics of temperament, adaptation to change, response to stress and degree of appropriate self-control.

4. Identity

Concerns the child's growing sense of self as a separate and valued being. Includes how a child views themselves and his abilities, feelings of belonging and acceptance by the family and wider society and strength of a positive sense of individuality.

5. Family and social relationships

Development of empathy and the capacity to place self in someone else's shoes. Includes quality of relationships with parents or caregivers, increasing importance of age appropriate friendships within peers and other significant persons in the child's life and response of family to these relationships.

6. Social presentation

Concerns child's growing understanding of the way in which appearance and behaviour are perceived by the outside world and the impression of being created. Includes appropriateness of dress for age, gender, culture and religion, cleanliness and personal hygiene and availability of advice from parents or caregivers about presentation in different settings.

7. Self care skills

Concerns the acquisition by a child of competencies required for increasing independence, from early skills of dressing and feeding, to opportunities to learn safe care beyond the family and independent living skills as older children. Includes encouragement to acquire skills and impact of disability and other special needs on how skills are gained.

Dimensions of parenting capacity

1. Basic care

This dimension involves providing for the child's physical needs, and appropriate medical and dental care.
    Includes provision of food, water, shelter, clean clothing and adequate personal hygiene.

2. Ensuring safety

Ensuring the child is adequately protected from harm or danger.
    Includes protection from harm or danger, and from contact with unsafe adults or other children and from self-harm.

3. Emotional warmth

Ensuring the child's emotional needs are met.
    Includes ensuring the child's requirements for secure attachment with significant adults and appropriate sensitivity; and responsiveness to the child's needs. Demonstration of affection and positive regard for the child and appropriate physical contact, comfort and cuddling sufficient to demonstrate warm regard.

4. Stimulation

Promotion of child's learning and intellectual development through encouragement and cognitive stimulation.
    Includes facilitating the child's cognitive development and potential through interaction, communication, talking and responding to the child's language and questions, encourage and joining the child's play, and promotion of educational opportunities. Ensuring school attendance or equivalent opportunity.

5. Guidance and boundaries

This comprises enabling the child to regulate their own emotional state, and develop an internal model of conscience and appropriate behaviour, while also promoting pro-social interpersonal behaviour and social relationships.
    The key parental tasks are *demonstrating* and *modelling* of appropriate behaviour, emotional regulation and interactions with others, and guidance with limit setting boundaries, so that the child is able to develop an internal model of moral values and conscience, and social behaviour appropriate for the society within which they will grow up. The aim is to enable the child to grow into an autonomous adult, holding their own values, and able to demonstrate pro-social behaviours with others, rather than having to be dependent on rules outside themselves.

Includes social problem-solving, anger management, consideration for others, and effective discipline and shaping behaviour.

6. Stability

Providing a *sufficiently* stable family environment to enable the above dimensions of parenting to operate reasonably consistently.

Includes responding in a similar manner to the same behaviours, providing consistency of emotional warmth over time.

Family and environmental factors

1. Family history and functioning

Who is living in the household and how are they related to the child?

Chronology of significant life events and their meaning to family members. Nature of family functioning and its impact on the child. Parental strengths and difficulties, including those of an absent parent.

2. Wider family

Who are considered to be members of the wider family by the child and the parents? This includes related and non-related persons and absent wider family. What is their role and importance to the child and parents and in precisely what way?

3. Housing

Does the accommodation have basic amenities and facilities appropriate to the age and development of the child and other resident members? Includes the interior and exterior of the accommodation and immediate surroundings. Basic amenities include water, heating, sanitation, cooking facilities, sleeping arrangements and cleanliness, hygiene and safety and their impact on the child's upbringing.

4. Employment

Who is working in the household and their pattern of work? How does this impact on the child? How is work or absence of work viewed by family members? How does it affect their relationship with the child?

5. Income

Sufficiency of income to meet the family's needs. Are there extreme financial difficulties which affect the child?

6. Family's social integration

Exploration of the wider context of the local neighbourhood and community and its impact on the child and parents. Includes the degree of the family's integration or isolation, their peer groups, friendship and social networks and the importance attached to them.

7. Community resources

Describes all facilities and services in a neighbourhood, including universal services of primary health care, day care and schools. Includes availability, accessibility and standard of resources and impact on the family.

There is little mention of sexual abuse within the *Safeguarding Children* document. There are two paragraphs on impact; four paragraphs on the need to restrict employment to those who do not pose a risk to children; three paragraphs on organised abuse; seven paragraphs on young sexual abusers (that exits them from the child protection system); four paragraphs on children involved in prostitution; three paragraphs on child pornography and the internet; two paragraphs on female genital mutilation; two paragraphs on the disclosure of information about sex offenders.

The Advantages and Disadvantages of this when Managing a Sexual Abuse Case

There are some positive elements of NAF: it adopts an ecological approach, expects us to build on strengths as well as identifying weaknesses, and moves us towards evidence-based interventions. Unfortunately these are insufficient to compensate for its application to circumstances of sexual abuse. The principal limitations of the framework in this area include:

- There is little commissioned research from the Department of Health to inform the required evidence base, other than a book on outcomes of treatment (Jones and Ramchandani, 1999).

- The reader (Horwath, 2000) that is designed to equip practitioners when applying the generic framework to sexual abuse cases contains only two chapters of 3,000 words each (Erooga and Print, 2000).

- There is no acknowledgement that sexual abuse cases present us with unique issues and dynamics that need to be addressed in a particular way. It is not viable or desirable to try and use the general approach when a specific one is indicated.

- It is a myth that there is an evidence-base in *all* the various sub-arenas of sexual abuse that could inform our intervention, even assuming the overarching framework was sound.

- The framework is premised on the need to shift cases from the child protection arena to the lower end of the children in need continuum. In doing so, it has jettisoned the concept of 'risk' as this was equated with Section 47 investigations. This is a misguided notion based on a misunderstanding of the term, and it has ostensibly re-framed 'risk' as 'need'. This is a dangerous development in the sexual abuse arena, and arguably provides a dilution to the notion of responsibility for the perpetrator. It is also at a time when the field of sexual abuse research is refining and extending the concept of risk assessment to provide us with a better structure through which we can effectively intervene. For adult male sex offenders, please refer to Grubin, 1998; Hanson, 1997; Hanson and Harris, 2000; Hanson and Thornton, 1999; and for young people who sexually abuse, please refer to O'Callaghan and Hackett, 1999a and b.

- The proforma assessment documentation does not fit with the core assessment tool developed for Youth Offending Teams (YOTs) (ASSET), thus leaving confusion. This is consistent with the lack of clarity over the future management of young people who sexually abuse (see Calder, 2000).

It is clear that the NAF does not immediately lend itself to sexual abuse work, given that a child may have many of their needs met other than that for protection in cases of sexual abuse, and that the parents may well be providing good parenting other than the sexual abuse. It is known that a child may well be sexually abused in an otherwise well-functioning family unit. Indeed, we know that it is nigh on impossible to prospectively predict sexually abusing families as they blend with the community in which they live without any problem. As Calder (1999a) has pointed out, what is consistently clear is that sex offenders do not present as remarkably different from others with social, personal or behavioural difficulties, except in the nature of their offending, rendering detection remarkably difficult.

It is essential that workers get the assessment stage right as the findings will inform any plan for future involvement and how best to undertake this work. The NAF should be viewed as a skeleton upon which we can add the flesh. The framework is sound in the sense it has been informed by evidence-based materials, but the parameters of sexual abuse and emotional abuse are such that further tailored materials will be needed to adapt the framework to the presenting family situation.

Evidence-based practice is where workers use knowledge critically from practice and research about the needs of children and families and the outcomes of services and interventions to inform their assessment and planning; gather, record and update information systematically, distinguishing sources of information e.g. direct observation, other agency records or interviews with family members; learn from the experiences of users of services; and evaluate rigorously the information, processes and outcomes from the worker's own interventions to develop practice wisdom. This book is an attempt to inform the worker on the issues that need to be addressed in the case of sexual abuse, although it does acknowledge that we are a long way from having detailed and reliable evidence upon which to practice. This clearly sets us up to fail when thinking about applying NAF in situations of child sexual abuse. There are also similar concerns in relation to other types of abuse, for which the author is also involved in producing a child care assessment manual (see Calder and Hackett, forthcoming).

One of the additional problems that we have is the lack of any real definition of sexual abuse. The current definition that appears in the latest guidance is:

> *sexual abuse involves forcing or enticing a child or young person to take part in sexual activities, whether or not the child is aware of what is happening. The*

activities may involve physical contact, including penetrative (e.g. rape or buggery) or non-penetrative acts. They may include non-contact activities, such as involving children looking at, or in the production of, pornographic material or watching sexual activities, or encouraging children to behave in sexually inappropriate ways.

(DoH, 1999: p6)

This differs from the criteria used to add a child's name to the child protection register under the category of sexual abuse, set down in DoH (1991). Here we refer to 'actual or likely sexual exploitation of a child or adolescent. The child may be dependent and/or developmentally immature'. This is concerning when the procedures have recently been extended to include children involved in prostitution (Calder, 1999c), child pornography and the internet (Calder, submitted) and female genital mutilation. Calder (1999a) has explored the importance as well as the difficulties of definitions in relation to sexual abuse. In this book various terms such as 'abuser', 'offender' and 'perpetrator' are used interchangeably. The difference between them is generally: an 'abuser' is someone not convicted; an 'offender' has been convicted; and a 'perpetrator' encompasses both other terms.

The NAF focuses on the needs of children and the capacity of their parents and families to respond to these needs in the short and longer term. A key principle of both the assessment framework and *Safeguarding Children* is that work with children and families will be informed by evidence about children's developmental progress and their parents capacity to respond appropriately to the needs of children within the family and environmental context. This means that those working with children will need to have a sound knowledge of the key developmental tasks at different stages in a child's life and to be able to use the information in relation to the particular circumstances of an individual child. Workers will be reassured to learn that this is an extension of the 'looked after' materials (see Parker *et al.*, 1991), which will now become a continuum.

The work of Jones and Ramchandani (1999) attempts to inform practice from research in relation to child sexual abuse. It presents findings on how best to help children who have been sexually abused and their families. The authors utilised an evidence-based approach coupled with the practice experience

of their advisory group. They set out to draw out implications for practice, based on various studies on *outcomes* for children, and they made recommendations on the most effective treatments available. This is to be expected given their practice background, remit and experience. What appears to be missing in this is a framework for assessing sexually abusing families in order to move cases on to where these authors start. This is a major omission when you consider one of the common pitfalls in assessments is to 'slide into therapy'.

Training materials have been developed which are intended to assist managers and trainers to develop a training strategy to promote effective use of the assessment framework. The training pack will consist of a reader, video and guide and training exercises. The reader will be sold separately (and thus should be able to 'stand alone') as it attempts to guide workers into how the framework can be adapted to certain areas. The reader is intended to 'assist practitioners, managers and trainers gain an overview of current knowledge, research and best practice in terms of child needs-led assessments' (Horwath, 1999).

Out of over 20 chapters only two (started as one) focus on sexual abuse. In 3,000 words each, Erooga and Print attempt to guide the worker through the complex web of sexual abuse assessments: embracing adult male and female sex offenders, adolescent sexual abusers and mothers in sexually abusing families. They were also asked to address issues of safe care, incidence, the current statutory framework, the effects of sexual abuse on children, theory, and reconstituting families. One could argue they were set up to fail, and it would appear that no guidance may have been better than diluted information that lacks detail and context. This is particularly true when they were directed not to use the term 'risk' in their contributions. In my books on adult male sex offenders, children and young people who sexually abuse, and mothers (Calder, 1997, 1999, forthcoming a) the materials covering the assessment framework cover approximately 150,000 words, and even these are summaries! It would appear that workers need materials to help them in the assessment of sexual abuse cases, if they are to have their 'hearts and minds' changed to embrace the framework.

The assessment framework makes recommendations on resources to assist effective assessment. In this section (pp66–81), only the work of Jones and Ramchandani (1999) is referred to in relation to sexual abuse.

In Figure 3, I set out a framework which workers rely on to get the job done. This shows that the assessment framework is just one, but very critical, part. In Figure 4, I provide a framework which highlights what workers might get from the assessment framework in child care, and this is contrasted to Figure 5 which they could use for sexual abuse assessments.

Figure 3: Tools for the frontline worker framework.

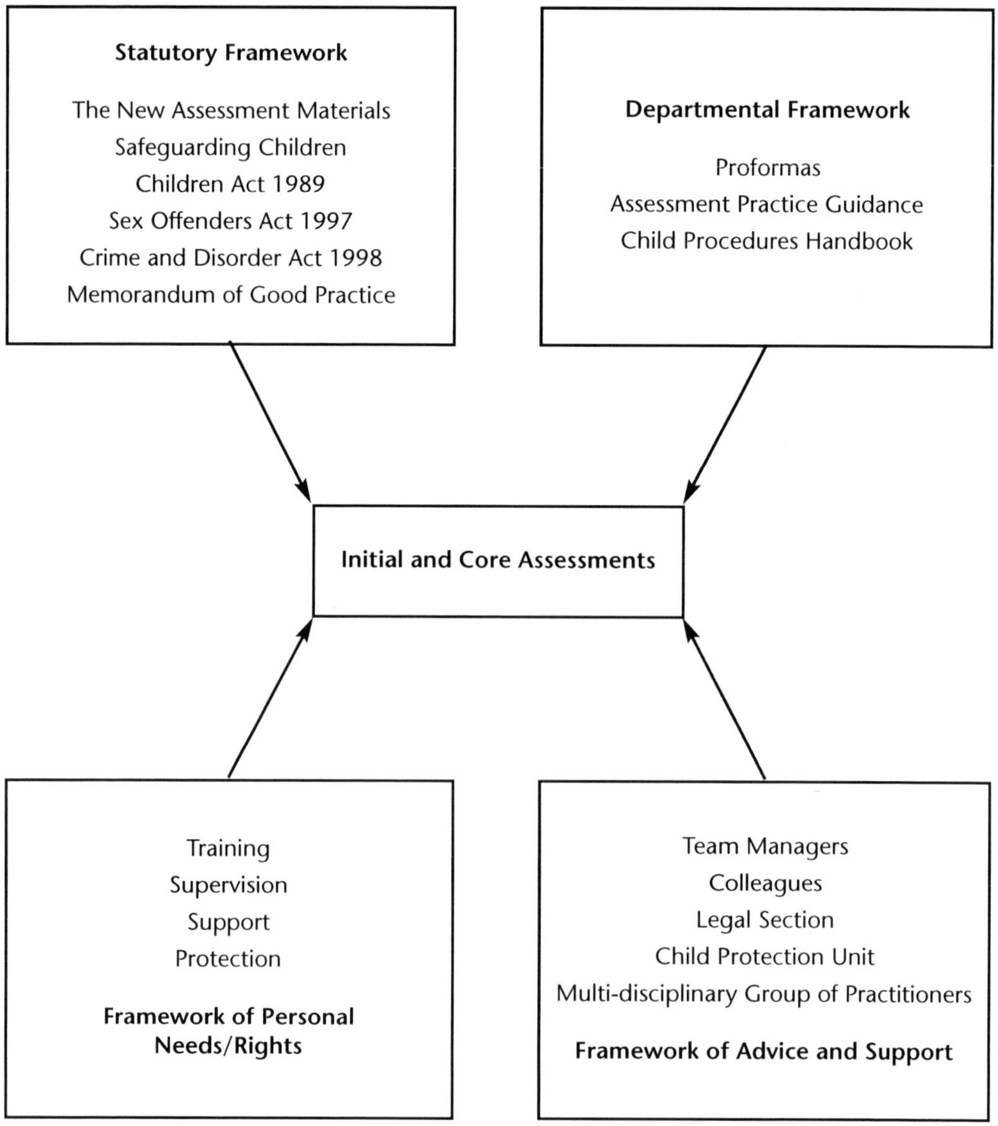

Statutory Framework

The New Assessment Materials
Safeguarding Children
Children Act 1989
Sex Offenders Act 1997
Crime and Disorder Act 1998
Memorandum of Good Practice

Departmental Framework

Proformas
Assessment Practice Guidance
Child Procedures Handbook

Initial and Core Assessments

Training
Supervision
Support
Protection

**Framework of Personal
Needs/Rights**

Team Managers
Colleagues
Legal Section
Child Protection Unit
Multi-disciplinary Group of Practitioners

Framework of Advice and Support

Figure 4: The new assessment framework: a vsual guide.

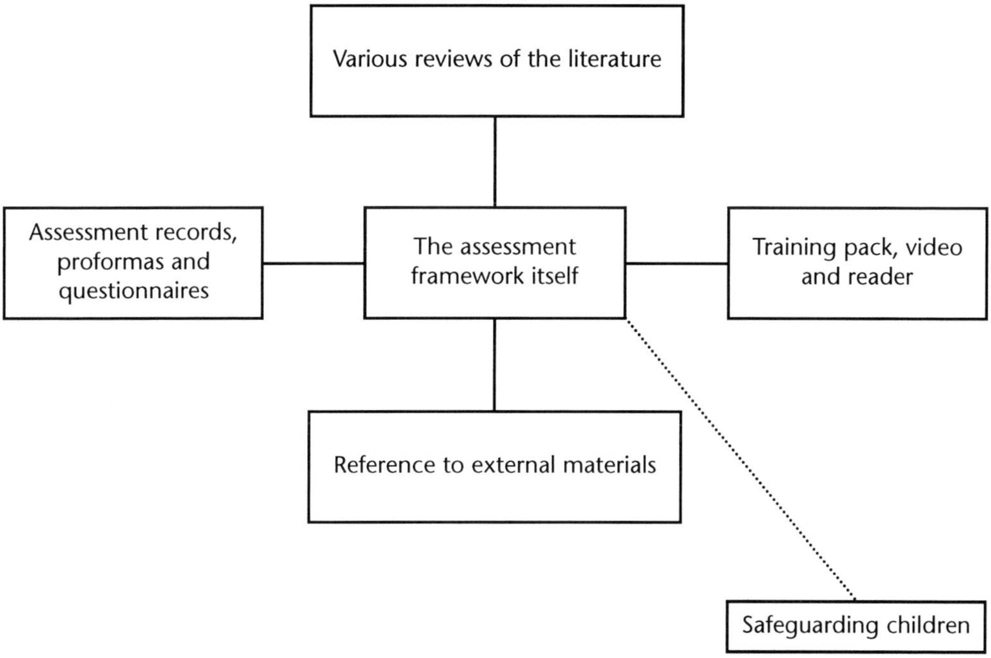

```
                    ┌──────────────────────────────┐
                    │ Various reviews of the literature │
                    └──────────────────────────────┘
                                  │
┌─────────────────┐    ┌──────────────────┐    ┌──────────────────┐
│ Assessment records, │──│  The assessment   │──│ Training pack, video │
│ proformas and      │    │ framework itself   │    │    and reader     │
│ questionnaires    │    └──────────────────┘    └──────────────────┘
└─────────────────┘         │        ·
                    ┌──────────────────┐  ·
                    │ Reference to external materials │
                    └──────────────────┘     ·
                                          ┌──────────────────┐
                                          │ Safeguarding children │
                                          └──────────────────┘
```

Figure 5: The assessment framework and its application to child sexual abuse.

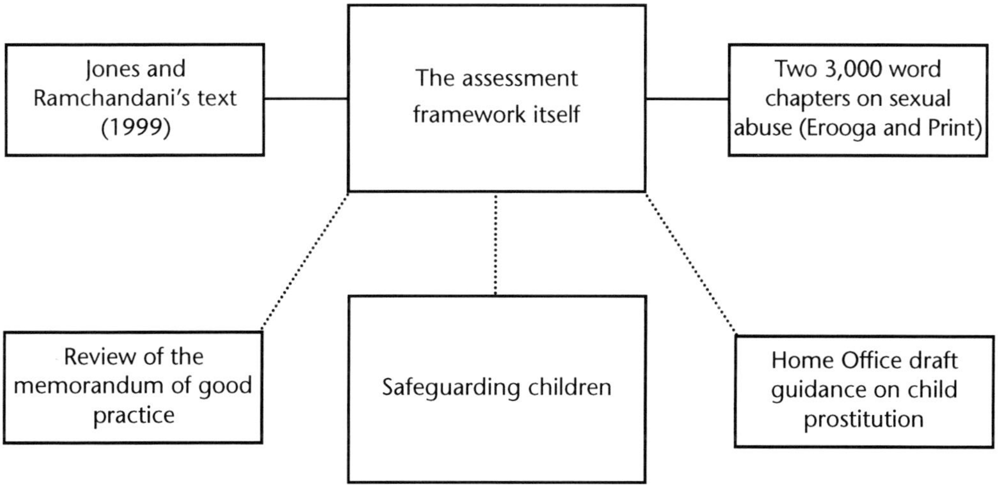

```
┌─────────────────┐    ┌──────────────────┐    ┌──────────────────┐
│    Jones and     │──│  The assessment   │──│  Two 3,000 word    │
│ Ramchandani's text │    │ framework itself   │    │ chapters on sexual │
│     (1999)       │    └──────────────────┘    │ abuse (Erooga and Print) │
└─────────────────┘                             └──────────────────┘

┌─────────────────┐    ┌──────────────────┐    ┌──────────────────┐
│  Review of the   │    │ Safeguarding children │    │ Home Office draft  │
│ memorandum of good │    │                  │    │ guidance on child  │
│    practice      │    │                  │    │    prostitution    │
└─────────────────┘    └──────────────────┘    └──────────────────┘
```

A further concern and potential constraint on workers are the strict time-scales set down for completing the initial assessment (seven working days) and the 'core' assessment (35 days maximum); particularly when there is a void of assessment materials, the thrust of inter-agency work appears to being lost; the workloads of social services personnel is rising, and may well be extended further given the move to 'need' from 'risk'; and the severe resource constraints on local authorities, restricting the commissioning of independent service providers to help them out. In this context, the goal has to be to equip workers to do the job properly and efficiently.

In child protection, there is reliance on close, inter-agency working in the child protection system. A major concern for some time was that the framework was going to be issued only to social services although it is relevant to all agencies: hardly a recipe for close inter-agency working (see Calder and Horwath, 1999). At the time of sending this book to press, the Department of Health had added other departmental logos to the front cover (DFEE and Home Office), but was unclear about what this means in terms of agency dissemination, training and responsibility. It appears to be a last minute attempt to promote corporate responsibility. We know that in the field of sexual abuse, the emergence of competing definitions and theories has largely reflected the fact that they have been developed by particular disciplines who tend to favour theirs over others. This has led to a great many single-factor theories being put forward to explain sexual abuse. Individual theories tend to restrict our vision, however, as we see things through a microscope rather than through a set of binoculars. Fortunately, there has been a move towards integrated models to explain sexual abuse (such as Finkelhor, 1984) and these have been very influential in practice. One of the best and most underused holistic frameworks is the ecological approach which offers us a very practical guide to understanding child abuse generally, and which can be superimposed upon the new assessment framework for sexual abuse with some guidance.

The Ecological Perspective and its Application in Cases of Child Sexual Abuse

Historically, each profession has developed their own theory of child abuse and neglect and adhered rigidly to it regardless of the presenting circumstances of a case. This is blinkered thinking and has led to a failure to offer a holistic framework within which respective theories could be located. The emergence of an ecological framework has offered the potential for conceptual unity across professions and professionals, although it has not explicitly been adopted or recommended to date. A shared knowledge base, originating from research is essential (Calder, 1992).

Ecology is a science, in which it explores how organisms interact and survive the environment in which they find themselves. It accepts that there are different levels in society where child maltreatment can occur—at an individual, family, community and society level. This approach is characterised by its prominent emphasis on the interaction between systems rather than on the properties and processes of any one system.

It allows for the dynamics of child abuse and neglect to be located in a framework which acknowledges that abuse frequently occurs in a socially unhealthy context, with factors such as isolation, poverty, and socially polluted environments acting as crucibles in which latent causal factors are identified (Calder, 1991). In my view, this has the potential as a comprehensive framework for organising knowledge of human behaviour as well as highlighting convergence among disciplines and integrating the diversity of theory, as seen in Figure 6 below.

Figure 6: An ecological framework (Calder and Waters, 1991).

Ecological levels	Levels of analysis/models
ontogenesis/individual	psychopathology
family micro-system	social-interactional
community exo-system	socio-situational
cultural macro-system	socio-cultural

There are some guiding principles within the ecological framework:

- The worker is holistic in their orientation, recognising that the ecosystem context is the foundation for every meaningful intervention into a troubled client system.

- The worker must place primary emphasis on relationships, recognising that every client is both part of a social environment for other individuals and a participant with others in a variety of social contexts.

- The client unit is also a system-in-transformation through an evolutionary process of intervention.

- The worker must pay attention to their own place in the total ecology of the client's presenting situation, choosing an appropriate ecological niche from which to make some useful contribution (Maddock and Larson, 1995). For further discussions on the ecological approach, the reader is referred to Belsky (1980), Bronfenbrenner (1977) and Garbarino (1977).

The current challenge is to see how well the ecological framework fits with sexual abuse and to see how useful it will be in structuring a core assessment. The following material attempts to guide the reader through this process. The framework that I will advocate views sexual abuse within a system of risk and protective factors interacting across four levels:

1. the individual or ontogenic level

2. the family micro-system

3. the community exo-system

4. the cultural social macro-system

We need to acknowledge that it is impossible to delineate precisely the boundaries between these levels.

Individual ontogenic factors

The literature on sexual abuse has traditionally focused on individual or familial aspects of abuse, hardly surprising given the strong sense of individualism in Western culture. The individual level consists of the experiences and characteristics of the individual, which may include interpersonal experiences such as a history of abuse, as well as personal conditions such as developmental level or health. The individuals include victims, abusers and non-abusing parents.

The literature on adult personality characteristics associated with sexual abuse is more extensive than that of other forms of abuse since the primary aetiology has been sought in the profile of the adult offender in contrast to other forms of abuse, which often focuses on parent-child interactions. Finkelhor (1987) has proposed four major theories to explain child sexual abuse: abusers obtain powerful, developmentally induced emotional gratification from the acts; abusers have deviant physiological sexual arousal patterns; abusers are blocked by arrested psychosexual development and emotional immaturity in their capacity to meet their sexual needs in more conventional ways; and abusers have problems in their capacity for behavioural inhibition.

The search for a biological basis for child sexual abuse has not been successful. It is clear that certain substances, such as alcohol and drugs, may have a dis-inhibiting contribution to sexual abuse, but they are not the cause of it.

Children are never responsible for inviting the sexual abuse: that is most certainly the sole responsibility of the adult abuser. There is some evidence that the impact of sexual abuse induces behaviours in some children which makes them more prone to re-victimisation (Friedrich, 1988).

For an excellent review of theory with young people who sexually abuse, the reader is referred to Epps (1999), and for adult male sex offenders see Calder (1999a).

As Fontes (1993) has pointed out, recent individualistic materials have focused on prevalence research, profiles of the effects of the abuse on victims or their characteristics after disclosure, case reports of treatment; accounts by victims or survivors themselves; reports on treatment outcome; abusers sexual and personal history, their arousal patterns, and their thinking patterns.

The family micro-system

The family level includes the victim or offender's family history, the interactions of family members, as well as family beliefs, norms, and practices.

The family is viewed as a crucial factor in the initiation and maintenance of sexual offences and is the primary context in which sexual victimising behaviour is learned and expressed. Research has focused on victims' accounts of their families; the views from treatment providers or members of the family other than the victim; the possible contributions of different family members to the occurrence of incest; and characteristics which may influence a family's denial of the abuse.

Family structure, functioning and relationships are all significant in sexual abuse cases. The way in which men and women are socialised maps the ways in which many families operate, with the female assuming a sole parenting role. They often become the target for intervention when sexual abuse occurs, as professionals tend to operate on the societal view that they must have known and thus failed to protect. This is an approach not grounded in current research, but the shift to empower women in such situations is slow in coming (see Calder, forthcoming a, for further discussion around these points). There is some evidence that stepfathers may be more likely abusers than biological fathers, and this may be related to the greater chance of role confusion in reconstituted families (Faller, 1990).

Family relationships that affect the quality of parent-child relationships have also been considered in developing the context for understanding child sexual abuse. Such factors include an estranged family; one in which the victim is closest to no one individual; a mother who is absent, ill, or otherwise not protective of the child; social isolation of the family; lack of supervision of the child; unusual sleeping or rooming conditions; the erosion of social networks; and the lack of social supports for the mother (Finkelhor, 1984). Factors in the child's behaviour, education, and relationships have also been considered, including the emotional security or social isolation of the child; knowledge about sexual abuse; the relationship of trust between the offender and the child; and coercion.

For further discussions around family issues relating to adolescent sex offenders, see Calder (1997, 1999b, forthcoming a) and for adult sex offenders see Calder (1999, forthcoming b).

The community exo-system

Individual and family characteristics do not function in isolation from the larger community that surrounds both abusing and non-abusing families. Although research on exo-system factors has concentrated on neighbourhood and community environments, other factors may affect individual or family functioning as well, including the criminal justice and child protection systems, the workplace, the media, the school, the church, ethnic culture, and peer groups. These are potentially powerful forces in shaping parenting styles and family functioning. Families reported for abuse often have multiple problems.

Factors such as poverty, unemployment, social isolation or the presence of social networks are central to sexual abuse considerations (see Calder 1999, forthcoming b for reviews)

The cultural social macro-system

This comprises the set of cultural and social values that pervade and support individual and family life styles and community services in today's society. A small number of studies and theoretical works have linked the occurrence, disclosure or treatment of child sexual abuse with factors in society at large. For example, Finkelhor (1982) discussed the possible influences of wider social trends including social isolation, patriarchal authority, divorce, the sexual revolution and male sexual socialisation.

This level is often the invisible layer in theoretical models of child abuse, yet its influence is increasingly recognised as important in understanding the hidden forces that govern personal and institutional behaviours. Social and cultural factors can foster or mitigate stress in family life and such factors have achieved new importance in emerging models of child abuse. It is important to note that the wider society does not impact uniformly on individuals, families, and members of ethnic cultural groups.

Historically, society has tended to deny and minimise the incidence, prevalence, and the impact of sexual victimisation (see Calder, 1999a for a discussion on the evolution of sexual abuse and the management response systems).

The way in which we view sexual abuse is changing and the recent raft of governmental activity (The Sex Offenders Act, 1977; the review of the criminal law concerning sexual crimes currently in progress; the guidance on children and young people involved in prostitution; the Waterhouse inquiry into sexual abuse in North Wales children's homes) has been a response to growing public disquiet about sex offenders remaining in the community. These measures offer us the illusion that sexual abuse will be controlled, when it is more likely to be maintained, and forced underground further. We provide the public with misleading information, such as focusing on stranger danger, when the principal risk lies much closer to home. We have allowed a sexually saturated culture to emerge and this is making the boundary between acceptable and unacceptable more difficult to define.

There is little attention paid to the impact of racism and oppression on many communities and in sexual abuse this has acted as a barrier to disclosure and treatment (Calder, 1999e). Fontes (1993) has provided us with an excellent review of ecology, sexual abuse and culture/ oppression.

Overall, I believe that the ecological framework can assist in our understanding of seemingly contradictory findings about characteristics of offenders, kinds of offences, and types of victims. It can provide the structure for the development of comprehensive causal model studies that include variables from several domains (e.g. individual, family, school, peer). It facilitates both/and, rather than either/or discussions which reduce complex social phenomenon to simplistic explanations. The reader will benefit from reading more detailed texts exploring the ecological framework and child sexual abuse. For example Bischof and Rosen, 1997; Fontes, 1993; and Maddock and Larson, 1995.

Superimposing existing models on the assessment framework

In order that practitioners begin to change the way they think about and conduct assessments they need to think about how to use existing models of sexual abuse and superimpose them onto NAF (see Figure 7). Given that the

ecological model has four components, I prefer to represent the NAF as a square rather than as a triangle. It is portrayed in such a way that there is interaction between the different components and the worker and their agency. This is important since the notions of motivation, resistance and co-operation are all interactive ones between worker and client, and this is essential when they have to comply with rigid time-scales to complete their assessments (see Calder, forthcoming). The models referred to are outlined in Chapter Seven.

A Framework for Understanding and Managing Initial and Comprehensive Risk Assessments

Risk assessment is not an exact science; prediction involves probabilities and that errors can be expected. Any model must have built into it a system for anticipating and dealing with false positives as well as accepting the inevitability of false negatives (Cleaver *et al.*, 1998).

The term risk assessment is used to define a number of different assessment and decision-making processes in various agencies. I believe that it is the systematic collection of information to identify if risks are involved, and if so, what these are; identifying the likelihood of their future occurrence (prediction); whether there is a need for further work; and what form this should take. It can also be used to predict the escalation of the presenting behaviour as well as the clients motivation for change.

The government appears to be jettisoning the concept of risk and risk assessment in their latest guidance in favour of a need-led assessment. The DoH assessment guidance of 1988 was built almost entirely on the notions of risk and dangerousness yet these do not appear to have been satisfactorily defined or applied in practice. This may be because it is a term which is often misused in social work because it focuses exclusively on the risk of harm, whereas in any other enterprise a risk equation also includes a chance of benefit resulting (Carson, 1994). Any risk assessment, should, therefore, be concerned with weighing up the pros and cons of a child's circumstances in order to inform decision-making as to what should happen with regard to intervention and protection. It involves examining the child and family situation to

Figure 7: Squaring existing models of child sexual abuse.

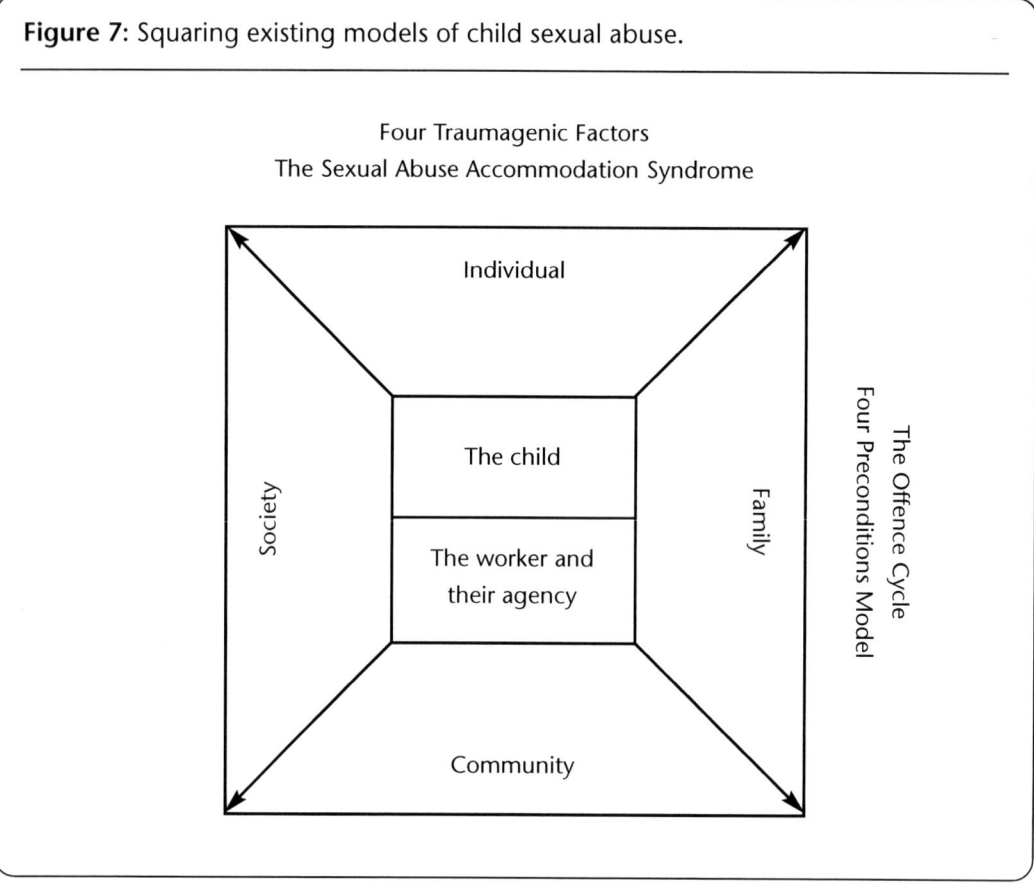

Four Traumagenic Factors
The Sexual Abuse Accommodation Syndrome

Individual

Society

The child

The worker and
their agency

Family

Community

The Offence Cycle
Four Preconditions Model

identify and weigh various *risk factors* (such as parents, family or other influences that increase the likelihood that a child will be harmed in a certain way), family strengths, family resources, and available agency services. This assessment information can then be used to determine if a child is safe, what agency resources are needed to keep the child safe, and under what circumstances a child should be removed from the family. The government thus appears to be redefining risk by utilising the component parts and framing them in the context of need. This is not convincing when there is repeated backtracking from needs-led assessments to a reminder that the child's safety is the primary objective of professional intervention.

One of the most confusing issues is that at a time in which the government is moving away from notions of risk, there are huge developments in risk assessments emerging in the field of sexual abuse. This is unfortunate for several reasons:

- Identifying risk is a central part of our work in sexually abusing families.

- It is an extremely difficult task for any professional, particularly given the lack of scientific evidence regarding predictions of human behaviour.

- There is a need to ensure that we construct our risk estimations based on theory and research in each sub category of sexual abuse and not rely on a transfer of knowledge from adult male sex offenders.

- There is a need to move from general risk estimations (high, medium or low risk) to the nature of the risk and the particular situations/contexts in which they apply.

- In the absence of a quantification of risk, then it is difficult to construct a plan to manage it. For a detailed resumé of risk assessments, see Calder (in press).

Developments in the Adult Field

Given the serious consequences of sexual abuse, special care is justified in the evaluation of sexual offenders. Future behaviour can never be predicted with certainty. Nevertheless, a growing body of research indicates that well-informed practitioners can predict sexual recidivism with at least moderate accuracy.

Hanson (1998; 1999) argued that risk assessments consider two distinct concepts: enduring propensities, or potentials to re-offend; and factors that indicate the onset of new offences. These offence triggers are not random, but can be expected to be organised into predictable patterns (offence cycles), some unique to the individual and some common to most sexual offenders.

Different evaluation questions require the consideration of different types of risk factors. Static, historical variables (e.g. prior offences, childhood maladjustment) can indicate deviant developmental trajectories and, as such, enduring propensities to sexually offend. Evaluating changes in risk levels (e.g. treatment outcome), however, requires the consideration of dynamic, changeable risk factors (e.g. co-operation with supervision, deviant sexual preferences). The relatively low recidivism rates of sexual offenders makes it difficult to detect dynamic risk factors. Over a 4–5 year period, approximately 10–15 per cent of sexual offenders will be detected committing a new sexual offence (Hanson and Bussiere, 1998). Although age is sometimes considered a dynamic factor, the most important dynamic factors are those that respond to treatment. Dynamic factors can further be classified as stable or acute. Stable factors have the potential to change, but typically endure for months or years (e.g. personality disorder) and, as such, represent ongoing risk potential. In contrast, acute factors (e.g. negative mood) may be present for a short duration (minutes, days) and can signal the timing of offending. Most risk decisions require consideration of both static and dynamic risk factors.

Hanson and Bussiere (1998) produced a meta-analysis of sexual offender recidivism studies in an attempt to predict relapse. This examined 61 different follow-up studies including a total of 28,972 sexual offenders. They found that the largest single predictor of sexual recidivism was the presence of deviant sexual preferences and they concluded that sex offender recidivism was closely related to sexual deviance. They suggested that this could be inferred in a number of ways:

- They had deviant sexual interests (PPG measurement).
- Had committed a variety of sexual crimes.
- Had begun offending at an early age, or had a lengthy history of sex offending.
- Had targeted boys, strangers, or unrelated victims.

This suggests that a sexual offending history contributes most to the successful prediction of recidivism. For example, they found that under 10 per cent of first offenders were re-convicted within five years of prison release, compared with a recidivism rate of over 30 per cent for those with any previous sexual offence convictions.

Whilst they found that over 20 variables contributed to the successful prediction of sexual recidivism, for the most part the magnitude of the relationship was so small that it was of negligible practical use. In the end they were able to identify about 10 variables that made some, mostly small, contribution to predictive accuracy, including being unmarried and failing to complete a treatment programme. They noted that risk scales that predicted general (i.e. non-sexual) recidivism well were related only weakly to sexual recidivism. Noticeably absent from the list of risk factors were any measures of subjective distress or general psychological symptoms (e.g. low self-esteem, depression).

Whilst dynamic risk factors are too important to ignore, there are no well-established dynamic risk factors for sexual offence recidivism. There are, however, some potential dynamic predictors of sexual assault recidivism:

- intimacy and attachment deficits
- negative peer influences
- attitudes tolerant of sexual abuse
- emotional/sexual self-regulation
- general self-regulation

Combining risk factors

Since no single factor is sufficient to determine whether offenders will or will not recidivate, practitioners need to consider a range of relevant risk factors. There are three plausible methods by which risk factors can be combined into overall evaluations of risk:

- Empirically guided clinical evaluations: which begins with the overall recidivism base rate, and then adjusts the risk level by considering factors that have been empirically associated with recidivism risk. The risk factors to be considered are explicit, but the method for weighting the importance of the risk factors is left to the judgement of the worker.

- Pure actuarial predictions: in contrast, explicitly state not only the variables to be considered, but also the precise procedure through which ratings of these variables will be translated into a risk level. In the pure actuarial sense, risk levels are estimated through mechanical, arithmetic procedures requiring a minimum of judgement.

- Clinically adjusted actuarial predictions: begins with a pure actuarial prediction, but then raises or lowers the risk level based on consideration of relevant factors that were not included in the actuarial method (see Quinsey *et al.*, 1995). As research develops, actuarial methods can be expected to consistently outperform clinical predictions. With the current state of knowledge, however, both actuarial and guided clinical approaches can be expected to provide risk assessments with moderate levels of accuracy.

Actuarial Risk Scales for Sexual Offence Recidivism

Note: all these are accessible on the Solicitor General Canada's website http://www.sgc.gc.ca

Rapid risk assessment for sexual offence recidivism (RRASOR) (Hanson, 1997)

This brief actuarial tool is intended to be used for screening purposes. The RRASOR score for any individual is based on the number of past sex offence convictions or charges he has, his age at the time of assessment, his relationship to his victims, and the sex of his victims, with additional weight given to his sex offence history. It is possible to score from zero to six points on this scale. The scoring procedure is illustrated below as Figure 8.

Nearly 2,600 sex offenders were rated with the RRASOR system and their re-conviction rates at five to ten years determined. Table 1 below illustrates that the system distinguished risk groups for sexual recidivism reasonably well, with a consistent increase in recidivism rates with higher scores. In addition, the majority of sex offenders were classified as low to moderate risk: 80 per cent of the population scored between zero and two, and in this group five-year sexual recidivism was under 15 per cent. Thus, if one relied on this system as a screening tool to identify a higher risk group for greater attention, it would be possible to focus on just 20 per cent of the sample.

Although RRASOR was based on both rapists and child molesters, separating the two groups out did not have any great impact on the results. It was also interesting that although child molesters are generally older than rapists, the effect of age was similar in two groups: in other words, contrary to expectations, it was the younger child molester who was at highest risk of re-conviction.

It should be noted, however, that although the risk of re-conviction is greatest in those who score three or higher, there are a much larger number of individuals who score zero to two. Therefore, in absolute terms, more of these latter individuals are re-convicted: at five years, 189 of the 2,075 men scoring zero to two are re-convicted compared with 154 of the 517 who score three to five.

Figure 8: RRASOR (Hanson, 1997).

Items	Points
Past sex offences	
0	0
1 conviction or 1–2 charges	1
2–3 convictions or 3–5 charges	2
4+ convictions or 6+ charges	3
Age	
Less than 25	1
Victim gender	
Any male	1
Relationship to victim	
Any non-related	1

Table 1: RRASOR accuracy over 10 years (Hanson, 1997).

Score	Number in group	Recidivism at five years	Recidivism at ten years
0	527 (20%)	4%	7%
1	806 (31%)	8%	11%
2	742 (29%)	14%	21%
3	326 (13%)	25%	37%
4	139 (5%)	33%	49%
5	52 (2%)	50%	73%
Total	2592 (100%)	13%	20%

Thornton's Structured Anchored Clinical Judgement (SACJ-Min) (Grubin, 1998)

This risk calculation algorithm was developed by Dr David Thornton of HM Prison Service in the context of the national prison Sex Offender Treatment Programme (SOTP). It is designed so that the assessment of risk can change over time as more and different types of information about an offender becomes available. This is an example of a structured approach to combining actuarial risk scales with other empirically based risk factors. It too is based on variables described in the sex offender literature as being predictive of sexual re-offending, but unlike RRASOR is not dependent solely on archival data. The SACJ risk classification is a three-step process, with risk reassessed at each step. Like RRASOR it is based on a simple point system with one point scored for each of the following:

- current sexual offence
- past conviction for a sexual offence
- non-sexual violent offence in the current conviction
- past conviction for non-sexual violence
- more than three past convictions of any sort

The risk level is then determined as follows: If offenders have four or more of the initial factors, they are automatically considered high risk. If two or more factors are present, offenders are considered medium risk, and zero or one factor indicate low initial risk.

Step two relates to aggravating factors. If two or more of the following are present, the individual is moved up one risk category level:

- male victim, any sexual offence
- stranger victim, any sex offence
- any non-contact sex offence
- substance abuse (not simply recreational)
- ever been in care
- never married

- deviant sexual arousal
- score of 25+ on the *Psychopathy Checklist* (Hare, 1991)

Step three is based on information that is unlikely to be obtained except for sex offenders who enter treatment programmes, and in this sample involves progress in prison. The risk category is increased if the offender fails to complete an offending behaviour programme, shows a deterioration while in treatment, or has displayed 'sex offending relevant behaviour' in prison within the last five years. Conversely, the risk category is decreased one level if there is successful programme completion, there is significant improvement in risk factors associated with offending, and there is acceptable performance on these risk factors.

The SACJ risk classification was tested on a cohort of 533 sex offenders (of whom 80 per cent had offended against children) released from prison in 1979 and followed up for 16 years. The results, based on information from step one and some from step two (victim gender, victim stranger, non-contact sexual offences, and marital status), a so-called 'low information' version of SACJ, are illustrated below in Table 2.

Table 2: SACJ results (Grubin, 1998).

Level	Number of offenders	Re-conviction
I	162 (30%)	15 (9%)
II	231 (44%)	53 (23%)
III	140 (26%)	64 (46%)
Total	533 (100%)	132 (25%)

Thus, like RRASOR, the SACJ risk assessment scale also appears to identify accurately three groups of sex offender:

- A lower risk group comprising about a third of the sample with a low rate of sexual re-conviction.
- A high risk group comprising about a quarter of the sample of whom nearly half are re-convicted for sexual offences.
- A middle group of about half the sample

amongst whom a quarter are re-convicted.

The SACJ has been adopted by many of the police forces in order to help them undertake their assessments as required under the requirements of The Sex Offenders Act (1997).

As screening tools, both the RRASOR and SACJ systems clearly have great potential, particularly if you accept that the average predictive accuracy of professional judgement to predict sex offence recidivism is only slightly better than chance (Hanson and Bussiere, 1998). There are some potential problems in the child protection arena given that:

1. There is likely to be an incongruence between re-conviction and re-offending rates.

2. The systems do not help us with those where there are allegations but no charges or convictions.

3. There is a need to look beyond frequency to severity of offending as the types of re-offences are not specified in their results.

4. They are unlikely to do well with respect to individuals who have committed their first sexual offence.

5. More refinement is needed if we are to identify the higher risk men in the middle group given they represent such high numbers of the population.

STATIC-99 (Hanson and Thornton, 1999; 2000)

This scale was developed by the authors of RRASOR and SACJ-Min by combining their items. Both these scales were intended to be relatively brief screening instruments for predicting sex offender recidivism. The scale is called Static-99 to indicate that it only includes static factors and that the version was completed in 1999 but remains work in progress. The actuarial risk scale will clearly benefit by including dynamic (changeable) risk factors as well as additional static variables.

The Static-99 is intended to be a measure of long-term risk potential. Given its lack of dynamic factors, it cannot be used to select treatment targets, measure change, evaluate whether offenders have benefited from treatment, or predict when (or under what circumstances) sex offenders are likely to recidivate.

Static-99 is intended for males aged at least 18 who are known to have committed at least one sex offence. Static-99 appears as Figure 9 (overleaf).

Table 3 below translates scores into risk categories:

Table 3: Translating Static-99 scores to risk categories

Score	Label for risk category
0–1	Low
2–3	Medium-low
4–5	Medium-high
6+	High

Predictive accuracy was tested using four diverse data sets from Canada and the UK (total n=1,301). The RRASOR and SACJ-Min showed roughly equivalent predictive accuracy and the combination of the two scales was more accurate than either original scale. Static-99 showed moderate predictive accuracy for both sexual recidivism and violent (including sexual) recidivism, but overall the incremental improvement over the two scales independently was small. It remains clearly more accurate, however, than unstructured clinical judgement.

The Sex Offender Need Assessment Rating (SONAR) (Hanson and Harris, 2000a and b)

There are no established scales that can be used to evaluate change in risk among sex offenders. SONAR was developed to fill this gap. The scale examines how well the dynamic risk factors identified in the Hanson and Harris (1998) study can be organised into a structured risk assessment. Evaluating change requires variables capable of changing, i.e. dynamic variables. It includes five relatively stable factors (intimacy deficits, negative social influences, attitudes tolerant of sex offending, sexual self-regulation, general self-regulation) and four acute factors (substance abuse; negative mood e.g. depression and anxiety; anger/hostility; opportunities for victim access). Acute risk factors are not necessarily related to long-term recidivism potential; instead, they are useful in identifying *when* sex offenders are most likely to re-offend.

Figure 9: Static-99 (Hanson and Thornton, 1999; 2000).

Risk factor	Codes		Score
Prior sex offences (same rules as RRASOR)	Charges	Convictions	
	None	None	0
	1–2	1	1
	3–5	2–3	2
	6+	4+	3
Prior sentencing dates (excluding index)	3 or less		0
	4 or more		1
Any convictions for non-contact sex offences	No		0
	Yes		1
Index non-sexual offence	No		0
	Yes		1
Prior non-sexual violence	No		0
	Yes		1
Any unrelated victims	No		0
	Yes		1
Any stranger victims	No		0
	Yes		1
Any male victims	No		0
	Yes		1
Young	Aged 25 or older		0
	Aged 18–24		1
Single	Ever lived with lover for at least two years?		
	Yes		0
	No		1
Total score	Add up scores from individual risk factors		

The SONAR scoring criteria is set out below as Figure 10.

Figure 10: SONAR (Hanson and Harris, 2000a and b).

Stable items		Score
Intimacy deficits	0 current lover, no troubles 1 current lover, troubles 2 no current lover	
Social influences	0 positive social balance of 2+ 1 balance of 0 or +1 2 balance less than zero	
Attitudes	0 no agreement with any 1 agree with some 2 agrees with many	
Sexual self-regulation	0 no entitlement or preoccupations 1 some entitlement or some sexual preoccupations 2 strong entitlement 3+ sexual preoccupations	
General self-regulation	0 no problem 1 some problem 2 serious problem	
Acute risk factors		
Substance abuse	-1 better 0 same 1 worse	
Negative mood	-1 better 0 same 1 worse	
Anger/hostility	-1 better 0 same 1 worse	
Opportunities for victim access	-1 better 0 same 1 worse	
Total		

Table 4: Translating SONAR scores into risk categories

Category	SONAR score
Low	-4 to 3
Low moderate	4–5
Moderate	6–7
High moderate	8–9

Overall, the scale showed adequate internal consistency and moderate ability to differentiate between recidivists and non-recidivists. SONAR continued to distinguish between the groups after controlling for well-established risk indicators, such as age, IQ, and scores on the Static-99 (Hanson and Thornton, 1999).

Comparing Young Abusers with Adult Sex Offenders

There is a need to question the application of adult risk assessment tools for this group. For example, Buckley and Brown (forthcoming) have questioned the use of static risk factors as there is a significant lack of historical information that will directly affect the findings and many, if not all, will come out as low risk, and intuition and practice experience tells us otherwise. The use of adult tools thus begs more questions than answers.

If we apply dynamic variables, then we find there are a lot of gaps in our knowledge base:

Table 5: Comparing young abusers with adult sex offenders across dynamic variables.

Variable	Adults	Adolescents
Denial	No	N/k
Cognitive distortions	High	N/k
Emotional loneliness	High	N/k
Victim empathy	Global deficits	N/k
Emotional congruence	High	N/k
Social competence	Poor	Poor (but retrospective evidence only)
Self-esteem	Poor	N/k
Treatment failure	Yes	Yes

Table 6: What do we know about risk assessment factors?

Variable	Adult sex offenders	Adolescent sex offenders
Sexual preference for children	Y	N/k
Previous sexual offences	Y	N/k
General deviant interests	Y	N/k
Extra-familial stranger victims	Y	Multiple/female
History of family breakdown	Y	N/k
Previous criminality	Y	Y*

*This debate is addressed further in Calder (forthcoming).

Characteristics of 'high risk' adolescent abusers

The multi-site research programme (Beckett and Brown, in progress) has identified the following risk factors in their interim analysis of data:

Peer sexual aggression/ sexuality

- psychopathy
- conduct disorder in childhood
- anti-social behaviour, delinquency, truancy, aggression and high impulsivity in adolescence
- association with delinquent peers
- high drug/alcohol use
- history of severe emotional neglect

Child sexual abuse

- previous sexual convictions
- expressed sexual preference/desires for children
- high levels of cognitive distortions
- major social competency problems
- emotional loneliness
- history of severe physical abuse

Practice Guidelines for Risk Assessment

First of all the bad news: there is no ideal risk assessment method or framework. Risk assessment is a feature of both the initial and the comprehensive assessments, as risk needs to be continuously reassessed as circumstances change and/or more information becomes available to the workers.

There have been many attempts to develop risk assessment models and guidance in order to assist professionals in making decisions about individual children. Whilst research-derived models are better than those built on professional consensus, both struggle to embrace the diversity of practice situations, particularly in sexual abuse situations. Since many models tend to err on the side of over-prediction, professionals need to accept that they represent a tool, which is not an end in

itself, merely an aid to professional judgement. The term risk assessment can thus refer to both a structured form of decision-making as well as to specific instruments or frameworks that are used in the process (e.g. Calder, 1997; 1999a and b; Calder, forthcoming a, b and c for sexual abuse assessments).

However, having reviewed the literature, I offer the following framework for conducting risk assessments:

- *Assess all areas of identified risk*: Write them each down and ensure each is considered separately, e.g. child, parent, family, surrounding environment, type and nature of maltreatment, intervention issues.

- *Then define the behaviour to be predicted*: Rather than focusing on the 'dangerous' individual. Assess each worrying behaviour individually, as each is likely to involve different risk factors.

- *Grade the risks, and be alert for especially serious risk factors*: e.g. previous corroborated or uncorroborated concerns; unwillingness or inability to protect. While numerical weighting is hard to give, some weighting has to be given to significance. A less likely event with a serious outcome if it occurred, would need to be weighted, e.g. injury, death, traumatic emotional impact. A more likely event with a high frequency, even though a not too serious outcome, would need to be weighted. Who is affected could add to the gravity, e.g. the harm to a child is often greater than if to an adult.

- *Be aware of risk factors that may interact in a dangerous manner*: e.g. a case of physical injury and the abuser is heavily drinking at present. Take into account both internal and external factors: almost all behaviour is the result of interaction between characteristics of the individual (e.g. attitudes, skills, controls) and those of the environment (demands, constraints, stresses, etc.).

- *Examine the nature of the risk factors*: How long have they been operating for? How severe are they? Risk factors that are long-term and relatively uncontrollable generally signal a higher level of risk.

- *Avoid focusing exclusively on the severity of the abuse*: We need to consider other factors that point to future risk not just commissioned harm. Distinguish between the probability and the cost of the behaviour—we need to distinguish between the likelihood of the behaviour occurring, from the seriousness of it if it does occur. Failure to do so makes any decision-making more problematic.

- *Assessing family strengths and resources*: While risk assessment is essentially a negative process, workers should be examining family strengths and resources that may be used to counteract the risk factors present. For example, good bonding; supportive networks. It is argued that the assessment process is incomplete in the absence of this dimension.

- *Use specific and descriptive terms to document the risk factors*: Do not rely on terms such as 'multi-problem family'.

- *Gather real and direct evidence whenever possible*: Do not rely on hunches, hearsay or circumstantial information.

- *Checking whether all necessary information has been gathered*: As in some cases, few sources of data may be needed to develop a strong understanding of the behaviour, whereas in others we may need to qualify any predictions made, due to the entirely inadequate or irrelevant material.

- *Identifying if/when specialists or other outsiders need to be involved*: Predictive accuracy is often improved when we utilise the combined skills across agencies and sometimes beyond. Where this is lacking, workers should explicitly state how their recommendations have been affected by such omissions.

- *Awareness of probable sources of error*: Which may come from the person being assessed (e.g. their poor reliability as an informant); the assessor (a difficulty in suspending personal values); or the context (such as an agency bias in favour of one or other party involved).

- *Planning key interventions*: Because a sound assessment of risk will be based on the formulation of the mechanisms underlying the behaviour, it will automatically identify those processes, which appear to be key elements in increasing or reducing such risk, e.g. within the individual or the couple.

- *Examine the overall level of risk to the child within the total context of risk factors, family strengths and agency resources*: This is an important step as it requires we try and assimilate all the identified risk factors as the basis of trying to determine the overall level of risk. Determining whether a case is low, intermediate, or high risk is a complex decision-making process where the worker considers the following conditions or criteria:
  - Number of risk factors (how pervasive are they?)
  - Severity of risk factors (how severe?)
  - Duration of risk factors (how long have they been present?)
  - Parent's or child's ability to control risk factors.
  - Family strengths and resources.
  - Ability of worker or agency to provide necessary services. Some possible courses of action may not be possible due to a lack of resources. Work first on including all that seems relevant. If necessary, list separately what appears realistic within the required resources. It may be that the decision is made to make the resources needed available. If not, then at least it is clear what is available and what is not. Lack of resources is not an automatic justification for not pursuing a course of action. If the result of using lack of resources as an excuse not to pursue a course of action is to add to the harm (risk), then the decision could be open to challenge. Furthermore, a review of resource use could show they were not being used efficiently enough.

- *Risk characteristics*: It is increasingly being accepted that we should not label any individual merely as high, medium, or low risk, as the level of risk is likely to change from situation to situation. The nature of the risk should be identified together with the particular situations/contexts in which they apply. For example, we may have a set of risk characteristics such as the offence, the social history, behavioural features, and attitudes, thoughts and feelings, with each being broken down into a continuum of high, medium and low risk. This should not be used as a checklist but as an aid to an overall consideration of risk. Some of the factors should be considered interacting as well as individually. There are no prescriptive ways of applying the factors, and the assessment of risk will always be down to the assessors overall evaluation of the individual's risk features, together with consideration of context and risk management strategies. As such, methods of managing the risks should be indicated and comment made on the overall impact of risk if particular strategies are adopted.

- *Likelihood of outcomes*: The aim here is for as accurate a prediction as possible. Bring together all known information about the particular situation and people involved. Identify what the likely error sources, gaps or limitations are in the available information, remembering that gaps in knowledge rarely indicate a decision cannot be made, only that it will need to be reviewed if that information becomes available.

- *Determine the child's degree of safety*: The central critical question throughout the process, both for the child and workers. Does this child need protection, and if so, what? What are the specific risks involved? What needs to be done and how soon to ensure the child has the protection needed from this risk of harm?

- *Make the decision*: If the harms are so significant that action is needed, then: ensure a monitoring system is in place that will receive all feedback rapidly, and have the capacity to act on an alternative plan if necessary; implement a decision for the agreed time period; and consider if a reduced time period for the risk and/or an alternative approach could manage the risk acceptably.

- *Prediction of factors likely to increase/decrease future risk*: A risk assessment is not a 'one off' snapshot of the current potential for harm, but rather a continuing process, to

be frequently modified and updated. If the formulation is comprehensive and sound, it should be possible to anticipate some of the events likely to occur in the future and how these would affect the risk posed. Some of these events may constitute warning signs that action is necessary by one or more of the supervising professionals; good practice would indicate that these should be identified to all concerned in advance (including, as far as is possible, the individual being assessed), and the reactions planned and agreed. Too often, entirely foreseeable developments trigger inconsistent, knee-jerk responses from workers who have an insufficient framework of understanding against which to measure events, and who therefore have to respond largely to their own anxieties, or those of their own supervisors (adapted from Calder and Skinner, 1999; Moore, 1996; Pecora *et al.*, 1992; and Stafford and Hardy, 1996).

Cleaver *et al.* (1998) identified a useful list of the blocks to identifying risk and include:

- The unknown—that is, knowledge of signs and symptoms and knowledge of the law that was not adequate.

- The known but not fully appreciated—the need to identify what is important from a 'flood of relevant data'.

- Interpretation—being able to correctly interpret information in the context of assessing risk.

- Objective and subjective information— failure to distinguish fact from opinion, being too trusting and uncritical.

- Unappreciated data—information may not be appreciated if it has come from a source which is distrusted.

- The decoy of dual pathology— information may be missed if the receiver is decoyed by a different problem.

- Certainty—investigators may have a false sense of security about a particular interpretation (e.g. medical assessments of sexual abuse in Cleveland).

- Competing tasks within the same visiting schedule, e.g. fostering and child protection.

- The known and not assembled—individuals may hold information which they can withhold or which is not pieced together with the rest.
- Not fitting the current mode of understanding—this has also been described as a loss of objectivity, and the importance of supervision is highlighted.
- Long standing blocks—assumptions made at an early stage, which influenced later interpretation of information (p9).

Summary and Way Forward

There is a very real danger that the new assessment framework will not adequately address the complexities of child sexual abuse. There has to be major concern about the lack of priority given to the commissioning of materials in relation to sexual abuse to accompany the assessment framework.

It does not auger well when the notion of risk has been ditched when it could be redefined in a more holistic and positive way to have the same impact as the much promoted 'need-led' assessment. It is worrying that we should intervene on the basis of our evidence base when it is lacking in so many ways in the sexual abuse arena. Sexual abusers do not come with flashing lights saying 'here I am, come and get me'. It is worrying that we have shaved a corner off the square-shaped ecological framework to consider only three dimensions. The lack of any interaction between the components and the worker is short sighted and completely disregards the centrality of engaging the client in any proposed work (Calder, forthcoming d). This has acute effects on mothers and sets up situations that could be avoided.

These things considered, the assessment framework is here and likely to stay for at least a few years until its flaws are acknowledged formally and redressed. This chapter has looked at how some of the central components of the assessment framework can be adapted to sexual abuse work, and how existing models in the sexual abuse arena can be superimposed on the framework to guide our thinking. Unless we respond in the practice situation with our own ideas the baby will have been thrown out with the bath water. It is in this context that I have constructed this book with the help of several eminent colleagues in the field. The aim

is to provide the reader with the basic information gathering requirements of both the initial and core assessments by providing suggested frameworks for practice. The only omitted chapter is the one that looks at the child victim in their own right. This is because the initial requirements are laid down in documents such as the Memorandum of Good Practice and the impact factors are detailed in the mother's chapter.

References

Adcock, M. (1995). Assessment. In Wilson, K. and Jones, A. (Eds.). *The Child Protection Handbook*, pp188–210. London: Bailliere Tindall.

Beckett, R., and Brown, S. (in progress). *Multi-site Research on Young People who Sexually Abuse*. Oxford Psychology Service.

Belsky, J. (1980). Child Maltreatment: An Ecological Integration. *American Psychologist*, 35: pp320–35.

Birchall, E., and Hallett, C. (1995). *Working Together in Child Protection*. London: HMSO.

Bischof, G.H., and Rosen, K.H. (1997). An Ecological Perspective on Adolescent Sexual Offending. *Journal of Offender Rehabilitation*, 26(1/2): pp67–88.

Bronfenbrenner, U. (1977). Toward an Experimental Ecology of Human Development. *American Psychologist*, 32: pp513–31.

Calder, M.C. (1991). Child Protection: Core Groups: Beneficial or Bureaucratic? *Child Abuse Review*, 5(2): pp26–9.

Calder, M.C. (1992). *Towards an Ecological Formulation of System Maltreatment: Identifying the Casualties*. Unpublished MA dissertation, University of Lancaster.

Calder, M.C. (1999a). *Assessing Risk in Adult Males who Sexually Abuse Children: A Practitioners Guide*. Dorset: Russell House Publishing.

Calder, M.C. (1999b). A Conceptual Framework for Managing Young People who Sexually Abuse: Towards a Consortium Approach. In Calder, M.C. (Ed.). *Working with Young People who Sexually Abuse: New Pieces of the Jigsaw Puzzle*, pp109–50. Dorset: Russell House Publishing.

Calder, M.C. (1999c). *Child Prostitution: An Evolving Framework of Response*. Presentation to a 1-day Infolog national conference, 'Child prostitution: tackling a massively underestimated problem'. The Barbican Centre, London, 11th November, 1999.

Calder, M.C. (1999d). *Eligibility Criteria: A Discussion Paper*. Children in Need Project: City of Salford Community and Social Services.

Calder, M.C. (1999e). Towards Anti-Oppressive Practice with Ethnic Minority Groups. In Calder, M.C., and Horwath, J. (Eds.). *Working for Children on the Child Protection Register: An Inter-agency Practice Guide*, pp177–209. Aldershot: Ashgate.

Calder, M.C. (1999f). *Young People who Sexually Abuse: Assessment and Practice Guidance.* Salford: Salford ACPC.

Calder, M.C. (1999g). Young People who Sexually Abuse: A Framework for Initial Assessment. *Child Care in Practice*, 5(3): pp262–80.

Calder, M.C. (2000). *The Evolving Management of Young People who Sexually Abuse: Towards Critical and Evidence-based Practice.* Keynote presentation to a national conference on adolescent sex offenders. London, 6–7th November, 2000.

Calder, M.C. (forthcoming a). *Mothers of Sexually Abused Children: A Framework for Assessment, Understanding and Support.* Dorset: Russell House Publishing.

Calder, M.C. (Ed.) (forthcoming b). *Work with Young Sexual Abusers 2001.* Dorset: Russell House Publishing.

Calder, M.C. (forthcoming c). *Juveniles and Children who Sexually Abuse: Frameworks for Assessment* (2nd edition). Dorset: Russell House Publishing.

Calder, M.C. (forthcoming d). The New Assessment Framework (NAF): A Critique and Reformulation. In Calder, M.C., and Hackett, S. (Eds.). *The RHP Child Care Assessment Manual.* Dorset: Russell House Publishing.

Calder, M.C. (in press). A Framework for Conducting Risk Assessments. *Child Care in Practice*, 6.

Calder. M.C. (Submitted for publication). *A Framework for Understanding and Assessing Sexual Abuse on the Internet.*

Calder, M.C., and Hackett, S. (Eds.) (forthcoming). *The RHP Child Care Assessment Manual.* Dorset: Russell House Publishing.

Calder, M.C., and Horwath, J. (1999). Policies and Procedures: A Framework for Working Together. In Calder, M.C., and Horwath, J. (Eds.). *Working for Children on the Child Protection Register: An Inter-agency Practice Guide*, pp46–80. Aldershot: Arena.

Calder, M.C., and Skinner, J. (1999). *Young People who Sexually Abuse: Risk Assessment and Community Management.* Workshop for NOTA North-West Training day, Chorley Medical Centre, 16th April, 1999.

Calder, M.C., and Waters, J. (1991). *Child Abuse or Child Protection: What's in a Name?* Paper presented to a conference on child abuse for the Association of Psychological Therapies, University of York, 18th June, 1991.

Calder, M.C., with Hanks, H., and Epps, K.J. (1997). *Juveniles and Children who Sexually Abuse: A Guide to Risk Assessment.* Dorset: Russell House Publishing.

Carich, M.S., and Calder, M.C. (forthcoming). *A Practice Guide to Contemporary Sex Offender Treatment.* Dorset: Russell House Publishing.

Carson, D. (1994). Dangerous People: Through a Broader Concept of 'Risk' and 'Danger' to Better Decisions. *Expert Evidence*, 3(2): pp21–69.

Challis, L., Fuller, S., Henwood, M., Klein, R., Plowden, W., Webb, A., Whittingham, P., and Wistow, G.

(1988). *Joint Approaches to Social Policy—Rationality and Practice.* Cambridge: Cambridge University Press.

Cleaver, H., Wattam, C., and Cawson, P. (1998). *Assessing Risk in Child Protection.* London: NSPCC.

DoH (1988). *Protecting Children: A Guide for Social Workers Undertaking a Comprehensive Assessment.* London: HMSO.

DoH (1991). *Working Together under the Children Act 1989: A Guide to Arrangements for Inter-agency Co-operation for the Protection of Children from Abuse.* London: HMSO.

DoH (1993). *Working with Child Sexual Abuse: Guidelines for Trainers and Managers.* London: HMSO.

DoH (1995). *Child Protection: Messages from Research.* London: HMSO.

DoH (1998). *Quality Protects: Transforming Children's Services.* LAC (98) 28. 11th November, 1998.

DoH (1999). *Working Together to Safeguard Children: A Guide to Inter-agency Working to Safeguard and Promote the Welfare of Children.* London: HMSO.

DoH (2000). *Framework for the Assessment of Children in Need and their Families.* London: HMSO.

Druacke, C.B. (1992). *Counselling Survivors of Childhood Sexual Abuse.* Newbury Park, CA: Sage.

Epps, K. (1999). Causal Explanations: Filling the Theoretical Reservoir. In Calder, M.C. (Ed.). *Working with Young People who Sexually Abuse: New Pieces of the Jigsaw Puzzle*, pp7–26. Lyme Regis, Dorset: Russell House Publishing.

Erooga M. (1994). Where the Professional Meets the Personal. In Morrison, T., Erooga, M., and Beckett, R.C. (Eds.). *Sexual Offending Against Children: Assessment and Treatment of Male Abusers*, pp203–24. London: Routledge.

Erooga, M., and Print, B. (2000). Assessing Parental Capacity when Intra-familial Sexual Abuse is a Concern. In Horwath, J. (Ed.). *The Child's World: Assessing Children in Need*, pp235–48. Reader. London: NSPCC.

Everitt, A., and Hardiker, P. (1996). *Evaluating for Good Practice.* London: Macmillan.

Faller, K.C. (1990). *Understanding Sexual Maltreatment.* Newbury Park, CA: Sage.

Farmer, E., and Pollock, S. (1998). *Sexually Abused and Abusing Children in Substitute Care.* Chichester: John Wiley and Sons.

Finkelhor, D. (1979). *Sexually Victimised Children.* NY: The Free Press.

Finkelhor, D. (1982). Sexual Abuse: A Sociological Perspective. *Child Abuse and Neglect*, 6: pp95–102.

Finkelhor, D. (1984). *Child Sexual Abuse: New Theory and Research.* NY: The Free Press.

Finkelhor, D. (1987). The Sexual Abuse of Children: Current Research Reviewed. *Psychiatric Annals*, 17(4): pp233–41.

Fontes, L. (1993). Considering Culture and Oppression: Steps Toward an Ecology of Sexual Child Abuse. *Journal of Feminist Family Therapy*, 5(1): pp25–54.

Friedrich, W.N. (1988). Behaviour Problems in Sexually Abused Children. In Wyatt, G.E., and Powell, G.J. (Eds.). *The Lasting Effects of Child Sexual Abuse*, pp171–91. Newbury Park, CA: Sage.

Garbarino, J. (1977). The Human Ecology of Child Maltreatment: A Conceptual Model for Research. *Journal of Marriage and the Family*, 39: pp721–35.

Groth, A.N., and Oliveri, F.J. (1989). Understanding Sexual Abuse Offence Behaviour and Differentiating Among Sexual Abusers: Basic Conceptual Issues. In Sgroi, S.M. (Ed.). *Vulnerable Populations* (Volume 2), pp309–27. Lexington: DC Health.

Grubin, D. (1998). *Sex Offending against Children: Understanding the Risk*. London: Home Office Research, Development and Statistics Directorate.

Hampson, A. (1993). *Annual Report of the Principal Officer—Child Protection*. City of Salford Social Services (Children's Division).

Hanson, R.K. (1997). *The Development of a Brief Actuarial Risk Scale for Sexual Offence Recidivism*. Ottawa: Department of the Solicitor General of Canada.

Hanson, R.K. (1998). *Using Research to Improve Sex Offender Risk Assessment*. Keynote presentation to the NOTA National Conference, University of Glasgow, 17th September, 1998.

Hanson, R.K. (1999). Sex Offender Risk Assessment. In Hollin, C.R. (Ed.). *Handbook of Offender Assessment and Treatment*. Chichester: John Wiley and Sons Ltd.

Hanson, R.K., and Bussiere, M.T. (1998). Predicting Relapse: A Meta-Analysis of Sexual Offender Recidivism Studies. *Journal of Consulting and Clinical Psychology*, 66(2): pp348–62.

Hanson, R.K., and Harris, A. (1998). *Dynamic Predictors of Sexual Recidivism*. Ottawa: Department of the Solicitor General of Canada.

Hanson, R.K., and Harris, A. (2000a). *The Sex Offender Need Assessment Rating (SONAR): A Method for Measuring Change in Risk Levels*. Ottawa: Department of the Solicitor General of Canada.

Hanson, R.K., and Harris, A. (2000b). Where Should we Intervene? Dynamic Predictors of Sexual Abuse Recidivism. *Criminal Justice and Behaviour*, 27(1): pp6–35.

Hanson, R.K., and Thornton, D. (1999). *Static-99: Improving Actuarial Risk Assessments for Sex Offenders*. Ottawa: Department of the Solicitor General of Canada.

Hanson, R.K., and Thornton, D. (2000). Improving Risk Assessments for Sex Offenders: A Comparison of Three Actuarial Scales. *Law and Human Behaviour*, 24(1): pp119–36.

Hare, R.D. (1991). *The Hare Psychopathy Checklist—Revised*. Toronto: Multi-health Systems.

Haugaard, J.J., and Reppucci, N.D. (1988). *The Sexual Abuse of Children*. San Francisco, CA: Jossey-Bass.

Hinnicks, (1976), as quoted in Morrison, I. (1995).

Horwath, J. (1999) Personal communication.

Horwath, J. (Ed.) (2000). *The Child's World: Assessing Children in Need*. The reader. London: NSPCC.

Horwath, J., and Calder, M.C. (1998). Working Together to Protect Children on the Child Protection Register: Myth or Reality? *British Journal of Social Work*, 28(6):

Jones, D.P., and Ramchandani, P. (1999). *Child Sexual Abuse: Informing Practice from Research*. Oxford: Radcliffe Medical Press.

Macleod, M., and Saraga, E. (1988). Challenging the Orthodoxy: Towards a Feminist Theory of Practice. *Feminist Review*, 28: pp16–55.

Maddock, J.W., and Larson, N.R. (1995). *Incestuous Families: An Ecological Approach to Understanding and Treatment*. NY: WW Norton and Company.

Mailick, M., and Ashley, A.A. (1989). Politics of Interprofessional Collaboration: Challenge of Advocacy. *Social Casework*, 62(3): pp131–7.

Margetts, T. (1998). Establishing Multi-agency Working with Sex Offenders: Setting up to Succeed. *NOTA News*, 25: pp27–38.

McFarlane, T., and Morrison, T. (1994). Learning and Change: Outcomes of Inter-agency Training for Child Protection. *Child Care in Practice*, 1(12): pp33–44.

Monck, E., and New, M. (1996). *Report of a Study of Sexually Abused Children and Adolescents, and of Young Perpetrators of Sexual Abuse who were Treated in Voluntary Agency Community Facilities*. London: HMSO.

Moore, B. (1996). *Risk Assessment: A Practitioner's Guide to Predicting Harmful Behaviour*. London: Whiting and Birch Ltd.

Morrison, T. (1992). Managing Sex Offenders: The Challenge for Managers. *Probation Journal*, 39(3): pp122–8.

Morrison, T. (1994). Context, Constraints and Considerations in Practice. In Morrison, T., Erooga, M., and Beckett, R. (Eds.). *Sexual Offending against Children: Assessment and Treatment of Male Abusers*, pp25–54. London: Routledge.

Morrison, T. (1995). *Learning, Training and Change in Child Protection Organisations*. Keynote presentation to the National Child Protection Trainers conference, 15 March 1995.

Morrison, T. (1996). Partnership and Collaboration: Rhetoric and Reality. *Child Abuse and Neglect*, 20(2): pp127–40.

Morrison, T. (1996b). *Making an Impact: Where Next with Adolescents who Sexually Abuse?* Keynote presentation to Barnardo's, 'Learning to change' conference, Liverpool Town Hall, 14th March, 1996.

O'Callaghan, D., and Hackett, S. (1999a). *Research Based Practice with Young People who Sexually Abuse*. Workshop presented at the 9th NOTA Annual Conference, University of York, 6–8th October, 1999.

O'Callaghan, D., and Hackett, S. (1999b). *Developmentally Sensitive Intervention with Sexually Abusive Youth: A Framework for Research Informed Treatment Planning*. University of Durham/G-MAP. Unpublished paper.

Parker, R., Ward, H., Jackson, S., Aldgate, J., and Wedge, P. (Eds.) (1991). *Looking After Children: Assessing*

Outcomes in Childcare. The Report of an Independent Working Party Established by the Department of Health. London: HMSO.

Parton, N. (1996). Social Work, Risk and the Blaming System. In Parton, N. (Ed.). *Social Theory, Social Change and Social Work*, pp98–114. London: Routledge.

Parton, N., and Small, N. (1989). Violence, Social Work and the Emergence of Dangerousness. In Langan, M., and Lee, P. (Eds.). *Radical Social Work Today*, pp120–39. London: Unwin Hyman.

Pecora, P.J., *et al.* (1992). *The Child Welfare Challenge: Policy, Practice And Research.* NY: Aldine de Gruyter.

Print, B., and Erooga, M. (2000). Young People who Sexually Abuse: Implications for Assessment. In Horwath, J. (Ed.). *The Child's World: Assessing Children in Need*, pp249–61. Reader. London: NSPCC.

Quinsey, V.L., Rice, M.E., and Harris, G.T. (1995). Actuarial Prediction of Sexual Recidivism. *Journal of Interpersonal Violence*, 10(1): pp85–105.

Skuse, D., Bentovim, A., Hodges, J., New, M.J., Williams, B.T., and McMillan, D. (1998). Risk Factors for the Development of Sexually Abusive Behaviour in Sexually Victimised Adolescent Males. *British Medical Journal*, 317: pp175–9.

Smith, G. (1993). *Systemic Approaches to Training in Child Protection.* London: Karnac.

SSI (1993). *Inspecting for Quality: Evaluating Performance in Child Protection. A Framework for the Inspection of Local Authority Social Services Practice and Systems.* London: HMSO.

Stafford, W., and Hardy, C. (1996). *Risk Assessment and Guardian Ad Litem.* Presentation to the 7th AGM and Spring conference of the National Association of Guardian *ad litem* and reporting officers. St William's College, York, 18th March, 1996.

Thornton, D. (1999). Keynote presentation to National NOTA conference, University of York, 6–8th October, 1999.

Chapter Two

Assessing Children who Sexually Abuse

Martin C. Calder

This chapter attempts to provide a framework to guide workers when a decision has been taken that the presenting behaviour goes beyond what may be considered 'normal' and further, more detailed assessments are needed (see Figure 11 overleaf). We know from work in the United States that this group is very small, although a full assessment of the child's sexually abusive behaviour is necessary when we have to:

- Determine what factors play a part in the presenting behaviour.

- Identify whether there are thought, feeling or behaviour problems for the child.

- Identify whether the behaviours are outside age-appropriate limits and part of an escalating pattern of behaviour.

- Determine whether treatment is indicated, and what components it should contain, e.g. areas for re-education and re-learning, for the child and/or the family.

It is important that we do not over-react to the presenting situation as this can have long-term adverse consequences for the child, as well as guarding against focusing on their victim status as this may allow them to contrive their behaviour. The younger the child, the more likely this becomes, although they are ripe for interventions given that their behaviour is less entrenched and sophisticated. It is important to follow a sequential response to any abusive sexual behaviour by children. When abusive sexual behaviour is first discovered, it is important for it to be labelled and for the child to be told that their behaviour has a negative impact on those involved. The primary goal is for children to stop abusive behaviour because they have learned that the behaviour makes others feel bad, not because they will get into trouble if they do not. It is important to respond consistently to the behaviour when it is reported rather than waiting for it to escalate to where no alternatives are available (Ryan et al., 1987).

The assessment work comprises two separate but inter-linking parts: work with the

parents and work with the abusing child. Both will be covered in this chapter.

Pre-assessment Tasks

- Workers need to collect all relevant background information (school, nursery, parents, carers, statements, etc.) Glasgow et al. (1994) found that children are more likely to admit to their behaviour than adults are when faced with some evidence.

- Workers need to ensure that issues of placement, contact and strategies for the day-to-day management of the child have been addressed.

- Workers need to establish an agreed language and words with the child—on sexual acts, language, body parts etc. Workers need to frame the assessment with the child at a level they can understand and engage with.

- Workers do need to acknowledge the centrality of the parents in work with this client group given their age and developmental level. It is thus wise to do some work with the parents first in order to get some idea of the child's developmental level which acts as a guide to constructing and undertaking the assessment work.

- A written agreement needs to be constructed with the parents to address the work, and should include:

  - A statement on why the assessment is needed.

  - A statement of intent, e.g. the goal is to avoid any repetition of problem behaviours, thoughts or feelings.

  - The areas that need to be covered in the work.

  - The number of sessions, the venue and times, and any practical arrangements such as transport.

  - The boundaries of the work need to be

Figure 11: The process of assessment with children who sexually abuse (Calder, 1997).

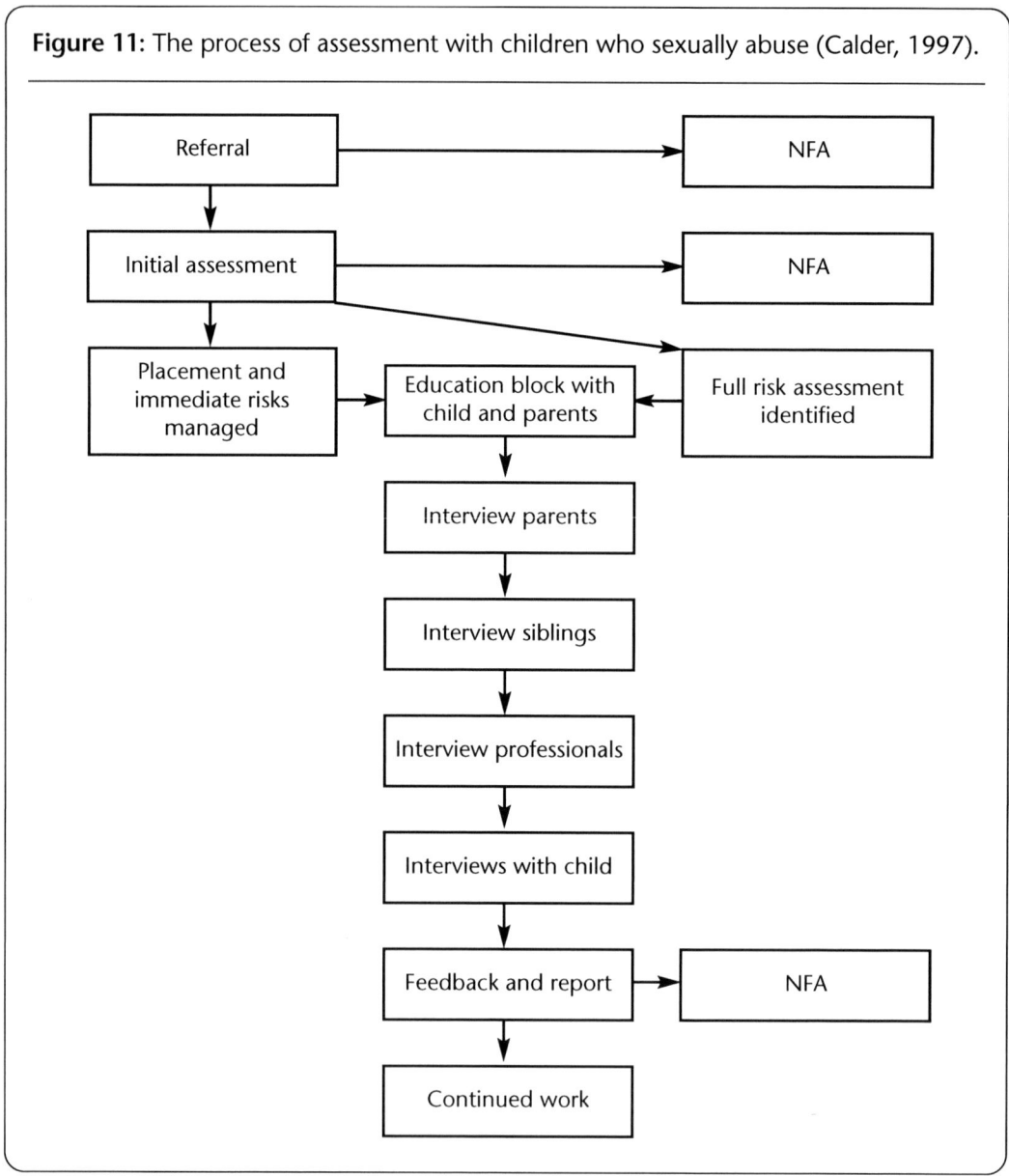

set with the parents and are non-negotiable with the child and needs to include any agreed management strategies if the child acts out verbally or physically in the sessions.

– The role of the parents needs to be clarified, e.g. they are not to be part of the interview, but their presence in the building may assist the child.

– The allocation and completion of homework assignments and the role of the parents with these needs to be clear—they can be framed as 'tests' which have no 'right' or 'wrong' answers, but are simply to provide more information on the child.

– The limits of confidentiality need to be explicit. With this age group it is difficult to grant any confidentiality, as the parents have a right to know the general information given. The specifics can usually be spared, other than where new information needs to be formally passed on, and

- Agree the child can bring a valued toy or something of their own choice to the sessions to comfort them during times of stress and which can help them regain their confidence and reassurance in the absence of the parents (Howard, 1993; p223).

- An education session should take place with the parents and the child as a preface to the work. Most parents are unaware of the dynamics of sexual abuse or about the developmental stages of their child. Education offers them a baseline from which to work. Many parents, given some insight, can offer a lot of support and encouragement to their child in the work that follows. They can be provided with explanatory booklets such as Ryan and Blum (1995) that they can take away and digest.

- The workers need to carefully plan any work with the child. Any programme of work needs to be constructed with a view to retaining the child's interest. As such, the materials used are as important as the content, so that cards, quizzes, games, glove puppets, and questionnaires need to be used. Using the right media to engage the child can offer a vehicle for the expression of feeling and emotions in the development of understanding of what is a very complex area of work, e.g. developing stories can help them access otherwise confused feelings and information; kaleidoscopes can offer altered images, thus helping the child with the concept of change; and the use of a glove puppet can act as a vehicle for communication and can remove the focus from the child, thus reducing the intensity of any psychological pressure on them (Howard, 1993; pp223–4).

Interviews with the Parents

It is important to see the parents separately as well as together, as their responses may be influenced by their partner's presence. It is also important to allow them an opportunity to raise issues on their own agenda, and to deal with any feelings of anger, denial and confusion. The areas which need to be covered with the parents include:

Social history

This needs to explore several key areas:

- The child's developmental history (sexual behaviours are only one part of their total being).
- The child's developmental needs.
- The medical and psychological background of the child.
- School history—performance, behaviour, attendance, relationships, etc.
- Peer relationships.
- What are their social skills?
- Hobbies, likes, dislikes.
- The child's strengths (what do they do well?) and weaknesses (what don't they do well?).
- Any history of separations, and in what circumstances?

Family composition, history and functioning

Understanding the child's broader family context is essential if we are to understand the origins of their behaviour. We need to help parents understand if any aspect of their family life of current family dynamics are contributing to the child's sexually abusive behaviour, and we also need to consider whether the child's behaviour is impacting on the family. The family dynamics can contribute to recidivist behaviours from the child, e.g. parental leniency with supervision or confused sexual messages/sexual climate in the home. Workers need to elicit what things can or cannot be changed, and why? We need to gather information around:

- A history of each family member.
- An overall family history—any problems, violence, sexual issues, parenting style and ability.
- Family composition, relationships, dynamics, rules, patterns, alliances, strengths and weaknesses.
- Any history of abuse in the family, and any links directly or indirectly with the presenting problem.
- Gender roles.
- Sleeping arrangements.
- Social supports and stresses.
- Any history of alcohol or substance abuse, psychiatric history, etc.
- Family approach to sex and sexuality, and
- Family secrets—here, families often have secrets that keep the unhealthy dynamics alive. There may be a silent or overt message to remain silent about relationships or about supervision issues such as sleeping arrangements, visitation, and recurrences of reactive behaviour. Parents may be silent about ongoing issues, but the children often are the family historians and will reveal the intimacies (Griggs and Bold, 1995).

The child's sexually abusive behaviours

This section needs to explore the history of the child's sexually abusive behaviours (number, types, whether they acted alone or with others, and whether any force was used or threatened).

The following offers a broad checklist of the areas that need to be covered:

- When did this behaviour first come to light? Was it a complaint? From whom?
- Has the child been approached about their behaviour? By whom? When? With what outcome?
- If there was a victim, what is their gender, age, relationship, ability level? Is there more than one victim?
- In what context did the behaviour occur, e.g. bathing, recreation, etc?
- Has the behaviour changed over time? In what way?

- Can they recollect any significant events or changes around the time of the abuse?
- Are they able to identify any antecedents to the behaviour?
- Was any force or threats used? Were they threatened themselves?
- What do they think is wrong with their son's behaviours? What are the high risk situations?
- Do they blame the victim for the problem? Themselves? The intervention?
- Has the child been abused themselves? By whom? And in what circumstances?
- Do they discuss sex and sexuality—At all? Openly? Can they discuss nudity, masturbation, etc.?
- Has the child ever had any 'consensual' sex to the parents' knowledge? Give details.
- Are they aware of any concerns about the child's behaviours in the past? If yes, what were they?
- Has the child ever expressed any interest in sexual matters? What have they asked?
- Do they show interest in sexual behaviours on TV, videos, magazines, etc? Do they have access to this material?
- Do they have any concerns about the child's attitude to women, sex or children?
- Has there ever been any concern about the child's sexual or physical behaviour towards others?

Parental attitudes towards the abuser and the victim

Most parents are overly concerned with any sign of sexuality in their child. Griggs and Bold (1995) found an interesting inversion of 'good' and 'bad' parents in this area. They found that 'good' parents tend to reject the need for intervention and deny the need to take full responsibility for their child's behaviour, whereas the 'bad' parents will often do anything to address their feelings of being defeated and hopeless (p153). Questions that need to be asked include:

- Are they obsessed with the information about the abuse?

- What is their concern and understanding of the risks?
- What is their reaction to the abuse? Do they identify with their son as a victim only?
- Are they projecting blame elsewhere? On to whom?
- Are they minimising the abuse, or denying any abuse took place?
- What feelings do they have towards the child who abused, the victim, the workers, etc?
- How will they respond to and manage any relapse by their child?
- What are their feelings towards the child?
- Do they feel contaminated?

We can remind the parents about the information on age-appropriate behaviours given in the education block, and we need to help them work through any of the negative feelings they have experienced, or else they become more entrenched in their denial, and this will be projected onto the child. What is clear is that the attitude of the parents is vital to a hopeful outcome.

Management strategies with the child

It is important that the parents are educated not to set their children up to continue their abusive behaviour. The aim of this block of work is for them to safeguard the home environment until the child has learned to develop internal controls. Such management strategies will be stressful to the parents. They need support themselves to prevent them from retreating further into isolation, depression, chemical dependency, etc., and ultimately framing themselves as the victim. We do need to acknowledge and work through any issues about their own abuse that may compromise their child's supervision. We should never underestimate or minimise the importance of supervising the child, particularly around any identified high risk situations, e.g. toileting, bathing, sleeping arrangements, etc.

Questions to be asked include:

- How did they manage the child—before and after the abuse was uncovered?

- Have they taken any steps to prevent any repetition of the abusive behaviour?
- What do they consider the high risk situations to be?
- How can they be managed or avoided?
- Can they identify any signals which may proceed the abuse?

Management strategies

Pithers *et al.* (1993) offered several steps for parents in the management of the abuser in the home:

- Decrease the opportunity to abuse.
- Don't leave your child alone with victim-age children.
- Don't have your child and a known victim bathe, sleep, or change clothes together.
- If your child is playing with another child, stay in the room or check on them frequently.
- Discourage games your child may have used to get another child to go along with the sexual behaviour (playing doctor, house, Simon Says, hide-and-seek, etc.).

Teaching sexual safety and privacy rules

- Bathrooms are private; others don't enter when someone is bathing or using the toilet.
- Doors are closed when someone is changing or using a bathroom.
- Bedrooms are private; other children enter only with an adult.
- Clothing is worn when one is in the presence of others.
- One should knock and wait for permission before opening a closed door.

Encouraging open communications

- Listen to your child when he/she shares feelings, problems or worries— compliment your child for sharing.
- Help your child figure out what to do about their worries. Avoid just saying 'Don't worry' or 'It'll be okay'.
- Give your child permission to share both negative and positive feelings.

Limiting experiences that increase sexual thoughts

- Don't expose your child to movies, soap operas, or music that show sexual or violent themes.
- Interrupt sexual jokes, stories, and language and describe how this can harm others.
- When adults engage in sexual behaviours, they should do so in private settings where they cannot be observed.
- Talk with your children about their sexual concerns and give clear, consistent messages about what is and is not okay.
- Give clear messages about when and where masturbation or touching one's own private parts is okay and having healthy, non-abusive thoughts while doing this.
- Videos and magazines containing graphic violence or sex should not be stored or used by adults at home.

Interrupting and redirecting misuse of power

- Discourage your child's bossiness or use of force to handle problems with another child. Help them problem-solve other ways to handle each situation.
- Encourage your child to feel good about their efforts. Discourage the belief that your child has to be best, the first, or have the most to be okay.
- Help your child say what they are feeling during acting-out behaviour. Help your child think about other ways to handle those feelings.
- Set limits and give clear messages that it is not okay to hurt someone else.

Correcting distorted thinking

- When you hear your child say something that supports their sexual behaviour problem, help your child to replace it with a corrected thought (such as replacing 'I can do what I want' with 'No, some things aren't safe, I have to follow some rules').
- Interrupt thoughts that allow your child to view themselves as being 'victimised' by

your discipline (such as, 'you don't love me because you said no' with 'I do love you; I don't want you to do this because…').

- Remind your child how others feel or are affected by their behaviours.
- Help your child say how they feel or are affected by problems that they experience.

Stay calm

- Help your child feel they can tell you about what occurred. You can let your child know you don't approve but want to help them not do it again.
- Let your child know that you want to hear when they are having sexual thoughts so you can help your child control the problem behaviours.
- If you observe your child starting to engage in a sexually abusive behaviour, calmly interrupt it, state why it is not okay, and help your child figure out how they can stop it or control it—stay with your child to provide control.
- If your child repeats a behaviour, let them know it is not okay but that you still want to work together to not let it happen again— know that your child may slip and it's a hard behaviour to interrupt because it 'feels good'.

Interviews with the Child

Social history

You will already have gathered considerable information in this area following the interviews with the parents. The aim of discussing this area with the child themselves is twofold: to build up some kind of rapport on a non-threatening topic as well as establishing whether any fundamentally different information has been given by their parents. It will cover developmental information, school information, peer relationships, areas of social competence, behaviour problems, and issues around their feelings. Despite differing views on many aspects of children who sexually abuse, there is consensus about the need to understand and then tackle the social aspects of the behaviour. Indeed, the younger the child, the more important this area of work becomes.

Family history and functioning

It is useful to cross-check information given by the parents, and the use of non-verbal exercises such as the ecomap and genogram can be useful engagement strategies.

Questions that need to be asked include:

- Any known history of abuse in the family.
- Family secrets/rules.
- How affection is shown and discipline administered.
- What solutions are applied to the presenting problems.
- Strengths and supports.
- Do they have secrets? That they are afraid of telling? Or threatened if they did? What would happen now if they were to tell?
- Has anyone touched them in a way they didn't like? When? Who? Did they tell anyone? Did it recur?
- Who are they frightened of, and why?

Sexual history and knowledge

It is important to follow a very simple format for collecting this kind of information, particularly as their abuse may be uncovered and relived by them. This is, however, a very essential block of the assessment work. To help us we can use the simple format offered by Smets and Cebula (1987):

Development

- What is your family's attitude about sex? Was (or is) it discussed easily or with difficulty?
- How old were you when you started to think about sex? Who did you talk to about it most?
- Tell us about the way you learned about sex. Who gave you your sex education? Do you feel you know everything? What questions do you still have?
- What kinds of sex play did you get involved in? With boys, girls? How much of the time that you spent with friends was spent on sex play, sex talk?
- How do they feel about the prospect of puberty? and masturbation ('playing with yourself')
- Have you ever had sexual contact during 'dating'?
- What was the most fun sexual experience you can recall?

About bad experiences

- Did someone else ever molest you sexually? How old were you when that happened? How often do you think back on that experience?
- Do you still feel angry about bad experiences? How so?
- Did you have other bad sexual experiences (other than being molested)? What did these experiences mean to you? (adapted from Smets and Cebula, 1987; p251).

We need to uncover whether the communication about sex and sexuality in the family is healthy or not. We then need to check out their level of knowledge and experiences about sex. Whilst we will have agreed names for body parts and language before the work begins, it is useful to take this a step further and assess their levels of understanding about them. This can be done by using body charts of males and females, or anatomically correct dolls, and get them to name all the body parts of each sex. We can then move on to consider which parts will be involved in sexual behaviours, and these may not correspond with what an adult or juvenile may identify. By asking them to explain why the parts are included on the list, we begin to understand how they view sex and sexuality. They can then be asked to describe the function of each of the sexual body parts they have identified, and this is helpful in assessing their level of understanding. We can use this session as an educational one by allowing them to ask questions of the workers. Any confusion can be clarified and we can reinforce any basic messages of privacy and their right to make all the decisions regarding their own private parts (Johnson, 1995; pp41–3). It is interesting that children can find it more difficult to know when a female is being sexually inappropriate or abusive towards them than they do with a male (Johnson and Freund, 1995; p68).

The nature of the child's sexually abusive behaviours

This work should be undertaken when all the available information has been collected and when some kind of relationship has been developed with the child. Cunningham and MacFarlane (1991) offered a very useful model for addressing the issue with the child, which I have adapted for this chapter.

Figure 12: A model for addressing children's sexually abusive behaviour (adapted from Cunningham and MacFarlane, 1991: pp31–5).

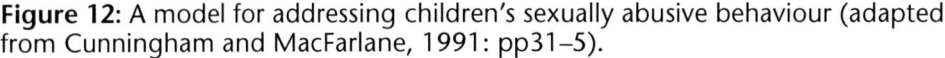

Does the child think they have a problem—other than being accused?

Do they admit to the sexually inappropriate or abusive behaviour?

Behaviour acknowledged	Behaviour denied

Details of incidents:
• who was involved (names, age, relationship)?
• who was touched/abused?
• why did they choose this particular child?
• what happened, where, number of times?
• was this their idea or did they copy it from someone? who?
• who initiated it?
• circumstances of the incident
  – where were the adults?
  – were they seen? by whom?
  – what led up to it?
  – was it a secret?
  – how did they silence the child?
  – was force threatened or used?
• was this incident similar to anything they have done before?
• had they had a drink and/or drugs before the incident?
• when did they stop and why?
• when and how were they caught?
• what was the reaction of their parents/family/others?
• what did they feel and do before, during and after the incident?
• what did the victim say? how did they get them to do it?
• what did they make the victim do?
• how do they feel now (e.g. remorse, guilt, shame, apathy)?
	• why would the other child(ren) lie about the incident(s)?
	• how do they feel about being accused?
	• what might have happened to them if they admit to anything?
	• what reasons do they have for denying the behaviour?
	
	N.B. Use any collateral reports or information to provoke discussions

From the information collected, is the sexual behaviour outside the normal range for their age? We do need to remember that children are capable of denial in much the same way as older abusers, so we need to guard against confrontation or punitive reactions. It is often much better to move on to a new area and return to the issue or point at a later time.

The child's attitude towards their sexually abusive behaviours

Questions that need to be asked include:
- Does the child accept any responsibility for their behaviour?
- Do they blame someone else for the problem? Who? For what?
- Do they accept and understand other people's concern about their behaviour?
- Are they frightened they have done something wrong?
- Who else knows about the child's behaviour? Does their child know this? How do others feel?
- What has the child said and done about their sexual behaviours?
- How do they feel about letting you help them?
- What areas do they want to change? Please list.
- What areas do they not want to change? Please list, and
- Will they let anyone help them in their effort to change? If so, who?

Motivation for their sexually abusive behaviours

Whilst it is important to try and isolate the individual motivators in each case, Pithers *et al.* (1993) set out some thoughts and emotions that accompany the behaviours:
- Some children feel more popular or grown-up when they engage in sexual behaviours.
- Some children believe they'll feel less weak or helpless if they can persuade another child to be sexual with them.
- Some children feel less worried about their problems when they experience sex.
- Some children feel excited doing something they know adults won't like, especially if they think they won't get caught.
- Some children are curious about sexual behaviours they have heard about or seen.
- Some children have been abused and repeat behaviours that were sexually stimulating, or they may be attempting to undo or understand the behaviour by repeating it.
- Some children like the way their body feels when their private parts are touched.
- Some children don't know that it's not okay to make another child do sexual behaviours.
- For some children, the behaviour has become a habit; they might feel unable to stop, and
- Some children think it's fun, not recognising how their behaviour affects others.

In a sexualised family environment, there may be a resulting preoccupation with sex or a need to dominate: either of these can result in sexual behaviours (Green, 1984). Neglected sibling groups sometimes become sexually interactive, whilst in others the motivating force may be curiosity. It is clear that the sexually saturated culture children grow up in is contributing to an alarming maturity about sexual matters in children (e.g. soaps and films) and when paired with the 'sexual revolution' (such as the relaxed standards on virginity) and the sexually charged home environment, the assessment task becomes acutely more difficult. The task for the workers is to differentiate whether the behaviour is the product of an overtly sexual, violent, emotionally barren family environment or wider influences beyond the control of the parents and others. It is easier to address issues within the family such as re-negotiating supervision, the physical and sexual rules and boundaries in the home, and the changes can be more speedily implemented and monitored.

Fantasy

Workers need to ask themselves what fantasies or daydreams may drive the child to act out sexually. It is often not the sexual sensation that drives them, and this was highlighted when Cunningham and MacFarlane (1991) gave examples of the kinds of cognitive distortions in children: 'my body is dirty; I can't feel anything; and I am a bad person' (p58).

Children who sexually abuse describe physiological arousal to a range of different emotions. Children who live in unstable and unpredictable environments frequently experience different states of physiological arousal. They seek to discharge such arousal quickly. The physiological arousal and feelings are paired with the environmental factors and the arousal is sometimes sexual or sometimes emotionally aggressive. Johnson (1993) also noted that sexually preoccupied children often have more highly developed fantasies than other children who molest, and are often reluctant to change their sexual behaviour (p3).

We can use a feeling journal or a fantasy/daydream log to capture the particular issues for the presenting child. Here, they can be asked to record the things that excite them, that scare them, that get them angry, turn them on, that they can't help thinking about, etc.

Victim issues

With children who sexually abuse there are different sets of victim considerations: to what extent does their own abuse contribute to their behaviour, how far are they able to empathise with the victim of their behaviour, and what part, if any, did the victim contribute to the incident?

Their own abuse as a contributing factor

Johnson and Freund (1995) found that less than half of sexually abused children manifest sexual behaviours of concern, whilst in the UK, the work of Dey and Print (1992) found that all of their sample had either been sexually abused or had witnessed sexual abuse in the home. Johnson and Aoki (1993) found that children who have been both physically and sexually abused engage in a greater variety of sexual behaviours than do those who only experienced sexual abuse. The work of Friedrich *et al.* (1988) differentiated between internalised and externalised behavioural responses in sexually abused children. They found that the frequency, severity, the sex of the abuser and the child, were factors most associated with internalised behaviour, whilst the duration, the abuser, and the sex of the child determined any externalised behaviour such as anger. Children under the age of seven are more likely to be victims of sexual abuse themselves (Friedrich *et al.*, 1992). Workers therefore need to be cautious when they assess this area as there are no sexual behaviours that are exclusively engaged in by sexually abused children.

Empathy with the victim

We need to understand how they feel towards their victim, how they begin to understand the impact of their behaviour on others, and how they can make up for what they have done.

The role of the victim in the abuse

Cantwell (1995) pointed out the need to assess the contribution (if any) the victim made to an instance of inappropriate sexual interaction. Some children who have been victims will try to re-enact their own abuse by getting another child to act the part of the abuser. One victim can involve others, who in turn involve others, and it can therefore be very difficult to identify the initial source of the behaviour. We also know that unchallenged, such behaviour is accepted as the norm by their peers. In the longer term, they need to develop empathy for their victims, recognise appropriate boundaries, and to master new skills in problem-solving, anger management and social skills.

Motivation to change

We need to be clear around several areas:

- Is there a need for continued work with the child? And his family?
- Have they tried to change in the past? What was the outcome?

- Are they willing and able to engage in further work? Are they able to generate any solutions to the identified problems?

- Are they able to effect any changes?

- Are they supported by the parents? Or constrained by them?

- Will a mandate be needed to ensure the continued co-operation of the child and/ or the family? Can one be secured? How?

- What are the contra-indications for treatment?

- What is the treatment prognosis?

- What is the prognosis without any further work?

Feedback and Report

The feedback needs to consider the concerns uncovered about the child, the families behaviour, any identified areas for future work, and whether a mandate or change of contact arrangements/placement are indicated. The headings in this section can be used as a framework for a report. The sessions with the child and the parents can be followed by an observational session of the family together to assess areas like interaction, communication, and behaviours. We can also discuss issues with siblings to try and uncover concealed information, or subsequently as part of a longer term child protection plan.

References

Calder M.C. (1997). *Juveniles and Children who Sexually Abuse: A Guide to Risk Assessment.* Lyme Regis, Dorset: Russell House Publishing.

Cantwell, H.B. (1995). Sexually Aggressive Children and Societal Response. In Hunter, M. (Ed.). *Child Survivors and Perpetrators of Sexual Abuse: Treatment Innovations,* pp79–107. Thousand Oaks, CA: Sage.

Cunningham C., and MacFarlane, K. (1991). *When Children Molest Children.* Orwell, VT: Safer Society Press.

Dey, C., and Print, B. (1992). Young Children who Exhibit Sexually Abusive Behaviour. In Bannister, A. (Ed.). *From Hearing to Healing: Working with the Aftermath of Child Sexual Abuse,* pp105–29. London: Longman.

Friedrich, W.H., Grambsch, P., Broughton, D., Kuiper, J., and Beilke, R.L. (1991). Normative Sexual Behaviour in Children. *Paediatrics,* 88: pp456–64.

Friedrich, W.H., Grambsch, P., Damon, L., Hewitt, S., Koverola, C., Lang, R., Wolfe, V., and Broughton, D. (1992). The Child Sexual Abuse Behaviour Inventory: Normative and Clinical Findings. *Psychological Assessment,* 4(3): pp303–11.

Friedrich, W.H., Urquiza, A.I., and Beilke, R.L. (1988). Behaviour Problems in Sexually Abused Young Children. *Journal of Paediatric Psychology,* 11: pp47–57.

Glasgow, D., Horne, L., Calam, R., and Cox, A. (1994). Evidence, Incidence, Gender and Age in Sexual Abuse of Children Perpetrated by Children: Towards a Developmental Analysis of Child Sexual Abuse. *Child Abuse Review,* 3: pp196–210.

Green, A.H. (1984). Child Abuse by Siblings. *Child Abuse and Neglect,* 8: pp311–17.

Griggs, D.R., and Bold, A. (1995). Parallel Treatment of Parents of Abuse-Reactive Children. In Hunter, M. (Ed.). *Child Survivors and Perpetrators of Sexual Abuse: Treatment Innovations,* pp147–65. Thousand Oaks, CA: Sage.

Howard, A. (1993). Victims and Perpetrators of Sexual Abuse. In Dwivedi, K.N. (Ed.). *Groupwork with Children and Adolescents: A Handbook,* pp220–32. London: Jessica Kingsley.

Johnson, T.C. (1993). Childhood Sexuality. In Gil, E., and Johnson, T.C. (Eds.). *Sexualised Children: Assessment and Treatment of Sexualised Children and Children who Molest,* pp1–20. New York: Launch Press.

Johnson, T.C. (1995). *Child Sexuality Curriculum for Abused Children and their Parents.* Self-Published.

Johnson, T.C., and Aoki, W. (1993). Sexual Behaviours of Latency-aged Children in Residential Care. *Residential Treatment for Children and Youth,* 11(1): pp1–22.

Johnson, T.C., and Freund, C. (1995). Assessing Young Children's Sexual Behaviours in the Context of Child Sexual Abuse Evaluations. In Ney, T. (Ed.). *True and False Allegations of Child Sexual Abuse: Assessment and Case Management,* pp49–72. New York: Brunner/Mazel.

Pithers, W.D., Gray, A.S., Cunningham, C., and Lane, S. (1993). *From Trauma to Understanding: A Guide for Parents of Children with Sexual Behaviour Problems.* Brandon, VT: Safer Society Program and Press.

Ryan, G.D., and Blum, J. (1995). *Childhood Sexuality: A Guide for Parents.* Denver, CO: Kempe Children's Centre.

Ryan, G.D., Lane, S.L., Davis, J., and Isaac, C. (1987). Juvenile Sex Offenders: Development and Correction. *Child Abuse and Neglect,* 11: pp385–95.

Smets, A.C. and Cebula, C.M. (1987). A Group Treatment Programme for Adolescent Sex Offenders: Five Steps Towards Resolution. *Child Abuse and Neglect,* 1: pp247–54.

Chapter Three

Young People who Sexually Abuse: A Framework for Engagement and Initial Assessment

Simon Goulding and Martin C. Calder

Children and young people account for at least one-third of all reported sexual offences in England and Wales, discounting those young people who do not get reported to the police. Whether or not they get a service is highly dependent on a number of factors:

1. Prosecution and admission of guilt.

2. Prosecution and finding of guilt.

3. Identification of behaviour as sexually abusive.

4. Willingness of child care/child protection system to accept responsibility and provide a service.

5. Availability of experienced staff to undertake work.

6. Agency willingness to purchase specialist services.

7. Existence of effective inter-agency procedures to ensure relevant children and young people come to the attention of the appropriate agencies.

The ability of the professional agencies to undertake assessments and provide effective intervention remain arbitrary, and prone to subjective issues regarding:

- Different and competing priorities within the interacting agencies.

- Different legislative and intervention requirements.

- Financial constraints.

- Conflicting value systems within the interacting agencies.

- Professional resistance to intervene rooted in lack of interest, knowledge or fear.

- Poor understanding of other agencies' responsibilities.

- Isolation of professionals and agencies.

- Unwillingness to provide resources to enable intervention.

Masson (1995) found that whilst child protection procedures regarding young people who sexually abuse others have become common, there is considerable variation in local arrangements. She notes that staff within agencies, involved at some level with young abusers, identified a set of concerns relating to systems, co-operation and communication between agencies. These concerns included:

- Lack of clarity as to responsibility.

- Lack of specialist services for assessment and treatment.

- Problems in the placement of young abusers.

- Inadequate training, supervision and managerial support.

Masson also found that unless the local arrangement was delivered via a dedicated project then practitioners reported a relatively low degree of time allocated and a limited amount of clinical experience gained. Many of these themes have recently been echoed by the Thematic Inspection undertaken by the Probation Inspectorate (1998) into services for sex offenders. Whilst praising the extensive development of services for adult offenders which has occurred almost entirely during the 1990s the report found that:

> The largest and most worrying gap in provision was for adolescent sex offenders, responsibility for whom did not lie solely or principally with the probation service. There appeared to be no coherent national strategic approach and in many of the areas inspected no provision specifically designed to tackle sexual offending by adolescents.
>
> (HM Inspector of Probation, 1998)

Calder (1999) identified a conceptual framework in an attempt to provide a unifying approach for Area Child Protection Committees (see Figure 13). Calder (1999) argues that each ACPC needs to develop shared aims and purposes about the work, which needs to be set in a local mandate, standards, structures and resources. This is essential because of the conflicting views held by the child care and youth justice systems.

Once a corporate baseline is established, a philosophy of intervention is required as well as clarity about respective roles and responsibilities. The next stage is to develop local policy, procedures and practical guidance.

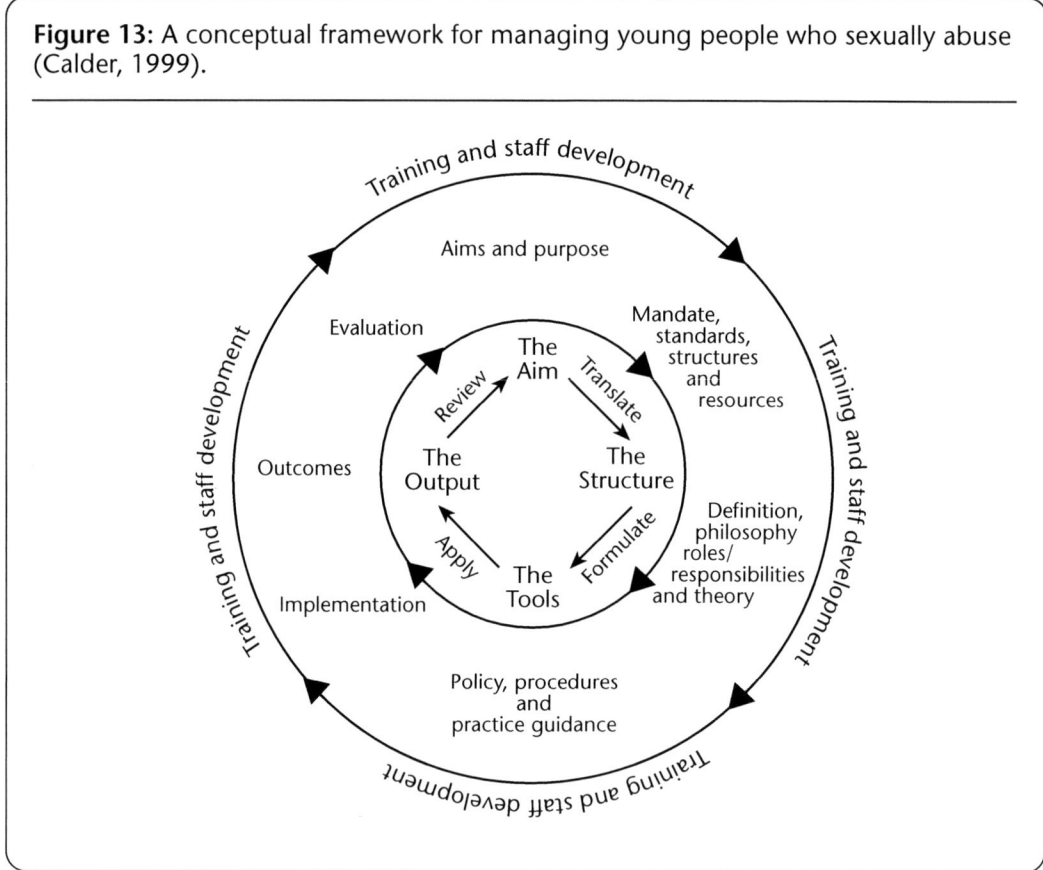

Figure 13: A conceptual framework for managing young people who sexually abuse (Calder, 1999).

Calder (1997a) (see Figure 14 overleaf) identifies the key conflicts between the two key systems charged with the management of young people who sexually abuse: child protection and criminal justice systems. These have the potential to become exacerbated by the development of Youth Offending Teams (with their ASSET documentation) and the introduction of NAF (DoH, 2000). This brings differences between *Children in Need* and *Children in Need of Protection*, with the first category allowing young people, their carers and families to refuse services. This leaves a gap in provision at a critical early stage in the intervention process, and this is unfortunate when there is a real potential for change if engaged in a tailored programme of work.

Figure 14: The battle for lead responsibility (adapted from Calder, 1997a).

	Child Protection	Criminal Justice
Principles	Interventionist. Grow into behaviour, which escalates over time. Legal mandate needed for the work to be completed.	Diversionary approach. Grow out of their behaviour. Innocent until proven guilty.
Supporting	*Working Together* (DoH, 1999) Diversion is collusion, allowing the abuser and their family to minimise their behaviour. Diverted cases are more likely to re-offend.	Practice wisdom (e.g. most young people stop offending at 16–17 years of age). 80% cautioned do not re-offend. Those referred to court most likely to re-offend. Court confusion over change of approach.
Benefits	Broadens the focus of intervention away from only those convicted. Widens the available options. Reinforces this group as children 'in need'.	Allows professional–young person partnership. Prevents stigma and labelling. Diversion avoids mixing delinquent youths together as peer group.

Working Together to Safeguard Children (DoH, 1999) identifies and recommends new procedures regarding children and young people who commit offences. The requirement to hold a child protection conference in respect of young abusers is removed unless they are a victim of abuse themselves. It also identifies the following:

Three key principles should guide the work with children and young people who abuse others.

● There should be a co-ordinated approach on the part of youth justice, child welfare, education (including education psychology) and health (including child health and adolescent mental health) agencies.

● The needs of children and young people should be considered separately from the needs of victims.

● An assessment should be carried out in each case; appreciating that these children may have considerable unmet developmental needs, as well as specific needs arising from their behaviour.

Area Child Protection Committees and Youth Offending Teams should ensure that there is a clear operational framework in place within which assessment, decision-making and case management takes place. Neither child welfare nor criminal justice agencies should embark upon a course of action that has implications for the other without appropriate consultation.

In an assessment of a child or young person who abuses other relevant considerations include:

● The nature and extent of abusive behaviour. In respect of sexual abuse, there are sometimes perceived difficulties in distinguishing between normal childhood sexual development and experimentation and sexually inappropriate, or aggressive behaviour. Expert professional judgement may be needed, within the context of knowledge of normal child sexuality.

● The context of the abusive behaviour.

● The child's development, and family and social circumstances.

● Needs for services, specifically focusing on the child's harmful behaviour as well as other significant needs, and

● The risk to self and others, including other children in the household, extended family, school, peer group or wider social network.

This risk is likely to be present unless:

The opportunity to further abuse is ended, the young person has acknowledged the abusive behaviour and accepted responsibility and there is agreement by the young abuser and his/her family to work with the relevant agencies to address the problem.

(DoH, 1999: pp70–1)

Given the clear shift in the way we are expected to manage young people who sexually abuse, it has become essential that we develop effective procedures which will enable work to be undertaken with this group, and that consideration is given to the development and training of specialist staff teams to undertake this area of work.

Goulding (1999) developed Lancashire's procedural response (see Appendix One) which are consistent with the requirements of Section 6 of *Working Together to Safeguard Children* (DoH, 1999). The procedures have been developed in the Chorley area in conjunction with Social services child care, youth justice, probation, and the police; and is expressed in flowchart form in Figure 15 below.

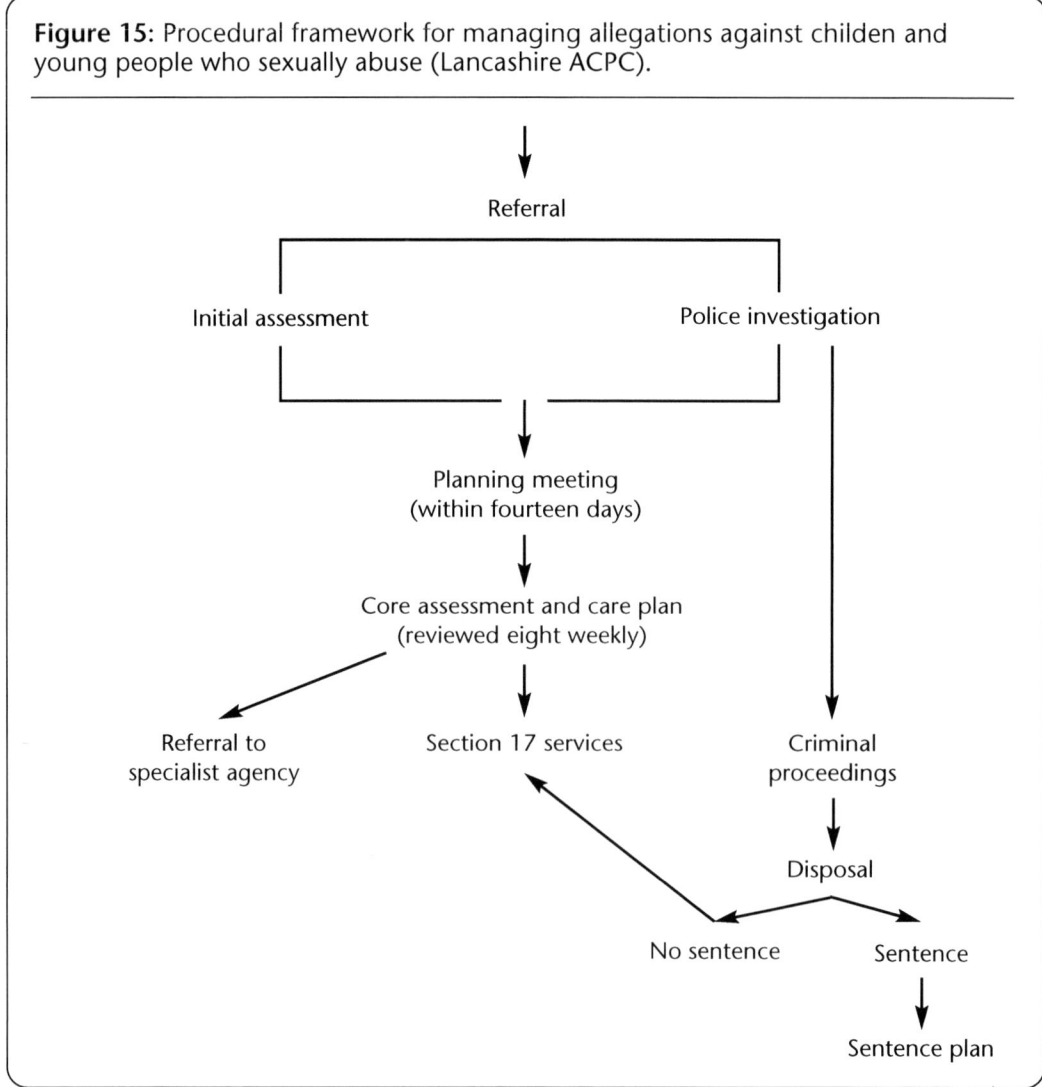

Figure 15: Procedural framework for managing allegations against childen and young people who sexually abuse (Lancashire ACPC).

Initial Assessment and Engagement

When approaching an initial assessment, it is important to consider the following: your philosophy of intervention; who the appropriate people may be to undertake the assessment; which source information is required and from where will it be accessed; the time-scale of the assessment; the primary purpose of the assessment; the parameters of confidentiality and with whom it is to be shared; and the decisions which are likely to be taken, and by whom, as a consequence of the assessment.

The impact on a child or young person's life who has sexually abused will have far reaching consequences in their immediate life and on their own emotional, psychological, sexual and educational development. Young people who commit sexual offences are often rejected by their families or carers; excluded from school, removed or rejected by their peer group, or placed in custody or the care system (LASOP, 1999). It is clear, therefore, that these young people feel a great sense of oppression. This is important when we look at the young people in the assessment process, so long as any acknowledgement of their experiences does not lead to a reinforcement of their distorted thinking or to collusion with any attempt to legitimise their behaviour. It is also important to acknowledge that we cannot import knowledge about interventions with adult abusers to work with children and young people who abuse or risk factors about future risk (Beckett and Brown, in progress).

Lancashire Adolescent Sex Offender Programme (LASOP) data collated between August 1998 and March 1999 in respect of 36 referrals found the following:

36 young people (12–16 years): 80 known victims

a) Legal orders made:

- No order   15
- Care Order   2
- Caution   3
- Supervision Order   8
- Probation Order   5
- Custody   3

b) Nature of offence:

- Incest   2%
- Rape   17%
- Unlawful sexual intercourse   9%
- Indecent assault   48%
- Gross indecency   10%
- Indecent exposure   14%

c) Relationship to victim:

- Babysitting (non relative)   3%
- Stranger   9%
- Brother   3%
- Sister   16%
- Half sister   6%
- Other relative   6%
- Both relative and non relative   9%
- Friend/acquaintance   48%

d) With whom young person had lived for majority of their life:

- Both parents   67%
- One parent   14%
- Other relative   12%
- Independent living   6%
- Custody   10%

e) Young person's placement following allegation:

- Looked after by local authority 36%
- With one or both parents   36%
- Other relatives   12%
- Independent living   6%
- Custody   10%

The most important factor in these figures to bear in mind is where young people lived before and after the disclosure of abuse and its impact on the assessment process.

Purpose and Process of Initial Assessment

The purpose of the initial assessment is:

- To collect information to inform the decision-making process about immediate management. For example, to consider the safety of the children the young person has ongoing contact with (home, school, community, extended family, etc.); and to consider where the young person should live (e.g. foster or residential care, extended family, or remain at home).

- Collect details about the nature of the abuse and the particular situational contexts in which it has occurred (such as in the house, at school, babysitting) and consider how the abuse was developed, i.e. grooming behaviours (game playing, use of bribes, threats).

- Consider any predisposing (e.g. family attitudes, friends, a history of abuse) or precipitating (opportunity) factors for the abuse.

- Consider the likelihood of repeat behaviours, (bearing in mind there are no predictive indicators from research).

- To identify the potential for the development of an appropriate 'treatment' programme.

- Future risk management based on a more comprehensive assessment.

- Consider whether a legal mandate is necessary for the work, or whether it is possible to engage the young person and their family/carers on a voluntary basis. It is important not to mistake compliance for

co-operation in making these decisions (adapted from Calder, 1999b).

The NAF (DoH, 2000), discussed and critiqued by Calder in Chapter One, identifies that assessment should not be regarded as an event but as a process, and that decisions should be made as part of the assessment process, not pending the outcome of the assessment. This is challenging to those undertaking an initial assessment since we know that, at best, the focus will be on the event(s) and possibly, the pattern. The assessment will not have had the opportunity to focus on the structure underpinning the abusive behaviour (Senge, 1990).

Senge (1990) distinguishes three levels of problem analysis and response.

- *Event*: looking at the immediate problem, treating it as a singular event, and applying a quick fix reactive solution that does not address underlying causes.

- *Pattern*: looking at trends, patterns of similar events in a wider context, assessing longer term implications, and learning to respond to changing situations.

- *Structure*: looking at the underlying structures, attitudes, perceptions, power relations, values and belief systems that enable the patterns, and identifying what support their continuance, and how this can be changed.

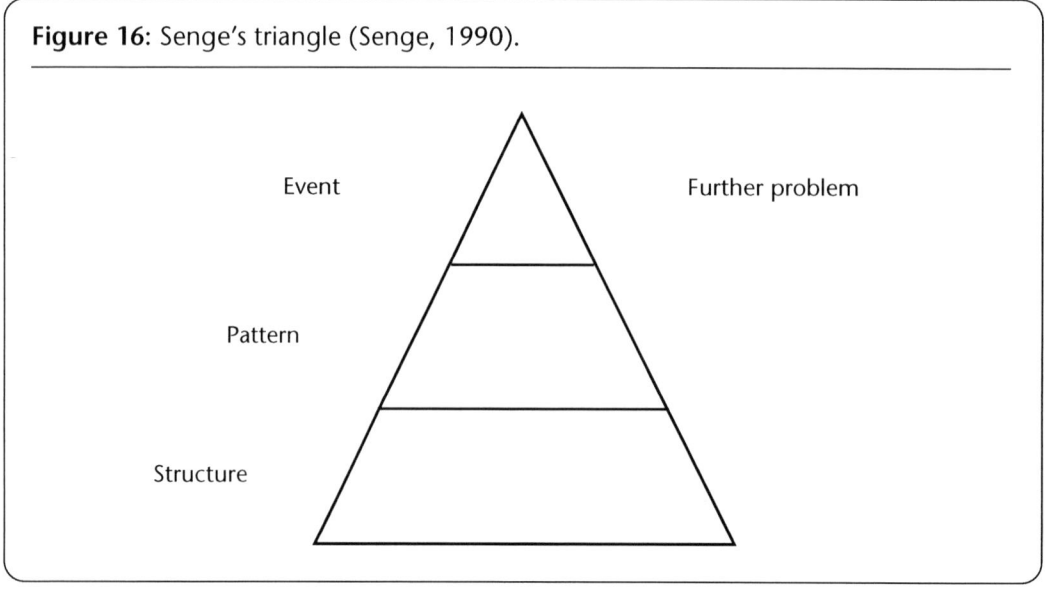

Figure 16: Senge's triangle (Senge, 1990).

Event   Further problem

Pattern

Structure

In considering factors associated with children and young people who sexually abuse, the following are key areas about which to gather information.

- Level of co-operation/compliance with assessment process.
- Family functioning and attitudes.
- Nature of sexual acts.
- Length of offending history, including non-sexual offending.
- Frequency of offending sexually (with reference to the amount of access to potential victims).
- Frequency and range of non-sexual offences, considering whether such offending could include any sexual motivation.
- Degree of inappropriate arousal/fantasy.
- Nature of cognitive distortions.
- Degree of aggression/overt violence present in offences.
- Victim selection characteristics.
- Availability/access to victims.
- Factors which precipitate offending.
- Degree of home, employment, school stability.
- Presence of other addictive or abusive behaviours.

- Honesty and degree of admittance of behaviours.
- Nature of social relationships.
- Internal motivation to change.
- External factors motivating change.
- Previous intervention regarding sexual offending.
- Personal responsibility for offending.
- Personality/psychopathic disorders.
- Level of intellectual abilities (Calder, 1997a).

The assessment is not to decide on the guilt or innocence of the young person or to employ subjective statements regarding the behaviour, i.e. 'I'm sure he won't do it again, it was a one off, it is out of character'. It is a consideration of the available information in order to enable agencies to take informed decisions. The process of collecting information should be viewed as a partnership between involved agencies; social services, health, police, Youth Offending Teams, as should the decisions made as part of the assessment process (Calder, 1999b). A consultation record for gathering initial information is produced as Appendix Two.

Calder (1999b) produced a framework, which utilises the respective skills of social workers and youth justice workers in the initial assessment process. The following framework provides child protection workers with some ideas about essential information required about the abuser:

Areas to be covered

Who has made the complaint–the victim or someone acting on their behalf?

How was the activity revealed?

Was the victim a sibling, friend or stranger? What are the implications for where the abuser lives? Are there contact implications?

The young person

Social history: serves three purposes–to gather developmental information that may help to explain their abusing behaviour; details of their recent history will help to identify contemporary factors which may have contributed to the current cycle of offending; and it unravels their personality style, their ability to recount events and their general willingness to disclose. It should include educational history, peer relationships, anger, assertiveness, self-esteem and self-contempt, social competence, health and medical history. The area of social skills is central to understanding the origins of the abusive behaviour, and the younger the child, the more important this becomes.

Patterns of their behaviour, or familial patterns of abuse.

Willingness to co-operate with the agencies involved? Reluctance should increase concern and may be an indicator that a prosecution is necessary.

Risk to the child exhibiting the behaviour

Dangerous networks.

Neighbourhood response to the behaviour–on behalf of the victim(s) as well as the abuser.

Legal consequences.

Exclusion from home, school or community?

Future life consequences.

Risk of suicide or self-harm?

Psychological or psychiatric assessment indicated?

View of parents or carers of the victims.

Family assessment

Full details of all members of the relevant present/past household?

What do the parents believe happened?

What are the family reactions to the behaviour? How supportive are the family? Do they deny or minimise the abuse or try to shift the blame? Will they support or hinder the comprehensive assessment of the young person? Is a prosecution necessary to ensure this happens? It is important to remember that the parents can be the biggest motivating factor for the young abuser facing up to their responsibilities for the abuse.

Family dynamics: interaction and differences.

Management of intra-familial abuse: balancing protection of victim and siblings with support to the abuser and the need for the abuser to undertake assessment work and face up to their responsibilities.

Family history: particularly any previous suspicion of abuse/reports of inappropriate behaviour?

What observations have they made of the young person's sexual attitudes and behaviour?

Care and control strategies: particularly any management strategies suggested or deployed.

Sexual attitudes and practices within the family, interaction, knowledge, etc.

Parental stress: environmental and employment.

Parental and sibling victim experiences.

The following framework utilises the skills of the youth justice workers and guides them through the information required to look at the offence(s) and the likelihood of repeat behaviours. The timing of this work is dependent on client admission or denial.

Nature of behaviour: e.g. any evidence of planning? Evidence of targeting vulnerable children (e.g. handicapped) or those with distinguishing characteristics (e.g. blond hair)? What, if anything, did the young person do to gain access to the other children (e.g. create opportunities)?

The act itself: How did the sexual contact take place? Is it through mutual agreement and negotiation, or is there covert aggression, coercion or bribery? If so, this usually indicates an abusive relationship, and may indicate that the abuser knew that their behaviour was wrong. The circumstances of the offence may give some clear indications of the degree of fear, humiliation and intimidation experienced by the victim.

What is the age difference between the persons involved? The greater the age difference, the more inappropriate the sexual activity. There could be a difference in functioning as well as chronological age—either emotional immaturity or intellectual functioning. The social relationship is therefore important, particularly if there are clear power differentials or if the abuser is in a position of authority over the victim, e.g. babysitting.

Consent needs careful examination: as consenting to sexual activity means giving informed consent, e.g. consent is freely given and implies a full understanding and a freedom to say no. Consent is different to co-operation or compliance. The lack of resistance does not imply that informed consent has been given.

Escalation: Has the young person committed previous sexual offences? Examine their previous record to determine any pattern or change in pattern. Has the abuse become more frequent or elaborate? Any increase in aggressions should increase concern.

Denial: Does the young person admit or deny the offence? How honest have they been regarding the details? What levels of responsibility are they accepting for what has happened? What distorted explanations are they presenting to justify their behaviour? Attempts to minimise or deny the offence or shift the blame should increase concern.

Level of empathy with the victim: How do they think their behaviour has affected the victim? Where is the victim now? How do they feel about that? Do they think about their victim now? Do they think about them often? Do they think they hurt their victim? If yes, in what ways? Do they think the victim was partly to blame? Why? Describe their feelings for the victim before, during and after the abusive incident. Get them to describe how they think the victim felt during and just after they had abused them.

Risk of repeat behaviour: Previous criminal history. Frequency: How persistent is the sexual activity? Has the frequency increased? Frequency is an important indicator of repeat behaviours. Patterns. Willingness to co-operate with the agencies involved? Reluctance should increase concern and may be an indicator that a prosecution is necessary. Sexual knowledge, experience, fantasy, attitudes, beliefs and behaviour. Consequences of their abusive behaviour versus benefits of continuing their behaviour.

Risk to the child exhibiting the behaviour: Dangerous networks. Neighbourhood response to the behaviour—on behalf of the victim as well as the abuser. Legal consequences. Exclusion from home, school or community? Future life consequences.

Crucial decisions need to be taken after the initial information has been collected. Calder (1997b and 1999b) has explored these and which might include:

Criteria for considering the need for a legal mandate and reasons for prosecution should include:

- There is no support for intervention, or collusion with the young person by parents/carers.
- The young person denies the behaviour.
- When the young person's behaviour elsewhere indicates poor impulse control, e.g. non-sexual offending.
- Where the young person does not have a stable base/home or stable positive supporting relationships.
- When they are abusing alcohol or drugs.
- When they have used force or violence in the commission of the offence.
- When the abuse has been of a serious nature and this needs to be reflected by a court appearance.
- When attitudes continue which justify the use of violence or force, and/or the belief that the young person has done nothing wrong.
- No agreement from the young person, family or carers to intervention.
- The need to hold the young person accountable for their behaviour.
- It registers the offence for future tracking and management purposes.
- It provides agencies with control over contact and placement decisions.

Placement decisions regarding the young person remaining in the home should take account of:

- The level of parental/carer co-operation, their acceptance of professional concern about the behaviour and their willingness to support and facilitate professional intervention with the young person.
- The parents/carers are willing and able to supervise and monitor the young person's behaviour and set safe and controlled boundaries.
- The degree of violence/force used in the offence.
- Any history of general anti-social or violent behaviour.
- Any evidence of psychopathy (psychosis, addiction, etc.) in the young person.
- The degree to which there is acknowledgement of the above by the young person and acceptance of intervention.
- The young person possesses enough social, intellectual, and psychological resources and skills to adequately manage their day-to-day life and can demonstrate conflict-free functioning in a number of areas of their life.
- There are dependable treatment and support services available in the community, and
- The victims are aware and any future risk can be contained.
- Whether it is reasonable to expect parents/carers to take responsibility for the safe management of the young person.

The placement of a young person away from their original home should be considered if:

- Issues of abuse in the family are not or cannot be resolved, and where denial and secrecy is maintained.
- The young person is already alienated from the family/carers or this occurs as a consequence of their offending.
- There is the clear potential or evidence that abuse within the home is likely to resume or is still taking place.
- The abusive behaviour demonstrates an escalation in frequency, type and/or use of threat or coercion.
- The young person denies the offence, or admits to it, but it is very serious in nature.
- There are victims within the immediate or extended family.
- The threat of retribution exists and there is

a need to remove the young person for their own safety or that of their family or carers.

- The parents/carers are unwilling or unable to contain and manage the young person's behaviour.
- The sexual abuse is one feature of a highly delinquent pattern of behaviour.
- There is a history of unresolved mental health problems or chemical dependencies.
- There is a known history of abuse within the home situation.

The choice of placement for a young person with extended family members, foster care, community home, residential placement, hostel accommodation, secure accommodation or custody should take account of the following:

- The level of denial from the young person and/or their family.
- The positive benefits or negative consequences to the young person of continuing to have contact with their family, peer group, etc.
- Community safety issues and the nature of the offence, i.e. the use of violence, use of weapons.
- Compulsive patterns in the history of offending.
- The degree and nature of substance and alcohol misuse.
- The degree and nature of previous delinquent or aggressive behaviours.
- The degree of psychopathology that limits their ability to understand or learn from the consequences of their behaviour.
- The availability of supportive family or community network.
- History of unsuccessful previous treatment programmes, taking into account why they did not meet set objectives.
- Potential risks that may be posed to other children/young people already living in the planned placement.
- The ability of carers/staff to manage the

young person and to provide them with appropriate support.

- The need to contain or restrict the young person's liberty commensurate with the nature of their general and sexually abusive behaviour. It is worth noting here that decisions to detain or restrict liberty should take account of Article 5 of the Human Rights Act (1998).

Decisions about continuing education placements

It is the responsibility of the education department to help individual schools reach a decision about whether to allow a young person who has an allegation or a conviction of a sexual nature back into the school setting. The following are some questions that should be considered when exploring the issue of educational placements:

- Did the abuse occur in school or against a pupil attending the same school and if so what are the views of the victim(s) and their family(s)?
- What are the known risks regarding further offences occurring in the school? Consideration should be given here to information gathered about the young person's offending history.
- Can the school or other agency provide adequate supervision to manage risk whilst enabling the young person to continue his/her attendance without such supervision causing unnecessary stigmatisation?
- Have any complaints been made by other parents against the young person? If so, when and in respect of what behaviour?
- Is the school willing to support a treatment plan that may require the young person to be absent on a regular basis?

Summary

Decisions about a young person's legal status, living arrangements and educational placement need to be carefully considered. A young person already facing the serious consequences of their abusive behaviour can, confronted by separation from family, friends and their known environment, suffer traumatic consequences that induce or reinforce conflict and resistance. Rather than reducing risk, this can have the effect of creating difficulties in motivating and engaging them in any future assessment or treatment work. The process of initial assessment at best is only likely to provide limited information upon which to base decisions regarding legal intervention and placement; the level of denial and minimisation that they hold regarding their abusive behaviour; and the possibilities for their engagement in a programme of work to address their abusive behaviour; and perhaps the starting point of such a programme.

Engagement and Motivation

The purpose of talking to young people as part of the initial assessment is not to gain a complete confession of their offending, develop victim empathy and to develop a relapse prevention plan. If this is the expectation then it is likely to fail and is likely to increase the young person's resistance to future intervention in the process.

The purpose of the initial assessment is to gather information, but more importantly to provide the young person with motivation to participate in a substantive assessment and treatment programme. This can be achieved by getting some degree of acknowledgement that either they or other people see the abusive behaviour as a cause of problems or difficulties that need to be addressed. As part of the motivational process, it is important to identify what may prevent them from talking about their behaviour and how they may benefit from talking about their abuse. The cost-benefit approach is presented by Figure 17.

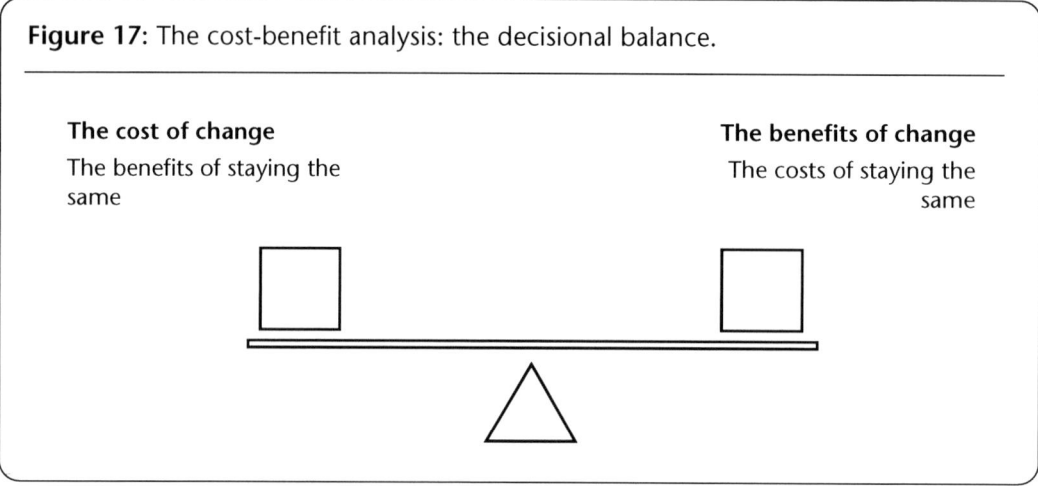

Figure 17: The cost-benefit analysis: the decisional balance.

The cost of change
The benefits of staying the same

The benefits of change
The costs of staying the same

Key ideas

- The worker style is a powerful determinant of client resistance and change.

- Confrontation is a goal, not a style.

- Argumentation is a poor method for inducing change.

- A young person's motivation can be increased by a variety of worker strategies.

- Motivation emerges from the interpersonal interaction between the young person and the worker.

- Ambivalence is normal, not pathological.

- Helping a young person resolve ambivalence is a key to change.

Individual work with young abusers should be undertaken by two workers. Less resistance is usually encountered when the workers involved in the process of assessment have not been involved in the decision-making process, i.e. as keyworkers or the authors of pre-sentence reports. The point at which the initial assessment focuses on the possibility of change is either at the pre-contemplation or contemplation stages of the cycle of change (see Figure 18) which is described in detail by Calder in Chapter Eleven. In attempting to persuade the young person in favour of change rather than staying the same, the motivational tasks for the workers should be:

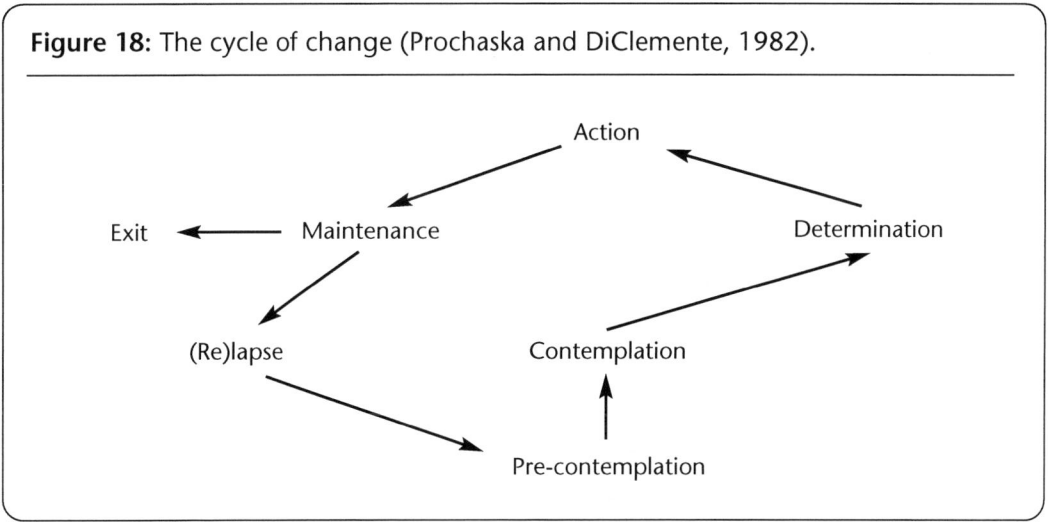

Figure 18: The cycle of change (Prochaska and DiClemente, 1982).

Pre-contemplation: raise doubts, developing the young person's understanding of risks and problems associated with their behaviour to either themselves, others or both (depending on resistance).

Contemplation: Identify and get the young person to identify reasons for change. These may be their own view of others about reasons for change. It is equally important to get them to establish what the risks of not changing are. Overall, the workers need to encourage the young person to believe in their own ability to change themselves and as a consequence of what happens to them.

Miller and Rollnick (1991) consider the five basic principles of motivational interviewing (see Figure 19).

Figure 19: The principles of motivational interviewing (Miller and Rollnick, 1991).

Express empathy	The worker needs to develop and communicate genuine empathy for the client's ambivalence. Empathy is generated when the worker develops an understanding of the process of change and learns that ambivalence is normal. Empathy is communicated though the skill of reflective listening.
Avoid argumentation	Argumentation—even in its milder form of direct persuasion—with an ambivalent client invariably produces defensiveness in the client, which is not a motivational success. Workers need to avoid argumentation at all times and be able to recognise the dangers of becoming trapped in a confrontation-denial discussion.
Roll with resistance	Too often resistance and denial in clients are seen as a personality characteristic inherent in offending. In fact resistance is simply an

	expression of ambivalence, and ambivalence is normal. In motivational interviewing, the momentum of resistance is seen as something to be used to good advantage through the application of various motivational strategies.
Deploy discrepancy	Discrepancy can be defined as that uncomfortable sensation that one is not where one would like to be. Particularly for clients at the pre-contemplation stage, ambivalence is characterised by a lack of discrepancy between what the individual is doing and what the individual wants to do. Another principle of motivational interviewing is that motivation develops as a sense of discrepancy between the present behaviour and important goals is created. Although the worker should encourage examination of discrepancy, it is essential that statements of discrepancy are made by the client only, not by the worker.
Support self-efficacy	Particularly for clients at the contemplation stage, what often holds a person back from change is a fear of not having the strength or ability to see it through. Consequently, it is essential that a worker demonstrates belief in the possibility of change, assists the client to identify their own problem-solving strengths, and gives the client hope by offering a range of alternative change strategies. Statements of self-efficacy should be drawn out from clients and should always be reinforced.

In considering what motivational interviewing should be, it is useful to identify what are not motivational questions or tactics. Miller and Rollnick (1991) suggest that the following responses do not constitute reflective listening:

- Ordering, directing or commanding.
- Warning or threatening.
- Giving advice, making suggestions, or providing solutions.
- Persuading with logic, arguing or lecturing.
- Moralising, preaching, or telling clients what they 'should' do.
- Disagreeing, judging, criticising or blaming.
- Agreeing, approving or praising.
- Shaming, ridiculing or labelling.
- Interpreting or analysing.
- Reassuring, sympathising or consoling.
- Questioning or probing.
- Withdrawing, distracting, humouring or changing the subject.

Interviewing young people requires the worker to be flexible and imaginative and to be able to develop an understanding of the young person's situations and problems. In preparing for the interview the workers should obtain information not only about the offences, but as far as possible other aspects of their life—family, friends, school; what has happened to them and where they are in the decision-making process; and what options are being considered for their future, their level of emotional/intellectual functioning. It is also important to know about what young people are interested in, i.e. computer games, television programmes, music etc. in order to develop rapport with them in the initial stages of interview.

As part of the initial interview workers should address the following:

- Ask the young person what their understanding is of why they are there.
- Ask the young person what their expectations of the assessment are and how they think it may affect them.
- Check out what the young person's expectations of others are, i.e. family, social worker, court, from the assessment.

- Describe the interview process, i.e. length of time of each session, how often, who else will be spoken to and why, with whom information may be shared, why, and rules regarding confidentiality.

- Describe interviewer's experience of this area of work indicating that you will not be shocked, angry, surprised, embarrassed etc. by anything which is said.

- Acknowledge that it may be difficult, upsetting, embarrassing, for the young person during and after the sessions.

- Check out what may prevent the young person from talking about their abuse i.e. fear of prosecution, rejection by their family/carers, rejection/victimisation by friends/peers, suspension from school, imprisonment, being put in a children's home.

- Ask about whom they have had positive relationships with in the past and whom they have had negative relationships with.

- Ask about who they have positive and negative relationships with/feelings towards now.

- Find out whom they want to have future positive relationships with. Do they think that negative relationships they have can become positive and how that might happen?

- Bear in mind that some of the above may already have occurred and check out how they feel about these issues.

- Explain that you have read the accounts given by the victim(s) and themselves and ask them to explain what happened before, during and after the abuse.

- Ask how it felt/how they felt.

- Ask how the abuse was discovered and what happened as a consequence.

- Ask how they felt about being caught/found out and what they feel about/towards the person(s) who made the allegations.

- Ask about who they feel is responsible for what is or has happened to them.

- Ask what they feel they have been responsible for in terms of their behaviour and what has happened as a consequence.

- Ask how much influence they feel they have over what is happening to them, the decisions and the people who are making decisions.

- Get them to consider how they might improve their position as a positive benefit of considering change.

- Provide information about what a treatment programme, i.e. individual or group work, might involve for them and ask how they might feel about undertaking such work.

Asking direct questions is not the only method of obtaining information and may create resistance and suspicion, so use alternative methods such as:

- Develop a family tree and ask about the nature of the relationships the young person has with the people identified.

- Draw a picture of the young person's social networks and life patterns to identify where they go and what they do and check out how they feel about peer and adult relationships and how they feel about their life experiences.

- Draw a lifeline with the young person to chart chronological experiences and ask them to describe these experiences and their effect on the young person, i.e. school, moving house, birth of siblings, etc.

- Draw a sexual history life line, identifying where they learnt about, heard about sexual behaviour, i.e. personal abuse, videos, TV, magazines, sex education, sexual relationships they have had and with whom. Situate the sexual abuse on the line and check out how this behaviour relates to their other experiences.

- Use cartoons to draw the offence(s) to develop a picture of what happened when the abuse occurred and develop the picture forwards and backwards in time to create an overall picture of what led up to the abuse, what happened and what occurred afterwards. Use this picture to identify how the young person controlled the situation to ensure they could avoid detection, what they said to the victim, how they overcame victim resistance, convinced themselves the abuse was OK, how they were feeling before, during and after the abuse.

- Draw a jigsaw, filling in some pieces with information which is known, and identify in the empty pieces of the jigsaw either the information or answers to questions which are needed in order to complete the jigsaw or picture. It is sometimes more effective to build this picture up over a series of sessions using one session to identify the missing pieces or questions and agreeing with the young person that they will answer the questions at the next session.

An alternative method as part of a motivational process is to identify the questions and discuss with the young person what may be difficult for them or what might prevent them from answering or talking about what happened in order to explore ways of 'tipping the balance' for them to feel they have more to gain than to lose. Again, it is sometimes more helpful to leave the answers to the questions to the following session, having gained an agreement from the young person about their willingness to think about the questions before the next session and provide answers.

Case Illustration

The following illustration demonstrates how some of these methods can be utilised and the importance of multi-agency agreement in developing an initial plan of assessment.

John was 13-years-old. At the age of 11 an allegation of indecent assault was made against him by a three-year-old girl. This was investigated jointly by the police and social services. The girl was unable, because of her age and understanding, to provide a clear account for evidential purposes. On interview John denied the allegation and was supported in this denial by his family. A year later a further allegation was made of indecent assault by a 12-year-old male with learning difficulties and again the boy could not provide a clear account and John denied the allegation.

A year later when John was 13 a further allegation was made of indecent assault by a 14-year-old boy, again police and social

services investigated but due to insufficient evidence and John's denial, no further action was considered possible criminally. Because John did not live in a household with other children it was not considered appropriate to convene a child protection conference.

Social services and the police agreed that intervention was appropriate and the police agreed that as long as John did not admit to any more serious offences than those he had already been investigated for they would agree to support a process of voluntary rather than legally mandated work with agreement that they would not re-interview or seek to prosecute John in respect of the previously made allegations.

The police agreed that it was more important to support the possibility of successful intervention than to increase resistance and denial by pursuing an investigation, which would ultimately be unsuccessful.

John's family agreed to his being involved in an assessment, although this agreement was based on their view that if they did not, there would be further intrusion into their lives by the police and social services, rather than an acceptance that there may be any validity in the allegations made against John. Despite this, they were willing to support John attending sessions to talk about the allegations.

The first session concentrated on what might be preventing John from talking about the abuse, why he should talk about the abuse and how he might benefit, and addressing his worries and fears about what might happen if he talked about the abuse. During the first session John identified the following:

Reasons why John won't talk about touching other children:

- Frightened of getting told off.
- John is embarrassed about talking about it.
- Worried that the police will be involved.
- Frightened what my dad might say.
- Worried what my mum might think.
- Worried I might be taken away from my dad and put into a children's home.
- Worried I might go to prison.

Reasons why John should talk about touching other children:

- It's really hard to carry on telling lies.
- Brian and Jane can help John if he talks to them.
- Talking to Brian and Jane will help me not to do it again.
- It will help me to stay out of trouble.

Because we had already made agreements with the police about prosecution and because John was living in a household with no other children we were able to address John's worries and provide him with reassurances about what would happen or not happen if he talked about the abuse.

Worries:

- Brian has told John that the police will not be involved.
- John will not go to prison.
- John will not go to a children's home. He will stay at his dad's.
- Brian and Jane are not embarrassed and will help John not to feel embarrassed.

This first session was concluded with an agreement that:

- In order to help John he would need to talk about what happened with the three children.
- John had touched the three children in a sexual way.
- And that at the next session John would talk about: Where did it happen? How often did it happen? How did John feel about what happened? Excited, worried, frightened about getting caught?

Having gained John's confidence and developed his willingness to engage in the assessment process by identifying the benefits of him doing so, and addressing his reasons for not doing so it was then possible to continue with further intervention to address his offending behaviour and to work with his family in order to help them accept and understand John's behaviour.

Conclusion

Initial assessment of children and young people who abuse is not rocket science, but because of the emotive nature of the behaviour and the risks involved concerning the continuation of such behaviour, this area of work, like other aspects of social work, creates anxiety amongst those asked to undertake such assessment. As long as a clear, shared, multi-agency plan is developed taking account of and ensuring that:

- Views and attitude of family carers are obtained.
- There are clear statements and accounts from victims and/or witnesses available.
- There is an agreed mandate and identified purpose for undertaking the assessment.
- Adequate time is allocated to property supported workers with access to consultation to plan and undertake the work.
- Expectations of the outcome of the initial assessment are not set too high.
- The assessment should as far as possible be taken at the child/young person's pace.
- The assessment is based in an understanding of the child/young person's previous and current life experiences and an understanding of their intellectual and emotional abilities.
- The process is based on the abilities of workers to motivate children and young people to overcome difficult issues.

The experience of workers and young people of the assessment process should be reasonably positive and meet required objectives and goals.

References

Beckett, R. and Brown, S. (in progress). *Multi-site Research Project*. Oxfordshire Psychology Service.

Calder, M.C. (1997a). Young People who Sexually Abuse: Towards International Consensus. *Social Work in Europe*, 4(1): pp36–9.

Calder, M.C. (1997b). *Juveniles and Children who Sexually Abuse: A Guide to Risk Assessment*. Dorset: Russell House Publishing.

Calder, M.C. (1999a). A Conceptual Framework for Managing Young People who Sexually Abuse: Towards a Consortium Approach. In Calder, M.C. (Ed.). *Working with Young People who Sexually Abuse: New Pieces of the Jigsaw Puzzle*, pp109–50. Dorset: Russell House Publishing.

Calder, M.C. (1999b). Young People who Sexually Abuse: A Framework for Initial Assessment. *Child Care in Practice*, 5(3): pp262–80.

DoH (1999). *Working Together to Safeguard Children*. London: HMSO.

DoH (2000). *Framework for the Assessment of Children in Need and their Families*. London: HMSO.

Goulding, S. (1999). *Good Practice Guide and Procedural Response to Working with Young People who Sexually Abuse*. Lancashire County Council Social Services Directorate.

HM Inspector of Probation (1998). *Exercising Constant Vigilance: The Role of the Probation Service in Protecting the Public from Sex Offenders. Report of a Thematic Inspection*. London: HMSO.

Jenkins, A. (1998). Invitations to Responsibility. In Marshall, W.L., Fernandez, Y., Hudson, S., and Ward, T. (Eds.). *Sourcebook of Treatment Programmes for Sexual Offenders*. NY: Plenum.

Lancashire Adolescent Sexual Offender Programme (1999). Annual review report.

Mann, R. (1996). *Motivational Interviewing with Sex Offenders: A Practice Manual*. Hull: Nota/Bluemoon Services.

Masson, H. (1995). Children and Adolescents who Sexually Abuse Other Children: Responses to an Emerging Problem. *Journal of Social Welfare and Family Law*, 17(3): pp325–36.

Miller, W., and Rollnick, S. (1991). *Motivational Interviewing: Preparing People to Change Addictive Behaviour*. NY: Guilford Press.

Senge, P. (1990). The Leaders New Work: Building Learning Organisations. *Sloan Management Review*, 32(1).

Abuse by Children and Young People (Lancashire ACPC)

Definition

Any child or young person under the age of eighteen years who is alleged to have committed an abusive act towards another person (including adults).

1. Referral

1.1 Allegation of any abusive act carried out by a child or young person should be referred to the relevant child care team.

Referrals regarding intra-familial will usually come via family, police family protection syndicate or other professionals.

Referrals involving a 'stranger' or abuse of an adult should come via the police, probation service, or youth offending team. Since these allegations are usually investigated by the CID, referrals should be made by the officer responsible for the investigation.

1.2 On receipt of a referral regarding allegations made in respect of a child or young person the case will be allocated by the case manager to an appropriate child care social worker.

1.3 In cases where referrals come directly to the social services directorate, the allocated social worker will make referrals to the relevant police department and local youth offending team to determine the most appropriate method of investigating the allegations.

1.4 A multi-agency planning meeting for children and young people who abuse will be convened (see Section 2) to consider the incidents; police investigation; management or risk and management of the alleged abuse. This meeting will usually take place after the initial investigation, and will be convened under Section 17 of the Children Act.

1.5 If the alleged abuser is aged ten or over the police may conduct an interview under PACE. Youth offending team workers may be required to act as an 'appropriate adult' where a parent or carer with parental responsibility is unable to attend the interview. In certain cases, e.g. intra-familial abuse, it may be desirable and in the alleged abuser's best interests for a youth offending team worker to act as the appropriate adult.

1.6 No youth offending team worker who has been involved in the assessment of a similar previous offence should act as an appropriate adult for the same young person.

2. Planning meeting to consider initial assessment and the management of risk

2.1 A planning meeting will be convened within fourteen days of the receipt of a referral. In respect of the final warning under the Crime and Disorder Act the planning meeting may need to be convened earlier.

2.2 Responsibility for convening a planning meeting will fall to the allocated child care team social worker. The meeting will be chaired by a representative of the child care team.

2.3 At the meeting relevant information gathered about the young child or young person and their family will be shared in order to manage issues of immediate risk posed to others as a consequence of the abusive behaviour. Issues such as the young person's level of understanding of the alleged incidents, as well as the response of their family or carers to the allegations should be considered. Possible immediate supervision should be considered. This information should be available from the social worker, police officer, probation officer or youth offending team worker.

2.4 A representative from the youth offending team will attend the planning meeting in order to:

a) Establish a youth offending team link with any ongoing work commissioned by the planning meeting.

b) Obtain information (initial assessment) that can contribute to any decision making regarding a final warning (Crime and Disorder Act).

c) Obtain information which may assist in preparing a court report regarding the child or young person.

d) In the case of a child aged under ten, enable the youth offending team to determine whether an application for a Child Assessment Order under the Crime and Disorder Act should be made to the relevant court.

2.5 The planning meeting will formulate a written plan (which will be reviewed on an eight weekly basis) regarding initial assessment of risk posed to others, placement, health and education provision and the implementation of an appropriate treatment plan.

Attendance will be expected from representatives of relevant agencies involved, i.e. health, education, youth offending team, probation and the police.

3. Situations when a child protection case conference may be convened in respect of an alleged abuser

3.1 An initial child protection case conference should be convened only when the child or young person is considered to be personally at risk of significant harm (i.e. they have been or continue to be likely to be a victim of abuse) and not that their own abusive behaviour placed them at risk from others (i.e. retribution).

3.2 In such cases a child protection conference and plan should only deal with the protection of the child or young person from further significant harm to themselves. A separate planning meeting should always be convened as per Section 2 to deal with their abusive behaviour towards others.

4. The assessment

4.1 Arrangements for an initial assessment will be made at the planning meeting. This assessment will usually be jointly undertaken by the allocated child care team social worker and youth offending team worker; following the guidance contained within the DoH framework for assessment and ASSET guidance for youth offending team workers.

4.2 The assessment should consider the following:

- The nature and extent of the abusive behaviours. In respect of sexual abuse, there are sometimes perceived to be difficulties in distinguishing between normal childhood sexual development and experimentation and sexually inappropriate or aggressive behaviour. Expert professional judgement may be needed, within the context of knowledge about normal child sexuality.
- The context of the abusive behaviours.
- The child's development, and family and social circumstances.
- Needs for services, specifically focusing on the child's harmful behaviours as well as other significant needs.
- The risks to self and others, including other children in the household, extended family, school, peer group or wider social network.

  The risk is likely to be present unless; the opportunity to further abuse is ended; the young person has acknowledged the abusive behaviour and accepted responsibility and there is agreement by the young abuser and their family to work with relevant agencies to address the problem.

4.3 A more comprehensive assessment of risk will be undertaken by practice team social workers and youth offending team social workers which may also include a referral to psychiatric or psychological services or other specialist agency.

4.4 Advice should be given to the young person at the commencement of the assessment process, that if further offences are disclosed, these will be reported to the police, but will retain the support of the social or youth offending team workers should the police decide to take further action.

Lancashire Adolescent Sex Offenders Programme Consultation Record

Consultation is available to any Lancashire based professional.

Topics for consultation may include case management, assessment or therapeutic issues for young people whose sexual behaviour is a cause for concern. Consultation meetings take place, by arrangement, at Calder House, Highfield Road North, Chorley, PR7 1PH on Fridays. Any person seeking a consultation should phone, E-mail or write to request an appointment.

The completed form must be received at LASOP no later than one week before the appointment.

Please attach recent court reports or depositions (if being charged with an offence) or a case summary together with details of the offences or concerning behaviour together with dates and outcomes.

1. **Referrer's name**

2. **Agency/Discipline**

3. **Address**

4. **Contact details**
    a) telephone
    b) fax
    c) E-mail

5. **What do you want to explore in the consultation meeting?**

6. **Who will attend the consultation meeting?**

7. **Young person's details:**
    Name
    DOB
    Address
    Racial and religious details

8. **Nature of placement:**

Parents home	( )	Foster care	( )	Residential est.	( )
Secure est.	( )	Hostel	( )	Independent	( )

    Other (specify)

    Legal status:

No order	( )	Care Order	( )	Supervision Order	( )
Secure Order	( )	Probation Order	( )	Cautioned	( )

    Other (specify)

Where applicable

Date of order   Duration of order

9.   **Criminal history**

Has young person ever been charged with an offence of any kind?

Yes   ( )   No   ( )

If yes what was the outcome?

NFA   ( )   Caution   ( )   Prosecution ( )   In process   ( )

If subject to criminal order:

Date of order	Type of order	Nature of offence	Date finished	Comments

If young person is due in court, detail when charges made, pleas made and any recommendations being considered:

10. **Have other family members criminal history?**

Yes   ( )   No   ( )   Not known   ( )

If yes please give details:

11. **History of victimisation**

Has young person suffered any form of abuse?

Yes   ( )   No   ( )   Not known   ( )

If yes please give details (including details of child protection measures):

12. **Have other family members been abused?**

Yes   ( )   No   ( )   Not known   ( )

If yes please give details (including details of child protection measures):

13. **Details of abusive behaviour**

Most recent concerns:

14. **Previous concerns:**

15. **Young person's response to discovery of abusive behaviour:**

16. **Parents or carers response to young person's behaviour:**

17. **Details of previous behavioural or psychological concerns not identified above:**

18. **In regard to referred behaviour has young person been subject to:**

    Joint police/SSD investigation   ( )
    Police investigation   ( )
    SSD investigation   ( )
    Own case conference   ( )
    Planning meeting   ( )

19. **Victims details:**

    Number of victims known: Age range (at offence):

    Gender of victim(s):   Length of abuse:

    Relationship to young person:

20. **Does young person have contact with victim(s)?**

    Yes   ( )   No   ( )

    If yes please give details:

21. **Are the victims receiving professional help?**

    Yes   ( )   No   ( )

    If yes please give details:

22. **Education and employment**

    Is young person in full time education?

    Yes   ( )   No   ( )

23. **Does young person have special educational needs?**

    Yes   ( )   No   ( )

    If yes please give details:

24. **If young person has gained or is taking exams give details:**

25. **Is the young person in or seeking employment?**

    Yes   ( )   No   ( )

    If yes please give details:

26. **Has young person had involvement with psychiatric or psychological services?**

    Yes   ( )   No   ( )

If yes please give details:

27. **Has young person history of chemical abuse?**

    Yes   ( )   No   ( )

    If yes please give details:

28. **Other health issues:**

    Advice given and recommendations made

    Further action required by LASOP consultants:

    Appointment for further consultation for:

    Signed: ....

    Name: ....
              LASOP Programme Worker   LASOP Programme Worker

    Date: ....

    Please use this space to feed back any corrections or comments to LASOP.

If you wish to forward feedback please copy this page and return to LASOP, c/o Calder House, Highfield Road North, Chorley, PR7 1PH

Chapter Four

The Comprehensive Assessment of Juveniles who Sexually Abuse

Martin C. Calder

It is important that each of the identified areas is addressed in the course of the assessment, which will normally take place over 8–10 sessions. Workers need to select the materials according to the specific circumstances of the presenting case.

The assessment needs to cover the following areas:

Individual Social History

Taking a social history serves three purposes: to gather developmental information that may help to explain their abusing behaviour; details of their recent history will help to identify contemporary factors which may have contributed to the current cycle of offending; and it unravels their personality style, their ability to recount events and their general willingness to disclose (Beckett, 1994: p63). Social and family histories in cases where juveniles sexually abuse are in general no different from those usually collected save that a more detailed exploration of a history of sexual and other abuse should be conducted in their immediate and extended family (Smith and Monastersky, 1986).

We should also gather information on the family, the individual's place within it, their memories, feelings individually and generally within the family, any alliances or enemies, any health, religious or financial issues, and how these impact on the individual. We need to explore their perceptions of their family life as we need to try and understand how they have integrated their experiences, e.g. how resilient are they? We also need to explore whether either of the parents has ever confronted them directly or indirectly about their sexually abusive behaviours. We can then break this component down into smaller, more specific parts for which more specific tools are available to elicit the necessary information. These include:

Educational history

It is important to establish their overall level of academic achievement, parental expectations, the presence or absence of problems within the school, either with relationships, disciplinary problems, attendance, isolation, scapegoating or rejection. It is helpful to gather positive as well as negative information, e.g. involvement in school activities, sports, plays, etc. Monck and New (1996) found that 33 per cent of the abusers in their sample had statements of special educational needs, which was significantly more than might be expected of a non-psychiatric adolescent population. James and Neil (1996) found that full attendance at secondary school is problematic for this group, only being achieved in 41.9 per cent of cases.

Peer relationships

We need to gather information that provides us with some idea of how they function within the school and outside, e.g. do they have a best friend or a number of friends? Are they in a gang? Are they of both sexes? Are their friends generally much younger, and if so, why?

Assertiveness

It is important to identify whether the juvenile exhibits assertive or non-assertive behaviour as a result of their feelings, thoughts and beliefs. This should not be confused with aggressive behaviour, which represents the inappropriate ways of expressing thoughts, feelings and beliefs. This is detailed more in Chapter Six.

Anger

Anger is an emotional reaction to certain kinds of stress, falling short of aggression. It needs to be understood in the context of the individual and their various contexts. This is detailed more in Chapter Six.

Self-esteem, self-concept and social competence

The significant factors are explored in detail in Chapter Six.

Health and medical history

This needs to include any experiences which may influence the behaviour, and self-harming behaviours and whether the young person might be suffering from depression (Gist *et al.*, 1994). James and Neil (1996) found that health concerns were either absent (67.7 per cent) or minor (29 per cent).

Non-sexual offending

It is useful to locate the sexually abusive behaviour within their overall pattern of delinquency. It should include their criminal record and anything for which they were not caught.

Drug and alcohol abuse

This needs to include the type (legal/illegal), method of use (oral/injection), frequency, etc. How they become involved with the substance(s), how they fund the addiction, whether they have had previous help to stabilise or withdraw from its use. What are the effects on the individual when 'high' or intoxicated? Workers should remember that these are key disinhibitors of sexually abusive behaviour. In taking detailed background information on the individual, the workers are starting to locate the sexually abusive behaviour within the overall pattern of delinquency and their family environment. The issues raised by this information are important as these influences in the short-term may have an impact on their longer term abusing pattern (NCH report, 1992: p14).

Family Composition, History and Functioning

The comprehensive assessment of the juvenile runs parallel to a comprehensive assessment of the parents, and a lot of information gleaned in each can be cross-checked in the course of the work. It is important that we establish clearly the family attitude towards both the abuse and the intervention, as well as considering their ability to protect. It is likely that the majority of the information in this section will derive from work with the parents and any observations or interactional assessments. The latter can be useful where there are concerns about who the abuser may be, but where their identity has not yet been disclosed by the victim.

Under family structure, we should cover:

- Flexibility regarding situational and developmental issues.
- How family decisions are made.
- How family members disagree and argue.
- How affection is shown.
- Who speaks for whom.
- Who protects whom.
- Secrets, what the family does not discuss.
- Level of comfort with individual differences.
- Recognition of conflicts and differences.
- How much input from outside the family is needed.
- Strength and consistency of the parent/executive system.
- How, or if, the children detour the conflict between the parents.
- Who else is closely involved with the family, e.g. church, grandparents, etc.
- Determine intra-familial alliances.
- Strength of boundaries between generations.
- Overt and covert family rules.
- Strength of sibling sub-system, and
- What is not working in the system that is producing sexually abusive behaviour.

Sexual History, Knowledge and Attitudes

The National Task Force on juvenile sex offending argued that the social and the sexual histories hold many keys to current functioning: their view of the world, behaviours and attitudes, self-image, and level of empathy. As such, this block is very important as it can generate useful information that will help us unravel what effect, if any, their early experiences may have upon their attitudes, values, knowledge and behaviour (Gist *et al.*, 1994). Saunders and Awad (1988) noted that few of us are trained in, or feel comfortable with, taking the kind of sexual history necessary in the assessment. This can be made easier by following two procedural steps: it is best taken after the workers have established a comfortable relationship with the juvenile, and it is important to have an outline of questions in mind prior to interview. We will each find our own questions and sequence with which we feel comfortable, and which matches the needs of the assessment (p574). The use of some structure allows the necessary information to be gathered at the same time that the workers stamp their control on the interview. We should always present as confident as the juvenile is not as likely to try things on as a result.

A structure for taking a sexual history:

- Any pre-pubertal sexual experiences
- The onset and impact of puberty—emotionally and behaviourally
- When were they aware of the changes that they would have to go through?
- Where, when, from whom and how did they learn about sex? Do they know everything? What questions do they still have? Can they easily talk about sex at home?
- Normal sexual experiences, e.g. ages of first non-genital and genital sexual experiences; number of sexual partners; when was their first sexual experience? Ask them to set out steps to making contact in a normal appropriate consensual way (meeting, going out, fantasy, petting, kissing, non-sexual cuddles, sex). Ask them to list everyone they have had a sexual experience with, including names, ages, gender, activity, etc. Does it include older partners?
- Histories of sexual abuse—Do they know what sexual abuse is? Tell them if they don't. Did anyone ever do any of these

things to them? Did they ever report it? To whom? What, if anything did they say or do about it? What happened to them? When? For how long, and how often? Was there ever more than one person abusing them? How do they think these experiences have affected their feelings/relationships/attitude to self/behaviour? Do they know anyone else who has been sexually abused?

- Questions regarding deviant sexual experience—Have they ever been punished for sexual activities? Have they ever sold sex? In what circumstances?
- Masturbation history and frequency—When did they start? Do they think it is harmful? When did they have their first wet dream?
- Sexual fantasy—Types used during masturbation as a sign of deviant arousal (Note: This is covered in detail in a later component).
- Sexual attitudes—individual and family. Who can they talk to most about sex?
- Effects of alcohol, drugs or pornography, if any, on sexual behaviour.
- Sexual orientation and any fears about homosexuality, particularly where males have abused males. Whilst this is an important area, we should clearly separate out sexual orientation from their abusive history, as there is no causal link. They can be asked about their most embarrassing sexual experience, or the one that they are most ashamed about. Have they ever had a sexual relationship with boys? Are they equally attracted to both sexes? If they feel they prefer boys, can or have they told anyone?
- Attitudes to women, men and children.
- Their understanding of consent, and
- Sexual deficiencies or abnormalities, e.g. no sexual education, impotence, premature ejaculation (adapted from Smets and Cebula, 1987).

The reader can also refer to formats for taking sexual histories of adults which may enhance this framework, e.g. Beckett (1994), Calder and Skinner (1999) and Faller (1990).

Sexual Fantasies, Cognitive Distortions and Arousal Patterns

Fantasy is defined as the 'product of creative imagination; mental pictures, images or representations of something not present' (National Task Force, 1993: p9). Sexual fantasies are defined as 'those thoughts and feelings that we have regarding sexual behaviour that we have done or would like to do, or sexual thoughts and feelings that turn us on, that arouse us' (Heinz *et al.*, 1987: p68). Exploring the nature of fantasies that precede or accompany sexual activity is often a problem with juveniles because they are too embarrassed to talk about them, and therefore co-operation is typically difficult to obtain. Insistence by the young person that they did not experience any sexual feelings or fantasies denotes minimisation and denial. These points will be covered later in this chapter.

Research has shown that sexual perpetrators approximate or rehearse sexual crimes through their sexual fantasies. Glueck (1956) reported that upward of 70 per cent of his subjects in sex offender groups reported having masturbation fantasies prior to acts of sexual aggression. Glueck also noted that the content of the sexual fantasies closely resembled the subjects' overt experiences, but that in fantasy, they became highly elaborated. Pithers *et al.* (1993) provided additional evidence that fantasy of sexual aggression almost always precedes the conscious plan and performance of sexual aggression. These masturbation fantasies can therefore indicate the purpose of an individual's sexually aggressive behaviour.

Dutton and Newton (1988) reviewed the recollections of sexual fantasies in eight adolescent males aged 13–17-years-old referred for sexual offences. They found that seven of the eight portrayed themselves as being in total control of their environment and other people in their fantasies. This needs to be considered alongside a general feeling of inadequacy and isolation outside of fantasy, where they are unable to deal with life's challenges and may be anxious over their penis size or inability to please the victims. They clearly viewed their environment as less threatening in fantasy.

Beckett (1994) offered us a range of working assumptions in assessing sexual fantasy:

- They are a guide to sexual arousal.
- They are constructed from memories attached to previous sexual experiences and also represent desired outcomes of future sexual encounters.
- The more long-standing the sexual fantasy, the greater the likelihood that it will be expressed.
- They are strengthened by masturbation.
- Deviant sexual fantasies may be more prevalent and accessible to assessment when self-esteem is low or threatened.
- Deviant and non-deviant sexual fantasies may co-exist. Thus, during masturbation, an individual may move between the two to sustain sexual arousal, and
- The relationship between deviant sexual fantasy and the behavioural expression of sexual deviancy is complex. While the presence of deviant fantasies increases the probability of sexual deviancy, it does not guarantee it (p75).

Wolf (1984) argued that sexual fantasy fulfils three roles:

- It acts as a disinhibitor towards the person being thought about.
- It reinforces the attraction towards the behaviour.
- It reinforces the rationalisations used in fantasy, which is the focus for masturbation.

In short, these fantasies serve as a cognitive rehearsal for deviant behaviour. The escape to fantasy puts them in control and they can then start targeting victims that match their deviant sexual interest. Indeed, if they fix their fantasy on a specific behaviour or individual, it will increase the need for, and attraction to, that behaviour or individual. Cognitively distorting the abuse allows them to overcome their own inhibitions and allows them to minimise and justify the abuse, thus making the unacceptable behaviour 'acceptable'. It is not unusual for guilt and embarrassment to follow (although this is often linked to their fear of getting caught), and this is usually pushed away quickly, reflecting a general inability to take any responsibility for themselves. As the process has not been broken, they continue in their pattern of abusive behaviour.

Cognitive distortions

A cognitive distortion is defined as 'thoughts which are based on erroneous perceptions; a misrepresentation of reality' (National Task Force, 1993: p8), or as 'a statement one makes to oneself which contains distorted information about the reality of the situation (e.g. an offender who sexually abuses children may say 'she seduced me', 'it's an education for the child', or 'it causes no harm' (Beck, 1976). To the outsider, such cognitive distortions amount to unreal excuses, although to the perpetrator they are functional as they control the level of guilt and anxiety they might otherwise experience as they repeat the abuse. When these distortions are processed by the juvenile, they are often represented as thinking errors, defined as 'patterns of thinking which are based on distorted perceptions, therefore seeming rational on the basis of some private logic but irrational in the light of societal reality' (National Task Force, 1993: p12). It can be said that this mode of thinking is the means by which the abuser is able to translate fantasy into action.

Steen (1993) pointed out that there are special kinds of distorted thinking common to most sex offenders. These include:

- Misinterpreting what their victim is thinking, such as believing the person is asking for sex when the person really isn't and doesn't want it.
- Excusing their sexual offences.
- Minimising the harm they have done, and
- Denying responsibility (pp25–6).

Most juveniles need to know that they made various types of thinking errors when committing their sexual abuse. Their thinking is not based on real facts. They may offer some of the following statements to justify their behaviour:

- They didn't stop me doing it.
- I think they liked it.
- I didn't hurt them.
- I only did it once or twice.
- I only touched them—nothing more.
- It happened on the spur of the moment.
- It happened to me.

- Someone has to teach them about sex.
- I was only showing her how to insert a tampon.
- I saw my friend doing it to her too.
- I get a buzz from doing it.
- I did it because I love them.

The abuser can be asked which of these apply to them, and what others they might want to add to this list. Steen (1993) has suggested that they be advised to ask the following questions of themselves if they are unclear about whether they are thinking correctly or incorrectly:

- Is this something someone might find harmful, embarrassing or unpleasant?
- Is this something I would feel uncomfortable telling my parents, teachers, friends about?
- Is this something I wouldn't like someone to do to me if I were their age or in this situation?
- Am I breaking any laws or rules by doing this?
- Would there be negative consequences if I were caught doing this? (pp27–8).

If they answer 'no' to all of the above then we might assume that their thinking is correct.

Research findings

- Becker and Abel (1985) have argued that cognitive distortions are a necessary prerequisite to the abuse as it allows the abuser to translate their fantasies into action. Despite this, Marshall *et al.*, (1991) found that only 21.7 per cent in their sample indicated that fantasies preceded their abuse. There is little clarity on the point at which fantasy of abuse actually occurs. It is clearly variable, and might only follow the abuse.

- Fantasies are most evident with those committing 'courtship-type' offences, such as voyeurism (Awad and Saunders, 1989). Rada (1978) confirmed that as high as 50 per cent of convicted rapists engaged in voyeurism, exhibitionism, fetishism or incest in their early adolescence.

- Most juveniles will probably not admit to masturbating, never mind admitting to fantasies that accompany it. Marshall *et al.* (1991) found that only 29.5 per cent recalled having deviant fantasies about children before they were 20 years of age.
- Marshall (1988) reported that those juveniles who reported usually or always using deviant sexual fantasies during masturbation had a higher number of victims than those who reported rarely or never engaging in deviant fantasising.
- Barclay (1973) studied male and female sexual fantasies and found that males mentioned visual aspects to their fantasies much more frequently, often reporting details about the appearance of female sexual characteristics such as pubic hair and breast size.
- Marshall and Eccles (1993) found that juveniles tended to show arousal to the children they abused rather than showing generalised arousal to all children.
- Freeman-Longo (1983) found that the average age at which sex offenders begin to have deviant sexual fantasies was 15. If they entertain them, then they develop a distorted thinking process that further condones the continuation of deviant thoughts, fantasies and behaviours. Longo (1982) found that the average age when juveniles who sexually abuse began to masturbate was 12.
- Pennell (1996) found no difference in cognitive distortions between juveniles who had been abused and those who had not. We can hypothesise that those who have, may well have more entrenched cognitive distortions.

Most juveniles are unwilling to discuss masturbation or fantasy. They may be far more willing to share dreams than fantasies. For those who deny dreaming, we should assume that most people dream whilst a small percentage may be unable to remember them (Breer, 1987: pp83–4).

The goals of the assessment are:

- To determine the content, duration, frequency and internal states that trigger or intensify the fantasies and how they find behavioural expression.

- To separate superficial distortions of defence from those that are more deeply entrenched, since the latter are commonly associated with a sexual preference for children and indicate an individual at greater risk of re-offending.
- To identify and elicit specific details of each distortion.
- To identify the perceived attributes, characteristics and behaviour of children which trigger such distortions.
- Whether certain moods or situations make such distortions more likely to occur.
- How they behave when they occur (Beckett, 1994: p68).

The identification of cognitive distortions is important, both to determine future risk as well as reinforcing to the juvenile that they feed their abusing behaviour which thus needs modifying (Jones and Lewis, 1990/91: pp44–5). Briggs (1994) advised us to be explicitly clear with ourselves and the abuser about the assessment of sexual fantasies. He recommended that we spend time educating the abuser and setting the scene before directly questioning them about their particular sexual fantasies. Here, we should explain that both masturbation and sexual fantasising are normal activities that often occur simultaneously. Sometimes several fantasies may be used within a single masturbatory episode. Sometimes, several fantasies will represent enactments of past relationships or will involve known partners but feature practices that have not been indulged in, and sometimes they will rehearse the abuse. It is realistic to target the control of, rather than the eradication of, such fantasies (p59).

Areas to cover

- Thinking patterns—What are they? When did they appear? How are they maintained? What part do they play in the development and maintenance of deviant sexual thoughts and fantasies?
- Attempt to obtain data on the content of their fantasies—being aware that most will be reluctant or completely unwilling to provide an accurate or correct account of their real fantasy activities.
- What percentage of their fantasies are deviant?

- Types of fantasies used during masturbation as a sign of deviant arousal patterns.

- Linking fantasy to the planning of the abuse, e.g. masturbating to a particular scenario, victim or behaviour. When did this start? How much planning went into the abuse? Has there been any change in their thinking since the abuse took place?

- Arousal patterns—are they present? When did they develop?

Tools to extract the necessary information include:

- Logging masturbation activities/fantasies over an agreed period, e.g. a week, recording date, time, fantasy and pleasure.

- Feelings journal—where we ask them to write down how they feel when they are having sexual fantasies, and how they enable the individual to get what they want.

Both these exercises allow us to gather information around how often each day they have a sexual fantasy, what type of sexual fantasy they are having most often, and what feelings they had before and after the fantasy. The goal is to help them understand the role of their fantasies in their behaviour, and for them to accept that they should not always act on them. Fantasies are normal, but acting on them is not. These can then be translated into a masturbation pie chart (Briggs, 1994) which displays the relative frequency of each fantasy as a segment and can highlight where any concerns exist.

- Brainstorm a list of excuses— rationalisations—distortions that they have used to 'justify' their sexually abusive behaviour.

- Rosebush fantasy exercise (Heinz *et al.*, 1987). On a piece of paper ask them to write a fantasy describing themselves as if they were a rosebush. Ask them to include the following:

  1. What you look like (describe your leaves, stems, and flowers).

  2. Describe in detail where you are growing.

  3. If a rosebush could see, what would you see? What sees you?

  4. Describe the weather today and most other days.

  5. Describe how you get nourished. Who feeds you, your roots, and the soil you are in; and where do you get your water?

  6. Describe those who care for you, if anyone does.

  7. Tell what is going to happen to you next week.

This exercise is helpful in getting the juvenile to understand the amount of detail that will be required when looking at more intimate fantasies. Workers always need to be aware that any materials used to elicit the necessary information can occasionally constitute a further source of fantasy stimulation.

Exploring the Alleged Abuse

This work should only be undertaken when some kind of worker/client relationship has been developed, and where the workers have collected and digested all the necessary information. In some situations, this may be reasonably quick, particularly if requested by the juvenile. If the assessment is being carried out with a young person who intends to plead 'not guilty' to a sexual offence, addressing the offence during the assessment is inappropriate. This should be deferred until after the court has established a finding of guilt. It is often useful to set aside two sessions for this crucial area of work, whilst also allowing the juvenile to change their information, based on either encouragement or direct challenge.

The workers need to prepare carefully for this session by obtaining, reading and digesting police statements, social services records, any criminal history and available psychiatric or psychological information. A good foundation of information is essential if we are to be in a position to challenge any denial, distortion, projection and/or rationalisations put forward by the juvenile. The availability of multiple sources of information means we are more likely to get somewhere close to the truth of what has happened. We have to accept that whilst we can use collateral sources to check any information given, it is unlikely this will extend to the sexual interest pattern of the juvenile. When all the information has been collected, it needs to be organised, e.g. the number of completed sex crimes by category, duration of deviant sexual interests by category, and reported ability to control deviant sexual interests (Becker and Abel, 1985: p111). Even here, we have to accept that we may be unable to identify types of sexual activity as they may be unknown or because we have inconsistent or incomplete accounts of the known offences (Howard, 1993: p228). The juvenile can be asked to prepare for the sessions by refreshing themselves with the details of their PACE interview.

The aim of this block is to compare the abusers account with that given by the victims (and others), and any changes that may appear as the process unfolds. It is the abuser's account that is more likely to be distorted. When asking the juvenile to tell their story in detail, we should ask them to describe:

- Aspects of preparation, e.g. fantasy/masturbation. Evidence of premeditation.
- Why and how they chose a particular victim (age, gender, race, ability, etc.), or could it have been anyone? Difference in age, physical stature and social status.
- How they created a situation in which they could abuse.
- Level of consent and power relationships.
- Whether drugs, alcohol, or both were a feature of the abuse.
- What they did to the victim. Full details of the nature of the sexual activity.
- What they required the victim to do.
- The response of the victim during and after the incidents.
- The extent to which persuasion, threats or coercion were used to obtain sexual contact, or how they convinced the victims to co-operate.
- Any co-abusers?
- What they did to try to keep from getting caught (e.g. lying). Level of emotional intimidation.
- How they ensured the victim maintained secrecy.
- How they themselves felt prior to, during and after the abuse.

- Whether they climaxed or later masturbated to climax whilst thinking about the abuse.
- The persistence and frequency of the sexual activity and whether there is any escalation in the nature and frequency of the abuse.
- Why they stopped when they did.
- Their understanding of how they were caught.
- Their feelings on getting caught, and
- The response of their family, friends, victims and others to the disclosure (adapted from Gist *et al.*, 1994; and Smets and Cebula, 1987: p250).

Saunders and Awad (1988) caution us to accept that the task of establishing the details of a sexually abusive incident is often quite difficult. DiGeorgio-Miller (1994) has argued that their comfort in discussing the intimate details relies on the comfort level of the assessors and the safe environment created by them. Desensitising ourselves pre-interview is one way of achieving this.

It is frequently useful to split the discussion around the sexual abuse into two sessions. For the juvenile, this allows them to reflect on what they have said, and allows them to return and provide further information, or clarify that already given. In the interim, they should be asked to go through their version of events with a parent to check their honesty outside of the assessment sessions. For the workers, this allows them the necessary space to go through the juvenile's version of the events and break it down into chronological segments, e.g. prior to the offence, the lead-up to the abuse, the incident itself, post-abuse and subsequent events. They can then work out a series of questions designed to take the juvenile through the blocks in minute detail, as well as identifying gaps that need to be plugged. Where the juvenile denies the abuse, the workers need to highlight loopholes and inconsistencies in the story, exposing to the juvenile that we believe the version given by the victims. Having stated this, it is often easier said than done. They are often very plausible and convincing in their denials, explanations and excuses, and it is not uncommon for workers to shift towards an acceptance of them, particularly where they are well articulated. The danger of collusion should never be overlooked or underestimated. Where denial persists, the workers have to decide whether to terminate the assessment or allow the discussion time on this block to be extended. The workers may also wish to seek further information from the victims in order to double check information, although this should never be relayed to the abuser as it is a breach of confidence, and may put them at greater risk. When moving into the second session where detail should be sought, we need to be very specific and refuse to accept vagaries. Examples of this include:

Aspects of preparation, e.g. fantasy/masturbation

- How old were they when they first attempted this kind of behaviour?
- Where did they get the idea for the offence?
- Did they plan it? To what extent? Premeditated, victim selected/premeditated, but no victim selected, or victim not known? How much time did they spend planning it? If not, was it opportunistic? How often did they masturbate around the time of the abuse? More than once a day? Once a week?
- When did they start fantasising about the abuse? The victim? The setting?
- Was the sexual abuse the primary intended offence?

Why and how they chose a particular victim

- Did they pick the victim, or could it have been anyone?
- How did they pick the victim? Behaviour they found sexually attractive (e.g. teasing or flirtatious)? Physical build, hair colour or style? Vulnerability? Clothes, jewellery, make-up? Unlikely to disclose given their ability to communicate?
- Was the victim simply available according to opportunity, e.g. babysitting, physical activity?

How they created a situation in which they could abuse

- Where did the abuse take place? Be specific. Why did they choose this place or setting? Was it isolated or dark?

- How did they approach the victim? What did you and they say?
- Did they create an opportunity where there was no adult or supervisor present?
- How did they get there and ensure the victim got there? Did anyone else know? Was anyone else there?
- Did you take them somewhere after they met? Why? How were they feeling? What mood were they in?

Were drugs or alcohol a feature of the abuse?

- If yes, what and how much was used? How was the drug taken—orally, intravenously, nasally?
- Was the victim drunk or high? Did you supply them? To what end? Did it induce compliance?
- Did the victim's presentation add to their sexual arousal?
- Do they think they have a drink or a drugs problem?

What they did to the victim

- What did they do and say to the victim? Before, during and after the abuse?
- How did it make them feel?
- What kind of games did they play with the victim?
- Did they kiss them? Where and how?
- Did they touch them? Where and why? How were they feeling at this point?
- Did they use a condom, lubrication, restraint?
- Did they take or use photographs?
- Was anyone watching them? Who and why?
- Did they both undress? Did they make them undress or did they do it for them?
- List all the different types of sexual activity they tried with the victims (e.g. exposing, oral, anal, vaginal sex, digital penetration, etc.).
- How many times did they abuse the victims?

- Over what period of time did this happen?
- Did they have an erection? Did they ejaculate? When? How many times?
- On a scale of 0–10, how strong were their sexual feelings during and after the abuse?
- Did the victim ask them to stop? When and why did they comply and why?
- What did they not do that they would have liked to have done?
- Why didn't they try these things out? Would they if they saw the victim again?
- Would they try these things with anyone else? Is there someone else they are attracted to now? What would they do if they were left alone with that individual?
- Were they successful in the abuse that they intended? If not, what stopped them from carrying it out?

The use of force in the abuse

- How did they get the victim to comply? What kind of threats did they use or act out?
- How sexually exciting was the use or the threat of using force?
- What instruments did they use, e.g. weapon? Did they show it to the victim?
- What did they say to them, e.g. threat to kill their pet, etc.?
- What prevented them from being more violent?

The sessions on the abuse undoubtedly place the workers in a powerful position compared to the juvenile, particularly where they are well prepared. This can induce considerable anger in the juvenile, particularly if they have to change their story a number of times. Their excuses and rationalisations need to be challenged and supplementary questions need to be constructed to add more detail. We should allow them the space and opportunity to ask questions of the workers. They should be allowed breaks where necessary, particularly where they are being challenged to fill in gaps or elaborate on partial information. Expect a distortion of belief and attitude when they are under pressure for a more detailed account. The aim has to be to challenge their distortions and help them move from a passive to an active account of their sexually abusive behaviour. In doing this, we are allowing them to accept the responsibility for, and the effects of, their behaviour. At the end of this block, we need to establish the degree of congruence between the accounts of the abuser and the victims. If others are identified in the abuse, then we need to establish the actions or words of the other person in the incident. This is not always a feature of juvenile sexually abusive behaviour, and this is represented by the findings of Monck and New (1996) who found that 72 per cent of their sample acted alone (p49).

Denial and Excuses

It is important to note that denial is not a fixed trait, but is expressed within the worker-abuser relationship. It is often motivated by fear of negative consequences, and can frequently be modelled on the behaviour of others. Workers have to understand the motivation for the young person using denial if they are to effectively tackle it in practice. There are many reasons why they may deny the allegations against them. These include the following, and are very similar to the list of consequences for admitting the abuse:

- I am afraid that I may be removed from my home.
- I am afraid that my siblings will be removed from home.
- I may be charged with a criminal offence.
- It may mean I can't get the job I want when I'm older.
- I may get called names, e.g. pervert.
- I may lose all my friends.
- I will get beaten up by some people.
- My parents may get into trouble.
- They will be humiliated, ostracised and blamed in the community.
- I will have embarrassed the family.
- I will be expelled from either my school or my employment.

Are these true for the juvenile you are working with? What others can you, or they, add to the list? Is there anything else they have trouble owning up to? Reframe these by asking them to list the reasons why they should tell the workers about what has happened. They might cite being better understood, accessing the right kind of help, removing secrecy, less likelihood of a punitive community and court response, etc. This exercise highlights the need to make slow and careful inroads into denial. Pithers *et al.*, (1989) developed several methods for assisting abusers admit to their sexually abusive behaviour, which include:

- Attempt to create 'yes' response questions.
- Demythologise stereotypes about sexual perpetrators.
- Mix confrontations with supportive comments.
- Emphasise the relief of acknowledging their secrets.
- Discuss the strengths demonstrated by disclosure.
- Stress the importance of not making a second mistake.
- Make use of any strong religious beliefs.
- Ask 'successive approximation' questions, e.g. they may deny a specific act occurred yet acknowledge that they approximated the act. By leading them by successive closer approximations to the act, they may reach the point of admitting it actually took place.
- Confront contradictions, and
- Repeat questions periodically (pp83–5).

Beckett (1994) made several further suggestions:

- Present as confident and familiar with the dilemmas they face in admitting the extent of their offending and the consequences of so doing.
- Convey that in your experience many offenders feel anxious about fully disclosing and co-operating, but will often feel relief having done so, and are subsequently able to change and rebuild their lives, albeit in a different way to before, and
- Explain the benefits of collaborating in the assessment and how it will open up the opportunity to access treatment.

A continuum of denial

Taylor (1996) offered us a very useful continuum of denial derived from work with juveniles who sexually abuse, and which highlights clearly what changes and shifts need to be made. It offers a visual guide to measure change both for the worker as well as the juvenile:

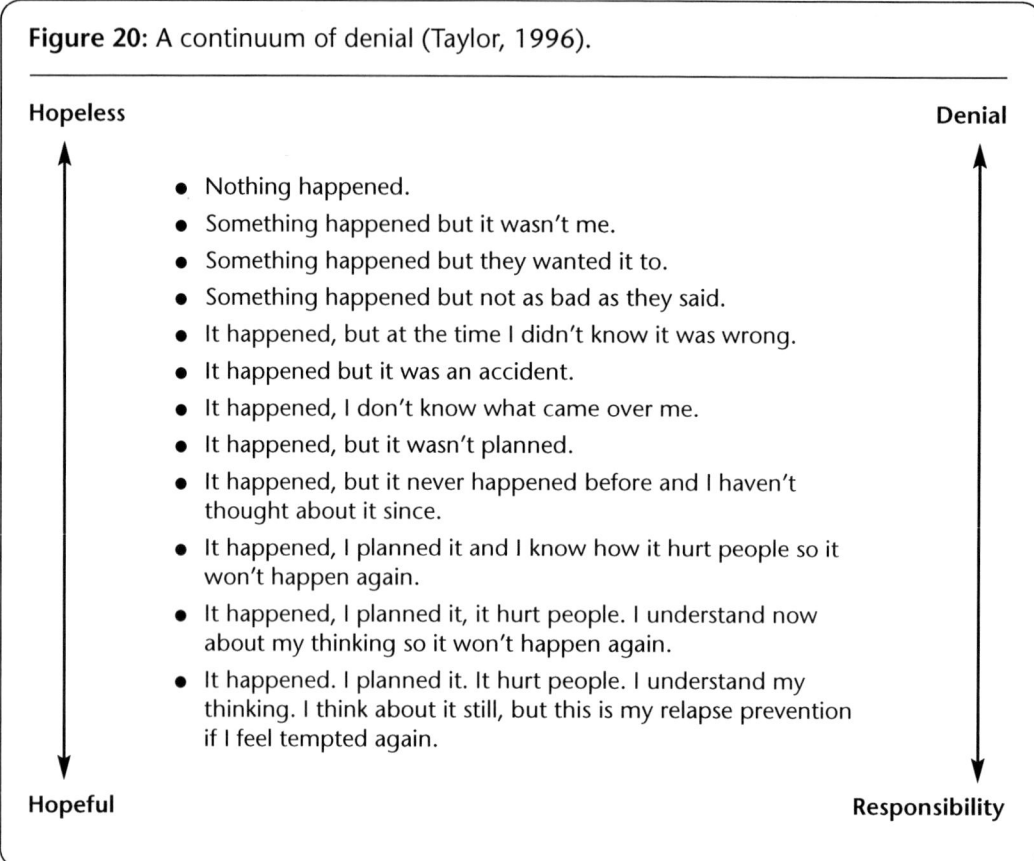

Figure 20: A continuum of denial (Taylor, 1996).

Hopeless   Denial

- Nothing happened.
- Something happened but it wasn't me.
- Something happened but they wanted it to.
- Something happened but not as bad as they said.
- It happened, but at the time I didn't know it was wrong.
- It happened but it was an accident.
- It happened, I don't know what came over me.
- It happened, but it wasn't planned.
- It happened, but it never happened before and I haven't thought about it since.
- It happened, I planned it and I know how it hurt people so it won't happen again.
- It happened, I planned it, it hurt people. I understand now about my thinking so it won't happen again.
- It happened. I planned it. It hurt people. I understand my thinking. I think about it still, but this is my relapse prevention if I feel tempted again.

Hopeful   Responsibility

Treatment of denial can take time and often needs to be measured in terms of months and years rather than days and weeks.

Victim Empathy and Awareness

It is important that we consider the young persons attitude to the victim, their empathy for the victim defined as an ability to accurately perceive and respond to the feelings of others, and their understanding of the short and long-term consequences of abuse. We should consider the young person's own experiences of abuse and how these might influence their thoughts and behaviour (Gist *et al.*, 1994). This can help them understand how the unresolved anger, fear and feelings of powerlessness, resulting from their own victimisation, was projected onto their victim.

This can be used as the basis of increasing their awareness of the negative impact of sexual abuse on their victim (Scavo and Buchanan, 1990: pp66–7). We also need to consider the extent to which they are taking full responsibility for their abusive behaviour. We should never overlook the possibility that victim retaliation may still be occurring, or the reality that the victim remains vulnerable to re-abuse.

Tools

Briggs (1994) outlined a framework for assessing empathy for victims. He draws our attention to the need to differentiate between cognitive and emotional empathy. Cognitive empathy is where they have an intellectual understanding of the feelings of others without necessarily experiencing any emotional change themselves, whereas emotional empathy is where they vicariously experience the emotion of others in response to their situation and feelings. He sets out the following questions that will assist the workers in judging the quality of victim empathy:

- The physical feelings of their victims before, during and after each offence.
- The emotional feelings of their victims before, during and after each offence.
- The thoughts of their victims before, during and after each offence.
- The physical and emotional state of each of their victims now.
- The impact of the offences upon the family members of each victim, and
- The physical and emotional state of those who dealt with the victims, e.g. friends, professionals, etc. (p65)

It is not unusual for abusing juveniles to start with a low level of empathy which usually means they are unable to understand how their behaviour has affected the victim. Poorly developed empathy can stem from their own victimisation in conjunction with repressed emotions (Becker, 1991: p162). By addressing their own victimisation, an enhanced sense of empathy can be created as they recall their own feelings. Continued victim blame precludes the development of victim empathy (Barbaree and Cortoni, 1993: p254). Kahn and Lafond (1986) have questioned how able juveniles are to acquire empathy with their victims at this late stage in their emotional development. The first step in helping the abuser to develop empathy involves teaching them to identify and communicate their own feelings (Perry and Orchard, 1992: p12). They went on to offer indicators of the abuser's capacity for empathy, which include a) the extent to which he blames the victims, b) the use of demeaning terms to describe his victims, and c) a failure to recognise either the short or long-term effects on the victims (p41). We should ensure they personalise the victims by calling them by their names. We should not disregard the possibility that their early life experiences have been characterised by a lack of empathic care, so the assessor can model empathy through their relationship with the juvenile. It is often through recognition of their pain that empathy is achieved. This should not excuse their abusive behaviour. The development of empathy for the victim and potential victims is arguably the most important variable to decreasing their potential to re-abuse (DiGeorgio-Miller, 1994: p124). Finally, the abuser is asked to identify their regrets about the abuse, then place them in order of importance (p35).

Motivation to Change

Morrison (1991) offered us a very useful continuum of motivation which can help us assess the level of motivation to change within the abuser (see Figure 21).

It is important to assess their motivation to continue into protracted treatment, and we can ask the following questions to this end:

- Why is it important that they change?
- Do they have the ability to change?
- What does change really mean? What will they have to do that they can't do now? What will they not have to do that they do now?
- Who can help them change, and in what way? and
- What have they tried to change in the past, and why wasn't it successful?

Feedback and Report

To ensure the young person does not acquire any aggravated distortion of their cognition, they need to be debriefed at the end of the assessment. They should be given the opportunity to hear the assessment feedback alone, before their parents are included, if that is what they want. A post-assessment interview should incorporate the information gathered from all the assessments, particularly where they are similar, different, or highlight more questions. The following issues should be covered in the feedback session:

- A report will be written to the commissioning body, although they will have sight of it.
- An appraisal of the assessments should be undertaken, with reference to any shifts in acceptance or attitudes noted, and any remaining concerns.

Figure 21: A continuum of motivation (adapted from Morrison, 1991).

Internal motivators

- I want to change.
- I don't like things the way they are.
- I am asking for your help.
- I have resources to help solve this.
- I think you can help me.
- I think things can get better.
- I have other supports which I will use to encourage me.
- I accept that I am doing something wrong.
- I accept what you say needs to change.
- I accept that others are right (family, friends, community, agencies).
- You defining the problem clearly helps.
- I understand what change will involve.
- I accept that if I do not change, you will take my siblings or me away.
- I can change if you do this for me.
- I'll do whatever you say.
- I agree to do this so the family can be reconstituted.
- It's your job to solve my problem.
- You are my problem.
- I am right and you are wrong.
- I don't have any problems

External motivators

- The viability of future work, with specific details, time-scale, and any mandate required.

- A treatment agreement could be discussed and some consensus on its content reached, and

- The family's response to the abuse is central to child protection planning and placement issues, and thus needs to be discussed. These are discussed more in Chapter Five.

The meeting to feedback often precedes the full assessment report and should always be done before a decision on disposal is made. The Coventry NSPCC have outlined a very thorough framework for the assessment report that addresses:

- Details of the young person.
- Details of their family.
- Reason for referral.
- Brief background information on the young person (individual and family profile).
- Engagement with the work (number of sessions, commitment and motivation).
- The assessment of their abusive behaviour.
- The sexual history, knowledge and attitudes.

- Victim awareness.

- Summary and recommendations.

- Involvement of the parents in the process (Gist *et al.*, 1994).

References

Awad, G.A., and Saunders, E.B. (1989). Adolescent Child Molesters: Clinical Observations. *Child Psychiatry and Human Development*, 19(3): pp195–206.

Barbaree, H.E., and Cortoni, F.A. (1993). Treatment of the Juvenile Sex Offender Within the Criminal Justice System and Mental Health Systems. In Barbaree, H.E., Marshall, W.L., and Hudson, S.M. (Eds.). *The Juvenile Sex Offender*, pp243–63. New York: Guilford Press.

Barclay, A.M. (1973). Sexual Fantasies in Men and Women. *Medical Aspects of Human Sexuality*, 7: pp205–16.

Beck, A.T. (1976). *Cognitive Theory and Emotional Disorders*. NY: Meridian.

Becker, J.V. (1991). Working with Perpetrators. In Murray, K., and Gough, D.A. (Eds.). *Intervening in Cases of Child Sexual Abuse*, pp157–65. Edinburgh: Scottish Academic Press.

Becker, J.V., and Abel, G.G. (1985). Methodological and Ethical Issues in Evaluating and Treating Adolescent Sex Offenders. In Otey, E.M., and Ryan, G.D. (Eds.). *Adolescent Sex Offenders: Issues in Research and Treatment*, pp109–29. Rockville, MD: US Dept. of Health and Human Services.

Becker, J.V., and Kaplan, M.S. (1988). The Assessment and Treatment of Adolescent Sexual Offenders. *Advances in Behavioural Assessment of Children and Families*, 4: pp97–118.

Beckett, R.C. (1994). Assessment of Sex Offenders. In Morrison, T., Erooga, M., and Beckett, R.C. (Eds.). *Sexual Offending Against Children: Assessment and Treatment of Male Abusers*, pp55–79. London: Routledge.

Bentovim, A., Elton, A., and Tranter, M. (1987). Prognosis for Rehabilitation after Abuse. *Adoption and Fostering*, 11(1): pp26–31.

Breer, W. (1987). *The Adolescent Molester*. Springfield, Illinois: Charles C. Thomas.

Briggs, D.I. (1994). Assessment of Sex Offenders. In Mcmurran, M., and Hodge, J.E. (Eds.). *The Assessment of Criminal Behaviours of Clients in Secure Settings*, pp53–67. London: Jessica Kingsley.

Calder, M.C., and Skinner, J. (1999). A Framework for Comprehensive Assessment. In Calder, M.C. *Assessing Risk in Adult Males who Sexually Abuse Children*, pp65–158. Dorset: Russell House Publishing.

Cook, S., and Taylor, J. (1991). *Working with Young Sex Offenders*. Liverpool SSD/Barnardo's North-West.

DiGeorgio-Miller, J. (1994). Clinical Techniques in the Treatment of Juvenile Sex Offenders. *Young Victims, Young Offenders*, 21(1/2): pp117–26.

DoH (1988). *Protecting Children: A Guide for Social Workers Undertaking a Comprehensive Assessment*. London: HMSO.

Dutton, W.E., and Newton, B.J. (1988). Early Recollections and Sexual Fantasies of Adolescent Sex Offenders. *Individual Psychology*, 44(1): pp85–94.

Faller, K.C. (1990). *Understanding Child Sexual Maltreatment*. Newbury Park, CA: Sage.

Freeman-Longo, R.E. (1983). *Developmental Histories in Sexual Offenders*. Unpublished Study.

Freeman-Longo, R.E. (1985). The Adolescent Sex Offender: Background and Research Perspectives. In Otey, E.M., and Ryan, G.D. (Eds.). *Adolescent Sex Offenders: Issues in Research and Treatment*, pp130–46. Rockville, MD: DHHS Publication.

Ginty, M., and Debelle, G. (1996). *Multi-centre Evaluation of Intervention Programmes for Juvenile Perpetrators of Sexual Abuse*. Presentation to the 11th ISPCAN Congress on Child Abuse and Neglect, Dublin, Ireland, 18th–21st August, 1996.

Gist, R., Taylor, J., and Fisher, D. (1994). *Assessment Programme: Assessment of Young People who Display Inappropriate Sexual Behaviour*. Coventry: NSPCC.

Glueck, B. (1956). *Final Report of the Research Project for the Study of Persons Convicted of Crimes Involving Sexual Aberrations. June 1952 to June 1955*. New York: State Department of Hygiene.

Hardy, K.Y., and Laszlotty, T.A. (1995). The Cultural Genogram: Key to Training Culturally Competent Family Therapists. *Journal of Marital and Family Therapy*, 21(3): pp227–37.

Heinz, J.V.V., Gargaro, S., and Kelly, K.G. (1987). *A Model Residential Juvenile Sex Offender Treatment Program: The Hennepin County Home School*. Orwell, VT: Safer Society Press.

Howard, A. (1993). Victims and Perpetrators of Sexual Abuse. In Dwivedi, K.N. (Ed.). *Groupwork with Children and Adolescents: A Handbook*, pp220–32. London: Jessica Kingsley, .

James, A.C., and Neil, P.C. (1996). Juvenile Sexual Offending: A One-year Prevalence Study Within Oxfordshire. *Child Abuse and Neglect*, 20(6): pp477–85.

Jones, C., and Lewis, J. (1990/91). A Pilot Prison Treatment Group for Sex Offenders at HMP Norwich. *Prison Service Journal*, 81: pp44–6.

Kahn, T.J., and Lafond, M. (1986). Treatment of the Adolescent Sex Offender. *Child and Adolescent Social Work Journal*, 5: pp135–48.

Longo, R.E. (1982). Sexual Learning and Experience among Adolescent Sexual Offenders. *International Journal of Offender Therapy and Comparative Criminology*, 26(3): pp235–41.

Marshall, W.L. (1988). The Use of Sexually Explicit Stimuli by Rapists, Child Molesters and Non-offenders. *Journal of Sex Research*, 25: pp267–88.

Marshall, W.L., Barbaree, H.E., and Eccles, A. (1991). Early Onset and Deviant Sexuality in Child Molesters. *Journal of Interpersonal Violence*, 6(3): pp323–36.

Marshall, W.L., and Eccles, A. (1993). Pavlovian Characteristics for Classifying Juvenile Sex Offenders. In Barbaree, H.E., *et al.* (Eds.). Op cit., pp118–42.

Monck, E., and New, M. (1996). *Report of a Study of Sexually Abused Children and Adolescents and Young Perpetrators of Sexual Abuse who were Treated in Voluntary Agency Community Facilities.* London: HMSO.

Morrison, T. (1991). Change, Control and the Legal Framework. In Adcock M., White, R., and Hollows, A. (Eds.). *Significant Harm: Its Management and Outcome,* pp85–100. Croydon: Significant Publications.

National Adolescent Perpetrator Network (1993). The Revised Report from the National Task Force on Juvenile Sexual Offending. *Juvenile and Family Court Journal,* 44(4): pp1–121.

National Children's Homes (1992). *Report of the Committee of Enquiry into Children and Young People who Sexually Abuse Other Children.* London: NCH.

Pennell, A. (1996). *The Link Between Child Maltreatment and Sexual Offending.* Paper Presented to the 11th ISPCAN Congress on Child Abuse and Neglect, Dublin, Ireland, 18th–21st August, 1996.

Perry, G.P., and Orchard, J. (1992). *Assessment and Treatment of Adolescent Sex Offenders.* Sarasota, FL: Professional Resource Press.

Pithers, W.D. (1990). Relapse Prevention with Sexual Aggressors: A Method for Maintaining Therapeutic Gain and Enhancing External Supervision. In Marshall, W.L., Laws, D.R., and Barbaree, H.E. (Eds.). *The Handbook of Sexual Assault: Issues, Theory and Treatment of the Offender.* NY: Plenum.

Pithers, W.D., Gray, A.S., Cunningham, C., and Lane, S. (1993). *From Trauma to Understanding: A Guide for Parents of Children with Sexual Behaviour Problems.* Brandon, VT: Safer Society Program and Press.

Rada, R. (1978). *Clinical Aspects of the Rapist.* NY: Grune and Row.

Salter, A. (1988). *Assessment and Treatment of Child Sex Offenders: A Practice Guide.* Beverley Hills, CA: Sage.

Saunders, E.B., and Awad, G.A. (1988). Assessment, Management and Treatment Planning for Male Adolescent Sex Offenders. *American Journal of Orthopsychiatry,* 58(4): pp571–9.

Scavo, R., and Buchanan, B.D. (1990). Group Therapy for Male Adolescent Sex Offenders: A Model for Residential Treatment. *Residential Treatment for Children and Youth,* 7(2): pp59–74.

Smets, A.C., and Cebula, C.M. (1987). A Group Treatment Program for Adolescent Sex Offenders: Five Steps Toward Resolution. *Child Abuse and Neglect,* 11: pp247–54.

Smith, W.R., and Monastersky, C. (1986). Assessing Juvenile Sex Offenders' Risk for Re-offending. *Criminal Justice and Behaviour,* 13: pp115–40.

Steen, C. (1993). *The Relapse Prevention Workbook for Youth in Treatment.* Brandon, VT: Safer Society Press.

Taylor, G. (1996). *Working with Denial.* Workshop at the Barnardo's Conference, 'Learning To Change', Liverpool Town Hall, 14th March, 1996.

Willis, G.C. (1992). *Unspeakable Crimes: Prevention Works with Perpetrators of Child Sexual Abuse.* London: Children's Society.

Wolf, S. (1984). *A Multi-factor Model of Deviant Sexuality.* Third International Conference on Victimology. Lisbon, Portugal, November, 1984.

Zussman, R. (1989). Forensic Evaluation of the Adolescent Sex Offender. *Forensic Reports,* 2: pp25–45.

Chapter Five

Family Assessments

Martin C. Calder

The assessment of the parents runs in tandem to the assessment of the young person. Before a comprehensive risk assessment can start, answers to certain questions designed to identify and contain initial risk will have been elicited:

- Can the children in the family be protected by the parents?

- Do the parents accept any responsibility for what has happened or for what could have happened? E.g. Have they contributed to the development of their son's sexually abusive behaviour?

- Do the parents supervise the abuser sufficiently, e.g. restricting babysitting?

- Can the parents balance support for the abuser alongside protecting the other children?

- Will the parents give active consent to the necessary work being suggested?

- Is there a history of abuse by the parents? If yes, and the abuse has been sexual, we should approach their involvement in any work in a fundamentally different way.

- Did the victim ever tell one or both of the parents about the abuse at the time? If yes, what was their reaction and response? E.g. 'that's quite normal', 'find your own solutions', or, 'it's only children's games'.

Regardless of the families ability and willingness to protect and co-operate, it is not unusual for them to respond to the allegations with strong negative feelings such as anger, guilt and despair. They may well be grieving the loss of their son's innocence, or they may be experiencing other impacts on family functioning such as relationship difficulties, difficulties in the adult sexual relationship, relating differently to their children for fear of their behaviour being misinterpreted, and their non-abusing children expressing confusion about what is happening and responding to them differently as a result (Gist and Taylor, 1994: pp23–4). They may be traumatised by a failure to respond appropriately to any direct disclosure or suspicion of the abuse. Parents cannot change overnight, particularly in the absence of any professional help. There will be situations where the parent's denial of the abuse feeds a continuing denial by the young person. In such situations, no work is going to be possible in the absence of a legal mandate. The majority of the work in the UK with this group will be achieved by working with the parents and eliciting their support and understanding as a means of education and monitoring. This is the best possible foundation for the assessment work, as any help they offer enhances the outcome. Indeed, it is far more difficult for the young person to deny if their position is not supported by their parents. They may also be less anxious about any response to what they have to say.

At this initial stage, therefore, we should be prepared for some response from the parents, and we should anticipate having to deal with their distress. Haase et al., (1990) outlined the stages of emotional response for parents: disbelief and denial that it could be possible; shock and alarm that may immobilise them; anger and rage accompanied by retaliatory urges, guilt and anguish where they blame themselves for the abuse; depression and loss which emerges as a result of emotional exhaustion combined with mourning the loss of a child's innocence; and recovery for the parents. Here, as the child improves, so do they. There are several useful mechanisms for eliciting the co-operation of the parents:

- Acknowledge their shock/numbness/shame/humiliation/feelings of failure and powerlessness, and give them space to feel uncertain and vulnerable.

- Give them information on abusing behaviour as well as the procedure and process of response.

- Advise them that they can be very influential in a discovery and recovery process.

- Encourage them to be a part of their son's assessment.
- Address their denial (if it exists), recognising that it is a common initial response, but becomes maladaptive if sustained. Denial is a block that they currently have about the need to change.
- Need to supervise/monitor their son if remaining at home, or during any contact periods.
- Stress the family strengths.
- Normalise without minimising.
- Watch for signs of depression.
- Identify intra-familial sources of support especially other parents who have shared their experience.
- Despite overt distrust, assume that they are searching for explanations and answers underneath. (Adapted from Gray and Pithers, 1993: pp313–4; and Morrison and Print, 1995: p31).

We should be clear that it will not always be possible or productive to involve the parents, as they may be either absent or dishonest. This has implications for the abuser, as it is far more difficult for a juvenile to change in a non-supportive family (Thomas, 1991, in Morrison and Print, 1995: p22).

As I have identified earlier in the book, several pieces of pre-comprehensive assessment work will have taken place, e.g. an educational block and the construction of an explicit written agreement. These will have contextualised the work, clarified the use of any sexually explicit material, and resolved any difficulties over practical arrangements such as transport, help with homework, the parental role in their sons assessment, and any arrangements for feedback and review.

The comprehensive assessment of the young person must consider the family context, and this section can be repeated and cross-checked with the parents responses. In broad terms, the aim of the assessment is to gain the fullest understanding of the juvenile; increasing the families understanding and commitment; identifying primary problems; assessing the immediate health and safety of the family; assisting in altering relationship patterns; maintaining a family perspective even where they will not participate, in order to break any

inter-generational cycle; identifying any discrepant perceptions; and gaining information from collateral sources (Thomas, 1991, in Morrison and Print, 1995: p22).

Aspects of the Family History and Functioning that may Predispose the Young Person Towards Engaging in Sexually Abusive Behaviour

We need to try and uncover and expose family secrets as the basis of trying to understand how these may have impacted on the young person, particularly how they may have contributed towards their abusive behaviour. The parents can begin to understand how some of their son's behaviour and other factors interplay to produce the abusive behaviour. Once secrets are exposed, it is not unusual for the family to grieve over the pain caused. We can then move into identifying what needs to be changed, and by supporting any attempts to break the dysfunctional behaviours, and continuing to challenge any denial (Heinz *et al.*, 1987: p112).

Information from police checks and collateral sources is helpful. It is not uncommon to find histories of physical, sexual and emotional abuse in the families of juveniles who sexually abuse. It is important to identify patterns of behaviour in the family, sanctions (physical or mental), approaches to discipline (style and enforcement), and any disagreements or inconsistencies. It is also important to establish whether there is a history of sexual abuse in the extended families, how this emerged, between whom and with what consequences, e.g. legally, within the family. What contact do they have with other children in the family? Has any professional help been offered to the family to resolve abuse issues? With what success? It is important to elicit how the parents view the child, as emotional harm is often defined through the range of parental behaviours rather than the obvious effects on the young person themselves. This has often to be drawn from more general discussions about the young person. In addressing this area, we can never discount uncovering abuse, which requires a broader protective intervention.

We need to explore the use of substances by the family, as they have an effect on their working life, social life, and the ways in which they handle conflict. It may also affect their ability to enforce sanctions in the home now to protect other children. We can be fairly sure the information they give will be misleading, wrong, or only partially correct. We need to cross-check with other agency records.

Alongside substance abuse, social network and work history are important, as children who are isolated are unable to seek help from their community. Other areas to cover include:

- What sorts of activities does the family engage in together?

- What regular quiet times do they have together as a family?

- How do they show affection in their family?

- What times do they have together away from the children?

- What interests do they share?

- What are the principal sources of support in the family?

- Have there been any separations/domestic violence?

- What is the power balance? Allocation of roles and responsibilities?

- How do they deal with disagreements? How do they reach decisions? List the situations that feature most in these areas, and compare with that given by the juvenile.

- What do they define the family problem to be? Do they accept one exists? (Adapted from Steen and Monnette, 1989: p157.)

Knowledge and Understanding of the Behaviour

Our goal here is to obtain a detailed understanding of what the parents believed happened:

- What is their understanding of the concerns? Get them to be as specific as they can be about their understanding of the allegations against their son.

- Where did they get the information from? Official or unofficial sources?

- Who else knows about their behaviour? Get them to draw up a list of who knows

as an indication of whether it remains a secret or whether it is well known.

- What information may be of further help to the parents? and

- What help can they be given? (Gist and Taylor, 1994: p28).

Family reactions to the behaviour

The aim of this block is to establish whether the family reactions have been helpful or unhelpful. The following questions will help elicit the answer to this question:

- Do the parents think that all or part of the allegations are true?

- What are their feelings towards their son? And the abuse? What has their son been told, or picked up about how they feel?

- Looking back, can they identify any worrying signs they may have picked up on?

- Who do they feel is responsible for their son's behaviour?

- Get them to list the reasons why they think their son acted in this way.

- Have they discussed the behaviour with their son? What was said? Most abusers want to discuss the issues with their parents. Kahn (1990) set out a series of questions that may assist parents when opening up lines of communication with their son, e.g. Why is what you did wrong? What are some reasons why you may be denying parts of your abusive behaviour? Give me some reasons why you want to tell the truth about what you did. How did you decide to act out what you were thinking? Are you having a hard time admitting that you still have sexual urges to re-abuse? And how do they think their behaviour has affected other people?

- Have they discussed the behaviour with the other children in the family? Who has been told? Who has not, and why? Has it been discussed with relatives or friends? Which ones? How were they told and what has been their reaction? What were they told?

- Has the abuse affected any relationships, either within or outside the family?

- Are there any major differences of opinion within the family about the abuse? How have these been dealt with?
- Have the parents acted appropriately in managing contact between their son and other children?
- What is the parents' view about the response of the professional agencies? Is it considered appropriate or excessively intrusive? (Adapted from Gist and Taylor, 1994: pp29–32.)

Family understanding of the victims experiences

- Is the victim another child in the family, or outside?
- What do they think the victim might be feeling about the abuse and about themselves? Do the family feel that the person who has abused is partly to blame? If so, in what way?
- Is there any disagreement or different views held by different family members? How is this expressed? What do the parents think the victim is feeling now? Do they understand the short and the long-term effects of the behaviour for the victim?
- Does the child know their parents' views? If so, what was said? Have they discussed the behaviour with the victim or their parents? What has been said to them?
- Is there any ongoing contact between the parents' and the victim, how is this contact managed?
- In what ways have they demonstrated concern for the victim? Are there any obstacles to them expressing this concern, e.g. they are victims themselves?
- What information can be provided to enhance the parents understanding around the effects on the victim (adapted from Gist and Taylor, 1994).

Providing Boundaries to Avoid Situations of Risk

Parents need to know that the behaviour will not necessarily stop during the assessment period, so monitoring and/or supervision remains an essential protective tool. How willing are they to assume these roles? Workers have to consider what limits the parents are able to place upon the young person to prevent further abusive behaviour occurring. Four areas need to be covered:

The setting and maintaining of family rules

- What are the family rules? Please list.
- Do the parents feel the young person is clear about the rules? Which children tend to adhere to the rules, challenge them, or break them? How often?
- What happens if the rules are followed? Or are broken?
- What members of the family tend to support each other?
- What behaviours do the parents particularly value amongst the children? How do they show this?

The parents knowledge of the young persons activities outside of the home

- List the friends the young person has. Are they family, close friends or acquaintances?
- Are they younger, older, the same age, male or female?
- What is the parents' view of these friends? What concerns do they have about them?
- Who has had regular, unsupervised contact with the young person—past or present?
- Can the parents complete a daily diary sheet to identify where, who with and how often the young person is involved in any given activity?

Boundaries within the home to ensure the protection of other family members

Defrances (1969) estimated that poor supervision by parents and failure to set proper controls for a juvenile is a contributing factor in over 70 per cent of all cases of sexual abuse and can inadvertently encourage further abuse by failing to supervise properly or reinstating the abuser in the child care role (Kahn and Lafond, 1986: p147).

- Where does everyone sleep in the home?
- Does the young person share a bedroom with anyone?
- Do any family members share beds at any time? Give details.
- Who cares for the children when the parents are not at home?
- What routines in the home allow the young person unsupervised contact with children?
- What is the level of privacy in the home? Do they lock doors when going to the toilet, getting undressed? Is there any shared bathing?

Contact issues

This is a difficult issue to resolve. If we allow the juvenile to have extensive contact with siblings, we often run the risk of deflecting the need for them to accept their responsibility for the abuse. On the other hand, restricting contact can isolate the juvenile from their family situation, and we may find that any work and progress with the juvenile is undone through the continuing denial by the parents. Supervision of contact becomes a very tiring and time consuming activity for the parents if the young person has remained within the family home, or for others if they have not. Parents often make initial offers with the best of intentions that are very difficult to sustain. Careful consideration needs to be given to the wishes and feelings of the children, particularly if they are the victims (adapted from Cook and Taylor, 1991: pp51–2; and Gist and Taylor, 1994: pp35–43). Workers do need to establish whether any of the siblings have any special needs that makes them more vulnerable.

Whilst parents may agree to abide by suggestions on containing their son in the home and the community, we have to be alert to the probability that these will not be transferred to the context outside of the professional work, e.g. allowing the abuser to play with the victims in the street. It is often useful to try and identify a network of support for these families who can offer guidance in between the formal work, e.g. friends, extended family. This often has the added bonus that their message is listened to more by the parents: same message, but different messenger.

Describing the Young Person

We can link this section with component one of the young person's assessment in Chapter Four. The following questions highlight some of the areas that need to be covered:

- Any significant life events.
- Unfolding memories of pregnancy, birth, early years—are there any concerns over health or development?
- Any separations or relationship problems? Any difficulties in peer or sibling relationships? Any behavioural or school problems? If yes, please list.
- What difficulties does the young person have now? Are they new problems or have they been developing and escalating over time?
- Have they ever been abused themselves? If yes, please give details, particularly if this has had any impact on them or the young person?
- Has the young person ever been charged or cautioned by the police? For what? When?
- Do they have any kind of drink or drug problem? Have they ever received help for this?
- Have they ever suffered from any mental health problems?
- Ask the parents to list the child's good and bad points.
- How might any of the information provided by the parents affect the young person's view of themselves? (Adapted from Gist and Taylor, 1994: pp44–50.)

Observing the Young Person's Sexual Attitudes and Behaviour

- Has the young person ever expressed any interest in sexual matters?

- Have they ever asked questions about sex and sexuality? What sort of questions were they?
- Do they show interest in sexual behaviour on TV or on video?
- Have they ever owned any sexually explicit material themselves? Give details.
- Have they ever had contact with sex or chat lines? Which ones?
- Do they have access to any other sexually explicit material? What are they?
- Does the young person ever get embarrassed about sexual matters?
- Has there ever been any concern about the young person's sexual or physical behaviour towards others?
- Does the young person tell 'dirty jokes', swear, or make sexual innuendoes?
- Does the young person like to watch others with few clothes on? In what context?
- Is the child's dress provocative?
- Do the parents have any concerns about the young person's attitudes towards the role of men, women and children?
- Has the young person ever written or drawn sexualised pictures or stories? When? What was their nature and content?

Attitudes Towards Sex and Sexuality within the Family

- Describe the words that the family uses for parts of the body/sexual behaviours.
- How does the family discuss sexuality in the home? Are there any views against homosexuality?
- Where are sexually explicit materials kept in the home? Are they secure?
- Does the family ever watch TV or video programmes, which contain scenes of violence or sexual behaviour? Give details.
- Do the parents check any computer disks their son has for pornographic material or contacts?
- What is the parent's view of masturbation? Does gender affect their views?

- What is an acceptable way of showing affection in the family?
- Have the parents ever offered or discussed sex education with the children? At what age and what was said? What materials, if any, did they use?
- How comfortable are family members talking about sexual matters? Is it any different with each other?
- Does anyone ever tease the children in a sexual way? If so, who and how?
- Has the young person ever witnessed any sexual activity? What? Where? And when?
- What messages within the home may predispose, precipitate or perpetuate the young person's behaviour or attitudes? (Gist and Taylor, 1994: pp54–69).

Motivation to Co-operate with the Work and Support the Young Person

- What level of support would the parents be able to offer? What is their level of involvement?
- What is the parents' perception of how long the work would take?
- How will their commitment be affected if the work exceeds six months?
- What can the parents offer to ensure that the work is completed?
- What support will the young person need and what problems can be anticipated?
- Has their position changed over time? Has it become stronger or has it withered?
- Are there any areas where they are 'stuck'? and
- Will they ever trust their son around children themselves? (Gist and Taylor, 1994: pp60–70).

After collecting the parents' information, we need to consider:

- The degree to which the parents have been able to reflect upon the information discussed and have modified their opinions.

- The family strengths and indicators of their support for the young person.

- Any areas of disagreement or differences of opinion.

- Any concerns about the parent's responses.

- Areas where further work or support might usefully be offered.

- The level of understanding about what is required of them, and

- The level of understanding about what family dynamics contributed to the abusive behaviour (Gist and Taylor, 1994: p162).

For an excellent general practice guide to family assessments, the reader is referred to the City of Salford (2000).

For an excellent guide for parents whose young person has sexually abused, the reader is referred to Hackett (forthcoming). This is a practical workbook in two parts. In part one, he explores issues of concern facing parents, whilst part two offers a range of therapeutic exercises to enable parents to work through the issues raised in part one.

References

City of Salford Community and Social Services (Family Support Service) (2000). *Conducting Family Assessments: A Practice Guide.* Dorset: Russell House Publishing.

Cook, S., and Taylor, J. (1991). *Working with Young Sex Offenders.* Liverpool SSD and Barnardo's North-West.

Defrances, V. (1969). *Protecting the Child Victim of Sex Crimes Committed by Adults.* Denver, CO: American Humane Association.

Gist, R., and Taylor, J. (1994). *Family Assessment Programme: Working with Parents and Carers of Young People who Display Inappropriate Sexual Behaviour.* Coventry: NSPCC.

Gray, A.S., and Pithers, W.D. (1993). Relapse Prevention with Sexually Aggressive Adolescents and Children: Expanding Treatment And Supervision. In Barbaree, H.E. (Eds.). *The Juvenile Sex Offender,* pp289–319. NY: Guilford Press.

Haase, C.C., Kempe, R.S., and Grosz, C.A. (1990). Non-familial Sexual Abuse: Working with Children and their Families. In Oates, R.K. (Ed.). *Understanding and Managing Child Sexual Abuse,* pp178–201. Marrickville: Harcourt, Brace And Jovanovich.

Hackett, S. (forthcoming). *A Guide for Parents of Children who have Sexually Abused.* Dorset: Russell House Publishing.

Heinz, J.W., Gargaro, S., and Kelly, K.G. (1987). *A Model Residential Juvenile Sex Offender Treatment Program: The Hennepin County Home School.* Orwell, VT: Safer Society Press.

Kahn, T.J. (1990). *Pathways: A Guide for Parents of Youth Beginning Treatment.* Orwell, VT: Safer Society Press.

Kahn, T.J., and Lafond, M. (1986). Treatment of the Adolescent Sex Offender. *Child and Adolescent Social Work Journal,* 5: pp135–48.

Morrison, T., and Print, B. (1995). *Adolescent Sexual Abusers: An Overview.* Hull: Bluemoon Corporate Services/Nota.

Steen, C., and Monnette, B. (1989). *Treating Adolescent Sex Offenders in the Community.* Springfield, IL: Charles C. Thomas.

Chapter Six

The Comprehensive Assessment of Adult Males who Sexually Abuse Children

Martin C. Calder and John Skinner

One of the most important messages to bring to the assessment itself is that many sex offenders present as 'ordinary men', 'normal' and heterosexual members of society, who cannot be typified in terms of class, profession, wealth or family status. They usually have the same emotional and psychological profile as people who do not abuse. As they do not present as remarkably different from non-sexual offenders, other than in the nature of their offending, it is remarkably difficult to detect them.

In this chapter, we will provide a comprehensive framework for assessing adult male sex offenders who target children. We present a complete and optimally desirable framework, which may be inappropriate if followed rigidly and prescriptively by workers in each case. Each comprehensive assessment needs to be tailored to the individual circumstance of each case, the requirements of the commissioning body and the time-scale allowed. It is for this reason, that a pic 'n' mix framework is proposed, allowing workers to select identified components as deemed appropriate.

Social and Family History

Anyone wanting to promote constructive changes in clients must first obtain a comprehensive under-standing of the total context in which the behaviours occur.

(Lazarus, 1976: p25)

This reinforces the reality that our identity is not exclusively sexual, and we should try and identify social factors, which may have contributed to the development of their sexual offending behaviour. Sex offenders as a group may not be relatively deficient in many aspects of social functioning, but what deficiencies they do have may be functionally related to their offending behaviour. Workers should acknowledge that a social history collected

under the guise of a sex offender assessment is fundamentally no different to that elicited in other situations, so we shouldn't be immobilised by the task. What is important is that we recognise that there is likely to be considerable variation among offenders concerning their social histories (Dougher, 1995). This block is a useful starting point as it is typically non-threatening to the offender and provides an opportunity to build a rapport with them. The following information should be sought from the offender and significant others (e.g. partner, previous partners, children, etc.) as part of the process:

The offender's family background and early home life and social support

There are two major reasons for speaking with the offender about his family of origin and social network: to get some sense of what it was like for them growing up, as well as wanting to assess the extended family and others as sources of social support.

Many factors related to their upbringing may shed light on the dynamics of sexual abuse and predict prognosis. We need to find out what kind of people his parents were and how he experienced them, particularly if there is a history of little nurturing, significant trauma, and deprivation; physical and/or sexual abuse; a lack of intimacy or attachments; no reference to sex (so they grow up with little sexual knowledge), or paternal modelling of patriarchy, exploitation and/or abuse; as well as social isolation and the absence of social supports—particularly as social isolation can have several functions: it may facilitate, prolong, or be the result of sexual abuse. Hanson and Scott (1996) researched the social networks of sex offenders and found that there is some evidence that sex offenders are likely to have friends and relatives who are also sex offenders.

Questions might include:

- The names, date of births and addresses of all immediate and extended family members—which do they maintain contact with and which do they avoid, and why? The names of past partners can also be helpful as an additional source of information, particularly where they can be traced and are willing to speak to us. They could reveal information about sexual deviancies and domestic violence. The names of children from previous relationships is also helpful as it may uncover information about parallel abuses and other concerns.

- The names, ages and descriptions of all the children in the family, including what pleases/displeases them and what, if anything, they do together? This helps us anticipate any other potential victims. The offender's responses should be assessed, according to: his ability to individualise children in the family so that they are described as separate people with personalities; the affective tone of the relationship with children; the accuracy of the offender's perception and description of the children, based upon the worker's contact with them and the opinions of others, and the presence or absence of inappropriately sexual descriptions of the children. The first two qualities, the ability to individualise and the quality of affect are important in determining whether the offender considers people, particularly children, as objects to be used or manipulated for his interests or needs, or whether he sees them as individuals with their own needs who are valued and loved for themselves. Workers should then look for perceptions of the child as being on either the same level as the offender, or as being described in negative terms or in a manner that suggests that they are to blame for problems associated with the allegation of sexual abuse. Finally, we should be alert to sexual connotations in their descriptions of victims: these may be speculations about the child's future sexual functioning or projections about how other men or boys regard the victim. In other situations, the victim's alleged sexuality provides an excuse to the offender for the abuse (Faller, 1988: pp196–7).

- Aspects of the family history and functioning that may predispose them towards sexually abusive behaviour. In particular, any evidence of sexual or associated abuse—either generally, or perpetrated against the offender themselves, and any demonstrable consequences, extent and duration of such behaviour.

- Any parental convictions for sexual or physical offences (schedule one status), including any episodes of imprisonment, or a child protection conference finding of harm.

- Any intervention for abuse by professional agencies, including domestic violence and any care episodes. (N.B. Care should be taken in evaluating the impact of this on the offender.) What success, if any, did they have in addressing the issues of concern?

- The nature and quality of family relationships (siblings, parent-children, etc.) and type and adequacy of role-modelling available.

- The stability and quality of their family life, including substance and alcohol use; separations/bereavements; family activities and interests; allocation of roles and responsibilities; support systems; and any mental illness histories.

- Methods of discipline (how and why), family rules and secrets, and sexual behaviour/attitudes/values.

- Means of resolving disagreements and conflict.

- Establish who they rely on when he or the family needs help. For example, who can they turn to when they have a financial problem? Who can they rely on when they have a problem with one of their children? And who would help out if there was a sickness in the family?

- The details of the offender's personal networks (names, dates of birth and addresses).

This information should begin to enable us to determine their perceptions of family life, and how they have integrated their experiences into their current make-up. Risk factors would include a history of abuse, substance abuse, criminal family, mental illness history, abandonment, denial of sexual offences, failure to protect children or violence in the home (Carich and Adkerson, 1995: p13).

Demographic data

Grubin (1992) points out that sexual offending is a culturally defined phenomenon. Definitions of sexual offences are located within dominant understandings of sexual behaviour and are considered to be serious the more they deviate from these understandings (Cowburn, 1996). Sexual offenders are driven by two inter-dependent engines: one internal to the offender, the other fuelled by social contingencies. Whilst we know quite a lot about the demographic features and make-up of individuals who sexually offend, much less is known about the extent to which characteristics of particular societies influence the amount and type of sex crimes that occur within them.

Clinical evidence suggests that there may be some variation in type of sexual abuse by subculture. For example, Pierce and Pierce (1984) indicated that, compared with other racial groups, in black families the offender is more likely to be someone other than the biological father and the family is more likely to take decisive action to protect the child. Thus, information regarding ethnicity can assist the workers in understanding the dynamics of the sexual abuse and alert us to any patterns that may be present (Faller, 1988: pp192–3).

Educational history

It is important to establish their school performance and academic achievement; classroom behaviour; the presence or absence of problems within the school (relationships with peers and teachers, attendance and any activity whilst truanting, isolation, disciplinary, suspension or exclusion, bullying or bullied with staff and/or peers, etc.); interests in school; aptitudes and abilities; special educational needs/services (ability or behavioural); school changes (including reasons); and any significant events.

Information about the offender's education tells workers a great deal about their overall functioning and is more important in terms of predicting treatment candidacy than sexual recidivism. School performance gives some information about the offender's ability to persist at long-term goals and his self-discipline and self-esteem (Dougher, 1995). The level of academic ability has a bearing on the type of assessment tools which can be used. Their school adjustment may offer some information about the development of peer relationships and their ability to relate to authority figures in a productive manner (Groth, 1979). As schooling is one of our first major life experiences that places demands on us to handle responsibilities, performance can be a useful predictor of subsequent difficulty or success in fulfilling life demands. Anyone who has failed at almost every major task is unlikely to benefit from any ongoing work (McGovern and Peters, 1988: p223). It is important to establish, and access if possible, any records of special educational needs as they contain contributions from the educational psychologist, school, parent and significant others. A number of studies have indicated that paedophiles have IQs that skew to the lower end of normal: often rendering detection more likely. Sex offenders with learning difficulties may have negative attitudes surrounding new learning and direction from authority as well as problems with language-based comprehension. Risk factors in this block include truancy and drop out, special education placement, discipline problems and any sexual offending or harassing (Carich and Adkerson, 1995: p20).

Questions might include:

- How did you feel when you started school? What was good about school? What was bad about it?
- Who were your friends at school? What did you do with them? What games or hobbies did you enjoy with other children?

- How did the teachers treat you?
- Did you enjoy schoolwork? Was any of it hard for you? What subjects?
- What did your parents want for you in school? Did they want you to do well in sports, schoolwork, or religion?
- Were there changes in your living arrangements or family during secondary school years? Financial changes? Deaths? Moves?
- Did your feelings about school or achievements in school change in your secondary school years?
- What friends and/or activities were you involved with during your secondary school years?
- What kind of future job dreams or plans did you think about in your secondary school years? What were your goals? (Schwartz and Cellini, 1995).

Occupational history

It is useful to obtain a record of the offender's work history, including types of jobs, job performance, level of responsibility and employment stability, job satisfaction, relationships with colleagues and their ability to support themselves and their family (Dougher, 1995; Groth, 1979). This information can throw light on their persistence, relationships, responsibilities and dependability—all keys to effective professional intervention and the creation of sustained change. Anyone who has been nomadic and created problems in work are unlikely candidates for treatment. Close scrutiny of their work record is essential as we may uncover inappropriate work, e.g. providing access to children. Other risks include excessive work hours, sporadic absenteeism, and frequent job changes (Cumming and Buell, 1997).

Religious beliefs

Religious beliefs should be thoroughly evaluated with this population, particularly any stability inconsistencies associated with their beliefs. We need to establish the meaning of religion for them, as it can have a role in the dynamics of their offending. Offenders frequently come from religious backgrounds that instil repressive sexual attitudes, fear of adult sexuality, and a lack of accurate sexual knowledge. We need to establish what their religious perspective is on sex and gender issues, plus whether there are any cult or unusual practices. Other individuals escape from the guilt and responsibility of their offending by suddenly becoming extremely religious. They often state that they no longer need an assessment to understand their behaviour as they have been 'forgiven' for their 'sins'. We need to establish, however, whether their reason for sanctuary in the church is a cover for access to children via church-related activities, particularly as there is not yet a police vetting system for screening volunteers.

Individuals of certain denominations may express religious objections to certain types of assessment or treatment procedures including the viewing of sexually explicit materials or techniques using masturbation (Dougher, 1995). Risk factors include the use of faith to justify offending (particularly if of their own invention); the use of a fall from faith to justify offending; a frequent shift in beliefs; the religious community supporting their denial or condemning any intervention; and any sexual abuse experiences associated with religion (Carich and Adkerson, 1995: p22).

Financial history

Financial history should include debts and assets. An individual's level of stability may be reflected in how they manage their finances (Cumming and Buell, 1997). Furthermore, Faller (1988) reported that over a quarter of cases of sexual abuse are marked with the onset of unemployment or some other factor which has an impact on the offender's self-esteem. It is therefore important to identify any such stresses, which may contribute to the dynamics of child sexual abuse.

Recreational interests

Groth (1979) pointed to the need for a description of the offender's leisure interests and activities, hobbies and clubs, and particularly where they involve contact with children, such as football coach or scout leader, as they indicate how the offender amuses himself as well as reflecting their social skills and self-image. Attention should be paid to solitary, high risk activities such as drinking or an obsession with weapons (Groth, p201).

Criminal history

A comprehensive understanding of the offender's criminal history and their attitudes towards their crimes can be useful in understanding the sexual abuse, developing a treatment plan, and in predicting prognosis—particularly if it indicates any other sex crimes. Sometimes the offender will be forthcoming and admit to his past history of criminal activity, but often the workers will have to rely upon a police check or data from other sources for this information, such as child protection conference minutes. We should always endeavour to elicit the circumstances of conviction, as it is not uncommon for 'plea bargains' to conceal the true nature and extent of their offending behaviour. This can be very difficult given the speed at which some agency and court records are destroyed.

Other offences are important indicators, such as arson, physical assaults or cruelty to animals. It is important to establish whether their sexual offending is unique or part of an extended pattern of criminal behaviour.

Once this history has been elicited, workers should explore anything unlawful that they didn't get caught for; any times the police were called to their house; and any arrests that didn't lead to a conviction, with reasons. The aim is for there to be a close match between the official records and the offender self-report. Valuable information can sometimes be elicited from the extended family and friends. It may also be appropriate to explore their experiences of custody—particularly if they have been on rule 43 (or equivalent if served as a young person)—as this may have a bearing on their sexual attitudes and behaviour.

In general, the best predictor of future sexual offences is the number of previous sexual offences. As such, the more sexual offences there are, the less optimistic workers should be regarding the prognosis for successful intervention. If there are previous offences, it is useful to determine whether the modus operandi and antecedent conditions or

behaviours are similar, and whether there has been any escalation in frequency and types of sexual deviancy. Chronic recidivists generally begin their deviant sexual behaviour at an early age and may avoid detection for years (see Calder 1997a and b; 1999a and b).

Psychiatric history

Between 5 and 10 per cent of sex offenders present with some form of identifiable mental illness (cf. Webster, Menzes and Jackson, 1982). It represents an important, minority factor, which must be addressed before any useful assessment of sexual offending behaviour can be completed. For example, an associated feature of anti-social personality disorder is persistent lying and other forms of deception which have a direct link to the usefulness of self-report questionnaires. It is important to know if a mental illness seen in the sex offender explains their sexual offending or is coincidental to it. The presence of an anti-social personality disorder is an important risk factor for acting out and hence re-offending (Langevin and Watson, 1996: p57), largely because they may have weak impulse control and may engage in inappropriate behaviour in exchange for the most fleeting gratification, without regard for the consequences (McGovern and Peters, 1988: p222).

Historically, many offenders may have been referred to mental health services as a direct alternative to pursuing any criminal prosecution, so a detailed trawl of psychiatric records can harness useful information of relevance. It is for this reason that permission for disclosure may be refused by the offender, and, as such, any refusal should be seen as significant by the workers.

There are three reasons for exploring the offender's history for mental illness:

- Mental problems must be taken into account in assessing overall functioning. The longer the mental illness and the more severe its presentation, the poorer the treatment prognosis.

- Certain kinds of mental illness are indicative of poor object relations, and can affect the offender's ability to relate to children and partners, and

- In a few cases, mental illness plays a key

role in sexual abuse. For example, a psychotic offender may have specific delusions, which justify his sexual abuse. In other circumstances, an assessment may be needed to establish whether it was the cause or the outcome of the sexual abuse, e.g. an offender suffering from depression. Here, the worker might query how long the depression has existed to determine whether it in part precipitated the sexual abuse or whether it is a result of the sexual abuse or its discovery. Furthermore, the offender's illness usually means he has few other positive experiences in life and also has impaired judgement, which may lead to repeated incidences of sexual abuse.

Questions might include:

- Have they have ever been hospitalised, and why? What medication have they taken previously? Or what are they currently taking? Have they ever felt anxious, easily upset or sad: and, if so, how have they managed such feelings? What views do they hold regarding both the victim(s) and the allegations?

- Observations of the offender may be diagnostic: poor responses in interview; information from the earlier education block regarding special educational needs, etc.; evidence of depression, persecutory beliefs, etc. These should be checked with significant professionals, family members or friends as there is often a continuum of mental health, and we need to know where they might have been at the time of the offences and the interviews.

- A psychiatric assessment is often needed and we should ensure the regional forensic psychiatry service are provided with all the relevant background information and concerns to allow them to comment both on their current presentation as well as their history.

Neurological and biological factors

Wherever possible, a neurological examination should be conducted since some disorders manifest as sexually deviant behaviours, whilst some neurological abnormalities can influence their sexual behaviour. For example, damage to the temporal and frontal lobe (involved in sexual behaviours) can lead to sexual offending. Epilepsy and brain damage is significant in the genesis of unusual sexual behaviour, and diabetes can mimic psychosis, with mood fluctuations, poor judgement and confused sexual behaviour (Langevin and Bain, 1992). Diabetics, like sex offenders, are often resistant to the prescribed regime. It is clear, however, that only a few sex offenders present with unusual sex hormone profiles (Langevin, 1988: p272).

Interpersonal relationships

Information about relations with significant others can be of benefit in understanding the dynamics and prognosis of sexual abuse. We will restrict our discussion here to relationships other than marital (sexual) as this will be explored in the next block under the notion of intimacy. A careful examination of the full range of sexual offenders' personal relationships is not only useful for identifying intimacy deficits, but may also reveal direct social support for sexual offending (e.g. paedophile rings, peer support for rape), (Hanson, in press). In a recent study of sex offenders in the community, Hanson *et al.*, (1997) found that the recidivists were more likely than the non-recidivists to have predominantly negative influences (43 per cent versus 21 per cent respectively).

Interpersonal communication is a dominant human function, and many of our problems stem from our concerns over the way we relate to other people, and the manner in which they respond to us (Lazarus, 1976: p42). It is not surprising, therefore, that interpersonal relations are a central part of dealing with a sex offender, particularly since the offence is an interpersonal act (Groth, 1979). The nature of their problems will vary from case to case and thus need to be isolated if we are to tailor our intervention to the individual.

Weiss (1974) identified six key areas which isolated people miss out on. They are: attachment, provided by close affectional relationships, which give a sense of security and place; social integration, provided by membership of a network of persons having shared interests and values; the opportunity for nurturing others, usually children, which gives some incentive for continuing in the face of adversity; reassurance of personal worth, which promotes self-esteem and comes both from those at home as well as from colleagues; a sense of reliable alliance, which is obtained mainly from kin; and obtaining help and guidance from informal advisors when difficulties have to be resolved. Examples of the items include: at present, do you have someone you can share your most private feelings with (confide in) or not? Who is this mainly? Do you wish you could share more with them, or is it just about right the way it is? Would you like to have someone like this or would you prefer to keep your feelings to yourself?

In exploring interpersonal relationships, we need to consider:

- The nature and quality of the offenders relations with peers.

- The nature, quality and duration of the offender's friendships.

- The relative age and gender and number of the offender's friends and the kinds of friends they select as associates. Are they susceptible to the influence of others?

- The nature and extent of social isolation— which may possibly indicate a more severe psychopathology.

- Whether the offender is active or passive in social relations e.g. social interests, activities

and memberships. Are they self-centred? Excessively controlling and competitive?

- The nature and stability in their relationships. Obtain a relationship history, including the ages and sexes of the ex-partners children (adapted from Dougher, 1995; and Groth, 1979).

Anger, aggression and assertiveness

Anger is a normal and natural emotion, which we all experience from time to time. Used constructively, it can motivate us to resolve problems. Alternatively, it can hurt us if repressed, as well as others if it is expressed uncontrollably. Many sex offenders have serious difficulties with the appropriate expression of anger. It is often a primary source of motivation for sexual offences, and the failure to manage anger does increase the likelihood of displacement through aggression toward others (Green, 1995).

Most sexual offenders have a pattern of anger that keeps them going in cycles, just like their sexual abuse cycle (see Figure 22). They get hurt and resent the pain. As they let themselves smoulder with resentment, they start thinking about getting even with whoever is around them. They think about how others have wronged them in the past, covering up their insecurity by establishing power as they have a need to control others. They repeat to themselves all the hurtful things anyone has ever said to them until, eventually, they take revenge verbally, physically, emotionally, or

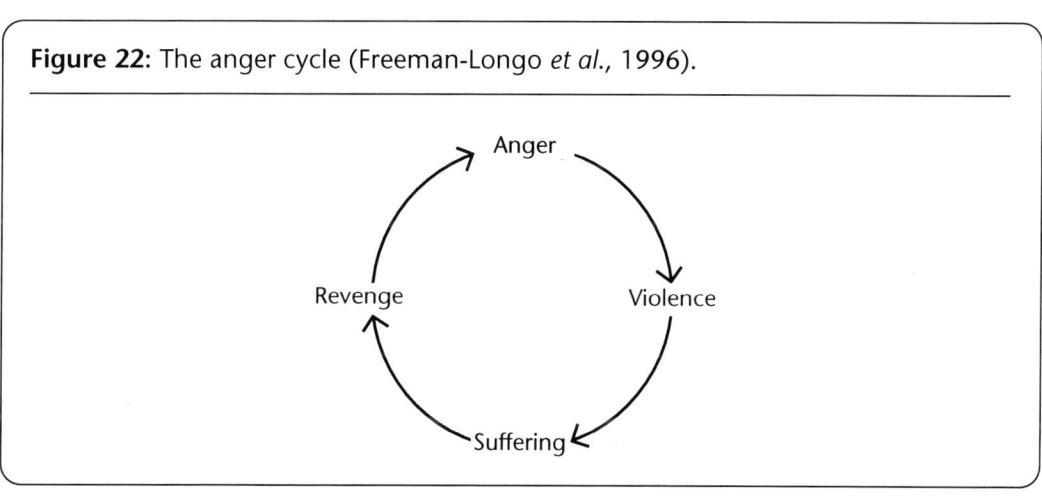

Figure 22: The anger cycle (Freeman-Longo *et al.*, 1996).

Anger

Violence

Suffering

Revenge

financially. In many instances, this can be physical and/or sexual abuse. The longer it goes on, the deeper they sink into the anger cycle (Freeman-Longo, Bays and Bear, 1996: p49).

Many offenders harbour substantial anger, often directed towards women. Pithers, Kashima, Cumming, Beal and Buell (1988) determined that in 88 per cent of rapes and 32 per cent of sexual attacks on children, generalised anger was evident in the offender. Anger is a motivator for sexual offences and to a higher degree for rapists.

Many sex offenders do have histories of physical or sexual abuse, conflict or trauma which has resulted in anger that has either been suppressed, repressed, or otherwise redirected. For those offenders who have unhappy backgrounds, the fusion of sex drives with violent ones can lead to a release in deviant sexual behaviour (Mayer, 1988). It can give the offender the illusion of having power and control. For the sex offender with feelings of inadequacy, it can be a comfortable emotion, providing temporary relief from the more painful feelings of vulnerability, fear and rejection, which lower self-esteem.

Aggression is a complex behaviour, and too narrow an intervention focus runs the risk of missing important information. Each assessment must establish the circumstances for the arousal of aggressiveness and carrying out a violent behaviour should be examined for each person, i.e. whether it occurs in the context of the family, or only under the influence of alcohol, etc. Sexual aggression is often related to the offender's developmental history. For example, the quality of early interpersonal attachments and the experience of sexual abuse as a child can play a significant role in sexual aggression in adulthood (Cerce *et al.*, 1984). Indeed, relationships in the family, and with significant others, during our formative years is crucial. Feelings of abandonment, of aggression, and often alcoholism in the parents are precursors of the adult sex offender of tomorrow.

There is an excellent resource from David Morran and Monica Wilson (1997) which sets out in detail a group work practice manual for men who are violent to women. It contains nearly 300 pages of materials, which can be readily adapted to work with aggressive sex offenders.

As Beckett *et al.*, (1994) pointed out, assertiveness is a multidimensional concept, covering such areas as an individual's ability to generally express feelings, stand up for their rights in public situations, initiate and maintain interaction with others, deal with criticism and pressure, and make requests and appropriate demands. Over-assertiveness/ aggression can interfere with constructive problem-solving and alienate others both generally and in intimate relationships, whilst a failure to assert can lead to them becoming socially and emotionally isolated, and can contribute to offenders being unable to extricate themselves from situations that may present a risk for further offences. Sub-assertive or passive communication patterns are often found among sex offenders who perceive themselves to be inadequate or inferior either to their peers or to authority figures. Fearful of expressing their thoughts or feelings, they often suppress their emotions, which can then manifest themselves through aggressive behaviour (Beckett *et al.*, 1994; Green, 1995). Individuals who are appropriately assertive are those who have skills in social perception, problem-solving and behavioural enactment. Sex offenders can therefore be either under-assertive or over-assertive.

It is important to identify whether the offender exhibits assertive or non-assertive behaviour as a result of their feelings, thoughts and beliefs. This should not be confused with aggressive behaviour, which represents inappropriate ways of expressing thoughts, feelings and beliefs.

Research findings

- Assertiveness deficits have assumed theoretical significance in a number of sexual anomalies (cf. Langevin, 1985). The rapist has been portrayed as unassertive, but aggressive, whilst the paedophile has been considered shy, unassertive, and lacking in masculinity, similar to incest offenders, and other sex offenders (Langevin, Wright and Handy, 1988a).

- The results of the assertiveness research on sex offenders, however, have been mixed. In some cases there are deficits and, in others, there are not (cf. Lang *et al.*, 1988; Langevin, Bain *et al.*, 1985; Langevin, 1983). Marshall, Barbaree and Fernandez (1995); Overholsen and Beck (1986); and Segal and Marshall (1985) have all found child molesters to be unassertive. Overholsen and Beck (1986) found child molesters to be less assertive than rapists, non-sex offenders, and community controls, and Stermac and Quinsey (1985) reported less assertiveness in rapists, but only in heterosexual situations. Abel *et al.*, (1985) found that 40.8 per cent of child abusers had deficits in assertiveness and 46.9 per cent of rapists also had problems of under-assertion. Inability to be appropriately assertive was implicated as the immediate precursor of sex offences in 42 per cent of rapists and general social skill problems were implicated as immediate precursors of sexual offences in 59 per cent of child abuses and 50 per cent of rapists (Pithers *et al.*, 1987).

- One significant confounding factor has been the prisoner status of the respondent. Segal and Marshall (1985) found that sexually aggressive incarcerated offenders were less assertive than community controls but they did not differ from other incarcerated non-sex offenders. Prisoners may be less willing to express their assertiveness while incarcerated to persuade a favourable parole application.

Self-esteem, sexual esteem and self-concept

Self-esteem is defined as the way in which a person perceives themselves, values themselves and rates themselves in relation to other people (Briggs *et al.*, 1998: p128).

Snell *et al.*, (1989) defined sexual esteem as 'positive regard for, and confidence in, the capacity to experience ones sexuality in a satisfying and enjoyable way'. They argued that the higher the sex offenders sexual esteem, the lower their sexual depression (e.g. the experience of feelings of depression regarding ones sexual life), and the more willing they would be discussing a variety of topics dealing with their sexuality with male workers.

Low self-esteem is a common presenting characteristic of sex offenders, and is believed to be a significant component accounting for both the development and the maintenance of sexual offending (Marshall and Mazzucco, 1995). Stephen Wolf (1984) has discussed the role of low self-esteem in sexual offenders 'cycle of offending' and described how some offenders with low self-esteem compensate by engaging in fantasies of emotional and sexual gratification with children. Many of these may have been the products of their own victimisation. Doing so contributes to such men then seeking association and sexual contact with children. Having committed a sexual assault, Wolf proposes that sex offenders, knowing that they have done wrong and fearing being apprehended, suffer a further fall in self-esteem, withdraw further from those adults around him and engage in more deviant compensatory fantasy, thus completing the cycle. Offenders with low self-esteem often have problems developing victim empathy (discussed later in this chapter).

Marshall (1989) and Marshall, Hudson and Hodkinson (1993) have suggested that low self-esteem in sex offenders results primarily from their experiences as children. More precisely, they claimed that if the parental attachments of male children were poor, (particularly if the parents were emotionally neglectful or rejecting), then the boy's self-esteem would suffer and they would be vulnerable to other influences that might lead them to become sexual offenders. These authors anticipated that many sex offenders would report parental rejection and that such rejection would be directly related to their current level of self-esteem. In fact, Marshall and Mazzucco (1995) reported that maternal rather than paternal rejection leads to lower self-esteem, whereas they would have expected the opposite. What remains unknown is how individuals take the next step from low self-esteem to sexual offending.

Social skills and competence

Deficiencies in the offender's social skills are frequently cited as playing a key role in both the origin and then the maintenance of sexual offending—by excluding them from access to appropriate sexual partners or preventing them from changing their mode of sexual expression to a more normative one (Marshall, Barbaree and Fernandez, 1995).

Social skills is a broad term used to describe a wide variety of behaviours and cognitive phenomena presumed necessary for effective functioning in social situations (Conger and Conger, 1986: p526). Sex offenders may present as being quite normal in their social functioning and beliefs, so the following summary needs to be read with this in mind. Many of the sections to this point will give us a clue as to the offender's social competency (e.g. interpersonal relationships, employment), but it is also important to assess areas such as their ability to manage interpersonal conflict.

Marshall (1971) argued that if we wanted to help sex offenders change their behaviour, then we needed to equip them with the necessary skills to be successful. He proposed deficits in conversational, assertive and relationship skills need to be addressed. For example, Lipton, McDonell and McFall (1987) found that rapists misconstrued women's cues on simulated first date situations. In particular, they misread cues from the women as positive and encouraging signs. Segal and Marshall (1985) found that child molesters were poorer than other sex offenders and non-offenders in predicting and evaluating their own performance in conversations with females. Barbaree, Marshall and Connor (1988) reported that although child molesters were as good as non-offenders at recognising a problem in a social situation and generating alternative solutions, they typically chose poor solutions and appeared not to consider the likely consequences of their choices. Decision-making skills involve being able to generate options, choose the best option and then evaluate the consequences of choosing that option (Fisher and Howells, 1993). These issues are often more profound in offenders with learning disabilities (cf. Murphy, Coleman and Haynes, 1983). Where the sex offender has learning difficulties, their level of social skills is often very low and this requires that we adapt the materials used as well as prioritising them for social skills training.

Tools

- The interview itself can provide clues as to the offender's social skills behaviours (verbal and non-verbal). Deficits may be indicated where they look away excessively, fail to listen, interrupt readily, lack social pleasantry, appear socially awkward, jump topics suddenly, become over-familiar with the worker or ask personal questions of the workers which are unrelated to the background relevant to the inquiry (Carich and Adkerson, 1995: p8). However, we need to be mindful of Segal and Marshalls' (1985) findings, as they reported that the offenders response and presentation within the interview situation may not accord with their behaviour elsewhere. Whilst role-play is advocated to counter this (Dougher, 1995), it is often difficult within individual sessions and maybe more practical in a group setting.

- It is also important to explore the relationship of any social skill deficiencies to their pre-assault cycle. In assessing the offender's perceptions, a number of questions need to be asked: Do they tend to be involved in insular activities? Do they value spending time with others? Has the influence of others been experienced primarily in negative or positive terms? Are there any differences in the way they describe interactions with children, same-sex adults, and opposite-sex adults?

Health and medical history

It should be routine to request the offender's medical history, which can be offset against any self-report questionnaires or interviews. It is important that this includes:

- Pre-natal, delivery and neo-natal development, including birth defects.

- Basic information about chronic and acute medical conditions, particularly any side-effects which may affect their sexual drive or performance.

- Illnesses or handicaps.

- Medication use, including conditions

necessitating it (past and present), and any non-compliance.

- Surgical history.
- Congenital disorders.
- Hospitalisations (and conditions necessitating this).
- Significant medical problems within the extended family.
- Self-harming behaviours/suicide attempts.
- Any major loss of schooling or periods of employment.
- Sexual diseases.
- Depression or mental illness.
- History of addictions (gambling, eating disorders, etc.). Any substance abuse accompanying medical treatment?
- Crime related injuries (adapted from Groth, 1979; Wincze and Carey, 1991).

Workers may wish to refer the offender for further medical evaluation, particularly if there are huge gaps in the history or where any outstanding concerns remain. The medical history may produce important clues regarding self-image, impulse management and control and feelings of self-worth and adequacy (Groth, 1979). Offenders may also use their medical conditions as a means of avoiding assessment work. An excellent source of questionnaires and scales for measuring health is McDowell and Newell (1987).

Sexual History

A sexual history is useful because:

- It may help in confirming a diagnosis of sexual abuse or understanding the dynamics of sexual abuse.
- It identifies their sexual development, experiences, habits and interests (e.g. sadomasochism), performance, satisfactions, blocks and dysfunctions.
- It identifies their sexual attitudes, values and orientations.
- It charts their sex education (formal or peer).
- It establishes how comfortable they are in discussing sex, N.B. Pay attention to their

non-verbal behaviour in addition to the content of their responses to your questions.

- It may offer an opportunity for them to discuss any sexual abuse they have experienced.
- It may highlight distorted family attitudes or practices regarding sex or sexuality.
- It may highlight sexual preferences, via patterns of behaviour.
- It may uncover the presence of other problems which are contributory to their sexual offending, and
- It is useful in assessing risk, making treatment recommendations and predicting prognosis and outcomes (adapted from Becker and Quinsey, 1993; Beckett, 1994; Faller, 1988; and Groth, 1979).

The following framework is our attempt to break down the sexual history into distinct, manageable parts.

Sex education and knowledge

Most people get their sex education from a variety of sources. Peer groups are usually a major source of information and young people may compare notes, borrow books from a friend, or pool scraps of information. Often the information from peers is inaccurate and facts do need separating from old wives' tales. Other children are more isolated and thus may have more problems accessing information, particularly as many parents find it difficult to provide their children with sex education. This is perhaps because they themselves received inadequate sex education and may be worried about revealing this, or they may simply be too embarrassed to talk openly about sex.

We all need sex education as we are growing up to help us make sense of the physical changes of puberty, such as menstruation and wet dreams, as well as the parallel emotional changes.

Despite the nature of their offences, it is not unusual for sex offenders to have limited sexual education and knowledge. This makes this block a crucial element of any sexual history. Many sex offenders also hold attitudes and myths, which reflect this lack of information. This can contribute to their avoidance of intimate, mutually consenting sexual relationships as well as their treatment of children as objects. The level of experience an offender has had sexually correlates positively with reported degrees of success and satisfaction in sexual relationships. These issues are often more acute in adult sex offenders with learning disabilities: they can be extremely deficient in their knowledge of both the biological and social aspects of sex, and many have extensive misinformation. In addition, many carers have adopted restricting or punitive attitudes towards sex for fear of promiscuity or sexual acting out, but this can lead to them denying their sexuality or experiencing guilt regarding sexual functioning (Murphy *et al.*, 1983: p39). Many sex offenders express concern that they were never able to talk about their sexuality with their parents.

Questions might include:

- Where, when and how did they learn about sex? (Peers, parents, TV, magazines, school, other, etc.)
- What were they taught? Elicit detail.
- What questions do they still have? Write these down and consider whether an education block is needed with the offender (see Calder, 1997a, for discussion on this issue).
- Ask them to describe the mechanics of sexual intercourse, masturbation, etc.
- Ask them to describe the developmental changes they experienced in adolescence. How did they feel about them?
- Was sex discussed at home? With siblings? Friends?
- What did their parents tell them about sex and masturbation?
- What was their parents' sexual behaviour like? How did they feel about it?
- Were their parents affectionate with them, their siblings, and each other?
- Understanding of sexual offences' legislation—homosexuality, consent, etc.
- Establish their knowledge of 'safe' sex, contraception, sexual diseases, etc.
- Establish how they would normally make

contact with a potential partner in a normal, appropriate, consensual way.

- What is their understanding of consent?
- When did they first realise that they were different sexually? E.g. developing patterns of sexually abusive behaviour?
- How old were they when their sexual problems began?

Sexual experiences

The exploration of sexual experiences is important as some offenders will claim that their behaviour is a poor attempt to get some sexual experience. Whilst the history of some offenders will reveal little or no sexual experience, there is ample evidence that this, in itself, is not a sufficient factor to sexually abuse. Those men who often feel inadequate sexually, or even overwhelmed by the prospect of a sexual experience with an adult, may fall into, or seek out, sexual relationships with young children.

Groth (1977) produced essential research that uncovered that 86 per cent of his sample had previous interpersonal sexual experiences prior to their sexual offence. Becker *et al.*, (1986) also found that the mean age of onset of non-deviant sexual behaviour predated the onset of deviant sexual behaviour. They found that some 95 per cent reported a prior, non-deviant, non-genital experience, whilst 59 per cent reported a prior, non-deviant, genital experience.

Workers need to be exploring the following with the offender:

- Their history of sexual encounters and the evolution of their sexual learning experiences, e.g. 'normal' sexual experiences—ages of first genital and non-genital experiences; sexual play with other children (playing doctor or 'show me' games; what sex games did they play as a child?; how did they feel about them?).

- The number of sexual partners: get them to list everyone they have dated and/or enjoyed a sexual experience with (male and female), including names, ages of both parties, activity, etc.

- Did they use any contraception? What kind?

- When did they start dating and what were their feelings about it?

- What was their most embarrassing sexual experience and which are they most ashamed about?

- Get them to describe their sexual and emotional relationships in their teenage years. What was their reaction to new physical developments in puberty?

- What was the expected sexual behaviour of men and women during their teenage years?

Workers can then move on to ask questions regarding any deviant sexual experiences, including the offender's own experience of abuse and its consequences, and homosexuality. Questions to ask may include:

- Did they have any sexual contact with other family members? Who? When?

- Did any other upsetting experiences happen to them as a child? Or to their siblings or friends?

- Was there ever more than one person abusing them?

- How did these experiences affect their feelings, relationships, behaviour, attitudes? (Note: While the role of childhood sexual abuse in the aetiology of sexual offending is debatable, there is some preliminary evidence that sexually abused sex offenders do often have problems that aren't found in non-abused offenders (Hanson, 1991). Despite this, the seriousness of the abusive behaviour of sex offenders is not mitigated by their having been sexually abused.)

- Was the abuse ever reported? To whom? Was anything ever done about it? If yes, what and when? What was their reaction?

- If they prefer boys, have they ever told anyone?

- Have they ever had any homosexual experiences? When? What were their feelings about that? How fixed are they in their sexuality? And sexual orientation? Are they attracted to both sexes?

- Have they ever sold sex? In what circumstances?

- Have they ever felt guilty or dirty about sex? What sexual outlets do they have (e.g. video, magazines, strip shows, etc.?).

Finally, workers should explore the offender's masturbation history and frequency, using such questions as:

- How do they feel about masturbation? And exploring their own body?

- Do they think it is harmful or enjoyable?

- When did they start masturbating?

- How often do they masturbate now?

- To what thoughts and/or fantasies do they usually masturbate to?

- Do they have different kinds of fantasies that they masturbate to? When? Have they changed over time?

- Describe their most common sexual fantasy. Do they reflect their behaviour or self-image?

- When did they have their first wet dream?

- Do they use their sexual experiences as a source of fantasy and masturbation? Or do they prefer pornography?

- What effects, if any, does alcohol, drugs or pornography have on their sexual practices and arousal?

Risk factors in this block include the lack of any history of relationships, a failure to initiate relationships, age-inappropriate partner choices, dysfunctional partner choices, lack of depth or stability in relationships, choosing partners with victim-aged children, a high anger level in relationships (or violence) or revenge and power themes in relationship interactions, e.g. revenge plans or stalking behaviours (Carich and Adkerson, 1995: p17).

Intimacy: sexual relationships and sexual satisfaction

Whilst we still have a long way to go before we are clear about the roles played by intimacy and relationship problems in the development and maintenance of sexual offending, it is clear from the work of Finkelhor (1984) that any blockage to the development of satisfying adult relationships is part of the offender's motivation to sexually offend. Such blocks might include there being little or no communication between the partners; and there being no sexual relationship between the partners or that it is not emotionally gratifying. Such problems in adult relationships may contribute to a gravitation toward children for emotional and sexual gratifications (Faller, 1988). On the surface, sexual satisfaction appears quite straightforward: either an individual is or is not satisfied with their sexual relationships. There are, however, a number of distinct, but related facets, relating to sexual satisfaction. These might include: frequency of sex and the degree of variation in sexual activities; communication between sexual partners about preference, such as foreplay; or broader factors such as the actual interpersonal relationship itself (Derogatis and Melisaratos, 1979: p256). Metts and Cupach (1989) argued that satisfaction in sexual relations is a function of the equitable nature of the relationship, (as well as being facilitated by effective communication about sex); and impeded by various dysfunctional beliefs and expectations, e.g. that simultaneous orgasm must occur if mutual satisfaction is to be secured, or sex is duty. It follows, therefore, that sexual satisfaction is related to levels of satisfaction in the rest of the relationship. It has been reported that men who are dissatisfied with sex in their relationship ask for an increase in the frequency of sex and for more variations and a greater degree of spontaneity (Hite, 1981), whereas women ask for more love, affection and caring during sex. Woman may argue, however, that they just want the men to learn to 'do it' properly.

Interpersonal dyadic relationships can be defined by three relatively independent dimensions: boundary, power and intimacy. Since the development of intimacy is a process, boundary and power cannot be isolated from any definition of intimacy (Waring and Reddon, 1983). A healthy intimate relationship is characterised by the capacity for constructive, respectful expression of positive and negative emotions. These expressions should be mutually acceptable and promote the psychological well being of the individuals involved; their function is primarily to define boundaries, to communicate concern and commitment, to negotiate roles, and to resolve conflicts (Coleman, 1987). Offenders with a history of being abused themselves have often lacked healthy role models, and boundaries

between family members are too weak or too firm. The boundary difficulties resulting from these factors may lead to two distinct problems with intimacy: they may be needy, intrusive, enmeshed, or controlling, resulting from a lack of clear boundaries between self and others, or the person may be avoiding and distancing, the outcome of boundaries too tightly drawn.

Intimacy is clearly important in establishing effective emotional and sexual relations with other adults (Brehm, 1992), and those who are able to develop it are seen to be warm and sincere; less aggressive, and better able to resist stress. Their relationships also provide them with a sense of security, emotional comfort, shared experiences, an opportunity to be nurturing plus a sense of self-worth (Marshall, 1993). Intimacy is a universal human characteristic. If thwarted in adult relationships, then sex offenders may seek intimacy in other less appropriate ways. This failure to achieve intimacy leads to the experience of emotional loneliness, which causes considerable frustration. If this frustration is experienced as emotional isolation from effective relations with women, adult females may be seen by these men as the cause of their loneliness (Marshall, 1989). Offenders who report a low sexual satisfaction with their adult partners are clearly more likely to overcome the resistance to sex with children (and therefore inappropriate partners) in their quest for intimacy.

Loneliness is usually split into social and emotional loneliness, with the latter proving the more difficult to endure. Social loneliness is a sense of isolation resulting from few social contacts. Emotional loneliness, the more severe condition, is at the heart of intimacy dysfunction, and arises when there is a lack of intimacy in personal relationships. Marshall *et al.*, (1996) defined emotional loneliness as 'what we feel when we are either separated for a prolonged period from our loved ones, or when a love relationship is terminated' (p230).

The association of the need for emotional closeness with the drive for sex can also lead to an increase in sexual behaviour as offenders escalate their attempts to achieve intimacy through sexual contact (Ward, McCormack and Hudson, 1997).This is likely to lead to sexual dissatisfaction, a gnawing sense of emptiness, and emotional isolation. As offenders arguably confuse sexual and intimacy needs, they may use sex as a way of coping with emotional loneliness and feelings of rejection arising from interpersonal difficulties. Sex becomes their way of coping or responding to negative affective states. Many offenders will therefore report feeling sexually dissatisfied when the crucial issue is actually a lack of intimacy. Their sense of loneliness may be aggravated by being processed as a sex offender due to the extensive negative responses by both the general public and other prisoners (Garlick, Marshall and Thornton, 1996). It is worth noting here, however, that intimacy deficits and loneliness are not the products of incarceration, they were present before and during their offences (Bumby and Hanson, 1997).

Whilst we all vary in our motivation for intimacy, many sex offenders do present as isolated loners or as having superficial or unsatisfying relationships. The assessment of intimacy deficits and loneliness may facilitate a more thorough understanding of the factors associated with the initiation and maintenance of sexually deviant cognition and patterns of behaviour.

Questions might include:

- A good way to approach this part of the assessment is to employ questions similar to those asked about children:

  - What is your partner like or what kind of a person is she?

  - What about her pleases you?

  - What displeases you?

  - What kind of things do you do together? Do you enjoy these?

  - Do you ever do things together without the children?

  - Are there things about your partner you would like changed?

  - Do you tell her things you don't tell anyone else?

  - How do you show her when she pleases you or you are happy with her?

  - How does she show you when you please her or she is happy with you?

  - How does she know when you are displeased?

  - How do you know when she is displeased?

  - What do you have arguments about?

  - Have you ever used physical force with each other? If yes, please describe (Faller, 1988).

- The marital relationship needs to be specifically targeted for information, eliciting how they met their partners; how they were attracted to them; how long it lasted (if it has ended, why and when); how many serious relationships they had before they married; why they decided to marry; how their relationship changed after marriage; what were the good and bad parts of the marriage; did they or their wives have other sexual relationships? Why? When? the number of children and their relationship with them; their attitudes and expectations regarding marriage; any history of rape, domestic violence, etc.; the quality of their relationships, their ability to see their spouse as a separate individual with her own needs, and the extent to which their descriptions correspond with information elicited from other sources. Marriage failures may reflect an inability to form lasting relationships, or to meet someone else's needs.

- How is their sexual relationship with their wife? Can they describe the kinds of sexual activity they engage in and their approximate frequency? How often do they engage in sexual activity? Has this relationship been more or less the same over the years or changing? Who initiates sex?

- Nature and age of partners (girlfriend, wife, child prostitute).

- Level of sexual satisfaction with different partners.

- The importance of sex to them in their relationships.

- The aspects of their sexual relationships they would change, and how.

- Their ability to discuss their sexual likes and dislikes with their partner.

- Their desired sexual competency.

- It is very important to establish what each individual offender understands by intimacy and relationships, any blocks or fears they have in these areas, and whether these are related to one or multiple relationship types (e.g. partner, friends, etc.). How do they communicate this, and the worker should always note any examples of inappropriate intimacy, e.g. with children or young people.

- How the offender reacts to the workers (and vice versa) may provide us with vital clues as to their ability to form adult relationships—as should parallel areas such as observations of supervised contact, joint interviews with their partner, etc. Workers do need to be conscious of the likelihood of different responses to the degree of loneliness and/or intimacy experienced by the offender at the time of their work, as compared to the time of their offending.

- Workers need to model, and stress the importance in understanding, the close relationship between emotions, behaviours and intimate relationships. It may identify 'chains' of emotions and behaviours associated with their intimate relationships and can lead to interventions tailored to them, e.g. addressing specific relationship deficits rather than the broader emphasis on social skills training (Ward *et al.*, 1996).

- It is well worth spending some time on this area as, once identified, there is the potential to help the offender make huge changes in the areas of relationships and intimacy deficits (Marshall, 1996).

Sexual attitudes

Sexual attitudes were defined by Lisak and Roth (1988) as 'predominantly consciously held thoughts or ideas, such as the best place for the woman is in the home' (p796). It is essential that we understand sexual attitudes as part of our understanding of sexual functioning. Derogatis and Melisaratos (1979) argued that in their 'value expressive' function, an individual's attitudes concerning sexual activities provide us with insight into their socio-cultural background. The mores of a society as a whole, and the significant sub-cultural units (e.g., family, friends) in which the individual holds membership, are communicated through attitude postures about sexuality. They also reported the role of attitudes acting as a 'gating' function in that they may act to screen selective information that is in conflict with the individual's predominant value orientation. Athanasion (1973) refers to this aspect of attitudes as their 'ego-defensive' function. This function relates attitudes to effects and thus may provide the workers with a window on the conflicted aspects of the offender's sexuality. It is important to have a valid appraisal of their attitudes about sex so that any communications are not presented in a fashion to produce a direct confrontation with value systems.

It is clear that there is a wide range of sexual attitudes just as there are a wide range of sexual behaviours. These will change over time as the wider culture changes also. Eysenck (1970) also confirmed that different personality types differ profoundly in their attitudes towards sexual issues. Marshall and Eccles (1991) have argued that many offenders hold attitudes, beliefs and distortions, which serve to both justify their offending and dehumanise women. This means that workers not only need to identify the inappropriate attitudes and beliefs but also the thoughts which underpin them if they are to understand their role in the commission of the sexual offences.

The most alarming finding is the lack of detailed research into the area of sexual attitudes in the sexual offending arena. Indeed, workers need to appraise themselves of the material in relation to rapists to try and unpick the issues that may arise in relation to the sexual abuse of children. Many rapists thus have negative views of women, endorse rape myths, condone violence against women, and are hostile toward women (Segal and Stermae, 1990). Feminists argue that sexual offending satisfies power motives, particularly of males over females. Abel, Blanchard and Becker (1978) claim that rapists display a 'hyperidentifcation with the masculine role' (p168), and more recently Muehlenhard and Falcon (1991) have found that males who endorse traditional sex role attitudes are more likely to have engaged in verbally and physically coercive sexual behaviours.

Questions might include:

- What were the attitudes within their family to sex and nudity?
- What are their attitudes towards men, women and children, particularly the division of roles and responsibilities?
- What are their attitudes towards masturbation, intimacy, relationships, prejudice, discrimination, etc.?
- How important is sex to them?

Sexual beliefs

All beliefs are ways of making sense of the world, or the sense that is made of the world (Horley, 1991). Ordinary beliefs have been described as 'expectancies (e.g. Rokeach, 1980) formed to deal with aspects of daily existence. Scheibe (1970), however, characterised expectancy beliefs as only one belief subclass, and he argued convincingly that many beliefs concern the present or the past only. Ordinary beliefs, then, refer to propositions about the nature of the world (past, present and future). They are typically expressed in the form 'S believes that P', where S (subject) is the believer and P (proposition) is that which is believed.' (Horley, 1991).

Abel, Becker and Cunningham-Rathner (1984b) investigated the role that certain beliefs and attitudes play in continued sexual involvement by adults with children. They focused on seven types of beliefs about children and sex they termed 'cognitive distortions'. These distorted beliefs were as follows: If children fail to resist advances, they must want sex; sexual activity with children increases sexual knowledge; if children fail to report sexual activity, they must condone it; in the future, sex between adults and children will be acceptable if not encouraged; if one fondles rather than penetrates, sex with children is acceptable; any children who ask questions about sex really desire it; one can develop a close relationship with a child through sexual contact. According to Abel and

his colleagues, the commonality among child molesters who hold these views is that they make no attempt to validate their beliefs against the experience of others. Other writers such as Stermac and Segal (1989) have confirmed this view. They found that child molesters, compared with normals, perceived more benefits for children as a result of adult sexual contact, greater complicity on the child's part, and less responsibility on the adult's part.

Beliefs supportive of sexually abusive behaviours are multidimensional and sexual conflict is often a means of supporting and reinforcing certain beliefs. For example, Briere, Malamuth and Check (1985) found that the absence of serious relationships with members of the other sex is associated with a belief that victims are responsible for their own rapes and the belief that women enjoy sexual violence. Another example can be found in the tabloid press, where a father reports having a sexual relationship with his 14-year-old daughter. He argued that he placed some of the blame squarely at the door of his wife because for the past four years she had denied him any sex, which is why he turned to his daughter. In more dubious pornographic magazines, there is material which reinforces a sex offenders belief that sex between an adult and a child is acceptable. It is not uncommon for sex offenders to hold exclusively rigid or puritanical attitudes and beliefs about sexuality. We also know that many hold irrational beliefs (about who is responsible for their offences and the impact of their actions on their victims) and these support their offending behaviour, along with cognitive distortions (dealt with in a later component). These irrational beliefs can often be concerned with what it is to be a man ('macho' or low in confidence) and beliefs about women, e.g. 'all' are rejecting. This has to be carefully managed if the workers are female. Some sex offenders believe that children benefit from, and enjoy, their sexual encounters with adult men. This is an area of importance in the assessment, but there is a surprising lack of material specifically about this component in the literature. Authors such as O'Carroll (1980) have provided material which supports the actions of offenders, challenging the assumption that sex between adults and children is morally problematic.

Questions might include:

- What, or how important was their religious background?
- What are their beliefs about sex? Masturbation? Relationships? Do they believe sex can only be legitimately expressed within marriage?
- Do they know what healthy or constructive beliefs might be?
- Can they identify any beliefs, which may have contributed towards their sexual offending?
- Get them to describe themselves as a) a man and b) as a sexual person, identifying any differences.

Sexual values

To talk of an individual's values is to refer to a system of learned beliefs concerning preferential objects, modes of conduct, and/or existential end states. Values include 'what is wanted, what is best, what is desirable or preferable, what ought to be done' (Schiebe, 1970: p42). Horley (1991) also noted that another generally accepted aspect of values is that they represent the essence of an individual. People come to see themselves, and others come to see them, by the standards that seem to guide their affairs. This is not to say that people always act according to their (ever-changing) standards of behaviour; they often find their own behaviour falling short of their ideals. Rather, the considered or expressed desires to see themselves and others act in a certain manner capture how people are, as individuals. Also, people's views on non-human matters, expressed by, say, a set of religious values, seem to make an important statement about essences. Self-knowledge and self-identity can thus be seen in terms of taking stock of values (p5). Rokeach (1973) defined the term moral values as 'those values that have an interpersonal focus, which, when violated, arouse pangs of conscience and feelings of guilt for wrongdoing' (p8). It follows, therefore, that values are a special type of belief.

Questions might include:

- What are their values? When, where and how did they learn them?
- Do they hold any unhealthy or inaccurate values, or stereotypes that are unhelpful?
- Is there any correspondence between their stated values and actual behaviours?

Sexual interests and sexual preferences

The sexual preference hypothesis is that sexual offending is driven by sexual desires for deviant sex (Marshall, 1996). It is criticised on the notion that you cannot always differentiate sex offenders from non-sexual offenders. Sexual preference is believed to be a relatively stable individual trait (Freund, 1981) and it is now considered to be an essential part of the assessment of sex offenders. It is a specialised component that needs the skills and expertise of psychologists, but we will explore the issues briefly here as we need to be clear about them as commissioning agents of the work. It is also important to have some knowledge of the issues as we may supplement any specialist assessment as part of our ongoing work with the offender.

Any assessment attempts to determine whether the offender shows an unusual sexual preference (e.g. for children), and as this escalates, the likelihood of them engaging in such acts. We will explore in a later block the reality that the offender, whatever the anomalous sexual preference, will fantasise and be driven by their unusual urges (Langevin, 1988: p270). There are repeated observations that sex offenders frequently ruminate over their sexual fantasies involving the types of behaviour in which they engage. The identification of some sexual preferences, such as sadism, is essential as, when aroused, they may want to rape and/or injure someone. There is a need, therefore, to identify the sexual preferences and then explore their relative strength, their duration, their potency for the individual, and if they are orgasmic in nature (Langevin, 1983). We have to remember that the offender may attempt to conceal their preferences either through guilt or fear of consequences such as imprisonment, and we need to acknowledge that the current charges or allegations do not always reflect the total map of their sexual preferences. Indeed, there may be other preferences unrecorded anywhere and there may be an overlap between the recorded sexual crimes. The common practice of inferring sexual preferences on the basis of index offences is thus very questionable. We know that many offenders have multiple victims over time: some younger, some older, and their current offence may not accurately reflect their true sexual preferences. Factors such as opportunity, disinhibiting effects of drugs or alcohol, social incompetence, or sexual frustration due to marital discord or dissolution, etc., may dispose men to commit a sexual crime with a child that is not sexually ideal in their mind (Langevin and Lang, 1990). It is therefore important to describe an offender's most desired partner (e.g. the victim's age and sexual features) and the desired victim response (e.g. admiration, fear, or pain) (Frenzel and Lang, 1989).

Determining sexual preferences is important because they imply cognitive and behavioural patterns that are long lasting and resistant to change. Thus, the male who has a preferential erotic attraction to children over adults may continue to be at risk for sexual offending throughout his life, although other factors such as age can be mitigating (Frenzel and Lang, 1989: p257). The identification of specific sexual preferences is an essential prerequisite for individualised, offender/offence-specific treatment programmes and relapse prevention plans.

It is also important to determine whether the sexual offending is down to either preference or opportunity, particularly as sexual preference patterns differ within the sex offender population; or whether it is the person or the activity they are attracted to. Some men have fixed sexual preferences whilst others are more transient.

Questions might include:

It is important to try and isolate each offender's particular sexual interests and preferences. Get them to write their reactions to each of the following:

Oral sex	Sex with children
Anal sex	Sex with older people
Sexual intercourse	Obscene phone calls
Foreplay	Massage parlours

Sex with animals (bestiality)	Group sex
	Rape
Different sexual positions	Sexual fantasies
	Sex in public
Exhibitionism	Partner swapping
Frottage	Homosexual
Extra-marital sex	experiences
Pornography	Sadomasochism
Prostitution	Voyeurism
Cross-dressing	Peeping

The worker can add to this list according to the requirements of each presenting case.

- We need to identify the sexual preferences of the offender and then explore their relative strength, their duration, their potency for the individual, and if they are orgasmic in nature (Langevin, 1983).

- What are the current charges and previous allegations/convictions, and what, if anything, do they tell us about their sexual preferences?

- Are their sexual preferences clearly identifiable? Are they fixed, transient, or is there evidence of crossover? Have they changed over time? If so, in what way?

- What would the worker expect to identify as their sexual preferences given the charges and the elicited history?

- What evidence of force is there?

- Does the worker suspect the offence is driven by opportunity or careful selection and grooming?

- What is their most desired partner and victim response?

Sexual arousal

This is linked closely with sexual preferences. One of the unique traits of the sex offender is the obsessive/compulsive nature of their deviant sexual arousal patterns for masturbation or other sexual excitability needs. When the compulsion is active, they are unable to get aroused to a normal sexual stimulus or fantasy regardless of how hard they try. If they do get erect, and a percentage do to anything that contains nudity or sexual suggestion, they are unable to reach orgasm unless they change the fantasy to include their own subjective deviant stimulus pattern (Prendergast, 1991:

p76). Fantasy is a guide to sexual arousal and, as such, their content can help to quantify the likelihood of recidivism. It is crucial to establish in what way arousal (fantasy) contributes to the origins and the maintenance of sexual offending. This is explored later in the chapter.

A major factor predisposing sexually abusive acts of some offenders is a distorted sexual arousal pattern. Indeed, dominance as a motivation for sexual activity can be a significant predictor of high sexual arousal (Malamuth and Check, 1983). Pithers *et al.*, (1987) found that 69 per cent of rapists and 57 per cent of paedophiles exhibited deviant sexual preferences during phallometric evaluation, whilst only 17 per cent of the rapists and 51 per cent of the paedophiles self-reported that they experienced greater sexual interest in abusive sexuality than affectionate sexuality with adults. Neglecting to evaluate an offender's arousal pattern may result in a failure to identify or address a central etiologic factor of that offender's abusive behaviours. If we do identify a disordered arousal pattern, it always indicates a need for specialist and focused treatment rather than it being used to exempt them from treatment (Pithers and Law, 1995). Indeed, Quinsey (1981) has argued that the best available predictor of long-term treatment success is the reduction of deviant sexual arousal coupled with an adequately high level of appropriate sexual arousal. To date, much more is known about the arousal patterns in rapists than in sex offenders against children or men in the general population.

Questions might include:

- It is important to differentiate arousal to gender (male, female, or both), ages, preferred sexual contact (e.g. anal sex; oral-genital contact, etc.), as well as sexual offences and behaviour type (e.g. frottage, exhibitionism, etc.).

- It is important to remember that subjective interviews may not accurately reflect physiological arousal, in that we only usually elicit partial or conservative estimates of their actual arousal.

- Link to the later section on fantasy and the earlier section on relationships for ideas on how to tackle this block.

Sexual blocks and sexual dysfunction

What exactly is dysfunctional is open to a wide range of interpretations, and has been thoroughly explored elsewhere (e.g. Jehu, 1979; Langevin, 1983). There are a number of theories as to the causes of sexual dysfunction. They may be due to anxiety, and this may be due to the new wave of women's sexual liberation, which has produced problems in the male partners, such as fear of competition or comparison. A second theory is that depression, anger and a loss of libido is contributory: anger and depression may induce impotence, whilst the associated impact on the self-esteem, sleep patterns and appetite may cause a loss of libido. Physical abnormalities, disease and chemicals are a third causal factor, lying in the psychological rather than the physical or the social domains. Some 90–95 per cent of sexual dysfunction are thought to lie in this domain (Langevin, 1983). There are a number of conditions that can result in impotence: diabetes, epilepsy, multiple sclerosis, bladder stones, sickle cell anaemia and leukaemia. Chemicals such as heroin addiction, tranquillisers, and chronic excessive alcohol results in temporary impotence. For a fuller discussion of sexual dysfunction, the reader is referred to Jehu (1979).

Questions might include:

Any history of sexual dysfunction should be elicited at the outset, particularly as blocks regarding the use of explicit terms such as anal sex can, unless resolved, render the assessment useless. It is important to explore the following areas:

- History of sexual offences and any other relevant, previous offences.

- Sexual deficiencies or abnormalities, such as impotencies, premature ejaculation, pain during sex, venereal disease, etc.

- How do they feel before, during and after sex? If happy, please describe. If not, how do they feel?

- Is there anything that has scared or humiliated them sexually? How? When?

- Why have their relationships ended?

- Do they experience and enjoy other stimuli, such as taste, auditory or visual, tactile pleasures? This is important as sensory sensations are often inter-linking.

Risk factors may include offending in response to sexual dysfunction; anger or blame of partner for their dysfunction; use of deviant fantasies to maintain arousal; or where the dysfunction is absent with the victim, but present with an appropriate partner (Carich and Adkerson, 1995: p25).

Summary and conclusions

At the end of the sexual and social history, the worker should be able to generate hypotheses about their sexual behaviours in areas such as:

- Sexual satisfactions, arousal, preferences, and dysfunction.

- Sexual beliefs and values, as well as their origins.

- Their approaches to sex, men, women and children.

- Any discrepancies between their responses and their behaviour.

For a fuller discussion of the role of hypotheses in the assessment process, the reader is referred to the stepwise model outlined in Samra-Tibbets and Raynes (1999).

Sexual Fantasies

Sexual fantasies are a component of normal sexual activities of most males and females, yet it is also considered important in the aetiology and maintenance of sexual offending. Wilson (1978) has pointed out that:

> ...nearly all of us have sexual fantasies at some time or another. They may occur as fleeting daydreams while at work, bizarre and intricate dreams during sleep, or exciting images accompanying intercourse or masturbation. Often they are things we would like to do in reality. Other times they are physically impossible or things we would have no desire actually to experience. Sometimes they appear in our heads spontaneously. Sometimes they are deliberate plans relating perhaps to the evening's activity. Mostly we enjoy our fantasies, but for some people they are disturbingly repetitive or a constant reminder of

> some frustration. Frequently they relate to actual events from our past, or things that we have seen or read which were experienced as very exciting at the time, and the memory retains the power to arouse us in the present. There are many kinds of sexual fantasy and the distinctions are difficult to draw.
>
> (Wilson, 1978)

In the past we tended to keep such thoughts very secret for fear of being seen as perverted. With the new permissiveness there is an increasing realisation that everyone is a little 'kinky' in their own way and if anything, this makes them normal rather than abnormal. Even so, our sexual fantasies remain a very private area of our mental life. Most of us would rather tell a stranger about them than a close friend or lover (p9).

Little research has been published about the common sexual fantasies and daydreams of the general public. It is known that young men engage in more sexual fantasies than older men and that more sexually experienced men engage in more sexual fantasies than less experienced men, regardless of age. Crepault and Couture (1980) addressed more specifically the issue of content. They were surprised by the diversity of fantasies reported. Paedophilic, voyeuristic, and rape fantasies were surprisingly common. Klein (1988) noted that deviant content often produces anxiety in the person who fantasises it and probably results in keeping these fantasies secret.

Sexual fantasies are linked to cognitive, affective and behaviour responses as fantasies can contain factual information, produce emotional reactions, and lead to overt responses (Byrne, 1977). Various functions of fantasy have been postulated: as an escape, as an outlet for anger, or as a means of regulating one's life (Rhue and Lynn, 1987). The following findings do help us understand how sexual fantasies might be translated into sexual offending behaviour:

Research findings

- The great majority of males fantasise while masturbating, although they may not fantasise on every occasion. Masturbation can reinforce fantasy.

- Broadly speaking, fantasy accords with the individual's overt experiences, but may become highly elaborated. Kirkendall and McBride (1990) found that 50 per cent of their college samples claimed that their childhood fantasies had been influenced by their childhood sexual experiences, with some non-sexual elements of early experience. They also found that some who had unpleasant sexual experiences had their fantasy inhibited. Many described their earliest sexual fantasy remaining their favourite fantasy. Those who have been sexually abused may begin masturbation earlier and use these experiences as the basis of their fantasy (Rhue and Lynn, 1987). Whilst the broad themes of fantasy appear to be laid down early in life, it can also embody a great deal of wish fulfilment that exceeds their actual experience (Gebhard et al., 1965). Many sex offenders generate fantasy through their offences.

- Gold and Clegg (1990) assessed the relationship between sexual fantasies and past coercive sexual attitudes or sexual experiences. They found that subjects with coercive experiences in their background had fewer emotions, greater explicitness in their fantasies, and a greater number of sexual partners. Malamuth (1986) also found that males with more sexual experience were more sexually aggressive. Respondents with a more coercive attitude tended to have more fantasies with the theme of extreme submissiveness, and to rate themselves less happy after their fantasies (Gold and Clegg, 1990: p471). They also found that force in sexual fantasies was associated with more explicit fantasies and less happy feelings after their fantasies. They were also less satisfied with their current sex life and more excited by their fantasies.

- Howitt (1995) found that only a few paedophiles actually reported orgasm as part of their offending, whilst many would masturbate to fantasy, at a later time, arising out of their offending (p176). This differs from Glueck's findings when he found that 70 per cent of males enjoyed masturbation fantasies before their offences (Glueck, 1956). Their sexual

fantasies of illegal acts seems to predispose them to enact these thoughts, through the associated excitement which also reduces inhibitions and guilt. In some cases, fantasies may become a necessary condition for sexual arousal.

- Whilst there is an assumption that fantasy is a prelude to action, particularly where it features over a period of time, it can also be a substitute for offending. Legal and illegal fantasies may co-exist, for example, they may fantasise about sex with a child during sexual intercourse with an adult.

- For offenders who lack social contacts and sexual experience, sexual fantasy becomes their primary (if not their only) source of sexual arousal. They may fantasise about their successful control and dominance of the world and this relieves any sense of failure they feel. It thus becomes easier and more pleasurable for the individual to retreat into their fantasy world (MacCulloch et al., 1983).

- For the habitual abuser, sexual fantasy is something which is activated at times of stress and strong negative (occasionally positive) emotional states. They retreat into their world of sexual fantasising, rather like an alcoholic might return to drink (Briggs, 1994) as a means of minimising their anxieties and ensuring that their stress becomes bearable.

- Howitt (1995) identified that there may also be substantial differences between offending and fantasy. Some men's fantasy includes sexual acts not to be found directly in their offending. A process of active negotiation may occur between fantasy and offending. For example, fantasies of buggery may be very arousing but its physical expression rejected because of the physical pain it might cause. In some cases, fantasy reverses reality. The offender who imagines himself the abused victim is a good example of this. Rather than being a script or plan for offending, fantasy engages with significant aspects of the experience and lifestyle before being expressed in action. In addition, it is often wrong to see offending as the source of sexual relief. Much sexual offending lacks immediate sexual release, and orgasm is not characteristic of all offences. In some cases sexual arousal and not sexual relief appears to be the main motive (pp186–7).

- Barclay (1973) studied male and female sexual fantasies and found that males mentioned visual aspects to their fantasies much more frequently, often reporting details about the appearance of female sexual characteristics such as pubic hair and breast size. He also reported that males tend to be active, impersonal and visually oriented in their fantasies, compared to women, whose fantasy themes are relatively passive.

- Fantasies are more evident with those committing 'courtship-type' offences, such as voyeurism (Awad and Saunders, 1989). Rada (1978) confirmed that as many as 50 per cent of convicted rapists engaged in voyeurism, exhibitionism, fetishism or incest in their early adolescence.

- Prentky *et al.*, (1989) found that the organised sex offender is more likely than the disorganised offender to be characterised by a fantasy life that drives their offences.

- Crepault and Couture (1980) identified three main themes in the male fantasies: confirmation of sexual power, aggressiveness, and masochistic fantasies.

- Wilson and Lang (1981) identified four main types of fantasy: exploration (group sex, promiscuity, homosexuality, mate-swapping); intimacy (oral sex, passionate kissing, outdoor love and masturbating a partner); impersonality (sex with strangers, fetishism, watching others, using objects for stimulation, looking at obscene pictures); and sadomasochism (whipping, being forced to have sex). They found that men were likely to be active in the fantasies and they were likely to be associated with dis-satisfaction (frustration?), possibly explained by difficulties in acting out their desires, and driven by the higher average level of libido. Men reported about twice as much fantasy as women.

Assessment areas

The assessment of masturbation fantasy often remains a taboo topic and workers need to acknowledge this when approaching the issue with the offender, and it can be helpful to be prescriptive when asking questions in order to maximise a likely response. Open-ended questions may lead to short, vague responses. Whichever approach is employed, accessing sexual fantasies, thoughts and masturbation remains difficult. Most offenders distort their perceptions in ways which psychologically justify their abuse. They also prefer to present their offences as momentary lapses, rather than a planned and erotic focus on children. Insistence by the offender that they did not experience any sexual fantasies or feelings denotes denial.

It is important to try and elicit information, which addresses the content of their sexual fantasies. It is important to differentiate between fantasy content. For example, homosexual, sadomasochism, sexual contact with animals, or residual contact such as peeping or exhibitionism (Gebhard *et al.*, 1965). The ages of the subjects should also be established. It is important to establish the number of sexual fantasies within each masturbation episode as well as their frequency and escalation. The role of stimulants such as pornographic magazines, videos, and television should be established, as should any internal states that trigger or intensify them.

- Logging masturbation activities and fantasies over an agreed period, e.g. a week, recording date, time, fantasy, pleasure sought and arousal. For example, did it involve a famous person or pop star? Or a complete stranger? Do they involve intercourse, oral sex, etc.? Does it involve violence or submission? Were any disinhibitors used, such as drink or drugs? Sexual fantasies are not a homogeneous phenomenon, and, as such, need to be addressed on a content basis.

- Masturbatory Pie chart (Briggs, 1994: p61)—where clients are asked to consider the last 100 times they have masturbated and to think about the range of different fantasies that they have used. These are then displayed as a segment of a pie chart to reflect the relative frequency of each fantasy.

- Feelings Journal—ask them to write down how they were feeling when they had sexual fantasies, and how they enabled them to get what they want.

- Rosebush Fantasy Exercise (Heinz *et al.*, 1987). On a piece of paper ask them to write a fantasy describing themselves as if they were a rosebush. Ask them to include the following:

  - 'What you look like (describe your leaves, stems, and flowers).

  - Describe in detail where you are growing.

  - If a rosebush could see, what would you see? What sees you?

  - Describe the weather today and most other days.

  - Describe how you get nourished. Who feeds you, your roots, and the soil you are in; and where do you get you water?

  - Describe those who care for you, if anyone does.

  - Tell us what is going to happen to you next week.'

Cognitive Distortions

Cognitive distortions related to sexual offending are learned assumptions, sets of beliefs, and self-statements about deviant sexual behaviours such as child molestation and rape which serve to deny, justify, minimise, and rationalise an offender's actions (Bumby, 1996). These beliefs and cognitive distortions function to avoid negative self-evaluation and social disapproval and facilitate the disengagement of the offender's inhibitions regarding sexual offending (Ward, Hudson and Marshall, 1995). For example, offenders may attribute responsibility for offending to their marital problems or a child's supposed seductiveness, or exclaim that they are entitled to satisfy their sexual needs no matter what the cost is to others (Hanson, Gizzarelli and Scott, 1994).

When these distortions are processed by the offender, they are often represented as thinking errors, defined as 'patterns of thinking which are based on distorted perceptions, therefore seeming rational on the basis of some private logic, but irrational in the light of societal reality' (National Task Force, 1993: p12). It can be said that this mode of thinking is the means by which the offender is able to translate fantasy into action, and subsequently to maintain their behaviour. Thinking errors become a way of life for sex offenders. They are tempting to the offender as, when these thoughts are used, they feel power and control, a sense of self-worth, and a general satisfaction. Cognitively distorting the offence allows the offender to overcome his own inhibitions and allows the offender to minimise and justify the offence, thus making the unacceptable behaviour 'acceptable'. Put simply, if the offender thought that there was nothing wrong with his behaviour, he would see no reason for stopping it (Jones and Lewis, 1990/1: pp44–5).

Cognitive distortions are arguably a partner for denial and minimisation for the offender. Most sex offenders deny the accusations against them, often despite overwhelming evidence to the contrary. Even in those who admit their guilt initially, there is often an effort to shift the blame from themselves. Related to this are the distorted perceptions related to the act itself. The sex offender typically sees the child as sexually provocative and as eagerly seeking sex with them. Innocent child-like behaviours (e.g. sitting in a manner which exposes the child's underwear or excessively seeking physical contact) are often construed as indicating sexual intent. Similarly, when the offender is engaging the child in sexual acts, he will typically see passivity on the part of the child as active agreement to participate in the behaviours (Ward, Johnston and Marshall, 1995).

Sex offenders also engage in covert planning (Laws, 1989; Pithers, 1990) in which they make decisions, which they see as justified and unrelated to any explicit plan to offend. It is as though they are deliberately suppressing full awareness of their intentions to gain access to the victim, by rationalising to themselves that their decisions, at each of the steps, serves a nobler cause and then, when the ultimate opportunity to offend arises, it is an accident rather than a plan. Such rationalisations obviously allow circumstances to unfold in a way that facilitates offending, but no doubt, once offending has occurred, serve to avoid any sense of guilt (Ward, Johnston and Marshall, 1995). Sex offenders frequently suspend self-regulation during their offence chain, failing to consider long-term consequences for short-term needs. As a consequence, they do not experience any emotional incongruity between their behaviour and their self-image, nor do they feel any distress concerning the responses of the victim.

Research findings

The following points have been gleaned from research and may help guide workers when exploring the issues in interview as well as deciding on their significance for further work:

- Becker and Abel (1985) have argued that cognitive distortions are a necessary prerequisite to the abuse as it allows the offender to translate their fantasies into action. Despite this, Marshall *et al.*, (1991) found that only 21.7 per cent in their sample indicated that fantasies preceded their abuse. There is little clarity on the point at which fantasy of abuse actually occurs. It is clearly variable, and might only follow the abuse.

- Freeman-Longo (1983) found that the average age at which sex offenders begin to have deviant sexual fantasies was 15. If they entertain them, then they develop a distorted thinking process that further condones the continuation of deviant thoughts, fantasies and behaviours.

- Pennell (1996) found no difference in cognitive distortions between young people who had been abused and those who had not. We can hypothesise that those who have may well have more entrenched cognitive distortions and that these findings hold true for adult sex offenders.

- Stermac and Segal (1989) examined the beliefs or cognitions of child molesters drawn from a treatment population and compared these to those of rapists, mental health clinicians, and lay persons. They found that child molesters perceived more benefits of sexual abuse to the child, attributed more responsibility to the child for the abuse, and attributed less overall responsibility to themselves for the offence than any of the other groups. Child molesters also endorsed more permissive attitudes about adult sexual contact with children than did the other groups. Differences of this sort suggest that the cognition of men who have had sexual contact with children may play a contributory or facilitative role in such behaviour.

- Anecdotal reports on the content of sex offenders' cognition do highlight many similarities, and include: ideas that children are informed and consent to, or refuse sex with an adult; that children are under no pressure to have sex with an adult; that children want sexual contact with adults; that sexual contact between adults and children is not harmful unless force is used; and that the prohibition against such activity represents an arbitrary social sanction (Finkelhor, 1984). These cognitions (and belief systems) are often modified by the offender in order to support and justify their deviant behaviour (Abel, Becker and Cunningham-Rathner, 1984a).

- Abel *et al.*, (1984a) hypothesised that as a child molester becomes aware of the discrepancy between sexual behaviour with children and the social mores of his culture, he begins to adjust by developing an idiosyncratic belief system of cognitions. The offenders continued sexual involvement with children is supported by the contribution of two factors: there are often no negative consequences for sexual involvement with children, such as arrest or discovery by peers, family and employers; and the offender never witnesses the negative effects suffered by their victims, since he leaves the site of the sexual involvement with the child.

- Abel *et al.*, (1989) found that cognitive distortions tend to increase as child molestation behaviours continue. The longer the offending goes on, the more cognitive distortions they endorse. They also found that child molesters do report beliefs and attitudes that are dramatically different from those of non-child molesters, suggesting that the normalisation of these faulty cognitions may be an integral part of the successful treatment of child molesters.

- Hayashino *et al.*, (1995), in a study embracing incestuous offenders, extra-familial offenders, rapists, incarcerated non-sexual offenders and lay persons, found that extra-familial sex offenders have a higher level of cognitive distortion than all other groups, whilst rapists and extra-familial sex offenders have a greater fear of negative evaluation. They may hold negative attitudes towards women that contribute to their maintaining a sexual and emotional interest in children. They were unable to establish whether these distorted beliefs were the cause and effect of their offending, but it did appear that they had a greater need to minimise and justify their behaviour. They also found that the lay persons' group endorsed several cognitive distortions. For example, at least a quarter of the lay persons believed that a child who does not resist an adult's sexual advances really wants to have sex with the adult; that a child's flirting with an adult means they want to have sex with the adult; and that if an adult has sex with a young child, it prevents the child from having sexual hang-ups in the future. In addition, 19 per cent of the lay persons reported some likelihood of engaging in sexual contact with a child if assured they would not be punished.

- Marshall and Eccles (1991) have noted that the problematic attitudes of these offenders concern not only their view of sex with children but also their more general views of children. For instance, Howells (1978) showed that child molesters saw children as non-dominant and compliant and viewed adults as dominant and threatening. They also tended to idealise children and to see them as having positive attributes that allowed the offenders both to feel more comfortable with children and to exercise non-sexual mastery over them. Gore (1988) also found that child molesters were more likely than other sex offenders and 'normals' to see children as seductive, as wanting sex with an adult, as able to consent to sex with adults, and as unharmed by such activities. Stermac and Segal (1989) essentially replicated these findings with the added observations that child molesters judged children to be more responsible than the offenders for sexual contacts with an adult and are more likely to benefit from the experience (p172).

- As we have already pointed out earlier, many sexual offenders may also have certain deficiencies or distortions which impair their ability to manage their lives responsibly or constructively. For example, they may have poor social skills and shyness, leading to avoidance of female or male peers. Feeling alone and perceiving themselves to be isolated from socially appropriate partners, they may seek primary social gratification and acceptance from children. They resort to children for intimacy and to gain a sense of competency and/or adequacy (Green, 1995).

- These points having been noted, most of us experience cognitive distortions, or errors in the way we think, at one time or another. We use them to push our point of view or to defend ourselves. However, when cognitive distortions continue or become extreme, they may poison our ability to function in a healthy manner. Steen (1993) pointed out that there are special kinds of distorted thinking common to most sex offenders. These include: misinterpreting what their victim is thinking, such as believing the person is asking for sex when the person really isn't and doesn't want it; excusing their sexual offences; minimising the harm they have done, and denying responsibility (pp25–6).

- There are always consequences for behaviour that is based on distorted thinking: what you think affects the way you feel and act and everything you do has many effects on yourself and others.

Distorted thinking can give you a false sense of being different from, more important than, or more deserving than others. It can lead to a belief that you have a right to do whatever you want (Freeman-Longo, Bays and Bear, 1996).

• Ward, Hudson and Marshall (1995) have proposed a theory on the role of cognitions in sexual offending that mirrors much of what was found in that study. Their theory suggests that offenders engage in a process of *cognitive deconstruction* related to offence events. According to Ward *et al.*, cognitive deconstruction is a process in which 'people attempt to avoid the negative implications of self-awareness in order to escape from the effects of traumatic or particularly stressful experience' (p71). In a cognitively deconstructed state, self-awareness is suspended or stunted and the person is typically focused on sensations in the here and now. While in this state, a person is not engaged in appropriate self-evaluative processes. This suspension of self-awareness may serve to help people reduce inhibitions and be more likely to violate their usual moral and personal standards. This theory of cognitive deconstruction may explain the offenders' lack of understanding of the child's or other's reactions to the abuse and their lack of fear about disclosure. Many offenders thus suspend their self-awareness of the impact or consequences of their behaviour so that this awareness would not inhibit them both beginning and continuing the abuse.

• There is likely to be a relationship between cognitive factors and the offence chain. Models of the offence chain (e.g. Ward, Hudson, Louden and Marshall, 1995) typically specify the cognitive, behavioural, motivational, and contextual factors associated with a sexual offence. These models make explicit the temporal component of offending and suggest that the functional role of cognitive distortions may change over the offence cycle. Some of these cognitive processes change markedly throughout the offending sequence as a result of increased sexual arousal and fluctuating mood states. The ways in which offenders interpret, explain and evaluate both victims' and their own actions can function to precipitate and entrench offending behaviour (Johnston and Ward, 1996).

• Ward, Fon, Hudson and McCormack (1998) provided us with a descriptive model to clarifying sex offenders' cognition concerning their offending behaviour. They argue that we need to extend our focus from post-offence cognition to all phases of the offending cycle, which consists of four sets of categories: offence chain; cognitive operations; cognitive content; and meta-variables. Given the detail of their arguments, the reader is advised to refer to the full paper for a detailed discussion of the points raised. The model aims to clarify statements made by the offender rather than to identify underlying distorting schemata. It offers the most advanced and dynamic conceptualisation of cognition.

• Ward, Hudson, Johnston and Marshall (1997) provided us with an excellent review of the available literature on cognitive distortions using a social cognition framework. They argued that the study of cognitive factors in sexual offending has been hampered by the lack of a theoretical framework. They note that there are a number of cognitive variables in addition to distortions (which they define as offence supportive beliefs or attitudes): such as cognitive structures (e.g. schemata); operations (e.g. information processing); and products (e.g. self-statements, attributions) and sex offenders may differ from non-offenders on some, but not all, of these variables. They argued that we need to assess more of these components if we are to effectively intervene to treat these sex offenders. That being stated, it is clear that specialist assessment is clearly needed in these areas.

• Bumby (1996) found that child molesters are likely to have more cognitive distortions about sexually offending behaviour in general and, thus, may tend to justify numerous forms of sexual deviance rather than exclusively holding distorted beliefs about child molestation.

The goals of assessing cognitive distortions include:

- To separate superficial distortions of defence from those that are more deeply entrenched, since the latter are commonly associated with a sexual preference for children and indicate an individual at greater risk of re-offending.

- To identify and elicit the origins, history and specific content details of each distortion.

- To identify the triggers that precipitate the offending cycle as the basis of offering alternatives.

- Whether certain moods or situations make such distortions more likely to occur (e.g. drinking), and

- How they behave when they occur.

- To isolate the origins of their cognitive distortions, e.g. seeing children as having adult characteristics, which enable them to be sexually provocative and being able to consent; beliefs about women (e.g. demanding); or social skill deficits.

- To list the offender's excuses for their behaviour and anyone they attribute any culpability to.

- To reinforce to the offender that these distortions feed their offending behaviour and need modifying.

- To determine future risk/relapse.

- To challenge the distortions and empower the offender to move from a passive to an active account of their offending.

- To allow the offender to accept the responsibility for their actions and to consider the harmful effects their behaviour has had on their victims.

- To use the cognitive distortions as an index of change, repeating assessments at various stages of the work.

- To determine treatment viability (adapted from Beckett, 1994; Briggs *et al.*, 1998; Jones and Lewis, 1991; and Moore, 1991).

For many offenders, the cognitive distortions they exhibit are essentially 'defence mechanisms' constructed during the course of the abuse to cope with guilt and anxiety associated with the abusive behaviour. Because of this, and because the legal system is more likely to increase the severity of punishment for those who fully disclose, workers need to recognise the investment the offender has in maintaining their defences. For this reason, workers may need to use direct confrontation, in the knowledge that this may not necessarily be productive, since it might serve merely to drive the distortions 'underground', where they are no longer accessible to exploration and change. It is appropriate, however, to be inquisitive and offer hypotheses as part of the work.

Adopting an approach which involves eliciting, rather than immediately confronting cognitive distortions can put considerable demands upon the worker, particularly where offenders are disclosing beliefs and attitudes which provoke anger and outrage in the worker. Moreover, it requires the worker to constantly be aware of the risk of collaborating with the offender in their distorted belief system. Few sex offenders will spontaneously abandon well-practised and emotionally satisfying cognition and actions simply because they have been discovered (Moore, 1991: p23).

Suggested materials to elicit required information include:

- Brainstorm a list of excuses, rationalisations or distortions that they have used to 'justify' their sexually abusive behaviour. We need to cover their pre-and-post-offence distortions as they may not necessarily be the same.

- Most offenders need to know that they made various types of thinking errors when committing their sexual offences. Their thinking is not based on real facts. They may offer some of the following statements to justify their behaviour:

  – They didn't stop me doing it.

  – They didn't say no.

  – I think they liked it. It gives her as much pleasure as it does me. She must like it, she responds.

  – I'll only go so far and then stop.

  – Sex can't hurt children.

  – I only did it once or twice.

  – I only touched them: nothing more.

  – It happened on the spur of the moment.

- It happened to me at that age.

- Someone has to teach them about sex.

- It comforts the child.

- I was drunk/ill/mad.

- I was only showing her how to insert a tampon.

- I saw my friend doing it to her too.

- I get a buzz from doing it.

- I did it because I love them.

- When women say no, they really mean yes.

- I deserve whatever I want.

- Rape is just forceful sex; women like being raped.

- Some children know more about sex than adults.

- Children can make me do things against my will.

- I was checking 'it' works.

- Unsatisfactory marital sexual relationships.

- Everyone wants to, but most don't dare.

- Somebody made me.

- I didn't know it was wrong.

- It's only the law that says its wrong.

- It's a good form of punishment.

- It's unlikely to be discovered.

- It's better me than someone else.

- She never told anyone.

- It's an urge no-one can control.

- It's an expression of love (adapted from Willis, 1993).

For a more extensive catalogue of common cognitive distortions used by sex offenders, the reader is referred to Abel *et al.*, (1984b); Abel, Rouleau and Cunningham-Rathner (1985); and Willis (1993).

- The offender can by asked which of the distortions listed above apply to them, and what others they might want to add to the list. Steen (1993) has suggested that they be advised to ask the following questions of themselves if they are unclear about whether they are thinking correctly or incorrectly: Is this something someone might find harmful, embarrassing or unpleasant? Is this something I would feel uncomfortable telling others about, e.g. work-mates or friends? Is this something I wouldn't like someone to do to me if I were their age or in this situation? Am I breaking any laws or rules by doing this? Would there be negative consequences if I were caught doing this? (pp27–8). If they answer 'no' to all of the above then we might assume that their thinking is correct.

- Thinking Error Journal (Green, 1995): this is the same as the masturbation log in that the offender is asked to keep a journal to record daily thinking errors. It should be completed daily embracing the thinking errors as well as the situations surrounding them. This is useful for the offender as it provides them with practice in identifying those errors whilst also providing the workers with an opportunity for assessing the offenders motivation and degree of self-awareness. Since many sex offenders are rather concrete in their thought structures, they find structures like this very helpful in effecting change and for holding themselves accountable. Anyone who is unable to recognise thinking errors is unlikely to benefit from further 'treatment' work. Conversely, just because they can recognise their distortions does not equate with them shifting in their beliefs, although it does at least indicate willingness to explore their cognitive process and assumptions (Willis, 1993: p51).

Denial and Responsibility

The single most powerful characteristic in child sex offenders is their capacity for denial. They deny their abuse not only to others but to themselves. They deny the true number of their offences, the number of children they have abused, and the true ages of the children abused (abuse of older children is more socially and legally acceptable). They minimise their offences in a multiplicity of ways. As if it was a one off, a coincidence, an accident; it just happened. They put the responsibility onto the children: she wanted it too; she really seduced me; these three-year-olds can be really provocative.

(Watts, 1989, in Gocke, 1991: p16)

Denial is therefore virulent in sex offenders, presenting itself in various forms. Leberg (1997) has defined denial as:

> *...all communication by the offender in which he insists that he did not commit the crime, gives reasons or 'proofs' intended to persuade others of his innocence, or attempts to minimise or distort the extent of his sexual deviance.*
>
> (p46)

Chaffin (1992) reminds us to be cautious in distinguishing 'denial' (a psychological defence mechanism) from 'lying' (a social behaviour). Lying is often motivated by fear of consequences, particularly short-term consequences, whereas denial might be thought of as motivated by a need to maintain a favourable image of self or important others or by fear of overwhelming aversive emotion.

Denial may be motivated by: anticipation of aversive events if responsibility is accepted, e.g. guilt, social stigma, marital breakdown, abuse, punishment, therapy; modelling, e.g. by other prisoners, group members, workers; reward, e.g. power over the worker; and ignorance.

Most sex offenders are referred for assessment via child protection conferences or the courts, and are therefore rarely co-operative or active participants in the assessment process. Whilst this will inevitably impact on the information provided, it may not extend to all the areas of information required. For example, it may be easier for them to admit to areas such as social incompetence or having a drink problem, than it is to acknowledge that they have committed sexual offences.

If we are to effectively respond to denial, it is important that we furnish workers with a detailed, yet practical framework, which sets out the offender's distorted representations of reality. Figure 23 sets out 15 different dimensions of offender denial, reflecting the reality that it is a spectrum and not a single state. Workers should find that offenders move

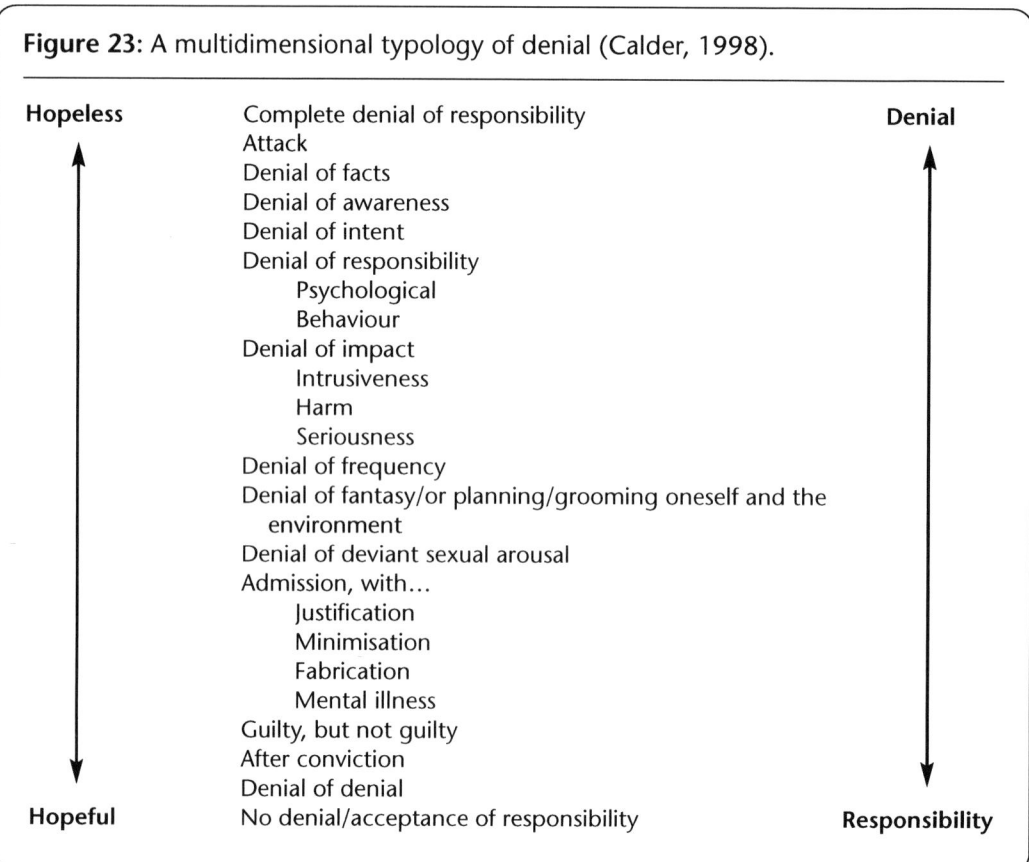

Figure 23: A multidimensional typology of denial (Calder, 1998).

Hopeless	Complete denial of responsibility	Denial
	Attack	
	Denial of facts	
	Denial of awareness	
	Denial of intent	
	Denial of responsibility	
	Psychological	
	Behaviour	
	Denial of impact	
	Intrusiveness	
	Harm	
	Seriousness	
	Denial of frequency	
	Denial of fantasy/or planning/grooming oneself and the environment	
	Denial of deviant sexual arousal	
	Admission, with…	
	Justification	
	Minimisation	
	Fabrication	
	Mental illness	
	Guilty, but not guilty	
	After conviction	
	Denial of denial	
Hopeful	No denial/acceptance of responsibility	**Responsibility**

between these dimensions as the assessment (and treatment work) unfolds (Salter, 1988). These dimensions are not neat compartments as they frequently overlap. Denial is not therefore a 'yes' or 'no' phenomenon, but is rather a continuum. Between the two extremes, offenders vary considerably on the level of responsibility they take for their behaviour. Offenders who can project blame on others and find excuses for their behaviour basically are blocked from truly recognising the impact their behaviour has on victims. The typology we present is not a continuum, given the real difficulty in grading the dimensions suggested.

Complete denial of responsibility

Here, the offender completely denies the behaviour described in the allegation, protests their innocence, and accuses others of fabricating lies about them. This is primary denial, and may include statements such as: 'I didn't do it, (even if I got blamed for it)'; 'I was out of the area at the time'; 'She's lying; she made it up'; and 'I was drunk, I must have blacked out'. This is the first reaction of most offenders: they act shocked, surprised, or even indignant about such an allegation. We should never be thrown by strong initial denial from the offender.

Attack

Some sex offenders can use this approach many times during an investigation or prosecution. This reaction consists of attacking or going on the offensive. The offender may harass, threaten, or bribe victims and witnesses; attack the reputation and personal life of the workers; attack the motives of the police or prosecutors; claim the case is selective prosecution; raise issues such as gay rights (if the child victim is the same gender as the offender); and enlist the support of groups and organisations. Physical violence also has to be considered a very real possibility (Lanning, 1986). These reactions are a severe example of denying the real truth of their abuse emerging and a denial of the process of justice.

Denial of facts

Denial of facts can take different forms. They may rationalise the fact that they have been convicted in a court by saying that they were framed. Alternatively, they may not deny that the sexual abuse occurred, they simply state that they were not the offender. It might occur when there is a denial of events on specific days and will often involve the use of alibis, which are clung to despite overwhelming evidence to the contrary. This denial may be aided by relatives, friends, neighbours, and others. They may claim that they did have sexual relations with the victims, but it was not an offence as they consented or did not resist, or because the victims received some emotional benefit from the sexual experience, or because they were tricked into thinking the victims were older. Another scenario is where they admit to the act but then go on to deny that the interaction was sexual in nature (e.g. they were administering cream). Typically, the offender will view himself as the victim and will protest his innocence with righteous indignation. The denial of facts position is often assumed by the family when they act as if the abuse has not happened or they ignore salient facts about the abuse. The offender may own the offence of which he is accused, but may represent this offence as the only deviant act committed.

Denial of awareness

This is a process in which the possibility of offending behaviour is considered, although conscious knowledge of the abuse is denied. This type of denial is demonstrated by an offender claiming lapses in memory or through alleged drug and alcohol-induced blackouts. They may claim that they know nothing about it or that they do not remember. They may claim their judgement, as well as their memory, was suspended for periods of time, when they were intoxicated.

Denial of intent

Here, the offender may admit some parts of the offence, but they deny that there was any intent on their part to commit the offence. Examples would include: 'It just happened', or

'I didn't want it to happen, things just got out of control', or 'Is it a crime to hug a child?'. Workers challenging this view will need to refer to the concept of pre-offence planning as set out very clearly by Finkelhor (1984).

Denial of responsibility

This describes a process of inappropriate displacement of responsibility onto non-offending objects. A range of behaviours, emotions, and cognition in which the offender and significant others blame people, substances, or circumstances other than the perpetrator of the abuse. Offenders displaying this position will often attribute their participation in the offence to seductive behaviour by the victim, problems with the spouse, or benevolent intentions such as educating the child for future sexual encounters (Winn, 1996). This might include:

Psychological

This is a more general form of denial of responsibility. It is where the offender does not focus on the concrete details of the alleged offence, as they maintain they are not the kind of person to commit such acts. This 'nice guy' defence is built on the premise that they are the pillar of the community, a devoted family man, with no prior arrests, and a victim of many personal problems. This tactic can be effective where people retain the belief that most sex offenders are 'strangers' or societal misfits (Lanning, 1986). They may try to discredit the victims by calling the victims liars or vindictive.

Behavioural

This is where external factors and mitigating circumstances are put forward to explain their offending. They may make the child responsible for the abuse saying that the child triggered the abuse by their behaviour, or they may say: 'Yes, I did it, but you can't blame me. If my wife hadn't left me, this wouldn't have happened'.

Denial of impact

This is a form of self-preservation in which the offender and significant members of his family or social network minimise or ignore the emotional, social, or physical ramifications of the offender's abusive behaviour. This process can relate to the offender's victims or to the impact of the crisis on the family as a consequence of disclosure (Winn, 1996). The offender may argue that the victim will fully recover and thus will not suffer any long-term effects, or that they will have other sexual experiences, thus rendering the abuse of no consequence. It might include:

Intrusiveness

Some offenders will admit some sexual acts and deny others. They may admit masturbating their victims and performing oral sex on them, but will deny actually penetrating them. Examples would include 'I only fondled her' or 'I didn't sodomise him, no matter what he says'. This is often noted when the offender minimises the extent of their previous offensive behaviour, the number of past victims, the frequency of their past offences and the degree of force they may have used.

Harm

This occurs when offenders may admit aspects of the offence, but deny that the victims were harmed. For example, they may say 'I did it, but it didn't hurt him, certainly not as bad as they say'; 'It didn't hurt me when I was abused'; 'When I had sex with my daughter I knew at the time it was my responsibility but I didn't hurt her'; 'She never asked me not to do it'; or 'It was a loving thing'. In this sense, they may portray the child as an active or willing participant in the abuse. They may deny any right of the child to say 'no'. The denial of harm allows the offender to pretend that their victims didn't suffer as well as preventing them from seeing their victims as people with thoughts and feelings about what happened to them. This will result in the offender seeing children simply as objects.

Seriousness

This follows on from where the offender has no concept of the severity of their acts, any long-term harm to their victims, or the difficulties involved in changing their pattern of offending behaviour. They may simply say 'It won't happen again', without accepting the likelihood of further abuse occurring; they may deny any abuse of power; they may deny any previous history of sexually deviant behaviour and/or any ongoing sexual problems. They may even present themselves as non-sexual beings. Offenders in this category are unlikely to want to change.

Denial of frequency

The offenders statement of how many times the abuse occurred may be much less than what the victim says occurred, for example, 'I did it, but only a few times, not the 20 times he says'. It is not unreasonable for the worker to double the frequency of admitted abuse, similar to a GP taking a history of alcohol or tobacco use.

Denial of fantasy or planning or grooming oneself and the environment

Some offenders admit the abuse, but deny any (internal) fantasy or (contextual) planning involved in organising the abuse. Offenders demonstrating this position will deny grooming themselves by fantasising deviant material or justifying the abuse to themselves. Similarly, they will deny any manipulation used in securing a victim. Rather, the abuse will be described as if it came 'out of the blue', with no warning to the offenders; or they may say 'I abused children, but the thought of it disgusts me' or 'I never get turned on when I think about it'. They may cite statements that the offence happened on the spur of the moment, for example: 'Her mother was out, she came downstairs in her night dress with no pants on, to watch her favourite TV programme and...' They may state that the offence was an isolated, inexplicable incident, or completely out of character, e.g. 'It's never happened before...it won't ever happen again...I don't behave like this, I'm happily married...'.

Denial of deviant sexual arousal

This describes a form of denial in which the offender and his family ascribe intentions for offending to non-sexual reasons. Instead of acknowledging the offence as sexual in nature, this position describes a range of thoughts, feelings, and behaviours which minimise or ignore the fact that the offender has a problem with paraphilic or inappropriate sexual behaviour (such as arousal, interest, or preferences), (Winn, 1996). Many offenders may deny only the sexual offence and intent and be candid about all the other requested information from the workers.

Admission, with...

Justification

A sex offender typically attempts to justify his behaviour to the police. This may be where the commission of the act is admitted, but where the extent and seriousness of the behaviour is often minimised and blame deflected onto life events or the victim. Consequently little guilt or blame is felt. This may involve pretending that the abuse was a normal or educational activity: 'I was teaching him about sex', or 'I was checking her out because she said she hurt down there'. They may outline the offence and argue that it included nothing unlawful (e.g. the child 'consented', or they did not know how old a certain victim was), or say that children often make up stories about being sexually abused. They may justify what they have done, saying 'She was sleeping with her boyfriend as well...'. They may argue that the victim encouraged them, initiating the process and taking the lead, as well as enjoying the sexual encounter. Many argue that the victim hasn't disclosed until now because of these factors. Even where the offender has been seduced by a victim, and they are promiscuous, a crime has still been committed, and such a justification has no meaning. Others will simply believe they have done nothing at all wrong. The offender might claim that he cares for these children more than their parent's do and that what he does is beneficial to the child.

Minimisation

If the evidence against the offender rules out total denial, the offender may attempt to minimise what they have done, both in quantity and quality. Offenders minimise their own responsibility for their offences in three ways: attributing blame to the victim, making external (situational) attributions (such as stressful circumstances, social pressure or provocation) and making irresponsible internal attributions (such as their deprived childhood, their hormones or sex drive). It is also important to recognise that even seemingly co-operative victims may also minimise the quantity and quality of acts. If a certain act was performed 20 times, the victim might claim it only happened ten, and the offender might claim it only happened once. Victims may also deny particular sexual acts, such as anal intercourse by adolescent males. Limited and highly selective admission is commonplace, with the all-important planning and fantasising frequently being denied. Here, whilst the offender admits the offence, they use the device of making it sound much less serious than other evidence shows it to be: e.g., 'I only brushed up against her just the once', 'I only touched her', 'It wasn't a big deal', or 'I only put the tip in'. When minimising the full extent of their behaviour, they frequently say that the child precipitated or collaborated with their own abuse. They may also minimise the full extent of their sexual problems. They may also be knowledgeable about the law and might, therefore, be motivated to admit to those acts that carry lesser consequences.

Fabrication

Some of the cleverest sex offenders come up with ingenious stories to explain their behaviour. For example, doctors saying they are researching male youth prostitution. A teacher claimed that his students had such a desperate need for attention and affection that they practically threw themselves at him and misunderstood his resulting affection for sexual advances. Another offender said that his sadomasochistic photographs of children were part of a child discipline programme. One offender claimed that some children made the sexually explicit videotape without his knowledge and he kept it only to show their parents. Workers clearly need to challenge such explanations and attempt to disprove them (Lanning, 1986).

Mental illness

When all other tactics fail, the offender may feign mental illness. Few do so until they are either arrested or charged. Such a diagnosis simply re-frames the need for treatment and never excuses their behaviour.

Guilty, but not guilty

This is where the offender will try to make a deal in order to avoid a public trial. Whilst this has the advantage of sparing the victim the trauma of giving evidence, it allows the offender to plead, in essence, to 'guilty, but not guilty'. In the UK, this can be plea-bargaining to a lesser offence. The offender might also say they are pleading guilty to spare the child, or that they cannot afford to contest the charges, but don't accept their guilt despite their pleas. This can confuse the victims further (Lanning, 1986).

After conviction

Post-conviction, and often incarceration, some offenders ask to speak to law enforcement officials in order to share information about organised abuse, including child sex rings, child pornography, abduction of children, etc., as this allows them to contextualise and minimise their abuses in the broader framework. It also allows them to plea for a reduced sentence (Lanning, 1986).

Denial of denial

Is a description of the offender's and the family's behaviour which minimises or disqualifies the fact that denial is a necessary means of psychological protection to cope with the shame generated in the maintenance of abusive behaviour. Accepting this fact often enables the offender to monitor themselves better, as they realise that denial has a purpose and cannot be cured but, rather, observed and managed (Winn, 1996).

No denial/acceptance of responsibility

This is where the offender's account of the events is essentially the same as the allegation.

Examples include: 'I did it. It's my responsibility'; 'I did everything s/he said I did, and there are things I did that s/he didn't mention'; 'I'm sure I hurt him, though I don't know how badly', and 'Even though I hurt him, sometimes I still get turned on when I think about it'. It is very important that we don't allow offenders who start at this point to avoid some detailed assessment work, as it can be a clever tactic to avoid detailed internal enquiry.

Research findings

- Research has highlighted specific differences with respect to the type of denial used by offenders. Rapists who deny their offence justified their behaviour by focusing on the victim and her role in the event (Scully and Marola, 1984), whereas rapists who admitted their offence characterised themselves as having substance abuse problems or emotional problems, but otherwise perceived themselves to be 'nice guys'. They focused on more socially acceptable personal difficulties that were of a temporary nature. In contrast, admitting child molesters used denial tactics in an effort to deny the impact of their behaviour (Lanyon and Lutz, 1984).

- Nugent and Kroner (1996) examined the correspondence of denial and level of admittance of offences among child molesters and rapists. They found a difference on both counts between the two groups, with child molesters admitting more frequently to the offence. Child molesters tended to deny the extent of the offence, while rapists denied the degree of force. Child molesters are significantly more concerned about what others think about them. For child molesters, they found that denial and lying about the offence went beyond self-protection to being an ingrained and pervasive response embedded in their lifestyle. More worryingly, many will remain unaware about the presence and extent of their denial. They also found that child molesters have a greater number of victims and commit several offences more repetitively than rapists.

- Barbaree (1991) found that among 114 incarcerated rapists, 59 per cent denied they had committed an offence and a further 41 per cent minimised either their responsibility for the offence, or the harm they had done or the extent of their offending (frequency, forcefulness or degree of sexual intrusiveness). Both groups presented justifications which were intended to support their denial or to minimise responsibility for the offence. For example, among those who denied their offence, 31 per cent reasoned that they had not committed an offence because the victim provoked them by being seductive. About one-third of those who denied their offence and one quarter of those who admitted their offence argued that their victims meant 'yes' even though they said 'no'. Of the deniers, 69 per cent claimed that their victims eventually relaxed and enjoyed the rape. The same argument was put forward by 20 per cent of the admitters. 69 per cent of the deniers and 22 per cent of the admitters alluded to the victims' unsavoury reputations as excuses for their crimes. 77 per cent of the admitters and 84 per cent of deniers excused their behaviour by attributing it to alcohol intoxication, while 40 per cent of deniers and 33 per cent of admitters explained their crimes by pointing to emotional problems caused by an unhappy childhood or current marital conflict. Treatment reduced the number of deniers who remained in therapy for the full programme, from 22 to three: but 15 of those deniers who admitted to having offended, were still minimising at the end of treatment. Of the 15 who initially admitted b1ut minimised their offence(s), only three gave up all evidence of minimising as a result of treatment.

- Bentovim (1994) reported that from his work in Great Ormond Street, only nine per cent of offenders accepted full responsibility; 15 per cent some responsibility; with 76 per cent refusing to accept any responsibility for their actions. These figures do highlight the centrality of the management of denial in any assessment or treatment work with sex offenders.

- O'Donohue and Letourneau (1993) explored the effectiveness of structured group treatment in reducing the denial of sexual offences in 17 males. Despite an average length of time of denial of nearly 2 years, by post-treatment, the majority of offenders had come out of denial. This supports the process of denial outlined earlier. As indicated by the pre-treatment clinical evaluations of subjects, almost all were in complete denial. One subject was rated as being in partial denial (e.g. he claimed to have no memory of the incident due to intoxication but allowed that it could have happened), and one subject fully accepted responsibility for the abuse, but refused treatment. At post-test, 13 (76 per cent) of the subjects were rated as being at least partially out of denial. Given the two subjects who were not in full denial pre-treatment, this indicates that 11 subjects (65 per cent) changed from 'denier' to 'admitter' status. In addition, one subject, (six per cent) maintained his denial but expressed interest in sex offender treatment in order to change his deviant arousal pattern. Of the 13 subjects who were out of denial at post-treatment, five (38 per cent) were rated as only partially admitting their guilt (e.g. admitting to the offence but minimising the impact of their actions of victims; or admitting to an earlier offence while maintaining innocence of the counts upon which they had been convicted). The other eight subjects fully admitted to the offence they were convicted of (e.g. gave details about the offence). Four subjects remained in denial.

- Langevin (1988) carried out a study of defensiveness in 100 sex offenders, 50 of whom were repeated sex offenders against children, and 50 of whom were sexually aggressive against adult women. He found a comparable degree of admission to the offence in question, less than one-third of the cases admitted both to their offences and their sexually anomalous preferences. Slightly more than a third admitted committing the offences but denied anomalous erotic preferences, and 13 per cent admitted both yet claimed special circumstances such as drunkenness, loneliness, or marital problems, as precipitators of the offences in question. Four men denied committing the offences but did admit to an anomalous sexual preference (i.e. for children or sexual aggression). 15 per cent denied everything, claiming mistaken identity or being 'framed'. He found that the sex offender differs from other defensive patients in a number of important ways. Most often, he presents a picture of a psychologically normal individual who attempts to minimise any attraction to children, sexual aggression, or other sexually anomalous outlets. He frequently denies the pending legal charges. He may deny a history of anomalous sexual behaviour or may attribute the offence to alcohol and drug abuse. In some cases, a partial denial occurs in which the current problems or substance abuse may be invoked as a contributing factor, even though the offender accepts his responsibility for the criminal behaviour.

- Sex offenders typically deny the true extent of both their sexual problems and offences. This becomes acutely obvious when we consider the full extent of their offending when granted confidentiality pre-disclosure. Abel *et al.*, (1987) found that this usually encourages a greater frequency and range of offences against the known victims, as well as admitting to previously undetected sexual offences and a wider range of paraphilic behaviour, for example, exhibitionism, stealing female underwear, etc.

Assessing denial

Most offenders are referred for assessment on a mandated or coerced basis, and the findings often have very important consequences for sentencing, child protection or custody disputes. Others do not want to give their behaviour up, so they present in a socially desirable way to impress the workers. It is not surprising, therefore, that offenders lie about their offences as a self-protective strategy.

As workers, we can easily become jaded hearing the excuses, minimisations, and denials from sex offenders and soon come to disbelieve every story; mostly with good cause (Maletzky, 1996). Assessing denial is important for two reasons. The degree to which an offender denies or minimises his behaviour will reflect his motivations to participate actively in the work. Secondly, by minimising in some way the significance of their behaviour, we are able to predict a likely recurrence more accurately (Murphy, 1990). If the offender surprises us and starts the work by openly admitting the offences and their responsibility for the crime, then that should not allow them to avoid facing the detailed introspection required to prevent relapse. Many offenders may admit in the hope that we will view the acceptance of responsibility as removing any future risks.

Workers need to understand the offender's motivation for using denial if they are to effectively tackle it in practice. Strategies for interviewing are considered in Chapter Five, yet it is important to look at this in relation to denial. Simplistically, if you believe that denial is a rationalising cognition, then you will be tempted to approach the offender in a confrontational manner in an attempt to separate out the truth from the lies. This approach can lead to denial entrenchment and there is rarely any progress made. If you believe that denial is a natural starting point when looking at the obstacles to accepting responsibility (such as the consequences socially, personally, financially, etc.), then you may be inclined to adopt a motivational interviewing approach. This approach views denial as simply a lack of recognition by the offender that they need to change. Schlank and Shaw (1996) set out the use of this approach in a group setting and provided some encouraging results, with some 50 per cent of the offenders modifying the denial to the point that they became eligible for treatment.

Denial is generally assumed to be anti-therapeutic in most cases as each side tries to disprove the other. Hartman and Reynolds (1987) identified five phases of movement with resistant clients: testing worker authenticity; checking the workers' values and experience; movement towards involvement with the workers; committing themselves to the work; and finally, engaging in problem-solving with the worker. If workers start by focusing on the sexual offences, then they may not get very far with the proposed work. It is an important area

to cover, but if you refer to the details needed in any comprehensive assessment, then you will have many other (non-threatening) places to start, such as social history, fantasy, beliefs and attitudes, etc. Ordering the work is an important consideration when anticipating denial, as workers need to create the right kind of environment in which the offender can think about change. Quite simply, we should encourage the offender to challenge their own denial and thus diminish detail by degrees (Maletzky, 1996): not only providing the offender with a springboard for change, but also providing the workers with some much needed job satisfaction.

Questions might include:

- The only credible and adequate method of assessing denial is by comparing the acts that offenders self-disclose to the acts recorded by more credible sources (e.g. victim reports, police records).

- What is the source of their denial? Is it overt or covert? What, if any, behavioural manifestations are present, such as body language, clothing, or dysfunctional behaviours? Once this information has been elicited, they may be useful for the worker to help the offender bridge resistance with alliance as a foundation for accepting responsibility for their actions.

- Get the offender to draw how they remember the alleged offence situation (or one of the many) and then get them to interpret it as well as offering your interpretation to them for their consideration.

- Ask the offender to list the reasons why they should tell us about what has happened. They might cite being better understood, accessing the right kind of help, removing secrecy, less likelihood of a punitive community and court response, etc.

- Ask them to describe the antecedents of their offending and the consequences of it.

- Many sex offenders say that they really didn't believe that they were doing anything wrong, or they didn't hurt the people they sexually abused. One way to test their honesty is to look at whether they told others about what they were doing. If they felt good about their sexual offences, or if they thought there was nothing wrong with what they did, they would have told others about their behaviour. Get them to list: Who they have told; listing names, relationship, order of who they told, why and when?

- As the offender talks about their offending, try to see the whole picture and how the pieces fit together. Listen for the defensive strategies being used and don't go along with them. He may say that he had been drinking beforehand and so can't recall what happened. Given the nature of the offending it is extremely unlikely that the most important details cannot be recalled, despite how much he had to drink! The motivation for the offending preceded the drinking. The drinking may have, in the words of one sex offender, given 'the courage to do what I really wanted to do'.

- Get the offender to construct a number of partial sentences that have a resemblance to their offences and ask them to complete them, for example, 'I use force when...', 'My attitude towards sex with women/ children is...'.

- Record of denial. We need to record what is being observed or said, how the attitude has been manifest, to whom, and under what circumstances. See Figure 24.

Figure 24: The record of denial (adapted from Briggs, 1994).

Type of denial	Yes/No	How manifested? In what context?
Complete denial		
Complete denial of responsibility		
Attack		
Denial of facts		
Denial of awareness		
Denial of intent		
Denial of responsibility		
Denial of impact		
Denial of frequency		
Denial of fantasy		
Denial of planning or grooming		
Denial of deviant sexual arousal		
Admission with:		
– justification		
– minimisation		
– fabrication		
– mental illness		
Guilty, but not guilty		
After conviction		
Denial of denial		
No denial		

Victim Empathy and Awareness

Empathy comprises multiple components and processes, which need to be understood as a preface to any work in this area. Empathy has been defined as a cognitive ability to understand and identify with another's perspective (Cronbach, 1955; Taguiri, 1969), an emotional capacity to experience the same feelings as another (Clore and Jeffrey, 1972) or an interplay of cognitive and affective factors (Aronfreed, 1968). Briggs (1994) noted that cognitive empathy is where the offender has an intellectual understanding of the feelings of others without necessarily experiencing any emotional change themselves, whilst emotional empathy is where they experience the emotions of others in response to their situations and feelings. Other writers have argued that it should embrace communicative and relational elements. Freeman-Longo, Bays and Bear (1996) have argued that it is not about being self-centred, harsh, indifferent, resistant, discouraging, unsupportive, impatient, angry, inconsiderate, hostile, irritated, selfish, mean, abusive, cynical (p7).

Sex offenders are thought to suffer from deficits in their capacity to experience empathy, yet the extent is in dispute, and this is considered to be important in the development, and particularly the maintenance, of their deviant behaviour. The lack of any empathy clearly has a significant impact on the likelihood of repeat and escalatory offending. For example, it is clear that those sex offenders who deny any responsibility for their offences will feel little remorse or shame for what they have done. Indeed, the use of mechanisms such as denial preclude empathic interactions or awareness of the victims rights, and they also fail to appreciate (or lack) the basic information regarding the consequences of their behaviour, other than for themselves. Far worse than this, many offenders argue that they have helped the child/ren they have abused, e.g. sex is educational and in the 'best interests' of the child. If the offender feels bad after abusing, the child victim, by simply surviving without psychological damage apparent to their offender, gives a covert message of 'its OK'. The offender thus feels better, and this can make it easier for them to offend again. Victims may subsequently perceive the bad feelings held by the offender and feel responsible, even reassuring him (White, 1992: p37).

Workers always need to consider whether the offender has been sexually abused themselves and how such experiences may affect their thoughts and behaviour. We should also not disregard the possibility that their early life experiences have been characterised by a lack of empathic care, so the workers can model empathy through their relationship with the offender. It is often through recognition of our own pain that empathy is achieved. Whilst this is important, workers can never overlook or excuse their abusive behaviour. The development of empathy for the victim and potential victims is arguably the most important variable to decreasing their potential to re-abuse (DiGeorgio-Miller, 1994: p124).

A model for understanding empathy

Marshall (1993b) argued that empathy involves four processes: recognition of the other person's feelings; the evocation in the observer of those same feelings; the recognition of those states by the observer; and the acceptance of the shared feelings. It is no surprise that our understanding of empathy is often confused given the complexity of the concept. In response to this, Marshall, Hudson, Jones and Fernandez (1995) offered us a multi-component model to help us better understand sex offenders. They argued that empathy is a staged process involving:

1. emotional recognition
2. perspective-taking
3. emotion replication
4. response decision

Stage 1: Emotional recognition requires that the offender be able to accurately discriminate the emotional state of the victim. The recognition of personal distress seems to be a necessary first step in the unfolding of an empathic response. Any failure to identify such distress prevents the subsequent stages of the empathic response following whilst also allowing a continuation of their sexually abusive behaviour.

In order for someone to 'feel' or experience the emotional state of another, they must first recognise the other person's emotional state.

Stage 2: Perspective-taking is the ability to put themselves in the victim's place and see the world as they do. In doing so, they are forced to recognise the unpleasantness of their actions, preventing any repetition from occurring. Those offenders who consistently offend against a particular group (e.g. children) or sex (male or female) may see them as quite different from themselves and, therefore, are unable to adapt the victim's perceptions.

Stage 3: Emotion replication involves the vicarious emotional response that replicates (or nearly replicates) the emotional experience of their victim(s). This requires some emotional repertoire by the offender to allow them to replicate the observed state. It requires that they recognise the emotion (stage 1) and adopt the perspective of that person (stage 2).

Stage 4: Response decision concerns the offender's decision to act or not to act on the basis of their feelings. They may have worked through the first three stages, yet decide against acting on their feelings (pp101–3).

Assessing victim empathy

An offender's failure to take responsibility for their actions or to empathise with the plight of their victims is a primary target both for assessment as well as treatment. It is important to consider the timing of this work, as commencement too early (e.g. when they have a low self-opinion) may lead to an even more acutely reduced level of victim empathy being developed. Victim empathy does not just happen, it must be learned by the offender feeling deeply and paying very close attention to the real feelings of others (Freeman-Longo, Bays and Bear, 1996: p 7). Sex offenders who lack empathy are likely to blame others for their problems, yet we need to continue to emphasise offender responsibility for controlling their feelings, thoughts and behaviours.

Questions might include:

- David Briggs (1994) has provided a useful framework for assessing an offender's empathy for their victims. He sets out the following questions that will assist the

workers in judging the quality of victim empathy:

- The physical feelings of their victims before, during and after each offence.

- The emotional feelings of their victims before, during and after each offence.

- The thoughts of their victims before, during and after each offence.

- The physical and emotional state of each of their victims now.

- The impact of the offences upon the family members of each victim.

- The physical and emotional state of those who dealt with the victims, e.g. friends, professionals, etc. (p65).

- Perry and Orchard (1992) offered several useful indicators of the offender's capacity for empathy which includes: the extent to which he blames the victims, the use of demeaning terms to describe his victims, and a failure to recognise either the short or long-term effects on the victims (p41). We should ensure that the offender personalises the victims by calling them by their names, and this can be modelled most by the workers when exploring the offences (dealt with later in this chapter).

- The offender can be asked to consider the feelings they experienced prior to, during and after each abusive incident. A range of feelings can be written on cards and they put face up those they experienced, whilst they place face down those they did not at each stage of the problem. They have to justify/articulate their choices. The cards should contain at least the following: planned, ashamed, sexy, in control, angry, confident, proud, turned on, secretive, terrified, macho, loving, determined, 'a buzz', powerful, drunk, satisfied, caring, guilty, worried, out of control, boastful. With the cards that are left, the worker can show the offender that many of the feelings that they experienced were less concerned with the sexual gratification, and more about the feelings about being powerful, in control and able to do what he wanted. A further set of cards can then be used to look at the abuse from the perspective of the victim; the cards contain both positive and negative feelings, and should be placed face up on the table. The offender is asked to turn face down any cards which they think the abused child did not feel at the time of the abuse. Any unacceptable cards picked up by the offender should be challenged by the worker, and any important cards should be structured to go through each stage of the abuse, with the task of dealing with the victim's feelings at each of the stages. *The victim's feelings on the cards should be*: guilty, in control, sick, confused, dirty, disgusted, powerless, sexy, scared, betrayed, alone, hurt, drunk, playful, threatened, angry, tense, weak, nervous, terrified, ashamed, turned on, unable to tell, out of control, embarrassed, and high spirited. The workers could go on to compare the feelings of the offender and the victim; usually highlighting the powerful-powerless relationship. The offender should be made aware that they have induced these feelings in the victim, which, in turn, may help them in the task of accepting responsibility for their actions.

- On a scale of 0–100 per cent how honest have they been with you regarding the sexual abuse?

- How can they explain their actions to the victim(s)? Why were they picked?

- How do they feel regarding the abuse: themselves, their families, friends as well as the victim(s)?

- The offender can be asked to identify their regrets about the abuse, then place them in order of importance.

- The workers can attempt to assess the offenders empathy in the clinical interview itself, looking at the impact of the abuse on the victim and their family; the consequences (short and long-term; temporary or permanent, etc.).

- Empathy can be assessed by analysing answers or observing reactions to reading material. For example, Bray (1997) offers several vivid accounts adaptable into case material; and the workbook on empathy by Freeman-Longo, Bays and Bear (1996) contains a wealth of useful information. Get

the offender to read materials setting out the consequences of their actions. Vizard (1988) has written an excellent paper on the child's experience of sexual abuse, and Freeman-Longo, Bays and Bear (1996) have set out the devastating experiences of being sexually abused: distrust of others and themselves; terror and anxiety; shame, guilt and self-hatred; alienation from their bodies; isolation and withdrawal from people and activities; powerlessness, depression and extreme passivity; anger; obsession with sex or complete aversion to it; questioning their sexuality and gender; drug and alcohol use, abuse and addiction; eating disorders; perfectionism and workism; mental illness and suicide. We should try to establish from the offender how reading about the things that can happen to victims affected them, how they think being sexually abused affects a child's relationship with his/her friends of the same sex and of the opposite sex? Why? Which stories do they identify with?

- Get them to think about things from their victim's perspective. Why did the other person do what s/he did? What role did the offender play in the person's behaviour? What does the offender think the other person really wants (more than getting even)? How can the offender help resolve the other person's problem? (Freeman-Longo *et al.*, 1996: p50).

- Get them to list at least five people (use their first names only and list what their relationship is to them, such as a friend, a sister-in-law, a neighbour) who have problems that are as great or greater than theirs. The people on their list might have severe problems with mental health, finances, children, parents, spouses, work, basic survival, or being harassed by someone. How do their problems affect their lives? If they did not have these problems, what could they do that they can't do now? (p14)

- Get them to list the difficulties they might have as they work on developing empathy. What are the things about them, their feelings and attitudes, their circumstances and life situation right now that might be roadblocks to developing empathy?

- Get them to give examples of 10 different times this week they thought of themselves first and either ignored or considered others a distant second. They can only give the same example once.

- Get them to give five examples of times in their life they helped others with no thought of reward or personal advantage, beyond feeling good within themselves for having helped. If they learned to be empathic, how would their family or friends benefit? How could they benefit?

- If they are known sexual abuse victims themselves get them to describe how this affected them and if not, ask them to imagine how it might be if their sister, mother or daughter was raped—or if they were raped by inmates in prison. If this induces some degree of upset, they can be reassured that this is empathy.

- Role reversal. Ask the offender to get into the role of the victim and then interview them and see how able and comfortable they are with changing roles. See how they would deal with cases if they were a judge or an investigating police officer.

- In order to reinforce their responsibility, they could be asked to write a letter as if they were writing to the abused child about the abuse, although they should be clearly told that it will not be sent. Alternatively, they could write a letter from their victim's perspective telling what happened to her or him during and after their assault. Include what their victim(s) thought, felt, and how she or he reacted to their aggression. This is often a very useful mechanism for evaluating the offenders' empathic abilities and can be regularly revisited to act as a measure of change, no movement, or regression.

Exploring the Current Sexual Offences (Allegations)

The aim of this block is to compare the offender's account with that given by the victims (and others), and any changes that may appear as the process unfolds. It is the offender's account that is more likely to be distorted. The workers also need to assess how the offender relates to them, as this is an additional and useful piece of information, e.g. open or manipulating, anxious or unconfident? (Zussman, 1989: p34).

An incremental approach to the work is often useful. Initial discussions are important to establish the offender's level of commitment to the work, the extent to which they are able to discuss their behaviour and others' expectations of it, and ascertaining their understanding of any concerns about their behaviour. It is always worthwhile detailing the allegations or charges against them at the outset. Becker and Kaplan (1988) ask the following questions about the sexual abuse in order to bring about the topic in a non-threatening manner:

1. Do you:
- Agree totally with the police report of these acts?

- Agree with most of the police report of these acts?

- Agree with some of the police reports of these acts?

- Disagree with all of the police reports about these sexual acts?

- Does not apply to me.

2. Concerning the alleged sexual crime you were charged with:
- The alleged victim initiated the involvement.

- Involvement was by mutual consent.

- I initiated the involvement, but the victim went along with it without resistance.

- I initiated, and the victim resisted.

- I initiated, the victim resisted, and I had to use force to commit the crime.

- I was not present at the alleged crime.

- None of these apply to me.

3. Concerning the alleged sexual crime you were charged with:
- I was involved just the way it was described in the statements.

- I was involved but wasn't responsible because I was under the influence of alcohol or drugs.

- I was present at the scene but committed no sexual offence.

- I was not present, but knew the victim.
- I was not present, and I did not know the victim.
- Does not apply to me (p108).

After these initial discussions, we can move into comprehensive discussions of the offending behaviour. This includes reconsidering the full details of the abuse, asking for details about all previous abusive incidents, and considering their thoughts, feelings and actions prior to, during and after the abuse. In approaching the abuse, we need to restrict the discussions to the allegations and not allow them to divert us to any mitigating or aggravating factors, which they will inevitably put forward to try and externalise the blame. Their account rarely provides an accurate picture of their behaviour, although it is often an indication of their current level of denial or distortion. Their account is best measured by reference to the victim statements, which usually contain details of the assailants behaviour, the degree and nature of any coercion, how the child was made vulnerable, the degree of immediate trauma suffered by the victim, and the situational circumstances surrounding the abuse.

We need to get them to describe in detail each of their sexual offences, even if they have not been charged with them as a crime. They should start with the abuse that has led to our current involvement, and which is usually the one we hold most information about. We should ask for a sequential description of everything that happened prior to, during and after the abuse, including their planning. They should be asked about all possible sexual deviations and not simply the presenting one. They should be specific, and we need to keep them on track by seeking clarification and pushing for detail. We should always point out any obvious minimisation and projection of blame onto others. If they are asked general questions, they are likely to respond with general answers, concealing the various behaviours they have participated in. In doing so, we have to be prepared for undisclosed sexual abuse which changes the assessment and the management of the case. We should always advise them that we are happy for them to discuss the abuse in any way they wish to express it, e.g. use of obscene language where the assessor is a female. We need to avoid

challenging or interpreting any responses at this stage, other than questions of clarification and seeking elaboration. It is important to hear their spontaneous thinking and feeling, and, by not interpreting, they are less likely to 'clam up' about the abuse. It may also furnish us with essential information about what their perception and rationalisation for the abuse may be, and it should allow the workers to check the similarities and differences in the statement to those held by the police. Our starting point has to be to elicit an overview of the problem before getting down to the specifics. When asking them to tell their story in detail, we should ask them to describe:

- Aspects of preparation, e.g. fantasy/masturbation. Evidence of premeditation.
- Why and how they chose a particular victim (age, gender, race, ability, etc.), or could it have been anyone? Difference in age, physical stature and social status.
- How they created a situation in which they could abuse.
- Level of consent and power relationships.
- Whether drugs, alcohol, or both were a feature of the abuse.
- What they did to the victim. Full details of the nature of the sexual activity.
- What they required the victim to do.
- The response of the victim during and after the incidents.
- The extent to which persuasion, threats or coercion were used to obtain sexual contact, or how they convinced the victims to co-operate.
- Any co-abusers?
- What they did to try to keep from getting caught (e.g. lying)? Level of emotional intimidation?
- How they ensured the victim maintained secrecy.
- How they themselves felt prior to, during and after the abuse.
- Whether they climaxed or later masturbated to climax whilst thinking about the abuse.
- The persistence and frequency of the sexual activity and whether there is any

escalation in the nature and frequency of the abuse.

- Why they stopped when they did.
- Their understanding of how they were caught.
- Their feelings on getting caught.
- The response of their family, friends, victims and others to the disclosure.

It is frequently useful to split the discussion around the sexual abuse into two sessions. For the offender, this allows them to reflect on what they have said, and allows them to return and provide further information, or clarify that already given. In the interim, they should be asked to go through their version of events to check their honesty outside of the assessment sessions. For the workers, this allows them the necessary space to go through the offenders version of the events and break it down into chronological segments, e.g. prior to the offence, the lead-up to the abuse, the incident itself, post-abuse and subsequent events. They can then work out a series of questions designed to take the offender through the blocks in minute detail, as well as identifying gaps that need to be plugged. Where the offender denies the abuse, the workers need to highlight loopholes and inconsistencies in the story, exposing to them that we believe the version given by the victims. Having stated this, it is often easier said than done. They are often very plausible and convincing in their denials, explanations and excuses, and it is not uncommon for workers to shift towards an acceptance of them, particularly where they are well articulated. The danger of collusion should never be overlooked or underestimated. Where denial persists, the workers have to decide whether to terminate the assessment or allow the discussion time on this block to be extended. The workers may also wish to seek further information from the victims in order to double check information, although this should never be relayed to the offender as it is a breach of confidence, and may put them at greater risk. When moving into the second session where detail should be sought, we need to be very specific and refuse to accept vagaries.

Questions might include:

Aspects of preparation, e.g. fantasy/masturbation

- How old were they when they first attempted this kind of behaviour?
- When did they first abuse the victim?
- Where did they get the idea for the offence?
- Did they start to plan it? What did they start to think? What did they start to fantasise about? How did these make you feel? To what extent? Premeditated, victim selected/premeditated, but no victim selected, or victim not known? How much time did they spend planning it? If not, was it opportunistic? How often did they masturbate around the time of the abuse? More than once a day? Once a week? What were they thinking/ imagining?
- When did they start fantasising about the abuse? The victim? The setting? What was the offence like in their mind? What did they hope it would be like?
- Was the sexual abuse the primary intended offence?
- What were their initial warning signs that they might abuse?

Why and how they chose a particular victim

- Did they pick the victim, or could it have been anyone? Was it opportunistic (the victim was in the wrong place at the wrong time)? Was it planned (the victim was known to the offender)? Are they related? Acquaintances? Friends?
- How did they pick the victim? Behaviour they found sexually attractive (e.g. teasing or flirtatious)? Physical attributes such as build, hair colour or style? Vulnerability, such as physical handicap? Clothes, jewellery, make-up? Unlikely to disclose given their ability to communicate? Age? Sex? Male or female only, or evidence of crossover? Emotional attributes? Naiveté or innocence?
- How old is the victim? How old were they when they started and then stopped the abuse? Is there a pattern to their age

choice, e.g. children, adolescents, or various ages?

- Get them to describe the victim in detail for you, including any crucial selection variables.

How they created a situation in which they could abuse

- Where did the abuse take place? Be specific. Why did they choose this place or setting? Was it randomly selected? Was it isolated or dark? How did they get there? Is the location always the same?

- How did they approach the victim? What did they say? What did the victim say?

- Did they create an opportunity where there was no other adult/supervisor present?

- How did they get there and ensure the victim got there? Did anyone else know? Was anyone else there?

- Did they take them somewhere after they met? Why? How were they feeling? What mood were they in?

Were drugs or alcohol a feature of the abuse?

- If drugs or alcohol was used, for what purpose: to entice the victim, to reduce victim resistance/incapacitate them, or to reduce the offender's own inhibitions?

- If yes, what and how much was used? How was the drug taken—orally, intravenously, nasally?

- Was the victim drunk or high? Did they supply them? To what end? Did it induce compliance?

- Did the victim's presentation add to their sexual arousal?

- Do they think they have a drink or a drug problem?

The offence itself

- Was the offence intra- or extra-familial?

- How old was the victim and the offender at the time of the offence?

- What were the specific behaviours acted out, i.e. intercourse (anal, vaginal),

simulated intercourse, rape, cunnilingus, fellatio, fondling, exhibitionism, voyeurism, fetishism, forced to watch pornography, etc?

- If the victim was male, did they make them ejaculate? If female, simulate orgasm?

- How long did the abuse last for?

- Was there any evidence of sexual dysfunction during the assault?

- Was the abuse committed under conditions of stress or in a particular psychological state such as depression?

- Was the abuse premeditated or spontaneous/impulsive? (Note. This is important if we are to identify the offender's cycle of offending and try to isolate the type of offences they may commit in future. For example, we need to know whether to target stress, substances or impulses as a regime for treatment.)

- What was happening in their lives just before the offences? How were they feeling? Happy/angry/sad/scared/hurt/rejected/lonely/sexually aroused/a failure? What sort of mood were they in? What was their state of mind at that time? What made them feel that way?

- What was the incident that triggered their sexually abusive behaviour? What antecedents led up to the offence being committed? What did they want from their behaviour?

- What evidence of escalation over time is there? How far did they take things?

Groth (1979) notes that we must view the offence against the background of their offenders developmental history, the social-environmental context of this development, the environmental-situational context of the crime, the current psychological and emotional life of the offender, and the social-environmental features of the life situation that the offender will probably remain in, or return to (post-incarceration).

What they did to the victim

- What did they do and say to the victim? Was it threatening, foul, or instructional language? Before, during and after the abuse?

- How did it make them feel?
- What kind of games did they play with the victim?
- Did they shave the victim? Where?
- Did they kiss them? Where and how?
- Did they touch them? Where and why? How were they feeling at this point?
- Did they use a condom, lubrication, restraint?
- Did they take or use photographs?
- Was anyone watching them? Who and why?
- Did they both undress? Did they make them undress or did they do it for them?
- List all the different types of sexual activity they tried with the victims (e.g. exposing, oral, anal, vaginal sex, digital penetration, etc.).
- How many times did they abuse the victims?
- Over what period of time did this happen?
- Did they have an erection? Did they ejaculate? When? How many times?
- On a scale of 0–10, how strong were their sexual feelings during and after the abuse?
- What was the victim's reaction? Did the victim ask them to stop? Was the victim scared, crying, passive, submissive or combative?
- When did they first notice that the victim was distressed by the abuse? How did that make them feel? How did they justify their behaviour to themselves?
- Did the offender stop at anytime because of the victim's reactions? Why? Or did their response arouse the offender further? How did they overcome the resistance?
- What did they not do that they would have liked to have done?
- What didn't they try these things out? Would they if they saw the victim again?
- Would they try these things with anyone else? Is there someone else they are attracted to now? What would they do if they were left alone with that individual?

- Where they successful in the abuse that they intended? If not, what stopped them from carrying it out?
- How did they feel after the abuse? Have they ever attempted to stop their abusive behaviour? How? Did they hope the victim would stop it, or did they try and stop themselves? Which of them tried the hardest? When? With what outcome?

The use of force in the abuse

It is essential that we assess the offender's history of violence and violence-proneness

- How did they get the victim to comply or submit? They might employ verbal threats, enticements, intimidation, trickery, physical abuse, a weapon or a threat to harm people close to the victim?
- What kind of threats did they use or act out?
- How sexually exciting was the use or the threat of using force?
- What instruments did they use, e.g. weapon? Did they show it to the victim?
- What did they say to them, e.g. threaten to kill their pet, etc.?
- What prevented them from being more violent?
- What injuries did the victim sustain in the abuse?

Post-abuse considerations

- How did they justify their abuse, initially, later on, and in the face of distress?
- How have they tried to stop people believing the victim?
- What are they doing now to stop their sexually abusive behaviour?
- How are they managing the consequences of disclosure?
- What other kinds of sexual problems might they develop if they don't get any help?
- Who would their next victim be?
- When did they last offend? When did they last plan to offend? How far had they progressed? Fantasy? Masturbation? Use of pornography or photographs?

- Do they accept responsibility for their behaviour, or are they maintaining that they are the victims of circumstances?
- What was the offence itself like?
- What did they say to themselves post-offence?
- What trends can they identify in their offending?

The sessions on the abuse undoubtedly place the workers in a powerful position compared to the offender, particularly where they are well prepared. This can induce considerable anger in the offender, particularly if they have to change their story a number of times. Their excuses and rationalisations need to be challenged and supplementary questions need to be constructed to add more detail. We should allow them the space and opportunity to ask questions of the workers. They should be allowed breaks where necessary, particularly where they are being challenged to fill in gaps or elaborate on partial information. Expect a distortion of belief and attitude when they are under pressure for a more detailed account. The aim has to be to challenge their distortions and help them move from a passive to an active account of their sexually abusive behaviour. In doing this, we are allowing them to accept the responsibility for, and the effects of, their behaviour. At the end of this block, we need to establish the degree of congruence between the accounts of the offender and the victims. If others are identified in the abuse, then we need to establish the actions or words of the other person in the incident.

Homework assignments may include:

- Describe how their sexually abusive behaviour is a problem and for whom?
- What efforts have they made or would want to make to stop this behaviour? Who can help them?
- Make a list of all the problems they had before they sexually abused.
- How did the sexual abuse affect them, their victims and their families?
- List why the victims would fabricate allegations of sexual abuse against them. What have they to gain from doing so?
- List all the needs (other than sex) that are

met for them through their sexual offending.

- Get them to rewrite their statements relating to the offences and then compare this with the original statement to the police. Any movement is a useful indicator of attitude change. It can, and should, be repeated as the work continues.
- Get them to describe a typical day (both before the allegations of sexual abuse, and now), beginning with when they get up in the morning, and including who is in the home, where they go, with whom, who might they meet, etc. What contact might they have with children with some other adults present, or alone? When do people go to bed, and with whom? Are there atypical days? Do weekdays differ from weekends? This might give us information on their access to victims, their overall functioning, and possible intervention strategies.
- Set out why they feel guilty/remorseful/sorry about their sexually abusive behaviour.

The Cycle of Abuse

The 'cycle of abuse' articulated by Steven Wolf (1984) is a very popular framework for workers when trying to understand offending patterns (see Chapter Seven for a detailed discussion). This is probably because it breaks down the offending pattern into a series of stages: the period leading up to the offence, committing the offence, reconstituting after the offence, leading back to the stage of committing further offences. This has many parallels with the notion of an addictive assault cycle, where the offender becomes more addicted to their behaviour over time. Whilst there are some sex offenders who fit neatly into Wolf's framework, there are many who do not. This being acknowledged, it is always best to proceed on the basis that you can identify a clear pattern of sexually abusive behaviour, as addictions can be very powerful and intractable, with a tenacious grip on behaviour that will persistently frustrate initiatives for change (Carnes, 1983). As the compulsion grows in intensity and severity of consequence, it comes to pervade virtually every aspect of the offender's life, with the result that their day-to-day routines often become organised around the offending (Gocke, 1991).

Some offenders have continuous cycles whilst others have inhibited cycles. Offenders with continuous cycles often have belief systems which legitimise their behaviour to the point where the cycle is only interrupted by their perceived risk of being caught, e.g. a faulty choice of victim. These offenders do strongly believe that they are in the right. For others, they may not be so secure, and their internal inhibitions interject to break their offending cycle. These inhibited offenders frequently question their own behaviour, and the strength of such questioning is directly linked to the length of their breaks. They do offend when they make excuses for their behaviour, such as feeling sorry for themselves and thus entitled to some small comfort. Wyre (1987) has also identified several different types of offending cycles: fixated paedophile; professional paedophile; anger rapist; and indecent assault. Please refer to the text for the detail.

More recently, Ward, Hudson, Louden and Marshall (1995) have provided us with a descriptive model of the offence chain for sex offenders, which provides an analysis of the offender's thoughts and behaviours preceding the offence. Comprising nine stages, the model incorporates offender type, offence type, and offers a description of the possible interactions between the various stages and factors. This does help to impress on the offender the process and not the spontaneity of their behaviour.

Questions might include:

- We would suggest that you take the offender through the questions set out in the last block, but being far more specific for each part of the cycle and for each offence they have committed. This should help identify any patterns of offending. It should also help identify which is their primary pattern (e.g. incest) and this can help clarify any degree of secondary patterns ('crossover'). Whilst the broad framework can be used in most cases, the

content and details will differ considerably. The frequency in which they complete the cycle is an integral consideration when predicting the likelihood of re-offending.

- Give the offender a blank offending cycle chart (see Figure 25 below) to fill in with their own details. Ask them to work backwards from the abuse and to identify any precursors to the abuse. Tell them we are assuming none are 'first-time' offenders. Get them to link all the component factors which have come together to allow the offence to have been committed, such as masturbation, fantasy, visual sexual stimulation and offending. Push for detail. If this is being completed with the workers present, the workers may have completed their idea of what the offenders cycle may look like, and they should get the offender to record the detail as it unfolds, for accuracy.

- Ask them to identify strategies, which might allow them to break out of the cycle that led to their offending.

- Post-assessment, get the offender to agree to masturbate first to a fantasy of some consensual sexual activity before then masturbating to their deviant arousal. This may play some small part in gradually decreasing their arousal to the deviant cues. Get them to identify personal strategies to avoid repeating their abusive behaviour. Whilst this exercise is most likely to be used in the treatment phase, it is potentially useful in the assessment phase with a willing offender.

Feedback and Outcomes

To ensure the offender does not acquire any aggravated distortion of their cognition, they need to be debriefed at the end of the assessment. They should be given the opportunity to hear the assessment feedback alone, before their partner is included, if that is what they want. A post-assessment interview should incorporate the information gathered from all the assessments, particularly where they are similar, different,

Figure 25: The offending cycle chart (Calder and Skinner, 1999).

Offender's name: ....

Full name of victim: ....

Date of offence: ....

Date form completed: ....

Each respondent is asked to complete their particular sexual abuse cycle in detail. This should include their fantasies, masturbation, arousal and offending, and a new cycle should be completed for each different offence.

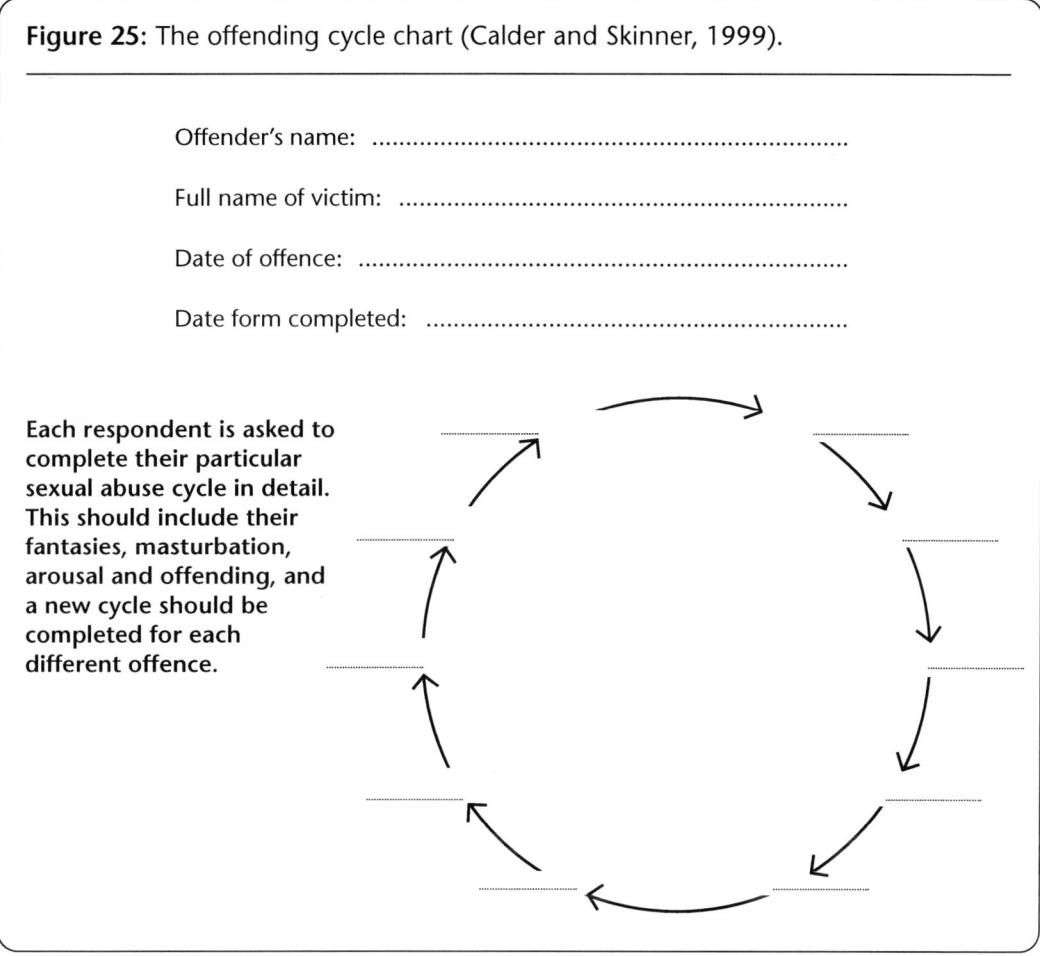

or highlight more questions. The following issues should be covered in the feedback session:

- A report will be written to the commissioning body, although they will have sight of it.

- An appraisal of the assessments should be undertaken, with reference to any shifts in acceptance or attitudes noted, and any remaining concerns.

- The viability of future work, with specific details, time-scale, and any mandate required.

- A treatment agreement could be discussed and some consensus on its content reached, and

- The family's response to the abuse is central to child protection planning and

placement issues, and thus needs to be discussed.

The meeting to feedback often precedes the full assessment report and should always be done before a decision on disposal is made. We would recommend the following framework for the assessment report that addresses:

- Details of the offender and their family.

- Reason for referral—summary of the offence. This should always describe in detail the behaviour, the location and duration of the offence, and how the offender gained access to the victim.

- Brief background information on the offender (individual and family profile).

- Engagement with the work (number of sessions, commitment and motivation).

- The assessment of their offending behaviour, including statements from the offender in their own words, covering the process of their cycle-in sequence. If they are denying, minimising or projecting blame elsewhere, this should be reported. Draw attention to any remaining discrepancies between the offender's statements and those given by the victim and any witnesses.

- Sexual history.

- Victim awareness.

- Summary and recommendations.

- Involvement of others in the process, including partners.

References

Abel, G.G., Becker, J.V., Cunningham-Rathner, J., Kaplan, M.S., and Reich, J. (1984a). *The Treatment of Sex Offenders*. NY: SBC-TM.

Abel, G.G., Becker, J.V., and Cunningham-Rathner, J. (1984b). Complications, Consent and Cognition in Sex Between Children and Adults. *Interpersonal Journal of Law and Psychiatry*, 7: pp89–103.

Abel, G.G., Becker, J.V., Cunningham-Rathner, J., Mittleman, R.S., and Rouleau, J. (1988). Multiple Paraphilic Diagnosis Among Sex Offenders. *Bulletin of the American Academy of Psychiatry and the Law*, 16: pp153–68.

Abel, G.G., Becker, J.V., Cunningham-Rathner, J., Rouleau, J., and Murphy, W. (1987). Self-reported Crimes of Non-incarcerated Paraphiliacs. *Journal of Interpersonal Violence*, 2: pp3–25.

Abel, G.G., Blanchard, E., and Becker, J.V. (1978). An Integrated Treatment Program for Rapists. In Rada, R. (Ed.). *Clinical Aspects of the Rapist*, pp161–214. NY: Grune and Stratton.

Abel, G.G., Gore, D.K., Holland, C.L., Camp, N., Becker, J.V., and Rathner, J. (1989). The Measurement of Cognitive Distortions of Child Molesters. *Annals of Sex Research*, 2: pp135–53.

Abel, G.G., Mittleman, M.S., and Becker, J.V. (1985). Sex Offenders: Results of Assessment and Recommendations for Treatment. In Ben-Aron, M.H., Hucker, S.J., and Webster, C.D. (Eds.). *Clinical Criminology: The Assessment and Treatment of Criminal Behaviour*, pp191–205. Toronto: M&M Graphics.

Abel, G.G., Rouleau, J., and Cunningham-Rathner, J. (1985). Sexual Aggressive Behaviour. In Curran, W., McGarry, A., and Shah, S. (Eds.). *Modern Legal Psychiatry and Psychology*. Philadelphia: EA Davis.

Alexandria Associates (ND). *Adult Sex Offender Program*. Oregon: Alexandria Associates.

Aronfreed, J. (1968). *Conduct and Conscience: The Socialisation of Internalised Control over Behaviour*. NY: Academic Press.

Athanasion, R. (1973). A Review of Public Attitudes on Sexual Issues. In Zubin, J., and Money, J. (Eds.). *Contemporary Sexual Behaviour: Critical Issues in the 1970s*. Baltimore: John Hopkins University Press.

Awad, G.A., and Saunders, E.B. (1989). Adolescent Child Molesters: Clinical Observations. *Child Psychiatry and Human Development*, 19(3): pp195–206.

Badgley, R. (1984). *Sexual Offences Against Children: Report of the Committee on Sexual Offences against Children and Youths* (Vols. 1&2). Ottawa, Canada: Ministry of Supplies.

Barbaree, H.E. (1991). Denial and Minimisation Among Sex Offenders: Assessment and Treatment Outcomes. *Forum on Corrections Research*, 3: pp30–3.

Barbaree, H.E., Marshall, W.L. and Connor, J. (1988). *The Social Problem-solving of Child Molesters*. Unpublished Manuscript, Queen's University, Ontario, Canada.

Barclay, A.M. (1973). Sexual Fantasies in Men and Women. *Medical Aspects of Sexuality*, 7: pp205–16.

Baxter, M. (1990). Flesh and Blood: Does Pornography Lead to Sexual Violence? *New Scientist*, 05.05.90: pp37–41.

Bays, L., and Freeman-Longo, R. (1995). Evaluation of Dangerousness for Sexual Offences. In Carich, M.S., and Adkerson, D. (Eds.). *Adult Sexual Offender Assessment Packet*. Brandon, VT: Safer Society Press.

Beck, A.T. (1976). *Cognitive Theory and Emotional Disorders*. NY: Meridian.

Beck, A.T., and Beck, R.W. (1972). Screening Depressed Patients in Family Practice; A Rapid Technique. *Postgraduate Medicine*, 52: pp81–5.

Becker, J.V., and Abel, G.G. (1985). Methodological and Ethical Issues in Evaluating and Treating Adolescent Sex Offenders. In Otey, E.M., and Ryan, G.D. (Eds.). *Adolescent Sex Offenders: Issues in Research and Treatment*, pp109–29. Rockville, MD: USA Dept. of Health and Human Services.

Becker, J.V., and Kaplan, M.S. (1988). The Assessment and Treatment of Adolescent Sexual Offenders. *Advances in Behavioural Assessment of Children and Families*, 4: pp97–118.

Becker, J.V., and Quinsey, V.L. (1993). Assessing Suspected Child Molesters. *Child Abuse and Neglect*, 17: pp169–74.

Becker, J.V., Cunningham-Rathner, J., and Kaplan, M.S. (1986). Adolescent Sex Offenders, Criminal and Sexual Histories and Demographics, and Recommendations for Reducing Future Offences. *Journal of Interpersonal Violence*, 1: pp431–45.

Beckett, R.C. (1994). Assessment of Sex Offenders. In Morrison, T., Erooga, M., and Beckett, R.C. (Eds.). *Sexual Offending Against Children: Assessment and*

Treatment of Male Abusers, pp55–79. London: Routledge.

Beckett, R.C., Beech, A., Fisher, D., and Scott-Fordham, A. (1994). *Community-based Treatment for Sex Offenders: and Evaluation of Seven Treatment Programmes*. London: HMSO.

Bentovim, A. (1994). *Is the Increasing Criminalisation of Child Abuse an Obstacle to Working in Partnership?* Keynote Presentation to the Second National Congress on Child Abuse and Neglect, University of Bristol, 5–8th July, 1994.

Bownes, I.T. (1993). Sexual and Relationship Dysfunction in Sexual Offenders. *Sexual and Marital Therapy*, 8(2): pp157–65.

Bownes, I.T., and Gorman, E.C. (1991). Assailant's Sexual Dysfunction During Rape Reported by their Victims. *Medicine, Science and the Law*, 31: pp322–8.

Bray, M. (1997). *Sexual Abuse: The Child's Voice. Poppies on the Rubbish Heap*. London: Jessica Kingsley.

Brehm, S.S. (1992). *Intimate Relationships* (2nd Edition). NY: McGraw Hill.

Briere, J., Malamuth, N., and Check, J.Y.P. (1985). Sexuality and Rape Supportive Beliefs. *Interpersonal Journal of Women's Studies*, 8: pp398–403.

Briggs, D., Doyle, P., Gooch, T., and Kennington, R. (1998). *Assessing Men who Sexually Abuse: A Practice Guide*. London: Jessica Kingsley.

Briggs, D.I. (1994). Assessment of Sex Offenders. In McMurran, A., and Hodge, J.E. (Eds.). *The Assessment of Criminal Behaviours of Clients in Secure Settings*, pp53–67. London: Jessica Kingsley.

Brownmiller, S. (1975). *Against our Will: Men, Women and Rape*. London: Penguin.

Bumby, K., and Hanson, D.J. (1997). Intimacy Deficits, Fear of Intimacy and Loneliness Among Sex Offenders. *Criminal Justice and Behaviour*, 24(3): pp315–31.

Bumby, K.M. (1996). Assessing the Cognitive Distortions of Child Molesters and Rapists: Development and Validation of the Molest and Rape Scales. *Sexual Abuse: Journal of Research and Treatment*, 8(1): pp37–54.

Burgess, A.W., Hartman, C.R., Ressler, R.K., Douglas, J.E., and Maccormack, A. (1986). Sexual Homicide: A Motivational Model. *Journal of Interpersonal Violence*, 1: pp251–72.

Byrne, D. (1977). Social Psychology and the Study of Sexual Behaviour. *Personality and Social Psychology Bulletin*, 3: pp3–30.

Calder, M.C. (1997a). *Juveniles and Children who Sexually Abuse. A Guide to Risk Assessment*. Dorset: Russell House Publishing.

Calder, M.C. (1997b). Young People who Sexually Abuse: Towards International Consensus? *Social Work in Europe*, 4(1): pp36–9.

Calder, M.C. (Ed.) (1999). *Working with Young People who Sexually Abuse. New Pieces of the Jigsaw Puzzle*. Dorset: Russell House Publishing.

Calder, M.C. (1999b). Young People who Sexually Abuse: A Framework for Initial Assessment. *Child Care in Practice*, 5(3): pp262–80.

Carich, M.S., and Adkerson, D.L. (1995). *Adult Sexual Offender Assessment Packet*. Brandon, VT: Safer Society Press.

Carnes, P.I. (1983). *Out of the Shadows: Understanding Sexual Addiction*. Minneapolis: Compcare Publications.

Carter, D.E., Prentky, R., Knight, R.A., Vanderveer, P.L., and Boucher, R.S. (1987). Use of Pornography on the Criminal and Developmental Histories of Sexual Offenders. *Journal of Interpersonal Violence*, 2: pp196–211.

Cerce, D., Day, S.R., Prentky, R.A., and Knight, R.A. (1984). *The Correlative Relationship Between Family Instability in Childhood and Sexually Aggressive Behaviour in Adulthood*. Paper at the 2nd National Conference for Family Violence Researchers. Durham: University of New Hampshire.

Chaffin, M. (1992). Factors Associated with Treatment Completion and Progress Among Intra-Familial Child Molesters. *Child Abuse and Neglect*, 16: pp251–64.

Chaffin, M. (1994). Research in Action: Assessment and Treatment of Child Sexual Abusers. *Journal of Interpersonal Violence*, 9(2): pp224–37.

Christie, M., Marshall, W.L., and Lanthier, R. (1979). *A Descriptive Study of Incarcerated Rapists and Paedophiles. Report of the Solicitor General of Canada*. Ottawa: Canada.

Clore, G.L., and Jeffrey, K.M. (1972). *A Descriptive Study of Incarcerated Rapists and Paedophiles. Report of the Solicitor General of Canada*. Ottawa, Canada.

Cohen, P. (1995). Sex, Lies and Videotapes. *Community Care*, 12–18.11.95: pp14–5.

Coleman, E. (1987a). Chemical Dependency and Intimacy Dysfunction: Inextricably Bound. *Journal of Chemical Dependency*, 1(1): pp13–26.

Conger, J.C., and Conger, A.J. (1986). Assessment of Social Skills. In Ciminero, A.R. *et al.* (Eds.). *Handbook of Behavioural Assessment*, pp526–60. NY: John Wiley and Sons.

Cowburn, M. (1996). The Black Male Sex Offender in Prison: Images and Issues. *Journal of Sexual Aggression*, 2(2): pp122–42.

Crepault, C., and Couture, M. (1980). Men's Erotic Fantasies. *Archives of Sexual Behaviour*, 9: pp565–81.

Cronbach, L.J. (1955). Processes Affecting Scores on 'Understanding of Others' and 'Assumed Similarity'. *Psychological Bulletin*, 52(3): pp177–93.

Cumming, G., and Buell, M. (1997). *Supervision of the Sex Offender*. Brandon, VT: Safer Society Press.

Day, K. (1994). Male Mentally Handicapped Sex Offenders. *British Journal of Psychiatry*, 165: pp630–9.

Deitz, S.R., Tiemann-Blackwell, K., Daley, P.C., and Bentley, B.J. (1982). Measurement of Empathy Towards Rape Victims and Rapists. *Journal of Personality and Social Psychology*, 43: pp372–84.

Derogatis, L.R., and Melisaratos, N. (1979). The DSFI: A Multi-dimensional Measure of Sexual Functioning. *Journal of Sex and Marital Therapy*, 5: pp244–81.

DiGeorgio-Miller (1994). Clinical Techniques in the Treatment of Juvenile Sex Offenders. *Young Victims, Young Offenders*, 21(1/2): pp117–26.

Dougher, M.J. (1995). Clinical Assessment of Sex Offenders. In Schwartz, B.K., and Cellini, H.R. (Eds.). *The Sex Offender: Corrections, Treatment and Legal Practice*. Kingston, NJ: Civic Research Institute, Inc.

Eldridge, H., and Still, J. (1995). Apologies and Forgiveness in the Context of the Cycles of Adult Males Sex Offenders who Abuse Children. In Salter, A.C. (Ed.). *Transforming Trauma*, pp131–58. Thousand Oaks, CA: Sage.

Eysenck, H.J. (1970). Personality and Attitudes to Sex: A Factorial Study. *Personality*, 1: pp355–76.

Faller, K.C. (1988). *Child Sexual Abuse: An Inter-disciplinary Manual for Diagnosis, Case Management, and Treatment*. London: Macmillan.

Finkelhor, D. (1984). *Child Sexual Abuse: Theory and Research*. NY: The Free Press.

Finkelhor, D., and Lewis, I.A. (1988). An Epidemiological Approach to the Study of Child Molestation. In Prentky, R.A., and Quinsey, V.L. (Eds.). *Human Sexual Aggression*. NY: New York Academy of Sciences.

Fisher, D., and Howells, K. (1993). Social Relationships in Sexual Offenders. *Sexual and Marital Therapy*, 8(2): pp123–36.

Fitch, J.H. (1962). Men Convicted of Sexual Offences Against Children: A Descriptive Follow-up Study. *British Journal of Criminology*, 3: pp18–37.

Freeman-Longo, R., Bays, L., and Bear, E. (1996). *Empathy and Compassionate Action: Issues and Exercises. A Guided Workbook for Clients and Treatment*. Brandon, VT: Safer Society Press.

Freeman-Longo, R.E. (1983). *Developmental Histories in Sexual Offences*. Unpublished Study.

Frenzel, R.R., and Lang, R.A. (1989). Identifying Sexual Preferences in Intra-familial and Extra-familial Child Sexual Abuse. *Annals of Sex Research*, 2: pp255–75.

Freund, K. (1981). Assessment of Paedophiles. In Cook, M., and Howells, K. (Eds.). *Adult Sexual Interest in Children*, pp139–79. NY: Academic Press.

Freund, K., and Blanchard, R. (1986). The Concept of Courtship Disorder. *Journal of Sex and Marital Therapy*, 12: pp79–92.

Freund, K., Scher, H., and Hucker, S. (1983). The Courtship Disorder. *Archives of Sexual Behaviour*, 12: pp369–79.

Garlick, Y., Marshall, W.L., and Thornton, D. (1996). Intimacy Deficits and Attribution of Blame Among Sexual Offenders. *Legal and Criminological Psychology*, 1: pp251–8.

Gebhard, P.H., Gagnon, J.H, Pomeroy, W.B., and Christerson, C.Y. (1965). *Sex Offenders*. NY: Harper and Row.

Gebhard, P.H., Gagnon, J.H, Pomeroy, W.B., *et al.* (1967). *Sex Offenders*. NY: Bantam Books.

Gilgun, J.F. (1988). Self-centredness and the Adult Male Perpetrator of Child Sexual Abuse. *Contemporary Family Therapy*, 10(4): pp216–34.

Glueck, B. (1956). *Final Report of the Research Project for the Study of Persons Convicted of Crimes Involving Sexual Aberrations. June 1952 to June 1955*. New York: State Department of Hygiene.

Gocke, B. (1991). *Tackling Denial in Sex Offenders. Probation Monograph 98*. Norwich: UEA.

Gold, S.R., and Clegg, C.L. (1990). Sexual Fantasies of College Students with Coercive Experiences and Coercive Attitudes. *Journal of Interpersonal Violence*, 5(4): pp464–73.

Gore, D.K. (1988). *Measuring the Cognitive Distortions of Child Molesters*. Unpublished Doctoral Thesis. Atlanta, GA: Georgia State University.

Green, R. (1995). Psycho-educational Modules. In Schwartz, B.K., and Cellini, H.R. (Eds.). *The Sex Offender: Correction, Treatment and Legal Practice*. Kingston, NJ: Civic Research Institute, Inc.

Groth, A.N. (1977). The Adolescent Sex Offender and his Prey. *Journal of Offender Therapy and Comparative Criminology*, 25: pp265–75.

Groth, A.N. (1979). *Men who Rape: The Psychology of the Offender*. NY: Plenum.

Grubin, D. (1992). Sexual Offending: A Cross-cultural Comparison. *Annual Review of Sex Research*, 3: pp201–17.

Grubin, D., and Gunn, J. (1990). *The Imprisoned Rapist and Rape*. London: Institute of Psychiatry.

Guttmacher, M.S., and Weihofen, H. (1952). *Psychiatry and the Law*. NY: Norton.

Hanson, R.K. (1991). Characteristics of Sex Offenders who Were Sexually Abused as Children. In Langevin, R. (Ed.). *Sex Offenders and their Victims: New Research Findings*, pp77–85. Toronto: Juniper Press.

Hanson, R.K. (in press). Sex Offender Risk Assessment. In Hollin, C.R. (Ed.). *Handbook of Offender Assessment and Treatment*. Chichester: John Wiley and Sons.

Hanson, R.K., and Scott, H. (1996). Social Networks of Sex Offenders. *Psychology, Crime and Law*, 2: pp249–58.

Hanson, R.K., Gizzarrelli, R., and Scott, H. (1994). The

Attitudes of Incest Offenders: Sexual Enticement and Acceptance of Sex with Children. *Criminal Justice and Behaviour*, 21(2): pp187–220.

Hanson, R.K., Harris, A.J.R., Fouruzan, A., McWhinnie, A.J., and Osweiler, M.C. (1997). Dynamic Predictors of Sexual Reoffence Project 1997. Presentation at the annual Research and Treatment Conference of the Association for the Treatment of Sexual Offenders, Arlington, VA.

Hartley, C.C. (1998). How Incest Offenders Overcome Internal Inhibitions Through the Use of Cognitions and Cognitive Distortions. *Journal of Interpersonal Violence*, 13(1): pp25–39.

Hartman, C., and Reynolds, D. (1987). Resistant Clients: Confrontation, Interpretation and Alliance. *Social Casework*, April 1987: pp205–13.

Hayashino, D.S., Wurtele, S.K., and Klebe, K.J. (1995). Child Molesters: An Examination of Cognitive Factors. *Journal of Interpersonal Violence*, 10(1): pp105–16.

Heinz, J.W., Gargaro, S., and Kelly, K.G. (1987). *A Model Residential Juvenile Sex Offender Treatment Program: The Hennepin County Home School*. Orwell, VT: Safer Society Press.

Hite, S. (1981). *The Hite Report on Male Sexuality*. NY: Knoff.

Horley, J. (1991). Values and Beliefs as Personal Constructs. *Construct Psychology*, 4: pp1–14.

Howard, A. (1993). Victims and Perpetrators of Sexual Abuse. In Dwivedi, K.N. (Ed.). *Groupwork with Children and Adolescents: A Handbook*, pp220–32. London: Jessica Kingsley.

Howells, K. (1978). Some Meanings of Children for Paedophiles. In Cook, M., and Wilson, E.T. (Eds.). *Love and Attraction*, pp57–82. Elmsford, NY: Pergammon.

Howitt, D. (1995). *Paedophiles and Sexual Offences Against Children*. Chichester: John Wiley and Sons.

Hudson, S.M., and Ward, T. (1997). Intimacy, Loneliness and Attachment Styles in Sex Offenders. *Journal of Interpersonal Violence*, 12(3): pp323–39.

Hudson, S.M., Marsall, W.L., Wales, D., Mcdonald, E., Bakker, L., and Mclean, A. (1993). Emotional Recognition Skills of Sex Offenders. *Annals of Sex Research*.Co: pp199–211.

Jehu, D. (1979). *Sexual Dysfunction: A Behavioural Approach to Causation, Assessment and Treatment*. Chichester: John Wiley and Sons.

Jenkins, A. (1990). *Invitations to Responsibility: The Therapeutic Engagement of Men who are Violent and Abusive*. Australia: Dulwich Centre Publications.

Johnston, L., and Ward, T. (1996). Social Cognition and Sexual Offending: A Theoretical Framework. *Sexual Abuse: A Journal of Research and Treatment*, 8(1): pp55–80.

Jones, C., and Lewis, J. (1990/1). A Pilot Prison Treatment Group for Sex Offenders at HMP Norwich. *Prison Service Journal*, 81: pp44–6.

Kanin, E.J. (1983). Rape as a Function of Relative Sexual Frustration. *Psychological Reports*, 52: pp133–4.

Kanin, E.J. (1984). Date Rape: Unofficial Criminals and Victims. *Victimology*, 9: pp95–108.

Kanin, E.J. (1985). Date Rapists: Differential Sexual Socialisation and Relative Deprivation. *Archives of Sexual Behaviour*, 14: pp219–31.

Kelly, L. (1992). Pornography and Child Sexual Abuse. In Itzin, C. (Ed.). *Pornography: Women, Violence and Civil Liberties*, pp113–23. Oxford: Oxford University Press.

Kirkendall, L.A., and McBride, L.G. (1990). Pre-adolescent and Adolescent Imagery and Sexual Fantasies: Beliefs and Experiences. In Perry, M.E. (Ed.). *Handbook of Sexology. Volume 7: Childhood and Adolescent Sexology*, pp263–86. Amsterdam: Elsevier.

Klein, M. (1988). *Your Sexual Secrets: When to Keep Them, When and How to Tell*. NY: EP Dutton.

Laflen, and Sturm, W.R. (1994). Understanding and Working with Denial in Sex Offenders. *Journal of Sexual Abuse*, 3(4): pp19–36.

Lang, R.A. (1991). Child Sexual Abusers who Use Pornography. In Langevin, R. (Ed.). *Sex Offenders and Their Victims*, pp53–75. Oakville, Ontario: Juniper Press.

Lang, R.A., and Frenzel, R.R. (1988). How Sex Offenders Lure Children. *Annals of Sex Research*, 1: pp303–17.

Lang, R.A., Black, E.L., Frenzel, R.R., and Checkley, K.L. (1988). Aggression and Erotic Attraction toward Children in Incestuous and Paedophilic Men. *Annals of Sex Research*, 1: pp417–41.

Langevin, R. (1983). *Sexual Strands: Understanding and Treating Sexual Anomalies in Men*. Hillsdale, NJ: Lawrence Erlbaum Associates.

Langevin, R. (1988). Defensiveness in Sex Offenders. In Rogers, R. (Ed.). *Clinical Assessment of Malingering and Deception*, pp269–90. NY: Guilford Press.

Langevin, R. (Ed.) (1985). *Erotic Preference, Gender Identity and Aggression in Men: New Research Studies*. Hillsdale, NJ: Lawrence Erlbaum Associates.

Langevin, R. (Ed.) (1991). *Sex Offenders and their Victims: New Research Findings*. Toronto: Juniper Press.

Langevin, R., and Bain, J. (1992). Diabetes in Sex Offenders. *Annals of Sex Research*, 5: pp99–118.

Langevin, R., and Lang, R.A. (1990). Substance Abuse Among Sex Offenders. *Annals of Sex Research*, 3: pp397–424.

Langevin, R., and Watson, R.J. (1996). Major Factors in the Assessment of Paraphiliacs and Sex Offenders. *Journal of Offender Rehabilitation*, 23: pp33–70.

Langevin, R., Bain, J., Ben-Aron, M.H., Coulthard, R., Day, D., Hardy, L., Heasman, G., Hucker, S.J., Pusins, J.E., Roper, V., Russon, A., Webster, C.D., and Wortzman, G. (1985). Sexual Aggression: Constructing a Predictive Equation: A Controlled Pilot Study. In Langevin, R. (Ed.). *Erotic Preference, Gender Identity and Aggression in Men: New Research*

Studies. Hillsdale, NJ: Lawrence Erlbaum Associates.

Langevin, R., Wright, P., and Handy, L. (1988a). Empathy, Assertiveness, Aggressiveness and Dangerousness Among Sex Offenders. *Annals of Sex Research*, 1: pp533–47.

Langevin, R., Wright, P., and Handy, L. (1988b). What Treatment do Sex Offenders Want? *Annals of Sex Research*, 1: pp363–85.

Lanning, K.Y. (1986). *Child Molesters: A Behavioural Analysis.* Washington DC: National Centre for Missing and Exploited Children.

Lanyon, R.I., and Lutz, R.W. (1984). MMPI Discrimination of Defensive and Non-defensive Felony Sex Offenders. *Journal of Consulting and Clinical Psychology*, 52: pp841–3.

Laws, D.R. (Ed.) (1989). *Relapse Prevention with Sex Offenders.* NY: Guilford Press.

Lazarus, A.A. (1976). *Multi-model Behaviour Therapy.* NY: Springer Publishing Co.

Leberg, E. (1997). *Understanding Child Molesters: Taking Charge.* Thousand Oaks, CA: Sage.

Lipton, McDonell, E.C., and Mcfall, R.M. (1987). Heterosocial Perception in Rapists. *Journal of Consulting and Clinical Psychology*, 55: pp17–21.

Lisak, D., and Roth, S. (1988). Motivational Factors in Non-incarcerated Aggressive Men. *Journal of Personality and Social Psychology*, 55(5): pp795–802.

MacCulloch, M.J., Snowden, P.R., Wood, P.J.W., and Mills, H.E. (1983). Sadistic Fantasy, Sadistic Behaviour and Offences. *British Journal of Psychiatry*, 143: pp20–9.

Malamuth, N.M. (1986). Predictors of Naturalistic Sexual Aggressor. *Journal of Personality and Social Psychology*, 56: pp953–62.

Malamuth, N.M., and Check, J.Y.P. (1983). Sexual Arousal to Safe Depictions: Individual Differences. *Journal of Abnormal Psychology*, 92(1): pp55–67.

Maletzky, B.M. (1996). Denial of Treatment or Treatment of Denial? *Sexual Abuse: A Journal of Research and Treatment*, 8(1): pp1–5.

Marshall, W.L. (1971). A Combined Treatment Method for Certain Sexual Deviations. *Behaviour Research and Therapy*, 9: pp292–4.

Marshall, W.L. (1988). The Use of Sexually Explicit Stimuli by Rapists, Child Molesters and Non-offenders. *Journal of Sex Research*, 25: pp267–88.

Marshall, W.L. (1989). Intimacy, Loneliness and Sexual Offenders. *Behavioural Research and Therapy*, 27: pp491–503.

Marshall, W.L. (1993a). The Role of Attachments, Intimacy and Loneliness in the Aetiology and Maintenance of Sexual Offending. *Sexual and Marital Therapy*, 8: pp109–21.

Marshall, W.L. (1993b). A Revised Approach to the Treatment of Men who Sexually Assault Females. In Nagayana-Hall, G.E., Hirschman, R., Graham,

J.R., and Zaragoza, M.S. (Eds.). *Sexual Aggression: Issues in Aetiology, Assessment and Treatment*, pp143–65. Washington, DC: Taylor And Francis.

Marshall, W.L. (1996). Assessment, Treatment and Theorizing about Sex Offenders. *Criminal Justice and Behaviour*, 23: pp162–99.

Marshall, W.L., and Eccles, A. (1991). Issues in Clinical Practice with Sex Offenders. *Journal of Interpersonal Violence*, 6: pp68–93.

Marshall, W.L., and Maric, A. (1996). Cognitive and Emotional Components of Generalised Empathy Deficits in Child Molesters. *Journal of Child Sexual Abuse*, 5(2): pp101–10.

Marshall, W.L., and Mazzucco, M. (1995). Self-Esteem and Parental Attachment in Child Molesters. *Sexual Abuse: A Journal of Research and Treatment*, 7(4): pp279–85.

Marshall, W.L., Barbaree, H.E., and Eccles, A. (1991). Early Onset and Deviant Sexuality in Child Molesters. *Journal of Interpersonal Violence*, 6(3): pp323–36.

Marshall, W.L., Barbaree, H.E., and Fernandez, Y.M. (1995). Some Aspects of Social Incompetence in Sex Offenders. *Sexual Abuse: A Journal of Research and Treatment*, 7: pp113–27.

Marshall, W.L., Bryce, P., Hudson, S.M., Ward, T., and Mott, B. (1996). The Enhancement of Intimacy and the Reduction of Loneliness among Child Molesters. *Journal of Family Violence*, 11(3): pp219–35.

Marshall, W.L., Hudson, S.M., and Hodkinson, S. (1993). The Importance of Attachment Bonds in the Development of Juvenile Sex Offending. In Barbaree, H.E., Marshall, W.L., and Hudson, S.M. (Eds.). *The Juvenile Sex Offender*, pp164–81. NY: Guilford Press.

Marshall, W.L., Hudson, S.M., Jones, R., and Fernandez, Y.M. (1995). Empathy in Sex Offenders. *Clinical Psychology Review*, 15(2): pp99–113.

Marshall, W.L., Jones, R., Hudson, S.M., and McDonald, E. (1993). Generalised Empathy on Child Molesters. *Journal of Child Sexual Abuse*, 2: pp61–8.

Mayer, A. (1988). *Sex Offenders: Approaches to Understanding and Management.* Holmes Beach, FL: Learning Publications, Inc.

McConaghy, N. (1993). *Sexual Behaviour: Problems and Management.* NY: Plenum Press.

McDowell, I., and Newell, C. (1987). *Measuring Health: A Guide to Rating Scales and Questionnaires.* NY: Oxford University Press.

McGovern, K., and Peters, J. (1988). Guidelines for Assessing Sex Offenders. In Walker, L.E. (Ed.). *Handbook of Sexual Abuse of Children: Assessment and Treatment Issues*, pp216–46. NY: Springer.

Mehrabain, A., and Epstein, N. (1972). A Measure of Emotional Empathy. *Journal of Personality*, 40: pp525–43.

Metts, S., and Cupach, W.R. (1989). The Role of

Communication in Human Sexuality. In McKinney, K., and Sprecher, S. (Eds.). *Human Sexuality: The Societal and Interpersonal Context*, pp139–61. NJ: Ablex Norwood.

Miller, P.A., and Eisenberg, W. (1985). The Relation of Empathy to Aggressive and Externalising/Antisocial Behaviour. *Psychological Bulletin*, 103: pp324–44.

Moore, J. (1991). Winds of Change. *Community Care*, 11.7.91: pp23–4.

Morran, D., and Wilson, M. (1997). *Men who are Violent to Women: A Groupwork Practice Manual*. Lyme Regis, Dorset: Russell House Publishing.

Muehlenhard, C.L., and Falcon, P.L. (1991). Men's Heterosocial Skills and Attitudes Towards Women as Predictors of Verbal Sexual Coercion and Forceful Rape. *Sex Roles*, 17.

Murphy, W., Coleman, E., and Haynes, M. (1983). Treatment and Evaluation Issues with the Mentally Retarded Sex Offender. In Greer, J., and Struart, I. (Eds.). *The Sexual Aggressor: Current Perspectives in Treatment*. NY: Van Nostrand Reinhold Co.

Murphy, W.D. (1990). Assessment and Modification of Cognitive Distortions. In Marshall, W.L., Laws, D.R., and Barbaree, H.E. (Eds.). *Handbook of Sexual Assault*. NY: Plenum Press.

National Task Force (1993). The Revised Report from the National Task Force on Juvenile Sexual Offending. *Juvenile and Family Court Journal*, 44(4): pp1–121.

Neate, P. (1990). The Unknown Quantity. *Community Care*, 8.11.90: pp17–9.

Nugent, P.M., and Kroner, D.G. (1996). Denial, Response Styles and Maintenance of Offences Among Child Molesters and Rapists. *Journal of Interpersonal Violence*, 11(4): pp475–86.

O'Carroll, T. (1980). The 'Molester' and his 'Victim'. In O'Carroll, T. (Ed.). *Paedophilia: The Radical Case*. London: Peter Owen Ltd.

O'Donohue, W., and Letourneau, E.J. (1993). A Brief Group Treatment for the Modification of Denial in Child Sexual Abusers: Outcome and Follow-Up. *Child Abuse and Neglect*, 17: pp299–304.

Overholsen, J.C., and Beck, S. (1986). Multimethod Assessment of Rapists, Child Molesters, and Three Control Groups on Behavioural and Psychological Measures. *Journal of Consulting and Clinical Psychology*, 54: pp682–7.

Pennell, A. (1996). *The Link Between Child Maltreatment and Sexual Offending*. Paper Presented to the 11th ISPCAN Congress on Child Abuse and Neglect, Dublin, Ireland, 18th–21st August, 1996.

Perry, G.P., and Orchard, J. (1992). *Assessment and Treatment of Adolescent Sex Offenders*. Sarasota, FL: Professional Resource Press.

Pierce, R., and Pierce, L. (1984). *Race as a Factor in Child Sexual Abuse*. Paper Given at the National Conference for Family Violence Researchers, Durham, New Hampshire.

Pithers, W., Kashima, K., Cumming, G.F., Beal, L.S., and Buell, M. (1988). Relapse Prevention of Sexual Aggression. *Annals of The New York Academy of Sciences*, 528: pp244–60.

Pithers, W.D. (1990). Relapse Prevention with Sexual Aggressors: A Method for Maintaining Therapeutic Gain and Enhancing External Supervision. In Marshall, W.L., Laws, D.R., and Barbaree, H.E. (Eds.). *Handbook of Sexual Assault: Issues, Theories and Treatment of the Offender*. New York: Plenum.

Pithers, W.D., and Laws, D.R. (1995). Phallometric Assessment. In Schwartz, B.K., and Cellini, H.R. (Eds.). *The Sex Offender*. Kingston, NJ: Civic Research Institute Inc.

Pithers, W.D., and Laws, D.R. (1988). The Penile Plethysmograph. In Schwartz, B.K. (Ed.). *A Practitioner's Guide to Treating the Incarcerated Male Sex Offender*, pp85–94. Washington, DC: Author.

Pithers, W.D., Beal, L.S., Armstrong, J., and Petty, J. (1989). The Identification of Risk Factors Through Clinical Interviews and Analysis of Records. In Laws, D.R. (Ed.). Op cit, pp1–31.

Pithers, W.D., Buell, M.M., Kashima, K.M., Cumming, G.F., and Beal, L.S. (1987). *Precursor to Sexual Offences*. Proceedings of the 1st Annual Meeting of The Association for The Behavioural Treatment of Sexual Aggressors. Newport, Oregon.

Prendergast, W.E. (1991). *Treating Sex Offenders in Correctional Institutions and Outpatient Clinics: A Guide to Clinical Practice*. NY: Haworth Press.

Prentky, R.A., Burgess. A.W., Rokous. F., Lee, A., Hartman, C., Ressler, R., and Douglas, J. (1989). The Presumptive Role of Fantasy in Sexual Homicide. *American Journal of Psychiatry*, 146: pp887–91.

Quinsey, V.L. (1981). *Prediction of Recidivism and the Evaluation of Treatment Programs for Sex Offenders*. Paper at Sexual Aggression and the Law: A Symposium. Vancouver, Canada.

Quinsey, V.L. (1986). Men who Have Sex with Children. In Weisstub, D.N. (Ed.). *Law and Mental Health: International Perspectives*, Vol. 2: pp140–72. NY: Pergamon Press.

Quinsey, V.L., Lalumiere, M., Rice, M., and Harris, G. (1995). Predicting Sexual Offences. In Cambell, J. (Ed.). *Assessing Dangerousness: Violence by Sexual Offenders, Batterers and Child Abusers*. Thousand Oaks, CA: Sage.

Rada, R.T. (1976). Alcoholism and the Child Molester. *Annals of the New York Academy of Justice*, 273: pp492–6.

Rada, R.T. (Ed.) (1978). *Clinical Aspects of the Rapist*. NY: Grune and Stratton.

Rhue, T.W., and Lynn, S.J. (1987). Fantasy Proneness: Developmental Antecedents. *Journal of Personality*, 55(1): pp121–37.

Rokeach, M. (1973). *The Nature of Human Values*. NY: Free Press.

Rokeach, M. (1980). Some Unresolved Issues in Theories of Beliefs, Attitudes, and Values. In Page, M.M. (Ed.). *Nebraska Symposium on Motivation 1979.* Lincoln: University Of Nebraska Press.

Salter, A.C. (1988). *Treating Child Sex Offenders and Victims? Assessment and Treatment of Child Sex Offenders: A Practice Guide.* Beverley Hills, CA: Sage.

Samra-Tibbets, C., and Raynes, B. (1999). Assessment and Planning. In Calder, M.C., and Horwath, J. (Eds.). *Working for Children on the Child Protection Register, an Inter-agency Practice Guide,* pp81–117. Aldershot: Ashgate.

Saunders, E.B., and Awad, G.A. (1988). Assessment, Management and Treatment Planning for Male Adolescent Sex Offenders. *American Journal of Orthopsychiatry,* 58(4): pp571–9.

Schiebe, K.E. (1970). *Beliefs and Values.* NY: Holt, Rinehart and Winston.

Schlank, A.M., and Shaw, T. (1996). Treating Sexual Offenders who Deny their Guilt: A Pilot Study. *Sexual Abuse: A Journal of Research and Treatment,* 8(1): pp17–23.

Schwartz, K.B., and Cellini, H.R. (Eds.) (1995). *The Sex Offender: Corrections, Treatment and Legal Practice.* Kingston, NJ: Civic Research Institute, Inc.

Scully, D., and Marola, J. (1984). Convicted Rapists' Vocabulary of Motives, Excuses and Justifications. *Social Problems,* 31: pp530–44.

Segal, L.E., and Stermac, L. (1990). The Role of Cognition in Sexual Assault. In Marshall, W.L., Laws, D.R., and Barbaree, H.E. (Eds.). *Handbook of Sexual Assault,* pp161–76. NY: Plenum.

Segal, Z.Y., and Marshall, V. (1985). Discrepancies Between Self-efficacy Predictions and Actual Performance in a Population of Rapists and Child Molesters. *Cognitive Therapy and Research,* 10(3): pp363–76.

Seto, M.C., and Barbaree, H.E. (1995). The Role of Alcohol in Sexual Aggression. *Clinical Psychology Review,* 15(6): pp545–66.

Snell, W.E., Belk, S.S., Papini, D.R., and Clark, S. (1989). Development and Validation of the Sexual Self-disclosure Scale. *Annals of Sex Research,* 2: pp307–34.

Steen, C. (1993). *The Relapse Prevention Workbook for Youth in Treatment.* Brandon, VT: Safer Society Press.

Stermac, L.E., and Quinsey, V.L. (1985). Social Competence Among Rapists. *Behavioural Assessment,* 8: pp171–85.

Stermac, L.E., and Segal, Z.Y. (1989). Adult Sexual Contact with Children: An Examination of Cognitive Factors. *Behaviour Therapy,* 20: pp573–84.

Taguiri, R. (1969). Person Perception. In Lindzey, G., and Aronson, E. (Eds.). *The Handbook of Social Psychology,* Vol. 3: pp. 395–449. Reading, MA: Addison-Wesley.

Thornton, D. (1994). Self-esteem Questionnaire. In Beckett, R.C. *et al.* Op cit.

Thornton, S., Todd, B., and Thornton, D. (1996). Empathy and the Recognition of Abuse. *Legal and Criminology Psychology,* 1: pp147–53.

Timnick, L. (1985). 22 Per Cent in Survey Were Child Abuse Victims. *Los Angeles Times,* 25.08.85.

Vizard, E. (1988). Child Sexual Abuse: The Child's Experience. *British Journal of Psychotherapy,* 5(1): pp77–91.

Ward, T., Fon, C., Hudson, S.M., and McCormack, J. (1998). A Descriptive Model of Dysfunctional Cognitions in Child Molesters. *Journal of Interpersonal Violence,* 13(1): pp129–55.

Ward, T., Hudson, S.M., and Marshall, W.L. (1995). Cognitive Distortions and Affective Deficits in Sex Offenders: A Cognitive Deconstructionist Interpretation. *Sexual Abuse: A Journal of Research and Treatment,* 7: pp67–83.

Ward, T., Hudson, S.M., Johnson, L., and Marshall, W.L. (1997). Cognitive Distortions in Sex Offenders: and Integrative Review. *Clinical Psychology Review,* 17(5): pp479–507.

Ward, T., Hudson, S.M., Marshall, W.L., and Siegert, R. (1995). Attachment Style and Intimacy Deficits in Sexual Offenders: A Theoretical Framework. *Sexual Abuse: A Journal of Research and Treatment,* 7(4): pp317–35.

Ward, T., Hudson, S.M., Louden, K., and Marshall, W.L. (1995). A Descriptive Model of the Offence Chain for Child Molesters. *Journal of Interpersonal Violence,* 10: pp452–72.

Ward, T., McCormack, J., and Hudson, S.M. (1997). Sexual Offender's Perceptions of their Intimate Relationships. *Sexual Abuse: A Journal of Research and Treatment,* 9(1): pp57–74.

Waring, E.M., and Reddon, J.R. (1983). The Measurement of Intimacy in Marriage. *Journal of Clinical Psychology,* 39: pp53–7.

Watts (1989). Quoted in Gocke, B. (1991). Tackling Denial in Sex Offenders. *Probation Monograph 98.* Norwich: UEA.

Webster, C.D., Menzes, R., and Jackson, M.A. (1982). *Clinical Assessment Before Trail: Legal Issues and Mental Disorders.* Toronto: Butterworths.

Weiss, R.S. (1974). The Provisions of Social Relationships. In Rubin, Z. (Ed.) *Doing unto Others.* Englewood Cliffs, NJ: Prentice-Hall.

White, C. (1992). A TA Approach to Child Sex Abusers. *Probation Journal,* 39(1): pp36–41.

Wild, N. (1989). Prevalence of Child Sex Rings. *British Medical Journal,* 293: pp183–5.

Willis, G.C. (1993). *Unspeakable Crimes: Prevention Work with Perpetrators of Child Sexual Abuse.* London: Children's Society.

Wilson, B.D., and Lang, R.I. (1981). Sex Differences in Sexual Fantasy Patterns. *Personality and Individual Differences,* 2: pp343–6.

Wilson, G. (1978). *The Secrets of Sexual Fantasy*. London: Jim Pert and Sons.

Wincze, J.P., and Carey, M.P. (1991). *Sexual Dysfunction: A Guide for Assessment and Treatment*. NY: Guilford Press.

Winn, M.E. (1996). The Strategic and Systemic Management of Denial in the Cognitive/Behavioural Treatment of Sex Offenders. *Sexual Abuse: A Journal of Research and Treatment*, 8(1): pp25–36.

Wolf, S. (1984). *A Multi-factor Model of Deviant Sexuality*. Paper at 3rd International Conference on Victimology. Lisbon, Portugal, November, 1984.

Wyre, R. (1987). *Working with Sex Abuse*. Oxford: Perry Publications.

Wyre, R. (1989). Workshop for Post-qualifying Diploma in Child Protection.

Wyre, R. (1992). Pornography and Sexual Violence: Working with Sex Offenders. In Itzin, C. (Ed.). *Pornography: Women, Violence and Civil Liberties*. Oxford: Oxford University Press.

Yates, E., Barbaree, H.E., and Marshall, W.L. (1984). Anger and Deviant Sexual Arousal. *Behaviour Therapy*, 15: pp287–94.

Zussman (1989). Forensic Evaluation of the Adolescent Sex Offender. *Forensic Reports*, 2: pp25–45.

Chapter Seven

Mothers in Sexually Abusing Families

Martin C. Calder

Introductory Comments

There is very little written on the position or dilemmas of the mother in sexual abuse cases, even less on a framework to guide practitioners in the task of assessing their needs at each stage of the child protection process, or on what components should be included in any 'ability to protect' assessment. The response to these areas has been low key, protracted, and incomplete. For example, the 'orange book' (DoH, 1988) and the new assessment framework (NAF) (DoH, 2000) do not acknowledge and redress the specific nature of sexual abuse assessments, and thus the worker is left to generate their own materials. The effect of this has been to generate intervention strategies built on stereotypical pre-determined views, disabling workers and generating resistance from the mothers. It has also prevented objective and comprehensive assessments to take place. This chapter aims to redress this by providing a broad assessment framework which focuses on the mother's needs and the professional needs. By doing so, the mother and the child become the central focus of the intervention process. The mother is a key figure in understanding the sexual abuse, and her role and functioning will have considerable influence on the professional decisions made. In most cases, the mother of the victim is not the perpetrator. As such, I make the assumption that the mother is the non-abusive parent. However, the closer her relationship is to the perpetrator, the more detailed the assessment of the mother needs to become.

The framework provided attempts to differentiate between those who believe and those who do not believe, as these polarised positions necessitate a different kind of assessment. There needs to be a differentiation between mothers whose children have been sexually abused and mothers whose partner presents as a risk to children. There is a need to differentiate between intra-familial and extra-familial child sexual abuse, as fathers are

devastated by the latter, and workers need to engage and work with both parents equally. The framework focuses primarily on *intra-familial* sexual abuse. The framework is a summary of more detailed guidance that will appear in Calder with Peake and Rose (forthcoming).

On a professional level the framework for understanding the conflicts and dilemmas faced by all mothers and carers moves beyond the point of focusing on the allegations of sexual abuse about their partners. I will explore how, for some women, assertions of denial initially of an allegation have led to an assumption of collusion and guilt and failure to engage with professionals. The outcome of this is often a long-standing history of social services involvement with families who have become increasingly alienated from the source of support they most need. As a result, I will propose a framework for individual assessments that enables women to move beyond a position of shock to regaining some control and focus on the future. Workers need to be aware that for most mothers, there are monumental impacts post-disclosure, and they cannot realistically be expected to be functioning at their optimal level. Mothers have to adapt to the dual impact of the effects on their children, as well as the losses associated with the perpetrator, who will often have created the opportunity to abuse, occasionally by splitting the mother-child relationship. Workers should expect, however, that some changes can be effected in the course of the assessment. In general terms, the more protective the mother becomes, the lower the future risks; the more suspicious or disbelieving the mother becomes, the higher the risk.

This chapter provides multiple components, which may be part of any assessment of a mother in a sexually abusing family. The aim is that the workers choose the appropriate components to the presenting family situation at an early point in the process, rather than attempt to cover them all without due consideration as to their appropriateness. The framework attempts to identify:

- A mother's ability to protect.
- The effects on the mother of the abuse.
- Her own needs and those of the children and how these might best be met.
- Identifying the family functioning—strengths and weaknesses.
- Strategies for managing the risks in the future.
- The areas where change is needed, in order of priority.
- Treatment needs, options and possible treatment programmes.

Engaging the mother in the work

The accuracy and extensiveness of the assessment of the mother will depend on the ability of the worker to successfully engage the mother in the process (Print and Dey, 1992). This can often be facilitated by offering the mother a worker of her own, with whom some degree of trust can be built. This helps to individualise the assessment and ensure the focus is very clearly on the mother's needs.

> *The purpose of the work with mothers is to empower them by recognising and developing strengths and thereby increasing their confidence to support and protect their children. This cannot be achieved if professionals merely mirror the behaviour of the abuser by making decisions about the child without involving the mother. If a mother is to increase her confidence and take responsibility for her child's welfare she must feel, and be, fully involved in planning for her child's future.*
> (Print and Dey, 1992: pp67–8)

For a fuller discussion of engagement issues the reader is referred to Calder with Peake and Rose (forthcoming) and Calder (forthcoming).

The written agreement

Any written agreement with the mother should be carefully negotiated and should enable her to exercise some control, within the context of the child's best interests. The agreement should include:

- The mother's feelings towards the abused child.

- The mother's ability to understand the offences and their effects on the child, siblings and herself.
- Her ability to give appropriate emotional support to the abused child.
- The mother's ability to protect the child (and siblings) from the perpetrator in particular.
- The degree to which the mother is financially, emotionally, or practically dependent on the perpetrator.
- The mother's support networks.
- Relevant issues from the mother's past, for example if she has been abused herself, that may inhibit her abilities to support the child.
- Medical and social factors that might be relevant. (Print and Dey, 1992: p68).

Defining the initial and core assessments

The initial assessment of the mother is likely to be based on the child's disclosure, the known history of the family, the child's wishes and feelings, and the reactions of other family members. It is designed to establish whether abuse has occurred, the likelihood of future abuse, the degree of protection available, the necessity of legal intervention, and the placement needs of the child.

The core assessment should be part of a broader child protection plan, often agreed at child protection conference. It is likely to sit alongside assessments of the child's wishes and feelings, the same of any siblings, and with the perpetrator. It is imperative that the process of assessment is a two-way one: with the professionals providing the mother with support, understanding and information. This variation from the norm often requires new techniques, which allow the mother to share their feelings and emotions as well as factual information. It is very important to assess a mother's ability to believe, support and protect the children. At no time, however, should the work with the mother, or her views, predominate over a consideration of the child's wishes and feelings and action deemed to be in their 'best interests'.

Possible assessment outcomes

The assessment processes are likely to produce one of the following conclusions:

- The mother can protect and support the abused child (and siblings) and does not require further professional intervention.

- The mother can protect and support the abused child (and siblings) if provided with sufficient resources.

- The mother denies the actual offences have been committed, but argues clearly that she will act protectively 'just in case'.

- The mother is ambivalent and the child's support and protection must be ensured by external sources, such as professionals, extended family, etc.

- The mother denies the abuse occurred or is very dependent on the perpetrator and so is unable adequately to support or protect the child. This invariably leads to removal from the family.

Recent experience tells us that many fall in the middle ground, and this makes planning and decision-making less clear, more anxious, and more prone to legal intervention. This position is often fuelled by the lack of any criminal prosecution and conviction for a recent offence, or where a previous allegation or schedule one conviction comes to light, and the mother has not seen any evidence of sexual abuse, or concerns about their role in the family, often over a significant period of time.

The Mother's Role in the Disclosing Process

The initial disclosure of a history of sexual abuse can come in a number of ways: from the child, possibly indicating that they are ready to address the secret; from the child already in therapy for some problem, and they have formed a trusting relationship with the helper; from medical evidence; from behavioural indicators; as a response to a direct question, or from some witness or other corroborating evidence.

The majority of children wish to tell their mother about the abuse. Many do so, some repeatedly. The likelihood of, and circumstances leading to, a child telling their mother vary and are dependent upon several factors. The younger the child, the more likely the first disclosure is to be to the mother. Younger children may have greater difficulty in comprehending the abusive experience, and the mother is usually the person to whom the child turns with physical soreness, etc. Younger children are also less likely to be fully aware of the negative consequences of disclosure and may disobey instructions by the perpetrator not to tell, impelled by their own developmentally inappropriate inability to contain their anxiety. The more distant the relationship between the mother and the perpetrator, the more likely the child is to disclose to her mother. There are also identifiable categories who are less likely to disclose to their mothers. These include older girls who are aware of the consequences of disclosure, often feeling protective of their families in the face of predicted disruption to family life that disclosure will bring. In addition, sexually abusive relationships, which bring a degree of enjoyment for the girl are less likely to be disclosed to the mother where the abuse is not a member of the immediate family. The girl may be getting some of her own unmet needs within the family fulfilled outside of it. The associated guilt may further deter the girl from disclosing.

A child's reluctance to tell of abuse should never be attributed as a fault in the mother, as this over-simplifies the difficulties of telling in sexual abuse cases. There are a number of reasons why children feel unable to tell:

- Children are dependent on adults for a lot of things e.g. food, warmth, shelter as well as love, laughter and discipline etc. Children learn to look to adults to meet these needs as part of growing up.

- Children are taught to obey parents and/or adults as having power and authority over them as a right.

- The perpetrator is probably someone who the child both likes and trusts. They may thus want to protect them.

- The child may not understand that what is happening is wrong as the perpetrator may tell the child that this happens to all children.

- The perpetrator may make threats or bribes to the child or be violent. The child will therefore be too scared to tell as they believe something worse will happen or they will be punished.

- The child may not know or understand the consequences of telling or they may feel such guilt and shame that they cannot tell. This may be especially true if their body responded to the sexual stimulation.

- The child may think they have told and nothing happened. This will give or make stronger the message that the child is at fault or has done something wrong.

- Generally, adults are not good at talking openly about sex, sexuality and most of all sexual abuse. The child might therefore have the message that this is something that they cannot talk about.

- The child may be passive because she believes the perpetrator when he says that the sexual abuse is acceptable.

- The child may feel there is no use in telling. If the parents are rarely around or are preoccupied with their own lives, the child may think that their parents simply do not care about what happens to them.

- The child who is sexually abused may receive many rewards from the perpetrator, both in terms of presents and affection/attention. The child will not want this part to stop, or are bribed not to say anything.

- They have a sense of loyalty and/or love for the perpetrator that makes it impossible for them to speak out against someone who is supposed to be protecting and caring for them.

- The child may not be getting love and cuddles and affection from other adults and so the abuse may be all the child receives in terms of these needs.

- The child may well fear the reactions of others, or has had unhelpful responses from people they told already.

- The child may feel too much guilt and shame to tell anyone.

- They fear they will be blamed.

- They fear breaking up the family.

(adapted from Engel, 1994; Hall and Lloyd, 1989; and Rose and Savage, 1995).

It is very important that mothers report the abuse once discovered. This is not a straightforward decision for many. Mothers' reports, as against those directly from children, are often viewed with particular suspicion (Humphreys, 1992). This has some origins in the professional perception of their culpability in the abuse (Hooper, 1989). A common reaction to learning about the abuse is to deny the need for outside help, feeling that the situation can be handled within the family unit. However, they must consider their sense of social responsibility to protect other children, desire for retribution, and fears that the court process will further traumatise the child (Regehr, 1990). The act of reporting sends a clear message to the child that what happened to them is very serious, must be stopped, and that the perpetrator needs to be punished or helped through legally-mandated treatment. To help them make the decision, mothers should be informed of the consequences of reporting and non-reporting, such as an inability to prosecute the perpetrator, and thus allowing the risk to remain untreated. It also prevents treatment being available either for the child or the mother.

Any significant delay in responding to a disclosure can have the following effects: the child feels that her history of sexual abuse is too shocking or disgusting for her to be helped; they may feel rejected after plucking up the courage to tell; they may minimise/deny/retract that they have been abused; they may feel that their abuse is not serious enough to warrant attention; and there is the potential for self-injurious behaviour (Hall and Lloyd, 1989).

The disclosure clearly represents the beginning of the crisis for the mothers (discussed in detail in a later component), often aggravated further by the professional expectations that they will focus all her energies on the safety of her child. Many mothers do not have sufficient resources to do this immediately. Professionals also approach mothers suspiciously, rather than with an open mind, until the extent of their involvement can be ascertained. Such an approach is one of seeing them as guilty until proven otherwise. The professional intervention thus pushes the mother and child apart at a time when they most need to be together. It is not surprising that many mothers who know of the abuse struggle to take the next step of reporting it to the authorities.

Research findings

Several studies show that fewer than half of victims tell anyone at the time of the abuse, and a large percentage never reveal the abuse until asked for research purposes. For example, Finkelhor (1990) found that only 40 per cent of both men and women had disclosed the abuse at the time it occurred, 24 per cent of women and 14 per cent of men told at a later time, and 33 per cent of women and 42 per cent of men had never told until the time of data collection.

Lawson and Chaffin (1992) found that disclosure was strongly associated with the attitude taken by the child's caretaker toward the possibility of abuse. Children whose caretakers accepted the possibility of abuse disclosed at a rate almost 3.5 times as great as those whose caretakers denied any possibility of abuse. They noted that parental or caretaker attitude towards sexual abuse disclosure is not necessarily a discrete post-disclosure event, but may be explicitly or covertly manifest during or even prior to the disclosure itself. As such, it may influence not only post-disclosure adaptation, but also the child's decision to disclose or not to disclose. In their sample, they found that 63 per cent of children with supportive caretakers disclosed compared with only 17 per cent of children with unsupportive caretakers.

Howarth (1999) reported that statistics from Childline showed that 22 per cent of girls who disclosed sexual abuse told their mothers, compared to 43 per cent who told their friends, 12 per cent who told both parents and extended family, and 3 per cent who told social services. She also noted that girls tend to be disclosing abuse at a much earlier stage than previously indicated, although there remains room for improvement in the 1–5 year age ranges. Furniss (1991) has noted that mothers are much more likely to become an ally for the child and the professionals if their own process of discovery is understood and facilitated.

Berliner and Conte (1995) in their research found that according to the parents, in only 43 per cent of cases did their children directly tell them about the abuse. They noticed physical evidence (4%), behavioural change (11%), or asked the child if anyone had touched them (10%). In the remainder of cases, they learned about the abuse of their child through others.

The children reported that they had told their mothers in almost half the instances (48%), and their fathers first in 5 per cent of cases. The next largest category of first person told was a friend (17%), while other relatives or professionals comprised the others to whom the children reported. Relief was the emotion most often expressed about telling (69%), with fear (16%), sadness (7%) and anger (3%) also mentioned. The majority of children characterised the initial reaction as supportive (54%). 26 per cent reported a reaction of shock/surprise, while 15 per cent described upset/sadness, 11 per cent anger, 8 per cent disbelief, and 1 per cent fear. The fact that many children did not report their experiences directly or did not tell their parents confirms that telling about the abuse is a difficult proposition.

Many children believe that their mothers were aware about their sexual abuse, and this makes it very difficult for them to disclose to them. Palmer *et al.*, (1999) found that 65 per cent of abuse survivors said that someone else knew about the abuse while it was happening. Only a minority (32%) had disclosed to one or more persons while the abuse was occurring. The distribution was disclosure to a non-abusive parent (41%), another relative (32%), a neighbour or friend (16%), a professional (8%), and others (3%). There were a range of reasons for non-disclosure: fear of the perpetrator (85%), fear of negative reactions from family members (80%), fear that no-one would believe them (72%), belief that they deserved the abuse (62%), and lack of awareness that the abuse was wrong or unusual (52%). Most survivors reported that no effective help was forthcoming from their disclosure or from someone knowing about the abuse. 60 per cent said it continued as before; 20 per cent said it became worse; 15 per cent said it stopped temporarily; and only 5 per cent said it stopped completely. The abuse stopped temporarily or completely 26 per cent of the time when mothers knew compared to 16 per cent of the time when others knew. Children reported 'ignoring' behaviour on the part of families and of larger communities, aggravated when they thought that professionals appeared protective of the perpetrators. The child may also fear disclosing as they will lose the affection that the perpetrator has given them in the grooming process, and worse still they may not be believed. Gomes-Schwartz *et al.*, (1990) found that the less loyalty the child feels towards the perpetrator, the more likely they are to tell, and they are least likely to tell when the perpetrator is a natural parent.

Issues to consider

One of the greatest professional (never mind maternal) fears is that a child chooses to disclose sexual abuse to them. They feel unskilled, and disabled by the experience, even though they probably have detailed guidelines on how to deal with such a situation, and have someone else who can be called upon to deal with it. Panic can easily set in. Some will construct their own defences to divert the disclosure elsewhere.

The reactions of those who the child first tells will determine whether they feel encouraged to seek or accept, further help. Indeed, the therapeutic work to overcome the effects of sexual abuse begins at this point. Positive responses to the child upon disclosure might include: acknowledging the difficulty of disclosing; relating the sexual abuse as linked to identified difficulties; offering immediate support; encouraging them to explore their feelings around the abuse; remaining calm, and not showing any feelings of shock, disgust or distress. It is important to understand and impart the reality that the abuse is never the child's fault. It is equally often not the fault of the mother, as she also may have been used by the perpetrator.

Unfortunately, it can also end there if the disclosure is managed in an insensitive or intrusive way. Unhelpful reactions might include ignoring or minimising the effects of being sexually abused; showing an excessive interest in the sexual details; or appearing very angry, shocked or disgusted by the disclosure. Unhelpful comments might include 'It's in the past. Do try to forget about it'; 'That is not as bad as some sexual abuse that I have heard about'; 'It only happened a few times, so maybe there isn't really anything to worry about'.

By using the information on why children do not tell, get the child to share with their mother the difficulties they had in telling, and why. If the mother is a survivor of sexual abuse, then get her to do the same and some comparisons may sow the seeds of empathy.

Help the child to understand they were never wrong. For example, compare photographs of the perpetrator and the child and compare size, age, etc.

Mothers need to know that if the child disclosed to them, they did so for a reason, e.g. as they will believe what they are saying, and will help them to sort it out. This does not negate the unexpected news when delivered, and the process that follows.

Questions that need answering include:

Did the child tell the mother? How? Is there evidence of changes in their awareness and understanding of the process of disclosure?

Position Regarding the Child's Disclosure

Belief or disbelief? Stand by your man, or your child? In this section, I will deal with the issue of maternal belief and support, given that they are inextricably linked.

Belief

> *The disclosure of incest differs from other family crises in that the mother is asked to believe something she may not want to believe, to interpret something that is at best difficult for her to comprehend, and to resolve the conflict between her roles as central support figure to both her child and her male partner at a time when her own social, emotional, and economic supports may be at risk.*
>
> (Everson *et al.*, 1989)

Humphreys (1992) has persuasively argued that in terms of belief in her child's sexual abuse, the mother's response was characterised by fluidity and change. The mother could move between feelings of ambivalence, strong belief, and disbelief about the abuse. The fluidity in her belief was ongoing from the earliest stages of discovery and was expressed in the mother's attainment of a stance of belief in the disclosure and then further in the maintenance of that position. The vulnerability of the mother of the sexually abused child in the aftermath of disclosure is underestimated by practitioners. There is dearth of services for mothers commensurate with the crisis they experience which indicates a failure to recognise their importance to the child victim and the fluid nature of belief. Understanding disclosure from the mother's perspective can be crucial as assumptions are often made about the mother's ability to believe, support and protect her child early in the investigation.

Mothers reported that the attainment of belief was inextricably linked to the process of disclosure and discovery. For some mothers, disclosure was the end point of a long-drawn-out process in which they had become increasingly concerned or suspicious about their children's behaviour. For others, disclosure was a 'bolt from the blue' for which they were completely unprepared. Regardless of the process of discovery, all mothers in this sample experienced a period in which they were unconvinced that the sexual abuse of their child has occurred. This may have been a period of five minutes while the evidence was placed before them or a more lasting state. Three mothers in this sample at the end of the six-month period could be said to have remained unconvinced that the abuse had occurred. However, each mother was left with some uncertainty.

All mothers also experienced periods of ambivalence in which they did not know whether to believe or disbelieve that the abuse of their child had occurred. This ambivalence took different forms for different women and included both emotional and cognitive aspects. For one group it was a time in which further evidence was gathered to support disclosure. For other mothers, the evidence was there, and the disclosure made. However, the mother was not emotionally ready to confront the abuse.

Ambivalence does not only refer to *attaining* a stance of belief. Seven mothers in this sample said that they believed that the abuse had occurred. However, they had difficulty *maintaining* protection and support for the child. For five mothers, this was due to the perpetrator's continued influence in their lives whereby he would continue to deny the abuse, seek their love and support, promise to reform and generally undermined the mother-child relationship. Three other mothers, all victims of childhood sexual abuse, experienced a breakdown in the relationship with their daughters following disclosure. As the mother's relationships changed, her stance of belief that the abuse had occurred, or that the

child was seriously affected or in danger, shifted.

Twenty-one of the twenty-two mothers also experienced a period at the other end of the continuum in which they were able to act congruently with the belief that the sexual abuse had occurred, and were able to communicate this to the child with protection and support.

This study showed that mothers throughout the sample period could move in either direction along the continuum from belief to ambivalence to disbelief and vice versa. Such movement suggests that the mother's perception of the event is not fixed and needs to be understood by practitioners who make judgements about the mother's position early in the assessment period. The process by which these changes occurred was complex, and experienced by women throughout the sample. The difficulties in sustaining a stance of belief, protection and support however, were much greater for women who were attached or who had ambivalent feelings towards the perpetrator who had been her partner prior to disclosure. This study indicated that three factors provided more powerful restraints to the mother's ability to comprehend that her child was being sexually abused. They were the power of the perpetrator over the child to keep the secret; the destruction of the communication between the mother and child that develops as a result of the imposition of the secret by the perpetrator; and the cleverness of the perpetrator in hiding his sexual abuse.

Without an admission of guilt and acceptance of responsibility, the path of the mother and the victim is doubly difficult. A particular problem is that the mother is left to judge whether the abuse has occurred or not. Calder and Skinner (Chapter Six) have explored in some detail the complexity and purpose of perpetrator denial.

Mothers also spoke of the emotional ingredients of 'belief' as against the more concrete elements mentioned in the previous section. It frequently occurred as a spontaneous emotional reaction: a natural defence against traumatic news, and parallels the evidence in the literature about a person's initial response of denial in the face of death or grief. Mothers spoke of functioning on at least two different levels as a means of coping with their aversion to the traumatic news: the mother was cognitively saying 'no, it's not happening', while at the same time having feelings congruent with belief. The women reported that this lack of congruence did not cease after the initial shock had worn off. Because belief is a fluid notion, different levels of understanding operate simultaneously. The initial response was not necessarily an indicator of how women would behave towards their children later.

There is a consensus that human beings react with some similarity in situations of acute stress. Twenty-one of the twenty-two mothers testified to being numbed by the blow. Then, as the full impact of the situation was confronted they experienced a downward slump in behaviour wherein they felt confused, disorientated and helpless. After a period of disorganisation, they attempted to reorganise their lives using whatever mechanisms were available including denial, minimisation, active involvement in 'the fight', and/or finding new strengths and support with which to confront the problem.

This description exemplified important aspects of the mothers' response. However, two important qualifications stemming from the mothers' reported experience need to be made. First, mothers did not experience this crisis once, but could track many occasions both prior to an event, if they had witnessed a marked inexplicable change in their child's behaviour, and in the months and years following disclosure. Their experiences suggested that for many women it was a life transition dotted with a number of active crisis states, rather than a single point of intensive crisis. It thus resembles a long, grieving process as mothers come to terms with the many losses which child sexual assault has wrought in their and their children's lives. Second, crisis was not a linear state but, through the necessity to reorganise, was connected to the construct of belief in both its cognitive and emotional aspects.

Thus, each time stresses were placed on the mothers by either the perpetrator, the child, or the legal, economic and social consequences of the disclosure, the subjective state of the mother could be affected.

Humphreys found that a constellation of factors assisted mothers in the process of lifting the blind which had hidden the child's reality of sexual abuse from them.

These factors included the age of the child, physical evidence of sexual abuse, police statements, past knowledge of the perpetrator's sexual deviance, the mother's own experience of child sexual assault, and professional and private support. As belief and support are not static states, these depicted areas are ones which may assist or restrain mothers in believing their child's disclosure. One factor in itself did not appear to be enough to confirm the mother's belief that abuse had occurred (*reproduced with the kind permission of Cathy Humphreys*).

There are a number of other factors relevant to the mother's response to any disclosure. These might include her relationship with the perpetrator; the nature of the child's relationship with the perpetrator; the power of the perpetrator in their life; the character of the intimate relationship between the mother and the perpetrator; the duration of the abuse; and the violation of trust. So, where they are powerless in their relationship with the perpetrator, they will respond to the disclosure with a proportionate sense of powerlessness. A good sexual relationship between the mother and the perpetrator can be a major restraint to women believing that sexual abuse could have occurred. The opposite is also true: mothers can find it easier to believe the disclosure if they know the perpetrator is sexually deviant in some way. Mothers may also be influenced by the child's age. Some mothers will not contemplate that their very young children have been abused, but tend to believe and sometimes blame older children.

There are some very clear obstacles to believing the child and these include: a parental history of abuse, which they promised would not happen to their child; a belief that they must terminate a relationship with the perpetrator once abuse is confirmed; excessive dependence on the perpetrator; or prior family rejection of the perpetrator, resulting in a situation where to believe is to accept family condemnation (Berliner, 1991). Where mothers have problematic relationships with their children and a lack of 'maternal protective behaviours', they are less likely to believe that abuse has taken place. This is even greater where there is a strong emotional tie between the mother and the perpetrator (Craig *et al.*, 1989).

Faller (1990) argued that there are a number of dynamics which may influence a mother's willingness to believe: acknowledgement of shortcomings as parent; acknowledgement of shortcomings as spouse; decision regarding leaving or staying with the perpetrator; facing practical consequences of that decision; coping with professionals' intrusions. A mother's shock (or numbness) associated with the disclosure may also contribute to a mother's difficulties around believing (Byerly, 1985).

Mothers may find the allegations totally unbelievable to themselves, either because the acts described are beyond anything they could ever imagine one person doing to another or because they care about the person against whom the allegations are made so much that they cannot believe they would do such a thing.

It is important to remember that children rarely lie about sexual abuse, except to minimise their involvement. Much more often, they are afraid to tell or, when they do tell, they tend to downplay the actual abusive episodes. We need to remember that younger children usually provide less complete and less detailed testimony than older children, and there can be incomplete recall or a lack of clarity about frequency, dates, times, etc. Older children are often more aware of the power of such accusations, and can thus use them as instruments of manipulation. There are some cases where children do distort the truth in some fashion, sometimes exaggerating details or making up stories that indirectly express their anger or provide satisfaction to a third party, e.g. their mother in custody dispute cases (Hillman and Solek-Tefft, 1988: p47).

We should remember that accusations of sexual abuse are very difficult to make as they go against basic human loyalties and attachments. Children usually have great anxieties as to whether they will be believed, and possibly fear the outcome, such as the splitting up of the family and, at least, the revelation possibly being unwelcome. Older children may have an appreciation of the fact that 'the authorities' take such allegations seriously, and therefore that making an allegation is a way of drawing attention to their predicament, or hurting somebody.

Support

Rollins and Thomas (1979) defined parental support as:

> ...the behaviour manifested by a parent toward a child that makes the child feel comfortable in the presence of the parent and confirms in the child's mind that he is basically accepted and approved as a person by the parent.
>
> (p320)

> The construct of support is made up of both belief and protective action. Belief involves validation of the child's account, placing the responsibility on the adult rather than the child, and conveying an attitude of concern for the child. Protective action is defined in various ways but basically involves the mother backing up her belief by behaviours that protect the child from further abuse and aid in recovery, such as co-operating with the child protection services and criminal justice agencies, removing the child from perpetrator access, and seeking counselling for the child.
>
> (Corcoran, 1998)

Humphreys (1992) differentiated professional from social support. She found that all the mothers required the help of professionals to confirm sexual abuse and to give appropriate information and encouragement to enable them to follow through with effective action. The importance of professional support is also illustrated by the mother's vulnerability to the perpetrator's definition of the situation when professionals withdrew the intensive involvement, which was present during the initial investigation. This was particularly so in cases where mothers were emotionally involved with the perpetrator. The mother's position is crucial for many children, since they may feel that she is the only person who can 'give permission' for them to disclose. The mother may find herself in an impossible dilemma: Butler-Sloss (1988, p8) comments that 'in the conflict between her man and her child, the relationship with the man, the economic and other support which she receives from him may disincline her to accept the truth of the allegation'. The problem is worse when the child cannot say anything directly or clearly to the mother about sexual abuse. It will seem to be a choice between the word of the professional and the possible perpetrator.

In Humphreys' study, mothers who were acting with belief and protection towards their victimised children were in receipt of a greater level of personal and professional support than those mothers who were at the stage of being unconvinced or ambivalent. However, the relationship between support and belief is complex. Mothers in this sample who moved to a position of consistent belief and protection for the child were not attached to the perpetrator. They were therefore less constrained by the perpetrator's tactics and relatively speaking had greater assistance from friends and family. The three mothers who were unconvinced the abuse had occurred, either named the perpetrator as their major source of support, together with a network of friends and family who did not encourage the child, or they had no close emotional support. A problem for mothers was that the very nature of child sexual assault structured their isolation and ability to talk with others. They named factors such as: the perpetrator's tactics to isolate them, both prior and post disclosure; protection of the child's privacy; protection of close friends and family who might themselves already be very distressed at the disclosure; time constraints imposed by the necessity of working to support themselves; and lack of understanding by friends and family of the ambivalent feelings they may have towards the abuser.

Support has different dimensions and levels, and appears to have measurable effects on the child's well being. Most mothers respond with some support to their children who disclose sexual abuse, although they frequently stop short of full support. One of the most commonly suggested adaptive responses is to convey a sense of belief in the child's report. It is also important that the mother conveys to the child that the abuse was completely the responsibility of the perpertrator, instead of becoming angry at the child or blaming him/her for the event. Instead of emphasising the child's victim status, it is important to stress that the child is a survivor (Esquilin, 1987). It is helpful for mothers to respond in a matter-of-fact manner while continuing their routine, as well as reassuring the child that no lasting harm will result from their experiences. Other suggested reactions have included protecting the child from further harm, acknowledging the courage it took for the child to disclose, accepting the child's feelings about the event, and reinforcing the child's disclosure by praising him or her for 'doing the right thing' (Wurtele and Miller-Perrin, 1992).

In many cases the mother is not in a position to offer support for reasons not always considered or clearly understood. Frequently, maladaptive responses would be to doubt the veracity of the child's report or to deny that the abuse has occurred. Overreactions can also contribute to the child's sense of stigmatisation or feeling as though they are different from others or 'damaged goods'. Other inappropriate actions include over-protectiveness (e.g. restricting usual activities), which may have the paradoxical effect of making children more vulnerable to abuse by disrupting their lives and lessening their ability to control their environment (Regehr, 1990). In addition, mothers may be reluctant to touch child victims, which may reinforce their sense of being 'damaged goods'. Professionals should be encouraged to provide normal expressions of affection to prevent these negative outcomes and to reassure victims that normal affection is quite different than abusive touching. Roberts and Taylor (1993) found that some mothers minimised the abuse, failed to act, and either blamed or rejected the child. They also emotionally withdrew and were inactive. Children are affected adversely when confidants do not support them, particularly where it is perceived by the child as nothing can be done.

Everson *et al.* (1989) found that negative chain events are set in motion when professionals perceive low maternal support. Children with blaming or rejecting mothers are much more likely to be removed from their homes; this may entail testimony in the court, changing schools, and otherwise being removed from familiar activities and friends. Furthermore, any support a child may be receiving from important others, or simply from familiar routine may be undermined by removal from home.

Research findings

Berliner and Conte (1995) found that the majority of children characterised the initial reaction as supportive (54%). 26 per cent reported a reaction of shock/surprise, while 15 per cent described upset/sadness, 11 per cent anger, 8 per cent disbelief, and 1 per cent fear.

Lyon and Kouloumpos-Lenares (1987) reported that though 70 per cent of the mothers believed in their children's sexual abuse, only 50 per cent responded with protective action, emotional support, and co-operation with protective agencies. Another 26 per cent were appropriately protective in action by getting the perpetrator to leave the home, providing only supervised contact, or making other child care arrangements. However, these mothers were also ambivalent, denying their children's need for treatment or additional support. 22 per cent of the victim's mothers were non-protective. In this study, belief and action toward protecting the child were strongly associated. Non of the non-believing mothers provided a protective response, while 58 per cent of the believing mothers were actively helpful.

A continuum of protectiveness was developed by De Young (1994):

- High protective: the woman behaviourally responds to the disclosure or discovery of the incest by removing the perpetrator from the home; calling the police or social services; and bringing her daughter for medical evaluation.

- Medium protective: the woman behaviourally responds to the disclosure or discovery of the incest by verbally confronting her husband; talking with her daughter to gather details about the incest; and/or seeking advice from an appropriate professional.

- Low protective: the woman behaviourally responds to the disclosure or discovery of the sexual abuse by seeking emotional support for herself, her daughter, and/or her husband from a person who is not a professional, and may include a member of the immediate or extended family, a friend, or a social acquaintance.

- Non-protective: the woman behaviourally responds to the disclosure or discovery of the sexual abuse by doing nothing; physically withdrawing from, or leaving the family or home; refusing to co-operate with, or lying to professionals with investigation responsibility; and/or punishing her daughter.

From this schema, 10 per cent of the women were evaluated as high protective; 25 per cent were classified as medium protective; 25 per cent as low protective; and 40 per cent as non-protective.

Everson et al., (1989) evaluated parental reactions within two weeks of victim disclosure. Parental reactions toward 88 victims (aged 6–17 years) were determined by combining clinical ratings in three areas, including:

1. Emotional support (ranging from commitment and support of child, to threats, hostility, and abandoning the child psychologically).

2. Belief of the child (ranging from making a clear, public statement of belief, to totally denying that the abuse occurred).

3. Action toward perpetrator (ranging from actively demonstrating disapproval of their abusive behaviour, to choosing them over the child).

Where all three criteria were met, the mothers were believed to have offered full support to the child. Results indicated that 44 per cent of mothers were rated as providing consistent support, 32 per cent as ambivalent or inconsistently supportive, and 24 per cent were rated as non-supportive or rejecting. Maternal support was not related to victim characteristics (i.e. age, gender, race), or mother's educational level, but was related to the perpetrator's relationship with the mother. Mothers were most supportive of their children when the perpetrator was an ex-spouse and least supportive when the perpetrator was a current boyfriend, as the child's disclosure appeared to be more of a threat to her emotional and financial security. Mother's disbelief might also have been associated with the fact that all boyfriends denied the sexual abuse, compared to two-thirds of the ex-husbands. Most studies tend to support the finding that mothers have less of a problem with divided loyalty when the perpetrator is not a family member. Everson et al., (1989) found that maternal support was a primary predictor of overall psychological functioning for the child.

The circumstances of the disclosure may also be related to maternal reaction. For example, if a child told the mother about the abuse soon after it occurred rather than delaying for a period of time, the mother was more likely to be concerned and protective (Tufts, 1984). More specifically, when the child told the mother about the abuse, she was more likely to believe that when it was revealed to professionals first. The gender of the victim may well be important, with mothers being more protective of sons rather than daughters (Tufts, 1984).

Salt *et al.*, (1990) found that the majority of mothers responded to the revelation of sexual abuse in a very appropriate manner. They expressed concern about the child's welfare and took appropriate steps to protect the child. They did find that for some mothers, their childhood histories affected how they responded after the disclosure. Those who reported having a poor relationship with either parent appeared to have less capacity to be concerned about their sexually abused daughters. Those mothers who did not protect their daughters seemed either to have experienced poor relationships with the maternal grandmothers or, as children, to have had mothers who were absent. Those mothers who described having poor relationships with their own parents were more likely to have their children removed from their care (Leifer *et al.*, 1993).

It is important that workers do retain a strong understanding that some mothers do not believe and therefore do not support their children post-disclosure. Where mothers are less supportive, the children are at greater risk of removal (Pellegrin and Wagner, 1990). For professionals, the key question is whether this is a temporary or a permanent situation.

Leifer *et al.*, (1993) studied various factors associated with supportive maternal behaviour toward sexually abused children, and found that mothers who abused alcohol and who had limited social support were least likely to be supportive of their children. They also found a relationship between low maternal supportive behaviour and low child functioning. The mother's reaction to, and belief in, the child's report of the sexual abuse may be very important to the child, and may well constitute a protective factor that could minimise the negative effects of the abuse.

The mother's support is an important factor in the recovery process due to the need of the girl to be loved and accepted by their mother; as well as telling them it was not their fault, thus removing some of the perceived guilt. In this study, the mothers who acknowledged

their own past childhood sexual abuse were perceived as more supportive than the mothers who reported that they had never been sexually abused. This has not always been the case, and Friedrich, 1990, found that mothers who were themselves victims of sexual abuse may be unable to support their own children because of their own unresolved sexual abuse issues. This may be explained by such factors as responding in a manner similar to how they would have wished their own mothers to respond to them. The results also show that the daughters perceived their mothers as less supportive than the mothers perceived themselves.

The research did identify similar perceptions of appropriate ways to show support, with the two most common themes being the need for the mother to believe the sexual abuse happened and the need for the mother to participate in the treatment process. The one area of disagreement centred on independence and space, with the adolescents wanting more of both, whilst the mothers thought this was just so they could have the total freedom to do what they want. This appears to be a consistent part of the developmental processes of the mother's struggle to set limits and the adolescents strive for freedom.

Issues to consider

This is an important component when workers are looking towards the way forward with a case, yet the expectations on mothers may differ slightly from the considerations applied for workers. Following Cleveland, professionals have been issued with very detailed guidance for the interviewing of child witnesses (Home Office, 1992), and this requires a very intensive training and accreditation programme. Mothers do not have this preparation although a great deal is expected of them, and they can be wrongly judged if they do not immediately espouse total belief with the child's disclosure. This is almost a case of double standards.

Signs that a mother has taken the abuse seriously include listening to what the child says about the impact of the experience, acknowledging the distress and pain for the child, placing responsibility for the abuse clearly with the adults involved, and taking all possible steps to ensure that the child is safe from further abuse by the same, or a different, perpetrator (Sayers, 1995).

A mother's response to the disclosure of sexual abuse appears to be influenced by many factors. Professional attention to the mother, however, can be limited and shaped by the fact that professionals feel intense pressure to quickly investigate and assess the situation for legal purposes and protection issues. Serious problems can arise when an initial maternal response is misunderstood and negatively interpreted by professionals with the authority to remove children from the home. It is questionable in this environment just how free a woman feels to respond in a fashion accurately reflecting her true emotional and mental state (Howard, 1993). In such a situation, assessment of her position with respect to belief or disbelief of the disclosure will be skewed at best, and is unlikely to strike at the true source of her problems or achieve the desired goals. Moreover, if the mother senses blame, her energies may well be deflected from supporting the child to defending herself. This in turn has the potential to confirm professional suspicions and negative judgements.

Many mothers sense that something is not quite right but do not dream that sexual abuse might be the cause. Those that might suspect sexual abuse as the cause often convince themselves they are reading too much into the situation. After the sexual abuse has been disclosed, they often ask themselves how this could have happened to their child, where were they to allow it to happen, etc? Ask the mother what she did when she thought something was wrong with her child, and then what she did when she found out about the abuse.

Questions that need answering include:

Did she believe straight away? Who had to tell her for her to believe it? Would she believe the child about further abuse? What does she think it would be helpful to know to keep her child safe/ to know if her child is being abused? What did she do when she found out about the abuse? Why did they respond in a particular way? What could they have done differently? Why?

Sometimes the mother hearing the child's account, particularly if they were not told directly, will help them conclude that sexual abuse has taken place. The mother can then tell the child that they have been told what they said and that they are glad about this and do believe them.

In assessing a mother's position, professionals need to consider whether the parent is minimising the extent of the abuse. This is understandable in the immediate crisis of discovery, but becomes less acceptable over time. More worrying are parents who disbelieve what the child has disclosed. In part, they may still be leaving open the possibility that, with additional information, they may believe the child's disclosure. This often needs to be the admission by the perpetrator or medical evidence or a criminal conviction. Where these are not available, workers need to actively help mothers try and make sense of conflicting information and in particular how to select the 'right' information. Using a child's statement can be helpful as it gives the mother the opportunity to come to terms with what the child has experienced. The same statement can then become the focal point of further work with the family.

Workers may want to adopt circular questioning to engage non-believing mothers into some areas of discussion. For example, they can be asked to think through what the child was alleging and consider what that experience may have been like. Why would they lie? It may also be appropriate for the mother to view the memorandum taped interview out of the presence of the child, and the transcript of the interview with the perpetrator (particularly where some partial admissions exist, or where there are known discrepancies and the mother will identify this and thus question any denial of the offences).

Craig *et al.*, (1989) suggest that workers who work with mothers who do not believe the abuse has occurred, face feelings of helplessness, despair and frustration, yet they must go on to assess why the mothers are unable to do this. The important thing is not so much to establish why the mother failed to protect, but one of establishing the expectations of mothers as responsible parents.

Workers should always allow the mothers time and space to effect some change to their originating stance at the point of disclosure, as reactions are often transitory.

It is important that workers discover what characteristics of the mother, her home situation and history, aspects of the abuse, or child characteristics determine her level of support for the child.

Rivera (1988) argued that given most mothers are confused post-disclosure, then they need someone to guide them through the process without blaming them or making them feel guilty. The assessment process thus needs to be conducted without insinuating that the mother is somehow responsible for the abuse.

The Mother's Role in the Sexual Abuse

Active participant, 'turning a blind eye', or innocent bystander? Whilst the role of the mother is repeatedly over-empathised, the literature suggests that it can play a contributing role in some cases. Rejection, ridicule, defiance, infidelity, the withholding of sex, as well as other behaviours, can trigger reactions in the perpetrator that increase the propensity to sexually abuse. Moreover, the desertion or absence of a partner and accompanying dynamics can enhance the risk for the sexual abuse of children (Faller, 1990).

Engel (1994) set out the following points, which may have left the opportunity for the child to be sexually abused:

- By denying the child attention and affection: causing the children to be vulnerable to someone who could exploit their needs.
- By leaving the children unsupervised—or poorly supervised—for lengthy periods of time: often necessary for the perpetrator to groom the situation for the abuse.
- By leaving the children with caretakers who were abusive: even though the mother may have been unaware about the real risks, they may have been aware that they drank or were emotionally disturbed.
- By abusing the children herself: can lead to the children not learning to value themselves and this opens up the pathways for the perpetrator to ask them to do almost anything.
- By ignoring obvious signs of abuse and cries for help: This may be due to their

own experiences of sexual abuse and their need to self-protect before having to take any action to stop the current abuse.

- By making the child feel that they would not be believed if she told: this may be a general message given to the child by the mother who has told the child they have exaggerated something or made it up.
- By showing other people that the children were not valued: by showing their disdain for the children, they imply they deserve what they get.
- By making the child feel that they could not, would not, protect them: maybe because the mother feels as helpless or as powerless as the child, thus making it impossible for them to do anything about the abuse (pp116–118).

There are cases where a non-abusing parent will have explicitly concealed the sexual abuse, and workers need to understand why, as there is still some potential to work with them later if they accept and believe the sexual abuse has taken place (Smith, 1995).

Research findings

Dietz and Craft (1980) examined the attitudes of 200 child protection workers in Iowa about mothers in families where sexual abuse had occurred. They found that 87 per cent of the respondents believed that mothers gave their unconscious consent to it and that 65 per cent believed that she was equally responsible. They also found that the professional attitudes were related to reading the professional literature. Indeed, this was moderately related to believing that mothers gave their unconscious consent to the abuse.

Faller (1991b) reported that, in a study of polyincestuous families, 38.8 per cent of her sample consisted of female abusers—mothers abusing with male partners. She states clearly that the possibility that a mother may be actively involved in sexually abusing her child cannot be overlooked. What should also not be overlooked is the fact that the mother will sense this, and her feeling that every move she makes will be scrutinised and judged will be intensified.

Scott and Flowers (1988) queried 24 adolescents and 26 adult female victims of father-daughter incest about their mothers' responses. 29 per cent of adolescent and 50 per cent of adult victims believed their mothers knew of the incest but failed to intervene. Maisch (1973) found that 12 per cent of mothers in their sample of 78 incest cases before the German courts knew of and tolerated an ongoing incestuous relationship and 3 per cent colluded with the incest.

Questions that need answering include

Was she involved? Was she coerced into involvement? It is important to explore with the mother ways in which they can apologise to the child for anything that they did to set her up for the abuse (consciously or unconsciously) and then as to any ways that they can now support them. The child may well be angry with the mother for lots of reasons, such as for failing to protect her, for looking the other way, for setting her up for the abuse, for blaming her, for not listening when she tried to tell the mother, for not believing her, for remaining with the perpetrator, or for not providing her with the necessary love and attention she needed.

Knowledge of the Abuse Taking Place

One of the key debates in recent years has been whether or not the mother has known or suspected the sexual abuse of their children. Historically, there was a strong belief that they *always* knew about it at some level (see Kempe and Kempe, 1978), although this is now beginning to give way to a recognition that they often did not. This is often because the sexual abuse takes place in their absence and the children are sworn or coerced into secrecy. Many children will go to great lengths not to let their mothers know (as well as others), although they often believe their mothers knew about the abuse, when in fact they did not. Conversely, some children do not believe that their mother knew, when in fact they did.

Friends may also insinuate that the mother must have known. Any insinuation from professionals that the mother is in some way to blame for what the perpetrator has done will deepen her emotional strife. Mothers caught in the tangled, dysfunctional web will find particular pain in such insinuations (Byerly, 1992).

There are some mothers who knew what was happening but were too intimidated or abused themselves to stop it. One mother who knew, slept with her child to protect her and put crackly paper under the bedroom door so she would wake when it opened. Workers do need to understand the devastating effect on mothers of learning of the sexual abuse. When the mother says 'I can't believe it' people think they are saying that they won't believe it. Mothers are either represented as collusive and offered no support, or else they are good mothers who believe in and protect the child so they are just left to get on with it. It is true that some children tell their mothers that someone has touched them and that the mothers don't believe them or act to protect their children from further abuse. It is more common that the mother knows that something is wrong with her child, but they are unclear about what that something might be.

Rickford (1992) noted that mothers of sexually abused children are frequently left alone to cope with assumptions of collusion. This may be coming from the child and only time and help will assist them in understanding that the mother did not know what was happening. As one mother indicated, 'She still hits and kicks me, and blames me. She said "You were cooking his dinner and let him come up and do the naughty things". She didn't realise that I didn't know'. Children see the mother as their protector, not the father or father-figure (Prendergast, 1991).

Todd (1989) in her sample in Sheffield found that many of the youngsters had attempted to tell their mothers of the abuse. One had said 'Tell me if it happens again'. Another came home unexpectedly and found her daughter with the stepfather dressing in the bedroom. She claims never to have known about the abuse. These cases show a profound level of denial by the mother, even when the evidence was overwhelming. In most of the cases, the mother put the perpetrator's needs first.

On occasions, the mother may have challenged the perpetrator about some of their behaviour (e.g. sharing a bath), only to be told they had the sexual hang ups. One of the key problems is that suspicion is characterised by the inaccessibility of clear information about events conducted in secrecy and uncertainty about the meaning of the information available.

In order to appraise a situation as potentially abusive, the mother must be sensitive to behavioural and/or mood changes or other clues. In some instances, indicators are fairly clear, such as genital injury. In other situations, the clues may be less obvious, such as atypical sexual curiosity. Professionals must remember that symptoms of abuse are more apparent to professionals than to the public at large (discussed in detail in a later component). With the increasing trend towards male involvement in child care, it is unfair to blame the mother for this shared responsibility if something like sexual abuse occurs, particularly when Herman (1981) argued that this is likely to reduce such abuse. It is possible that denial may be a defence mechanism that protects mothers from confronting the emotional consequences of acknowledging that abuse is occurring, particularly if the mother was sexually abused herself. Mothers may also be overwhelmed by financial, marital, or other concerns and thus not notice clues that might be obvious under less stressful conditions.

There have been a number of lists developed to explain why it would have been difficult for a mother to know at the time their child was being sexually abused. These include:

- Most of the TV, videos, newspapers etc. tell us that sexual perpetrators are strangers or weirdos and monsters, not people one knows.
- The perpetrator is usually someone known or trusted by them and would be the last person they would suspect.
- The perpetrator often manipulates the situation so they can give the 'love' and 'affection' to the child and prevents closeness between the mother and the children.
- The perpetrator often brings lots of presents and is seen as genuine in their care and concern for the children. This can easily deceive the mother. A family may find themselves financially dependent on the perpetrator.
- The public is not provided with sufficient information, which would alert them to the possibility of sexual abuse.
- The 'warning signs' (if they exist) are often non-specific signs of sexual abuse e.g. stomach aches, nightmares, fears and phobias, may put the thought in the back of their mind, but it is hard to see an overall picture. Also, the cause for these things could be any number of reasons.
- The perpetrator may have a reasonable explanation for some of the child's behaviour and this may stop the mother looking for other reasons or cause them to lose faith in their own judgements of the situation.
- The perpetrator may rationalise the child's behaviour so the mother loses faith in her own judgement.
- The mother may be a lone parent and there may be other children in the family. Lots of time and energy will therefore be taken up looking after lots of needs.
- The mother may have their own difficulties e.g. recent bereavement, financial problems etc. A change in a child's behaviour could be explained as due to these reasons.
- The mother may be blamed by the perpetrator for not satisfying him or being sick etc. This may make them feel like they have no power to change anything and the situation is their fault. The mother may lack self-esteem.
- The abuse will be well planned and hidden, highlighting that the perpetrator is aware that what they have done is wrong. It will be very difficult for the mother to detect. The perpetrator will go to great lengths to ensure that the child does not tell. Please refer to the later section on the modus operandi of the perpetrator and Calder (1999).
- The perpetrator may be violent and oppressive and it may be too frightening to speak about.
- Even if abuse is suspected, it may be hard to approach any professional about this for fear of what might happen.
- The perpetrator may control the mail and phone so it is impossible for the mother to communicate with others.
- In society, as a carer, mothers are not well listened to and the job is not always seen as worthwhile.
- There is limited support for carers who want to take their children away from abuse (Rose and Savage, 1995).

Peake and Fletcher (1997) provided some stimulating debate around this subject, geared at helping mothers explore some ideas around the issue. They organise their section (pp16–20) around three ideas: the sexual abuse of a child is always the responsibility of the perpetrator; it is never the fault of the child victims; and mothers rarely know at the time that their child is being sexually abused by someone they know and trust. In relation to this final point, these authors highlight four reasons that underpin this for most mothers:

- Children cannot tell about the sexual abuse: they are either too young and/or do not have the language to tell what is happening to them. They may also have been threatened, bribed or tricked by the perpetrator and may see no reason to tell their mother.

- Society has been slow to recognise that sexual abuse of children does occur and that the principal perpetrators are those close to them, not strangers. Society and not just mothers have defences that maintain that sexual abuse couldn't happen.

- There is no public education about child sexual abuse and its warning signs and thus mothers have no basis on which they could have known.

- Perpetrators are clever. They often groom the mother as well as the child, and the mother finds it difficult to accept that the person they know, need and trust so much has abused their child.

Research findings

Whilst it has often been argued that mothers always know when a child is being sexually abused within the family, research more recently has been challenging this. For example, Jane Gilgun (1984) found that sexual abuse of one family member can take place for several years and no-one but the perpetrator and the victim know about it.

Hooper (1989) found that all the sexual abuse in her sample was committed when the mother was not in the home. She suggested that it may be more productive, therefore, to explore the process of discovery (over time)

rather than categorising women into those who did, and those who did not, know. There are many different levels of knowledge between total ignorance with no suspicions, through to full knowledge and understanding of the events. The level of knowledge depends on the available sources of information and on the coping strategies mothers adopted in response to the trauma discovery involves for them. Sources of information within the family include signs of distress in the child, observations of the perpetrators or child's behaviour, the child telling directly or more often giving indirect and conflicting messages, and the perpetrator confessing. Sources of information from outside the family might include the media, or the experiences of family or friends. For the mothers, the discovery process was rarely straightforward and often chaotic, involving for some suspicions, confrontation and denial, conflict over the meaning of behaviour, self-doubt, and sometimes uncertainty about who the perpetrator was. Women may alternate between resisting the recognition of abuse for fear of the consequences and trying to gather proof and assess the evidence. This process may continue over months or years.

Disclosure can either be a specific, single event or a cumulative process over time. For example, Hooper (1992) argued that discovery of the abuse is:

> *an active and interactive process which develops over time and has no clear beginning or end.*
>
> (p54)

It may involve the mother and child only, or more commonly a range of others, both within and outside the family. It may involve a period of not knowing about the abuse, followed by a period of suspecting, followed by a period of knowing, or one or both of the first two stages may be omitted if the mother finds out fairly quickly after the abuse starts. The process is interwoven both with the woman's own response to loss and with decisions taken about family relationships and is not therefore a straightforward linear one. In some circumstances, suspicions can only be entertained where the mother has harnessed sufficient resources to address the possibility, particularly around her self-worth. The ability to confirm suspicions is dependent not only on the mother's motivation, but also on her interaction with both the child and the perpetrator, and the child's ability to confirm or refute (age and language issues). Where the child was unable to verbally confirm their suspicions, this impacted on the mother's ability to verify their concerns.

Hooper (1992) found that many mothers spoke of not knowing, accompanied by reasons as to why they did not, as well as those who felt that something was wrong, and of suspecting abuse, but needing their suspicions confirmed (p54). There is a clear link between a mother's motivation to find out when compared with the losses accompanied with verification of sexual abuse. Some mothers did become preoccupied with the need to find out and this contributed ultimately to their failure to protect. Many mothers may now consider statements that the victim has imparted at earlier points, and with the benefit of hindsight now believes them to have been an indirect or unspecific attempt at disclosure. Some mothers may have had their suspicions, but were unclear as to who the perpetrator might be.

In her sample, Hooper found that 66 per cent of the women where the perpetrator lived in the home, did not know of the abuse for a substantial period of time (ranging from 1–5 years). Within this group, 62 per cent found out in a sudden, clearly identifiable incident, although that was often followed by a period of reassessment, recurring confusion or ambivalence.

Kelly (1988) argued that women's responses to their own experiences of sexual abuse include 'forgetting and minimising', and they may employ similar strategies when their children are sexually abused. Such responses are better understood as coping strategies rather than as collusion with the abuse itself.

Breckenbridge and Berreen (1992) reported that between 40 and 60 per cent of workers believe that mothers 'know about' the incest. Their answers revealed that 10.3 per cent of them felt that a mother would know in most cases and 60.8 per cent felt that a mother would know in some cases. This means that overall 71.1 per cent of workers would have in their minds when dealing with a disclosure of incest that mothers know; at least in some if not all cases. Whilst this does not equate with them being responsible for the abuse, it does lead to the view that they failed to act

protectively towards the child. Conversely, some 28.9 per cent of workers believed that the mother would rarely know that incest was occurring before disclosure.

Johnson (1992) noted that there is considerable disagreement about how much a mother knows of the sexual abuse while it occurs. She found that some mothers in her sample suspected abuse (i.e. had suspicions, especially if they had been victims of sexual abuse themselves), whilst others did not know (some may have been absent through work, or were unaware of the clues that might induce some concerns). She acknowledges that it is difficult for persons outside the incest family to believe that a mother does not know that her child is being sexually abused by her partner. Yet it is not a simple matter of whether the mother knew or did not know, consciously or unconsciously. Society expects mothers to be all knowing about what goes on in the family and the home. Johnson found that:

> there are complex explanations for why any mother may not recognise, see, acknowledge, interpret, understand, or know a multitude of things that happen to her children.   (p25)

Other salient points from research has included that the perpetrator admitted to 22 per cent more sexual involvement than children disclosed (thus the mother would not have known about the true extent of the abuse previously Terry, 1990); and gender differences did emerge in that there was a higher rate of disclosure among girls, although once boys had disclosed, they provided as much detail about alleged abuse as girls did (DeVoe and Faller, 1999).

Bagley and Naspini (1987) found that in a sample of 44 mothers of sexually abused children only four had any knowledge that sexual abuse had taken place before the child disclosed and those four felt powerless to stop it. Thirty-eight of the women when informed of the abuse took immediate action to protect their children.

Issues to consider

One of the key elements of a social work assessment is to establish whether the mother knew or not about the abuse. This is unlikely to be a simple question, as there are multiple possible combinations of awareness, and it cannot be concluded that because a child thinks the mother knows she does or because a child thinks the mother does not know that she does. Hooper (1992) argued that 'the question of knowing itself is over-simplistic since it is possible to know of events without understanding their meaning, to be confused over the boundaries between normal and abusive behaviour but open to help which clarifies definition' (p77).

Questions that need answering include:

How aware of the abuse was she at the time? What does she now believe happened? On reflection, was she suspicious before?

Position Regarding Responsibility for the Abuse (What am I Responsible for?)

Several writers have tried to charge mothers with indirect responsibility for the abuse. For example, by failing to provide the sexual gratification for their partners, mothers in incestuous families may indirectly foster father-daughter abuse. A considerable amount of the early written material suggested that:

> When a mother withdraws from her family, her children and husband may turn to one another for support, practical assistance or comfort and the foundations of an incestuous relationship are laid. In other cases a man deprived of his conjugal rights may turn to the nearest available source of gratification— a dependent child.
>
> (CIBA, 1984: p9)

Justice and Justice (1979) have similarly portrayed mothers of abused children as 'frigid' and not wanting sex with their husbands. If you follow this line, then you will clearly attribute responsibility to mothers without assessing the individual cases.

In many cases, the responsibility for the sexual abuse is not focused for long on the perpetrator, and is often filtered quickly down onto the mother or the child, or both. Most mothers remain wedded to their responsibilities of maintaining the family and relationships even after the form of the family had changed (Orr, 1995). She found that there were many prescriptions for women post-disclosure (courts, counselling appointments,

parenting courses) but very few for the men. The mothers also projected forward to assume the role of protectors of their grandchildren.

Mothers are **never responsible** for the sexual abuse unless they actively or consciously encouraged it. It is important, however, that workers do not absolve mothers of their responsibilities, but rather to bring their expectations and judgements into a realistic perspective.

Mothers need to be clear that the perpetrator is responsible alone for what they do. They demonstrate each day an ability to control their behaviour in their work place and with others, so it follows that they must accept responsibility when they do not. However, next to denying the childhood sexual abuse entirely, the most common thing that perpetrators do is to make excuses for their behaviour (see Calder and Skinner, Chapter Six for a fuller discussion in this area). They may blame the child, the mother, or someone else. Often, even those who do admit to their actions never actually accept responsibility for them.

As Sgroi (1982) has noted, the ability to be an effective ally for the child depends on allocating responsibility clearly to the perpetrator. Women should never be held accountable for someone else's behaviour nor should they have imposed on them unrealistic expectations about constant vigilance or ascribe to them the power to protect which they simply do not have. Yet we do have to consider what children have a right to expect within the family setting and this must include some measure of protection and nurture from their mother. The crucial issue is that women have some responsibility for protecting their children but all too often this is interpreted as sole responsibility (Todd and Ellis, 1992).

The issue of responsibility is a key one for mothers, and this needs to be addressed quickly by workers. Mothers will often feel guilty about allowing the abuse to have happened in the first place and for allowing it to continue. They need to be told that the perpetrator has abused his position of power and responsibility by sexually abusing the child. It is the perpetrator who is responsible for cognitively distorting the child's behaviour as provocative, and the mother is often not responsible for what has happened. The mother may need to work through her feelings of guilt for her to shift responsibility for the abuse from herself to the perpetrator. This is important as it challenges her positive picture of the perpetrator and forces her to reassess her view of him, often with painful consequences.

Smith (1994) notes that the mother's position regarding the responsibility for the abuse is of less importance than her belief that it happened. Indeed, if she is able to discuss who is responsible for the abuse, then there is at least an acknowledgement that it has taken place. There are situations where the blame is targeted on the child, and this is indicative of their likely removal from the family. The perpetrator often denies the abuse, and their admission is a prerequisite for the mother attributing total responsibility with the perpetrator. The mother then needs to know how the perpetrator manipulated the situation to make it appear that the child was responsible for the sexual abuse.

Many child victims feel responsible for the abuse. Indeed, the perpetrator encourages this to encourage the child's sense of entrapment that facilitates the continuation of the sexual abuse. The child's sense of responsibility can become distorted. They can feel overly responsible even for things that are clearly not their responsibility. They may feel they are guilty and need to be punished (self-harm). If it is the child and not the perpetrator who is removed from the family home, then this further complicates the issue of responsibility. Many children also locate responsibility with their mothers and so a lot of work is needed to help them shift their view on this. The mother and the child are never responsible for the perpetrator's actions.

There needs to be a differentiation between responsibility for protecting the child and responsibility for or involvement in the abuse itself. A mother has five possible responsibilities towards her daughter, and Hall and Lloyd (1989) offered a useful continuum for understanding the mother's role in the sexual abuse:

- The mother did not know about the abuse: either because of her reactions to the disclosure or from circumstances in which the abuse took place. Mothers may have known nothing about the abuse because: they were not in the home when it was taking place; she was caring for other children; the perpetrator ensured

silence; it occurred in the context of normal family situations, such as bathing or putting to bed; and each incident took a very short time and no-one else could possibly have known about it. Mothers are helped if the child states they believe that the mother did not know about the abuse.

- The mother suspected that sexual abuse was taking place but could not acknowledge it: some mothers pick up signals from their daughters that something is amiss, only to block or disregard the information. The mother may also doubt her perceptions, believing herself to be crazy for believing that such a thing could happen. Children who tried to tell their mother only to have the information ignored will conclude that her mother failed to protect her from further abuse.

- The mother knew of the abuse but did nothing to stop it: the child may have told the mother on more than one occasion, only to be responded to with disbelief, anger, or resigned acceptance. The child would conclude that the mother failed to protect her.

- The mother knew of the abuse and condoned it: the mother may even have set up the abuse by putting her in situations where she would be alone with the perpetrator, or by making her available for child prostitution or pornography. The child will blame her mother for failing to protect her, be very angry towards her, as well as struggling to understand her mother's behaviour.

- The mother sexually abused her child, in which case the child will experience intense feelings of isolation and betrayal and feel that the mother has abdicated her maternal role. Few children disclose sexual abuse by their mother and they are likely to be met with a greater potential for disbelief (Hall and Lloyd, 1989).

Laing and Kamsler (1990) approach their work with mothers and children grounded in an appreciation of the perpetrator's central role in shaping the beliefs and perceptions of the other and victim/s themselves, each other, and the issue of responsibility. Secrecy enables the perpetrator to avoid taking responsibility for the abuse, for its impact, and for the consequences for the rest of the family. A major ploy he uses to shift responsibility away from himself is to give the victim the message, either covertly or overtly, that the sexual contact is the child's fault. This shifting of responsibility from the perpetrator to the child creates a context in which the child will experience feelings of guilt and shame about the abuse, and these feelings will create a further barrier to her ability to overcome secrecy. In many instances, the perpetrator will go even further in his attempts to shift responsibility for his behaviour and seek to implicate the mother. This has the effect of the child becoming angry with the mother and even blaming her for the perpetrator's actions and her suffering. This shifting of responsibility by the perpetrator creates a situation in which the victim is encouraged to feel responsible for protecting the mother from learning the truth. The mother will be unaware of the ways in which the child has been coached by the perpetrator to keep secret what occurred. These tactics are likely to have a devastating effect on the mother-daughter relationship, creating division and mistrust.

Research findings

Orr (1995) found that although the mothers were angry with the perpetrators, they also felt that it was their responsibility to help the perpetrators change.

Sirles and Franke (1989) found that the majority of perpetrators (77.8%) denied the abuse, thus potentially displacing the responsibility from them onto the mother. This may well be reinforced through the professional intervention.

Bagley and King (1990) noted that the question of responsibility versus blame is a common theme of the literature. Kroth (1979) found that women were able to resolve their own feelings very quickly in therapy, either accepting any responsibility for their role in a failing marriage or, in other cases, realising they were in no way responsible for the husband's actions. The complexity of this dilemma is clarified by understanding that people often tend to marry spouses with

different but often complementary needs and problems. Both spouses may project concerns to distract themselves from their own pain: at the same time both need to prevent abandonment by the other partner, and settle into an uneasy equilibrium, waiting for the other to change.

In an attempt to make sense of the involvement between fathers and daughters, mothers would often attempt to apply a logical explanation for what happened—they denied any accountability themselves. They did not acknowledge responsibility as they had not verbally sanctioned the behaviour: therefore they believed somehow that it was the daughter's fault. In the mothers' perceptions, the fathers responded sexually because the children made sexual overtures (Hubbard, 1989).

Hooper (1992) found that a key factor enabling women to leave abusive partners was a clear sense of the perpetrator's responsibility for the abuse. While mothers have often been observed to blame children for abuse, self-blame is also a problem. She also identified several other issues, which influence the degree of responsibility accorded to the perpetrator. First, if the perpetrator is framed as being sick, then illness is seen as being beyond their control, although they should assume responsibility for ensuring their recovery. Second, when the perpetrator indicated they would seek such corrective (curative) help, they are accorded diminished responsibility and this can affect the woman's judgement of future options. The moral responsibility for the perpetrator's actions (e.g. 'they are old enough to know right from wrong') is lost. This differs starkly from the mother who usually emphasises the responsibility for their own response, which can only be reviewed when the perpetrator has either accepted the responsibility or it has been firmly located with him. The latter does not always mean that the nature of the abuse is fully understood.

Issues to consider

Get the mother to list all the responsibilities a parent has towards their children. For example, protection from harm, caring for the children and allowing them to mature in a safe environment. Then get them to compile a list about the perpetrator, and compare the two to establish which responsibilities he met and which ones he abdicated (Hall and Lloyd, 1989). For example, perpetrators are well aware of the emotional needs of children, but they fail as a responsible adult by using this awareness to manipulate a child into sexual activity. This may challenge an idealistic view of the perpetrator, which the mother has built up over time, and this will allow her to formulate a more realistic and probably ambivalent view of him. It is important for the worker to remind the mother of the perpetrator's responsibilities when she lapses into self-blame.

Definition of Risk Compared to Professionals, Abuser and Extended Family/Community

Mothers need some definition of sexual abuse as a starting point so they have a reference point for the allegations. For some mothers, they may not correlate an incident with being sexual abuse, and they may need some time to reconsider whether the incident was indeed abusive. The length of this process will vary enormously depending on the individual. There are a number of potential areas for confusion: the relationship between pleasure and harm if the child appeared to enjoy the sexual contact, the significance of the power relationship between adults and children in defining abuse, and the indirect relationship between harm and visible effects (Hooper, 1992: p78).

Defining risk is an important starting point in work with mothers. Wherever social workers 'intervene' with families, they start with a view about why they are there and what the best outcome could be. Achieving these outcomes can be relatively straightforward, i.e. where a child has been sexually abused by a stranger, the family believe and are sensitive to the needs of family members. The worker's view of the needs is most likely to be mirrored by the family's view and everybody is agreed about what needs to happen.

Alternatively the perception of the risk may not be immediately shared, e.g. a woman whose partner has offended outside the home, may view her own children to be perfectly safe (Rose and Savage, 2000).

There is also a group of women who do take the decision to remain with their partners, the perpetrators. Whilst they would not be defined as traditional 'safe carers', neither were they the principal risk. They are women who need to learn to 'live with risk'. Rose and Savage helped them to develop an understanding that it is possible for some women to choose to continue their relationship, in some shape or form, with partners who are schedule one offenders. However, in doing this, they can also remain carers of their children. Their belief remained that, if the 'risk' presented by the continuing relationship between the women and their partners could be managed safely for the children, then this was the best outcome for them in the longer term.

The most significant confusion lay in workers failing to define with the women what the risk was, or where the differing responsibilities lay for managing that risk. The use of the child protection and court system only served to reinforce the position of fight rather than adding clarity to the plan. The final, and additional, task for the worker is to assess whether the suggested management of the risk is safe for the children. If it isn't, where this process has been followed, it should be relatively easy to be clear about why not.

All the women accepted and agreed that putting the children's safety and well being first was the most important thing. Equally, all the women agreed on some level that continuing a relationship with this man posed some risk (even if women were saying they felt sure he wouldn't re-offend within the family now, the women acknowledged they were often kept awake at night worrying about, 'What if?'). Once the risk to all family members had been named, the women were able to acknowledge that they were willing to accept this level of risk and move to develop ways of managing this risk.

Even in situations where involvement results in being unable to agree on a risk existing, the process of exploring this can enable women to gain some insight and information into why protective action was necessary. Rose and Savage found that the process of defining the risk was resolved much more quickly than they had imagined, with many of the mothers reaching a point by the third session where they were asking for more information and clarification in order to develop ways of managing their households. The conclusion for many was that they were dependent on the honesty of their partners and the focus then became one of developing rules for safe caring within their own situations, based on the assumptions that they would be unlikely to know prior to their partner's re-offending. The enormity of trying to manage this risk was realised when the women began to think about their daily routine. For example, the simple task of bathing the children—the sounds may, for their partner, trigger distorted thinking without being involved in the bathing itself.

Research findings

Smart (1997) studied parents and professional perspectives in abuse situations. The study looked at the differences in information gathered from social work records and from interviews with families that had received protective services. Although factual matters were generally agreed, impressions and judgements were often different. In terms of continued risk to children records noted more concerns than were acknowledged by parents. In follow-up interviews, researchers heard no parental reports of further abuse whereas official records showed that 19 per cent of families had received further services and another 18 per cent had been scrutinised following concerns for the child's welfare. Thus, social workers are more likely than parents to view the child as being 'at risk' and to regard preventative action as having been taken (Cleaver and Freeman, 1995).

Issues to consider

What is her definition of sexual abuse?

Does the mother know how workers make informed estimates of perpetrator risk, so they are familiar with some of the risk situations? It is important that workers make this information available to mothers in a straightforward manner. Whilst Calder (1999) explores perpetrator risk in some detail, the following summary may be useful in discussions.

Assessing risk accurately is difficult when we know that perpetrators lack any distinct profile, and there is an absence of longitudinal studies post-offence to accurately predict recidivism. The task is compounded further if the perpetrator is selective in the provision of information, or where the information derives solely from a single source.

Risk factors place the individual at risk to re-offend. They are guidelines only and not absolute predictors. A risk factor is defined as 'any experience, event, environmental influences/parameters, internal/external behaviour, historical factor, situations, that presents or enhances the offender's chances of re-offence. These may or may not be cycle behaviours and triggering events' (Carich, 1994).

In determining the risk a sexual perpetrator presents we need to consider the types of offences committed, sexual history, treatment history, and amenability to treatment. McGrath (1992) suggests that we focus on five factors, in order to look at perpetrator risk: probability of re-offence; degree of harm most likely to result from a re-offence; conditions under which re-offence is most likely to occur; likely victim's of a re-offence; and the time-scale within which a re-offence is most likely to occur. These are dealt with below:

1. **Perpetrator risk:** cannot be exclusively defined by the nature of the problem for which the perpetrator has been referred, when we are aware of potential crossover of acts, the genders and ages of the victims, and the context of the offence, e.g. inside or outside the family. For example, Abel *et al.*, (1985) also found that 75 per cent of recidivists crossed both age and sex in their choice of victims. The incest perpetrator has the lowest recidivism rates (although they are known to offend against more than one child), whilst untreated exhibitionists have the highest recidivism rates. The younger the incest victim, the higher the risk of re-offence (Williams and Finkelhor, 1992). Perpetrators who abuse unrelated boys have higher recidivism rates than those who abused unrelated girls (McGrath, 1991); whilst the probability of recidivism rises with each offence. The degree of force is associated with an increased risk to re-offend, especially those who are sexually aroused by aggression. Deviant

sexual arousal is also associated to recidivism. Repeated sexual crimes remain an important predictor of future behaviour. The sexual abuse may well not be the only concern that needs to be resolved before rehabilitation can be effected. Stermac *et al.*, (1995) found that 55 per cent of incest perpetrators demonstrated non-sexual forms of violence and abuse within their homes. As such, issues of anger, power, and control need to be addressed. A perpetrator's specific beliefs about his own behaviour is likely to be predictive of future behaviour (Marshall and Eccles, 1991), as is their general attitude to sexual aggression (Segal and Stermac, 1990). Serin *et al.*, (1994) found that psychopaths are at higher risk of re-offending than non-psychopaths, they re-offend sooner, and they are likely to become increasingly violent.

2. **Harm from the offence:** is again correlated with the use of weapons or force, and any escalation in the patterns of offending is significant.

3. **Conditions associated with re-offending:** embraces their response to the assessment, degree of co-operation or compliance with any requests or conditions set down; the opportunity to access victims, either through family, friends or leisure interests, e.g. football coaching; the use of substances; availability of sexually stimulating material; level of mobility, e.g. through work, leisure outlets such as train-spotting; and any anger related to job loss or restricted contact with their birth children.

4. **Likely victims:** through preference in previous offences, or as admitted by the perpetrator in the work to date.

5. **When?** Many perpetrators act when they have opportunity, or they actively create them. The degree of supervision the perpetrator receives from professionals and others, such as the family, will have a bearing on this point. In broader terms, research does suggest that the risks from sexual perpetrators against children is over a significant length of time and it is a

myth that the risk reduces over time (particularly in the absence of treatment).

The Effects of 'Knowing' on the Mother: The Mother's Distress to the Disclosure

Salter (1988) maintains that for the mother the impact of the disclosure that her child has been sexually abused is like an 'emotional earthquake' (p56). Yet it is these women, even though they are in the midst of a crisis, on whom so much relies. They are the key person on whom depends their child's protection and recovery. They are crucial to the social services ability to fulfil their statutory responsibilities to protect children whilst allowing them, if at all possible, to remain in their family (Walton, 1996).

When a mother is faced with sexual abuse, she faces simultaneous and overlapping tasks: assessing the accuracy of the information, determining the meaning of incest to her and her family, deciding what to do with the new information, and locating and using resources (Elbow and Mayfield, 1991).

The area of the mother's behaviour following disclosure is important as it is often used to gauge their ability to protect/support their sexually abused child. Workers need to move beyond the outdated descriptive accounts of mothers as pathological, and being unable to meet their child's needs because of their own unmet needs (Crawford, 1999). Although some mothers respond calmly and decisively, others exhibit symptoms of crisis such as shock, confusion, and disbelief, any of which can limit their ability to take immediate protective action. Against this background, many take heroic actions to protect their children, which may well be overlooked by professionals, thus weakening the mother's support for the child. Many want to explore whether clues they have noticed are indicators of sexual abuse.

Professionals should not expect a 'new-world' to spring fully developed and put into operation within moments of a disclosure just in time for the mother to fully support and protect her child victim. Rather, they should consider how they help both the mother as well as the victim to progress through the disclosure process.

Reactions to shocking news have been found to follow a predictable pattern of denial, anger, bargaining, depression and acceptance, and any variation is one of degree rather than kind (Milner and Blyth, 1989). In relation to child sexual abuse, mothers will find that it is inextricably linked to their lives—both in terms of what might have happened to them in the past and what they might not have done; and in the future in terms of the need to do something for the children but balanced by a fear of the consequences if they get it wrong.

The emotional and behavioural impact on mothers mirrors what is experienced by the victims themselves. There is also a correlation between the level of distress in the child and that of the mothers (Massatt and Lundy, 1998). The emotions stirred up by sexual abuse have effects that can be both positive and negative. On the positive side, if the child is being abused, the mother's emotional reaction gets them started on the road to protection. On the negative side, the emotional reaction that is natural for any loving parent can cloud clear thinking and cause them to jump too quickly to conclusions (Myers, 1997). Emotions are not wrong or a sign of weakness, although they can frequently be used against mothers. They are interpreted by judges and others (mostly men) as a sign of weakness, instability, and even hysteria or mental illness.

The reactions of mothers to the sexual abuse may vary according to whether they have been sexually abused themselves. Irrespective of their own history, however, the reactions they have may well parallel those of the victims in many ways, as a consequence of living with a controlling and abusive husband. They may feel socially stigmatised, isolate themselves from extended family and friends, and even wish to leave their community of origin to avoid exposure.

Dwyer and Miller (1996) applied the concept of 'disenfranchised grief' (Doka, 1989) to our understanding of the experiences of non-abusing mothers in incest families. They pointed us to the fact that the experiences of mothers and daughters are often intimately entwined, like 'hand and glove'. They argued that the complexity of this experience provides a powerful constraint to the recognition and resolution of grief. Those directly involved may struggle with confused and conflicting feelings; the need to take action in the face of disclosure may leave little room for reflection;

and the number of people involved and the diversity of opinions held, can be traumatising in itself. Doka defined disenfranchised grief as

> …the grief that persons experience when they incur a loss that is not or cannot be openly acknowledged, publicly mourned, or socially supported. The concept… recognises that societies have sets of norms—in effect 'grieving rules'—that attempt to specify who, when, where, how, how long, and for whom people should grieve.
>
> (p4)

He argues that grief may become disenfranchised for three reasons:

- The relationship between the grieved and the griever is not recognised: Grief at the loss of a relationship between family members is recognised and accepted. It is usually accompanied by a ritual such as a funeral. However, the act of sexual abuse is expected to invalidate the relationship between the perpetrator and other family members, and any expression of grief may be unacceptable both to the family and professionals. As such, no ritual exists after incest.

- The loss itself is not recognised: As many argue the mother is better off without him. As such, the grief cannot be sanctioned by others, and the mother may be unable to recognise their own grief given their self-blame and shame.

- The griever is not recognised: This may well be the siblings or extended family members who are not seen as being directly involved in the abuse with the consequence that their own needs may be overlooked.

As a consequence of these, disenfranchising grief may complicate and exacerbate problems in coping with the loss, demonstrated through feelings of isolation, anger, self-blame, sadness, and fear. Dwyer and Miller (1996) argue that

> …these losses occur on many levels including: the loss of 'family', both nuclear and extended; loss of innocence; loss of faith in themselves and their judge-ments; material losses such as homes, jobs/schools, and financial security; loss of dreams and hopes for the future, to name but a few.
>
> (p138)

Once mothers accept that their children have been sexually abused they go through a succession of reactions similar to a complex grief reaction, and which may include denial, guilt, depression, anger and finally acceptance. This makes sense when one considers that the non-abusing mother's world has, at the very least, suffered a serious blow and may very well be dying.

Whilst the parallel experience of grieving a death may be useful, it also has its limitations. For example, sexual abuse is not, like death, a clearly defined event with an end and from which the mother then recovers and returns to normal, but one which tends to have ongoing and unpredictable ramifications for years and years (Hooper, 1989). Hopkins and Thompson (1984) developed a 'reaction to loss' continuum. For losses at the 'highly acceptable' end of the continuum, society has established routine and ritualistic patterns of response (cards, expressions of sympathy, flowers, food, calls, extra attention) which legitimise the loss and grief and provide comfort for the bereaved and the giver. This is most evident in cases of 'normal' death and serious illness. Such clearly established recognition, acceptance and reaction patterns do not yet exist for the grief resulting from other types of losses such as divorce, redundancy, or suicide, although conventional forms of response to these losses are emerging. There are no generally recognised socialised responses to losses resulting from sexual abuse, which fall at the 'non-acceptable' end of the continuum.

Responses to disclosure from the mother

Every mother will respond differently to the disclosure of sexual abuse of their daughter. There are, however, some common threads worth mentioning, which many will recognise to be similar to those of the primary victims.

Shock

Shock is a common reaction to disclosure although it does vary in its intensity. It is often compounded by stress and anxiety, inducing confused and ambivalent feelings towards both the child as well as the perpetrator. This often renders decision-making by mothers impossible in the short-term. It is important that workers do not dismiss the mother as

being an un-protecting or an unfit mother, but rather they concentrate on helping her to meet her child's needs. This has the potential to encourage more informed and positive maternal responses. If this is not facilitated, then mother's can get 'stuck' in the process and never overcome denial. Since many mothers will be in a state of shock after learning of the sexual abuse, they are therefore unlikely to be able to make decisions and assume responsibility and it is unfair if workers expect them to do so.

Denial

A mother's denial is to be seen as a normal and healthy reaction to this kind of news as it gives them time to assimilate the shock and build up the strength to deal with it. The problem comes if the mother does not move to the next stage of the reactive process. Many will move on as the reality niggles away but may slip temporarily into denial whenever they need to feel safe. For some, the denial is short-lived: within moments they accept the unpleasant reality and mobilise themselves to respond. These tend to be psychologically healthy mothers. For others, refusing to believe that the abuse could have taken place may persist for a longer time. Some are never able to acknowledge the abuse and resist all efforts to engage them in treatment. They never complete the process. Most, however, are able, with help, to support the child during the difficult process of resolving the sexual abuse situation.

Denial is likely to be expressed in a number of ways by mothers: denial that sexual abuse took place; accepting that sexual abuse took place but denying that it was harmful to the child; denial that there is a need for any external help to resolve the crisis; that the partner was drunk; that the child seduced him; or that he has been so stressed lately that he didn't know what he was doing, etc. The extent of a mother's losses may become a compelling aspect of their denial. These being stated, workers cannot dismiss the link between denial and the children's safety. They need to use empathy as the most effective strategy for engaging the mother in this state.

Anger

Mothers may then feel angry and want to blame the perpetrator, but they are often inaccessible for the expression of feeling. The perpetrator will often do anything to ensure they do not have a sexual conviction or sexual stain on their character. Mothers often end up selecting someone else to blame when faced with these issues. This may be the child, or the system. Anger is a common reaction of mothers, to the perpetrator, the child and the workers and it tends to be specific and triggered by a particular incident, person or object (Trotter, 1998). There may be anger towards the mother herself. For example, the child may be angry at the mother's failure to protect them, and they may be joined by members of the extended family as well as the professionals. A mother's anger is often associated with seeking a reason for why the abuse occurred. It can also manifest itself in depression, stress responses, etc. The person who the mother believes has caused the abuse will become the focus of her anger. This could be herself, the perpetrator or the child. Anger is legitimate, but it is how it is dealt with and expressed that is important. If it is expressed as revenge and she takes the law into her own hands, or uses her children as a tool against her partner, then it is inappropriate and may even place the children at greater risk.

When mothers respond to the disclosure with either *denial or anger*, this is simply their way of protecting themselves and is to be expected. They may feel betrayed by their partner as he has been living a lie by keeping the relationship with the daughter quiet or they may feel angry and jealous of the daughter if they perceive her as a threat or rival. She will be confused because she wants to help the child on the one hand, but also maintain the relationship with the perpetrator. Their feelings will not be changed or reversed overnight, and this often means that they will be faced with two sets of conflicting feelings. The mother may also be repulsed by the perpetrator and even hate him for the consequences of his behaviour. She may even feel she has failed as a wife. These are very powerful feelings that will often take some considerable time to resolve.

Guilt

When anger expires, mothers may well enter the bargaining stage—'maybe if...' Here, the range may be to do nothing as to do something might make it worse, to a fairly sophisticated rationalisation about limiting damage. Guilt is an inevitable maternal response to the discovery of child sexual abuse, and may feature heavily in her initial responses and decision-making. For example, she may act to protect the child without reference to the personal implications, such as dealing with her own emotions, or with more practical consequences such as where to live and how to support herself financially. Many mothers try to conceal their own fears or confusion from others as well as from themselves, and this can have knock-on effects post-disclosure, e.g. being unable to confront any subsequent issues of pain. A mother's guilt will often be intensified if the abuse continued over a long period of time and she did not know about it. Once the mother learns of the child sexual abuse, this will lead to guilt either if they had their suspicions, or they did not know. They will relive any previous episodes of disbelief to the child. They will experience a continuing sense of loss, isolation and rejection as emotional accompaniments to the discovery. This will be aggravated if they have been isolated in the process of disclosure. They will often be faced with multiple, conflicting and changing versions of events and they may struggle to construct a single explanation. They will consider what they can remember of past events, with what they think they know about the perpetrator, to help them.

Guilt is a form of anger directed at oneself. This is most apparent when mothers believe that they should have known. The mother's feelings of guilt may be influenced by the child's age, the duration of the sexual abuse, and symptoms in the child which preceded the disclosure or discovery of the abuse. Mothers and daughters need to realise that every time they blame each other for the abuse, they absolve the perpetrator of their responsibility. Mothers with a history of sexual abuse themselves will have acute feelings of guilt thinking they should have recognised it happening.

Many parents of sexually abused children are racked with guilt. When a mother finds out that their child has been sexually abused, a thousand questions race through their mind, including: What is child sexual abuse? How common is it? How can I tell whether my child was abused? What will happen to them if they were abused? Who can I turn to for help? Will my child ever be normal again? What are the short-and long-term effects of child sexual abuse? Will my child grow up to be an abuser? Will my child blame me for the abuse? What could I have done differently? Why did I not see the signs that something was wrong? How could I let this happen to a child that I love so much? Why does my child still want to see the man who sexually abused her? Professionals need to facilitate the answering of these, and probably many other questions, if they are to equip the mother to help the child. They need to remind them that they did not commit the abuse, but rather are the one trying to protect them. Sexual abuse often occurs in secret and there are no witnesses. Mothers need to be cautioned against judging things retrospectively as hindsight is always a more exact science. They need to be reminded that they did nothing wrong. When they learned about the abuse, they took action. That is all that they can ask of themselves (Myers, 1997).

Depression

Many mothers then become overwhelmed, feeling helpless, inadequate and depressed, and this can lead to apathy and despair, and may lead to the mother's effectiveness as a mother being compromised, and becoming less able to respond to the distress of the child.

Acceptance

The next stage might be an acceptance that the reality of sexual abuse is awful (and not passive resignation) and that it is difficult to tackle single-handedly.

Other reactions

Sexual offences are something that families are *ashamed* of so the mother may choose to lead a double life to conceal the facts from others. This is increasingly true in a culture that is adopting punitive attitudes towards the

problem. The ensuing hysteria is something the mother and the remainder of her family has to deal with, often alone. Many experience overwhelming feelings of stigma and shame due to the nature of the offence, and mothers become dishonest to conceal the offence.

It is important not to interpret a mother's initial *hesitation* as not wanting to protect her child. Once she has made the decision to protect her child, she may be faced with having to provide for the child alone. It is also important to assess the mother on the basis that they can only do their best with what they know at the time. We should work with them to emerge after the professional intervention stronger and wiser.

The fact that the perpetrator may still be at large in the local community often instils *fear* into the mothers. Fear of their environment follows the discovery that nowhere is safe. The closer the mother's relationship with her child and partner, the greater the fear. This is important for professionals to understand so they do not slip into labelling the mother as unco-operative. They need to understand her fear of what has happened and what may happen next. This leads professionals to provide a context where the mother can assume a greater understanding and control over her life. Clear explanations are needed of each option and stage of the process to facilitate working through her fears, recognising that it will take some time.

Grief and loss

Mothers may want to protect their child from loss of their father and this may be their motivating drive in keeping contact between father and daughter alive. This does not mean they are not anxious about this continuing relationship. Mothers do need to list all the losses they have experienced post-disclosure and this forms the basis for them understanding the complexities of grief and will help them map a strategy for resolution.

Powerlessness

May come from a sense that events now control her life. She may feel that the situation will not go away and that things may not get better. There are a range of possible manifestations of this, perhaps rage in an attempt to gain control or apathy and withdrawal. Workers may want the mother to articulate those areas of her life where she does and does not have power to provide a framework within which her powerlessness can be explored. A schedule for successes can be set and reviewed quickly so positive strokes are provided. Workers need to be conscious of this dynamic when they are intervening. Partnership is the key rather than being 'told' what they must do (Ovaris, 1991).

Mothers described a range of *feelings* to match the devastation of disclosure, including sleep disturbances, psychological difficulties, difficulty in expressing their feelings, shame and embarrassment, letting their children down, an inability to trust, poor self-esteem, limited social skills, depression, inadequacy, frustration and ongoing distress (Trotter, 1998).

Research findings

The mothers own behaviours at the time of disclosure may be related to the emotional stress brought on by the disclosure itself. Some mothers may experience shock and denial (Myers, 1985), and the symptoms may resemble those of post-traumatic stress (Timmons-Mitchell *et al.*, 1996). Deblinger *et al.*, (1994) found that those mothers who had been sexually abused as children may experience more severe symptoms at disclosure. Those who are overwhelmed by confusion and turmoil often find they persist over time (Hubbard, 1989), and it is important that professionals intervene quickly to help the mothers achieve a way of adapting and managing the abuse.

Burgess *et al.*, (1977) reported that the reactions will vary according to the site of the abuse. For example, where the abuse takes place on 'home territory' that is considered to be 'safe ground', then the adults will have a stronger reaction, such as outrage, when that space is invaded. The authors identified several situations in which the mother was absent from the home: medical needs, recreation, errands, work, etc., showing that it is increasingly difficult to trust adults to care for, and protect, their children.

Those mothers who appear to be psychologically healthier at the beginning have more inner resources to draw on, and can accept and be offered more appropriate support, will be better able to gain access to and express the full range of emotions necessary for the resolution of the crisis. Research does show that at disclosure, those mothers who have been sexually abused themselves displayed more distress than those who had not been sexually abused (Deblinger *et al.*, 1994).

Manion *et al.*, (1996) also found that the severity of distress was related to their own perceptions of themselves as parents, rather than to any variables about the abuse. The fact that many blame the mother rather than the perpetrator for the sexual abuse only compounds and complicates their reactions further.

Miller and Dwyer (1997) argued that there has been little recognition of the impact on mothers, and they would prefer them to be seen as *secondary victims*. More than the issues of grief and loss are the maternal suicide attempts as well as the ongoing psychological distress.

Fong and Walsh-Bowers (1998) found that all mothers reported feelings of helplessness and depression while they were dealing with the abuse. On the one hand, they were angry at their husbands for betraying them and hurting their daughters, but on the other hand they felt guilty for not knowing what happened and being unable to help their daughters to stop the abuse.

De Jong (1988) found that supportive mothers were more likely than non-supportive mothers to express anxiety about the effects that the experience would have on their children. Feelings of guilt, fear of repeat victimisation, and beliefs that friends or family members would not support them were more common in supportive mothers who noted emotional changes in themselves. Non-supportive mothers were often frustrated that the professionals were doing too much, whereas supportive mothers complained that they were doing too little.

De Francis (1969) suggested that the initial parental reaction to child sexual abuse may be either child, self, or perpetrator-oriented. Peters (1973) reported that the self-oriented reaction of the parent may be more common in household abuse; however, mixed feelings toward the perpetrator or external pressures not to file charges against a family member or friend may produce a perpetrator-oriented response.

Cohen and Mannarino (1996) found a strong correlation between parental emotional distress related to the abuse and treatment outcome in sexually abused pre-school children. It is possible that the strong relationship between parental emotional distress and child outcome measures were in part due to modelling, in that the child may learn fewer adaptive coping behaviours from a parent who is having difficulty coping with his or her own emotional distress. It is very likely that such a parent would be less emotionally and/or physically available to the child to provide needed emotional support. It is also possible that a biological factor may play a role in coping style or capacity, such that the capacity to recover from emotional distress is in part genetically transmitted. This reiterates the importance of addressing parental distress related to the abuse in providing effective treatment to sexually abused pre-school children.

Salt *et al.*, (1990) found that the actions a mother took in response to the abuse were strongly linked with their emotions. Those mothers who were more concerned about the child were also more likely to take protective action. Similarly, mothers who were angry were more likely to punish the child, possibly as they blamed the child for threatening her relationship with the perpetrator. They found that the mother's attitudes and actions were shaped by their relationships with perpetrators. Mothers were least protective and most angry and punitive toward the child when the perpetrator was not the natural father, but a stepfather or boyfriend. This may be because they find it difficult to believe that a father would hurt his own child.

Issues to consider

Workers need to acknowledge the extreme stress facing mothers at the point of disclosure and should not confuse her stress responses with how she behaved in the family whilst the incest was occurring. Mothers frequently apportion blame to themselves for the abuse, e.g. 'if only I had…', but this does not take account of the secrecy surrounding sexual abuse and the sophisticated modus operandi of the perpetrators. Mothers need to think through the consequences of self-blame when they need to be looking to move forward.

The mother will often face a flood of recurring memories for some considerable time after the abuse has come to light, as they are haunted by the story, and in particular how they may have prevented it. This is most noticeable where incest has occurred. These memories will strike at all times of day and in all places, such as shopping or driving, and strategies need to be constructed to deal with these when they arise. For example, having a 24-hour contact agreement with a close friend.

Many mothers will consider the fact they should have known retrospectively, as do many professionals. This can affect their ability to recover and move on. It is not always true that time heals.

The mother is faced with a need to review the sequence of events to make sense of them. This process of review will include past knowledge of the child's behaviour problems, of the perpetrator's propensity to violence, the child's age and access to other sources of knowledge about sex, awareness of the reasons children find telling about sexual abuse difficult, and information from friends and public sources about sexual abuse in general. The mother may often make premature judgements in an attempt to protect their child, overlooking the need to attend to her grieving and the need for external support.

Questions that need answering include:

Can the mother work through her feelings of guilt/anger/shock/shame/denial? How quickly? How safe is the child while she does so? Does she understand that hers is a stress response?

There is no single formula for getting through the emotional tangle although identifying an intelligent sounding board is recommended. The resolution of these reactions does not always pave the way to protective action, although support or pressure from outside authorities sometimes makes it easier for a mother to initiate and follow through with protective action. It can also make a mother's choices easier (Johnson, 1992).

Consequences of Disclosure

The last section highlighted the multiple processes that mothers will experience and those that they need to help the victims manage also. It is essential that every worker have some understanding about the imbalance between the negative and the positive consequences of accepting, and working with the allegations, for the perpetrator and his family. Figure 26 sets out the feared negative consequences of disclosure for all family members.

Figure 26: The feared negative consequences of disclosure for all family members.

	Perpetrator	Mother	Child
1. Legal	• Imprisonment	• Care order on child and other siblings	• Care order
2. Family being	• Marital separation • Loss of children/ restriction of contact • Loss of support by other relatives	• Loss of partner • Loss of children • Loss of co-parent • Loss of support by other relatives	• Loss of father • Loss of mother • Loss of siblings • Fear of not being believed • Fear of retribution • Fear of violence and punishment • Fear of violence within the family • Fear of perpetrator's and others' well (e.g. perpetrator's threat of suicide)
3. Psychological	• Suicide • Guilt over effects • Let down of partner • Self-respect • Self-esteem and identity • Own history of sexual abuse • Fear of loneliness and isolation • Inability to cope • Inability to face addiction and tension relief through abuse	• Self-respect • Let down of child • Self-blame • Having married a perpetrator • Own history of sexual abuse • Fear of loneliness and isolation • Need to care without partner • Desperation, fear, anger and loneliness	• Fear of being blamed • Fear of being scapegoated • Self-blame • Fear of loneliness and isolation • Loyalty • Desperation, fear, anger and loneliness
4. Social	• Reprisal • Reputation • Stigma	• Reputation • Stigma • Isolation	• Reaction of peers • Treatment at school • Loss of friends

	• Isolation • Overcoming shame	• Problems of being a single parent	• Behavioural changes, e.g. becoming beyond control • Assumption of parenting role
5. Financial and Professional	• Loss of job • Loss of earnings • Loss of professional licence • Loss of reputation	• Financial hardship and stress • Effects on own work and professional career • Legal expenses	• Doing part-time jobs to help (e.g. paper rounds)

(adapted from Furniss, 1990, p245; and Wright, 1991)

For the mother

Mothers who are faced with a disclosure of sexual abuse have a great number of potential consequences: they have the impact of the sexual abuse itself to deal with; the choice between their partner or their children; the possible resurfacing of their own abuse; and the financial and associated consequences. They may feel they are to blame for the abuse. They also have to face the influx of professionals who will be watching her closely and making seemingly impersonal decisions. They will decide the disposition of the case and making decisions based on her ability to make 'good' decisions and whether or not she colluded with the perpetrator. They will be recommending a series of assessments for the child victim, other children in the family, and possibly herself. She will also be learning of the duration of protracted treatment (possibly years). She may face the prospect of the perpetrator being interviewed, possibly arrested and prosecuted, and that her child may have to testify in court. Should a custodial sentence be the outcome for the perpetrator, then the mother may be facing a significant loss of finances. This may result in her need to try and supplement her income, often via her extended family, or re-enter the workplace. This requires potential retraining and then she is faced with the difficult idea of safe child care to facilitate this. This trust will clearly be at an all time low given the recent events.

The available information suggests that mothers continue to suffer from the consequences of the abuse for years after the disclosure. For many these remain invisible given the professional management of the situation. For example, those mothers who act 'appropriately' in protecting their children do not receive much follow-up, even though they may have lost practically (their partners, homes, income, support networks) and emotionally (their faith in people, their dreams for the future, and the loss of faith and trust in the world). In short, they put their lives on hold until the child is grown up (Dwyer and Miller, 1996). If a mother chooses her partner, then she faces a potential backlash from the professionals and she could lose her child and potentially her grandchildren. The perpetrator becomes her sole support, and this renders her isolated and lonely. While many may see the decision between child and partner as 'either/ or', the mother may wish to support both. This option is rarely understood by the child or the professionals, who may push her to make a choice.

It is thus very important that we get the perpetrator, their families, as well as professionals, to look at any positive consequences of disclosure. These might include:

For the perpetrator

- An understanding of how their behaviour has developed as this is the start of repairing the damage and working at controlling any future repetition of their behaviour.

- It allows the workers to identify and work on the most dangerous areas.

- It shows the perpetrator they are able to accept responsibility for their behaviour and the need for change.

For their partner

- It allows them to make a more informed decision on the risk their partner poses and whether they are to continue with, or end the relationship.
- It can encourage the perpetrator to complete the necessary work.

For the child/ren

- It allows them to have a safe home environment.
- It allows them to have their views regarding contact heard.
- It allows them to have safe contact with their father.

It is important that the workers encourage the families they are engaged with to identify all the positive consequences of working on the sexual abuse, as otherwise they will be overwhelmed by the negative consequences (Calder and Skinner, 1999).

Research findings

Mothers often face loss at a number of levels: loss of self, loss of roles (as mother and wife), and loss of ideas about the future (for themselves and their family). The evidence suggests that anywhere between 40 per cent and 73 per cent of sexually abused children are removed from their homes post-disclosure (Hunter *et al.*, 1990; Jaudes and Morris, 1990). The mother also has to manage the reality that many children thus blame themselves for the outcome, seeing removal as a form of punishment.

Homelessness is also a potential outcome for some families faced with an abrupt drop in income (see Shinn *et al.*, 1991). Pellegrin and Wagner (1990) in their sample found that 58 per cent of mothers were working and 42 per cent were unemployed at the point of disclosure. They did not find that the unemployed mothers were more available to their daughters and being unemployed was associated with a greater probability of victim removal. They suggested that this may be due to their financial dependence on the spouse. Those of us who have never lived alone or been a single parent need to consider what an overwhelming prospect that is for the mother to contemplate. As such, it may seem easier to live with a 'child who lies' than to confront the issue of a partner who sexually abuses against children; or to accept that minimisation and rationalisations from the perpetrator and believe that it will not happen again; or hope that now it is out in the open it will cease (Smith, 1995b). Most women do not have viable economic choices after the child has disclosed the sexual abuse, with many quitting their jobs to protect their children's needs from the abuse or because they feared that their children would be abused again (Carter, 1993).

Mothers may face deteriorating mental health (McIntyre, 1981). A study by Goodwin (1981) suggests that following a child's disclosure, mothers are at increased risk of attempting suicide, whilst Bagley and King (1990) uncovered a range of mental health difficulties, including depression, anxiety attacks and engaging in acts of self-harm. They may also feel that they have failed in their duties as a wife, mother and a woman. De Jong (1988) found that some mothers required hospitalisation for somatic disorders.

Bagley and Naspini (1987) found that mothers of sexually abused children may also experience suicidal tendencies when their daughter reveals the abuse. Briere and Runtz (1986) studied 195 women seeking help from a community health centre and found that former child sexual abuse victims were more than twice as likely to have attempted suicide than non-abused clients. Factors of impaired self-esteem and self-blame; powerlessness including vulnerability to depression; interpersonal dysfunction, and attempts to escape the abuse seemed to be important antecedents of self-destructive behaviour (Bagley and King, 1990). These issues are explored in more details in the social history section.

Mothers are frequently required to review their perceptions of significant others, including the child, the perpetrator and extended family members. This can be difficult and anxiety provoking, reflecting the reality that we tend to feel threatened and vulnerable when our beliefs are challenged (Engel, 1994).

Issues to consider

Johnson (1992) found that:

> *...the coins of consequences for the mothers sometimes has two sides: punishment and betrayal on one side; relief, vindication, a way out, and new opportunities on the other. Crisis can be an opportunity for new growth and opportunities, and for some of the mothers this was true in terms of them individually. But when talking about their families, the consequences of the incest violated their illusions of family life.*
>
> (p98)

The Mother's Needs Post-disclosure

> *The field is beginning to realise that the needs of the non-abusing mother are as important as the needs of the children.*
>
> (Massatt and Lundy, 1998)

Byerly (1992) set out the following list of needs experienced by mothers following disclosure:

- Someone to talk to: to express trust and belief in them, often for weeks or months afterwards.
- Someone to counsel them about their own abuse: as the child's disclosure may have resurrected memories of their own abuse.
- To know what happened: as this is essential as well as painful: they need to know the nature, the frequency, extent, the time and place, the child's feelings, etc.
- To know they weren't the first mother this had happened to: so they are not alone, and can possibly meet and learn from shared feelings.
- To have a break from him: they need space away from the perpetrator in order to gain a perspective, consider their feelings about the relationship, etc.
- To be treated as a person: to have their feelings listened to seriously, to feel respected, to be acknowledged when they are present, etc.
- To regain control of their lives and minds: particularly in incest cases where they need to resume control over the day-to-day events and their personal thoughts.

- To obtain basic information on survival: to embrace new aspects of their life, such as courts, police, treatment, etc.
- To understand how domestic violence and sexual abuse were related: and to understand they are separate issues that need to be addressed.
- To make basic life decisions: to move away, separate or divorce their husband, tell people, etc.
- To know options regarding contact and custody: both in relation to their partner, but also if the child has been removed from home by the local authority.
- To know how their child/ren will react: as everyone will be affected to some degree by the trauma.
- To ensure this will not happen again: taking steps to safeguard the child from continued sexual abuse is important, such as no contact or supervised contact.

The needs of non-abusing parents can be neglected as professional responses focus on the children who have been abused, their siblings, and on the perpetrators of the abuse. In this sense, the professional response system is insensitive to the needs of women. However, both for the women's emotional survival and growth and so that they can provide appropriate parenting for their children, thereby reducing the need for their children to be removed from their care, or remain there long-term, these women need the therapeutic opportunity to deal with their feelings about what has happened and to adjust to the major change that has taken place in their lives.

Initial intervention with the mother following disclosure needs to include a functional assessment of her need both for psychological support, and for concrete services such as interim safety, financial needs, and support in living independently (Byerly, 1985). The needs of the mother are often the same as the child: impaired self-image can be repaired through teaching women to recognise and respond to their own nurturing needs. Denial can be confronted as they learn to ventilate conflicting motivations and loyalties. Focus on universal dimensions can help shape reasonable expectations of their husbands and children. Practice in limit setting is required to overcome failures in establishing and enforcing limits. Anger needs to be recognised and validated, with appropriate outlets found (Bagley and King, 1990).

Walton (1996) found that help was not forthcoming from the child protection services for most of the mothers following the disclosure. The professionals concentrated on the needs for protection of the child, not the needs of the mother. Once workers impose a judgement on a non-abusing mother, they make decisions about what she needs and what she will do. In doing so, attempts may be made to make her fit the professional understanding and abilities. It might be more productive to approach her with the understanding that they know only some of what she has experienced, and this may then lead to the gathering of information required to make more informed decisions. Workers often have a temptation to 'know' why it happened which can override the objective of gathering information and understanding the uniqueness, needs and circumstances of the individuals involved (Ovaris, 1991).

Women in our society are expected to meet the needs of men and of children before their own needs. Orr (1995) pointed out that women develop differently to men and have a greater emphasis on continuity and connection with others rather than separation and autonomy. Indeed, women's sense of self becomes organised around being able to make and then maintain affiliation and relationships. Thus, when a mother's self-worth comes from keeping the family together, the impact and consequences of sexual abuse can shatter her and make the meeting of her needs very difficult to achieve. Many experience disorganisation in their lives, both internal and external, and struggle to keep things together. The disintegration of the family and loss of roles and relationships within the family can be disorientating. What is interesting is that at the point of disclosure, is that women are asked to make choices that will inevitable result in the dissolution of their family, and which thus opposes her socialisation. Many need to work through their feelings of being lost or confused to find out who they are and to get to know themselves better. Many mothers are ostensibly attempting to identify and then meet their own needs for the first time.

Following disclosure, many of the mothers become single parents. This often means that they are unable to cope with their children's needs given that so many of their own needs remained unmet. It is logical that in order to help the children, some attention must be paid to the mother's needs. More importantly, professionals need to ensure that they offer services that will fulfil the needs of the mothers as they saw them, rather than as the professionals saw them.

Research findings

Mitchell (1985) identified that some mothers have suffered multiple forms of physical and emotional abuse from their male partners. They may require help themselves before they can move on to assist their children. For example, children do not need to be victims: they need help so they can move to becoming survivors. Mothers are an integral part of the creation of an environment where their experiences are acknowledged without stigma, suspicion, shame, guilt and fear. Unfortunately, this is often not a feature of professional intervention. Many writers have articulated the feelings of mothers in such situations, who found themselves discounted and misunderstood. For example, Rivera (1988) found that mothers were often left to deal with the abuse alone. They also found that the court system was inadequate in securing justice and protection for victims, especially when the victims were under eight years of age. As such, no criminal charges were levelled, no prosecution undertaken, no conviction secured, and no admission of culpability made. Johnson (1992) argued that mothers were immobilised by the poor professional response, needing time alone to sort things out before they could take action. Whether the mothers sought help or not depended largely upon their feelings about the abuse, their sense of obligation, the social pressure they encountered, and the kind of resources available to them.

Salt *et al.*, (1990) found that 50 per cent of the mothers in their sample were as preoccupied with the effects on themselves as with those on the child. De Jong (1988) found that although some of the mothers reported on appeared disturbed by their child's behaviour changes, many appeared more concerned about how they themselves were going to be able to cope with their own feelings and the responses of family, friends, and the agencies involved.

While the importance of family support for the sexually abused child is clear, there is some suggestion that children may benefit if their mothers are also receiving support. For example, Leifer *et al.*, (1993) found a significant positive relationship between inadequate social support of the mother and the lack of maternal support to the child, as well as the increased likelihood of foster care placement for the child. Newberger *et al.*, (1993) have explored the emotional functioning of mothers post-disclosure, and noted that they also should be identified as victims and provided with treatment. It is conceivable that the level of support the mother can provide is associated with their own emotional well being. Lipton (1997) explored the emotional distress of the primary caretakers of sexually abused children, as well as the relationship between maternal distress and the emotional well being of her child. When comparing biological parents with foster or adoptive parents, she found that the biological caretakers were significantly more distressed; and that there was a significant positive relationship between the distress of the child and the distress of the caretaker. It may be that the marked differences in marital and economic status between the two groups could explain the variation in distress levels. By supporting the mothers, professionals might well create a mediating factor to the combined distress of the mother and the child.

It is well reported that mothers have extensive needs for support in the aftermath of abuse. Humphreys (1995) explored the needs, and unmet needs, of mothers in the aftermath of child sexual abuse disclosure. She argued that the experience of the sexually abused child is highly dependent upon the support extended to the child's mother in the aftermath of abuse. Mothers identified the need for individual support and counselling to help them deal with their own crisis, particularly when their normal avenues of support were unavailable. This is acute in mothers from non-English speaking backgrounds. Disclosure of sexual abuse was experienced as undermining central beliefs about themselves, particularly in their role as parent. They were acutely aware that their ability to manage the crisis affected their children. Others found support through a self-help group where they met with mothers in similar situations. They spoke of a lack of support from their partners which manifested in different ways, particularly the different reactions to the disclosure. For example, men were far more likely to react by retribution against the perpetrator, and this became the source of conflict between the couples; as was their sexual relationship, which was affected. This was exacerbated when the mothers wanted to talk through their feelings, and was magnified when the mother was blamed for the abuse by her husband. Overall, mothers needed ongoing support for themselves as individuals, couples and parents.

Issues to consider

The mother has a crucial role to play in helping her abused child, and it is to them that the child will often turn for support, reassurance and future protection. Workers thus need to provide mothers with the support, understanding and assistance that will help them to respond appropriately to their children. Furniss (1991) has noted that mothers are much more likely to become an ally for the child and the professionals if their own process of discovery is understood and facilitated.

Mothers need their own source of support and it is important to find a trusted adult, who will not judge them, with whom they can talk things through. They need to be able to discuss honestly past and future risks and strategies for managing them. This requires that mothers become selective as they do not want the conversation disseminating in the local community. The problem will not simply disappear and if the mother tries to keep the problem contained within the family alone, then they remain vulnerable to the perpetrator's tactics of persuasion, and ultimately convincing themselves that the abuse did not happen, or that it has indeed stopped. However, mothers do need to remember that support from the extended family has the advantage that they have some knowledge of everyone involved, coupled with a slight distance from the situation, that does make it easier for them to be helpful (Smith, 1995b). Respite by looking after the children occasionally is also helpful.

Too often the professional response reinforces the reality that the needs of men and children come first and that mothers have no needs but to meet the needs of others.

Professionals need to slow the process down and lessen the trauma for women, giving them space to think. They need to create an environment where the mother can mobilise her own resources for recovery whilst shielding them from either a lack of support or conditional or cutting support. Mothers need some distance from the criticism and judgements of others whilst feeling they can regain a sense of control over their lives.

Smith (1994) pointed out that there is a need for mothers and workers to explore the available options in order to agree priorities for change.

Perceived Options or a 'No-win' Situation?

A considerable amount of the literature points to the reality that no matter how hard mothers try or what they do, they are in a 'no-win' situation, and are still blamed for their actions and choices.

When a mother discovers or is told that her partner has sexually abused her child, she is faced with conflicting images of herself, her child, and the perpetrator. She will need to decide whom to believe, whom to continue a relationship with, and whom to maintain a loyalty to. It also leaves her having to sort though various options that may conflict with her view of marriage, parenting, and sense of competence as a wife and a mother. Unfortunately, professionals frequently want her to make life-changing decisions immediately upon discovery of the abuse. She must either separate from the perpetrator or lose her child: a difficult decision under the best of circumstances, but an overwhelming one for someone in the throes of a situation that forces her to view her life in new ways (Elbow and Mayfield, 1991). Where social services alienate the mother in the investigation of the case, then they are increasing her vulnerability to pressure from the perpetrator. If the abuse is within the family, the mother is often left to make the choice about who to believe and stand by, and

by implication, is taking sides against others. It is impossible to find some middle ground. Separating from the perpetrator requires resources that are often not immediately available. This concern about her material well being may be re-interpreted as denial, greater loyalty to the perpetrator, or dependence upon him. This is unfair when incest is over-represented in low-income families (Julian and Mohr, 1979).

Beneath what may be a mother's disbelief or denial is the reality of what they will have to do, and this means making hard choices. Mothers may well be less able to initiate and follow through with protective action if they have to confront their partners alone. Likewise, they may find it more difficult to move from disbelief and denial toward belief and acceptance and subsequent action without support and assistance of professional outsiders.

The mother may be very fearful that fully supporting the child will lead her to lose both her future security and her relationship with the perpetrator. This creates a dilemma of loyalty about whom to support and the mother may feel overwhelmed by confusion about what action, if any, to take. Burgess *et al.*, (1978) looked at the social pressures and the psychological stress involved in making a decision about where to place one's loyalty post-sexual abuse. This is especially true in cases of sexual abuse within the family. The question that the family must face is, should we be loyal to our child and react to the perpetrator as we would react to any perpetrator basing this decision on our duty as community members to bring such a person to the attention of the law? The alternative to this choice is to make an exception for the family perpetrator and be loyal to the family ties rather than bring him to an outside group's attention. The family must choose one of the two courses of action.

There is a large personal cost for the women in making a decision that conflicts with a traditional notion of a 'good mother'. This decision places these women in conflict with the child protection system. The consequence of this conflict is that women are perceived as unco-operative and unable to protect their child.

Post-disclosure, mothers are required to reassess their marriage, although many expect this to only conclude with her decision to reject the man and support her child. This pressure from professionals comes from their benefit of experience and hindsight (of practice and research, which highlights how the perpetrator targets and grooms the situation), and they only view the male as a sexual perpetrator. The mother often sees things very differently. They may see the man as her partner and as a father. They are thus asked to consider the information against their history of being with them and these often conflict in every sense. Even when they hold their partner entirely responsible, they may be wracked by a sense of failure they had chosen this individual. Many mothers are perplexed at why their choices are so difficult and they may be shocked that they still feel something for the man or find themselves unable to separate (Dwyer and Miller, 1996). However, this needs to be seen in the context that at a time in which they feel most vulnerable and uncertain, they are asked to be responsible and decisive.

Boulton and Burnham (1989) consider the process of social work intervention and the conditions that affect the response of the mother to that intervention (see Figure 27). It is always a legitimate question to ask, 'Who is responsible for the abuse?' However, enshrined within the question that often follows, 'Who will the non-abusing carer choose, their partner or their child?', there are inevitably assumptions by professionals about the women, based on their choice. The authors suggest that women who have low self-esteem are poorly nurtured themselves, experience financial and environmental stress and/or are socially isolated, and are inevitably more likely to have a greater need for the support their partners provide. Research into perpetrators would indicate that it is often families in this position that increase child vulnerability and attract potential perpetrators (Finkelhor and Baron, 1986.) The likelihood is that in being asked to choose, many women opt to continue their relationship with their partner in some way, either overtly or covertly. During the course of their work, Rose and Savage (2000) commonly heard professionals attach negative labels to these women. They have been described as collusive of the abuse, in denial, unfit mothers, minimising of the effects of the abuse, and so on.

When professionals fail to recognise the feelings of the women and the context within which they are asked to make a choice, the assumptions about the 'sort' of mothers they are, appears to follow. The perceived hostile responses of professionals to women in this position often serve to strengthen the relationship between the women and their partners (where the women feel needed). The responses of workers to the women commonly took the form of the children's names being placed on the Child Protection Register as well as initiation of care proceedings. This action supported the concept of these carers as unsafe, and further entrenched the position of warring sides.

The social worker has the difficult job of helping the mother to overcome or contain her reactions, to help her accept the need for a possible choice between child and the perpetrator; and to encourage her to maintain a benevolent and supportive attitude toward the child. It is important, and appropriate, to allow the mother a short period of time in which to collect herself and make a decision (Glaser and Frosh, 1988).

Research findings

Hooper (1992) found that 40 per cent of women who discovered the sexual abuse in a clearly identifiable incident were those who decided to stay or reunite with their partners later. Of the five women faced with persistent denial from the perpetrator, 80 per cent had separated from the abusive men, although 40 per cent not by their own choice.

Salt *et al.*, (1990) found that the most difficult situation for mothers to deal with was a perpetrator who would not leave the child's home. When asked to do so, only 22 per cent of the mothers could make this demand on the perpetrator.

De Jong (1988) found that the child's parents or mother will frequently have mixed feelings about the perpetrator and may be pressured not to file charges by relatives or friends. The supportive mothers who did not press charges usually expressed concern about the stress of the legal proceedings on the children and themselves and the fear that the perpetrator might not be convicted. Overall, 17 per cent of the supportive mothers did not press charges, and 12 per cent of the non-supportive mothers did press charges. The latter group expressed a desire for the perpetrator to share the blame,

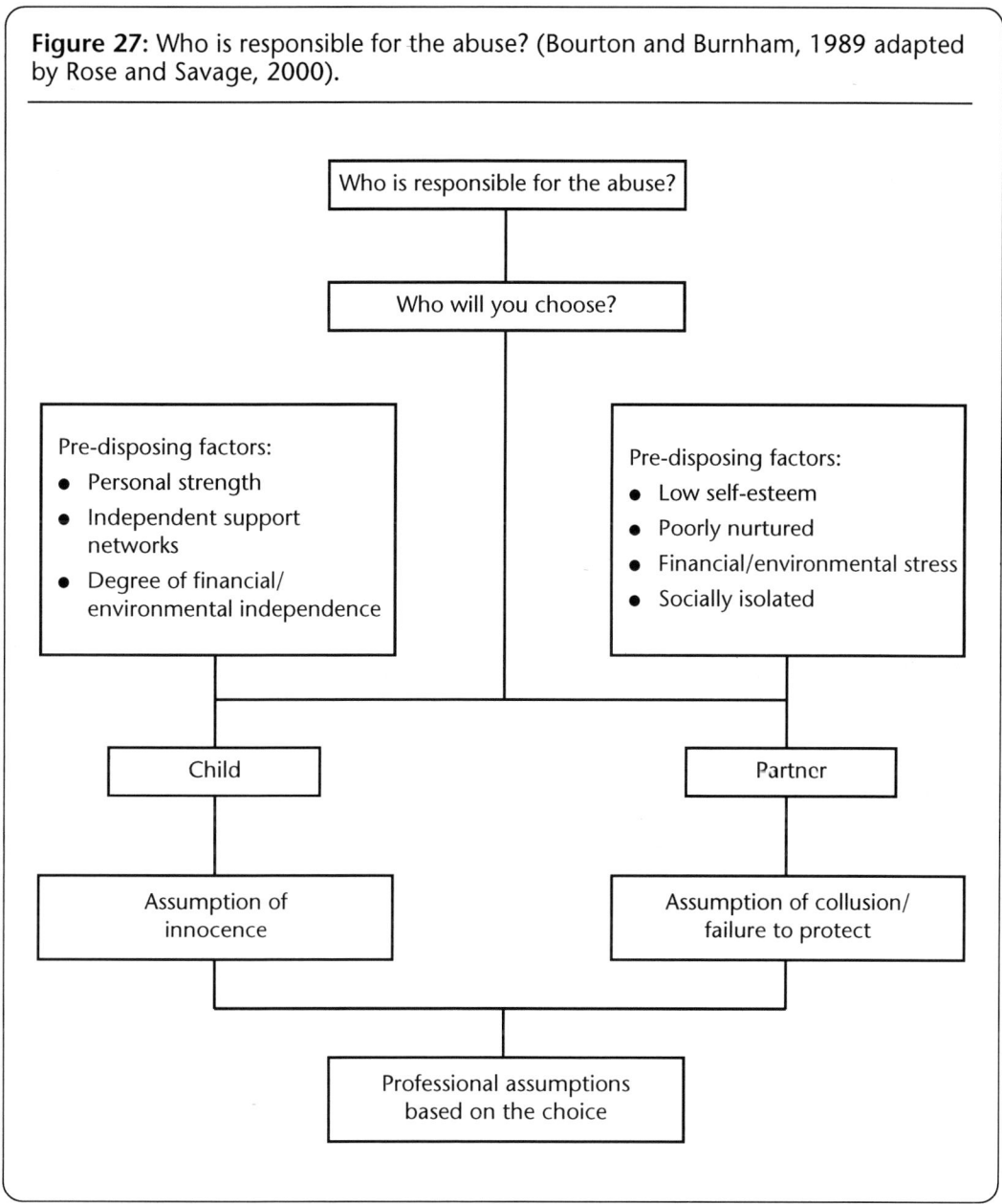

Figure 27: Who is responsible for the abuse? (Bourton and Burnham, 1989 adapted by Rose and Savage, 2000).

although each believed that the child had initiated or caused the contact.

Because of conflicting expectations, the victims and their families often find it difficult to decide whether or not to press charges against the perpetrator. The agony of making this decision is increased when he is a family member. Here, families are caught between two conflicting expectations: universalistic versus particularistic. Should they be loyal to the child victim and treat the perpetrator as they would treat and assailant—thinking of their duty as citizens to bring such an individual before the law? Or should they be loyal to them and make an exception for him because he is a family member and let their duty to him as a particularistic individual prevail? They cannot honour both expectations, and the choice is often a difficult one (Burgess *et al.*, 1977). In their sample, just over half resolved in favour of the child. Even when a decision is made, this can be hard to bear, particularly if pressure is applied to reverse it, e.g. from the perpetrator's extended family. The low rate of action by the criminal justice agencies is often a factor in families' decisions. For example, Palmer *et al.*, (1999) found that in only 6 per cent of the 384 cases in their sample was the perpetrator charged by the police, and he was only convicted in half of these cases, that is, 3 per cent. This compared with 85 of children being removed from their homes due to the abuse and a further 17 per cent being removed for another reason.

McLurg and Craisatti (1999) found that in their sample 80 per cent of the partners stayed together. In half of the families where they did so, the victim was the daughter of the alleged perpetrator and in one-third of cases the victim was the step-daughter of the alleged perpetrator.

Fong and Walsh-Bowers (1998) explored the responsiveness of mothers to father-daughter incest. Of the six women interviewed, half of the incestuous relationships occurred while the mother was still living with her partner (type A family), whereas the other half occurred after the women separated from their partner (type B family). For women from type A families, the disclosure of the abuse was complicated by the stability of family relationships. On the one hand, they were socialised to take the responsibility for keeping the family intact and helping their partners as well as their daughters to deal with the crisis. Because incest was an alien concept to them, they needed time to consider what to do. On the other hand, the professional system expects them to act immediately so as not to feed the view of them as either unfit mothers or as condoning the abuse. Type B families found that because their children were too young to be listened to seriously and the physical evidence was not considered sufficient to diagnose sexual abuse, their reports were not considered credible. When they tried to protect their daughters by denying the perpetrator access, they felt abused further by the court process, and the threat of contempt of court for failing to comply with judgements.

Sirles and Lofberg (1990) noted that mothers often have much to lose and little to gain by separating from their partners. In their research they found that the families that broke up were more likely to have young child victims and have additional problems with domestic violence. The child was likely to have revealed the abuse to the mother and was believed by her.

Wright (1991) explored the family effects of perpetrator removal from the home. Given that intervention and choices can have varied and unexpected consequences, it is important to state these to understand how the decisions on choice for the mother may be loaded. They uncovered a powerful picture of the emotional, structural and financial changes in the lives of all family members when the perpetrator is removed. They found two main themes: financial effects and structural effects. They expressed desperation, fear, anger, and hopelessness about their financial condition (which often predates the offender removal from home, but is aggravated by overwhelming treatment and legal expenses). This can impact on the children if they have to lose college education, whilst mothers reported working long hours in multiple jobs just to make ends meet, and older children also took jobs of their own to help out financially. The ongoing psychological aspects of financial trauma need to be handled as any other trauma, particularly when affluent people have been demoted to joining lower classes.

Forty per cent of the adults believed that perpetrator removal had contributed to marital dissolution. They noted that boundary ambiguity (Boss and Greenberg, 1984) is a consequence of the situation they find themselves in. So when workers are trying to teach families about appropriate boundaries, couples are forced to experience a major boundary ambiguity situation—is the perpetrator 'in' or 'out'? Are they married or not? Are they a family or not? Another contributing factor to the marital dissolution may be the structure of the treatment programme if it calls for a logical, linear progression through individual issues, couple work and then family therapy. People do not live their lives linearly and relationships do not remain static or on hold while individual issues are resolved.

Hooper (1992) found that decisions to separate permanently from their partners were related to previously considering whether to leave on the grounds of domestic violence or earlier sexual abuse. This is a common pattern to women's response to domestic violence, with recurring hopes and promises of reform, together with self-blame and the desire to make their marriages work, thus bringing women back until the relationship deteriorates still further. The sexual abuse became the 'last straw'.

Issues to consider

Todd and Ellis (1992) explored the issue of divided loyalties following an abuse disclosure. Professionals with responsibility to protect children look very closely at a mother to inform their judgements about how the situation is best handled. Those who end their relationship with the perpetrator may be allowed to care for the child. Unfortunately, few women are able to immediately adopt such a position. Furthermore, any pressure to make a choice between the perpetrator and the child forces the mother into a corner, which is at best unhelpful, and at worst disastrous. Mothers need time and space in order to make decisions on anything. Workers have an important role in constructing an environment where women are enabled to express a whole range of changing feelings, There is also the added guilt that women feel at rendering their partner homeless if they 'choose' their daughter. The challenge for workers is how to assist women to meet their parental responsibilities without reinforcing the sense of blame and how to ensure that professional responsibility for responding to sexual abuse is not abdicated. The mothers in their study are testimony to their resourcefulness and capacity for trust in that they retained some hope and belief in the possibility of embarking on new relationships in the future which would offer something positive both to their children and themselves.

One option open to workers is to try and introduce the mother to others who have had to endure the process previously, to facilitate informal avenues for identifying the choices to be made, with positives and consequences.

Smith (1995) noted that if a mother had options available to them and did not use them, or, worse, perceives no options and thinks sexual abuse is an inevitability which requires endurance skills rather than escape mechanisms, the prognosis is poor. However, if the mother believes the child, then the interventions should increase the options rather than persecute them for not perceiving those options in the first place.

Relationship and Co-operation with the Agency (Throughout the Process)

There is a need to establish a good working relationship with mothers from the outset. Most women state that their first contact from social services shapes their relationship from then on. Parental willingness to co-operate with the process of child protection influences social worker's judgements. When it is forthcoming, children are perceived to be less threatened; conversely, unco-operative attitudes raise social workers' uncertainty about parental motivation towards their children. There is often the middle ground, where parents may be at odds with each other about whether to volunteer information, or may be prepared to go along with the investigation of the allegedly abused child.

It is often difficult for mothers to co-operate closely with agencies whose intervention alienates them and subjects them to prescribed societal expectations. Many mothers have reported the services provided to be inadequate. For example, those mothers who were sent onto parenting courses were confused as to the reasoning behind this and why the focus was on them. This appeared to be consistent with the view of women's responsibility being to protect the children.

Most mothers are willing to co-operate in the necessary assessment and treatment work once they trust that they are not being criticised or labelled for their confused and conflicting feelings.

Research findings

It is important to accurately assess the family's level of co-operation with the work as this will have a direct correlation with the level of partnership proposed with the family, and the type of mandate needed. Co-operation will often fluctuate and will need to induce a more or less authoritative role from the workers in response to the presenting situation. This may occur when progress is slow or non-existent and a review of the plan is required.

Pellegrin and Wagner (1990) found that 40 per cent of the mothers in their sample attended appointments about 90 per cent of the time while 30 per cent attended less than 20 per cent of the time. Overall, 67 per cent of the mothers were deemed by the workers to be at least average in their compliance with the recommended plan. They noted that eliciting the co-operation of non-compliant or non-believing mothers was difficult to obtain. In these circumstances, the children were often removed from home as they could not be assured protection at home. This action confused just what the mothers were not co-operating with, either the allegation or the removal. Workers also need to be alert to the reality that mothers of sexually abused children are not a homogeneous group, and thus a variety of techniques are needed, as what works with one will not necessarily work with another. Resistance will be induced where workers try and fit the mother to the technique and not the reverse of this.

Gilgun (1984) argued that where the professionals assume that the mother knew of the abuse, then this is correlated with the source of maternal resistance to working with professionals. Conversely, where the professionals squarely placed the responsibility with the perpetrator, then they were more amenable to such an approach.

We know from *Messages from Research* (DoH, 1995) that plans made at conference do not necessarily mean they will be accepted or processed by the family. It is important to make a distinction between co-operation and compliance. Sayers (1995) noted that:

> ...*our understanding of a mother's ability to protect is helped by carefully considering the extent to which she has taken seriously the child protection requirements of the agencies involved. However, we do need to think carefully about the extent to which the demands of the agencies on the mother are realistic. It would, for example, be unrealistic to expect that a mother could protect her child from a perpetrator who creates opportunities for contact with the child outside the home. We must ask ourselves whether the demands for protection that we make of the mother could be met by anyone, whatever their relationship with the child or however determined they are to ensure the child's safety and protection.*

Smith (1994) noted that it is difficult when a mother simply complies with the involvement (e.g. the removal from the home of the perpetrator is a professional and not a maternal decision).

Jones and Ramchandani (1999) explored the question 'how do professionals manage the dilemma of discovering whether a child is safe, while also not alienating potential carers, who may eventually work in partnership with the professional?' They found that the way in which a case is handled initially can affect the entire subsequent process. Where handled well and sensitively, keeping the non-abusing parent informed and involved, there can be a positive effect on the eventual outcome. Conversely, poorly handled initial contact can alienate both the child and carer, making later work more difficult. The variation in initial approach may reflect a worker's underlying beliefs about the way in which an investigation should be carried out. They found that some professionals approach parents on the basis of supportive acceptance, whilst others require parents to accept responsibility. The majority favour the latter. This has implications in the case of sexual abuse, where the wide range of parental reactions are often difficult to interpret accurately, particularly at the time when they were also considering placement issues. There is thus a wide difference in perspectives between the parents and the professionals. Parents were typically shocked, frightened, or became withdrawn, whereas for the professional this was a 'routine' job. In these circumstances, professionals sometimes misjudged parental capacity to understand allegations or protect their children.

They found that parents retained a strong expectation of help despite the quality of the initial contact, showing that the prospect of working in partnership is not necessarily lost forever, particularly with mothers who remained open and receptive to advice given their predicament. Workers face the difficult task of balancing the need to obtain the non-abusing parent's commitment to help protect the child, while also being responsive to that parent's needs for understanding, information and psychological treatment. Fortunately, many believe it possible to balance a supportive and accepting stance with one of encouraging parental responsibility, seeing them as a tension that can be maintained rather than a dichotomous choice.

Parents who were not kept well informed were marginalised when they attended the initial child protection conference. They wanted professionals to consider all the family history and not just the sexual abuse in order to take decisions on the way forward. For example, issues of finances, supports, general parenting ability, previous domestic violence with its potential repercussions were all central to such decisions. Families have broad needs that require services and a focus in the assessment. Farmer (1993) has noted that the conference has an important role in ensuring the mother does not feel blamed, as this can be a block to partnerships later. It has an important role in helping the mother become equal with the professionals.

Most clients value courtesy and respect, being treated as equals, as individuals and as people who can make their own decisions; they value workers who are experienced, well informed and reliable, able to explain things clearly without condescension, and who really listen; and they value workers who are able to act effectively and make practical things happen. Workers who deal with their clients in these ways empower them. This can become more difficult in some situations of child protection, where workers have considerable power, which makes the relationship inherently unequal.

Issues to consider

With these points in mind, it is useful to have a framework for assessing the client's co-operation with the workers and tasks:

1. **Client is fully and actively involved in case planning, services and/or treatment:**
   - Accepts and actively uses suitable services, including following through on tasks or on referrals to other service providers.
   - Keeps appointments, makes self available as needed, and follows directions to best of their ability.
   - Shows concern about impact of services or treatment; complains about inadequate service when warranted.
   - May not agree with everything suggested, but tries to be constructive in proposing alternatives.
   - When problems in co-operation develop, there tend to be extenuating circumstances.

2. **Involved in planning and services, but lacks initiative and tends to hold back:**
   - Not as fully or actively involved in case planning or services as they could be. This may be because they are rather disorganised or somewhat ambivalent about the services.
   - Accepts and uses suitable services, but doesn't always make best use of them, or drops them too early; follows through on referrals, but sometimes not in a timely manner.
   - Makes appointments, but often postpones them and sometimes doesn't keep them at all.
   - May co-operate satisfactorily with services for other family members, but may co operate less well with personal services focused on self.
   - Tends to wait for caseworker to suggest and act, may complain without proposing alternative, but does accept advice.

3. **Only minimally involved in planning and services:**
   - Passively resists co-operating or is argumentative at every stage.
   - May accept services verbally, but doesn't use them or follow through on referrals or tasks without constant prodding and direct assistance (e.g. has to be taken there every time, even though their own transport can be arranged).
   - Often has to be cajoled, coerced and/or 'chased after'.
   - Makes appointments, but rarely keeps them; doesn't reschedule in advance, even if there are extenuating circumstances.
   - When services are used, participates without much enthusiasm or at the minimum acceptance level but generally doesn't refuse to accept services, doesn't

act consistently hostile, and doesn't actively sabotage services.

- Agency is able to remain in contact with client.

4. Rejects any involvement with agency:

- Actively or passively rejects any agency contact or involvement.

- Refuses to accept any service, or actively sabotages services when persuaded or coerced into using them.

- May threaten service providers, or otherwise discourage them from engaging in services, may not accept even being 'led through' tasks; may have no reaction to admonitions or criticism at all. May display psychosomatic symptoms when confronted with the need to act.

- May be very difficult to contact or remain in contact with. (Magura *et al.*, 1987: p27).

Jones and Ramchandani (1999) set out some useful factors influencing a mother's co-operation with agencies:

- It is important to attempt to work in partnership with parents, especially with mothers who refer many, if not most, cases of suspected sexual abuse.

- Parents, and especially mothers, require clear information in an attempt to work as openly as possible, in order to keep them engaged in the process.

- Informing parents as swiftly and as completely as possible after children have been interviewed is necessary to enable trust to be maintained. Parallel sessions interviewing parents and children in tandem may prove useful.

- If conflict occurs between potentially jeopardising the partnership with parents and on the other hand fully protecting the child from harm, it is clear that the child's needs are paramount.

- Few specialists are currently involved and thus it may be useful to identify cases that need specialist help at an early stage.

- The early planning stage, following the initial referral, would be the most useful point to identify issues of race, culture, or language, which may require addressing (p25).

Openness Regarding the Sexual Abuse

Because of the stigma attached to sexual abuse, families affected by it often do not want to share with others. They thus run the risk of becoming isolated and overwhelmed, even where they have believed the child and protected immediately. Many mothers will not want to broach the sexual abuse with family members for some time following the discovery or disclosure. Hesitant and tentative discussions are the norm. If this persists then it clearly places the child at greater risk. There is a need to try and replace secrecy with openness within the family as a whole, particularly if rehabilitation is being considered.

Research findings

A mother's willingness to discuss the sexual abuse in the wider family may be dependent upon a number of factors. If she previously looked to them for support and guidance when any prior suspicions came to light, and they disbelieved, then this is unlikely to be replicated once substantiation has occurred. Trotter (1998) found that not all the mothers denied the reality of the abuse, but many of their families and friends disclaimed or rejected it to some extent or other. It was then very difficult to persuade them that the abuse had in fact happened. According to Berliner (1991) family members may also avoid imagining or thinking about what actually happened to reduce their own painful feelings. Unfortunately, this may lead to a lack of empathy for the child's experience and reinforce avoidance as a primary coping strategy.

Burgess *et al.*, (1977) looked at how families decide whether or not to tell outsiders once the sexual abuse has been disclosed. Three possibilities exist: do nothing; handle it only as a family matter and tell no outsiders; or tell an outside group. Where the latter option is chosen, it prompts decisions being made by people often without any input from the victim. In their sample, nine of the 44 cases handled the matter as a family matter. Of these, two mothers explicitly severed family ties with the perpetrator's side of the family. In three cases, the perpetrators were lectured by another family member. In two cases the perpetrators were sent to live with the grandmother. In two cases, the perpetrator continued to live in the same home as the child.

It is probable that many attempts to stop the sexual abuse by the mother do not come to the attention of the professionals. If these attempts fail, then they will probably work against the mother if the matter is eventually reported to the child protection agencies, as they may see her actions as denial or attempts to conceal the sexual abuse to protect the perpetrator. Elbow and Mayfield (1991) argued that the decision by the mother to report the matter requires considerable problem-solving skills on the mother's part. For example, she may be considering the impact of the process on the child even though it may appear that she is protecting the offender. It may be that she has been intimidated by threats of or actual physical abuse: thus fear and isolation may preclude both reporting and other attempts to limit the perpetrator's abuse of the child.

Issues to consider

The mother of a newly disclosing incest victim must test out the extent to which they can rely on their own social network. Myers (1985) noted that this can be difficult when the family members may blame her for allowing the abuse, often reinforced by the intervening professionals. This is also linked to the escalation of stress for the mother if she cannot rely on the family in the short to medium term financially as well as emotionally and practically.

Most people do tend to cope with stressful life events within the family or their informal social network before seeking help from formal service providers (Golan, 1981). They may even then turn first to the clergy or their doctor. Mothers will often weigh the efficacy of their own resources against the consequences or availability of external sources of help.

Engel (1994) explored how to break the news to the extended family. There is a need to acknowledge that the news will affect other family members, and that their immediate response may not be all the mother hoped for, e.g. they respond with questions and doubt, if not disbelief. Do not set such a situation up. Acknowledge that they will need time to absorb the information and process their feelings. Some will understand much more and provide the necessary support. It is thus important to consider how to elicit the latter response, and this may be through first approaching the family member the mother feels closest to.

There is a need to consider the motivation to tell: to force an alleged perpetrator to confess, to share it so they do not feel alone, or to displace the responsibility for addressing the aftermath with someone else.

Present Attitude and Relationship with the Perpetrator

Faller (1988) has indicated the merits of exploring the mother's relationship with her partner. First, it is an indicator of the mother's overall functioning. Second, her information regarding the perpetrator can help the worker judge her level of dependence on him, his personality and functioning, and his treatment prognosis. Third, the worker may discover a pattern in the mother's relationships with men that are related to the dynamics of the sexual abuse and her prognosis for protecting her children. Faller also cautions workers to filter the information on the perpetrator provided by the mother depending on her reactions to the abuse, and in particular relating to her belief or disbelief of the allegations. For example, if she has decided to support her partner, she may well obscure his faults and lie about material related to the sexual abuse. Conversely, if she is supporting the child, then the information about the perpetrator may be very negative. It is more important therefore to explore her history of relationships. In doing so, workers should explore how the couple met, the length of time between meeting and sexual intimacy, the division of labour in the relationship, the quality of the relationship, good aspects versus bad ones, their sexual relationship, the partner's relationship with the children, any violence with her or the children, his work history, his use of drugs or alcohol, his involvement in criminal activity, and the reason they parted, if they have.

Loyalty is a highly valued feature of relationships, and is often understood to mean supporting and trusting a person at a time of adversity. The mother thus finds herself in a huge dilemma with incest, since being called upon to be loyal to one family member, her child, is at the cost of withdrawing her support from another, her partner. If the adult relationship remains intact, then it is likely that the mother will show some semblance of commitment towards her partner.

The future relationship the mother chooses to have with the perpetrator is the litmus test of whether she will be able to offer her children any protection from further abuse. This often depends on the nature of the mother's relationship with the perpetrator. For example, offering protective action to the child and separation from the perpetrator usually presents relatively little difficulty if the perpetrator is a stranger to the family. The mother's protective abilities may similarly be mobilised if she learns of abuse, of which she was previously unaware. For example, when the perpetrator was a family friend or is in a relationship with the child that exists relatively independently of the family.

The difficulties of ensuring protection for the child multiply as the perpetrator's emotional proximity to the family increases. This is particularly true when there is a close relationship between the mother and the perpetrator, leaving the mother with an extremely painful choice—break the relationship with the perpetrator or lose the child. This can be where the perpetrator is the partner or a valued relative, such as a grandfather. Only a minority of perpetrators agreed to leave the home as an expression of their responsibility for the abuse. Any mother that undertakes to exclude the perpetrator from the home will need considerable professional support to maintain the decision in the face of emotional and economic strains and stresses, and even threats of violence from the perpetrator and his family or friends (Glaser and Frosh, 1988). In cases where the perpetrator is the stepfather, the decision for the mother is complicated by the fact they have probably had a failed relationship already and are facing another one.

Mothers who are able to confront the perpetrator and are more able to exist independently from him are more likely to be able to effectively protect their children from further abuse. Those who are more dependent will require considerable external support to protect the child.

In response to the disclosure, the mother may become alarmed and distressed for her child and she may immediately feel very angry toward the perpetrator. She may have previously harboured suspicions, particularly if abused herself, possibly by the same man. The confirmation of her suspicions might lead to relief and enable her to pursue the protection of her child. When there is a continuing relationship between the mother and the perpetrator, the mother's natural first move will be to approach the perpetrator, who is likely to strenuously deny the abuse. This may lead to the mother gaining awareness of her pre-existing and now exceedingly uncomfortable position between the perpetrator and her child. The confusion and turmoil engendered in the mother by disclosure, particularly when faced by denial from the perpetrator, may lead the mother to disbelieve the child. Some mothers, themselves suspecting the abuse of the child, pursue their suspicions by questioning the child and the perpetrator. If the suspicions are confirmed, then outside help may be sought. Conversely, if the mother is deterred from pursuing help because of the consequences, then this becomes an obstacle to protecting her child (Glaser and Frosh, 1988).

Many mothers of sexually abused children may have been sexually abused themselves in childhood, and this may lead to them selecting emotionally inadequate partners (Cammaert, 1988) as a result of their low self-esteem. This can combine with their socialised role as being dependent on others and passive.

There is some controversy about the significance accorded to the mother's attitude towards the perpetrator and the apparent dependence by social services on them to protect children from sexual abuse. Whilst this is an important consideration, it should be considered alongside the perpetrator's willingness to address their behaviour as well as the child's ability to protect themselves. If the mother's position is considered in isolation, then it runs the risk of drawing the responsibility away from the perpetrator (MacLeod and Saraga, 1988). For many mothers, they simply maintain their relationship with their partner as a means of survival. Workers thus need to draw a careful line to facilitate the mother's participation in the process of assessment and determination of outcomes, without either holding women solely responsible for the safety of their children or blaming them for what has happened.

Women have increasingly been encouraged to separate from abusing partners to prevent sexually abused children being removed from home. However, such women have the right to remain with the sexually abusive partner, although this clearly challenges the traditionally held beliefs about safe parenting (Smart, 1997). There are ways in which the 'risk' presented by the continuing relationship between the women and their partners can be safely managed, and this can be seen as the best outcome for them in the longer term. Experience has shown that if women feel pressurised into ending their relationships, the outcomes for children are rarely satisfactory and many continue the relationship, albeit in a clandestine way. For a fuller discussion around this area, please refer to the chapter on safe care by Rose and Savage, (1999).

Byerly (1992) set out some important factors for mothers to consider when making decisions about how and whether to maintain interaction with the perpetrator. They include:

- Proximity: to the perpetrator can make them feel trapped, threatened or resentful, e.g. if they are an immediate or extended family member. The mother needs to consider how to create and sustain space between them if desired.

- Emotional attachment: is central to the mother's future relationship with the abuser, e.g. Are they in love? What are their views about divorce? His willingness to undergo change and treatment? All of these take time. Where the mother wishes to remain with the perpetrator, they need to face issues such as re-establishing trust, sexual contact, openness, and a relationship based on equality (in terms of respect, shared responsibility, and privileges).

- Re-establishing sexual relationships with sexual perpetrators: is often much more difficult than deciding to stay with him,

and often takes time and counselling to achieve. This is often a part of the overall treatment package and needs to address how sexual boundaries and needs will be achieved and maintained.

Research findings

Very little information is available regarding mothers who protect their children by leaving their partners but who do not go on to report the abuse to the authorities.

Todd (1989) found that the mother's loyalties often remained with the perpetrator, whose needs predominated. This may be in part due to their history of abuse and their investment in their current relationship was often great. If the children have picked up on this, then they may well have accepted their subordinate role and acknowledged the importance of the adult union. In all the Sheffield cases, the mother could not escape the needs of the male partner. His triumph and control continues in that the child knows and understands that their disclosures have caused the devastation of the family. If this is the case, then reintroducing the perpetrator back into the home would present an unacceptable level of risk, and as such the safety of the child cannot be guaranteed.

For a mother to take action, she must feel strong enough to make a stand against the perpetrator, who is usually her male partner. Workers need to consider the co-existence of domestic violence with the sexual abuse, and how this impacts on the mother's choices. There is increasing evidence that domestic violence is more prevalent in sexually abusive families than in the general population (Truesdell *et al.*, 1986), and thus workers need to acknowledge that any effective intervention will need to address the domestic violence before she can cope successfully with her child's victimisation (Dietz and Craft, 1990). Where the mother's partner tends to be violent, the mother's fear may compromise her ability to be supportive of a child who discloses. Even where her partner is not violent, a mother may be understandably reluctant to take action that may result in her partner being arrested, becoming alienated, or leaving the home. These inhibiting influences are reflected in the studies that show mothers are more likely to be supportive when they are no longer living with the perpetrator and that mothers who take action tend to divorce their partners (Faller, 1991).

Trepper *et al.*, (1996) found in their sample that almost one half, 49 per cent, of the perpetrators and non-abusing spouses indicated a marital relationship in which extreme emotional separateness was the modus vivendi. An additional 40 per cent of couples displayed a moderate emotional separateness in their marital relationship. Only 11 per cent of these couples reported being more emotionally close than emotionally separate. The communication patterns of perpetrator and non-abusing spouses reflected estrangement between the two. Some 90 per cent of perpetrators exhibited poor communication with their partner; that is, communication that was unclear, incongruent, and void of empathy. In fact, only 10 per cent of perpetrators displayed some effort to communicate effectively with their spouses. The majority of perpetrators, 63 per cent, rated the alliance between themselves and their spouse as unhappy. Two-thirds of this group rated the relationship as very unhappy, whereas one-third rated their marital relationship as somewhat unhappy (i.e. more discontentment than contentment). The remaining one-third of perpetrators, 38 per cent, ranked the relationship with their spouse as satisfactory and none reported being happy in their marriage. However, two per cent of non-abusing parents classified the marital relationship as very happy although a quarter, 26 per cent, viewed their marriages as satisfactory. 72 per cent of the non-abusing respondents appraised the couple's relationship as unhappy whilst 46 per cent of the total referred to their marital association as unhappy.

Massatt and Lundy (1998) found that the loss of the relationship with the perpetrator, whether that be through divorce, separation, or incarceration, and regardless of any history of physical and emotional abuse, came as a shock and loss to them. They found that the number of non-abusing parents married to and living with the perpetrator dropped from 35 to two post-disclosure. The level of intimacy with him moved from 35.7 per cent reporting being 'not at all close in any way' before disclosure to 87 per cent reporting being 'not at all close in any way'.

Walton (1996) explored the issue of interpersonal role conflict for mothers between the perpetrator and the child. In this, the mother may well attempt to fulfil more than one role simultaneously and in so doing will find that they must satisfy multiple sets of expectations. Todd and Ellis (1992) reported on children who had been sexually abused in the family and had been removed by the local authority. The mothers, on learning about the abuse, had decided to 'support and remain with (their) partner with the consequence that their children were admitted to care and in some instances expelled from the family completely' (p14). They argued that the choice made by these mothers was due to forcing her to decide whom to support at such a time of emotional upheaval, placing her in an impossible position. In addition, the mother's isolation may be a critical factor in her management of events, in that they may have to turn to the person whom they traditionally rely on for their support—the perpetrator.

Eaton (1993) highlighted the way in which perpetrators groom mothers as well as the children, and Salter (1988) referred to the 'cognitive dissonance' to be reconciled by most mothers in order to believe their child and disbelieve their partner is enormous. Despite this, a significant proportion of mothers do find the time to make the choice of the child, with others requiring time and help to achieve the emotional and cognitive 'leap' of believing that their child has been sexually abused.

Dempster (1993) found that all 34 women in her sample took some action towards ending the abuse and protecting their children when they found out about the abuse. For some, this was done in the face of complete denial by the perpetrator, disapproval or even harassment from the perpetrator's friends, from relatives and sometimes even the surrounding community.

Sirles and Lofberg (1990) studied factors associated with divorce in cases of intra-familial child sexual abuse. They noted that the decision about divorce is but one of the many and complex issues facing mothers. Often they have much to lose and little to gain by divorcing their husbands. In their sample of 128 cases, they found that 48 per cent ended in divorce. They identified significant relationships for the following variables:

- Age of the victim: with 72.7 per cent of the children being pre-school compared to 33.8 per cent of teenage victims. This suggests that a protective bond exists between the mothers and their children.

- Who the abuse was revealed to: with 66.7 per cent of cases leading to divorce being reported initially to the mother, reducing to 33.3 per cent when reported to a friend and 34.5 per cent to a professional.

- The mother's reaction: 66.1 per cent were believed by their mothers compared to 33.9 per cent who were met with disbelief. Of those cases where the child was believed, 64 per cent of cases ended in divorce. In the majority of cases, the matter was reported to a professional agency immediately.

- A history of physical abuse of the mother: was present in 68 per cent of the cases that ended in either separation or divorce, compared to 32 per cent that remained intact.

- Duration of the abuse: They found that victims whose families remained intact were abused for longer periods (n=37.09 months) than for families that broke up (n=25.65 months).

Overall, they found that there were differences between child sexual abuse cases that elected to stay together and those that divorce. Those who divorced had sufficient power and autonomy to take assertive action. They were not easily intimidated by their husband's physical abuse and threats of intimidation. They chose to place the protection of their child above the many negative consequences of separation.

Bagley (1995) found that mothers who had themselves been sexually abused often saw the marriage in unrealistic terms, as ideal relationships which contrasted with their unhappy childhood. Some of the women were also probably trapped in the cycle of learned helplessness. They rarely knew of the sexual abuse of their daughter, but often it was not difficult for their husbands to browbeat and deceive them. He noted that husbands of the mother group were on average 4.5 years older than their wives, significantly higher than the age difference of 3.1 years in the controls.

Issues to consider

Some mothers wish their lives to return to how it used to be pre-disclosure. In order to achieve this, the mother may seek to normalise the perpetrator's behaviour by believing that: his promises never to repeat the behaviour are valid; he is a good father in every other way; the impact of the abuse was not serious; or that herself or the daughter was responsible.

We need to explore the mother's current position regarding the perpetrator, bearing in mind his position regarding the abuse (admits, minimises or denies), and the tactics he will deploy when he now needs his partner more than ever before. For example, he may plead remorse and promise to change his ways as a means of blocking any information being provided to the professionals involved. This is necessary regardless of whether he continues to have contact with the child, because the crisis of the disclosure and of professional intervention may produce numerous changes in the non-abusing parent as well as in the perpetrator. For example, as the crisis of the disclosure recedes, the mother's previous, perhaps intensely held, feelings for the perpetrator may re-emerge. On the other hand, a mother may become more autonomous and less dependent in relation to the person who may have been her husband or cohabitee (Glaser and Frosh, 1988). If the mother and the perpetrator are to continue their relationship, in the context of rehabilitation, very careful work will be required.

Questions to be asked:

- What is expected of a mother who learns that her child has been sexually abused by a man who she thought she loved and trusted?

- It is very important that workers establish just how the couple met, in what circumstances, and how much he has groomed the mother. This can be reflected in how much her cognitive distortions mirror his. We also need to establish whether she has been abused by him— sexually, emotionally or physically?

- What is her motivation for continuing her relationship with him?

- Where is her primary alliance—with the child or with the perpetrator? The less predictable or less sympathetic the mother is to the child's interests, the greater the vulnerability to the child. The younger the child the greater the risk becomes.

- What is her complicity or non-complicity with the perpetrator post-disclosure?

- What are the mother's dilemmas?

- What do we as professionals need to offer practically? What do we need to understand ourselves?

Roberts (1992–93) argued that it is the notion of the couple as 'one', and the mother's fear of collapse at separation, which offers some clues to individual work with non-believing mothers. By giving them time to consider what qualities they find lacking in themselves and which they value in their partners, it is possible to convey clearly that their predicament is accepted and the reasons for their defensive behaviour understood. At a later stage, and at their own pace, they may also begin to assert themselves in the areas they regarded themselves as deficient, e.g. self-worth, setting limits, communication skills. They can become far less dependent upon their partner in those areas and much less likely to regard separation as losing a part of themselves. Coupled with the time to reflect upon their unenviable situation, and the provision of whatever practical help that is available, there can be at least some partnership and further exploration of the many confused and painful feelings they are experiencing (p269). We will not successfully convert all mothers to choosing their child, and legal intervention to protect the child is often needed where the mother will safeguard their adult relationship at all costs. A woman's allegiance to her partner may well be to avoid losing an important part of themselves, and, rather than acknowledge having misjudged their man, will try all sorts of denials or strategies to put the most favourable interpretation on what has happened.

Knowledge of Sexual Offending Behaviour—Generally and Specific to their Partner

The abusive adult understands children better than the rest of us. The child can come to depend on

victimisation with terrible assurance, much more surely than our protection. It is the perfect fit between the child's needs and the adult's desires that we must consider if we are to comprehend the incomprehensible and empower our interventions on behalf of the powerless.

(Summit, 1990: p60)

Mothers often ask many questions about the sexual perpetrator and which might include:

- How often is sexual abuse committed by strangers, and how often by people the child knows?

- How much sexual abuse is committed by fathers and stepfathers?

- How much sexual abuse is committed by teenagers?

- Do women sexually abuse children?

- Why do men sexually abuse children?

- What is paedophilia?

- Do sexual perpetrator's have one or more victims?

- How do they get the trust of the child?

- What help do they need?

- What help is available?

- How can such help be accessed?

- Does treatment work?

- Can we ever live together again as a family? How? When?

This section will offer some basic information, which might help workers answer the mother's queries. Those interested in more detail should refer to Chapter 6 (this volume), or Calder (1999).

Our current level of understanding

It has taken some time to begin to shift the responsibility for the abuse from both the victim and the mother to the perpetrator, although there is still some way to go. There are many problems associated with a comprehensive knowledge base on child sexual abuse, not least the secrecy in which it is perpetrated, and the common invisibility of harm. Despite these problems, there is now a fairly broad knowledge base and level of insight with regards to how sexual perpetrators select their victims and perpetrate the abuse.

It is now generally agreed that there is a process to sexual offending and that perpetrators go through a number of stages prior to committing the offence (Finkelhor, 1984; Wolf, 1984). It is also known that individuals who perpetrate sexual offences against children plan their abuse and that they will undertake a variety of roles to enable them to gain access to potential victims. In certain circumstances, this will involve 'targeting' women who are single parents. It is significant that perpetrators can target vulnerable children as well as mothers (e.g. single parents) and then groom them in order to gain access to the children. It is not difficult for a man who is intent on abusing children within his family to distance a child from its mother. His power in the family would allow him to effectively use physical or emotional threats. He may also 'groom' the child by offering special treatment or manipulate the child emotionally, for example telling the child that their mother would place her in care if she found out. Mothers should thus be regarded as vulnerable and in no way responsible. This is important as workers need to understand the continuing influence of the perpetrator on the mother and the children. For example, if he is adept at denying responsibility for the abuse, displacing emotional responsibility and putting blame onto others in the immediate environment.

Most, but not all, perpetrators do have a cycle of behaviour, which may go from masturbatory fantasy to contact with the victim. Each cycle is unique, which, if identified, allows work to focus on how it can best be interrupted and managed. Perpetrators can identify the points at which they are able to control and divert their thoughts and actions and consequently avoid offending. Workers need to understand that the stages are not necessarily distinct, and the sequence is not rigid: there is considerable overlap between the stages and smaller, repetitive cycles operate within the longer cycle. The length of the cycle may vary, and this is important as the frequency is an important indicator of risk. Perpetrators can travel through their cycle in a matter of hours, or it may take a few weeks or even years for others to reach the point of re-offending. The cyclical nature of the behaviour reinforces that it is continuous unless challenged.

Steven Wolf (1984) provided a theory of the cycle of offending which links factors known frequently to occur in the lives of individuals identified as sexually deviant. His paper builds on earlier research to suggest a comprehensive model to explain (in part) the development and maintenance of sexually deviant orientations. His hypothesis is that there exists a positive and increasing relationship between specific environmental and developmental experiences and the acquisition and maintenance of sexual deviance. He describes a multidimensional model linking factors known frequently to occur in the lives of individuals identified as sexually deviant and a learning model describing the relationship between inhibition and deviant arousal.

Wolf identified a category of 'potentiators' which simplistically relate early experiences of the perpetrator influencing their later attitudes and behaviour. The range of the latter includes witnessing sexual violence or abuse, family dysfunction, isolation, or being a victim themselves from some kind of violence or abuse. He found that this group of perpetrators experienced significant abuse and deprivation at a rate approximately twice that of the general population. These potentiators seem to have a direct impact on the form of adult personality. These areas include low frustration, tolerance and poor social adjustment. They had a tendency to form interpersonal relationships that were shallow and lacking in true intimacy. They also commonly projected blame for whatever current difficulties they were experiencing. In terms of sexual preoccupation, Wolf noted that these individuals had developed a coping strategy for dealing with internally felt stress by translating it into sexual fantasy and behaviour. Under pressure, the sex offender will give way first in the weakest area of his personality membrane e.g. his sexuality.

Wolf then moved on to consider disinhibitors which he defined as transitory environmental factors or internal states that act to lower the person's inhibitions against a specified behaviour. These have an important role in weakening the inhibition (social controls) against, and strengthening the attraction to, sexually deviant behaviour. Disinhibitors also have a role in terms of justification or rationalisation, which serve to further the individual's development and continuation of their sexual deviation.

Wolf also considers the role that sexual fantasy plays. Firstly, it acts as a disinhibitor towards the person being thought about. Secondly, it reinforces the attraction towards the behaviour, and finally it reinforces the rationalisations used in the fantasy, which is the focus of masturbation. Fantasy acts to desensitise the perpetrator to the behaviour. The consistent repetition of the deviant theme in association with the pleasant sensations of sexual arousal and/or ejaculation serves to reinforce the attraction to the deviance, so that the overall arousal and attraction to the deviant focus increases.

After the sexual fantasy the person may have to deal with a sense of guilt and embarrassment, so that a pattern of rationalisation is incorporated—a process known as 'cognitive distortion'. To the outsider such cognitive distortions amount to unreal excuses, although to the perpetrator they are functional as they control the level of guilt and anxiety that the offender might otherwise experience as he repeats the abuse. Wolf points to how strong this belief system can be.

Wolf then looks at the addiction cycle, which has the advantage of being easily used in any direct work, and can be used for those who cannot read or write. Wolf developed the cycle of addiction after having looked both at the perpetrator's past history and his presenting behaviours.

Wolf's cycle of offending can be expressed as follows:

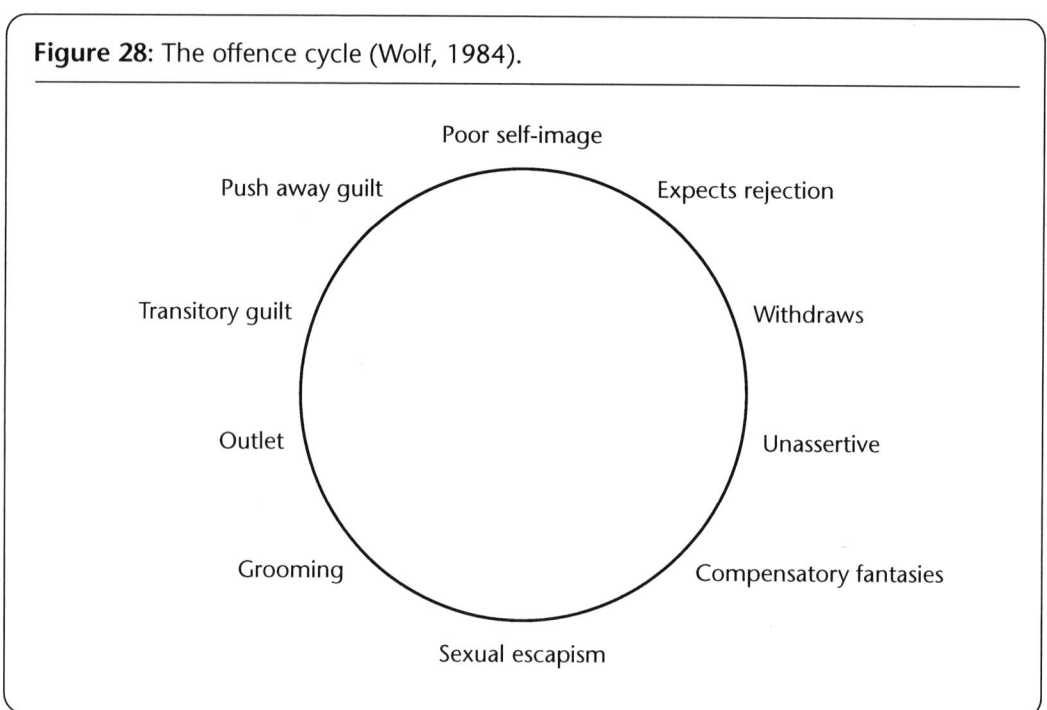

Figure 28: The offence cycle (Wolf, 1984).

Poor self-image

Push away guilt   Expects rejection

Transitory guilt   Withdraws

Outlet   Unassertive

Grooming   Compensatory fantasies

Sexual escapism

This addiction cycle charts the entry level, then all the points the perpetrator must go through in order to sexually abuse, and then rationalise and continue their behaviour. The entry point of poor self-image is often related to their early life experiences and to a general dissatisfaction with their life. Indeed, Koester-Scott (1994) referred to the fact that perpetrators frequently present with a significantly disturbed developmental history; early feelings of emotional and social isolation, often combined with physical and sexual abuse, which leads them to distort cognitively about themselves, others and the way in which the world operates. They often present in a state of 'victim posture'. They expect rejection, so they withdraw. They compensate through needs fulfilment fantasies, which often have a sexual dimension or tone. This 'escape to sexuality' can be understood as a learned coping mechanism, which develops fairly early in life out of a realisation that sexual gratification is a way of displacing other more painful feelings. These belief systems form the beginning components of the 'offence cycle' as the perpetrator develops a habit of using fantasy in order to manage emotional needs unmet because of a lack of connection with others. These fantasies serve as a cognitive rehearsal for deviant behaviour and may include aspirations of wealth, power, control and revenge. The escape to fantasy places the perpetrator in control and they then start targeting victims that match their deviant sexual interest. Indeed, if they fix their fantasy on a specific behaviour or individual it will increase the need for, or attraction to, that behaviour or individual. The result is that the fantasy begins to 'groom' the environment, as

the perpetrator rehearses sexual behaviours and this reinforces their belief that the primary goal of sexual relations is to feel better about themselves. Behaviourally, compulsive masturbation often follows, as does the incorporation to their fantasy of rationalisation and justification. Although guilt and embarrassment follow, particularly relating to the possibility of being caught, it is quickly pushed away, and this is symptomatic of their general inability to take responsibility for themselves. They externalise responsibility and often promise never to do it again, although we need to note that they rarely learn from their mistakes. Since the perpetrator has not really changed and been unsuccessful in applying discontinuation strategies they are again at step one and the whole process begins anew.

Finkelhor, (1984) developed a multi-factor model to explain child sexual abuse by integrating a variety of single factor theories. It incorporates characteristics of the perpetrator, disinhibitors, the environment and the victim (see Figure 29). It operates at a high level of generality, thus allowing its use across a wide range of sexual perpetrators, whilst also encouraging analysis of the relative significance

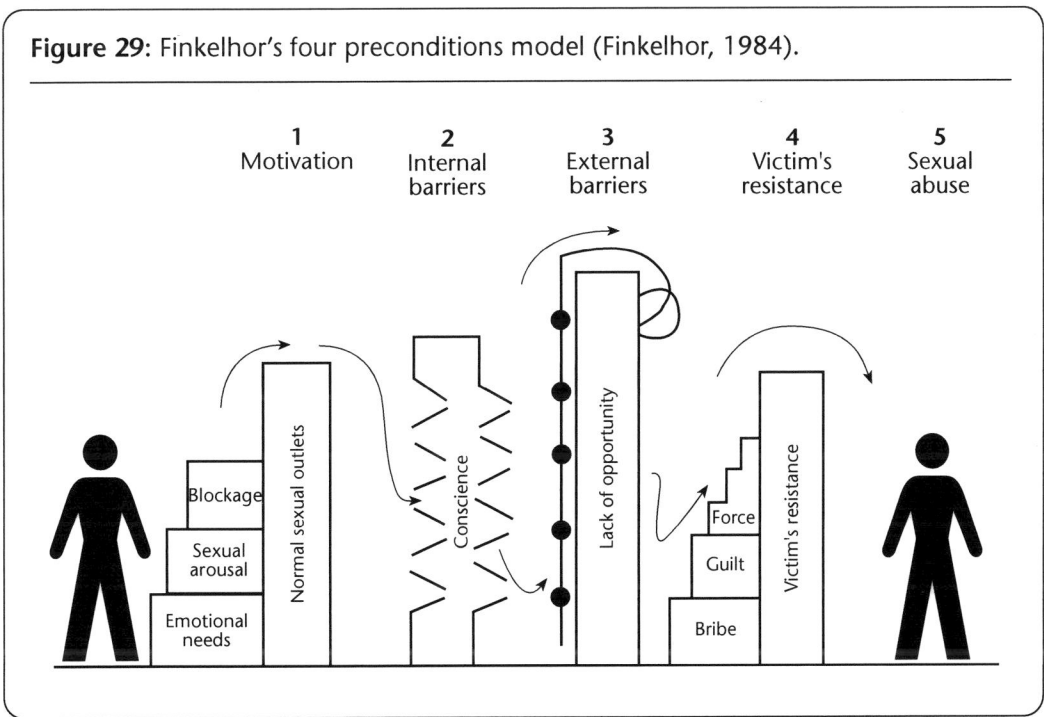

Figure 29: Finkelhor's four preconditions model (Finkelhor, 1984).

of the different factors in individual cases. It allows individual cases to be examined in detail, moving a perpetrator on from asserting that his behaviour 'just happened', to an understanding of the thoughts, feelings and conscious manipulation of people and events which he undertook before the offence could take place (Lancaster, 1996). It thus emphasises that sexual abuse only takes place if the perpetrator already has sexual feelings towards the child, and this firmly locates responsibility with the perpetrator. Finkelhor's model accounts for both familial and extra-familial child sexual abuse, and, although widely used, there remains a paucity of hard evidence to support the model or risk factors (Oates, 1990).

Finkelhor argues that all the known factors contributing to child sexual abuse can be grouped into four preconditions, which need to be met prior to the instigation of child sexual abuse. The four preconditions are:

1. *Motivation*: The potential perpetrator needs to have some motivation to sexually abuse a child. Thus, he will need to find children erotically and sexually desirable.

2. *Internal inhibitions*: They must overcome internal inhibitions that may act against his motivation to sexually abuse.

3. *External inhibitions*: They also have to overcome external obstacles and inhibitions prior to sexually abusing the child.

4. *Resistance*: Finally, they have to overcome the child's possible resistance to being sexually abused.

All four preconditions have to be fulfilled, in a logical, sequential order, for the abuse to commence. The presence of only one condition, such as a lack of maternal protection, social isolation or emotional deprivation is not sufficient to explain abuse.

1. Motivation to sexually abuse

Finkelhor argues that there are three functional components subsumed under the motivation to sexually abuse children:

1. *Emotional congruence* in which sexual contact with a child satisfies profound emotional needs.

2. *Sexual arousal* in which the child represents the source of sexual gratification for the perpetrator.

3. *Blockage* when alternative sources of sexual gratification are not available or are less satisfying.

As these components are not actual preconditions, not all three need to be present for sexual abuse to occur. They are, however, important in explaining the variety of motivations perpetrators may have for sexually abusing children. The three components explain not only the instance of those who aren't sexually motivated but enjoy degrading victims by wielding power, but also the paedophile, and the sexually motivated perpetrator who looks towards children for variety, even though he has access to other sources of sexual gratification. In some instances elements from all three components may be present to account for whether the motivation is strong and persistent, weak and episodic, or whether the focus is primarily on girls or boys, or both.

2. Overcoming internal inhibitors

To sexually abuse, the perpetrator needs not only to be motivated but also to be able to overcome his internal inhibitions against acting on his motivation. No matter how strong the sexual interest in children might be, if the perpetrator is inhibited by taboos then he will not abuse. Arguably, most people do have some inhibitions towards sexually abusing children. Dis-inhibition is not a source of motivation, it merely releases the motivation. Thus an individual who has no inhibitions against child sexual abuse, but who is not motivated, will not abuse. The second precondition aims to isolate the factors that account for how inhibitions are overcome, and whether they are temporary or not. The element of dis-inhibition is an integral part of understanding child sexual abuse.

3. Overcoming external inhibitors

While preconditions one and two account for the perpetrator's behaviour, preconditions three and four consider the environment outside the perpetrator and child which control whether and whom he abuses. External inhibitors that may restrain the perpetrator's actions include family constellation, neighbours, peers, and societal sanctions, as well as the level of supervision that a child receives. Although a child cannot be supervised constantly, a lack of supervision has been shown in the clinical literature to be a contributing factor to sexual abuse, as has physical proximity and opportunity. External inhibitions against committing child sexual abuse may easily be overcome if the perpetrator is left alone with a child who is not supervised.

4. Overcoming the resistance of the child

One limitation of much of the research literature is the failure to recognise that children are able to resist, or avoid abuse. The focus in the clinical literature is on children who have been sexually abused, while ignoring those who although approached were able to avoid it or resist. The feminist argument proposes that insufficient attention is paid to the fact that children do have a capacity to resist. This capacity may operate in a very subtle, covert way, and does not necessarily involve overt protestations. Perpetrators may sense which children are good potential targets, who can be intimidated, and can be exhorted to keep a secret. They report that they can almost instinctively pick out a vulnerable child (and mother) on whom to focus their sexual attentions, while ignoring those who might resist. Frequently these children may not even be aware that they are being sexually approached, or indeed resisting such advances.

Some of the risk factors that inhibit the capacity to resist include emotional insecurity and neediness, lack of physical affection, lack of friends, lack of support and interest from parents, age, naïveté, and lack of information. Knowing which factors make children vulnerable is essential in formulating prevention programmes. Isolating behaviours that continue a risk, while emphasising those that enhance resistance or avoidance, can empower children to protect themselves. This is not to say that children who are not vulnerable do not get abused. Many children may be forced or coerced despite displaying resistance or avoidance behaviours. In such instances the factors overcoming a child's resistance has nothing to do with the child, or the child's relationship with the offender, but is the result of force, threat or violence. No matter how much resistance is manifested by the child, this may not necessarily prevent abuse.

Precondition four has three possible outcomes: the child may resist overtly by saying no and running away, or covertly by presenting a confident, assertive demeanour which conveys a strong message to the perpetrator not to attempt abuse for fear of detection or exposure; the child may resist but still be abused through the use of force or violence; or a child may resist but be overcome through coercion.

Acknowledging the child's capacity to resist or avoid abuse enhances our understanding of child sexual abuse. The notion that children can resist, albeit frequently covertly, is a positive one which could usefully generate more empirical research on the content of resistance behaviours, and how these can be incorporated and adopted in the preventive programmes which aim to teach children how to avoid sexual abuse (Sanderson, 1990).

Perpetrators: what they tell us

There are a growing number of papers which set out the findings of research into why sexual perpetrators commit sexual offences against children—in their own words. These are essential developments in our understanding and are given some status as the respondents are frequently offered confidentiality, thus removing the fear of further consequences.

Selection of victims

Elliott *et al.*, (1995) found the following selection characteristics used by sexual perpetrators:

42 per cent felt the child had to be pretty.

27 per cent cited the way the child dressed was important.

18 per cent reported being young or small was significant for them.

13 per cent focused on innocent or trusting children.

49 per cent reported an attraction to those

who lacked confidence or had low self-esteem.

Conte *et al.*, (1989) interviewed a sample of adult sexual perpetrators who claimed a special ability to identify vulnerable children, and to manipulate this vulnerability as a means of sexually using them. Vulnerability was defined in terms of children's status (e.g. living in a divorced home or being young), and in terms of emotional or psychological state (e.g. a needy child, a depressed or unhappy child). This can be extended to include handicapped children, particularly those with a physical or learning difficulty, those in poor parenting situations who are not assertive or outgoing, and who are trusting or withdrawn. Many claim that they can almost instinctively pick out vulnerable children, whilst ignoring those who might resist.

Age of victim

Elliott *et al.*, (1995) found that the child victim age ranged from 1–18 years. The mean age of the youngest victims was 8.5 years: the mean age of the eldest victims was 13 years. 6.6 per cent also assaulted victims aged 19–45; one offender abused a 65-year-old victim (pp583–4).

Gender of victim

Elliott *et al.*, (1995) found that the perpetrators generally had a preference for the gender of their victims: 58 per cent targeted girls, 14 per cent preferred boys, 28 per cent targeted both boys and girls (p583).

Relationship of victim to perpetrator

Sexual offences are often perpetrated by someone very familiar to the victim. Elliott *et al.*, (1995) found that 46 per cent of the perpetrators felt that a 'special relationship' with the child was vital. They found that 66 per cent knew their victims. Most can be divided into three groups based on their relationship with the victim: family members, friends or acquaintances, and strangers.

- Family members: Waterhouse *et al.*, (1993) found that 40 per cent of perpetrators

were related to the victim. In their earlier research, Waterhouse and Carnie (1992) found that they were the natural father in 31 per cent of cases, stepfathers in 21 per cent of cases, and co-habitees in 11 per cent of cases. Kelly *et al.*, (1991) found that close relatives (father-figures, siblings, grandfathers, uncles and aunts) offended in 14 per cent of cases, compared to 68 per cent perpetrated by distant relatives, known adults and peers. Oates (1990) found that in 75 per cent of cases the perpetrator was known to the child and vice versa. In 50 per cent of the cases, they were a member of the child's own family, whilst 50 per cent were trusted friends who had access to the children.

- Friends or acquaintances: Elliott *et al.*, (1995) found that 66 per cent of perpetrators knew their victims through their families, friends or acquaintances, e.g. babysitting. Waterhouse *et al.*, (1993) found that 60 per cent of the men in their sample were not biologically related to their victim.

- Strangers: The range of perpetrators unknown to the child pre-abuse ranges from 18 per cent (Kelly *et al.*, 1991) through 25 per cent (Oates, 1990) to one-third (Elliott *et al.*, 1995).

Location of offence

Elliott *et al.*, (1995) found that perpetrators often used more than one location to abuse children. 61 per cent reported abusing in their own home compared to 49 per cent in the victims home. 44 per cent reported abusing in public places such as toilets or parks, compared to 13 per cent in the homes of friends, 6 per cent in the vicinity of the perpetrator's home and 4 per cent in the car. It is highly significant that 48 per cent of them isolated their victims through babysitting.

Strategies used

- Offering to play games, teach them a sport or play a musical instrument.

- Giving bribes, taking them on outings, or giving them a lift home.

- Using affection, understanding and love.
- Telling stories involving lies, magic or treasure hunts.
- Asking a child for help (Elliott *et al.*, 1995).

They found that 84 per cent used a strategy that had been previously successful compared to 16 per cent who adapted theirs over time. 30 per cent replayed their own experiences, whilst 14 per cent were influenced through pornography, television, films and the media.

Types of offences

Elliott *et al.*, (1995) found that all the perpetrators in their sample indecently assaulted their victims, sometimes in more than one way. 72 per cent of them reported that this included masturbating the child and being masturbated by the child. 31 per cent engaged in mutual oral sex and 57 per cent attempted or actually engaged in full sexual intercourse, either vaginal or anal. Eight per cent murdered or attempted to murder the child victim during or after the sexual assault. 85 per cent committed the sexual acts with one victim at a time although the remaining 5 per cent had multiple victims present. 93 per cent acted alone.

The first abusive action often involved one or two immediate sexual acts, such as sexual touching or genital kissing, whilst others desensitised the child by asking them to do something that would help them, such as undressing. The majority carefully tested the child's reaction to sex, by bringing up sexual matters or having sexual materials around, or by subtly increasing sexual touching. This 'normalised' sexual setting could be achieved by using sexually explicit videos, or magazines, or sexualised talking.

The use of force

Perpetrators can use one or a combination of methods to secure a child's compliance. Elliott *et al.* found that 19 per cent used physical force with a child, 44 per cent used coercion and persuasion, and 46 per cent used bribery and gifts in exchange for sexual touches. 39 per cent were prepared to use threats or violence to control a resisting child. 61 per cent used passive methods of control such as stopping the abuse and then coercing and persuading once again. 33 per cent specifically told the child not to tell compared to 24 per cent who used threats of dire consequences, whilst 24 per cent used anger and the threat of physical force, and 20 per cent threatened the loss of love or said the child was to blame. 61 per cent were 'very worried' about the child disclosing.

The Waterhouse research reported on a wide range of means used to procure sex from naïve children. Actual physical coercion and force was used in some 20 per cent of cases, verbal inducements or bribes in 14 per cent and coercion by verbal threats of violence in 6 per cent of cases. Margolin (1992) shattered the myth of the friendly and 'gentle' grandfather approaches reported earlier by Goodwin *et al.*, (1983), finding evidence of explicit threats and overt physical coercion (p740). Conte *et al.*, (1989) also noted that verbal threats are based on an understanding of the child and what will be an effective threat against them. Waterhouse *et al.*, also recorded that most sexual abuse was severe. In 40 per cent of cases children were subjected to sexual manipulation of their genitals either beneath or above their clothing, vaginal intercourse occurred in 20 per cent of cases, whilst four per cent of the sample were subjected to oral sex, four per cent to sodomy, and five per cent to non-contact abuse. Conte *et al.* found that those relatively non-violent men in their sample had employed a range of coercive behaviours, e.g. conditioning through the use of reward and punishment, and letting the child view violence towards their mother (p299).

Crossover

Sexual offending can occur within and outside the family, with male and female victims, of varying ages, and there can be a variety of sexually deviant behaviours. They are not always discrete or compartmentalised. Those perpetrators who are caught offending inside the family are potentially a threat to children living outside the family as a preference for that kind of behaviour develops (Wolf, 1984; Abel *et al.*, 1987). It is important to provide such information as it is a central part of how professionals manage the perpetrator and assess risk. Most professionals assume a generalised risk to all children unless narrowed down through assessments.

Research findings

- Abel and colleagues found that whilst there are clearly some men that only abuse inside or outside families, some 65 per cent of intra-familial perpetrators also abused outside the family.

- Research by Abel *et al.*, (1987; 1988) has significantly influenced our approach to this group, as their work demonstrated that sexual perpetrators have a larger number of victims, acts, and multiple paraphilias than had previously been assumed. Few of the men were found to have a single paraphilia or to have only abused a single child. Indeed, extra-familial men were found to have an average of 19.8 victims (for those molesting a girl) and 150 victims (for those molesting a boy). The figures for incest perpetrators were significantly lower, with approximately two victims. However, over half or more of them were noted to have abused outside their families, and 70 to 95 per cent were noted to have engaged in another paraphilia, most commonly rape or exhibitionism.

- Earlier research (Abel, Mittleman and Becker, 1985) also established that many incest perpetrators who avowed no attraction to same sex children disclosed a history of abusing children of both sexes and 44 per cent of them also revealed an astonishing number of child victims in addition to numerous other paraphilias. Abel *et al.*, (1987) reinforced this cross-over between different sexually deviant behaviours. Indeed, they revealed that 23.3 per cent offended against both family and non-family members, 20 per cent offended against both sexes whilst 26 per cent offended against both sexes and 26 per cent used touching and non-touching behaviours.

- Freund and Blanchard (1986) also pointed out that those who have committed more than one type of sexual offence or deviation belonged to the group called 'courtship disorders': exhibitionism, voyeurism, obscene calls, toucherism, and sadistic rape. Freund *et al.*, (1983) found that 45 of the 86 exhibitionists, 11 of the 22 touchers, and two of the seven voyeurs reported co-occurrence of these deviations. Abel, Becker, Cunningham-Rathner, Mittleman, and Rouleau (1988) investigated 561 male sexual perpetrators and found that at least 72 per cent of them (other than transsexuals) reported additional deviations.

- Day (1994) reported that mentally handicapped perpetrators are more likely than non-handicapped perpetrators to commit offences against both males and females, against both same-age and older victims, and are less likely to know their victims, to commit violence, or to commit penile penetration of the vagina.

- The principal implications of crossover relate to the number of children at risk, the possibility of an indiscriminate sexual arousal, as well as the practical difficulties surrounding where they live and whom they see.

Issues to consider

Sexual abuse is not a random activity. It is overwhelmingly based within relationships where the perpetrator is in a trusted position of power and where the child is dependent, at least at times, on that person. The betrayal of loyalties by the perpetrator impacts on the mother who internalises the devastation of the betrayal, often leaving her truly damaged.

Workers need to explore how the perpetrator manipulated the situation and the mother's perceptions to facilitate the opportunity to abuse. The mother needs to understand how the perpetrator may have taught the child that the experiences they have undergone were normal and unimportant, and how the professionals will have advised them that they are significant and unusual. As such, the child has to adjust their viewpoint. The mother also needs to understand the processes by which the perpetrator has elicited victim loyalty: they often do not name their perpetrators.

Children who have been sexually abused will almost certainly have been told not to tell. Moreover, the perpetrators will have singled out the mother for exclusion. For example, threats will have been made about what will happen if they do tell, such as not being believed, being removed from home, or their pets or friends being hurt. Mothers need to be aware of the chameleon like nature of the perpetrator: they will be charming when they are in control, but they can change dramatically when the allegations are made, becoming bullying and intimidating.

The men who sexually abuse children are not weird and bizarre strangers who suddenly appear in the lives of children, nor are they outcasts of their communities. Instead, these men are often known and trusted fathers, husbands, and relatives or 'respectable' neighbours and friends. The information from perpetrators themselves shows their behaviour to require motivation, intention, and planning. It is unfair to expect mothers to know when these trusted individuals pose a serious threat to the safety of their children. As the earlier research material has clearly indicated, they were unaware on most occasions that their children were being victimised. Perpetrators are adept at prevailing upon the children to keep the sexual abuse a secret from the mothers by just telling them to do so, and, because of the unequal power relation between them, the children obey. They can also persuade the children from telling their mothers by using bribery and threats. The perpetrator, by undermining the relationship between the mother and the child, is able to maintain the child's loyalty after the abuse.

Mothers and victims of sexual abuse are rarely aware about the compulsivity and repetitiveness of sexual abuse: their behaviour is not an accident that happens to perpetrators. It is not an illness that descends on them and then mysteriously passes. It is not a behaviour that necessarily gets better over time.

Mother's Relationship with her Child/ren

Hubbard (1989) defined the mother-daughter relationship as any thoughts or feelings about the relationship, description of the quality of the relationship, or any activities engaged in together.

Incest produces a crisis in a mother's relationship with her child. They have to deal with the anger of the children. The victim will have ambiguous feelings about the perpetrator. While they may have been afraid and disliked the sexual contact from the outset, there will have been dependence and usually affection for the perpetrator in other contexts. The threat from the perpetrator that maintained the child's secrecy may have been that the mother would become very angry and the family would have been destroyed. From the child victim's perspective, a mother removing the children from the home or forcing the father to leave will be a fulfilment of that prophecy. In this confusion and pain, the child may project anger onto the mother, especially if the father has presented himself as a victim of circumstances. In the mother's decisions and actions following disclosure of the abuse, the child will again feel powerless, further fuelling anger toward the mother. The mother is likely to feel that she is being challenged 'on all fronts' when this anger is expressed. In her own stress and frustration, she may retaliate 'in kind' only to chastise herself even more severely after the fact (Ovaris, 1991).

The child's relationship with the mother is a critical one, within which there may be difficulties predating the abuse and which will be compounded if the abuse was intra-familial and of long duration. This relationship may have a distant or a conflicting quality, which militated against disclosure and allowed the abuse to continue. The child may previously have tried unsuccessfully to tell her parent about the abuse, and anger about a perceived lack of protection may only emerge after disclosure. The mother may harbour feelings of resentment against the child for attracting the perpetrator, or for 'causing' a separation from him which has physical, emotional or economic consequences for the whole family (Glaser and Frosh, 1988). These authors advocate intervention which aims to help both mother and child to express their feelings, ensuring that the child is protected from excessive parental anger, while being able to recognise the mother's predicament. Resolution requires the mother's open acceptance of the child's feelings, which may include some continuing fondness of the abuser. The mother's acknowledgement of their often inadvertent contribution to the child's emotional discomfort is part of the healing process. Bridging the distance that may have arisen between mother and child and enabling each to learn about and comprehend the feelings of the other is a process that can be substantially helped by the presence of two workers, with each adopting a supportive position for each participant and attempting to avoid mutual recriminations. The principal professional goal is the restoration of the mother-child relationship and not meeting the mother's needs, which may well emerge and highlight the necessity for further individual support.

Because the mother may well be in acute shock post-disclosure, this affects her availability for her children. Mothers who have been sexually abused themselves may have some difficulties relating to children. They may have lacked a good parenting model, they may have their own memories resurrected by the abuse, feeding their own neediness. They may turn to the child for support to deal with their distress, aggravating the child's sense of guilt about the abuse. They may also become over-protective of their own children. For example, keeping them in the house, not allowing them to do childhood things, ensuring the child has their body covered at all times, etc. Over-protectiveness may be most pronounced in mothers who see characteristics of themselves in the child.

Emotional sensitivity can be affected from the mother if the child's reaction to the sexual abuse does not conform to expectations. If the child does not show distress and reject the abuser, then this is confusing for her. However, they should be careful not to condemn the perpetrator as a person since the child may well have confused feelings about them.

Mothers need to acknowledge the impact on the child's self-esteem and they need to expect an angry response. Whilst anger can be a legitimate and positive expression of emotion and necessary for the child's emotional growth, it can be misdirected onto the non-abusing carer if the perpetrator is not there ('kick the cat' syndrome). The mother has to understand that the child needs to be angry in order to trust again, and it is comforting to know that the child has a relationship with the mother, which is worth being angry about. In time, the child may come to forgive the mother as they see her also as a mutual survivor. The child may well be angry with the mother for lots of reasons, such as for failing to protect her, for

looking the other way, for setting her up for the abuse, for blaming her, for not listening when she tried to tell the mother, for not believing her, for remaining with the perpetrator, or for not providing her with the necessary love and attention she needed. In lots of ways, the child has to be given free licence to work through all of these things in order to release the anger.

Tinling (1990) noted that victims often hold bitter, confused feelings against the mother, even more intense than those they hold against the father. She reviewed victim accounts of sexual abuse to identify several distinctive characteristics of the mothers: that they are in conflict, having misplaced priorities, being a chronic avoider, and perceived by victims as a hopeless victim herself. The victim often perceives the mother to have made destructive choices. The 'martyr' is the most commonly described type of mother by victims. Their goal is to attain nobility by silently enduring and suffering. The 'inadequate' mother, through her own default, gets others into her service. They manipulate their daughters into assuming the mother's responsibilities by the mother's inability to deal with the overwhelming position she is in or has put herself in.

As many victims believe their mother to have been aware of their sexual abuse, they may well be angry towards them. They may believe the lies the perpetrator told the child about the mother so they would be disliked. They may even have tried to give out 'indirect' messages (acting out or withdrawal). In sum, they may feel the mother approved of what happened. Mothers have to work against feeling jealous towards their daughter as this serves the perpetrator's motives, and the child may well choose him if faced with a choice.

The response of adult caretakers to abused children is critical to the child's perception of the experience (Adams-Tucker, 1982). In addition, having an opportunity to ventilate feelings about the abuse has been identified as central to the recovery process (Wyatt and Mickey, 1988). In this light, the mother's relationship with the child is going to be influenced by her reaction to the abuse disclosure or discovery.

Depression in either the child or the mother can lead to low levels of communication about anything. This lack of availability is often aggravated by a maternal preoccupation with personal survival where adult domestic violence, often to the point of repeated hospitalisation, is a feature of family life.

Mothers must be aware not to seek to apportion blame to others, particularly their children, for the sexual abuse and the grief that follows their loss of innocence.

Mothers have often been self-critical about their relationship with their children, as compared to that of their partner. This can be the product of a close father-child relationship on the surface, but which can mask a grooming process.

Research findings

Avery *et al.*, (1998) discovered a frequently profound bitterness of survivors of intra-familial abuse toward the non-abusing parent. The negative feelings expressed were often more severe toward the non-abusing parent than toward the perpetrator. The mother may well need to understand the child's feelings, particularly if they expect anger at the perpetrator, rather than the apparent attachment to him.

Burgess *et al.*, (1977) pointed to the feelings child victims will experience post-disclosure, and which need to be harnessed and understood by the mother if she is to enhance her relationships with the children. Perpetrators, if they are successful in gaining access to the child sexually, will continue to press for more activity with the child. For the perpetrator to keep his dominance and sexual control over the child, he must ensure that the secrecy of the behaviour is maintained. Thus, when the secret is disclosed, the tension surrounding the secret is broken and his power over the child is disrupted.

Gomes-Schwartz *et al.*, (1990) considered the mother's relationship with the child. They formed four scales made up of ratings of the mother's relationship with the child: 'caring', meaning that the mother displayed love and concern for the child; 'depending', meaning maternal intrusiveness and reliance upon the child as a source of support; 'burdened', meaning the mother was not emotionally available; and 'hostile', meaning the mother was angry at the child and saw her as bad. 97 per cent of all mothers had moderate to high caring attitudes towards their children. Yet 43 per cent did show some tendency to be dependent on the child and 41 per cent felt burdened. They also found positive correlation between caring relationships and level of concern and protection upon disclosure. Hostile relationships correlated negatively with concern and protection; they correlated positively with anger and with punishment toward the child upon disclosure. Burdened mothers tended to punish and be angry and not to protect. Depending mothers tended to express concern for themselves.

Fong and Walsh-Bowers (1998) found that almost all the mothers in their sample claimed that they had a better and closer relationship with their daughters after the disclosure.

Finkelhor (1984) found in his sample of college women that those who were at highest risk were the ones who said they were not close to their mother or received little affection from their mother. One hypothesis for this might be that when victimisation occurs, it alienates a girl from her parents. For example, because they have had to keep the abuse secret or because they felt betrayed by the failure of the parents to come to their support when they reveal it (Meiselman, 1978).

Rickford (1992) found that some women have great difficulty relating to the child physically—being unable to touch their child—and they need space to talk this through before looking at strategies to remedy this.

Meiselman (1978) found that three years after the incest had ended that 40 per cent of the victims continued to experience negative feelings towards their fathers, while 60 per cent were described as 'forgiving'. In contrast, 60 per cent of the mothers were definitely disliked by their daughters and only 40 per cent were regarded positively. Herman and Hirschman (1977) found that the daughters who perceived their mothers as weak, helpless, and masochistic women, could barely care for themselves, let alone their children.

Hooper (1992) highlighted two purposes for the child directing their anger towards their mother. First, anger at the mothers enables girls partially to break their own identification with their mothers, and hence with powerlessness, and to feel worthy of protection from abuse. Second, it is generally easier to direct anger at women than men.

Johnson (1992) identified two mother-daughter relationship patterns when talking to mothers: peer relationships and parent-child relationships.

1. Peer relationship patterns fell into two patterns, that of pals and rivals. When pals, they would share sexual jokes and sex education together, advise on how to dress and wear make-up, and generally acted as 'one of the gang'. When rivals, their relationship was characterised by estrangement and misunderstanding rather than malice or jealousy. Both experienced a peer relationship with their daughters. While they may not be true role reversal, they saw their daughters in adult roles in the father-daughter relationship and themselves more as child-wives to their husbands. In both family configurations, the mother was outside the boundary around their husband and daughter.

2. Mother–daughter, parent–child relationship patterns also fell into two patterns, loving-close, and strict-distant. In loving-close, both parents were overjoyed at the pleasure brought to them by the child, and this did not change as they got older. Indeed, they can view the child as mature and independent, but never parentified them or exchanged the parent role. The mother presents as more of a mother-wife than a child-wife and sees the daughter more as a peer to the husband than as an adult and herself as a mother to them both. In this family configuration the family boundary did not leave anyone outside, but enclosed all members in loving closeness. In the strict-distant, the mother is overprotective with her daughter because of her own childhood memories, fearing her daughter might do the same. The mother functioned here more as a mother-wife than as a child-wife and saw herself as a mother to both her daughter and her husband. She also saw her daughter as a child to her husband. In this family, the mother drew the boundary around herself and her daughter, leaving the father on the outside.

These findings confirm that mother-daughter relationships are complex. What is unclear is how the mother's portrayals of family relationships compare or differs from other family members.

Todd and Ellis (1992) found an enormous complexity in the mother-daughter relationship. Mothers struggled with their ambivalence towards the child, their anger and need for the allegations to be untrue alongside the fearful prospect of losing their man, their child, or both. The fact that mothers were thrown into turmoil or immobilised by their experiences inevitably has serious consequences for the mother-daughter relationship. Daughters are engaged in strategies, which will enable them to endure and survive their experiences. Mothers, on the other hand, have to negotiate a process of knowing and not knowing, of confronting the possibility that the man they married is molesting their child.

Wright (1991) found that there are consequences for the mother-daughter relationship of the perpetrator's removal from the home. They noted that one justification for removing him from the home is the hope that this will allow weak mother-daughter bonds to become stronger. Only two-fifths of the victims went on to establish healthier relationships with their mothers, with the remainder declining. They also found another change was the lack of control mothers experienced over their children. Where the mother and daughter had a history of strained or remote relationships and where mothers sometimes felt that they had something to make up to their daughters, maintaining effective parental control was difficult. In some cases, the male had been the disciplinarian in the family; whilst in some cases the mother was too overwhelmed with financial and emotional stress to be firm; whilst others became stronger than ever before and children were reacting to this new strength. Another consequence was that some children assumed a parent role (mild or moderate).

Issues to consider

Hall and Lloyd (1989) identified a number of issues for mothers and daughters (see Figure 30) which need to be acknowledged and then embraced in an agreed work programme.

The development of a trusting relationship with their mother is often the key to helping

Figure 30: Issues for mothers and daughters (Hall and Lloyd, 1989).

Mothers	Daughters
Acknowledging that the abuse has occurred.	Did she know about it? How could she not have known?
Feelings of guilt and failure to protect her child, of not being a good enough parent.	Why did she not see that something was wrong? What did she do/could she have done to stop it?
Vulnerability when confronted with the facts about the abuse.	May want to protect mother from details of the abuse.
Finds it difficult to cope with daughter's feelings.	May want to protect mother so disguises her true feelings.
Is she able to let her daughter know what it was like for her, especially in her relationship with the perpetrator.	May not want to hear. Finds it difficult to acknowledge mother's own difficulties.
Mother may have been abused by the same man.	Why didn't she protect me from him? She knew what he was like

the child recover from their experience of sexual abuse. This can take many forms, such as the establishment of flexible and negotiated routines in the home that they feel comfortable with, and which encourage physical comfort, emotional security, love, affection and belonging, achievement and self-esteem, and self-actualisation, to working with professionals to provide future safety, supports outside the home, and strategies for overcoming their trauma. Some agreements need to be reached about safety rules, such as it never being acceptable for the child to hurt themselves or others, it being important that the family share with each other their whereabouts, and that it is never right to keep secrets.

The ability of the mother to communicate with the child is central to achieving these goals, particularly since many victims are resistant to relationships, having experienced betrayal from the perpetrator. The crisis can provide the mother with the opportunity to engage with the child and connect with what they are experiencing, although it is also the time when they will feel most fearful about

making a mistake. It can open the door to emotional vulnerability that allows the child to accept the connection with the mother.

Workers need to get some sense of the quality of the mother's relationship with each of her children, and any positive or negative feelings around. It is important to note whether the mother can see the child as an individual having needs separate from the mother's and to assess the accuracy of the mother's perception of the child by comparing it to their own and that of others (Faller, 1988b). Where the mother is unable to emotionally support the child at all, then a period of separation may be indicated until she can.

Brown (1998) argued that it is important for the mother to appreciate that her relationship with the child may need to develop over time: it is easy for the mother and the child to become stuck in their relationship. It may be that the abuse has left the mother less able to express physical affection. This can be hard for the child, and be experienced as a sense of rejection and a confirmation of the stigma borne. There will be layers of different emotions for both parties in this relationship and many aspects of the abuse as well as the role of the mother may need to be examined repeatedly. Even where the child has disclosed to the mother, there may remain a residual tension about what has happened.

Workers may want to work with the child to enable them to tell their mother, thus increasing the availability of information, e.g. through a story or letter.

The mother and the children may need to set out a list of points describing how they see the mother-child relationship, the good and the bad, and how it may change for the worse or the better in the future. They then may move on to set out an action list of points they will change in the future, being realistic and setting small, attainable changes out first.

The needs of both the children and the mother need to be listed as they often conflict, and workers need to be alerted quickly to situations where they need to arbitrate and possibly conciliate.

Workers need to consider the answers to the following questions when talking with the mother and observing the mother and child together: what is the mother's response to the information around the sexual abuse: is she angry with the perpetrator or the child? Does she believe that this could have taken place? What is her attitude towards the child? The mother's responses will help the worker assess the mother's relationship with the victim and her ability to perceive the child's needs, which will probably be very different to her own and those of the perpetrator.

Knowledge of the Effects of Child Sexual Abuse on the Victims Generally, and Specifically to their Children (Empathy)

Once a child is safe, the mother will want to know the short and the long-term effects of the sexual abuse. Hooper (1989) found that many of the mothers in her sample were unaware about the effects of sexual abuse, leaving them with vague worries and little idea of how to help. Common questions from mothers will concern their children's sexual development, the impact on their current and future relationships with adults and other children, and the duration of current symptoms of stress (such as bedwetting, nightmares, etc.). Workers

need to provide mothers with this information and also the stages of their child's recovery.

Although there is ample evidence about the *potential* negative impacts of sexual abuse on the victim, such victimisation does *not necessarily* have inevitable or massive impact on victims. There is no universal or uniform impact of child sexual abuse and no guarantee that any one person will develop any post-traumatic responses. Some children do not show any outward signs of harm or distress. The word asymptomatic is used to describe such children. In fact, up to 40 per cent of sexually abused children did not appear to have any of the expected abuse-related problems in several studies (such as Kendall-Tackett *et al.*, 1993). This does not mean that the child is not suffering. Some children who keep the abuse 'bottled up' inside may become symptomatic at some future date.

It is important that we advise mothers of potential variance between the consequences on male and female victims. For some time, much of the information derived from work with female victims (set out below) and only in more recent times are we finding the particular issues that impact on the male victim (addressed later).

Short-term effects of sexual abuse

These may vary from child to child, although certain symptoms may be seen in many victims. Short-term symptoms are usually the result of the anxiety, stress, and fear caused by the abuse. They include:

Anxiety: is a state of heightened emotional arousal. The abused child may be preoccupied and worried about the abuse and unable to stop thinking about it.

Fear: every threat possible has been made to children to keep them quiet. The fear induced by such threats is responsible for much of the child's anxiety.

Nightmares and sleep problems: are often a terrifying re-enactment of the abuse or of dreams involving monsters of other frightening events. Children may stay awake to prevent any recurrence of the abuse.

Acting out and general misbehaviour: sexually abused children are often seriously distressed and their unhappiness can lead to acting out and misbehaviour at home and in school. Their academic performance may deteriorate. Older children may run away, abuse drugs or alcohol, become promiscuous, or engage in illegal conduct.

Withdrawal: Some children withdraw rather than acting out, retreating into their own shells.

Regression: to an earlier stage of development, such as returning to wetting the bed.

Poor self-concept: occurs when they think the abuse was their fault and they feel damaged by that as well as the abuse itself.

Depression: Sexual abuse makes children sad. For some children, they become clinically depressed and this is a serious psychiatric problem that goes beyond transitory sadness.

Inappropriate sexual behaviour: some children develop sexually developmentally inappropriate behaviour as a result of their sexual abuse.

Post-traumatic stress disorder: children with symptoms of PTSD may repetitively act out their abuse in play. They may have stomach aches and headaches. They try to avoid people and things that remind them of the abuse (Myers, 1997: pp30–2).

Long-term effects of child sexual abuse

A great number of difficulties may lie ahead for children who have been sexually abused. The following information highlights just how sexual abuse can take its toll in the victim's lives. Briere (1992) has set out seven psychological disturbances found in adult and adolescent survivors:

Post-traumatic stress disorder: as above.

Cognitive distortions: embrace the feelings of helplessness, chronic danger, self-deprecation and pessimism about the future.

Dissociation: is a defensive disruption in the normally occurring connections between feelings, thoughts, behaviour and memories, consciously or unconsciously invoked in order to reduce psychological distress.

Altered emotionality: includes depression, fear and anxiety.

Impaired self-reference: refers to the difficulties the victims' experience relating to themselves.

Disturbed relatedness: includes problems with interpersonal relationships, especially intimate and sexual.

Avoidance: many adults avoid pain by engaging in behaviours that consciously or unconsciously lessen their distress. These include the use of alcohol, drugs, self-mutilation, compulsive sexual behaviour, and eating disorders.

Mothers do need to be advised that no-one has the ability to accurately predict the long-term consequences of abuse, and that there is a great risk of attributing all the problems of the abused child on to the sexual abuse. They need to hear that most victims can and do recover to become survivors.

The impact of sexual abuse on male victims

It is important to record at the start of this section that there are a great many similarities between male and female victims of child sexual abuse: both are likely to be abused by older males or siblings, and the range of the sexual assaults are similar; both are equally reluctant to report the abuse; both are equally fearful of the disclosure and its aftermath; both exhibit acute problems from the effects of the abuse; and both need considerable support to recover from their experiences.

Bolton *et al.*, (1989) noted that male victims are less likely to report their sexual abuse, thus creating a situation of self-victimisation for themselves. The least reported abuse is actually that by their mothers, although the focus of much writing is on the effects of abuse by other men. If and when they disclose their abuse, this may be followed by them minimising the impact to distance themselves from homosexual labelling whilst preserving their macho image. This feeds the public perception of the abuse being less traumatic than that for females. Male children are often sexually abused more outside the family (Finkelhor, 1984) and in the presence of other victims. Coercion becomes a very real feature for older male victims.

Although males and females suffer from the same long-term effects, males tend to react somewhat differently from females to the abuse itself. This is because we raise boys and girls differently, have different expectations of them, and tend to view male and female victims slightly differently. Males are supposed to be dominant and aggressive, while females are traditionally viewed as submissive and passive. We can have more difficulty empathising with male victims, as we believe they should protect themselves in any situation, and any failure to do so is seen as a sign of weakness. This ostensibly creates a situation in which the male victim of child sexual abuse is revictimised by his culture and his own tendency to be critical of himself. He may see himself as a coward for allowing it to happen in the first place and for not avenging the crime. Many male victims may feel they did something to encourage the advances and this can lead to them questioning their sexual orientation. Homosexuality is an added burden in today's society. Some males are unable to define themselves as sexual beings at all, because sexuality has become associated with abuse in their minds. If the perpetrator was their role-model then they may conclude that 'being a man' means being abusive. They may feel less masculine than other males, and believe that no female would want to know them now. Adult male victims can have a variety of sexual problems, including an inability to achieve or maintain an erection, premature ejaculation, fears of specific sexual acts, particularly those performed on them. Some become sexually controlling of women and become daredevils, risking their lives to prove their manhood.

Unless a boy who has been sexually abused by a man also had access to non-abusing males, they may assume that all males become perpetrators as they grow up. They may want to convince themselves that they have not been damaged by what would be considered by many to be a homosexual encounter, and he may then become deliberately sexually aggressive towards women. Fears about issues relating to homosexuality are thought to be one of the main reasons boys are reluctant to disclose sexual abuse by men, despite that there is a high degree of crossover between gender.

Friedrich *et al.*, (1986) found that boy and girl victims exhibit different responses to abuse and have different factors associated with

severe effects. For boys the risk factors are abuse of a longer duration, a closer relationship between the perpetrator and the victim, and a longer duration since the last incident. For girls, the risk factors are abuse which is more frequent, more severe, and which involves a closer relationship between the perpetrator and the victim.

Briere (1992) writes that:

> *Treatment should also address sex differences in how child abuse is cognitively processed. Because boys and men are expected to be strong and aggressive, victimisation may be more of a sex role violation for them than it is for girls and women. This additional trauma can result in somewhat different cognitive responses to abuse for male and female survivors… Many sexually abused males have sexual concerns related to theory molestation. Heterosexual boys and men may believe that childhood sexual abuse by another male has caused them to be latently homosexual—a fear that, in a culture as homophobic as ours, may result in compensatory masculinity or over-involvement in heterosexual activity. Conversely, homosexual men who were sexually abused by males may be concerned that their sexual orientation somehow caused them to be abused by men, or that their abuse somehow caused them to homosexual conclusions that can lead to feelings of guilt, shame and self-betrayal.*

Much of the research on the effects of sexual abuse focus on the sequels in women and not men. It is important to note the particular issues as they differentially impact on male victims. Research has shown that only one in three boys with a history of child sexual abuse disclose in comparison to two in five girls (Finklehor, Hotaling, Lewis and Smith, 1990). Finkelhor (1979) postulates that our society casts men as sexually active and women as sexually passive, thus attributing more consent and less exploitation into male victims. Indeed, Pierce and Pierce (1985) in a sample of sexual abuse victims found that 12 per cent of boys compared to 3 per cent of girls were believed to have encouraged their sexual abuse.

Lessons for professionals

Workers need to have some understanding and awareness about the impact of socialisation on the possible presentation of boys, its effects on victims and thus indicators; the impact dimensions peculiar to male victims; the need to address their potential to become

Figure 31: The short-term effects of sexual abuse on males.

Initial effect categories	Presenting symptoms
Emotional and psychological distress (similar to females)	• Fear • Problems with self-concept and self-esteem • Guilt and shame • Marked anxiety • Depression • Sleep disturbance • Withdrawal and isolation • Anger and aggressiveness • Suicidality • Dependency
Behaviour problems	• Homophobic concerns • Aggressive and controlling behaviour • Infantile behaviour • Paranoid or phobic behaviour • Sexual language and behaviours • Dreams of being chased, punished, or isolated • Body image concerns • Setting fires • Running away • Failure to develop trust and intimacy • Enuresis and encopresis • Prostitution • Suicide attempts or ideation • Hyperactivity • Regressive behaviours (thumb sucking) • Declining school performance and school avoidance • Drug and alcohol abuse • Delinquency
Sexual problems and concerns	• Confusion or anxiety over sexual identity • Inappropriate attempts to reassert masculinity • Recapitulation of the victimising experience • Sexualised behaviour • Difficulties with interpersonal relationships • Problems with sexual performance

Figure 32: The long-term effects of sexual abuse on males.

Subsequent effect categories	Presenting symptoms
Emotional and psychological disorders	• Anger or rage • Self-concept or self-esteem problems • Relationship problems • Suicidality • Depression • Self-mutilation • Fantasies of retribution • Focus on confrontation • Shame • Inability to protect themselves
Relationship difficulties	• Difficulties in establishing and maintaining intimate relationships • Difficulties talking about feelings • Promiscuity/unfaithfulness • Inability to form relationships with other men • Involvement in abusive relationships in adulthood
Sexuality and sexual problems	• Dissatisfaction with sexual interactions • Avoidance of sexual interactions • Poor sexual self-esteem • Preoccupation with sexual thoughts • Fascination with pornography • Compulsive masturbation • Multiple sexual partners • Sexual dysfunction (difficulties with erections; impotence; ejaculatory problems, etc.) • Inhibited sexual desire • Prostitution
Sexual orientation	• Masculine identity confusion • Sexual identity confusion • Homosexuality
Addictive behaviours	• Chemical dependency • Alcohol use • Compulsive overeating • Compulsive overworking • Compulsive spending • Compulsive sexual behaviour • Compulsive relationships
Cyclical victimisation	• Sexually abusive behaviours towards others

perpetrators; and the need to provide them with considerable time as well as written information about others so they do not feel alone in their journey towards recovery.

Theoretical Models

Traumagenic dynamics

This model was developed by Finkelhor and Browne (1985; 1986; 1988) and is probably the most influential and important framework for understanding the impact of sexual abuse. It is an eclectic, comprehensive model that suggests a variety of different dynamics to account for the variety of different types of symptoms (Finkelhor, 1988: p68). They offer us four traumagenic (trauma-causing) dynamics, defined as:

> ...*an experience that alters a child's cognitive or emotional orientation to the world and causes trauma by distorting the child's self-concept, worldview, or affective capacities.*
>
> (Finkelhor, 1988: p68)

The model allows sexual abuse to be conceptualised as a situation or a process rather than simply as an event, and this is important as different parts of the process contribute different traumagenic dynamics. The latter are not restricted to one part of the process, operating before, during, and after the sexual contact. Most of the effects that have been noted in the literature can be conveniently categorised and explained by one or two of the dynamics. Whilst the fit is not perfect, it does offer a plausible framework for the variety and diversity of impacts noted (Finkelhor and Browne, 1988: p77). They also note that different traumagenic dynamics lead to different types of trauma, and that each of the dynamics themselves are ongoing processes.

The experiences of sexual abuse can be analysed in terms of four traumagenic dynamics: traumatic sexualisation; betrayal; powerlessness; and stigmatisation. Each dynamic is a clustering of injurious influences with a common theme. There are no direct correlates between effects and dynamics, although there are many affinities. The issue of gender is an important one here, given the differential impact that victims experience. As always, there are differing views on impact across the sexes. Barbaree, Hudson and Seto (1993) in a review of the literature found the effects to be broadly similar whether the victim is male or female (p8), although Friedrich (1988) found real differences, finding that boys tend to externalise their responses whilst girls internalise theirs. Girls who do not follow this pattern tend to have a close relationship with the perpetrator and have suffered a higher frequency and more serious forms of sexual abuse (Print and Dey, 1992). Whatever is accepted, one needs to acknowledge that the knowledge base is drawn almost entirely from female victims. Mendel (1995) argued that whilst it seems reasonable to hypothesise that the four traumagenic dynamics are present in male victims, it is likely that several differences exist between males and females in terms of the salience or potency of the four: it would appear that the degree of stigmatisation surrounding male sexual victimisation is far greater than that experienced by females, and the dynamic of powerlessness holds different meanings for each sex, standing at odds with the male role expectation of powerful competence and self-reliance (p77).

Having reviewed the positive aims of the model, let us move on to consider the individual traumagenic dynamics individually and in more detail:

1. *Traumatic sexualisation:*

was defined by Finkelhor and Browne (1986) as:

> *A process in which a child's sexuality (including both sexual feelings and sexual attitudes) is shaped in a developmentally inappropriate and interpersonally dysfunctional fashion as a result of the sexual abuse.*
>
> (p181)

Finkelhor (1988) offered us several distinct processes, which combine to contribute to traumatic sexualisation:

- Sexually abused children are often rewarded, by perpetrators, for sexual behaviour that is inappropriate to their level of development.

- Because of the rewards, sexually abused children learn to use sexual behaviour, appropriate or inappropriate, as a strategy for manipulating others to get their needs met.

- Because of the attention that they receive, certain parts of sexually abused children's anatomy becomes fetishised and given distorted importance and meaning.
- Children become confused and acquire outright misconceptions about sexual behaviour and sexual morality as a result of things that perpetrators tell them or ways that they behave.
- A child's sexuality can become traumatised when frightening and unpleasant memories become associated in the child's mind with sexual activity (p69).

Finkelhor noted that these were among the most important of the dynamics that traumatise a child's sexual capacities. He also noted that they are among the dynamics unique to sexual abuse. We have to accept that experiences of sexual abuse will vary dramatically in terms of the amount and kind of traumatic sexualisation that they provoke (Finkelhor and Browne, 1986). The same authors went on in a later article (1988) to explore the debate on what kinds of abuse are more or less traumagenic (p60). Groth (1978) contends that sexual abuse generates the greatest trauma when:

- it continues over a long period of time
- it occurs with a closely related person
- it involves penetration
- it is supported by aggression

There are several other important considerations that should be added to this list:

- evoking a sexual response from the child
- it depends on the degree of the child's understanding (Finkelhor and Browne, 1986: p182)
- non-disclosure of the abuse (Finkelhor, 1979)
- the age of the victim (Finkelhor and Browne, 1988: p61)
- the gender of the perpetrator (males being the most traumatic) (Russell, 1986)
- the age of the perpetrator—with adults being more traumatic than juveniles (Russell, 1986)
- parental reaction—is more traumatic

when negative (Finkelhor and Browne, 1986: p61)
- removal of the victim from their home

Sexual abuse experiences can vary dramatically in terms of the amount and kind of traumatic sexualisation they provoke. It is plausible to hypothesise that it is associated with impacts on sexual behaviour, where the effects would include sexual dysfunctions, promiscuity, sexual anxiety, and low sexual self-esteem (Finkelhor and Browne, 1988: p 65). Children who have been traumatically sexualised emerge from their experiences with inappropriate repertoires of sexual behaviour, and their experiences may initiate the motivation to abuse. Child sexual abuse has the capacity to arouse juveniles sexually before they have the appropriate developmental capacity to cope. Certainly sexual aggression can present as a behavioural manifestation of early traumatic sexualisation (Elliott and Butler, 1994).

2. Betrayal:

Refers to the dynamic in which children discover that someone on whom they are vitally dependent has caused them harm, this could be the actions of the abuser through their manipulation or lies, or by the failure to protect or believe the victim by a family member.

(Finkelhor and Browne, 1986: p182)

Betrayal is present to some degree in most abuse situations, and can operate in several ways e.g. at the time of the abuse itself or belatedly in the realisation that they were tricked into doing something bad. Abuse by family members or trusted persons have the greatest potential for betrayal, particularly when the closeness of the relationship is considered. Regardless of the relationship, the degree of harm experienced by the child will be related to how taken-in they feel by the abuse (Finkelhor, 1988: p70), as well as the family's response to the disclosure. Where the child is disbelieved, blamed or ostracised, the degree of betrayal will be perceived to be higher than those who were supported (Finkelhor and Browne, 1986: p183). The greatest sense of betrayal often comes when the mother's are unwilling or unable to believe and protect them. Even where parents do believe and support the child, they may still feel betrayed as they assumed that they were capable of warding off all harm (Finkelhor, 1988: p70).

Finkelhor and Browne (1988) linked this factor with effects such as depression, dependency in extreme forms, impaired ability to trust and to judge the trustworthiness of others, and anger. Some of the manifestations of these might be a vulnerability to subsequent abuse and exploitation (p65).

3. Powerlessness:

> *Refers to the process in which the child's will, desires, and sense of efficacy are continually contravened.*
> (Finkelhor and Browne, 1986: p183)

Finkelhor (1988) argued that there were two main components to the traumagenic dynamics of powerlessness:

- A child's will and wishes are repeatedly overruled and frustrated.
- The child experiences the threat of injury or annihilation (p71).

Many aspects of the sexual abuse experience can contribute to powerlessness, but certain of them are particularly significant and particularly common:

- A basic kind of powerlessness occurs when a child's fantasy and body space are repeatedly invaded against their will, regardless of whether this occurs through force or deceit. The latter may exacerbate the powerlessness experienced.
- The experience of violence, coercion and a threat to life is the second core form of powerlessness, which is again exacerbated and reinforced when their attempts to halt the abuse are frustrated. It is increased when the child feels fear, and they are unable to make adults understand or believe what is happening, or when they realise how conditions of dependency have them trapped in the situation. Children are arguably powerless whether or not force is used (Finkelhor and Browne, 1986: p183). Ongoing vulnerability, entrapment, and the associated emotions of fear and anxiety also contribute to the dynamic (Finkelhor, 1988: p72).

Clearly, the dynamic of powerlessness distorts the child's sense of ability to control

his or her own life (Finkelhor, 1988: p68). This can be offset by trying to give them some say in the way in which the abuse ends. Finkelhor and Browne (1988) relate this factor to various manifestations, which include nightmares, somatic complaints, depression, running away, school problems, employment problems, vulnerability to subsequent victimisation, aggressive behaviour, delinquency, and/or becoming a perpetrator (p68).

4. Stigmatisation:

> *Refers to the negative connotations (e.g. badness, shame and guilt) that are communicated to the child in the surrounding experiences of molestation and that then become incorporated into the child's self-image.*
> (Finkelhor and Browne, 1986: p184)

These negative messages are communicated in several ways:

- They can come directly from the perpetrator, who may blame the victim ('you seduced me') or denigrate ('you bitch') or shame the victim about the behaviour.
- From attitudes that the victim hears from other persons in the family or community, or from people in their environment who may impute other negative characteristics to the victim (loose morals, spoiled goods, or 'queer' in the case of boys) as a result of the abuse.
- Perpetrators may say it indirectly through their furtiveness and pressures for secrecy.
- Stigmatisation may grow out of the child's prior knowledge or sense that the activity is considered deviant and taboo.
- It is reinforced if, after disclosure, people react with shock or hysteria or blame the child for what has transpired (Finkelhor and Browne, 1988: pp64–5).

The dynamic of stigmatisation clearly distorts the child's sense of his or her own value of worth (Finkelhor, 1988: p68). It occurs in various degrees in different abuse situations. We therefore need to consider this as a possibility in each presented case. An example would be that some are told that it is their fault, whilst others are not (Finkelhor and

Browne, 1988: pp64–5). Others may be too young to have much awareness of social attitudes and thus suffer little stigmatisation as a result. Others may have to manage powerful religious and cultural taboos on top of the usual stigma. Having to retain the abuse as a secret may increase the sense of stigma, since it reinforces the sense of being different. In contrast, children who find out that such things happen to many children may have some of their stigma assuaged (Finkelhor and Browne, 1988: p64). These authors relate this dynamic to long-term effects such as guilt, poor self-esteem, a sense of differentness and isolation, and secondary problems such as drug and alcohol abuse, criminal involvement, suicidal ideation, and attempts (p65). Any accommodation of the perpetrator's own

distorted rationalisations can lead to the victim's personal stigmatisation (Ryan, 1991: p166).

A Practical Framework
Ten impact areas (Porter et al., 1982)

The following framework highlighting the ten impact areas has been very influential in the field of practice (see Figure 33). The authors note that the first five impact areas are likely to affect all children who have been sexually abused, regardless of the identity of the perpetrator. The last five issues are much more likely from intra-familial sexual abuse victims, although they cannot be excluded from other groups.

Figure 33: Ten impact areas (from Porter *et al.*, 1982).

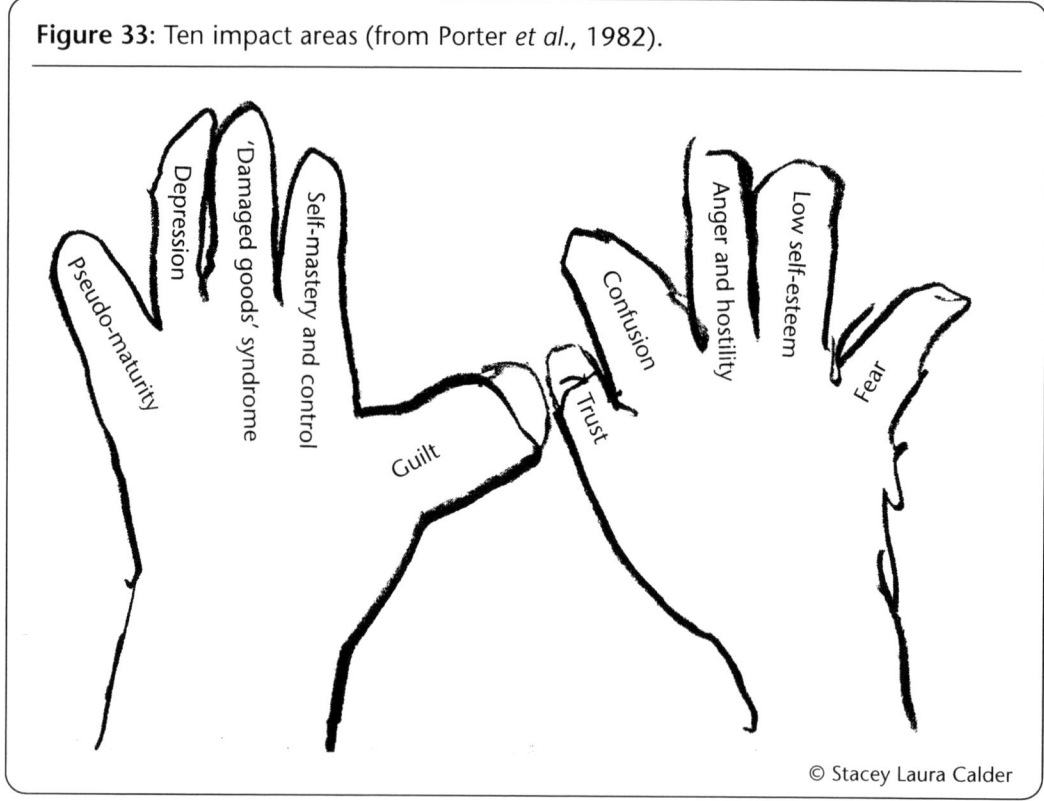

'Damaged goods' syndrome

In most cases, a child victim of sexual abuse feels damaged by their experiences. The 'damaged goods' syndrome is an amalgam of reactions:

- physical injury or fear of physical damage
- societal responses, particularly those of the immediate family who may reinforce the victim's feelings of damage

Guilt

Some sexually abused children do not feel guilty about their behaviour prior to the disclosure of the secret of the sexual activity. However, intense guilt feelings following disclosure of sexual abuse are practically a universal victim response. Children who have been sexually abused usually experience guilt on three levels:

1. responsibility for the sexual behaviour
2. responsibility for the disclosure
3. responsibility for the disruption to all the family members

Fear

All child victims of sexual abuse can be expected to be fearful of the consequences of the sexual activity as well as the disclosure. Child victims may also fear subsequent episodes of sexual abuse both before and after the disclosure as well as reprisals by the perpetrator after disclosure. These fears may be expressed on a conscious level or they may be manifested by sleep disturbance, especially in the form of nightmares.

Depression

Nearly all victims will exhibit some symptoms of depression after the disclosure of sexual abuse. Children who are victims of ongoing sexual abuse may appear depressed prior to disclosure as well. There may be overt signs of depression with the child appearing sad, subdued, or withdrawn. Or it may be masked and expressed as complaints of fatigue or physical illness. Some children may act out their despair with self-mutilation or suicide attempts.

Low self-esteem and poor social skills

Fear of physical injury, societal response to the sexually abused child, experiencing guilt and shame for participating in the sexual behaviour, for disclosure and the subsequent disruption—all these feelings tend to undermine the victim's self-esteem. Low self-esteem combined with a feeling of being somehow spoiled or damaged in turn tend to undermine the child's self-confidence. Many victims of intra-familial child sexual abuse have been pressured by their parents to limit outside relationships and to depend only upon interaction with other family members to meet their social needs: thus causing them to possess few social skills. This is aggravated further if they have attempted, and failed, to make friends of the same age band. Victims often feel helpless and are rarely assertive on their own behalf. They also often describe themselves in derogatory terms. Some find themselves so unappealing that they will initiate a series of sexual relationships to prove they are 'desirable'.

Repressed anger and hostility

Although they may appear outwardly passive and compliant, most sexual abuse victims are inwardly seething with anger and hostility. They are angry at the perpetrators for abusing them; they are angry with non-abusing parents for their failure to protect; they may be angry at neighbours, extended family and friends, possibly for their responses to the disclosure. In most cases, the anger is repressed rather than expressed or acted out. It may be characterised by depression or withdrawal, and occasionally in psychotic symptomatology.

Inability to trust

A child who has been sexually victimised by a known and trusted person can be expected to have difficulty in developing trusting relationships thereafter. The degree of impairment will depend on a variety of factors which might include:

- The identity of the perpetrator.
- The relationship between the victim and the perpetrator.
- The age of the young person when the abuse began and the duration of the abuse.
- The extent of the abuse.
- The type of sexual activity involved in the abuse.
- The degree of pleasure or discomfort experienced as a result of the abuse.
- The degree of force used to coerce the child.
- How others responded to the child's disclosure.
- The support persons that were available to the child post-disclosure.
- The point at which the abuse was disclosed.
- The personality structure and coping style of the victim (adapted from Tower, 1989).

The significance of these will vary from child to child. Frequently, the child's inability to trust is a direct consequence of broken promises from the perpetrator and others. No two children are alike and thus every child's reaction to their experiences of abuse will be unique. One child may fall apart whilst another will not.

Blurred role boundaries and role confusion

Child sexual abuse is disorientating because the victims frequently experience role confusion due to the inevitable blurring of role boundaries between the perpetrator and the child. For an adult who occupies a power position to turn to a relatively powerless child for a sexual relationship implies a profound disregard for the usual societal role boundaries. Although the sexual activity is primarily in the service of non-sexual needs, the premature and inappropriate sexual experience with an adult generates a great deal of role confusion for the child victim. If the adult is a parent then the role confusion is magnified. Blurred boundaries in incestuous families also tends to increase the likelihood

that sexual abuse will occur since more opportunities for sexual abuse are thereby created and the stage is set for incest.

Pseudomaturity and failure to complete developmental tasks

Child sexual abuse is disruptive because the extensive stimulation and preoccupation with the sexual relationship tends to interfere with the accomplishment of age-appropriate developmental tasks of childhood and adolescence. In addition, role confusion often leads to the child's premature assumption of an adult role in the incestuous family. As sexually abused children assume more adult responsibilities, the gap widens even further between them and their peers. If this is identified by peers then this isolation becomes permanent.

Frameworks for Understanding the Process of Sexual Abuse

The sexual abuse of children follows a predictable pattern of stages or phases, and mothers will have an increased ability to understand the impact of sexual abuse when they understand the process through which sexual abuse usually progresses. It will also help them to understand why it is often so difficult for the child to tell.

The child sexual abuse accommodation syndrome (Summit, 1983)

The syndrome includes five categories, two of which are preconditions to the occurrence of sexual abuse and define basic childhood vulnerability, whilst the remaining three are sequential contingencies following sexual abuse.

Secrecy

Sexual abuse mostly occurs when the perpetrator and the child are alone and it must never be shared with anyone else. The perpetrator often attaches a danger to breaking this secrecy, such as 'Do not tell your mother: she will…(hate you, kill you, send me away, etc.)'.

This usually alerts the victim to the fact that this is something bad and dangerous. Unless the victim can find some permission and power to share the secret and unless there is the possibility of an engaging, non-punitive response to disclosure, the child is likely to spend a lifetime in what comes to be a self-imposed exile from intimacy, trust and self-validation.

Helplessness

Children are basically helpless within authoritarian relationships. They are advised to avoid the attention of strangers, but are required to be obedient and affectionate with any adult entrusted with their care. This is ironic given that children are three times more likely to be harmed by a trusted adult than a stranger. The fact that the adult is often in a trusted and loving position only increases the imbalance of power. Children cannot consent to such a sexual relationship, and it is unfair to expect them to resist the abuse given the difference in size and strength. Children are powerless in these situations.

Entrapment and accommodation

Once sexual abuse has started, it frequently assumes a compulsive, addictive pattern and continues over a period of time, often until they are autonomous or until discovery. Since few cases are believed to come to the attention of family or professionals, the only healthy option for the victim is to learn to accept the situation and survive. They learn to accommodate the sexual abuse, which frequently escalates and this is coupled with a realisation by the victim of the betrayal from the perpetrator. They do so by employing a number of accommodation mechanisms which might include delinquency, self-mutilation and concealing any sign of conflict or distress.

Delayed, conflicted and unconvincing disclosure

However the sexual abuse comes to light, the child has to cope with the process of investigation, either by the family or by professionals, and the subsequent consequences of the disclosure/discovery.

There are often many barriers to belief of the allegations, particularly that the abuse has been going on for some time and they never reported it. How could the child wait so long before telling their mother? The perpetrator is rarely successfully prosecuted or convicted, and some children may be removed from home. Mothers and workers need to assume a position of believing, accepting, supporting and protecting the child.

Retraction

Whatever a child says about sexual abuse, they are likely to reverse it. They experience guilt if the family has disintegrated and the outcome is a reflection of the perpetrator's threats. They frequently bear the responsibility for the abuse and the outcome. As a result, they become aware that it is better to capitulate and restore a lie for the sake of the family. For many, a retraction of the allegations follows. The lie carries more credibility than the most explicit claims of incestuous entrapment, restoring the precarious equilibrium in the family. The child learns not to complain, and the adults learn not to listen. The professionals learn not to believe rebellious children who try to use their sexual power to destroy 'well-meaning parents'.

Children are thought to recant either because they have been subjected to pressure from the perpetrator or family members or because their report has produced negative consequences to themselves or others. Many children report fears about telling or regret the disclosure because of the outcome (Sauzier, 1989). Even when children do report abuse that is later confirmed, their accounts frequently are marked with inconsistencies and tentativeness (Sorenson and Snow, 1991). Recantation can occur in between one-fifth (Sorenson and Snow, 1991) to one-third of cases (Sahd, 1980). Whilst not diagnostic of abuse, recantation is a typical reaction of a child who has been abused and has disclosed the abuse.

Issues to consider

Whilst information on the impact of sexual abuse on children is important, workers need to establish whether the mother can empathise with her children. Victim empathy does not just happen, it must be learned by the mother feeling deeply and paying very close attention to the real feelings of others.

Get them to think about things from their victim's perspective. Why did the perpetrator do what he did?

Get them to list the difficulties they might have as they work on developing empathy. What are the things about them, their feelings and attitudes, their circumstances and life situation right now that might be roadblocks to developing empathy?

The mother will probably need basic information about what is meant by sexual abuse, what is known about its effects, the way that children retract as part of the process, etc. in order to enable them to understand the situation and judge their response.

Get the mother to look at the effects of sexual abuse as set out in this component and get her to tick off or detail those that apply to her child, and herself if she is a victim of sexual abuse.

Get the mother to write an account of how the sexual abuse has affected the child, the siblings and herself.

Siblings

Siblings are often a neglected group. It is important that professionals recognise how greatly the siblings, as secondary victims, are affected, in order that we may appreciate their need for and use of survival strategies. Workers first need to establish the degree to which the siblings may have been aware of the sexual abuse. They may do this by talking with the children or by exploring their behaviour patterns previously and now. These may give some indication as to whether they were abused themselves or whether they may have witnessed the abuse. Both may result in the same range of responses being noted.

It is important to establish whether a sibling has been the first to learn about the sexual abuse, and whether this was from the victim, or from an adult using them as a secondary mechanism of silence. If they are unaware, then the mother needs to be involved in telling them, as this allows them to make some sense of the disruption as well as empowering them to act if the perpetrator acts inappropriately towards them—either in contact or if eventually returned to the family. Talking to

the children has to be age-appropriate and in ways they understand (using terminology they are familiar with). It can then lead into useful discussions around secrecy, privacy and confidentiality (Smith, 1994) (see self-protection component later).

If the perpetrator has moved out of the home whilst the situation is being investigated, then there should be serious consideration as to telling them why: in an age-appropriate fashion. There may be consequences to this, in that the victim may be blamed. This is more likely where the mother has adopted this position. We cannot discount that the siblings also have been sexually abused but have chosen not to disclose that information at this stage. This can provide some insight into the strong reactions exhibited by siblings.

Siblings may well feel responsible or guilty concerning the abuse for several reasons: they knew what was going on and felt they should have told to stop the abuse continuing; they may have repeatedly breathed a sigh of relief when the victim was chosen rather than themselves; they may also have been jealous by the attention the abuser gave to the victim; or they may have been angry with the victim and felt that they deserved the abuse.

Research findings

Anthony and Watkeys (1991) found that, of the siblings in their sample who were investigated because of residing with an alleged perpetrator or having a victim sibling, over half had been abused compared to eight per cent who had been harmed in the home of the alleged perpetrator. Overall, this may be considered as an indication that siblings of abused children must be treated as possible victims and as such included in the investigation and assessment.

Attention must be given to the needs of children within the family who may not have been sexually victimised, but who suffered the consequences of disordered family dynamics before and after revelation. For example, there may be problems about relating to each other, role reversals, collusion, secrets, etc. The results for other siblings can be numerous. Rivalry and jealousy may result from all children in the family craving love and attention, and not realising the price of special favours. Collusion may result when other children are socialised to be the next victim; or they may experience a combination of guilt and gratitude that they were not chosen. A climate of premature sexual stimulation within the family may result in the children being more susceptible to abuse by older persons outside the family (Bagley and King, 1990).

The other children in the family may feel different from the child who has been abused and perhaps begin to act distant, jealous, because the victim sibling is getting so much attention now, or otherwise differently than before. Depending on the age and knowledge of the other children, they may also exhibit confusion over what is happening. If they are very young, they may not grasp what has happened, even if it is explained to them. If the siblings identify strongly with the victim, then they will exhibit traumatic responses similar to the victim. Talking to them and giving them appropriate information is important. They need to be updated as new events occur to help them understand why so much attention is focused on their sibling. They need to understand the necessity to be especially kind to the victim at this juncture (Byerly, 1992).

Monahan (1997) studied the attributions of incestuously abused and non-abused sisters. She explored the attributions of participants regarding the general sibling group, victim selection and non-selection, as well as attributions regarding jealousy, protection, and guilt within the sister relationship. She found that all participants harboured ambivalent feelings such as relief and then guilt for not being chosen for the abuse, and then anger at the targeted sister. Competition and antagonism were commonplace in a chaotic environment filled with distance, violence, and unpredictability. All participants presented clear perceptions of the family as dysfunctional and, very often, pathological. They articulated the following regarding the context of the abuse in their family:

- Attributions regarding context: siblings were often totally unaware of the nature of the abuse being endured. There were often reports of solidarity among the siblings, even though it was unison against an unspoken enemy. Several participants remembered having their sister stand guard at the bed until she fell asleep in a valiant effort to protect her from her father.

- Attributions regarding victim selection: were related to factors such as parenting perceptions of the child, inviting self-blame from many victims, compared to 'incest envy' from the non-abused siblings because of their 'special status'.

- Attributions regarding the sister relationship: all indicated that the incest had affected their sister relationship in some way, with many spending a great deal of time thinking about how much their relationship had suffered, and quite often, had spent just as much time trying to repair the sibling relationship. Each child had experienced the family in different ways. Whilst the normal development of a sibling will not be permanently disrupted, it is expected that a crisis will occur which will cause at least temporary cessation of normative experiences for the sibling. A non-abused sibling could be regarded as a secondary victim of the incest: as whilst not directly abused, she may nonetheless learn that trusting men, or people in general, is not the safest thing to do. Additionally, they will learn which behaviours will keep her safe and which ones might subject her to possible abuse. The non-abused sibling, unlike her abused counterparts, were able to blame the perpetrator rather than toward themselves. While some of that blame was also projected at the abused sister, it can be viewed as a coping mechanism and therefore assisted the non-abused sister in rejecting a self-view as victim. It was noteworthy just how the non-abused women readily identified how and why they needed to take evasive action from their father, and were able to identify and process the predatory styles of the male caretaker within their familial environments. They learned how to be assertive and how to sense danger. Several attributed their assertiveness or knowledge to remaining free from abuse. Many of the women, although motivated and optimistic about repairing the sister relationship were also ambivalent, demonstrating the incest may have left its mark by making a supportive, trusting and functional adult relationship difficult, at best.

Engel (1994) explored how siblings cope with the news of the abuse. Where the abuse has been allegedly perpetrated by someone they care about, denial may be the first response. The sibling may then have an investment in protecting the image of the perpetrator rather than in being there for the victim. Alternatively, the sibling may have been abused by the same person, in which case their response may be angry, anxious or upset. This could be aimed at the perpetrator, or if they have tried to block their own abuse out, towards the victim for reminding them of things they would have preferred to remain buried. The sibling may also have reasons for not wanting to believe the news: they may have known what was going on, but felt helpless to prevent it. This may induce feelings of helplessness, guilt, shame and inadequacy. They may experience some of these feelings as they are glad it happened to someone else and not themselves. Others resent the attention the abused child received, thus feeling jealous towards them. This can create problems as the victim feels betrayed and abandoned, similar to siblings who refuse to believe or side with the perpetrator.

Fong and Walsh-Bowers (1998) found that mothers reported that siblings were also affected by the abusive relationship in different ways. Some children felt that because more attention was focused on the victim, they were left out; thus, mothers had to deal with the children's anger and disruptive behaviour. Other children sympathised with the victim and thus were more willing to show emotional support.

Dwyer and Miller (1996) have noted that siblings may experience disenfranchised grief (see the earlier section on the 'effects of knowing' for a discussion of this concept). They found that many women perceive the interests of the child who has been abused as conflicting with those of other children in the family, who may still want and need their father. In these cases, the dictates of a 'good mother' are not easily defined.

Wright (1991) found that siblings were peripheral to the family as a whole. When they were talked about as important people, they were cherished for the roles they could fill, not for themselves. Despite this, the inclusion of siblings is important as they are undergoing enormous change and stress: they are losing their fathers, their mothers are changing, the whole world seems suddenly to be involved in the private lives of their families.

Issues to consider

Professionals need to be sensitive and responsive to the needs and issues of children not involved in the incest directly, and offer them support. They are *secondary victims* like their mother. They also need to be included in the healing or recovery process and assume the status as a survivor. Siblings who are affected by the abuse will increase their demands on the parent. Mothers will often seek advice about what to tell the children and the only basis of response is honesty and openness:

> Children make up what they don't understand and they are especially vulnerable to the gossip or interpretations of others outside the immediate family.
> (Ovaris, 1991)

It may take some considerable time for siblings to work through the issues as they affect each individual, and this must be done at their own pace. Nobody should try to push them to face particular issues unless they are happy to do so. The sibling may well have experienced the abuse and family life very differently from the victim—by either playing a different role in the family or having developed their own method of coping. Workers do need to consider whether there are preferred children in the family and what this means for them and for the other children, e.g. have they been scapegoated and marginalised?

Workers need to encourage siblings who have experienced sexual abuse by the same person to open up some dialogue in which they piece together their histories and childhood to enable some mastery to be gained over a lost past. Where the siblings are experiencing problems working together, then simple supportive opportunities need to be created, such as stating they care for each other, even if they cannot offer what each needs at the present time. Siblings need to be careful not to accept any responsibility for not protecting the victim, not telling someone, feeling jealous of the attention the victim was getting from the perpetrator, or taking his side.

Mothers need to consider and devise strategies for managing and protecting siblings.

At some point, the siblings need to be forgiven for the feelings of responsibility for the abuse they have harnessed. For example, siblings may not have been responsible for the abuse, and may have been unable to stop it, but they still feel that they have failed the child victim.

Position Regarding Self-protection Work: What do their Children Know Now?

Self-protection work does not refer to physical self-defence but rather to the complex of mental and behavioural skills that children of all ages employ to seek assistance in times of threat. The child's increased self-confidence will serve both healing and preventive functions (Orten and Rich, 1993). Whilst Regan (Chapter Nine) provides us with a generic framework in this area, I will provide some specific guidance in the context of this chapter.

A mother's first role in preventing any recurrence of harm is to permit their children to participate in a programme of self-protection. By teaching children strategies to avoid sexual abuse in no way implies that the child is any way responsible for the sexual abuse. It is a sad indictment on society today that they have to be prepared for such an event.

Research findings

Palmer *et al.*, (1999) found that there were a number of very real reasons why children did not disclose earlier than they did. These included the fact that they were unaware that the abuse was wrong or unusual, as well as fear of the perpetrator. The latter is not uncommon given the range of tactics deployed by the perpetrator, such as threats of harm to the child or other family members. Not knowing the abusive behaviour was wrong was a feature of many children. Their self-protection to this included not remembering, acknowledging, or discussing the abuse. Some blocked it out completely. These authors found that preventive education to school-age children has a limited influence on their ability to respond to familial abuse, compared with the child's relationship with the perpetrator. First, abusive patterns in the family tend to

begin so early for many children that the patterns would be established before the child's consciousness could be raised by a school programme. Second, respondents indicated that they were often as inhibited by fears instilled by the perpetrators than by their own inability to perceive the abuse as wrong or unusual. To counter the strong influence of the family perpetrator, child education programmes could include survivors' experiences about how perpetrators blocked them from understanding and disclosing. Advance knowledge of typical rationalisations and methods of instilling fear, including death threats, may alert children and help them to recognise when they are being manipulated and to react in a self-protective way.

We know that relatively few parents opt to discuss child sexual abuse with their children (ranging from 22 to 60 per cent, Wurtele and Miller-Perrin, 1992), and this may be because: it is a difficult subject to discuss; the topic might frighten the child; the need for discussion has not occurred to the parent; the child is either too young for discussion, is in little danger of abuse, or is reluctant to discuss the topic; parents may lack the confidence in their own ability, and this may be linked to a lack of knowledge, vocabulary, or materials.

Children may not recognise that they are being abused because they lack knowledge of social norms, and their awareness may be blocked by self-protective defence mechanisms. Perpetrators of sexual abuse often use a deceptive process of grooming, pressure for secrecy, and distortion of reality and morality, leaving the child confused about what happened (Berliner and Conte, 1990).

De Jong (1988) found that 31 per cent of the supportive mothers were not interested in counselling for their children, whereas 9 per cent of non-supportive mothers sought such help for the child whom they had blamed for initiating the sexual contact with the perpetrators. De Jong argued that minimal counselling should include and address all the emotional, medical, social, environmental, and legal issues involved, as well as the treatment implications. At least one session with the entire family, including siblings, is recommended to clear the air and bring fears and concerns to the surface.

Elrod and Rubin (1993) reviewed the materials in relation to parental involvement in sexual abuse prevention education as well as establishing what parents know and need to know about child sexual abuse. They noted that parents are not typically given an opportunity to be involved in the planning of a child's curriculum on sexual abuse and often do not understand the issues or seriousness of the problem because of their own fear or lack of knowledge. These factors can lead to the parents denying their children access to important prevention information and increasing the susceptibility of children to sexual abuse and exploitation. In addition, if parents are not involved in prevention education for themselves, they may not perceive the reality or extent of sexual abuse or the need to be aware of the risks and the possibilities of prevention. They noted that most programmes on sexual abuse tend to target mothers. They found that the agreed topics for children's curriculum on prevention education for pre-schoolers included: good/bad touches; how to tell if you are being abused; who to tell if someone abuses you; the importance of telling; abuse is not the child's fault; who abusers are; how to protect yourself; why abuse happens; what happens when you tell; what a child can do when they know someone else is being abused; and the likelihood of abuse happening to the child. The need for a professional involvement in the work was supported when they found that over half of the parents planned not to discuss several of the emotionally laden topics (e.g. who abusers are), although mothers planned to discuss significantly more topics than did the fathers.

Issues to consider

Many children will be very angry with their mothers for failing to protect them sufficiently, and it is important that they be given the time and the space to work through this. Both the child and the mother could be asked to list all the reasons each of them are angry with each other, the perpetrator, and others (such as siblings and extended family members or professionals).

It may take some considerable time for workers to get the trust of the victim or other children involved in the intervention process. Children may harbour feelings of guilt, shame

and helplessness; and fear disbelief, blame and rejection once more. The experience of sexual abuse by the child is surrounded by secrecy. It involves a misuse of power, betrayal of the child's trust, and compounds the child's helplessness and lack of control over the situation. Workers thus need to be very careful in exploring how they will engage the young person in the work as well as its content. Strategies might include being empathic, responding warmly, with interest and support, working at their pace, and respecting their right to remain silent about any issue, such as the detail of the abuse. It may take several months for a secure and trusting relationship to be forged and to allow any meaningful work to begin. We need to be aware that they may feel worse before they begin to feel better.

An initial disclosure of sexual abuse may only be the tip of the iceberg. Thus, workers who are engaged in work with a child need to be aware about the possibility of subsequent disclosures, and in many cases, should actively facilitate them. In order to do this, they should use a range of materials so the child has a choice of method of disclosure, e.g. writing, drawing or artwork, or talking face-to-face with the helper. They should encourage disclosure by reminding them that by breaking their silence they will lose some of their pain. Workers do need to be mindful of the requirements of criminal courts if such disclosures are to lead to convictions, and they need to negotiate any self-protection work with the Crown Prosecution Service (CPS), so as not to prejudice any incomplete legal proceedings.

It is important that consideration is given to the role of the mother in the process, particularly since we know that mothers are important for clarifying concepts and applying their new knowledge in daily life. Mothers should be available for the child should they wish to disclose anything further in the future. In contrast, uninformed parents may not be able to answer questions, may contradict accurate information, and may not know how to correct any misconceptions their children may have (Adams and Fay, 1981).

Techniques and strategies to help children and young people avoid falling prey to perpetrators of sexual abuse must take into account a variety of factors. Children are sexually abused by young people in a range of different settings, usually by boys well known to them, such as brothers or family friends, but sometimes by complete strangers. The type of relationship between the perpetrator and the victim will influence the way in which the child is engaged in sexual activity. Thus, a perpetrator who has regular contact with the victim has the opportunity to persuade and groom the victim, introducing him or her to sexual behaviour gradually over a period of time, whilst gaining the child's trust and confidence. This type of approach is frequently used by adult paedophiles and occasionally by experienced adolescent perpetrators, especially those who have themselves been groomed by adult perpetrators (Epps, 1997).

Some perpetrators, however, have no regular contact with children, or have made a conscious decision not to abuse children known to them, perhaps through fear of being caught. These men are more likely to prey on unfamiliar children, having no desire to engage victims in a longer term relationship. Findings from community surveys show that boys are more likely than girls to be sexually abused outside of the home, especially boys from low-income families who have also been subjected to physical abuse (Finkelhor, 1984). These stranger assaults are more likely to be accompanied by the use of threats, physical coercion and violence in an effort to force the child to participate in sexual activity. It is also likely that perpetrators of stranger assaults more often offend in an opportunistic way, not carefully planning the offence, and using excessive force in their desperation to engage the victim, perhaps with little thought as to the consequences. There is some evidence to suggest that perpetrators of sexual abuse are more likely to be reported to the police if they are strangers than if they are known to the victim (Finkelhor, 1979). It follows, therefore, that intra-familial assaults are least likely to be reported to the police (Finkelhor, 1984; Russell, 1984).

West (1991) recognises that some children are more vulnerable to abuse, especially those who have previously been abused. Victims of childhood sexual abuse sometimes exhibit sexualised and 'seductive' behaviours (Yates, 1982), making them vulnerable to further abuse by those adolescents and adults with a proclivity for sexually abusing children. Finkelhor (1988) refers to this effect as 'traumatic sexualization', caused by premature

and inappropriate sexual learning. Sexually abused children are often rewarded by their perpetrators with material goods, such as sweets and money, and may come to view sex as a way of manipulating people. According to Finkelhor (1988), children who have been abused under conditions of danger, threat and violence are especially likely to be traumatised.

Children are usually unaware of the distorted way in which perpetrators interpret their behaviour, and are therefore oblivious to the fact that they may be placing themselves at further risk.

Broadly speaking, two types of sexual abuse prevention programmes can be identified: those aimed at all children (primary prevention) and those targeted towards 'at-risk' children, including children who have already been abused (secondary and tertiary prevention). However, Elliott (1992) makes the important point that targeting specific children suggests that they are somehow responsible for their abuse or for being unable to stop it. Thus, she suggests that programmes should be aimed at all children, not just those that have been abused. In addition, programmes should aim to educate all parents and carers, raising awareness about the risks of sexual abuse, and encouraging the use of books and materials within the home which enhance self-protection. A range of books and videos are now available, aimed at different age groups. Many of these can easily be obtained through good bookshops and toyshops, or through charities such as KIDSCAPE. For example, *Feeling Happy, Feeling Safe*, written by Michele Elliott (1991), is aimed at ages 3–7. A brightly illustrated, colour picture book, it aims to teach children how to deal with bullies, how to keep safe, and how to react to advances by strangers and known adults.

Primary prevention programmes assume that all children are potentially at risk and will therefore benefit from self-protection strategies. Programmes usually provide classroom-based instruction for children of all ages on how to protect themselves from sexual assault and what to do if they experience actual or threatened abuse. Children are taught a variety of techniques, including: how to distinguish between 'good' and 'bad' touching; how to be assertive, ranging from repeatedly saying 'no' to the use of self-defence techniques; and the importance of not keeping secrets. Most programmes aim to reduce the risk of abuse by changing the child's behaviour. By teaching children to avoid risky situations, to recognise inappropriate touching, to say no (if possible) when anyone tries to do something which makes them frightened or confused, to refuse to keep secrets, and to seek adult help, it may be possible to help children to avoid abuse.

Research suggests that boys exposed to prevention education programmes perceive themselves as less likely to be abused, perhaps because they feel more able to control potentially abusive situations (Dziuba-Leatherman and Finkelhor, 1994). However, doubts have been expressed about the ability of such programmes in preventing sexual abuse (Gilbert, 1988). Outcome research in this area is lacking and must be a priority for the future.

Ability to Identify Indicators in Both the Perpetrator and the Child/ren

Whilst it is important to educate mothers in the signs that may be indicators of sexual abuse, we need to also caution against overreactions which instigate a protective process which uncovers a false allegation. Symptoms of sexual abuse do not follow a set pattern: there is no single behaviour or symptom or combination of behaviours or symptoms that always proves abuse, nor do all child victims display the same kinds of behaviour.

Every child is unique, and every abuse experience is unique (Myers, 1997). In some cases, there are no demonstrable changes in behaviour. Despite this, it is important to provide mothers with a framework to help them watch for any possible signs of abuse. In doing so, readers should refer back to the component on the effects of child sexual abuse on the victims, and also acknowledge that it is impossible to detail all the possible behavioural changes and psychological symptoms in a book of this kind.

Several guidelines have been suggested which should help parents identify circumstances where they should be concerned:

1. Any radical change in behaviour, particularly where it is a dramatic change from a usual pattern of behaviour.

2. When any symptoms are chronic and fail to respond to the usual methods of management, then child sexual abuse should be considered.

3. Any pattern of three or more symptoms and behaviours should indicate more likely harm or risk to the child.

4. The severity of the symptoms.

5. Even where child sexual abuse is not proven from these, it should require an investigation for the cause of the behaviour (Wurtele and Miller-Perrin, 1992).

Mothers should document the changes and symptoms immediately in detail and in writing, along with when they first appear. They should note anything that might explain behaviour changes or psychological symptoms.

Mothers are often provided with information to alert them to the many behavioural indicators of child sexual abuse. These indicators have been established from victim accounts and with the benefit of hindsight. They are not always helpful checklists as they refer to behaviours fraught with value judgements and most children exhibit some of these behaviours at some point without necessarily being subjected to sexual abuse. Indeed, recent research shows that attempts to assess risk and dangerousness are in themselves risky (Clark *et al.*, 1990). We must avoid the error of assuming that retrospective studies can be used to predict sexual abuse with any degree of accuracy. What mothers do need to be clear about is that the checklist is not the key feature, it is the picture which builds up around it which is important.

Given that there are often no distinct signs of sexual abuse, victims are often extremely hard to distinguish from any other children. Given that the essential human instinct is survival, it may be much better to identify signs of sexual abuse that we look for in survivors rather than victims. The least common survival method is disclosure that abuse has taken place. Brown (1998) has usefully set out the most obvious survival strategies utilised by children following the abuse:

- Forgetting: this might take the form of repressing the memory (either during or following the abuse), storing it in the subconscious, as this may seem like the only way to continue to live. This is only a short-term strategy as it can create other difficulties, such as aspects of recall through smell or touch, etc.

- Pretending: this can take the form of children fabricating an alternative and idealised picture of their actual experience, e.g. seeing the perpetrator as the best parent in the world.

- Denying what has happened is a natural response, combined with the awfulness of what has happened, the fear of the consequences of relating the abuse, and of telling what has happened.

- Distancing themselves physically from the perpetrator by either running away or staying with a friend's family is only a viable option for a few, particularly when the child is very young.

- Transcending: is a psychological distancing, such as leaving their body throughout the abuse.

- Numbing: allows the child to immunise the pain at both a physical as well as at an emotional level.

- Rationalising: includes excusing the behaviour of the abuser, e.g. 'they have their own problems.'

- Minimising: plays down the importance and significance of the abuse, e.g. 'it wasn't that bad'.

- Justifying: is rationalisation with accompanying self-blame, e.g. 'I deserved it'.

- Compartmentalising: is where the child stores the abuse away from other aspects of life, freeing them to function well in other social settings, such as school.

- Striving for perfection: only by being the best will the child survive. They compensate for the abuse by creating outlets to escape from the abuse, and this is seen in workaholics. The child may become obsessed with achieving success: academically, sporting, etc.

- Finding faith: here, the child looks for something more powerful (than the abuser) to place their trust in, although this can be due to a belief that the abuse was justified and they are working to find forgiveness for their part in the abuse.

Any lists for recognising signs and indicators of sexual abuse should be used as a guide only. It is most likely that if sexual abuse is happening there will be a number of signs and indicators from all of the categories that have been present for quite some time.

When assessing indicators of sexual abuse, it is important to take into account the child's current development. For example, what may be appropriate behaviour for an older child, may indicate a problem for a younger child or vice versa. Sexual abuse may even stop growth at the developmental stage in which the abuse began. Many young people will regress to earlier developmental stages following abuse. They are seeking comfort, safety and reassurance from the adults around them, but have difficulty in re-establishing trust in relationships. Those who cannot function at the developmental level that corresponds with their chronological age will encounter a variety of difficulties in their daily life experiences. They may struggle to bond well with others. Many adults will interpret immature or unco-operative behavioural responses as a sign of unwillingness, rather than inability and they will often respond harshly in return. They may then perceive themselves as failures when they are unable to meet the expectations of the adults around them, and their self-esteem suffers. Social problems develop as they encounter relationship difficulties with their peers: they may feel different from and inferior to others their own age; they may withdraw from social contact in shame, or become aggressive, venting their anger and frustration; they may experience anxiety in situations that are competitive, or require them to measure themselves to the standards of others; communication and problem-solving may be weak and present increased levels of frustration in expressing feelings and needs, and in having needs met; there may be limited ability to show empathy or a caring attitude toward others; and intolerance or indifference shown by other children can greatly heighten anxiety of children and young people who long to belong or fit with their peer groups (Croll, 1994).

Behaviours need to be assessed in the context of the child's total life situation, and some questions that are helpful to ask include: 'What needs does this behaviour meet?' 'Is this behaviour developmentally appropriate?' 'Is there a pattern to this behaviour?' 'What other behaviours have been noticed?' 'How does the child understand the behaviour?'

Ordinary/normal sexual development, knowledge and behaviour

It is important for mothers to be clear about age-appropriate sexual behaviour, knowledge and development if they are to be able to differentiate the 'abusive' from the 'normal'. Hanks (1997) offered a very useful baseline from which to work.

From birth to 2 years of age

Sexual development	Sexual behaviour	Sexual knowledge
Gender established.	Erect penis.	Limited language for body parts (including genitals).
Newborns are capable of erect penis (male) and lubrication (females).	Recognition/experience of pleasurable feelings when touching genitals.	
Physiology for arousal is present.	Touching self, sometimes looking at and touching others.	
Spontaneous penile erection.		

From 2 to 6 years of age

Sexual development	Sexual behaviour	Sexual knowledge
Children grow. Boys testicles descend.	Touch their own and other (peer) genitals. Look and play doctor, nurses, mum games with peers.	Language develops. They become more inquisitive and verbal about some functions; imitate without understanding; limited knowledge about childbirth and where babies come from. Know gender differences as they get older.
Erections and lubrication for boys and girls.	Peer exploration.	
	Masturbates self.	
	Experiences pleasurable feelings.	
	Interest in own faeces. Watches with interest when others use the toilet and bathroom.	Child asks about genitals, breasts, intercourse and will name body parts more accurately; using slang words for bathroom/toilet functions, genitals and sex.
	Mimicking having babies in their tummy.	Little understanding of sex.
	Rubs genitals, masturbates when uncomfortable/ unhappy, tense, excited or afraid.	
	Practices kissing.	

From 6 to 12 years of age

Sexual development	Sexual behaviour	Sexual knowledge
For some children of 8–9 years pubertal changes may begin. Some children are capable of childbirth. Menstruation, wet dreams, develops sexual fantasies.	Masturbation in private. Shows guilt/embarrassment about sexual activities. Simulates intercourse, kissing, petting with peers. May have actual intercourse without knowing consequences properly. This age group cannot give informed consent.	Language for genital parts. Increased knowledge of sexual behaviour and sexual language and slang (derived from media and peers). Confused about sexual behaviour and causal effects. Unclear about intercourse and pregnancy.

'Normal' sexual behaviours in juveniles include

Joint activity with partner	Individual activity
• Embracing and kissing. • Close bodily contact. • Fondling. • Mutual petting and masturbation. • Simulated intercourse. • Intercourse.	• Masturbation. • Highly eroticised fantasies. • 'Wet' dreams.

These indicators show the need to properly assess the age-appropriateness and behavioural appropriateness of the juvenile's sexual development and functioning. We then need to compare the sexual development alongside their physical, emotional, intellectual and social development, and highlight any significant discrepancies between the two. On the basis of such an assessment we should be better able to distinguish between: normal developmental sexual experimentation between age-mates, and abusive experimentation which involves a pre-pubertal child; and abusive exploitation of a child by a juvenile who is sexually knowledgeable and is knowingly abusive, and sexual assault and violence (Richardson, 1990: p153).

Calder (1997) then went on to offer a framework for differentiating the 'normal' from the 'abusive' in young people.

• What is the age relationship between participants?

• What is the social relationship? In what context did the abuse occur?—Are they related?

• What type of sexual behaviour is exhibited?

• What is the experience of the victim?

- How does sexual contact take place?
- How was the sexual activity revealed?
- How persistent is the sexual behaviour?
- Evidence of escalation.
- Sexual fantasies.
- What are the characteristics of the victims?

Johnson (1994) has produced 21 red flags in children's sexual behaviour that mothers might find useful:

1. The children engaged in the sexual behaviours do not have an ongoing mutual play relationship.
2. Sexual behaviours which are engaged in by children of different ages or developmental levels.
3. Sexual behaviours which are out of balance with other aspects of the child's life and interests.
4. Children who seem to have too much knowledge about sexuality and behave in many ways more consistent with adult sexual expression.
5. Sexual behaviours which are significantly different than those of other same-age children.
6. Sexual behaviours which continue in spite of consistent and clear requests to stop.
7. Children who appear to be unable to stop themselves from engaging in sexual activities.
8. Sexual behaviours which occur in public or other places were the child has been told they are not acceptable.
9. Children's sexual behaviours which are eliciting complaints from other children and/or adversely affecting other children.
10. Children's sexual behaviours which are directed at adults who feel uncomfortable receiving them.
11. Children (four years and under) who do not understand their rights or the rights of others in relation to sexual contact.
12. Sexual behaviours which progress in frequency, intensity or intrusiveness over time.
13. When fear, anxiety, deep shame or intense guilt is associated with the sexual behaviour.
14. Children who engage in extensive, persistent, mutually agreed upon adult-type behaviours with other children.
15. Children who manually stimulate or have oral or genital contact with animals.
16. Child sexualises non-sexualised things, or interactions with others, or relationships.
17. Sexual behaviours which cause physical or emotional pain or discomfort to self or others.
18. Children who use sex to hurt others.
19. When verbal or physical expressions of anger precede, follow or accompany the sexual behaviour.
20. Children who use distorted logic to justify their sexual actions (she didn't say 'no').
21. When coercion, force, bribery, manipulation or threats are associated with sexual behaviour.

Mothers who are aware of these frameworks and how children change developmentally over time, should be in a better position to identify any victims.

Indicators in the perpetrator

It is very difficult to predict with any certainty those who will abuse and those who will not. There are, however, certain behaviours and personality characteristics that are common among men who sexually abuse children. These are warning signs, or red flags, that they may be more likely to sexually abuse a child. These indicators should not be singled out but seen in their entirety, as a unit (Engel, 1994). They include:

- Poor impulse control.
- Low self-esteem.
- Selfishness and narcissism.
- Neediness and a tendency to make demands on the mother's time and attention.
- Timidity, lack of assertiveness, feelings of inadequacy, social awkwardness, poor social skills, difficulty developing adult social and sexual relationships.
- Alcohol abuse, alcoholism, and drug addiction.
- History of being sexually abused as a child.

- History of being abusive (physically, verbally, sexually) as an adult or older child.

- History of mental illness.

- Dependent personality (unable to support oneself financially or emotionally).

- 'Loves' to be with children, relates to children much better than adults, acts more like a child than an adult.

- Anti-social behaviour (does not believe in society's rules, has own set of rules that seem to accommodate his desires). Aggressive, abusive behaviour.

- Withdrawal into one's own world, an extremely active fantasy life.

- Inability to have a successful relationship with an adult woman.

- Overly sexed, preoccupied with sex, needs to have sex daily or several times a day, masturbates compulsively.

- Does not seem to have any limits when it comes to sex—anything goes (such as sadomasochism, wife swapping, etc).

- Overly involved in pornography: constantly reads porno magazines, watches porno movies.

- Exposure to and interest in pornography involving children.

- Showing more interest in children than the mother.

- Sexual repression, moralistic behaviour, feeling guilty about sex.

- Sexual impotency or other sexual dysfunction with adult females.

- Need to feel powerful and controlling (Engel, 1994: pp40–1).

Behaviour changes to be observed in the perpetrator when they return home include:

- Starts to abuse alcohol or drugs.

- Stresses the impossibility of re-offending.

- Interested in pornography.

- Stresses the innocence of his sexual contact with children.

- Begins to minimise the impact of his past offending.

- Keeps leaving the house for no apparent reason.

- Lies in other areas of his life.

- Gets involved in youth activities.

- Wants to be left alone with the children.

- Changes noticeably in his sexual functioning.

- Discusses sexual issues in front of the children.

- Starts to use innuendoes.

- Becomes paranoid and stresses the fact that you don't trust him (Wyre, 1987).

Research findings

Hubbard (1989) found that many mothers believed they would recognise the signs in their own children. Without exception, this was not the case, although with hindsight there were clues, which could have served as stimuli for the mothers to question what was occurring. As many of the clues went with no response and were avoided, it strengthened the mother's denial pattern and further dissociated themselves from their own sexual abuse.

Issues to consider

What does she think it would be helpful to know to keep her child safe/to know if her child is being abused? What would she notice if there was a risk to her child in the future?

Advise the mother that if the child has a number of indicators, then they should start asking questions of the child, rather than the perpetrator.

Mothers do need to be aware that they can often be confronted with contradictory messages from their child, which makes it very difficult to know how to respond. The child may describe something that suggests it is very distressing but they exhibit no signs of distress. These children have become adept at smothering their true feelings as a protective mechanism.

General Parenting

The issue of general parenting is important for a number of reasons. There is a correlation between a lack of confidence in their own parenting and a reduced awareness of risks for their children (Hooper, 1992). There are a number of potential problems for those mothers who were either sexually or otherwise abused as children, particularly the lack of any good parenting model. Many mothers feel that they are inadequate parents for allowing the sexual abuse to take place.

The moment the professional agencies become aware of the alleged sexual abuse, the person who comes under the greatest scrutiny is the main carer, the mother. It seems a little unfair that at a time when she is preoccupied with the consequences of the disclosure she is required to make a super-human effort to be a model parent (Peake and Fletcher, 1997). This is often not the same for the perpetrator who may leave the home and not face up to the sexual abuse.

They may often find themselves referred for parenting courses or assertiveness training. We have to question the appropriateness of retraining them after they failed to prevent their partners from sexually abusing their child. It often appears that the women are slotted into pre-existing programmes open to professionals, rather than being tailored to this group generally, or to individual cases.

The current practice of assessing risk centres around issues of parenting and the needs of the children. Many mothers think that this is the focus of the work from social services, particularly as they have received the message that by remaining with their partner means that they are a bad parent. Mothers may become confused about what is expected of them if they are not prepared to change their decision. The consequence of this is that they feel isolated and can react with conflict and confrontation. This has the potential to result in stalemate. If this is perceived as non co-operation, it is possible that legal proceedings might be considered. The process thus confirms that they are inadequate parents (Rose and Savage, 1998).

Research findings

Tamraz (1996) noted that non-abusing mothers are often reported to lack mothering skills. They may be characterised as detached and distant, or as over-attentive and over-involved.

Some material contends that the mothers may never have received the mothering they needed in their childhood and accordingly lack the skills or the ability to provide their daughters with what they never had. They may go on to recreate their own childhood experience by repeating their own mother's lack of protectiveness and so deprive their daughters of a strong sense of self, thereby facilitating incest.

In their exploratory study of parenting attitudes among women who were sexually abused as children, Cole and Woolger (1989) found that both incest victims and those abused by unrelated men had similar child-rearing attitudes regarding nurturance and control of their children, but that the incest victims had more stringent attitudes towards autonomy promotion. Their responses reflected a high interest in their children becoming self-sufficient as early as possible. As such, a possible indication of incest is that the victims distance themselves from the demands of parenting. The authors compared this against their practice experience when they found that mothers with a history of incest often reported positive attitudes towards child rearing, but often seemed hostile, resentful, and jealous when describing actual parenting situations. This raises a question as to whether the central problem is coping with the emotional demands of parenting or is an attitudinal problem. Many do not want to replicate the mistakes of their parents and most endorse the expectations of good parenting. Incest survivors may struggle most at times of acute emotional stress in parenting given that their history has taught them to flee from the feelings of inadequacy and confusion rather than moderate their feelings in ways that mothers typically do. Benedek (1959) has argued that confidence in one's own parenting is a protection against the inevitable frustrations of parenting.

Cole et al., (1992) examined the quality of the self-reported parenting experiences and practices of women who were incest victims as children, and compared them to families where alcohol but not sexual abuse was a feature. They found that incest survivors reported significantly less confidence and less sense of emotional control as parents than non-risk mothers. In addition, they reported significantly less support in the parental partnership with their spouses, and reported being less consistent and organised, and making fewer maturity demands on their children. Overall, being an incest victim as a child was related to their feelings of adequacy as parents.

Issues to consider

Reder and Lucey (1995) explored the significant issues in the assessment of parenting. They provided a framework for the assessment of parenting under various headings/themes, each of which come together to provide an overall picture. They are set out below.

1. The parent's relationship to the role of parenting

- Does the parent provide basic essential physical care?
- Does the parent provide age-appropriate emotional care?
- Does the parent encourage development of the attachment dynamic?
- What attitude does the parent have to the tasks of parenting?
- Does the parent accept responsibility for their parenting behaviour?
- Is the child expected to be responsible for his/her own protection?
- If there are problems, does the parent acknowledge them?

2. The parent's relationship with the child

- What feelings does the parent have towards the child?
- Does the parent empathise with the child?
- Is the child viewed as a separate person?
- Are the child's essential needs given primacy over the parent's desires?

3. Family influences

- What awareness and attitude does the parent have regarding their own parenting experiences?
- Is the parent able to sustain a supportive relationship with a partner?

- Is the child over-involved in the family's discordant relationships?
- How sensitive is the family to relationship stresses?
- What is the meaning of the child to the parent?
- What is the child's contribution to the parenting relationship?
- What attitude does the child have to his/her caretakers?

4. Interaction with the external world

- What support networks are available?
- What is the pattern of the parent's relationships with professional workers?

5. The potential for change

- What is the potential to benefit from therapeutic help?
- What responses have there been to previous offers of help?

These authors clearly believe that parenting is not a quality that someone does, or does not, possess, but is a relationship that responds to fluctuations in other relationships. The assessor needs to consider all such influences.

Social and Family History
Current family home environment

The literature strongly supports the belief that incestuous families are dysfunctional families with multiple stressors. It is not typical for sexual abuse to occur independently of other aspects of family dysfunction. It occurs with greater frequency in homes disrupted by parental absence or separation, or in those in which standards of parental care are punitive, confused, and rejecting (Bagley and King, 1990). However, we must also remember that sexual abuse does occur in seemingly normal families, including the seemingly upright, religious and respectable ones. Judges, lawyers, doctors, school teachers, and social workers are all represented in the perpetrator population. Perpetrators are infrequently entirely bad parents. They have good sides too. Many children want the abuse to stop, but they want to retain the good father as they love them when the abuse is not happening. Herman and Hirschman (1980) noted that when sexual abuse is carried out in the context of a caring relationship that almost all the victims expressed some warm feeling towards their fathers.

An assessment of current family functioning and level of support is needed to determine what kinds of supportive and therapeutic services mothers will need. Testa *et al.*, (1992) hypothesised that children who did not disclose sexual abuse or who received negative support following victimisation were more likely to come from distressed families than those who are able to obtain support.

Workers need to consider the co-existence of domestic violence with the sexual abuse, and how this impacts on the mothers' choices. There is increasing evidence that domestic violence is more prevalent in sexually abusive families than in the general population (Truesdell *et al.*, 1986), and thus workers need to acknowledge that any effective intervention will need to address the domestic violence before the mother can cope successfully with her child's victimisation (Dietz and Craft, 1980). Nelson (1992) reported that in 40 per cent of divorces, women cite domestic violence as a factor. 90–97 per cent of domestic violence is from men to women.

Despite under reporting, we do know that:

● One in four women experiences domestic violence in her lifetime, and it is estimated that at any one time between one in eight to ten women will experience domestic violence at any given time.

● Every week two women in England and Wales are killed by their current or former partners.

● Domestic violence accounts for a quarter of all violent crime.

● UK figures suggest that between 40–60 per cent of separated or divorced women experienced domestic violence.

● Women aged 16–29 are at greatest risk of experiencing domestic violence.

● Domestic violence often starts, or escalates, during pregnancy.

● A woman on average will approach over ten different agencies before she receives an appropriate response, and receives the help she needs.

● Domestic violence seriously impacts on women. It affects their physical health, mental health, and all other aspects of their lives, and the lives of their children (Rose, 2000 and forthcoming).

Research tells us that child abuse is most likely to occur where abuse of mothers is present (Stark and Flitcraft, 1988) and that these mothers are the most likely to seek help to protect their children. Conclusions reached from research indicate that:

● Abused mothers do not usually come from disorganised, or violent families of origin, casting doubt on the myth that family history predisposes women to domestic violence or their children to abuse.

● Mothers experiencing domestic violence are more punitively treated (i.e. their children are far more likely to be removed) than mothers not experiencing domestic violence, even when the abuse of the child is not physical.

● Professionals often fail to acknowledge the existence of abuse, and its impact on women, at the same time as blaming them for the abuse of their children. Very often women are accused of 'failure to protect' when agencies are themselves failing to protect them.

The presence of other problems in the home needs to be explored. For example, Server and Janzen (1982) in a study of 48 incestuous families, found a 71 per cent rate of alcohol abuse and a 31 per cent rate of drug abuse. If denial exists in relation to these, then it will easily be extended to defend the sexual abuse.

Palmer *et al.*, (1999) found that in their study of abuse survivors, only 6 per cent had experienced sexual abuse alone. Many had experienced a combination of different kinds of abuse: physical, emotional and sexual (45%), physical and emotional (21%), or sexual and emotional (17%). This highlights the need to assess the family functioning broadly. They also found that the age of onset was very young: for physical abuse, 4.7 years; for emotional abuse, 6.3 years; and for sexual abuse, 6.3 years. The abuse tended to persist for many years. Emotional abuse had an average duration of 20.3 years, physical abuse 11.2 years, and sexual abuse 8.1 years. These findings were replicated in DeYoung's study (1994), where she found that many of the woman described having been sexually, physically and emotionally abused by their husbands.

Family dynamics may contribute to sexual abuse through improper supervision, poor choice of babysitters, inappropriate sleeping arrangements, and blurred role boundaries. Mothers who were themselves victims of . sexual abuse may even set up their own children for abuse and then require additional help working through the prior unresolved incest experience before they can be supportive of their children (Goodwin *et al.*, 1982).

About one in six British families is now headed by a lone parent, the vast majority of them women. The risks from babysitters are heightened in this group, particularly as they rarely have choices about whom they employ—especially as many are struggling on low incomes, and lack a support network of family or friends. Research tells us that perpetrators target single mothers to gain access to children (Nelson, 1992).

Hoagwood and Stewart (1989) reported on children's perceptions of family functioning in sexually abusing and non-sexually abusing families. They found that there were differences on three dimensions: problem-solving, roles, and general functioning. Sexually abused children were more likely to report poorer problem-solving skills in their families, more role confusion, and more general pathological functioning than children in the non-abused group. Differences in the problem-solving dimension is consistent with reports of chaotic family structure and concomitant dysfunction. The victim's feelings of isolation, anxiety, and lack of support that many victims experience may also be reflected in this dimension. Difficulties in establishing and maintaining effective role boundaries often has a diagnostic significance regardless of whether the abuse is inside or outside the family. The greater overall dysfunction in families of abused children may reflect greater general unhappiness that the child victims experienced in their families. There were two differences between children sexually abused inside and outside the family: affective

responsivity and affective involvement. Victims of intra-familial abuse reported more pathological affective responsivity and affective involvement within their family than those abused extra-familially. This shows that victims who are abused by a family member perceive more pathological affective intimacy and lack of emotional boundaries.

Issues to consider

We will never know the true number of women who experience domestic violence, as many women do not report violence to agencies for many reasons. These include the lack of awareness about or access to available services; concern that agencies will not be sympathetic; sensitive or provide the help that is needed, fear of agencies having different agendas from their own, particularly with regard to their children; and fear of retribution from their perpetrator. Some women approach services, but do not necessarily disclose violence as the source of their problems. For example, many women seek medical help and are not asked how their injuries were inflicted, or by whom. Many women do disclose and still fail to get adequate, appropriate responses. If the opportunity for intervention is lost, violence may continue and women and children may be at significant risk.

Even after separation women are at considerable risk from their former abusive partners. Contact with children is often used as an opportunity to further abuse women, and children may be abused directly or indirectly by the man also. All women are vulnerable regardless of colour, race, nationality, ability, sexuality, lifestyle, class and income. However, women already experiencing oppression may find it more difficult to seek or access help. For example, black women, women with disabilities, women working in prostitution, will find additional barriers which agencies need to be aware of and work hard to remove if we are to safeguard the safety of all women and children.

Domestic violence between parents seriously compromises the protective capacities of both parents. Children can be frightened to let possible protectors know about sexual abuse for fear of the repercussions, both for themselves and for their mothers. If children have witnessed their father beating their mother, it is unlikely that they will perceive their mother as someone who could protect them. They are more likely to perceive her as a victim like themselves.

Where domestic violence and/or child abuse occurs in a family it is important to examine the wider picture. It is important to be aware that violence continues after separation, often when women are most at risk and receive least support. This is also true where contact between violent fathers and their children occur.

It is important to ensure that questions about domestic violence are asked and framed in a non-blaming and sympathetic manner. The worker should explore the issues with the mother and from this develop an understanding of what risks there are for the child. The risks, both immediate and longer term, should be discussed with the mother including the need for protection of the child and how this can be achieved, who is responsible for providing this and what support can be given. Within this a view of the mother's immediate and longer term capacity to understand the risks and to protect her child with support should be gained, including her awareness of the impact on the children. A safety plan should then be formed and agreed with the mother, reflecting the capabilities of the mother and the positive survival strategies that may already be in place.

Women living in situations of violence may be immobilised through shock or fear. Remaining in a violent relationship does not mean that the care and protection of the children is not a primary concern. Pressure to leave by professionals places the onus of responsibility for the violence on the woman. If a woman is not able to leave, she faces the possibility of being labelled a bad parent and as colluding with the violence. Thus begins the 'fight' with professionals at a time when information and time to assimilate this is most needed. Women in violent relationships may be acutely aware that leaving does not mean the violence will cease. Thus they may be constantly weighing up the safety issues on a day-to-day basis. Women will be employing complex strategies to avoid violence in the home. Mental ill health, alcohol and drug misuse can be as a result of ongoing violence.

Women need to know they are not being judged by workers for the actions of their partners. If we can agree that the children's protection is a shared and primary concern, it is more likely that a creative solution can be found. In order for this to begin we need to believe women are not helpless victims.

We need to know who is living in the household and how family members are financially supported. This will help workers assess whether there was opportunity for sexual abuse, possible abusers (if unclear), other potential victims, the adequacy of the living situation, and how independent the mother is, or has the potential of becoming, of the alleged perpetrator (Faller, 1988c).

Mothers need to look at the dynamics in their families and to identify the power the perpetrator wielded.

Family background

Faller (1988c) indicated that the family background can be quite useful in providing indicators of overall functioning, in understanding the dynamics of the sexual abuse, and in making treatment plans. She advised that workers assess the discipline techniques of each parent, the nature of the relationship with each parent, and the relative closeness to each parent.

There are two major reasons for speaking with the mother about her family of origin and social network: to get some sense of what it was like for them growing up as well as wanting to assess the extended family and others as sources of social support. Many factors related to their upbringing may shed light on the dynamics of sexual abuse and predict prognosis. We need to find out what kind of people her parents were and how she experienced them, particularly if there is a history of little nurturing, significant trauma, and deprivation; physical and/or sexual abuse; a lack of intimacy or attachments; no reference to sex (so they grew up with little sexual knowledge); social isolation and the absence of social supports—particularly as social isolation can have several functions: it may facilitate, prolong, or be the result of sexual abuse.

Research findings

Hanson and Scott (1996) researched the social networks of perpetrators and found that there is some evidence that they are likely to have friends and relatives who are also sexual perpetrators.

Salt *et al.*, (1990) found that a significant number of mothers reported having indifferent to overtly hostile relationships with their maternal grandmothers. Testa *et al.*, (1992) explored comparisons between women in treatment and a comparison group. They found that those in the treatment group were more likely to have been physically abused by one or both parents (62% versus 35%), to have had a parent with alcohol problems (56% versus 34%), and to be a member of a minority group (37% versus 13%). Treatment sample women came from families with lower socio-economic status and experienced more childhood family changes (e.g. divorce, remarriage, death) than women in the comparison group. Of the women who had been sexually abused, those in treatment were more likely to have experienced penetration (60% versus 29%) and exposure (83% versus 69%). They also experienced more sexually abusive incidents (31.82 versus 13.62).

Salt *et al.*, (1990) found that mothers from lower social classes tended to be less protective of their children, more punitive, and less concerned for the child's welfare. Non-white mothers were more likely than white mothers to punish and blame the child for the abuse. These differences may be explained in part by the heightened stresses in the lives of poor families.

Trepper *et al.*, (1996) examined the family-of-origin factors of both the perpetrator and the non-perpetrator in intact incestuous families. One-third of perpetrators and their non-abusing partners acknowledged some form of abuse or neglect. The perpetrator was more likely to experience physical and emotional abuse compared to the non-abusing partner who was more likely to have experienced sexual abuse.

Issues to consider

Child sexual abuse is intergenerational. That means that if one person in their family was

sexually abused then the likelihood is that someone else was also. Does the mother know anyone else in the family who was sexually abused? Did anyone have a mental disorder, use drugs or alcohol, have a criminal record or have allegations made against them?

Educational history

Faller (1988c) pointed to a mother's education as a good indicator of ability. A mother who reports she was the subject of a statement of special educational needs or was excluded from school or schools for long periods has clearly had difficulties in a major arena of childhood functioning.

It is important to establish their school performance and academic achievement; classroom behaviour; the presence or absence of problems within the school (relationships with peers and teachers, attendance and any activity whilst truant, isolation, disciplinary, suspension or exclusion, bullying or bullied with staff and/or peers, etc.); interests in school; aptitudes and abilities; special educational needs/services (ability or behavioural); school changes (including reasons); and any significant events.

Information about the mother's education tells workers a great deal about her overall functioning. School performance gives some information about her ability to persist at long-term goals and her self-discipline and self-esteem. The level of academic ability has a bearing on the type of assessment tools which can be used. Their school adjustment may offer some information about the development of peer relationships and their ability to relate to authority figures in a productive manner. As schooling is one of our first major life experiences that places demands on us to handle responsibilities, performance can be a useful predictor of subsequent difficulty or success in fulfilling life demands. Anyone who has failed at almost every major task is unlikely to benefit from any ongoing work.

Research findings

Carter (1993) found that 38 per cent of the mothers in her sample had not completed high school, 38 per cent had and gone on to complete additional education, and 24 per cent had attended universities.

Deblinger *et al.*, (1993) found in their sample that 28.3 per cent of mothers had completed at least some college; 35.4 per cent were high school graduates; and the remaining 36.4 per cent had not completed high school.

Issues to consider

Questions to ask include:

- How did you feel when you started school? What was good about school? What was bad about it?
- Who were your friends at school? What did you do with them? What games or hobbies did you enjoy with other children?
- How did the teachers treat you?
- Did you enjoy schoolwork? Was any of it hard for you? What subjects?
- What did your parents want for you in school? Did they want you to do well in sports, schoolwork, or religion?
- Were there changes in your living arrangements or family during secondary school years? Financial changes? Deaths? Moves?
- Did your feelings about school or achievements in school change in your secondary school years?
- What friends and/or activities were you involved with during your secondary school years?
- What kind of future job dreams or plans did you think about in your secondary school years? What were your goals? (Schwartz and Cellini, 1995).

Occupational history

Faller (1988) pointed to the work history as a further measure of the mother's overall functioning as well as being an indicator of her ability to act independently of the perpetrator. If she has a means of supporting herself, she will probably be more independent in other ways, including resisting his sexually abusive behaviour, extricating herself from the relationship with him, and supporting herself

and the children. A history of employment commensurate with her skill level suggests to the worker that she can hold her own in the work arena.

Research findings

Trepper *et al.*, (1996) found that approximately half of the families in the study defined the highest level of parent's employment as skilled, at 47 per cent. 22 per cent were classified as unskilled, 13 per cent were professional, and in 17 per cent of families both parents were unemployed. Two-thirds of families reported a middle-class income for the household with the majority of the remaining one-third of families reporting low-income.

Carter (1993) found that the work patterns of the mothers changed post-disclosure, with some mothers going from part-time jobs to no job at all, some taking part-time or full-time jobs when they had not been previously working, and others quitting to attend to their child's needs. Their options were limited and dictated by economic needs for survival. Mothers who decided to share the information of the sexual abuse at work largely received little or no emotional support or consideration.

Deblinger *et al.*, (1993) reported that 52.5 per cent of the mothers in their sample reported that they had been employed at least sporadically during the last year, whereas 47.5 per cent were unemployed throughout the year.

Issues to consider

It is useful to obtain a record of her work history, including types of jobs, job performance, level of responsibility and employment stability, job satisfaction, relationships with colleagues and their ability to support themselves and their family. This information can throw light on their persistence, relationships, responsibilities and dependability: all keys to effective professional intervention and the creation of sustained change.

Financial history

Financial history should include debts and assets. An individual's level of stability may be reflected in how they manage their finances. Furthermore, Faller (1988c) reported that over a quarter of cases of sexual abuse are marked with the onset of unemployment or some other factor that has an impact on self-esteem. It is therefore important to identify any such stresses, which may contribute to the dynamics of child sexual abuse.

Research findings

This has been partially covered in the earlier 'options' component. Carter (1993) found that the majority of two-parent families had incomes of over $40,000 per year, whereas the majority of single parents were living near the poverty line, of $20,411, while several mothers were attempting to support their children on less than $10,000 per year. Most women do not have viable economic choices after the disclosure of the sexual abuse.

Deblinger *et al.*, (1993) found that 36.7 per cent of the mothers in their sample reported annual family incomes greater than $20,000; 31.1 per cent between $10,000 and $20,000; and 32.2 per cent reported $10,000 or less.

Financial stress can be a risk factor for incest (Van der Mey and Neff, 1986). Much of the financial stress predates the incest but becomes compounded after it has been disclosed (see consequences and options section for a further discussion around this area).

Health and medical history

Mothers in violent families frequently exhibit anxiety-related health problems prior to the discovery of child sexual abuse. Kinard (1996) noted that the detrimental impact of stress and inadequate social support on psychological well being in adults has been well documented in research, with depression receiving the most attention as an outcome. The cumulative evidence suggests that inadequate social support is one of the strongest predictors of depression. Maternal deficiencies in social competence and interpersonal social skills may be the most important personality factors associated with the ability to develop and maintain social support networks. Indeed, deficiencies in these areas are likely to increase the risk of depression. Kinard explored this and found that at the first interview, mothers of abused children reported less perceived support from family and partners and greater depressive symptomatology than did mothers of non-abused children. The abuse and the non-abuse groups did not differ on perceived support from friends, neighbours, co-workers, or organisations. At the second interview one year later, the abuse and non-abuse groups continued to differ on family and partner support, but did not differ on competence. The depressive symptoms declined over time for mothers in the abuse group, although they remained higher than that of the non-abuse group. This may be due to improvements in family circumstances, to cessation of abuse, or to intervention services.

There are three reasons for exploring the mother's history for mental illness:

- Mental problems must be taken into account in assessing overall functioning. The longer the mental illness and the more severe its presentation, the poorer the treatment prognosis.

- Certain kinds of mental illness are indicative of poor object relations, and can affect the offender's ability to relate to children and partners, and

- In a few cases, mental illness plays a key role in sexual abuse. For example, Finkelhor (1984) found that having an absent or ill mother was an important predictor of the likelihood of sexual abuse. Kaplan *et al.*, (1988) found that the increased risk of parental depression in abusing families extends to mothers who were not the perpetrators of the abuse. Belsky (1984) concluded that the most important determinant of parenting skills is the parents' psychological well being. Although low social support, lack of self-competence, and depression have been noted as common characteristics of parents in abusing families, the links between them have seldom being examined. Trepper *et al.*, (1996) found that 31 per cent of the mothers in incest families had some type of recognisable psychopathology. They were more likely to display a passive-dependent personality and to experience depression than was the offender or the victim. They also scored highly on seeing themselves as the victim, being introverted and having poor self-esteem.

Faller (1988c) notes that the mother's mental illness can have a range of functions. Occasionally a mentally ill parent who has some sexual dysfunction will develop delusions that her partner is sexually abusing the child. There are some circumstances where her mental illness may lead her to facilitate the sexual abuse. Another possibility is that the circumstances of the marriage and the sexual abuse may precipitate mental illness on the part of the mother. They may also be psychologically unavailable to others (partner and children). Where the mother needs periodic hospitalisation, she is physically unavailable to protect. Some mothers tend to focus on getting their own needs met and the needs of the child become secondary. The same techniques used for ascertaining the abuser's mental state can be used with the mother.

Depression can be a very disturbing and frightening experience. People often feel that depression descends on them from nowhere and they feel powerless to understand or change that feeling. Whilst it can cause physical changes such as tiredness or loss of appetite, it is primarily a problem about feelings. For example, people may feel worthless, inferior, or unlovable; or they may feel negative about themselves in response to a particular event.

Newberger *et al.*, (1993) found that a mother's level of depression may be an aspect of her emotional reaction to the disclosure of the sexual abuse itself. The findings regarding depression are important, because if chronic or recurrent, may affect her post-disclosure ability to parent and protect her children. This is important when we know that depression in mothers is a significant predictor of children's subsequent functioning (Forchand *et al.*, 1987).

Depressed mothers have been shown to report increased behavioural symptoms in their children (Deblinger *et al.*, 1997). They may have less energy and tolerance than non-depressed parents and experience their children's behaviour as more symptomatic than they otherwise might. At the same time,

distressed mothers may be less emotionally available for their children, thereby setting the stage for the development of increased child symptomatology.

Herman (1981) also found that over half of the incest survivors in her sample remembered that their mothers had had periods of disabling illness which resulted in frequent hospitalisations or in the mother living as an invalid at home. 38 per cent of the daughters had been separated from their mothers at some time during their childhood either because their mothers were hospitalised or because they felt they could not cope with looking after their children. Depression, alcoholism and psychosis were among the most common problems that these mothers had.

Substance abuse may have a variety of functions in sexual abuse. Using either drugs or alcohol may cause the mother to lose her attractiveness to the abuser. She may not be sexually responsive to him because of her intoxication, and this renders her unavailable to protect her children also. Drug use inevitably impacts upon the finances and she may involve herself in illegal activities to obtain money for drugs. This may extend to prostitution, which also exposes the children to men who may exploit them.

Leifer *et al.*, (1993) found that a maternal history of childhood abuse and of poor childhood attachment relationships were strongly associated with current maternal substance abuse. In turn, maternal substance abuse and dissatisfaction with current social supports were highly related to the lack of maternal support to the sexually abused child, and to a higher frequency of abuse incidents.

Issues to consider

The task for professionals is to assess whether these mothers are capable of showing concern for their children and whether they have the potential to learn how to protect. If there are some promising indicators, such as the mothers feeling able to express concern for the child, then professional intervention of an intense nature may help them move on.

It is important that people set and keep to a routine, which involves contact with people so they can begin to work with the positives around them and explore how to learn to enjoy themselves again. Exercise is also a good stimulant.

The mother's recovery of mental health is an essential part and even preface to effective treatment, particularly since it has often been affected by the disclosure and then the subsequent intervention (Bagley, 1995).

Interpersonal relationships

This section explores more than the mother's relationship with the perpetrator, covered in an earlier section. This section is designed to explore relationships with significant others and what this means for the mother in terms of networks and support.

Information about relations with significant others can be of benefit in understanding the dynamics and prognosis of sexual abuse. Interpersonal communication is a dominant human function, and many of our problems stem from our concerns over the way we relate to other people, and the manner in which they respond to us (Lazarus, 1976: p42). It is not surprising, therefore, that interpersonal relations are a central part of dealing with sexually abusing families.

Weiss (1974) identified six key areas which isolated people miss out on. They are attachment, provided by close affectionate relationships, which give a sense of security and place; social integration, provided by membership of a network of persons having shared interests and values; the opportunity for nurturing others, usually children, which gives some incentive for continuing in the face of adversity; reassurance of personal worth, which promotes self-esteem and comes both from those at home as well as from colleagues; a sense of reliable alliance, which is obtained mainly from kin; and obtaining help and guidance from informal advisors when difficulties have to be resolved. Examples of the items include: at present, do you have someone you can share your most private feelings with (confide in) or not? Who is this mainly? Do you wish you could share more with them, or is it just about right the way it is? Would you like to have someone like this or would you prefer to keep your feelings to yourself?

Interpersonal dyadic relationships can be defined by three relatively independent dimensions: boundary, power and intimacy. Since the development of intimacy is a process, boundary and power cannot be isolated from any definition of intimacy (Waring and Reddon, 1983). A healthy intimate relationship is characterised by the capacity for constructive, respectful expression of positive and negative emotions. These expressions should be mutually acceptable and promote the psychological well being of the individuals involved; their function is primarily to define boundaries, to communicate concern and commitment, to negotiate roles, and to resolve conflicts (Coleman, 1987). Mothers with a history of being abused themselves have often lacked healthy role models, and boundaries between family members are too weak or too firm. The boundary difficulties resulting from these factors may lead to two distinct problems with intimacy: they may be needy, intrusive, enmeshed, or controlling resulting from a lack of clear boundaries between self and others, or the person may be avoiding and distancing, the outcome of boundaries too tightly drawn.

Intimacy is clearly important in establishing effective emotional and sexual relations with other adults (Brehm, 1992), and those who are able to develop it are seen to be warm and sincere; less aggressive, and better able to resist stress. Their relationships also provide them with a sense of security, emotional comfort, shared experiences, an opportunity to be nurturing plus a sense of self-worth (Marshall, 1995). Intimacy is a universal human characteristic. If thwarted in adult relationships, then sexual perpetrators may seek intimacy in other less appropriate ways. This failure to achieve intimacy leads to the experience of emotional loneliness, which causes considerable frustration.

Research findings

Courtois (1988) found that incest survivors often lack friendships due to anger, mistrust, and a general devaluation of women, including themselves. Herman (1981) also noted that they favour men for their privileged position and resent woman for their powerlessness. Alexander (1992) suggested that they present with a consistent pattern of insecure attachment that interferes with their establishment of peer relationships.

Lubell and Peterson (1998) found that the closest relationships reported by incest survivors lasted an average of seven years less than those of the comparison participants. They also reported lower levels of interpersonal competence. Survivors of incest viewed their relationship with their mother as poor. They reported less satisfaction, less compatibility, less intimacy, more conflict, and less assurance in the continuity of these relationships. They spent less time with their mothers and desired even less contact with them than they had. They viewed their mothers as more isolated and lonely than the comparison groups. Perhaps this was due to the mothers being victims of sexual abuse themselves in their families of origin and/or experienced domestic violence in their current family environments. Perhaps they distanced themselves from others because they were reluctant to discuss their own experiences of incest or domestic violence. This finding contributes to understanding why mothers and daughters in families where incest occurred experienced poor interpersonal relationships— the family system was, and is, problematic.

Issues to consider

Questions to be asked include:

- What is your partner like or what kind of a person is he?
- What about him pleases you?
- What displeases you?
- What kind of things do you do together? Do you enjoy these?
- Do you ever do things together without the children?
- Are there things about your partner you would like changed?
- Do you tell him things you don't tell anyone else?
- How do you show him when he pleases you or you are happy with him?
- How does he show you when you please him or he is happy with you?
- How does he know when you are displeased?
- How do you know when he is displeased?
- What do you have arguments about?

- Have you ever used physical force with each other? If yes, please describe (Faller, 1988c).

In exploring interpersonal relationships with the mother, we need to consider:

- The nature and quality of her relations with peers.
- The nature, quality and duration of her friendships.
- The kinds of friends they select as associates. Are they susceptible to the influence of others?
- The nature and extent of social isolation— which may possibly indicate a more severe psychopathology.
- Whether the offender is active or passive in social relations e.g. social interests, activities and memberships. Are they self-centred? Excessively controlling and competitive?
- The nature and stability in their relationships. Obtain a relationship history, including the ages and sexes of the ex-partners children.

The marital relationship needs to be specifically targeted for information, eliciting how they met their partners; how they were attracted to them; how long it lasted, and if it has ended, why and when; how many serious relationships they had before they married; why they decided to marry; how their relationship changed after marriage; what were the good and bad parts of the marriage; did they or their wives have other sexual relationships? Why? When? The number of children and their relationship with them; their attitudes and expectations regarding marriage; any history of rape, domestic violence, etc.; the quality of their relationships, their ability to see their spouse as a separate individual with her own needs, and the extent to which their descriptions correspond with information elicited from other sources. Marriage failures may reflect an inability to form lasting relationships, or to meet someone else's needs. How is her sexual relationship with her partner? Can they describe the kinds of sexual activity they engage in and their approximate frequency? How often do they engage in sexual activity? Has this relationship been more or less the same over the years or changing? Who initiates sex?

Self-esteem

Self-esteem is defined as the way in which a person perceives themselves, values themselves and rates themselves in relation to other people (Briggs *et al.*, 1998: p128).

If individuals grow up in a loving and supporting environment, then they learn to trust their own judgement; to feel 'safe' in the world; that they can be liked for themselves; that they can make their own decisions; that they are valuable; and that they deserve to be treated with love and respect.

When mothers have been sexually abused themselves or where their children have been sexually abused, their self-esteem may suffer as they learn that the world is a dangerous place where trusted people take advantage of them and use them for their own ends. This can lead to problems like not being able to say 'no' to people; always putting other people's needs first; not being able to make decisions; waiting to see what happens rather than making a choice; staying in bad relationships; and having a sense of no choices or control. Workers do need to create space to listen to mothers and assist in problem-solving that promotes their self-esteem.

Mothers' self-esteem is acutely affected by domestic violence and a controlling partner whose interaction is telling them what they can and cannot do, as though they were children themselves.

Every mother will react differently to the disclosure of child sexual abuse, and is linked to her personal characteristics and resources. Her self-esteem will affect and be affected by: what she believes her alternatives might be in the presenting situation; how she perceives her relationship with the child and with the offender; what fears and losses she faces; what meaning she gives to the situation; and how she responds to therapeutic interventions (Ovaris, 1991: p14). These forces will become more apparent as the crisis evolves.

Research findings

Bagley (1995) found that mothers and controls have identical levels of self-esteem. The most likely reason for this is that the time mothers have spent in therapy has enabled them to develop normal levels of self-esteem, even though in the recent past they experienced crises which were associated with devastated mental health, depression, suicidal feelings and, in some cases, actual suicidal behaviour. He argued that the longer the time that has elapsed since the revelation, the better the mother's self-esteem level is likely to be.

Cammaert (1988) found that many mothers in families where their child had been sexually abused had low self-esteem. This finding was echoed in the research of Leifer *et al.*, (1993), and they found it was linked to the fact that 52 per cent of the mothers in the study had been sexually abused themselves.

Sgroi and Dana (1982) reported that low self-esteem is a common feature of mothers in incest families. An important task for workers is for them to attempt to rebuild self-esteem as well as helping to mobilise support networks and providing practical advice to enable the mother to cope more positively with her own needs and those of her children. Hooper (1989) noted that a focus on self-esteem has important implications for intervention: attempting to reinforce women's performance in their family roles may produce guilt about the parts of their life, which actually provide sources of autonomy and self-worth.

Issues to consider

Most mothers experience some loss of self-esteem when their child is harmed. Low self-esteem is not the cause of the sexual abuse. *Self-esteem is an indicator of one's psychological resources and feelings of competence.* A lack of confidence in a mother's ability to parent can make the simple tasks seem very complex. Mothers often feel overwhelmed by the demands placed on her, which add to her perceived sense of failure. Mothers need to be given some permission to be overwhelmed and to talk through their feelings as they are experienced.

Mothers need to work on their thoughts and feelings about the abuse that will help them to feel better in themselves, thus encouraging a growth in their self-esteem. They need to challenge any negative thoughts they have. For example, they may divide a piece of paper into negative thoughts and more positive thoughts. They then complete this task as though it was a diary, articulating the thoughts they have when they feel low. When they feel more positive, reflect on their thoughts and ask themselves whether this is very true or not, articulating counter-thoughts on the opposite side of the paper. They may want to do this with a friend or counsellor if there are more low moments than high ones at any given time. Another alternative is to simply keep to the positives and write a list of all the positive things about themselves, whether they be things they like about themselves or what they are good at. They reaffirm these to themselves as frequently as they feel is necessary.

Many mothers seek a speedy resolution to the problem and this can affect their self-esteem if she believes it is not possible and that that is her fault. Low energy levels and eroded self-esteem are not a good recipe for recovery. Indeed, a mother's self-esteem level will be critical to how she copes.

Social skills

Social skills is a broad term used to describe a wide variety of behaviours and cognitive phenomena presumed necessary for effective functioning in social situations.

A lot of the literature on mothers of sexually abused children highlights them lacking self-esteem and social skills (Sahd, 1980). A woman's very sense of who they are may be sorely damaged by the discovery of sexual abuse, which challenges every aspect of her identity. They may question their judgement of the world, as their previous perceptions of reality, family relationships, partner and children are all thrown into turmoil (Hubbard, 1989).

Research findings

Salt *et al.*, (1990) found that 19 per cent of the mothers in their sample had serious problems in social interaction with others.

Issues to consider

The interview itself can provide clues as to the mother's social skills behaviours (verbal and non-verbal). Deficits may be indicated where they look away excessively, fail to listen, interrupt readily, lack social pleasantry, appear socially awkward, jump topics suddenly,

become over-familiar with the worker or ask personal questions of the workers which are unrelated to the background relevant to the inquiry (Carich and Adkerson, 1995: p8).

Do they tend to be involved in insular activities? Do they value spending time with others? Has the influence of others been experienced primarily in negative or positive terms? Are there any differences in the way they describe interactions with children, same-sex adults, and opposite-sex adults?

Social support

Understanding the mother's support system is a central area of assessment as it may help in the understanding of the dynamics of the abuse, be of assistance in treatment planning, and aid in predicting prognosis. Indeed, social isolation can play a role in causing or prolonging sexual abuse. Conversely, if the mother does have a support system she will usually be better able emotionally to manage the abusive situation. In particular, she will probably be less dependent on the perpetrator and more able to seek out what is best for herself and her children.

It is not uncommon for the mother to lose extended family and support networks after the disclosure. This can happen even when they choose the child rather than their partner, as they may not wish to burden others and they are often overwhelmed by shame and grief. Other mothers may be shocked that friends or family may accuse them of over-reacting and rally to support the man. Conversely, others may see her grieving for someone believed to be undeserving as unacceptable and this can make it more difficult for her to gain the support needed to understand her own conflicting feelings.

There is often a need for an increased level of support following disclosure. This is important if the mother is to harness sufficient resources to cope with the presenting situation and look forward to protective strategies in the future.

We also need to be aware that where the mother has herself been the victim of physical and sexual abuse, particularly from her partner, then they may have great difficulty in asking for help, assuming rejection, disbelief and hostility; they fear regression when addressing the abuse, both due to any re-activation of the abuse, or the associated terror and despair; and they have concerns over confidentiality, particularly if they remain in contact with the perpetrator.

Research findings

Following the disclosure of sexual abuse, family members may become more socially isolated as contact with relatives and/or friends decreases or terminates entirely (MacFarlane and Bulkley, 1982). This is unfortunate since this is the time when the mother needs help in order to create some degree of stability in the family. It is always better when families work this problem out together. They too have to go through the same time-consuming, painful process before they can admit exactly what happened. As such, mothers may find that the extended family is believing, and understanding about feelings one day, only to reverse their position the next. Mothers need to understand that other family members may have very good reasons for not wanting to believe. For example, they may not want to end their relationship with the perpetrator, or they may have had memories of their own abuse resurrected for them. This understanding on the part of mothers should lead to them allowing some space for the family to work through the issues as they affect individuals differently. In all families, the process of change remains an extremely difficult one to achieve. Over time, families must learn different ways of communicating so that there is a lot more listening and a lot less blaming.

Immediate changes can take place in the relationships between the perpetrators and other members of the children's families when relatives, trusted friends, or neighbours were the perpetrators. Formerly friendly relationships disappeared. Many mothers were ostracised in and by their communities. In those families where the perpetrator was a relative, the disclosure of the sexual abuse invariably split families up as members took sides, leaving women whose social lives revolved around their families isolated. The most significantly lacking aspect for most mothers is the emotional support from significant others (Carter, 1993). The best support for mothers frequently came from female friends and sisters.

Fong and Walsh-Bowers (1998) reported that following disclosure, mothers tried to look for help from both formal and informal sources, but were often disappointed. This may be linked to their physical and psychological health becoming affected. They found that whether the women received support from their extended families depended upon the depth of the previous relationships they had with them. Some women felt supported, but others felt that their extended families would not want anything to do with such a family scandal, and thus they never tried to discuss it with them.

Trepper *et al.*, (1996) found that families are vulnerable to incest because the members are socially isolated from the outside environment. 36 per cent of the families in the study were described as extremely socially isolated with another 43 per cent identified as moderately socially isolated. Overall, three quarters of the families were more insulated from the social environment than not.

Issues to consider

Child sexual abuse is an isolating and frightening experience for both children and women. Where mothers are offered their own worker, they often act more supportively towards their child and with less hostility to the professionals acting on behalf of the child.

There is a need to identify her supports and other means of validation in her life.

Workers need to explore the mother's relationships with her family, her partner's family, friends, work mates, neighbours and professionals. Has she been able to ask anyone to mind the children in the midst of the crisis? Who would she usually turn to if there is a crisis, e.g. needing to take one child to hospital? What has failed her to allow the abuse to take place, if anything? What can be mobilised to support the mother and child now, or in the future?

Many mothers identified isolation as a common factor with feelings of being unable to deal with all of the issues around the abuse. This often links to the mother needing something for themselves in order to cope as well as to offload. They need time out from the pressure and all the responsibilities. Many mothers felt that they had been let down by the agencies involved and the system, and could rarely see any light at the end of the tunnel.

Sexual History

Dual vulnerability: the mother's own history of sexual abuse

> *Non-offending mothers are not likely to seek help for resolving their childhood trauma until there is an external reason for doing so. This is due, at least in part, to a lingering belief that they were responsible for the abuse experienced in their childhood.*
> (Ovaris, 1991: p60)

Hubbard (1989) defined a history of sexual abuse in mothers as any reference to sexual abuse experienced by the mothers, or the after effects of that sexual abuse, including references to the mothers' inability to establish intimate relationships with family members.

The possibility that the mother herself is a survivor of childhood sexual abuse cannot be overlooked. Many mothers will, when asked, identify incidents of sexual abuse in their own lives, and most will never have told anyone about it, may not have been supported if they did, and have probably not received adequate treatment. As such, they are probably still using coping strategies developed to contend with the original trauma. They may thus experience anxiety attacks, flashbacks, deepened depression, and dissociation when confronted with the sexual abuse of their own child.

A classic response for many mothers to their own abuse is one of either forgetting or denying. It is not surprising, therefore, that they face huge dilemmas when they discover sexual abuse, and they may choose against actively pursuing such information in relation to their children. Hooper (1989) sees these as coping strategies rather than collusion.

For some mothers, their history of sexual abuse has remained hidden, sometimes even to themselves, until an event in adult life brings the past to the surface. This can include the discovery that her child is being sexually abused by either the same perpetrator or another family member, such as her partner. Some factors which facilitate disclosure lie within the mother herself and include: whether she has learnt to dissociate herself from the abuse as a child; the reactions of others to previous attempts to disclose as a child and as an adult; whether she has told anyone before; the extent of her recall of the abuse; her emotional reactions to the memories of the abuse; and whether she has had close relationships with non-abusive adults during childhood (Hall and Lloyd, 1989).

Research findings

There is evidence that mothers of children who have been sexually abused experience greater distress than mothers of children who have not been abused (Kelley, 1990; Manion *et al.*, 1996). It has also been noted that mothers of sexually abused children frequently have a history of sexual abuse and further, that this history interferes with their ability to deal with the current abuse of their children (Carter, 1993).

Cole *et al.*, (1992) have also found a relationship between being an incest victim and reported feelings of inadequacy as a parent, especially a lack of confidence and control. Furthermore, they also expressed higher expectations of themselves as mothers than did their non-abused counterparts. The authors suggest that problems coping with intense emotion induce withdrawal from immediate parenting situations, leaving children with less consistency and direction, and mothers feeling overwhelmed or inadequate. The mother who is herself an incest survivor may feel an intensity to a greatly magnified degree and respond by emotionally withdrawing from the immediate situation. This is often *not* their final response to the disclosure.

Tinling (1990) argued that women who were abused sexually as children go on to marry child abusers and then become mothers of sexually abused children. Things are never that clear cut, but there is some evidence to show that sexual abuse histories can signal increased vulnerability to having children who are sexually abused. For example, a woman who has been sexually abused may feel uncomfortable with normal adult sexual relationships and choose a partner who does not make sexual demands upon her because his primary sexual attraction is to children. In addition, a woman who has a background of sexual victimisation may either not be as sensitive to risk situations as other woman and unwittingly place her children at risk, or conversely becomes over-protective and hyper-vigilant towards them.

Current research does indicate that a significant proportion of mothers in families where sexual abuse has occurred report having experienced sexual abuse during childhood. Faller (1989) examined the histories of mothers where their child had been sexually abused in the family, and found that 49.9 per cent of the sample recalled having sexually abusive experiences as children; whilst 42.2 per cent reported having experienced direct sexual victimisation.

Sroufe *et al.*, (1985) found that women who suffered sexual abuse as children tended to behave in sexualised ways with their young male children, controlling them in seductive, over-intimate ways. Their relationship with their daughters was very different: they were distant and somewhat rejecting.

Bagley and King (1990) found that half the mothers of abuse victims had experienced serious sexual abuse within their family, compared with 18 per cent of controls in comparable periods of family life. They hypothesised that these mothers failed to suspect sexual abuse as they had escaped their abusive homes by entering idealistically into new relationships which they assumed must inevitable be better. A combination of naïve optimism and continued powerlessness and subordination to male dominance had resulted in an emotional and cognitive framework which made it very difficult for them to understand what might be going on (p168).

Burkett (1991) explored the links between a childhood history of childhood sexual abuse and current parenting behaviours of school-aged children. She found that there were blurred boundaries between parent and child sub-systems, with a greater percentage of self-focused rather than child-focused messages from abuse-history mothers. The children had clearly taken on board their parent's expectations that they take a leadership role in meeting the adult's needs for caretaking (role reversal). She identified two main parenting categories. The first category appeared to consist of women who struggle with depression, chemical abuse and despair. These women function marginally as parents, having little energy or emotional resources available

for raising children. Women in this category are sometimes unable to provide their children with protection. These women could be called 'under-functioning' in regard to parenting. In the second category, mothers felt positive, excited, and enthusiastic about their parenting. These women were generally functioning better in various areas of life than those in the previous category. They had the energy and motivation to actively emphasise excellent parenting as a major personal goal, but seemed over-focused on their parental role, and dependent on their children for emotional closeness. Many appeared to be caught up in a smothering, over-controlling kind of pseudo-nurturing. Women in both these categories were markedly more likely to meet their companionship needs through their children and rely on their children for emotional support than were comparison-group women.

Deblinger *et al.*, (1994b) found that mothers with a history of sexual abuse felt more alone in the crisis than did mothers without a history. But, even with higher distress levels and feelings of aloneness, mothers with a history of abuse believed the allegations concerning their children and acted as advocates for their children to the same extent as mothers without such a history. They argued that a mother's history of sexual abuse is important, not because it is a risk factor for her child, but rather because it points to critical issues to address in treatment, such as symptom distress and the sense of isolation. They believe that a maternal history of child sexual abuse should be included as a moderating variable in future investigations examining the effectiveness of interventions for sexually abused children and their parents. Muram *et al.*, (1994) explored the personality profiles of mothers of sexual abuse victims. They found that they did not display noteworthy psychopathology in any sphere. They were only marginally less outgoing than control mothers and nothing suggested that they were a markedly passive or apathetic group.

Newberger, Newberger and Gremy (1991) compared the psychiatric responses of women with and without sexual abuse histories to disclosures of their children's sexual abuse and to assess the relationship of these histories to the nature of the child's victimisation. They found that neither the duration nor the use of force in the child's abuse appeared to exert an effect independent of the mother's own abuse history. Whether the child's abuse was intra-familial also did not appear to contribute to the victimised mother's psychiatric responses. A marginal relationship was found, however, with the presence of intercourse in the child's abuse and the severity of the mother's psychiatric symptoms after 12 months. One specific aspect of the mother's own victimisation, its duration, was strongly associated with the nature of the children's abuse experience. The longer the mother's abuse the greater the likelihood that force would be used in the abuse of the child. They were unable to explain how the experience of child sexual abuse translates to the later vulnerability of women and their children. They did note, however, that it may be expressed as a panoply of troubles. These may include vulnerabilities in the domain of interpersonal relationships and the capacity to recognise people who would be hurtful to herself and her children and to protect against them. In comparison to the children who were not sexually victimised in childhood, these women's children suffered abuses which were substantially more severe. This suggests that women and children may be vulnerable to domination by intrusive men, a *dual vulnerability*, which may be associated with the womens' childhood victimisation experience. They proposed that from this set of connections that child sexual abuse in subsequent generations may be partly or largely explained by the enduring impacts of coercive control and powerlessness deriving from protracted abuse in the early years. Maternal powerlessness deriving from protracted abuse in childhood may be associated with later relationships of a coercive and intrusive nature. Support for such a formulation is suggested by the finding that the longer the mother's childhood abuse endured the greater the likelihood that force would be used in the abuse of the child. Overall, the emotional burdens of a maternal history of child sexual abuse appear to be substantial, continuous, and connected to a child's vulnerability.

The Intergenerational Nature of Sexual Abuse

The intergenerational model of child abuse has attracted considerable interest in the literature (see Buchanan, 1996). The transmission rate has ranged from 7 per cent to 70 per cent in various studies. Belsky (1993) maintained that approximately one-third of former victims become abusive parents themselves. The relationship between a parent's past history and current parenting behaviour is of particular interest in studying child sexual abuse given that most females are victims, yet most perpetrators are male. There has not been any research conducted that examines a connection between mothers who were sexually abused and the sexual abuse of their children.

Kreklewetz and Piotrowski (1996, 1998) explored how mothers' own sexual abuse influences her parenting perceptions and behaviour. The key findings included:

Mothers' fears and protective behaviours

All the mothers described themselves as protective parents, with some describing themselves as 'overprotective'. The most frequently mentioned protection strategies were communication, education and information sharing. Mothers felt that the more information they could gain about parenting and the more open the communication channels were with their children, the more protected their daughters would be. Implicit in this strategy was a strenuous effort to promote good communication with their daughters. Mothers also supervised the contact with certain individuals and situations and developed safety plans. They withheld contact with family members who refused to acknowledge the mother's own past abuse, and they stopped contact with their own perpetrators and the molester of their child (if different). They felt they had less control over the child's safety outside of the home. Mothers developed 'monitoring behaviours' of their daughters both in the home as well as their social activities with peers. Mothers who perceived certain situations to be high risk expressed concern about their daughter's safety, say, if drinking or staying over at a friend's house. Most mothers agreed that their children were at greatest risk for harm when they were younger, smaller, and were less able to protect themselves. They made repeated reference to their child's physical size and suggested that their small stature left them more vulnerable to harm. Interestingly, some mothers even judged their daughter's age of vulnerability to be around the same age as when they themselves had been abused. In contrast, other mothers felt that very young children were at little risk, because they were easier to monitor closely. Finally, while some mothers acknowledged that their early adolescent daughters were now older and physically larger, the fact that they were more difficult to monitor closely contributed to maternal fears and anxiety that puberty was a high risk period for sexual abuse.

Mothers' coping ability

Fourteen of the sixteen mothers described earlier periods during which they were emotionally or physically absent from their children, especially when they were pre-school aged or younger. These were periods of illness, depression, heavy drinking, 'nervous breakdowns', or when they 'just couldn't function'.

Parentification

All the mothers current beliefs scored within the normal range, and half were not aware that parentified behaviour had taken place.

Remembering their abuse

Many mothers began remembering their abuse during counselling. Those that did, expended a lot of energy towards protecting their daughters. There is a potential, therefore, that mothers that have little or no recall of their own abuse may be at higher risk for the recurrence of incest. Mothers often became more confident after counselling, having worked on their own feelings from the past which had, in turn, opened the doors to communication between themselves and their children. Their self-esteem had also improved.

Effects on mothers' parenting and influences of counselling

Mothers unanimously felt that their parenting had been affected by their past incest experience. These included: repeating patterns, inability to experience emotional physical closeness with their daughter, and pervasive anger and feelings of powerlessness as a parent. Most mothers found that resolving their abuse through counselling was instrumental in making them less fearful, less withdrawn, less depressed, and more actively protective of their daughters. This change in parenting focus points to the need to focus on survivors of sexual abuse prior to or early in their parenting years, and further work is needed to determine what factors play a role in this transition.

Partner trust issues

Five of the seven women who were married or living with a partner expressed some ambivalence, worries, and concerns about trusting their partner and others.

Kreklewetz and Piotrowski found that no clear link has been made between a mother's own history of incest and her ability to protect her daughter from incest. They uncovered several strengths in the mothers responses, which included having appropriate methods of the control of children, use of disciplinary methods other than corporal punishment, and having a clear understanding of the role of 'parent' and 'child'. The mothers usually displayed strong sensitivity to their children's needs.

McMillen *et al.*, (1995) recorded four principal benefits of being sexually abused after interviewing 154 women. 46.8 per cent reported perceiving some benefit from child sexual abuse. 24 per cent felt they received quite a bit or lot of benefit. 22.7 per cent felt they received a little or some benefit. 88.9 per cent also reported perceptions of harm. The reported types of benefit included: protecting children, self-protection, increased knowledge of child sexual abuse, and having a stronger personality.

Protecting children

29.2 per cent reported that they felt they were better able to protect children from being sexually abused as a result of being sexually abused themselves. Many mentioned a general caution they take with their children. Others mentioned more concrete strategies used to protect children from abuse, such as teaching their children about child sexual abuse or controlling access to their children. Some women reported trying to keep an open, stronger relationship with their children, in the hope that they would tell them if someone did try to touch them inappropriately.

Self-protection

Women described themselves as less naïve, less trusting, more careful in their relationships, and trusting their instincts more.

Increased knowledge of child sexual abuse

The knowledge women elicited from their own sexual abuse experiences seemed to be of two types: a general knowledge of sexual abuse and paedophilia, and increased empathy with victims of sexual abuse. This information sometimes led to self-protection or protection of children.

Strength

Some women described themselves as being a stronger, better person and being much more self-sufficient.

These findings are important as they suggest that women may be empowered by their abuse experiences to take concrete actions to protect themselves and their children. There may be a trade-off between self-protection and satisfying adult relationships. A lack of trust in people, especially men, resulting in strained romantic relationships may be a common long-term consequence of child sexual abuse (Alexander, 1993).

Oates *et al.*, (1998) studied whether mothers who were sexually abused in their own childhood are at increased risk of their children being sexually abused and to see if prior sexual abuse in mothers affected their parenting abilities. They found that sexual abuse in a mother's own childhood was related to an increased risk of sexual abuse occurring in the next generation, although prior maternal sexual abuse did not effect the outcome in children who were sexually abused. They found that there was no significant difference of intra-familial sexual abuse occurring between those mothers who had, and those who had not, provided a history of being sexually abused themselves.

Cohen (1995) found that adult female survivors of sexual abuse were less skilful in their maternal function, particularly in role support, communication and role-image than mothers who had not been sexually abused as mothers.

Role support

She found that mothers who were incest victims function generally on a lower level than mothers who were not exposed to this trauma in their childhood.

> *Indeed, the general plight of women who were incest victims, and the specific difficulties they experience as mothers may well be linked to the past abuse. Incest and child sexual abuse is above all the betrayal of the child's trust, and as such may hinder a victim's developing ability to protect others. In addition, these mothers may experience a constant fear that their children may also become victims, a fear which contributes to their seclusion. The past abuse may thus inhibit the victims from enlisting the support of husbands and friends in sharing child care responsibilities, leaving them overburdened and over-extended with the unavoidable result of physical as well as emotional depletion.*
>
> (Cohen, 1995)

Role image

Future difficulties in the mother's perceived role image can be traced to past sexual abuse and the family dynamics. Motherhood is a socially learned role and so past parentification and especially mother-daughter role reversal and alienation may contribute to a general distortion of the psychological capacities for mothering, and also to future unrealistic perception and expectations regarding this role.

Communication skills

Communication skills may be adversely affected by past sexual abuse and specifically linked to its secretive nature: the ensuing subjective experiences of the child victim are ones of isolation, inadequacy and guilt over the past abuse, and the adult women may continue to feel responsible for past occurrence as well as its continuation long after its cessation. The resulting reluctance, shame and fear to share her past abuse, coupled with 'learned submissiveness' in her family of origin, may well interfere with her developing ability to communicate freely and openly, thus constricting her capacity in general, and eventually hinder open and spontaneous expression of feelings towards her children.

Issues to consider

Mothers do need to be aware that having a history of sexual abuse themselves does not impact negatively on their capacity to protect. Rather, they should be more alert to the signs and indicators that their child is being sexually abused.

Mothers who remain in denial about their own abuse are not able to protect their children from the same or other perpetrators. They have such an investment in protecting themselves from their own memories that they cannot see the abuse or the indicators in their own children. There are issues for mothers who have faced up to their own abuse if this has not been in the context of therapy, as they may still have an investment in denying that the same thing is happening to their child and they also have to face up to their feelings about it.

Questions: what are her survivor issues? Explore with the mother how she survived her childhood trauma and focus her attention on potential and actual strengths and previously used coping strategies: those that were successful and those that were not. Also, explore any unresolved issues for them and assess how these may impact on her and the child's recovery. Unfortunately, by focusing on the weaknesses of her unresolved problems, the worker is most likely to engage the mother in treatment. Utilise her experience to focus on her ability to empathise with the child.

Summary

This chapter has set out a detailed framework for assessing a mother's ability to protect in a way that encourages workers to think more about the knowledge and value base that structures their intervention style. There is a need to embrace more recent research and practice experience to inform an approach which considers impact, support and dilemmas facing the mothers when the sexual abuse is intra-familial in nature. This chapter forms the basis of a more detailed book that is currently in preparation (Calder with Peake and Rose, forthcoming) and which looks more at messages for professionals, more detailed exercises to elicit the required information, treatment issues, a review of the literature, causation, separate considerations for extra-familial abuse, and detailed frameworks for determining outcome. This chapter offers some preliminary guidance and should go some way towards equipping workers when they are faced with assessing a mother in a situation of intra-familial sexual abuse.

References

Abel, G.G., Becker, J.V., Cunningham-Rathner, J., Mittleman, R.S., and Rouleau, J. (1988). Multiple Paraphilic Diagnosis Among Sex Offenders. *Bulletin of the American Academy of Psychiatry and the Law*, 16: pp153–68.

Abel, G.G., Becker, J.V., Cunningham-Rathner, J., Rouleau, J., and Murphy, W. (1987). Self-reported Crimes of Non-incarcerated Paraphiliacs. *Journal of Interpersonal Violence*, 2: pp3–25.

Abel, G.G., Mittleman, M.S., and Becker, J.V. (1985). Sex Offenders: Results of Assessment and Recommendations for Treatment. In Ben-Aron, M.H., Hucker, S.J., and Webster, C.D. (Eds.). *Clinical Criminology: The Assessment and Treatment of Criminal Behaviour*. Toronto: M and M Graphics.

Adams, C., and Fay, J. (1981). *No More Secrets: Protecting Your Child from Sexual Assault*. San Luis Obispo, CA: Impact Publishers.

Adams-Tucker, C. (1982). Proximate Effects of Sexual Abuse in Childhood: A Report on 28 Children. *American Journal of Psychiatry*, 139: pp1252–6.

Alexander, P.C. (1992). Application of Attachment Theory to the Study of Sexual Abuse. *Journal of Consulting and Clinical Psychology*, 60: pp185–95.

Anthony, G., and Watkeys, J. (1991). False Allegations in Child Sexual Abuse: The Pattern of Referral in an Area Where Reporting is not Mandatory. *Children and Society*, 5(2): p. 111–22.

Avery, L., Massatt, C.R., and Lundy, M. (1998). The Relationship Between Parent and Child Reports of Parental Supportiveness and Psychopathology of Sexually Abused Children. *Child and Adolescent Social Work Journal*, 15(3): pp187–205.

Bagley, C. (1995). *Child Sexual Abuse and Mental Health in Adolescents and Adults. British and Canadian Perspectives*. Aldershot: Avebury.

Bagley, C. and King, K. (1990). *Child Sexual Abuse: The Search for Healing*. London: Routledge.

Bagley, C., and Naspini, O. (1987). *Mothers of Sexually Abused Children*. Unpublished paper.

Barbaree, H.E., Hudson, S.M., and Seto, M.C. (1993). Sexual Assault in Society: The Role of the Juvenile Offender. In Barbaree, H.E. *et al.*, (Eds.). *The Juvenile Sex Offender*, pp1–24. NY: Guilford Press.

Belsky, J. (1984). The Determinants of Parenting: A Process Model. *Child Development*, 55(1): pp. 83–96.

Belsky, J. (1993). Etiology of Child Maltreatment: Developmental–Ecological Analysis. *Psychological Bulletin*, 114: pp413–34.

Benedek, T. (1959). Parenting as a Developmental Phase. *Journal of the American Psychoanalytic Association*, 7: pp389–417.

Berliner, L. (1991). Therapy with Victimised Children and their Families. *New Directions for Mental Health Services*, 51: pp29–46.

Berliner, L., and Conte, J. (1990). The Process of Victimisation: The Victim's Perspective. *Child Abuse and Neglect*, 14: pp29–40.

Berliner, L., and Conte, J. (1995). The Effects of Disclosure and Intervention on Sexually Abused Children. *Child Abuse and Neglect*, 19(3): pp371–84.

Bolton, F.G., Morris, L.A., and MacEachron, A.E. (1989). *Males at Risk: The Other Side of Child Sexual Abuse*. Newbury Park, CA: Sage.

Boss, P., and Greenberg, J. (1984). Family Boundary Ambiguity: A New Variable in Family Stress. *Family Process*, 23: pp535–46.

Boulton, A., and Burnham, L. (1989). Stand By Your Man: Or Your Child? *Social Work Today*, 14th September, 1989, p20.

Breckenbridge, J., and Berreen, R. (1992). Dealing with Mother Blame: Workers Responses to Incest and Child Sexual Abuse. In Breckenbridge, J., and Carmody, M. (Eds.). *Crimes of Violence: Australian Responses to Rape and Child Sexual Assault*, pp97–108. North Sydney: Allen and Unwin.

Brehm, S.S. (1992). *Intimate Relationships* (2nd edition). NY: McGraw Hill.

Briere, J. (1992). *Child Abuse Trauma: Theory and Treatment of the Lasting Effects*. Newbury Park, CA: Sage.

Briere, J., and Runtz, M. (1986). Suicidal Thoughts and Behaviour in Sexual Abuse Survivors. *Canadian Journal of Behavioural Sciences*, 18: pp413–23.

Briggs, D., Doyle, P., Gooch, T., and Kennington, R. (1998). *Assessing Men who Sexually Abuse: A Practice Guide*. London: Jessica Kingsley.

Brown, K. (1998). *Surviving Sexual Abuse*. Crowborough, East Sussex: Monarch Books.

Buchanan, A. (1996). *Cycles of Child Maltreatment: Facts, Fallacies and Interventions*. Chichester, West Sussex: John Wiley and Sons.

Burgess, A.W., Holmstrom, L.L., and McCausland, M.P. (1977). Child Sexual Assault by a Family Member: Decisions Following Disclosure. *Victimology*, 11(2): pp236–50.

Burgess, A.W., Holmstrom, L.L. and McCausland, M.P. (1978). Divided Loyalty in Incest Cases. In Burgess, A.W., Groth, A.N., Holmstrom, L.L., and Sgroi, S.M. (Eds.) (1978). *Sexual Assault of Children and Adolescents*, pp115–26. Lexington, MA: Lexington Books.

Burkett, L.P. (1991). Parenting Behaviours of Women who were Sexually Abused as Children in their Families of Origin. *Family Process*, 30: pp421–34.

Butler-Sloss, E. (1988). *Report of the Inquiry into Child Abuse in Cleveland*. London: HMSO.

Byerly, C.M. (1985). Mother Survival in the Incestuous Family. *Sexual Coercion and Assault*, 1: pp11–3.

Byerly, C.M. (1992). *How to Survive the Molestation of your Child*. Kendall-Hunt Publishing Co.

Calder, M.C. (1997). *Juveniles and Children who Sexually Abuse: A Guide to Risk Assessment*. Dorset: Russell House Publishing.

Calder, M.C. (1999). *Assessing Risk in Adult Males who Sexually Abuse Children: A Practitioners Guide*. Dorset: Russell House Publishing.

Calder, M.C. (forthcoming). The New Assessment Framework: A Critique and Reformulation. In Calder, M.C., and Hackett, S. (Eds.). *The RHP Child Care Assessment Manual*. Dorset: Russell House Publishing.

Calder, M.C., with Peake, A., and Rose, K. (forthcoming). *Mothers of Sexually Abused Children: A Framework for Assessment, Understanding and Support*. Dorset: Russell House Publishing.

Calder, M.C., and Skinner, J. (1999). A Framework for Comprehensive Assessment. In Calder, M.C. *Assessing Risk in Adult Males who Sexually Abuse Children: A Practitioners Guide*, pp65–158. Dorset: Russell House Publishing.

Cammaert, L. (1988). Non-offending Mothers: A New Conceptualisation. In Walker, L.E.A. (Ed.). *Handbook on Sexual Abuse of Children: Assessment and Treatment Issues*, pp309–25). NY: Springer Publishing Co.

Carich, M.S. (1994). A Review of Different Risk Factors. *INMAS Newsletter*, 7(4): pp3–10.

Carter, B. (1993). Child Sexual Abuse: Impact on Mothers. *Affilia*, 8(1): pp72–90.

CIBA (1984). *Child Sexual Abuse Within the Family*. London: Tavistock Routledge.

Clark, B., Parkin, W., and Richards, M. (1990). Dangerousness: A Complex Practice Issue. In Violence Against Children Study Group's *Taking Child Abuse Seriously*, pp143–66. London: Unwin Hyman.

Cleaver, H., and Freeman, P. (1995). *Parental Perspectives in Cases of Suspected Child Abuse Studies in Child Protection*. London: HMSO.

Cohen, J.A., and Mannarino, A.P. (1996). Factors that Mediate Treatment Outcome of Sexually Abused Pre-School Children. *Journal of the American Academy of Adolescent Psychiatry*, 34(10): pp1402–10.

Cohen, T. (1995). Motherhood Among Incest Survivors. *Child Abuse and Neglect*, 19(12): pp1423–9.

Cole, P.M., and Woolger, C. (1989). Incest Survivors: The Relation of their Perceptions of Parents and their Own Parenting Behaviour. *Child Abuse and Neglect*, 13: pp1–8.

Cole, P.M., Woolger, C., Power, T.G., and Smith, K.D. (1992). Parenting Difficulties Among Adult Survivors of Father-daughter Incest. *Child Abuse and Neglect*, 16: pp239–49.

Coleman, E. (1987). Chemical Dependency and Intimacy Dysfunction: Inextricably Bound. *Journal of Chemical Dependency*, 1(1): pp13–26.

Conte, J.R., Wolf, S., and Smith, T. (1989). What Sexual Offenders Tell us About Prevention. *Child Abuse and Neglect*, 13: pp293–301.

Corcoran, J. (1998). In Defence of Mothers of Sexual Abuse Victims. *Families in Society*, July–August 1998.

Courtois, C.A. (1988). *Healing the Incest Wound: Adult Survivors in Therapy*. NY: WW Norton.

Craig, E., Erooga, M., Morrison, T., and Shearer, E. (1989). Making Sense of Sexual Abuse: Charting the Shifting Sands. In Wattam, C., Hughes, J., and Blagg, H. (Eds.). *Child Sexual Abuse: Listening, Hearing and Validating the Experiences of Children*, pp59–77. Harlow: Longman.

Crawford, S.L. (1999). Intra-familial Sexual Abuse: What We Think We Know About Mothers, and Implications for Intervention. *Journal of Child Sexual Abuse*, 7(3): pp55–72.

Croll, L. (1994). *Caring for Children and Young People who have been Sexually Abused*. Basildon, Essex: Breakthrough for Youth.

Day, K. (1994). Male Mentally Handicapped Sex Offenders. *British Journal of Psychiatry*, 165: pp630–9.

De Jong, A.R. (1988). Maternal Responses to the Sexual Abuse of their Children. *Pediatrics*, 81: pp14–21.

Deblinger, E., Hathaway, C.R., Lippmann, J., and Steer, R. (1993). Psychosocial Characteristics and Correlates of Symptom Distress in Non-offending Mothers of Sexually Abused Children. *Journal of Interpersonal Violence*, 8: pp155–68.

Deblinger, E., Lippmann, J., Stauffer, L., and Finkel, M. (1994). Personal Versus Professional Responses to Child Sexual Abuse Allegations. *Child Abuse and Neglect*, 18(8): pp679–82.

Deblinger, E., Stauffer, L., and Landsberg, C. (1994b). The Impact of a History of Child Sexual Abuse on Maternal Response to Allegations of Sexual Abuse Concerning her Child. *Journal of Child Sexual Abuse*, 3(3): pp67–75.

Deblinger, E., Taub, B., Maedel, A., Lippmann, J., and Stauffer, L. (1997). Psychosocial Factors Predicting Parent Reported Symptomatology in Sexually Abused Children. *Journal of Child Sexual Abuse*, 6: pp35–49.

DeFrancis, V. (1969). *Protecting the Child Victim of Sex Crimes Committed by Adults: Final Report*. Denver: American Humane Association, Children's Division.

Dempster, H. (1993). The Aftermath of Child Sexual Abuse: Women's Perspectives. In Waterhouse, L. (Ed.). *Child Abuse and Child Abusers*. London: Jessica Kingsley.

DeVoe, E.R., and Faller, K.C. (1999). The Characteristics of Disclosure Among Children who may have been Sexually Abused. *Child Maltreatment*, 4(3): pp217–27.

DeYoung, M. (1994). Immediate Maternal Reactions to the Disclosure or Discovery of Incest. *Journal of Family Violence*, 9(1): pp21–33.

Dietz, C., and Craft, J. (1980). Family Dynamics of Incest: A New Perspective. *Social Casework*, 61, pp602–9.

DoH (1988). *Protecting Children: A Guide for Social Workers Undertaking a Comprehensive Assessment*. London: HMSO.

DoH (1995). *Child Protection: Messages from Research*. London: HMSO.

DoH (2000). *Framework for the Assessment of Children in Need and their Families*. London: HMSO.

Doka, K. (1989). *Disenfranchised Grief: Recognising Hidden Sorrow*. Lexington, MA: Lexington books.

Double, R. (1999). Hidden Victims. *Community Care*, 15th–21st April.

Dwyer, J., and Miller, R. (1996). Disenfranchised Grief After Incest: The Experience of Victims/ Daughters, Mothers/Wives. *Australian and New Zealand Journal of Family Therapy*, 17(3): pp137–45.

Dziuba-Leatherman, J., and Finkelhor, D. (1994). How Does Receiving Information About Sexual Abuse Influence Boys' Perceptions of their Risk? *Child Abuse and Neglect*, 18: pp557–68.

Eaton, L. (1993). Mother's Helpers. *Community Care*, 967: pp16–7.

Elbow, M., and Mayfield, J. (1991). Mothers of Incest Victims: Villains, Victims, or Protectors? *Families in Society*, February 1991: pp78–85.

Elliott, C.E., and Butler, L. (1994). The Stop and Think Group: Changing Sexually Aggressive Behaviour in Young Children. *Journal of Sexual Aggression*, 1(1): pp15–28.

Elliott, M. (1991). *Feeling Happy, Feeling Safe: A Safety Guide for Young Children*. London: Hodder and Stoughton.

Elliott, M. (1992). *Protecting Children: Training Pack for Front-line Carers*. London: HMSO.

Elliott, M., Browne, K., and Kilcoyne, J. (1995). Child Sexual Abuse Prevention: What Offenders Tell us. *Child Abuse and Neglect*, 19(5): pp579–94.

Elrod, J.M., and Rubin, R.H. (1993). Parental

Involvement in Sexual Abuse Prevention Education. *Child Abuse and Neglect*, 17: pp527–38.

Engel, B. (1994). *Families in Recovery: Working Together to Heal the Damage of Child Sexual Abuse*. Los Angeles, CA: Lowell House.

Epps, K.J. (1997). Pointers for Carers. In Calder, M.C. *Juveniles and Children who Sexually Abuse: A Guide to Risk Assessment*, pp99–109. Lyme Regis, Dorset: Russell House Publishing.

Esquilin, S.C. (1987). Family Responses to the Identification of Extra-familial Child Sexual Abuse. *Psychotherapy in Private Practice*, 5(1): pp105–13.

Everson, M., Hunter, W., Runyon, D., Edelsohn, G., and Coulter, M. (1989). Maternal Support Following Disclosure of Incest. *American Journal of Orthopsychiatry*, 59: pp197–207.

Faller, K.C. (1988). The Myth of the 'Collusive Mother': Variables in the Functioning of Mothers of Victims of Intra-familial Sexual Abuse. *Journal of Interpersonal Violence*, 3(2): p190

Faller, K.C. (1988b). Decision-making in Cases of Intra-familial Child Sexual Abuse. *American Journal of Orthopsychiatry*, 58: pp121–8.

Faller, K.C. (1988c). *Child Sexual Abuse: An Inter-disciplinary Manual for Diagnosis, Case Management, and Treatment*. London: MacMillan.

Faller, K.C. (1989). The Role Relationship Between Victim and Perpetrator as a Predictor of Characteristics of Intra-family Sexual Abuse. *Child and Adolescent Social Work*, 6: pp217–29.

Faller, K.C. (1990). *Understanding Child Sexual Maltreatment*. London: Sage.

Faller, K.C. (1991). Possible Explanations for Child Sexual Abuse Allegations in Divorce. *American Journal of Orthopsychiatry*, 61: pp86–91.

Faller, K.C. (1991b). Poly-incestuous Families: an Exploratory Study. *Journal of Interpersonal Violence*, 6: pp310–22.

Farmer, E. (1993). The Impact of Child Protection Interventions: The Experiences of Parents and Children. In Waterhouse, L. (Ed.). *Child Abuse and Child Abusers: Protection and Prevention*. London: Jessica Kingsley.

Finkelhor, D. (1979). *Sexually Victimised Children*. NY: The Free Press.

Finkelhor, D. (1984). *Child Sexual Abuse: New Theory and Research*. NY: The Free Press.

Finkelhor, D. (1988). The Trauma of Child Sexual Abuse: Two Models. In Wyatt, G.E., and Powell, G.J. (Eds.). *Lasting Effects of Child Sexual Abuse*, pp61–82. Newbury Park, CA: Sage.

Finkelhor, D. (1990). Early and Long-term Effects of Child Sexual Abuse: An Update. *Professional Psychology: Research and Practice*, 21: pp325–30.

Finkelhor, D., and Baron, L. (1986). Risk Factors for Child Sexual Abuse. *Journal of Interpersonal Violence*, 1: pp43–71.

Finkelhor, D., and Browne, A. (1985). The Traumatic

Impact of Child Sexual Abuse: A Conceptualisation. *American Journal of Orthopsychiatry*, 55(4): pp530–41.

Finkelhor, D., and Browne, A. (1986). Initial and Long-term Effects: A Conceptual Framework. In Finkelhor, D. (Ed.). *A Sourcebook on Child Sexual Abuse*, pp143–79. Beverly Hills, CA: Sage.

Finkelhor, D., and Browne, A. (1988). Assessing the Long-term Impact of Child Sexual Abuse: A Review and Re-conceptualisation. In Walker, L.E. (Ed.). *Handbook of Sexual Abuse of Children: Assessment and Treatment Issues*, pp55–71. NY: Springer-Verlag Publishing Co.

Finkelhor, D., Hotaling, G., Lewis, I.A., and Smith, C. (1990). Sexual Abuse in a National Survey of Adult Men and Women: Prevalence, Characteristics, and Risk Factors. *Child Abuse and Neglect*, 14: pp19–28.

Fong, J., and Walsh-Bowers, R. (1998). Voices of the Blamed: Mothers' Responsiveness to Father–Daughter Incest. *Journal of Family Social Work*, 3(1): pp25–41.

Forehand, R., McCombs, A., and Brody, G. (1987). The Relationship Between Parental Depressive Mood States and Child Functioning. *Advances in Behaviour Research and Therapy*, 9: pp1–20.

Freund, K., and Blanchard, R. (1986). The Concept of Courtship Disorder. *Journal of Sex and Marital Therapy*, 12: pp79–92.

Freund, K., Scher, H., and Hucker, S. (1983). The Courtship Disorder. *Archives of Sexual Behaviour*, 12: pp369–79.

Friedrich, W., Urguiza, A., and Berlke, R. (1986). Behaviour Problems in Sexually Abused Young Children. *Journal of Pediatric Psychology*, 11: pp47–57.

Friedrich, W.N. (1988). Behaviour Problems in Sexually Abused Children: An Adaptational Approach. In Wyatt, G.E., and Powell, G.J. (Eds.). *Lasting Effects of Child Sexual Abuse*, pp171–91. Newbury Park, CA: Sage.

Friedrich, W.N. (1990). *Psychotherapy of Sexually Abused Children and their Families*. NY: WW Norton.

Furniss, T. (1990). Dealing with Denial. In Oates, R.K. (Ed.). *Understanding and Managing Child Sexual Abuse*, pp242–57. Marrickeville: Harcourt Brace Jovanovich, .

Furniss, T. (1991). *The Multi-professional Handbook of Child Sexual Abuse*. London: Routledge.

Gilbert, N. (1988). Teaching Children to Prevent Sexual Abuse. *The Public Interest*, 93: pp3–15.

Gilgun, J.F. (1984). Does the Mother Know? Alternatives to Blaming Mothers for Child Sexual Abuse. *Response*, Fall 1984.

Glaser, D., and Frosh, S. (1988). *Child Sexual Abuse*. London: MacMillan.

Golan, N. (1981). *Passing Through Transitions*. NY: Free Press.

Gomes-Schwartz, B., Horowitz, J.M., and Cardarelli, A.P. (1990). *Child Sexual Abuse: The Initial Effects*. Newbury Park, CA: Sage.

Goodwin, J. (1981). Suicide Attempts in Sexual Abuse Victims and their Mothers. *Child Abuse and Neglect*, 5: pp217–21.

Goodwin, J., Cormier, L., and Owen, J. (1983). Grandfather–Grand-daughter Incest: A Tri-generational View. *Child Abuse and Neglect*, 7: pp163–70.

Goodwin, J., McCarthy, T., and DiVasto, P. (1982). Physical and Sexual Abuse of the Children of Adult Incest Victims. In Goodwin, J. (Ed.). *Sexual Abuse: Incest Victims and their Families*, pp139–54. Boston: John Wright.

Groth, A.N. (1978). Guidelines for the Assessment and Management of the Offender. In Burgess A., Groth, A.N., Holmstrom, L.L., and Sgroi, S. (Eds.). *Sexual Assault of Children and Adolescents*. Lexington, MA: Lexington Books, pp25–42.

Hall, L., and Lloyd, S. (1989). *Surviving Child Sexual Abuse: A Handbook for Helping Women Challenge their Past*. Basingstoke: The Falmer Press.

Hanks, H. (1997). 'Normal' Psycho-sexual Development, Behaviour and Knowledge. In Calder, M.C. *Juveniles and Children who Sexually Abuse: A Guide to Risk Assessment*, pp16–23. Lyme Regis, Dorset: Russell House Publishing.

Hanson, R.K., and Scott, H. (1996). Social Networks of Sex Offenders. *Psychology, Crime and Law*, 2: pp249–58.

Herman, J. (1981). *Father–Daughter Incest*. Cambridge, MA: Harvard University Press.

Herman, J., and Hirschman, L. (1981). Families at Risk for Father–Daughter Incest. *American Journal of Psychiatry*, 138: pp967–70.

Hillman, D., and Solek-Tefft, J. (1988). *Spiders and Flies: Help for Parents and Teachers of Sexually Abused Children*. Lexington, MA: Lexington Books.

Hite, S. (1990). I Hope I'm not Like my Mother. *Women and Therapy*, 10: pp13–30.

Hoagwood, K., and Stewart, J.M. (1989). Sexually Abused Children's Perceptions of Family Functioning. *Child and Adolescent Social Work*, 6(2): pp139–49.

Home Office (1992). *Memorandum of Good Practice*. London: HMSO.

Hooper, C.A. (1989). Alternatives to Collusion: The Response of Mothers to Child Sexual Abuse in the Family. *Educational and Child Psychology*, 6(1): pp22–30.

Hooper, C.A. (1992). *Mothers Surviving Child Sexual Abuse*. London: Routledge.

Hooper, C.A. (1992b). Child Sexual Abuse: Working with Mothers. *Childright*, 86.

Hopkins, J., and Thompson, E.H. (1984). Loss and Mourning in Victims of Rape and Sexual Assault. In Hopkins, J. (Ed.). *Perspectives on Rape and Sexual Assault*. London: Harper and Row.

Howard, C.A. (1993). Factors Influencing a Mother's Response to her Child's Disclosure of Incest. *Professional Psychology: Research and Practice*, 24(2): pp176–81.

Howarth, V. (1999). Presentation to sex offender review team conference. York: Stakis Hotel, 28th June, 1999.

Hubbard, G. (1989). Mothers' Perceptions of Incest: Sustained Disruption and Turmoil. *Archives of Psychiatric Nursing*, 3(1): pp34–40.

Humphreys, C. (1992). Disclosure of Child Sexual Assault: Implications for Mothers. *Australian Social Work*, 45(3): pp27–35.

Humphreys, C. (1995). Counselling and Support Issues for Mothers and Fathers of Sexually Abused Children. *Australian Social Work*, 48(4): pp13–9.

Hunter, W.M., Coulter, M.D., Runyan, D.K., and Everson, M.D. (1990). Determinants of Placement for Sexually Abused Children. *Child Abuse and Neglect*, 14: pp407–18.

Jaudes, P., and Morris, M. (1990). Child Sexual Abuse: Who Goes Home? *Child Abuse and Neglect*, 14: pp61–8.

Johnson, J.T. (1992). *Mothers of Incest Survivors: Another Side of the Story*. Indianapolis: Indiana University Press.

Johnson, T.C. (1994). *Children's Natural and Healthy Sexual Behaviours and Characteristics of Children's Problematic Sexual Behaviours*. Self-published.

Jones, D.P., and Ramchandani, P. (1999). *Child Sexual Abuse: Informing Practice from Research*. Oxford: Radcliffe Medical Press.

Julian, V., and Mohr, C. (1979). Father–Daughter Incest: Profile of the Offender. *Victimology*, 4: pp348–60.

Justice, B., and Justice, R. (1979). *The Broken Taboo*. NY: Human Sciences Press.

Kaplan, S.J., Pelcowitz, D., Salzinger, S., and Ganeles, D. (1988). Psychopatholgy of Non-violent Women in Violent Families. In Anthony, E.J., and Chiland, C. (Eds.). *The Child in his Family: Perilous Development: Child Raising and Identity Formation Under Stress*, pp503–14. NY: Wiley.

Kelley, S.J. (1990). Parental Stress Response to Sexual Abuse and Ritualistic Abuse of Children in Day-Care Settings. *Nursing Research*, 39: pp25–9.

Kelly, L. (1988). *Surviving Sexual Violence*. Cambridge: Polity Press.

Kelly, L., Regan, L., and Burton, S. (1991). *An Exploratory Study of the Prevalence of Sexual Abuse in a Sample of 16–21 Year Olds*. London: Child Abuse Studies Unit.

Kempe, R.S., and Kempe, C.H. (1978). *Child Abuse*. London: Fontana/Open Books.

Kendall-Tackett, K.A., Williams, L.M., and Finkelhor, D. (1993). Impact of Sexual Abuse on Children: A Review and Synthesis of Recent Empirical Studies. *Psychological Bulletin*, 113(1): pp164–80.

Kinard, E.M. (1996). Social Support, Competence, and Depression in Mothers of Abused Children. *American Journal of Orthopsychiatry*, 66(3): pp449–62.

Koester-Scott, L. (1994). Sex Offenders: Prevalence, Trends, Model Programs and Costs. In Roberts, A.R. (Ed.). *Critical Issues in Crime and Justice*, pp51–76. Thousand Oaks, CA: Sage.

Kreklewetz, C.M., and Piotrowski, C.C. (1996). *Towards a Theoretical Model of the Recurrence of Incest: Perspectives from Incest Survivor Mothers*. Poster presentation to the 11th International Congress on Child Abuse and Neglect, August 1996, Dublin, Ireland.

Kreklewetz, C.M., and Piotrowski, C.C. (1998). Incest Survivor Mothers: Protecting the Next Generation. *Child Abuse and Neglect*, 22(12): pp1305–12.

Kroth, J.A. (1979). Family Therapy Impact on Intra-Familial Child Sexual Abuse. *Child Abuse and Neglect*, 3: pp297–302.

Laing, L., and Kamsler, A. (1990). Putting an End to Secrecy: Therapy with Mothers and Children. In Durrant, M., and White, C. (Eds.). *Ideas for Therapy with Sexual Abuse*. Adelaide, Australia: Dulwich Centre Publications.

Lancaster, E. (1996). Working with Men who Sexually Abuse Children: The Experience of the Probation Service. In Fawcett, B., Featherstone, B., Hearn, J., and Toft, C. (Eds.). *Violence and Gender Relations: Theory and Interventions*, pp130–46. London: Sage.

Lawson, L., and Chaffin, M. (1992). False Negatives in Sexual Abuse Disclosure Interviews: Incidence and Influence of Caretaker's Belief in Abuse in Cases of Accidental Abuse Discovery by Diagnosis of STD. *Journal of Interpersonal Violence*, 7(4): pp532–42.

Lazarus, A.A. (1976). *Multi-modal Behaviour Therapy*. NY: Springer Publishing Company.

Leifer, M., Shapiro, J.P., and Kassem, L. (1993). The Impact of Maternal History and Behaviour upon Foster Placement and Adjustment in Sexually Abused Girls. *Child Abuse and Neglect*, 17: pp755–66.

Lipton, M. (1997). The Effect of the Primary Caretaker's Distress on the Sexually Abused Child: A Comparison of Biological and Foster Parents. *Child and Adolescent Social Work*, 14(2): pp115–27.

Lubell, A.K., and Peterson, P. (1998). Female Incest Survivors: Relationships with Mothers and Female Friends. *Journal of Interpersonal Violence*, 13(2): pp193–205.

Lyon, E., and Kouloumpos-Lenares, K. (1987). Clinician and State Children's Services Worker Collaboration in Treating Sexual Abuse. *Child Welfare*, 67: pp517–27.

MacFarlane, K., and Bulkley, J. (1982). Treating Child Sexual Abuse: An Overview of Current Treatment Models. *Journal of Social Work and Human Sexuality*, 1: pp71–93.

MacLeod, M., and Saraga, M. (1988). Challenging the Orthodoxy: Towards A Feminist Theory of Practice. *Feminist Review*, 28: pp16–55.

Magura, S., Moses, B.S., and Jones, M.A. (1987). *Assessing Risk and Measuring Change in Families: The Family-risk Scales*. Washington, DC: Child Welfare League of America.

Maisch, H. (1973). *Incest*. NY: Stein and Day.

Manion, I.G., McIntyre, J., Firestone, P., Ligezinska, M., Ensom, R., and Wells, G. (1996). Secondary Traumatisation in Parents Following the Disclosure of Extra-familial Child Sexual Abuse: Initial Effects. *Child Abuse and Neglect*, 20(11): pp1095–109.

Margolin, L. (1992). Sexual Abuse by Grandparents. *Child Abuse and Neglect*, 16: pp735–41.

Marshall, W.L. (1995). The Role of Attachments, Intimacy and Loneliness in the Aetiology and Maintenance of Sexual Offending. *Sexual and Marital Therapy*, 8: pp109–21.

Marshall, W.L., and Eccles, A. (1991). Issues in Clinical Practice with Sex Offenders. *Journal of Interpersonal Violence*, 6: pp68–93.

Massatt, C.R., and Lundy, M. (1998). 'Reporting Costs' to Non-offending Parents in Cases of Intra-familial Child Sexual Abuse. *Child Welfare*, 77(4): pp371–88.

Mayer, A. (1983). *Incest: A Treatment Manual for Therapy with Victims, Spouses and Offenders*. Holmes Beach, FL: Learning Publications Inc.

McGrath, R.J. (1991). Sex Offender Risk Assessment and Disposition of Planning: A Review of Empirical and Clinical Findings. *Interpersonal Journal of Offender Therapy and Comparative Criminology*, 35(4): pp328–50.

McGrath, R.J. (1992) Assessing Sex Offender Risk. *American Probation and Parole Association Perspectives*, 16(3): pp6–9.

McIntyre, K. (1981). Role of Mothers in Father–Daughter Incest: A Feminist Analysis. *Social Work*, 26: pp462–6.

McLurg, G., and Craissati, J. (1999). A Descriptive Study of Alleged Sexual Abusers Known to Social Services. *The Journal of Sexual Aggression*, 4(1): pp22–30.

McMillen, C., Zuravin, S., and Rideout, G. (1995). Perceived Benefit from Child Sexual Abuse. *Journal of Consulting and Clinical Psychology*, 63(6): pp1037–43.

Meiselman, K. (1978). *Incest: A Psychological Study of Causes and Effects with Treatment Recommendations*. San Francisco: Jossey-Bass.

Mendel, M.P. (1995). *The Male Survivor: The Impact of Sexual Abuse*. Thousand Oaks, CA: Sage.

Miller, R., and Dwyer, J. (1997). Reclaiming the Mother–Daughter Relationship After Sexual Abuse. *Australian and New Zealand Journal of Family Therapy*, 18(4): pp194–202.

Milner, J., and Blyth, E. (1989). *Coping with Child Sexual Abuse: A Guide for Teachers*. London: Longman.

Mitchell, A. (1985). Child Sexual Assault. In Guberman, C., and Wolfe, M. (Eds.). *No Safe Place: Violence Against Women and Children*. Toronto: The Women's Press.

Monahan, K. (1997). Crocodile Talk: Attributions of Incestuously Abused and Non-abused Sisters. *Child Abuse and Neglect*, 21(1): pp19–34.

Muram, D., Rosenthal, T.L., and Beck, K.W. (1994). Personality Profiles of Mothers of Sexual Abuse

Victims and their Daughters. *Child Abuse and Neglect*, 18(5): pp419–23.

Myers, J.E. (1997). *A Mother's Nightmare: Incest. A Practical Legal Guide for Parents and Professionals.* Thousand Oaks, CA: Sage.

Myers, M. (1985). A New Look at Mothers of Incest Victims. *Journal of Social Work and Human Sexuality*, pp47–58.

Nelson, S. (1992). Power Failure. *Social Work Today*, 11 June, 1992.

Newberger, C.M., Gremy, I.M., Waternaux, C.M., and Newberger, E.H. (1993). Mothers of Sexually Abused Children: Trauma and Repair in Longitudinal Perspective. *American Journal of Orthopsychiatry*, 63: pp92–102.

Newberger, E.H., Newberger, C.M., and Gremy, I. (1991). *Dual Vulnerability of Sexually Victimised Mothers and Sexually Victimised Children: A Longitudinal Study.* Paper presented to the 7th Annual Convention of the International Society for Traumatic Stress Studies, Washington, DC, 26th October, 1991.

Oates, R.K., Tebbutt, J., Swanston, H., Lynch, D.L., and O'Toole, B.I. (1998). Prior Childhood Sexual Abuse in Mothers of Sexually Abused Children. *Child Abuse and Neglect*, 22(11): pp1113–8.

Orr, T. (1995). *No Right Way: The Voices of Mothers of Incest Survivors*. London: Scarlet Press.

Orten, J.D., and Rich, L.L. (1993). A Model for Assessment of Incestuous Families. In Rauch, J.B. (Ed.). *Assessment: A Sourcebook for Social Work Practice*, pp227–39. Milwaukee: Families International Inc.

Ovaris, W. (1991). *After the Nightmare: The Treatment of Non-offending Mothers of Sexually Abused Children.* Holmes Beach, FL: Learning Publications Inc.

Palmer, S.E., Brown, R.A., Rae-Grant, N.I., and Loughlin, M.J. (1999). Responding to Children's Disclosure of Familial Abuse: What Survivors Tell Us. *Child Welfare*, LXXVIII(2): pp259–82.

Peake, A., and Fletcher, M. (1997). *Strong Mothers: A Resource for Mothers and Carers of Children who have been Sexually Assaulted.* Lyme Regis, Dorset: Russell House Publishing.

Pellegrin, A., and Wagner, W.G. (1990). Child Sexual Abuse: Factors Affecting Victims' Removal from Home. *Child Abuse and Neglect*, 14: pp53–60.

Pierce, R., and Pierce, L. (1985). The Sexually Abused Child: A Comparison of Male and Female Victims. *Child Abuse and Neglect*, 9: pp191–9.

Porter, L.S., Blick, L.C., and Sgroi, S.M. (1982). Treatment of the Sexually Abused Child. In Sgroi, S.M. (Ed.). *Handbook of Clinical Intervention in Child Sexual Abuse*, pp109–45. Lexington, MA: DC Heath.

Prendergast, W.E. (1991). *Treating Sex Offenders in Correctional Institutions and Outpatient Clinics: A Guide to Clinical Practice.* NY: Haworth Press.

Print, B., and Dey, C. (1992). Empowering Mothers of Sexually Abused Children: A Positive Framework. In Bannister, A. (Ed.). *From Hearing to Healing with the Aftermath of Child Sexual Abuse*, pp57–81. London: Longman.

Reder, P., and Lucey, C. (1995). Significant Issues in the Assessment of Parenting. In Reder, P., and Lucey, C. (Eds.). *Assessment of Parenting: Psychiatric and Psychological Contributions*, pp3–17. London: Routledge.

Regehr, C. (1990). Parental Responses to Extra-familial Child Sexual Abuse. *Child Abuse and Neglect*, 14: pp113–20.

Richardson, G. (1990). Inadequate Intervention. *Social Work Today*, 6th December, 1990: pp19–21.

Rickford, F. (1992). You Must Have Known. *Social Work Today*, 23rd January, 1992: pp14–5.

Ringwalt, C., and Earp, J. (1988). Attributing Responsibility in Cases of Father–Daughter Incest. *Child Abuse and Neglect*, 12: pp273–81.

Rivera, M. (1988). Social Systems' Intervention in Families of Victims of Child Sexual Abuse. *Canadian Journal of Community Mental Health*, 7(1): pp35–51.

Roberts, J. (1992–93). Non-believing Mothers of Sexually Abused Children. *Practice*, 6(4): pp268–70.

Roberts, J., and Taylor, C. (1993). Sexually Abused Children and Young People Speak Out. In Waterhouse, L. (Ed.). *Child Abuse and Child Abusers: Protection and Prevention*, pp23–37. London: Jessica Kingsley.

Rollins, B.C., and Thomas, D.L. (1979). Parental Support, Power, and Control: Techniques in the Socialisation of Children. In Burr, W., Hill, R., Nye, F.I., and Reiss, I. (Eds.). *Contemporary Theories About the Family*, Vol 1: pp317–64. NY: The Free Press.

Rose, K. (2000). *Practice Guidance on Domestic Violence.* Salford ACPC (unpublished).

Rose, K. (forthcoming). Domestic Violence. In Calder, M.C., and Hackett, S. (Eds.). *The RHP Child Care Assessment Manual.* Lyme Regis: Russell House Publishing.

Rose, K., and Savage, A. (1995). *Who Cares?* Kaleidoscope Project, Salford Area Child Protection Committee.

Rose, K., and Savage, A. (1998). *Stand by your Man.* Presentation to a one-day conference, 'A betrayal of trust: who abuses children and why' at the Dalmeny Hotel, Lytham St Annes, 21st January, 1998.

Rose, K., and Savage, A. (2000). Living with Risk. In Wheal, A. (Ed.). *Working with Parents.* Lyme Regis: Russell House Publishing.

Russell, D.E. (1984). *Sexual Exploitation: Rape, Child Sexual Abuse and Workplace Harassment.* Beverley Hills, CA: Sage.

Russell, D.E. (1986). *The Secret Trauma: Incest in the Lives of Girls and Women.* NY: Basic Books.

Ryan, G.D. (1991). Consequences for the Victims of Sexual Abuse. In Ryan, G.D., and Lane, S.L. (Eds.). *Juvenile Sex Offending: Causes. Consequences and Corrections*, pp163–74. Lexington, MA: Lexington Books.

Sahd, D. (1980). Psychological Assessment of Sexually Abusing Families and Treatment Implications. In

Holder, W. (Ed.). *Sexual Abuse of Children: Implications for Treatment*. Englewood, CO: American Humane Association.

Salt, P., Myers, M., Coleman, L., and Sauzier, M. (1990). The Myth of the Mother as 'Accomplice' to Child Sexual Abuse. In Gomes-Schwartz, B., Horowitz, J.M., and. Cardarelli, A.P. (Eds.). *Child Sexual Abuse*, pp109–31. Newbury Park, CA: Sage Publications.

Salter, A.C. (1988). *Treating Child Sex Offenders and Victims: A Practical Guide*. Thousand Oaks, CA: Sage.

Sanderson, C. (1990). *Counselling Adult Survivors of Childhood Sexual Abuse*. London: Jessica Kingsley.

Sauzier, M. (1989). Disclosure of Sexual Abuse. *Psychiatric Clinics of North America*, 12: pp445–71.

Sayers, T. (1995). Issues for and about the Non-abusing Parent. In Hollows, A. (Ed.). *Rebuilding Families After Abuse*, pp28–36. London: National Children's Bureau.

Scott, R.S., and Flowers, J.V. (1988). Betrayal by the Mother as a Factor Contributing to Psychological Disturbance in Victims of Father–Daughter Incest: An MMPI Analysis. *Journal of Social and Clinical Psychology*, 6(1): pp147–54.

Segal, L.E., and Sterma, C.L. (1990). The Role of Cognition in Sexual Assault. In Marshall, W.L., Laws, D.R., and Barbaree, H.E. (Eds.). *Handbook of Sexual Assault*, pp161–76. NY: Plenum.

Serin, R.C., Malcolm, P.B., Khanna, A., and Barbaree, H.E. (1994). Psychopathy and Deviant Sexual Arousal in Incarcerated Sex Offenders. *Journal of Interpersonal Violence*, 9(1): pp3–11.

Server, J., and Janzen, C. (1982). Contraindications to Reconstitution of Sexually Abusive Families. *Child Welfare*, 61: pp279–88.

Sgroi, S.M. (Ed.) (1982). *Handbook of Clinical Intervention in Child Sexual Abuse*. Lexington, MA: Lexington Books.

Sgroi, S.M., and Dana, N.T. (1982). Individual and group Treatment of Mothers of Incest Victims. In Sgroi, S.M. (Ed.). Op cit, pp191–214.

Shinn, M., Knickman, J., and Weitzman, B. (1991). Social Relationships and Vulnerability to Becoming Homeless Among Poor Families. *American Psychologist*, 46: pp1180–7.

Sirles, E.A., and Franke, P.J. (1989). Factors Influencing Mothers' Reactions to Intra-family Sexual Abuse. *Child Abuse and Neglect*, 13: pp131–9.

Sirles, E.A., and Lofberg, C.E. (1990). Factors Associated with Divorce in Intra-family Child Sexual Abuse Cases. *Child Abuse and Neglect*, 14: pp165–70.

Smart, P. (1997). *Child Sexual Abuse: Non-abusing Parents Perspectives of Social Work Intervention*. Unpublished BA Research Project. University College, Salford.

Smith, G. (1994). Parent, Partner, Protector: Conflicting Role Demands for Mothers of Sexually Abused Children. In Morrison, T., Erooga, M., and Beckett, R.C. (Eds.). *Sexual Offending Against Children: Assessment and Treatment of Male Abusers*, pp178–202. London, Routledge.

Smith, G. (1995). Assessing Protectiveness in Cases of Child Sexual Abuse. In Reder, P., and Lucey, C. (Eds.). *Assessment of Parenting: Psychiatric and Psychological Contributions*, pp87–101. London: Routledge.

Smith, G. (1995b). *The Protector's Handbook: Reducing the Risk of Child Sexual Abuse and Helping Children Recover*. London: Women's Press.

Sorensen, T., and Snow, B. (1991). How Children Tell: The Process of Disclosure in Child Sexual Abuse. *Child Welfare*, 70: pp3–15.

Sroufe, L.A., Jacobvitz, D., Mangelsdorf, S., De Angelo, E., and Ward, M.J. (1985). Generational Boundary Discussion Between Mothers and their Pre-school Children: A Relationship Systems Approach. *Child Development*, 56: pp317–25.

Stark, E., and Flitcraft, H. (1988). Women and Children at Risk: A Feminist Perspective on Child Abuse. *International Journal of Health Services*, 18(1): pp97–118.

Stermac, L., Davidson, A., and Sheridan, M. (1995). Incidence of Non-sexual Violence in Incest Offenders. *International Journal of Offender Therapy and Comparative Criminology*, 39(2).

Summit, R. (1983). The Child Sexual Abuse Accommodation Syndrome. *Child Abuse and Neglect*, 7: pp177–93.

Summit, R. (1990). The Specific Vulnerability of Children. In Oates, R.K. (Ed.). *Understanding and Managing Child Sexual Abuse*, pp59–74. Marrickville: Harcourt Brace Jovanovich.

Tamraz, D.N. (1996). Non-offending Mothers of Sexually Abused Children: Comparisons of Opinions and Research. *Journal of Child Sexual Abuse*, 5(4): pp75–99.

Terry, W.T. (1990). *Perpetrator and Victim Accounts of Sexual Abuse*. Paper presented at the San Diego Conference on responding to sexual maltreatment. San Diego, CA.

Testa, M., Miller, B.A., Downs, W.R., and Panek, D. (1992). The Moderating Impact of Social Support Following Childhood Sexual Abuse. *Violence and Victims*, 7(2): pp173–86.

Timmons-Mitchell, J., Chandler-Holtz, D., and Semple, W.E. (1996). Post-traumatic Stress Symptoms in Mothers Following Children's Reports of Sexual Abuse: An Exploratory Study. *American Journal of Orthopsychiatry*, 66(3), pp463–7.

Tinling, L. (1990). Perpetuation of Incest by Significant Others: Mothers who do not Want to See. *Individual Psychology*, 46(3): pp280–97.

Todd, I. (1989). When There's Nowhere to Run. *Community Care*, 23rd September, 1989: pp18–9.

Todd, I., and Ellis, L. (1992). Divided Loyalties. *Social Work Today*, 25th June, 1992: pp14–5.

Tower, C.C. (1989). *Understanding Child Abuse and Neglect*. Boston: Allyn and Bacon.

Trepper, T.S., Niedner, D., Mika, L., and Barrett, M.J. (1996). Family Characteristics of Intact Sexually Abusing Families: An Exploratory Study. *Journal of Child Sexual Abuse*, 5(4): pp1–20.

Trotter, J. (1998). *No-one's Listening: Mothers, Fathers and Child Sexual Abuse*. London: Whiting and Birch.

Truesdell, D.L., McNeil, J.S., and Deschner, J.P. (1986). Incidence of Wife Abuse in Incestuous Families. *Social Work*, 31: pp138–40.

Tufts New England Medical Centre, Division of Child Psychiatry (1984). *Sexually Exploited Children*. Unpublished manuscript.

Van der Mey, B.J., and Neff, R.L. (1986). *Incest as Child Abuse: Research and Applications*. NY: Praeger.

Walton, P. (1996). *Partnership with Mothers in the Wake of Child Sexual Abuse. Social Work Monograph 154*. Norwich: University of East Anglia.

Waring, E.M., and Reddon, J.R. (1983). The Measurement of Intimacy in Marriage. *Journal of Clinical Psychology*, 39: pp53–7.

Waterhouse, L., and Carnie, J. (1992). Assessing Child Protection Risk. *British Journal of Social Work*, 22: pp47–60.

Waterhouse, L., Carnie, J., and Dobash, R. (1993). The Abuser Under the Microscope. *Community Care*, 24th June, 1993: p 24.

Weiss, R.S. (1974). The Provisions of Social Relationships. In Rubin, Z. (Ed). *Doing unto Others*. Englewood, Cliffs, NJ: Prentice-Hall.

West, D.J. (1991). The Effects of Sex Offences. In Hollin, C.R., and Howells, K. (Eds.). *Clinical Approaches to Sex Offenders and their Victims*. Chichester: Wiley.

Williams, L., and Finkelhor, D. (1992). *The Characteristics of Incestuous Fathers*. Unpublished manuscript: University of New Hampshire Research Laboratory.

Wolf, S. (1984). *A Multi-factor Model of Deviant Sexuality*. Paper at 3rd International conference on victimology. Lisbon, Portugal, November, 1984.

Wright, S. (1991). Family Effects of Offender Removal from Home. In Patton, M.Q. (Ed.). *Family Sexual Abuse: Frontline Research and Evaluation*, pp135–46. Newbury Park, CA: Sage.

Wurtele, S.K., and Miller-Perrin, C.L. (1992). *Preventing Child Sexual Abuse: Sharing the Responsibility*. Lincoln: University of Nebraska.

Wyatt, G.E., and Mickey, M.R. (1988). The Support by Parents and Others as it Mediates the Effects of Child Sexual Abuse: An Exploratory Study. In Wyatt, G.E., and Powell, G.J. (Eds.). *Lasting Effects of Child Sexual Abuse*, pp211–25. Newbury Park, CA: Sage.

Wyre, R. (1987). *Working with Sex Abuse*. Oxford: Perry Publications.

Yates, A. (1982). Children Eroticised by Incest. *American Journal of Psychiatry*, 139: pp482–5.

Chapter Eight

Females who Sexually Abuse: An Approach to Assessment

Helga Hanks and Jane Wynne

Introduction

In the early 1980s the Leeds team began to work with children who had been sexually abused. Initially, it was expected that the abused children would be teenagers, or girls abused by stepfathers, and early clinical material reinforced this belief, as well as seeing the traumatised, colluding mother as central. It was soon evident that child sexual abuse (CSA) began in early childhood and the perpetrator was commonly the birth father, and boys as well as girls were victims. The reality that CSA occurs in families and perpetrators are not easily identified was, and remains, difficult in a society which would prefer to have a quick method of the identification of, and consequent vilification of, paedophiles.

Data was collected in Leeds and published in 1987 of 357 children who had been sexually abused. Some four per cent of the known perpetrators was the child's mother. The relationship of female perpetrators to the child was the same as for males: that is, they were known to the child, were usually within the household and the birth mother was the usual perpetrator. CSA involving the child's mother appeared to the clinicians to be particularly damaging.

Work on the Leeds Sex Rings in 1986 also involved women as perpetrators, albeit a minority, but teenage girls were very much involved in the running of the groups. The spectrum of abusive behaviours involving women was wide and the background of perpetrators showed that they came from an equally wide variety of homes: nuclear families, extended families, gay couples, children in day care, sex rings, parents prostituting their children, babysitters, children in foster-care and in all types of institutions. It was very difficult to discuss the 'unthinkable, which was the reality': women, and mothers, not only physically and emotionally abused and neglected children, they also sexually abused children. It became important to put

this 'new' knowledge into a historical framework. It was only in 1961 that Kempe gave his first paper on child abuse and in 1962 published *The Battered Child*. Recognition of physical abuse rapidly increased, and in 1978 Henry Kempe mapped out the stages a society would pass in the recognition of other forms of abuse.

The focus of child protection in the UK remained on physical injuries, albeit recognised as caused by parents or carers, until the mid-80s and inter-agency guidelines reflected the need to protect. After the events in Middlesborough in 1987 (*Inquiry into Child Abuse in Cleveland*, 1988) there was a plethora of guidelines and advice. Ongoing research has shown that women physically abuse more children than men; which is not surprising as women remain the main carers of children, but woman are not expected to be violent, especially towards children. It is important to recognise that abusive relationships may develop between any members of a family and not to over sentimentalise the mother-child relationship.

Allen (1991: pp11–20) in his comparative analysis about women and men who sexually abuse children makes a succinct and interesting argument when he highlights three important points which show how we have come to mislead ourselves and avoid the inevitable recognition that women are capable of sexually abusing children. This is important to consider when assessing whether children have been sexually abused by women. He had a sample of 65 women in his study taken from a much larger female perpetrator sampling frame. The three points are as follows:

1. Over-estimating the strength of the incest taboo

Allen (p11) says that the incest taboo was thought 'by anthropologists to be 'the foundation of all kinship structures its purpose the preservation of the human social order'. Having given women this position Allen argues that the 'breach of the incest taboo by a woman, consequently, is viewed as a far greater deviation than incest committed by men'. Meaning that females are less likely to sexually abuse children.

2. Over-extending 'feminist' explanations of child sexual abuse

Here Allen argues that researchers and theory makers in the area of child abuse have understood the sexual abuse:

> ...to be a direct result of culturally based socialisation processes that lead to male dominance and promote the sexual exploitation of women and children.

He is careful to point out that while:

> ...male dominance, differential socialisation, and sexual exploitation may help to explain a substantial proportion of child sexual abuse, they can also form barriers to the recognition of female perpetration.

These barriers of recognition develop:

> ...when feminist perspectives are presented as the only viable explanations for child sexual abuse, and female sexual abuse is, consequently, considered non-significant.

3. Over-generalising the lack of reports of child sexual abuse by women

By making this point Allen highlights that we may have become confused by interpretations which have been extrapolated from the low reports of female sexual abuse.

> Two types of misinterpretations lead to such conclusions about female sexual abuse of children: the assumption that reports in the literature accurately reflect rates of female perpetration, and the assumption that low rates of occurrence mean low absolute numbers of instances.

The use of Allen's three points has proved helpful in discussion with professionals in all areas to make sense of women as perpetrators (sexual). Another area of increasing concern is that of female child perpetrators who involve other children, usually younger children, in inappropriate sexual activity. Few cases have been reported but Johnson (1989) described the 'sexual perpetrating behaviour of 13 female child perpetrators between 4 and 13 years of age'.

Case history

The child was first seen because of physical abuse when she was six-years-old. Two years later her sister was referred because of frequent and vigorous masturbation against furniture, staff's knees etc. This child was four years old and she complained of 'soreness'. The mother had lived for several months with a Schedule 1 offender.

On examination both children had signs consistent with penetrative sexual abuse. The mother told her partner to leave and undertook to protect the girls. Over the next few months the girls were unhappy at school, wetting and sad. They also had 'too many bruises' a professional said.

A further investigation revealed that an 'uncle', who had a record of sexually abusing pre-pubertal girls, had moved in with the family. The girls mother did not believe that her partner had abused her daughters and did not co-operate with social services.

After two years, when in a pre-adoptive placement, the younger girl started to make disclosures of sexual abuse involving both her mother and the partner. The child described how '...mummy used to laugh...but she and uncle...hurt me'. Meanwhile, the older sister became very angry and difficult to manage and several months later also disclosed her abuse and confirmed what her sister had previously said. The Crown Prosecution felt there was not a realistic chance of a criminal conviction and the case was dropped.

This case history affirms the complex and prolonged abuse of two young girls and the apparent active involvement of their mother, as when 'mummy used to laugh'. It is important to note that it was over two years before the girls felt safe enough to disclose. The denial that surrounds the sexual abuse by women, and mothers in particular, remains considerably bolstered by comments given with great authority such as Mathis (1972) who declared 'women as harmless' when the subject was brought to his attention and said about mothers: 'That she might seduce a helpless child into sex play is unthinkable, and even if she did so, what harm can be done without a penis?' (p54). The idea that without a penis no harm could be done was an attitude which prevailed widely well into the 1980s.

Since when, much has been written about the CSA perpetrated by women and the damage done (Elliott, 1993; Finkelhor and Russell, 1984; Mayer, 1992; Salter, 1995; Saradjian and Hanks, 1996; and Welldon, 1988).

There continues to be considerable denial by some professionals, which makes working together difficult, particularly in the assessment of relationships. Use of the rapidly expanding literature is needed to back up the opinion that CSA, whilst primarily perpetrated by men, shows that in 15–20 per cent of cases, the perpetrator is a woman. Finkelhor and Russell (1984) in reviewing the literature, estimated that 20 per cent of CSA of boys and five per cent of girls were abused by women and these percentages have increased with investigation of day care, sex rings and organised abuse. Clinically, the range of sexually gratifying behaviours is extensive.

Case history

A 20-year-old single mother was fleeing from violence and moved with her four-year-old son to a women's refuge. The little boy was traumatised by the violence, which had involved the last male partner attacking both the mother and child. But, he had confided to his nursery worker that he '…knew how to make his mummy feel nice…'. His mother readily said that she had taught him how to masturbate her. The mother's background was one of violence, CSA, and self-harm before she ran away and became involved with drugs and prostitution. After initial engagement with a voluntary social work agency the mother and son left abruptly.

The Focus of this Chapter

The brief for this chapter is to concentrate on children who have been sexually abused by women, both adult and adolescent, and consider the assessment process. Saradjian's (1996) research has led to an assessment protocol for women who have sexually abused children and have gone through the court system. However, since few women perpetrators are charged and fewer still criminally convicted this paper will address this dimension in the assessment of alleged female perpetrators:

- The children have disclosed and many have clearly been abused (there is medical evidence, psychological evidence, sometimes corroboration).
- Few cases will have been thoroughly investigated under the auspices of the care system, let alone the criminal court system.
- Several individual cases will be discussed to illustrate strategies for assessment which may lead to better protection for children in the future.

Case history

A mother in her late 20s came to the clinic with her two children, a boy and a girl, both under five years old. The issues around the original referral centred on physical abuse and failure to thrive. The children's mother admitted the physical abuse and co-operated with plans to improve the children's nutrition. She was depressed but accepted support and this was recorded in the child protection conference minutes. There was also a brief note that there had been concern that the girl of the household had been sexually abused. An investigation did not find the perpetrator and, despite a clearly abnormal physical examination, the investigation was dropped. The children's names were briefly on the child protection register. However, the children continued to be seen for regular paediatric and psychology appointments and appeared to be making progress.

The mother then asked for an opportunity to talk for herself and began to discuss her own sexual abuse as a child and the guilt she felt having abused young children when she was about 10 years old. She said after one of the paediatric attendances, during which the children had a physical examination '…I did not realise that my daughter still has the injuries caused by me abusing her and I do sometimes wish I'd never said anything because it is easier to lie and say nothing happened than to try and explain why I did what I did'. She started writing down the events because she felt she could do this more easily than speak. In her writings she detailed the progression of her own sexual abuse which led her to the sexual abuse of other children when she was still a child herself, and subsequently to the sexual abuse of her own children. In her writings she detailed her arousal pattern and specific ways in which she abused sexually.

The above case history shows how the cognitive distortions, well known in the literature (Calder, 1999; Salter, 1995) had become part of this mother's thinking and acting. Her assessment was complicated by the fact that she had been told not to go to a white person or a professional and talk about her difficulties. When she was asked outside the therapeutic sessions whether she was abusing her children she would say 'no'. She was never prosecuted for the sexual abuse of her children. The children never made disclosures. She fitted the description (Saradjian and Hanks 1996) of many of the women interviewed.

In the case of this mother:

- She was abused as a child, physically, emotionally and sexually.

- She was lonely and not very sociable as a child and adult.

- She was aroused by her children.

- She was depressed, at times phobic.

- She was at times violent to her children.

- She denied to herself and others that she did sexually abuse her children.

- She showed cognitive distortions.

- She disclosed and retracted the disclosures.

- She was an intelligent women with excellent writing skills.

- She spoke very little.

Not all CSA perpetrated by women is of their own children and case studies will describe individual histories. Assessment leads to an understanding of the patterns, the consequences of such abuse, the denial and disbelief so prevalent in family, professional systems, and the public domain. The assessment of female perpetrators encompasses many aspects and procedures used in the assessment of male perpetrators. The chapter dealing with the assessments of non-abusing mothers (Chapter Seven in this book) should be used in conjunction with what we suggest to assess mothers who abuse their children sexually.

Characteristics of Female Abusers

There is contention in the literature when it comes to discussions about whether male sexual perpetrators have been sexually abused when they were children. The evidence seems to be somewhat different when it comes to adolescent female perpetrators of sexual abuse. Faller (1987) found that 47.5 per cent of her sample were sexually abused as children, whilst Bumby, Halstenson and Bumby (1995) found that all the female adolescents who had sexually abused were found to have been sexually abused when they themselves were children. Hunter *et al.*, (1993) reported that all the female juvenile sex offenders in their study had been sexually abused as children. Johnson (1989) conducted a study about children who molest other children and found that all of their subjects had been sexually abused when they were younger. Mathews *et al.*, (1997) conducted research on juvenile female sexual offenders, a larger study with a cohort of 67, and found that 52 (77.6 per cent) juveniles had a history of child sexual abuse themselves. In addition:

71.6 per cent had previous mental health treatment

43.9 per cent had suicidal ideation and or made suicide attempts

33.3 per cent were 'runaways'

25.4 per cent were abusing alcohol or drugs

23.4 per cent had a learning disability

77.6 per cent had a history of sexual abuse

60.0 per cent had a history of physical abuse

Mathews *et al.*, (1997) when discussing the issues about typologies of these young people said:

> *The range of offending reported suggests that juvenile female sexual offenders, similar to youthful male offenders, are a diverse group and can be classified into subtypes that may prove useful to clinicians and criminal justice offenders.*
>
> (p195)

Consequently, there is no simple system of the characterising of either male or female perpetrators.

Finkelhor and Russell (1984) and others take the view that sexual abuse is culturally based, and is emphasised by strong social mores which demand that women and children are perceived as sexually exploitable and that men are dominant and sexually aggressive. Finkelhor (1984) stated that:

> ...especially since contact with female children occurs at least twice or three times the frequency as those with male children, the presumption that sexual abusers are primarily men seems clearly supported.
>
> (p177)

As Saradjian and Hanks (1996) point out, the result of this model being applied led to the assumption that:

> ...women who sexually abuse children are highly sexually active or promiscuous or have a history of indiscriminate or compulsive sexual activity.
>
> (p126)

Saradjian's research (Saradjian and Hanks, 1996) does not indicate that these women were promiscuous and in addition those women who sexually abused children coerced by a male partner did not rate themselves as having a high sex drive (p127). In this study all the women who abused children sexually as sole perpetrators reported that they were sexually abused themselves. Some 75 per cent of the women who sexually abused by being coerced by men, reported that they were sexually abused themselves as children (p51). It has to be recognised that sexual relationships between adults and children may take place under actual or threatened violence, or may be non-aggressive. However, this behaviour towards children is insidious, collusive and secretive, and unwanted and disliked by the children who are powerless to stop it. It also leads to consequences in their development which need to be addressed and recognised in the assessment process.

Typologies

There are a number of varying typologies emerging and this highlights the infancy of this area of work and the lack of any kind of consensus to date.

Case history, harmful genital practices

A girl aged five years was referred to a paediatrician because of vulval soreness: she had no vaginal discharge but the mother complained the child had 'an offensive body odour'. Numerous urine samples had been sent to the microbiology laboratory but there was no infection. She had been treated repeatedly with creams. Examination showed that the child was 'sore' but there was no sign of other trauma. The mother volunteered that the child had always been susceptible to 'infection'. Over the next two clinic appointments the child's mother told the paediatrician that she had stopped putting disinfectant in the bath, and now limited washing in the bidet to three times a day: previously it was 10–12 episodes of 'washing' a day.

Allen (1991) described women in the US being registered as sex offenders when they have not protected a child knowing that the child was being sexually abused. In clinical practice a descriptive definition of the actions and behaviour of the women towards the children is still the most valuable way to identify and assess whether abuse has taken place. Mayer (1992) described types of women who have sexually offended against children.

- female rapist
- female sexual harassment
- mother molesters
- mother–son incest
- mother–daughter incest
- triads (co-offending)
- mothers

Mayers classification requires further refinement, and a recent paper by Graystone and De Luca (1999) divided the characteristics of female sexual perpetrators into the following categories:

- characteristics of offences
- characteristics and dynamics of female sex offenders
- demographic characteristics
- personal characteristics and experiences
- psychiatric impairment
- deviant perceptions regarding sexual abuse
- deviant arousal and interest patterns
- domestic violence
- family and marital dysfunction

This provides a more detailed format for describing the perpetrator and whilst it still remains unclear as to why some women abuse, the collection of data in a systematic way is helpful in assessment and clinical research. In this context it is interesting to note that Graystone *et al.*, (1999) agree with most workers in the field that psychiatric impairment of women who sexually abuse children is not common. They point out that '…up to the 1980s these women would have been described as psychotic or grossly disturbed'. The majority of the research carried out more recently shows clearly that the psychiatric label applies to only a small number of women who sexually offend against children. Faller (1987) showed that 7.5 per cent fell into that category.

Saradjian and Hanks (1996) proposed a typology as follows:

- women who target pre-pubescent children
- women who offend initially against children
- women who are coerced by men
- women who co-offend either with men or women
- women involved in ritual abuse groups

The typologies that Matthews (1993) proposed were slightly different and related to their sample of sexually abusing women. Interestingly they did find teachers in amongst their subjects, and divided their subjects as follows:

- **Teacher/lover:** who is considered to have initiated and carried out the abuse, and to have taken advantage of the child. These offenders tend initially to target adolescent children.
- **Pre-disposed:** who also initiate and carried out the abuse but whose background is considered to be a very influential element. These women tended to target younger children.
- **Male coerced offender:** who was under the influence of a male or who was forced to abuse the child. These women may abuse children of any age.

This description is slightly different from a previous typology Matthews published (Matthews *et al.*, 1991). It may be inevitable that there is no consensus given the complexity of this behaviour. However, although there are aspects which are common to male and female perpetrators there are also differences (for a fuller discussion of these points the reader is referred to Allen (1991) for adults, and Blues *et al.*, (1999) for adolescents).

The definitions proposed for male sexual perpetrators have some important common aspects, repeated in female sexual offending, e.g. sexual fantasies. Particularly as research continues it becomes clear that there are more categories that need to be added. A descriptive model seems at present to be the best way forward.

Welldon (1988) wrote a most important account of her clinical experience of working with women who sexually abused their children. The provocation we experience when reading the title *Mother, Madonna, Whore: The Idealisation and Denigration of Motherhood*, is an introduction to the way she examines the role of the mother and her psychological profile which may lead her to sexually abuse. It also describes the experiences and consequences of the 'children', many of them adults by the time the book was written, and gives some clear accounts of what happens in these abusive relationships. Speltz, Matthews and Mathews (1989) first wrote about their research into women who sexually abused and found that there are different groups of women who can be recognised when they sexually abuse children. Elliott (1993) brought together professionals who had helped women to talk about their being sexually abused by their mothers or female carers when they were children.

Case history (CSA involving a neighbour)

A boy of four years, we'll call him Carl, ran into his house crying, and his mother noticed blood on his shorts. When she asked him what had happened he would only cry inconsolably and point to his penis. The foreskin had been forcibly retracted and torn. The child had delayed language and was not able to verbalise what had happened clearly.

The following day Carl was playing with another four-year-old friend (Danny) and both boys raced into Carl's house. Danny was crying but could say 'old women' and later pointed out the house where 'she…hurt me'. Danny had a similar injury to Carl's (i.e. a torn foreskin frenulum). Danny's mother complained to the police. Carl's mother had a social worker but did not mention the incident because she was living with a Schedule 1 offender and was frightened he would be blamed. The elderly neighbour denied any contact with the boys and the investigation was inconclusive.

Mathews, Hunter and Vuz (1997) discussed the clinical characteristics and treatment issues relating to children and adolescents. These authors state that there is now data available which shows that juvenile female perpetrators of sexual abuse are far more common than had previously been recognised. Their study looked at 67 girls (juveniles) in treatment for sexually abusing other children. They compared this group with 70 boys who had also sexually offended and were in treatment. They found that 100 per cent of these girls had been sexually abused as children and that force and aggression were part of their abuse experience. They also found:

> …that most juvenile females who sexually perpetrate frequently have had disruptive and tumultuous childhood's replete with high levels of trauma and exposure to the modelling of interpersonal violence and aggression.
>
> (Mathews, Hunter and Vuz, 1997: p194)

Clinical experience in the UK mirrors this with recognition that violence plays a large part in the abuse but also in management as the girls' own behaviour results in placement in residential units. The girls' violent behaviour precipitates placement as the violence spills over from the CSA to everyday living. The clinical anxiety remains as to whether the CSA is tackled or the violence takes over and the cause is forgotten.

What happens to the girls and adolescents who do not have violent behaviours? They are perpetrators but appear well behaved and compliant? Some of the children who have themselves been sexually abused through bribery, gentle coercion, persuasion, and generally by non-violent means may continue that pattern when they repeat the cycle and sexually abuse. There is very little documented about this group of 'less violent' offenders, even though their victims may disagree with the 'non violent' tag, as mis-use of power is

universal and a small victim *is* frightened. In this 'secret' behaviour, society does not see the violence which has not been generalised .

Another study about juvenile female perpetrators of sexual abuse by Hunter *et al.*, (1993) examined the psychosexual, attitudinal and developmental characteristics of these young females. Though the study is small, with only ten girls, it highlights the profiles of these children. An interesting finding from the study shows that all of them were sexually abused as children by several perpetrators and that six out of the ten children were also sexually abused by females. It would be interesting to know whether having been sexually abused by a female in childhood produces a pattern that leads females to abuse sexually in later life, and there does appear to be an increased risk.

Questions at the beginning of an assessment

Adcock (1995) wrote a comprehensive chapter on the assessment of children and their families, and highlights the difficulties and differences that occur in bringing together a variety of professionals in an attempt to assess an abusive, or possibly violent situation. The same principles apply when female sexual perpetrators are to be assessed.

Calder in Chapter One has explored the changing central framework for assessment and child protection and identified some of the key limitations when attempting to apply them to sexual abuse (see also Calder, forthcoming).

The Assessment

'Why is the assessment being done?' is the single most crucial question before beginning any assessment.

Assessment is beset with hazards which attack the accuracy of the evaluation; the most important of these being the limited knowledge base in relation to the aetiology of sexual offending in general, and in particular, of sexual offending by women.

The questions that need to be asked at the beginning are:

1. To give an opinion on whether a women is likely to have sexually abused a child.

2. To consider the risk a women who is known to have sexually abused a child has of re-offending.

3. To consider the areas that need to be worked on in therapy to reduce the risk of re-offending, including most importantly the women's motivation to change.

4. To gain information from the women perpetrator that may inform the therapy of her victims.

(Saradjian and Hanks, 1996: pp203–4)

Following on from that the assessor needs to be clear about:

- Why is an assessment taking place? (i.e. for court, child protection conference, etc.)

- Who (which agency) has requested it and who will make the principal use of it?

- Is it a risk assessment, needs' assessment, a social or psychological/psychiatric assessment? Or is it a combination of the above?

- Is it a joint assessment which pools together information from different professions or do several professionals do their specific piece of assessment?

- If the latter is taking place: who is co-ordinating this?

- What multidisciplinary support is available and how is that co-ordinated?

- Where is the assessment to take place?

- How many different assessments are to be undertaken?

The different aspects of female sexual perpetrators

A model has evolved out of clinical experience which categorises the abusing women. It is based on a cascading model of questions that need to be asked. A pathway developed which allowed the therapist to gain some understanding of the situation of each case and to make an initial analysis. By following a path as described, a structured assessment of the women who have allegedly sexually abused and the circumstances in which this abuse took place becomes clear or better understood. A continuum of the part played by women was recognised and it is this understanding that is pivotal in the last analysis.

The spectrum of the involvement of the women is represented:

convicted women on their own	women abuse on their own	women abuse willingly with another	women coerced into sexually abusing	women who know of CSA and do nothing	women who know a little or suspect and do nothing	ordinary women
/_____/_____/_____/_____/_____/_____/___						

There are of course other dimensions which are used. Whether there was violence, alcohol or drug abuse. Whether there was one child involved or more, whether the children were the birth children of the women or not. Did the abuse take place in an institution (school, nursery, children's home)?

Collecting this information and recording it is helped by the use of a flowchart. The questions can often be answered with a simple yes or no. However, assessors should not feel restricted from answering the questions more descriptively. Having identified the position of the women on the continuum the next step was to identify different groups:

1. Adult women

2. Women who had and had not been convicted of sexually abusing children

3. Teenage girls

4. Children

Further questions resulting from Group 1 are:

- Was the women a stranger to the child?

- Was the women related to the child?

- Was the child the birth child of the mother?

- Was the child abused:
  - sexually?
  - emotionally?
  - physically?

- Was more than one child abused by the woman and if so:
  - Are the children siblings?
  - Are the children related otherwise?
  - Do the children know each other ?
  - Are the children aware of each other?

- Did the women sexually abuse on their own?

- Who else was present when the sexual abuse took place?

- State the relationship of that person to the women:
  - A casual acquaintance?
  - A stranger?

- Did she sexually abuse willingly with another:
  - male?
  - female?
  - both male and female?

- Did she sexually abuse under threat from another:
  - male?
  - female?
  - group of people?

- What threat was used?

- Were the children the women abused disabled:
  - physically?
  - have learning difficulties?
  - both?

Questions relating to Group 2 are:

- Has the woman had a conviction of sexually abusing children?

- Has the woman been known to, or been suspected of, sexually abusing children in the past? (If the answer is yes, give details

of the number of convictions, where they took place, dates, who was involved etc.).

It is necessary to ascertain the positions they hold in life.

- Age now.
- Age when she first sexually abused.
- Has she got children (how many boys and girls)?
- Is she a carer of other children?
- Does she live alone or with a partner (male or female)?

Chapter Seven in this book, on the assessment of mothers who are the non-abusing party, contains many of the components which are useful for the assessment of abusing mothers. The reader is referred to this chapter when planning the assessment.

Questions for Group 3 are:

- In what position vis-à-vis the child victim was this teenager:
  - A sibling (state whether brother or sister)?
  - A relative other than sibling (state relationship)?
  - Was the child victim a friend's child?
  - A child doing a job?
  - 'unusual' child?

- When the sexual abuse took place was the sexually abusing adolescent:
  - On her own?
  - With others?
  - An adult parental figure (mother or father)?
  - An adult known to the family?
  - An adult known to the adolescent only?
  - A sibling?
  - A relative?
  - A stranger?

- What was the family and social background of the child or adolescent:
  - Did she come from a violent home?
  - Did she come from a non-violent home?

- Did she come from a home that was otherwise abusive or malfunctioning?
- Was she violent with the child she sexually abused?
- How can her background be characterised (silent, isolated, easy going)?
- How did she get to the position of sexually abusing a child?

Female children and adolescents who sexually abuse other children are not uncommon and the assessment of their involvement has to be as clear as that of older women. This is particularly so that the child can be helped to stop the abusing pattern.

Vizard's (1997) paper on adolescents who sexually abuse, though written with both sexual groups in mind gives a clear insight into the youngsters behaviour. Vizard *et al.* (1996) also wrote a paper detailing the assessment issues for juvenile sexual offenders and again, while this includes males and females who are abusing, they offer important points to be considered when assessing juveniles. Calder (forthcoming b) also extends his risk assessment frameworks of children and young people to embrace females as well as those with learning disabilities.

Questions for Group 4 are:

- Was the child on her own?

- Was the child with other sexually abusing adults?

- Was the child with other sexually abusing children/adolescents?

- Was the sexually abused child a:
  - sibling?
  - relative?
  - friend?
  - stranger?

- Was the child violent to the victim?

The problem of young children sexually abusing other children is not new, but remains a difficult situation. Particularly when discussing the cycle of abuse, researchers and clinicians have long recognised that children from an early age on can behave sexually towards other children. Whether their behaviour is intentionally hurtful or abusive or takes place for less malicious reasons needs to be assessed. With all sexual perpetrators the question about their own abuse is important. When children abuse each other the question of their own abuse, and who taught or initiated them into how to behave in this sexually abusive way needs to be addressed.

Case history

A mother came for consultation in a paediatric clinic. She had a three-month-old baby and a four-year-old boy. Her concern was with the boy who had both been poorly, had sleep disturbances and difficult behaviour patterns which included considerable distress at times. The mother put the baby in a blanket on the carpeted floor in the consulting room and the doctors and the mother entered into an intense conversation where the mother voiced her concern over the little boy. When asked what she thought was happening to her son she said she did not know. A moment later the baby started crying and as the mother and professionals turned their attention to the baby they saw that the little boy had positioned himself on top of the baby and was performing quite violent rhythmic movements (sexual mounting) on top of the baby. The mother was distraught and said he had done this before and when one of the doctors asked the boy why he was doing this to the baby the little boy said ; 'because my daddy does it to me and he hurts my bottom. I show you', and with that he went over to the baby, now in the mother's arms, and tried to take her clothes off. Both mother and the little boy became very distressed when she tried to stop him. Just from this brief description the value of the child's spontaneous disclosure and the value of observing the behaviours was shown.

Professionals need to recognise the effect, the emotional intensity, as well as the words and pictures that the children may use to communicate about what has been happening to them. Professionals who assess children need to have a thorough knowledge of the developmental stages children go through, physically and psychologically.

Bremer (1993) described the treatment of children and adolescents with what she called 'aberrant sexual behaviour'. She points out that even for small children the issue of taking responsibility for their behaviour and, in a developmentally appropriate way be guided to take personal accountability of the behaviour, is a vital step in the attempts to change these children's way of conducting themselves. It is important to recognise this even at the assessment stage. Bremer (1992) described three groups of 'child sexual offenders' and grades them roughly by age. Though she devised these groups for the assessment of treatment for the children, they are helpful guides to the general assessment too.

Group 1: The sexually reactive children:

- The children are very young (pre-school to six years of age).
- Boys and girls are equally represented.
- They show hyper-sexualised behaviours.
- They do not respond to limit setting and boundaries at school or at home.

Group 2: The incipient child perpetrators:

- Children are 5–13 years of age.
- Boys and girls.
- Showing hyper-sexualised behaviours.
- Show victimising behaviours.

Group 3: Maximum intervention group:

- School-aged children.
- Boys and girls.
- Their behaviour includes aggressive sexual acts.

The assessment of adolescents has to be carried out with equal rigor to that of the adult assessment. Vizard *et al.*, (1996) lay down some of the assessment procedures for adolescents but the position of the female offender has to be attended to. The assessment also needs to include ways to help the adolescent break the cycle of abuse and identify treatment programmes in the area. For young children, those between 5 and 13 years, the assessment again has to be very detailed to ascertain what stage in the cycle the child has reached. Treatment can be effective at this stage because the child might be able to undergo change. The support and co-operation of parents or parental figures will have to be assessed because their role will be vital. It will be important to know whether the child has been sexually abused in the past, or is still being

sexually abused in the present. Bremer's (1993) model can be a helpful adjunct to the assessment documents produced by the Department of Health.

Disclosure

A brief word about disclosure of the sexual abuse in these cases is all we intend to do for this chapter. In terms of assessment the question about how the disclosure, if any, came about and who did the disclosing, is important.

Children's disclosure

Young children who have been sexually abused may make spontaneous disclosures about all forms of abuse, including that by their mothers. The older the child is, the more complex becomes the disclosing by the child, since he/she are much more aware of the constraints of their relationship with their mother and of the position they may put their mother in. In many cases the mother would have warned them or threatened them with what would happen if they disclosed.

Elliott and Briere (1994) found that children who have great difficulties in disclosing were more likely to have non-supportive mothers, and they were more likely to have been victimised by someone who abused them in their home. They were also more likely to have experienced longer and more severe abuse. The authors concluded that the child's willingness to disclose will be influenced by parental support which, in turn, is linked to the caretaker's relationship with the perpetrator in cases were the father is the abuser it would be the mother they turn to. Our clinical experience tells us that children find it harder to disclose their sexual abuse when it is their mother who is abusing them.

Female perpetrators' disclosure

Female perpetrators of sexual abuse have the professional and public 'support' in their denial of what they have done. On the one hand this makes it easier to stay silent and on the other hand it makes it much harder to be heard when they do disclose. Their disclosures are also often not believed. Many women in this position have said that it was much, much easier to stay silent and lie than to speak up and disclose their abusive behaviour.

Disclosure and retraction follow one another with regularity and are in a pattern much more like children disclosing abuse than perpetrators disclosing. Professionals are often split and argue for or against the abuse having been perpetrated by the female, and if it is a mother the doubts and recriminations are increased. We have often recognised that the child can easily be forgotten in this tug-of-war over the position of the mother. The need to protect a mother who has disclosed her sexual abuse on her children seems overwhelming. The behaviour or deed seems so unthinkable that professionals often side with the retracting statements the mother makes. Observing such systems and trying to make sense of it can be very hard work.

When we consider the position of paternal sexual abuse on children we hope that the child has a mother who can provide some protection and safety. When we have a situation where the mother is the perpetrator of the sexual abuse the child is often left without any support whatsoever.

Bentovim (1996) pointed out that:

> An extension of the issue of responsibility for direct abusive action is the attitude of the other parent in child abuse. Often the trauma organised system means that not only is a child abused, but a partner is intimidated or threatened into a dominating story. A parent might frequently telephone a child in care saying that unless she changes her story the father will commit suicide, or that he cannot tolerate life without a partner. It is very difficult to be certain of a protective parent maintaining a caring stance in the face of the pressure of her own needs, or those of a powerful partner.
>
> (Bentovim, 1996)

What has to be considered in children who are abused by their mothers or female carers is that they rarely have a non-abusing parental figure and one has to wonder what that means for the child. Saradjian (1997) talks about some of these issues but we have much more to learn.

Denial is a First Line of Defence

Denial and minimalisation are common aspects in most of the perpetrators of sexual abuse, whether they be male, female or adolescents.

When there is some evidence that a women has abused a child sexually but is denying this, Saradjian and Hanks (1996: p209) advocate that 'all the possible hypotheses must be considered':

1. She has done so, knows she has, and is lying.

2. She has done so, but sincerely does not recognise that her behaviour towards the child constitutes sexual abuse.

3. She has abused but due to dissociation genuinely does not recognise or recall that she has sexually abused the child.

4. She has not sexually abused the child.

It is important that the final possibility is always considered along with the others. In paediatric clinics where children are seen when there is a suspicion that sexual abuse has occurred, the pattern of denial can be clearly observed. We recognise that it is at times extremely hard for the professionals to stay focused and work towards protecting the child. It must also be said that we are not always successful in protecting the child.

Case history

A mother brought her five-year-old daughter to a paediatric clinic because the child had been complaining of a sore tummy for a long time. The child had been investigated and nothing had been found 'wrong'. She was thin and very withdrawn but otherwise not ill. The child had also started wetting and soiling and the mother said that was the final straw. On medical examination the child was found to have signs of genital and anal abuse. When these findings were discussed with the mother she did not seem surprised and said she thought her husband had sexually abused the child when she was a baby. He had committed suicide two years previously. When it was pointed out that the abuse seemed to be recent the mother could not find an explanation. She said the child never left her side except to go to school. At that point the child said; 'it does not happen at school'. The paediatrician asked where does it happen? She said 'at home'. At that point the mother became distraught and cried. The child became extremely solicitous, said she was sorry she had said anything and then turned to us and said 'it is not true'. The mother regained her composure and said she was sure we were thinking that she was the perpetrator.

An investigation with social services was undertaken, but apart from finding the mother unusual in some of her behaviours, isolated and socially not very active, no perpetrator of the sexual abuse could be isolated.

The mother then came to further paediatric appointments and said that she wanted to talk because it was she who was abusing her daughter sexually. She gave a description of what she did which included inserting objects and washing the child's private area very vigorously. The mother's disclosure was spontaneous and the child, who was present, nodded affirmatively. Repeated investigations produced nothing because the mother said she had never said anything to the doctors. When the child was asked she did not speak.

The mother became very distressed and depressed. She agreed that the child should go into respite foster care for a short while. The child stayed with foster parents for four weeks. The mother hardly visited and was supervised when she did. The vaginal and anal signs healed and on examination had returned to normal.

The child returned home and after a very short time complained of being sore in her genital area. Signs of sexual abuse had recurred. The mother now said she thought the child was inflicting the injuries herself by scratching. The child said she did not scratch herself, and that her mother knew that because she had to wear mittens all night long, had to wear two pairs of pyjamas and had her hands tied together by mother.

The child's mother again made a disclosure of her abuse on the child but retracted it when she talked to the social worker. It was interesting as well as frustrating to watch how well this mother was able to manipulate the various professionals involved in the case and have them argue with each other. The child was never protected. The outlook for this girl is likely to be poor, not least because of the dishonesty and ambivalence of the mother.

Bremer (1992) said about adolescents that: 'Denial is the sex offenders first line of defence' and also the strongest. Confronting denial is a painstaking process. It involves taking apart, detail by detail, all the justifications the adolescent has learnt and relied on to make sense of his/her nonsensical world.

The working through of the 'minimisation' of the behaviour, leading to the acceptance of what the offender has done is the point where the treatment process can begin. This is for the perpetrator. For the child the treatment should start long before that.

Conclusion

Despite the fact that far more is written and understood about female sexual abusers, children are still unprotected when it comes to acknowledging that women can and do sexually abuse children or, that denial of women as potential abusers exists. It is now over ten years since the Inquiry into Child Abuse in Cleveland but denial of the existence of the sexual abuse of young boys and disabled children still exists. Equally, it is still denied that middle class men, let alone upper class ones, are capable of sexually abusing young children and that they do so. The notion of women and teenagers as abusers is a step too far. It seems still much easier to believe that child abusers are rare, evil and wicked and are not to be contemplated.

Teenage girls may be told to '...pick on someone your own size' or, come down on the child heavily with the aim of punishment. But their sexual abusive behaviour is often not addressed.

Saradjian and Hanks (1996) and Saradjian (1997) felt that concentrating on the research questions is most certainly one important step further in gathering information and understanding about this subject. Saradjian (1997) and Sgroi and Sargent (1993) as well as Welldon (1988) discuss the effects and trauma female sexual abuse and particularly maternal sexual abuse has on children. Unfortunately, the subject is still in the realm of 'the unthinkable' and change will occur only once society as a whole is prepared to undergo change and relinquish the denial patterns so firmly entrenched.

This chapter has attempted to give a flavour of how one might begin the task of assessing female sexual perpetrators of abuse on children. The chapter is housed in a book which discusses the issues of assessment and the reader is encouraged to make use of the various and different techniques and ideas which may help in assessment.

References

Adcock, M. (1995). Assessment. In Wilson, K., and Jones, A. (Eds.). *The Child Protection Handbook*, pp188–210. London: Bailliere Tindall.

Allen, C.M. (1991). *Women and Men who Sexually Abuse Children*. Orwell, VT: The Safer Society Press.

Bentovim, A. (1996). *Trauma-organised Systems*. London: Karnac Books.

Blues, A., Moffat, C., and Telford, P. (1999). Work with Adolescent Females who Sexually Abuse: Similarities and Differences. In Masson, H., and Erooga, M. (Eds.). *Children and Young People who Sexually Abuse Others: Challenges and Responses*, pp162–82. London: Routledge.

Bremer, J.F. (1992). Serious Juvenile Sex Offenders: Treatment and Long-term Follow-up. *Psychiatric Annals*, 22(6): pp326–32

Bremer, J.F. (1993). Children and Adolescents with Sexually Abusive Behaviour. *Bailliere's Clinical Paediatrics*, 1(1): pp269–82

Calder, M.C. (1999). *Assessing Risk in Adult Males who Sexually Abuse Children: A Practitioners Guide*. Lyme Regis: Russell House Publishing.

Calder, M.C. (forthcoming). *Juveniles and Children who Sexually Abuse: Frameworks for Assessment*. (2nd edition). Lyme Regis: Russell House Publishing.

Calder, M.C. (forthcoming b). The New Assessment Framework: A Critique and Reformulation. In Calder, M.C., and Hackett, S. (Eds.). *The RHP Child Care Assessment Manual*. Lyme Regis: Russell House Publishing.

Elliott, D.M., and Briere. J. (1991). Multivariate Impacts of Parental Incest, Physical Maltreatment, and Substance Abuse. In Salter, A.C. *Transforming Trauma*. Thousand Oaks: Sage.

Elliott, M. (Ed.) (1993). *Female Sexual Abuse of Children*. UK: Longman.

Etherington, K. (1995). *Adult Male Survivors of Childhood Sexual Abuse*. London: Pitman Publishing.

Faller, K.C. (1987). Women who Sexually Abuse Children. *Violence and Victims*, 2(4): pp263–76

Finkelhor, D., and Russell, D. (1984). Women as Perpetrators. In Finkelhor, D., and Associates. *A Sourcebook on Child Sexual Abuse*. Beverley Hills, CA: Sage.

Finkelhor, D., Williams, L.M., and Burns, N. (1988). *Nursery Crimes*. Newbury Park: Sage Publications.

Graystone, A.D., and De Luca, R.V. (1999). Female Perpetrators of Child Sexual Abuse: A Review of the Clinical and Empirical Literature. *Aggression and Violent Behaviour*, 4(1): pp93–106

Hunter, J.A., Lexier, L.J., Goodwin, D.W., Browne, P.A., and Dennis, C. (1993). Psychosexual, Attitudinal, and Developmental Characteristics of Juvenile Female Sexual Perpetrators in a Residential Treatment Setting. *Journal of Child and Family Studies*, 2(4): pp317–26

Johnson, T. (1989). Female Child Perpetrators: Children

who Molest Other Children. *Child Abuse and Neglect*, 13: pp571–85

Kempe, H. (1978). Paediatric Implications of the Battered Baby Syndrome. *Archives of Diseases in Childhood*, 46: pp28–37

Kempe, R., and Kempe, C. (1978). *Child Abuse*. London: Fontana.

Lawson, C. (1993). Mother–Son Sexual Abuse: Rare or Under-reported? A Critique of the Research. *Child Abuse and Neglect*, 17: pp261–9

Mathews, R., Hunter, J.A., and Vuz, J. (1997). Juvenile Female Sexual Offenders: Clinical Characteristics and Treatment Issues. *Sexual Abuse: A Journal of Research and Treatment*, 9(3): pp187–99

Mathews, R., Matthews, J.K., and Speltz, K. (1991). Female Sexual Offenders: A Typology. In Patton, M.Q. (Ed.). *Family Sexual Abuse: Frontline Research and Evaluation*. London: Sage.

Mathis, J.L. (1972). *Clear Thinking About Sexual Deviation*. Chicago: Nelson-Hall.

Matthews, J.K. (1993). Working with Female Sexual Abusers. In Elliott, M. (Ed.). *Female Sexual Abuse of Children*. UK: Longman Group.

Mayer, A. (1992). *Women Sex Offenders*. Holmes Beach, FL: Learning Publications Inc.

Salter, A.C. (1995). *Transforming Trauma*. Thousand Oaks: Sage Publications.

Saradjian, J., and Hanks, H. (1996). *Women who Sexually Abuse: From Research to Practice*. Chichester: John Wiley and Son.

Saradjian, J. (1997). Factors that Specifically Exacerbate the Trauma of Victims of Childhood Sexual Abuse by Maternal Perpetrators. *Journal of Sexual Aggression*, 3(1): pp3–14

Sgroi, S.M., and Sargent, N.M. (1993). Impact and Treatment Issues for Victims of Childhood Sexual Abuse by Female Perpetrators. In Elliott, M. (Ed.). *Female Sexual Abuse of Children: The Ultimate Taboo*. UK: Longman Group.

Speltz, K., Matthews, J.K., and Mathews, R. (1998). *Female Sexual Offenders: An Exploratory Study*. Orwell, VT: Safer Society Press.

Travin, S., Cullen, K., and Trotter, B. (1990). Female Sex Offenders: Severe Victims and Victimisers. *Journal of Forensic Sciences*.

Vizard, E. (1997). Adolescents who Sexually Abuse. In Welldon, E., and Van Velsen, C. (Eds.). *A Practical Guide to Forensic Psychotherapy*. London: Jessica Kingsley.

Vizard, E., Monck, E., and Misch, P. (1995). Child and Adolescent Sex Abuse Perpetrators: A Review of the Literature. *Journal of Child Psychology and Psychiatry*, 36(5): pp731–56

Vizard, E., Wynick, S., Hawkes, C., Woods, J., and Jenkins, J. (1996). Juvenile Sexual Offenders: Assessment Issues. *British Journal of Psychiatry*, 168: pp259–62

Welldon, E.V. (1988). *Mother, Madonna, Whore: The Idealisation and Denigration of Motherhood*. London: Free Association Books.

Chapter Nine

Self-protection/Personal Safety Skills

Lynda Regan

What is Self-protection

Undertaking a piece of self-protection work with a child who has been sexually abused can often be perceived as a solution to a problem.

With the increasing demands placed on social workers, practice becomes more and more reactive, leaving little time to reflect, research and consider wider issues about effective methods of intervention. Evaluation becomes a little visited luxury.

Children are, by their very nature, dependent on adults to meet their basic needs, one of which is to be protected.

Working in the field of child sexual abuse highlights children's vulnerability on all levels. All children will have different experiences as they grow and progress towards adulthood. Their transition can be aided by parenting that recognises the child's basic needs for food, shelter, warmth, etc.; on developmental levels where a child is encouraged to learn safely about their world, themselves and their environment; and on an emotional level where their thoughts, fears and feelings are acknowledged and guided towards insight and further understanding.

When a child has been sexually abused they have experienced physical abuse, an abuse of their body that often, but not always, will have involved pain, and an abuse of their emotional, social and cognitive developmental processes that can subsequently affect how they view themselves and how they relate to others.

For some children whose experience of being parented has not been generally supportive or positive, sexual abuse adds yet another layer of confusion and distortion to their already mixed up world.

It is against this diversity of backgrounds, of experiences, levels of development and understanding that add to the dilemmas faced by adults in considering appropriate information for children, to help keep them safer.

Children are taught from an early age to trust, respect and accept adult authority, often without question, especially if the adult is someone well known to the child. Being obedient equates with being good.

Children are incapable of understanding adult motives of tricks, bribes and subtler emotional manipulation used by abusive adults to gain co-operation.

It would seem to follow that to give a child limited information about body safety in isolation from wider issues about trust, assertiveness, choices, feelings and without support to test these out in safe relationships, places responsibility for their future safety solely on the child's shoulders.

Self-protection work is never a solution to a problem. It cannot make everything safe for a child. It can only be a starting point for identifying what each individual child needs and what they need from the safe adults around them.

There are other labels for this type of work—personal safety skills is perhaps the most common alternative and one which at least takes the notion of responsibility away from the child.

Developing Sexuality

Human sexuality is socially constructed and as such is influenced by country, culture (which may change over time) and religion:

> In the course of development from infant to adult in any society, individuals learn the current social rules, which determine the sexual behaviour of men and women in their culture. These form a system of meaning, which is made up of language, symbols and both explicit and implicit rules about behaviour. The developing individual becomes aware of how they are viewed within the sex and gender structure by other people of both sexes and thus becomes fundamental to their development and ideas of identity.
>
> (Ennew, 1986: p26)

The developing child becomes aware of their gender role from a very early age by the words and actions of adults around them.

A young child has no understanding of the social meanings of behaviours until this is given to them by adults through their reactions, attitudes, language, rewards or disapproval. Adults may feel they face a moral dilemma when considering providing a child with information on sex and sexuality. In reality are we protecting children from knowledge that may allow them to be safer, or are we protecting them from what they may choose to do with that knowledge. Is it better to preserve a child's innocence? Is it putting ideas into a child's head? If they are given information, what will they do with it? Getting the balance right can seem to be a daunting task. However, any child who is uninformed is at risk because they have no notion that someone may want to hurt them and may have no notion of how to tell someone they need help. As long as sexuality is seen as something distinct from other aspects of learning about relationships, and communicating with each other, it retains the idea that it is solely about sex rather than about a development of ourselves.

The natural development of a child's sexuality is at the pace of the child, and is not just about sex or gender, but about assertiveness, choices, feelings, and trust in a much wider context. Having a safe carer who can support the child to learn and grow naturally provides a protective environment within which the child can learn at their pace about who they are in relation to in the world around them.

Children who have been sexually abused have experienced distorted adult sexuality that they will not be able to fully understand and have received confusing messages about sex, sexuality, relationships, boundaries and power.

Why Children Need Safety Skills

- All children are vulnerable to sexual abuse.
- All children are powerless.
- Uninformed children trust all adults.
- Young children are incapable of assessing adult's motives.
- Children are taught that goodness equates with obedience to adults.
- Children are curious about their own bodies.
- Children are deprived of information about their own sexuality.

- Uninformed children do not realise that abusive behaviour is wrong.
- Sexual abuse is often presented as evidence of affection.
- Children are even at risk in their peer groups.
- Children are confused by sexual misbehaviour.
- Children are seldom encouraged to express their anxieties and fears (Briggs, 1995).

The above list highlights children's vulnerability and conversely shows us what our work needs to address.

However, this is only one aspect of what a child needs to be safe. Even with some extra knowledge and understanding, children will be unable to recognise some of the techniques abusive adults use to gain co-operation and it is both unrealistic and unfair to expect the child to take responsibility alone for their safety.

For these reasons, self-protection work or safety skills work is only one part of the information a child needs to help them make some sense out of what happened, to unlearn some of the destructive patterns of responding in relationships generally, and to help keep themselves safer, within an effective and protective support system.

Current practice in relation to self-protection work would seem to have been developed from conceptual frameworks relating to some of the specific conditions we are aware of that allow sexual abuse to thrive, and a knowledge of impacts (see Chapter Seven for further details).

Often, workbooks are specifically designed for this focus on identified issues, for example, good and bad touches; body awareness and body safety. Whilst these resources are useful to have they seldom provide a complete piece of work within themselves.

When considering working with a child it is important to address the issue of timing.

Recent disclosure: if matters have only recently been investigated, criminal proceedings may be pending. It is essential to discuss any proposed work with the Crown Prosecution Service (CPS) and investigating officers. In relative terms work with a child may fall into two areas at this stage.

Stage one: the child may be experiencing distress, sleep disturbance, behaviour problems or other reactions that can be addressed in the short-term by providing immediate coping strategies for the child and their family. It is important to discuss this with others involved and to record what is being done and why.

Stage two: if the child's behaviour is continuing over a period of time to cause serious concerns, if coping strategies have not been successful and the child is unable to continue their day-to-day life in a reasonable manner, more in-depth therapeutic help may be required. This should always be discussed fully with the child protection unit, investigating officers and with the person the child is being referred to. However, the child's needs are paramount and any decisions taken should be a reflection of their needs.

Past issues: sometimes we work with families where sexual abuse has been a feature in the family's past history. It may be that issues were not addressed at the time, that the child or family could not accept help to work through the issues at that time or that something from the past experience has re-surfaced at the present time.

In these circumstances it is important to clarify who needs the help or support. A safe carer may request work with a child, when it could be the carer who has not worked through their own issues in relation to the child's abuse.

Some trigger questions to consider are:

- Who is referring the child?

- What is being requested?

- Are there issues for siblings?

- Why is it being requested now?

- Whose problem is it?

- Is the child aware their carer has concerns?

- Does the child want some time (at this stage) to explore why their behaviour is worrying their carer, what is troubling them or perhaps why things seem to be going wrong at home; school; with friends etc.?

Not all children need or benefit from direct work. It will only be meaningful to the child if it is provided at a time when they feel it is useful to them. Sometimes it is more constructive to work with the safe carers. To help them understand what sexual abuse is, and how it happens. Sometimes, having provided knowledge and support to work through their own issues, it can

be possible to provide them with the skills to help the child learn assertive body safety skills.

Issues for Safe Carers

Child development theories tell us that adverse social relationships in childhood can affect a person's sense of well-being, self-worth, confidence, and ability to form satisfying, conflict-free relationships.

The child who doesn't disentangle some of the distorted patterns they have learnt can carry these effects into adulthood. If a child has been sexually abused by a known and trusted adult they have received distorted messages about trust, adults, relationships, sex, sexuality, giving and receiving affection—attention, boundaries, self-worth. The impacts are much wider than focusing on the physical sexual experience.

Once the child has spoken of the abuse, investigations have taken place and the child is placed with a safe carer (either within the immediate family or within the care system), there can be the assumption that they 'know' they are safe and as a consequence should be relieved, feel safe and be socially co-operative.

However, it is more common for destructive behaviours to emerge, at times, putting placements at risks. Carers need to have some basic information about the impact of sexual abuse on a child emotionally, and be given an opportunity to reflect on how the child may have processed their experience.

For example, if the abuser was a parent or carer the child may have experienced inner confusion and conflict:

The child is rejected, abused or hurt and feels they have 'lost' parents love/interest.

↓

The child feels anxiety.

↓

When anxious or upset the child would usually seek reassurance from an attachment figure.

↓

Child's attachment figure is responsible for raising the anxiety.

↓

Child experiences internal conflict and has to deal with this alone.

↓

This anxiety has to be dealt with psychologically and may mean the child uses *defence mechanisms* to cope.

A range of superficial behaviours may emerge which can lead to the child being labelled difficult, attention seeking, bad, distant etc. The child may have learnt that to get attention you must give affection to an adult. This may lead a child at times of inner confusion about what is expected of them, trying to please other adults by being sexual and may lead to a misinterpretation of the of the child's behaviour as precocious, flirtatious etc.

Providing clear, basic information to the safe carers may help them understand that the behaviour presented by the child is not the whole problem. The underlying fear or confusion can create immediate behaviours and the child needs help with both.

In working with children over time what becomes clear is that for any child who is actively listened to, whose feelings and views are validated, who can learn to see the good within themselves and know that others see it too, and experience some level of control in small situations, then this child gains self-confidence, self-worth and the destructive behaviours decrease.

At times adults can be helped to resolve their confusion or lack of knowledge and can then help the child move forward in a positive way with insight and understanding.

Whatever the plan of work is, the safe carer is a crucial element. It is within the day-to-day experience of life with family and friends that the child will take their new knowledge. They can only do so if the safe adults around them make space for the changes and allow them to be themselves. If a safe carer has no information about body assertiveness work with the child, how do they encourage the child to practice this within the home. If they have no understanding of cycles of abuse, grooming methods or of how difficult it actually is for children to tell when something is happening, how can they support and encourage the child, or how do they build on this in order to provide a support network to and for the child.

For a fuller description of safe care, the reader is referred to Rose and Savage (1999).

A Framework to Help Focus on what Specific Work May be Needed and Why

If our intervention is to help the children we work with to be 'safer' in the future we need to construct an individual framework from the knowledge we already have for each child, and then we must help the child take any new skills or information back into their family and wider relationships.

In a simplified form we can try to create our own 'menu' that considers each child's situation individually and which may allow us to target a more thorough support package for the child.

The menu should be constructed after considering:

a) The circumstances that were present that allowed the child to be sexually abused.

b) The impact on the child.

c) The reasons why all children need safety skills.

d) What current support networks the child has got.

If we focus on each of these areas in some depth we can effectively create our own checklist from which to begin to prioritise and shape our work with a child. Please refer to Appendix One for an operational framework with the child.

The circumstances that were present that allowed the child to be sexually abused

If we consider Finkelhor's (1986) four preconditions for sexual abuse we start to identify the specific circumstances for each child.

1. The presence of someone with a predisposition to sexually abuse a child.

2. Their ability to overcome their own internal inhibitors.

3. Creating opportunity (manipulating safe carers and the child).

4. Overcoming the child's own resistance.

Without apportioning blame to anyone other than the perpetrator, focus objectively on the specific set of circumstances and identify where the distortion or manipulations occurred. If the safe carer and the child trusted the abusive adult there are dual issues about trust and responsibility that can yo-yo back and forth. How does the safe carer help the child to learn to trust appropriately again (and who helps the safe carer)? What needs to happen to allow the safe carer to be able to check out with the child how they feel in other peoples company in the future? What will issues of concern be? How will the child let the carer know they have worries?

What were the child's own strengths (coping strategies), what were the child's fears about telling, who did they think would help/already knew etc. Were they protecting siblings?

The impact on the child

> Effective treatment of the sexually abused child requires an understanding of the significant impact issues for the victim. Helping the child to overcome the effects of sexual victimisation is not easy; however, it is not impossible, either. Unless the child victim is psychotic (fortunately a rare occurrence), the treatment goals will usually be a reflection of the impact issues.
>
> (Porter, Blick and Sgroi, 1982: p 109)

When considering the impacts of sexual abuse on a child it is important to recognise that there is fluidity within the process. Children can be affected in different ways at different times and will move between identified areas dependant on internal and external factors.

To help to identify immediate issues it may be helpful to refer to Porter *et al.*'s (1982) list of ten impact issues. Allow yourself to focus on the 'here and now' for the child. How are they behaving; how does the child interact with carers, friends, wider networks; what concerns are people expressing about the child; what does the child think of the concerns expressed: regardless of actual behaviours it is useful to get both the child and adult views to ensure that the child is aware that you will listen to their view of what is happening. This process may also be helpful in identifying whose problem it is.

Refer to the list and try to identify the issues presented from the knowledge you have about the child and the particular circumstances:

Damaged goods syndrome: is an amalgam of reactions. The child may believe that because there was pain there must be an injury, or that some part of them has been damaged and as time passes they may develop worries about whether they have healed; whether they will be able to have children; whether a partner will 'know'

something has happened to them etc. They also highlight that externally, societies' attitudes towards sexual abuse and sexuality may compound the view of sexual abuse as the 'damaged goods syndrome'.

Guilt: it is widely recorded and accepted that all children who have been sexually abused carry feelings of guilt. It is suggested that this is experienced on three levels:

1. Responsibility for the sexual behaviour: children need to hear externally why they were not responsible and need help to understand their dependence and vulnerability at the time.

2. Responsibility for disclosure: given the secrecy and the deception, deceit and manipulation used by the perpetrator it is more amazing that children ever have the courage to tell.

3. Responsibility for disruption: the child needs help to understand that the resultant effects on themselves, their family and siblings are the responsibility of the perpetrator, and are not a response to the child's disclosure.

Fear: of consequences, reprisals, threats coming true.

Depression (sadness and loss): children may exhibit signs of sadness, withdrawal, or may appear excessively tired, have repetitive 'illnesses'. Some children may act out their despair by self-harming.

Low self-esteem (and social skills): the abusive experience on a physical and emotional level may reinforce the child's notion that they are bad or unworthy and serves to undermine confidence and self-esteem.

Anger and hostility: anger can either be acted out against 'safer' adults or peers, or more often is repressed to become problematic at some future time.

Trust: a child who has been sexually abused by someone they trusted and cared for is likely to experience difficulty developing further trusting, mutually rewarding relationships.

Confusion: a child may experience confusion because of the distortion of boundaries, trust and roles. If the abuser is also a parent or carer this confusion is magnified, because the person causing the hurt is also the person the child is dependent on for their survival, food, shelter, clothes, warmth, protection, care etc.

Pseudo-maturity: a child whose healthy sexual development has been prematurely interrupted may have confusion and conflict about sexual behaviours, boundaries, roles and expectations of theirs and other people's behaviours.

Self-mastery and control: the child who has been sexually abused has been taught that they have no rights, no privacy and no power. Learning that they can be appropriately assertive, can have rights and maintain rights over their own body, can help towards gaining some confidence, self-mastery and control.

Go through the list of impacts and identify areas most significant for the child at this stage. You may also wish to note secondary issues that are currently bubbling under the surface or which are present but (as yet) appear to have a lesser immediate impact. Please refer to Appendix Two for a framework for operational use.

We know from research that the impact on males includes some of the same issues as for females but there are also some distinct differences. It is acknowledged in research that it is much harder for young men to disclose sexual abuse, that anger may be more overtly extreme, or that depression and suicidal thoughts more intense. There are often fears around sexuality and some young males feel the need to over-compensate for their experience by 'proving' they are male, others may act out aggressively or sexually as they identify with the 'aggressor' as opposed to the 'victim'. For a fuller discussion of impact issues for males, the reader is referred to Calder in Chapter Seven. Please also refer to Appendix Three for an operational framework.

The reason why all children need personal safety skills

Refer back to all the reasons why. We know that all these reasons are important for children, but which of these statements would seem to be a priority for the child you are working with. Please refer to Appendix Four.

The child's current support networks

What is the child's current ecosystem? Who cares for the child, who does the child depend on, trust, tell how they are feeling? Who does the child go to if they are hurt or upset? Who offers support in wider settings, school, nursery, extended family and who does the child relate to in these settings? Do they have a favourite auntie, uncle, teacher, neighbour, friends or parent? Consider who is there for the child when you aren't. What do their safe carers know about sexual abuse? How they help to keep the child safe? How will the child test out new information and skills in their wider networks, and will the networks allow this to happen? What are the links that need strengthening to ensure this support (not everyone needs to know what has happened).

In working with the child to help them keep safe in the future we also have a responsibility to promote and strengthen networks that will consolidate any new skills learnt or information gained.

On learning new skills and information, to enable the child to use these when appropriate, the child needs to be able to take them into their main relationships, with safe adults. In doing so the child may gain in confidence and may get back some notion of self-mastery and control. The safe carer or other trusted adults involved are most likely to ensure the child has the opportunity of being listened to when it really matters.

It is worth considering that in all other forms of abuse, services are usually targeted at altering adult behaviours. Yet somehow within child sexual abuse there seems to have developed a notion of teaching the child in isolation to be responsible for their future safety. By taking this wider perspective we try to place responsibility at a more realistic level and acknowledge that the work with the child can really only have a chance of success if the child has a knowledgeable protective safety network that they can access with confidence. Please refer to Appendix Five.

Can Young Children Learn Personal Safety Skills?

In America where CSA prevention programmes are the strategy of choice used by communities to protect children, it is stated that 25 per cent to 35 per cent of all sexually abused children are under the age of seven years, (Cupoli and Sewell, 1988; Eckenrode, Munsch, Powers and Doris, 1988). There has been an ongoing debate about ages at which children can cognitively process information about CSA prevention concepts (Reppucci and Haugaard, 1989; 1993; Webster, 1991). Studies which compared responses of children from different age groups found that older children knew more initially and learn more of the concepts than younger children (Laing, Bogat and McGrath, 1993; Nemerofsky, Carran and Rosenberg, 1994; Saslawsky and Wurtele, 1986). However, recent research by Wurtele and Owens (1997) focusing on the effectiveness of safety skills programmes for pre-school age children suggests that within a wider framework some children can increase their knowledge of body safety skills and can translate this into practice. Their findings indicated that children who participated in the programmes demonstrated greater knowledge about sexual abuse and also improved their skills of recognising, resisting and reporting inappropriate touch requests.

Despite some measure of success with younger children understanding at a basic level body safety and assertiveness skills there were a small group of children within the research who were unable to grasp prevention concepts and the one skill that was identified as being particularly difficult for young children to acquire was 'reporting' i.e. telling someone when something inappropriate had occurred.

These findings are encouraging on one level but also contain a note of caution. They serve to remind us that children are only a part of their own prevention network and that they cannot protect themselves, by themselves. Also, that knowledge evolves and so has to be built on as the child's understanding grows.

Children with Disabilities

American and Canadian studies suggest that children with disabilities are from three to seven times more likely to experience sexual abuse than non-disabled children (Briggs, 1995).

Children with developmental disabilities are at highest risk of sexual abuse. A summary of studies by Senn (1988) states that:

- 68 per cent of intellectually disabled girls were victimised before the age of 18 years.
- 25 per cent of adolescent girls with intellectual disabilities had experienced rape or attempted rape. One-third of the perpetrators were their fathers or father figures.

It is also known that sexual abuse of deaf or non-verbal children is also significantly higher than in the non-disabled population.

Summary of the reasons why disabled children are at higher risk of sexual abuse than non-disabled children

Children with disabilities are at higher risk of sexual abuse than non disabled children when they are:

- In the care of adults who have accepted the myths relating to the abuse of children with disabilities.
- Kept ignorant of their rights.
- Devalued and dehumanised by society.
- Not adequately protected by child care, education and justice services.
- Deprived of information about their sexuality, the limits of acceptable adult behaviour and their rights to reject unwanted touching.
- Dependent on adults for day-to-day care, becoming compliant and malleable and unlikely to know that they can take control of some aspects of their lives.
- Deprived of parental affection and approval.
- Over-protected with few opportunities for independence and problem-solving.
- Unable to receive or communicate information about sexual matters.
- Lacking the confidence and assertiveness needed to complain.
- Unable to distinguish between acceptable and unacceptable touching due to the quantity of touching involved in their everyday care. (Briggs, 1995).

Despite increasing knowledge of the risks for children within the disabled population, there are as yet no significant resources with which to address this problem in a child centred manner. Like many others I continue (and still have a long way to go) to learn more about this aspect of child sexual abuse, but have no answers to give to practitioners, other than to seek out colleagues or other professionals who have experience in whatever form of communication is appropriate for the child and to work together to put the safest framework possible in place. I am aware that this offers little realistic application as the crucial area is lack of recognition or appropriate response to concerns in this complex area initially.

Children from Non-white British Mainstream Culture

Again, there is little practical information to hand that will advise practitioners working with a specific set of circumstances, and for each of the children and families the impact of sexual abuse will have a specific significance in their lives. Some of the impacts will be common to everyone, some will bear specific relation to cultural or ethnic norm.

It is for individual workers to seek out this information before being able to respond in the most helpful way for the child and family. However, it is nothing magical, just more information that is needed to help the process of understanding how to help a child heal and be safe. It may be possible to make your own checklist of what extra information you need, some suggestions might be:

- How is sexual abuse viewed within the family/culture?
- What support can the young person expect from the family network?
- What support can the safe carer expect?
- What may be the response to the child/family/wider networks?
- What may be the child/families biggest worries/fears?
- Are there financial/accommodation implications?
- Is the child likely to be able to get support from peers/school friends/teachers?

A Framework for Direct Work with a Child

It is important to acknowledge that the work discussed here in play work/direct work is short-term focused intervention, and not an in-depth therapeutic treatment programme.

The purpose of direct work as outlined in this context is to explore alongside a child the impact of their experiences and untangle some of the confusion within themselves.

> *At every age, direct work can be used to help strengthen current relationships, to understand the child's needs and perceptions, and to prepare him/her for transitions. However, when it comes to coping with the effects of earlier traumas and parental separations and losses, the child's cognitive abilities will strongly influence what can be accomplished.*
>
> (Fahlberg, 1994: p334)

Whatever you name the work, any work with a child involves communicating and takes on the same basic principles:

- Every child's experience is unique and as such needs an individualised response.
- Some knowledge and understanding of child development is important. Children's abilities and methods of communication vary according to age and stage of development, both cognitive and social. There are added complexities for children who have a disability or who are from a different culture, where there may be language differences or different cultural norms which would need to be understood at the planning stage.
- An understanding of some basic principles in communicating with children is needed. Through play children may be able to communicate what they cannot express in words. Children are seldom comfortable with an interview type situation, as their responses are often guarded and direct eye contact may feel quite oppressive to a child.
- Communicating with a child is a dynamic process. Our aim should be to complete the task alongside the child, at his/her pace in a way that allows the child to feel accepted, gain an insight into parts of

his/her struggles, and to test out feelings and responses against new information/skills acquired during the process.

- A child does not come to us in isolation. The child has a family, safe carers, social networks and a history. They have his/her own ecosystem. If the child is to learn new information/skills and incorporate them into their life how will they do this, who needs to know, help and support the child in the process of change?

Before starting any piece of work with a child we need a clear framework (see Figure 34 below). Plans may need to be adapted as work progresses and dependant on what the child brings to the sessions, but without any frame of reference for the boundaries of the work there is a danger that it will be unfocused, unclear and ultimately less helpful to the child.

Figure 34: Some questions to ask before starting a piece of direct work.

Worker

Why

...*am I considering doing this now?* (is there a specific reason/focus)

...*choose direct work?* (is this the best way?—have other options been considered?—can I give the time energy and commitment?)

...*should this child trust/invest in me?*

What

...*is it for?* (is it primarily for the child's needs?—is it for court/planning? etc.—representing child's views in a specific forum?)

...*do I want to achieve?* (my needs or child's needs?—what do I need to help the child work through? etc.—what do I need to find out?)

Child

Why

...*would I want to spend time with my social worker now?*

...*do they think I need to do this?*

...*am I suddenly important?* (makes me very nervous!)

What

...*do I get out of it?*

...*is it all about?*

...*happens if I don't want to do it?*

...*what happens when its all over?* (will I still be important or will I feel let down/rejected?). Will I know when/why?

Planning

Think about:

1. **Time to plan and complete the work.** If you cannot commit to the sessions consider whether starting the work is appropriate. Often the children we work with have experienced rejection, loss, hurt and pain. Don't be another adult who lets them down.

2. **Clear aims.** A clear framework is essential to be able to stay on track. However, be adaptable and creative and notice what is important for the child in sessions. Be aware that some children have learnt to respond and survive in chaos. Responding to each and every issue a child brings up may be helpful to some children but not to others. Some immediately presented needs might require attention—perhaps this could be built into the work, by mutual agreement with the child, at a later date.

   Some immediately presented needs might not be appropriate to include in the sessions. If this is the case explain to the child:

a) Why not?

b) What do you both think might be the place/time/person the child could take the problem to?

It is important to remember you cannot make right the whole of the child's confusion in one piece of direct work, but helping a child through one identified area allows them to also recognise that some parts of their lives are manageable and with help to gain insight they can regain some of their confidence, self-worth and self-mastery.

3. **Venue.** Where will the child feel comfortable and safe?

4. **Agreement.** Do children and young people always know why we are seeing them, what will happen when we see them, how long will we be seeing them for, when, where and how, and what will happen afterwards. A useful way of addressing these issues with children and young people is through a written agreement? Given that this is most beneficial in the initial stages of work, it can also be a 'tool' for establishing safety, trust and a working relationship.

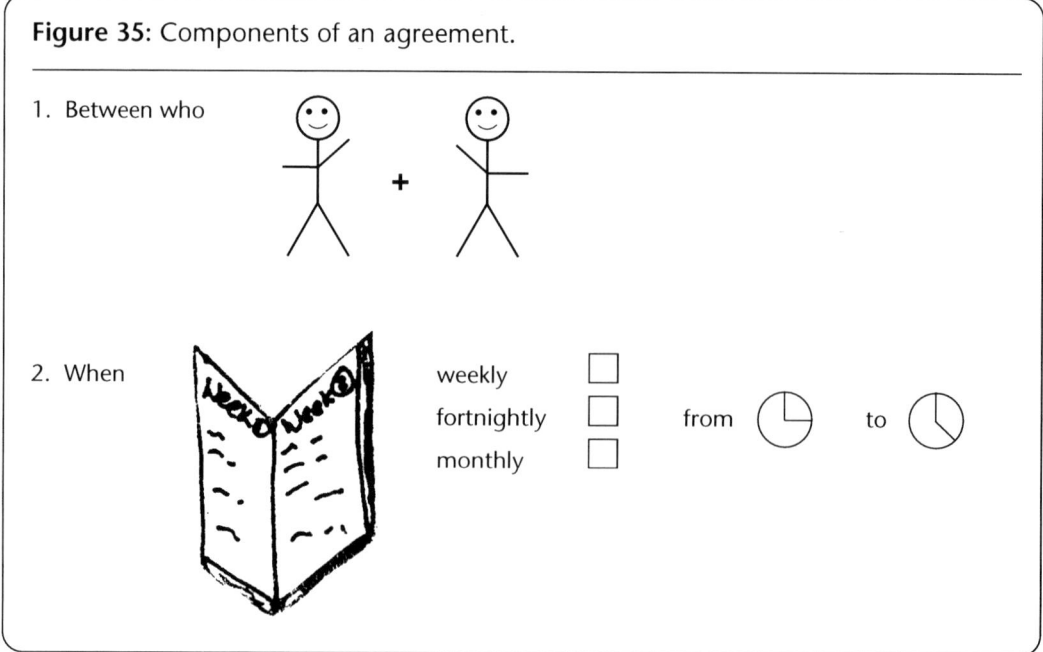

Figure 35: Components of an agreement.

1. Between who +

2. When weekly ☐ fortnightly ☐ from ◷ to ◷ monthly ☐

Figure 35: cont.

3. Where  or

4. Who will  +

deliver   collect

5. Where will  +   + others be

female and/or male
carer   carer

6. Why are you there

1) To look at any worries or troubles

2) To talk about why ....

3) To find a reason for ....

7. What are 'the rules'
   – It's OK to say no
   – Don't have to talk about anything you don't want to
   – Don't have to stay
   – OK to be angry/sad/happy/loud/quiet
   – How will worker know if x is any of the above.

8. Who will you be talking to about sessions

Police
Courts

'boss' in supervision   family members   others

Figure 35: cont.

9. What will happen if a child/young person talks about them or other children being hurt non-accidentally or abused in some way.

10. The young person can see the notes you make. Maybe read and sign at beginning of each session

11. Complaints—What can happen if the child is not happy with the work? Who can they contact? Who can help them to make a formal complaint if they want to?

12. How long will this go on for
- [ ] forever
- [ ] 100 years
- [ ] few months
- [ ] few weeks etc.

13. Need to review regularly and check out that it's still clear and OK for the child/young person. It is always helpful for the child/young person to check out about half way through the sessions what they are feeling; what still needs to be covered and whether they feel it is still the right work plan or do changes need to be made.

14. How can it be fun/not boring. What could be a fun thing to do to prove we are human and can have a laugh.

15. Who can the child tell if they want to stop coming to sessions. This should be someone easily accessible to the child. The child needs to know they don't have to give reasons, but they do have a choice.

5. How many sessions will I need. Always at the beginning consider what happens at the end.

If a child is made to feel important for a time, if they share their inner feelings and emotions, their best/worst memories, if they begin to trust then how do they feel when they can no longer receive your time or attention.

If a child is involved in the planning they must know what the rules and boundaries are. They know that for the agreed amount of sessions it is their special time, they have some involvement in the process, content and reviewing of these areas. It allows them to share the control of the work—to feel included, involved and confirms that what they have to contribute is important. It also acknowledges that the work has a focus and time limit (which may or may not be reviewed and flexible).

The initial sessions can be used as ice breakers. Get to know what the child likes, dislikes, what makes them laugh, what their perceptions on life/family/

friends/relationships/adults etc. are. Check out what they do and don't know, and what developmental level they are at.

Engaging a child is the start of sharing something with a child: part of a journey.

Initial sessions are about conveying a message to the child; that they are important, that you want to know more about them, their views, opinions, ides, even if these are different to your own; that you enjoy spending time with the child, validating their 'self', acknowledging that they are worth being listened to.

At the outset of the piece of work you will have a framework for what it is you hope to achieve.

The child should have some knowledge of sessions and purpose, but will experience a very simple level in the initial session, whether you are really interested in them or not. Whether you are interesting to be with, to a child, doesn't mean having to entertain them, be funny, clever or witty, it simply means using all of your senses to notice what they enjoy doing—noticing, listening, allowing a child to show you who they are.

We all like to feel valued as people, to be listened to, acknowledged, and included. Children are no different, but they are not mini-adults.

6. **Have some information about the child.** What do they like and dislike, interests, hobbies. Are they active or quiet, do they like drawing, making things, being creative. What are they good at?

7. **Inform the child's carer of the plan and explain the aims of the work:** The carer can then support the child if any difficulties arise e.g. upset, answer questions. Agree with the child and carer what level of information will be shared with the carer.

8. **Recording the work:** departmental guidelines. Who is the information for? case files, planning, courts etc.

9. **Supervision:** perhaps ask for a consultation with another more experienced worker/or resources within the department.

Self-care

As social workers we are trained to value each child's individuality and recognise their strengths. We are often acutely aware of the multi-faceted nature of abuse, and of the courage each child displays facing every new uncertainty, fear and confusion without the benefit of adult concepts to help understanding or measurement of progress.

Sharing part of a child's journey, experiencing with them their feelings, thoughts, emotions, both happy and sad, takes its toll on workers.

It is important to acknowledge that although we all communicate daily with children in our work, not everyone is comfortable undertaking pieces of planned direct work with a child, particularly if the issue is around body safety. Equally, for the child's sake, issues of gender, race or culture can sometimes be the driving force behind choice.

It might in some cases be more appropriate for a co-worker to complete the jointly planned work with the keyworker acting as consultant (perhaps in return you may be able to complete a separate piece of work on your colleagues case, a kind of planned case-swap intervention, so be creative).

A worker who cannot look after themself will not be able to effectively meet a child's needs in a reliable, consistent, clear and beneficial way.

A child does not come to us with a single problem. There may be a multitude of issues to be resolved in their complex and complicated lives. It is not helpful to try to deal with them all together. This could mean jumping from one thing to another as the child brings out 'here and now' issues and may actually mirror the confusion in the child's life.

Working directly with children in a focused way can be challenging, demanding, time-consuming, tiring and emotionally draining. It can also be fun and very rewarding.

Workers need to put a framework of support in place for themselves prior to embarking on pieces of work, just as they put a clear, thought out framework in place for the child.

As we plan work with a child we do so with our thoughts focused on trying to understand and be empathetic to their needs, and respectful of their struggle to survive and find a way through the situations they find themselves in, often with no sense of positive control or long-term expectation. Children live in the 'here and now'.

As workers we owe ourselves the same consideration, thoughtfulness and support.

Support in planning and during delivery of direct work helps us to keep focused on whatever issues are a priority at the current time. This does not mean ignoring other things of importance to the child, but these can often be planned into further work with the child if appropriate, or reasons given to the child why these issues will not be dealt with at this time.

It also gives an opportunity to reflect on practice. To share feelings, ideas, discuss concerns, focus on the child's interactions within sessions, explore difficulties that have arisen and also, very importantly, provides a forum to share the good experiences as well.

Support networks enable workers to keep some perspective in relation to the work. We don't have magic wands or the ability to make everything alright for a child. What we can do is help the child learn to cope and negotiate their way through situations in a more positive way. Some of the work may not impact on the child immediately, sometimes it is after the event that a child uses the skills and knowledge acquired. A child must negotiate life at their own pace. All we can do is help them acquire less destructive patterns of behaviour by encouraging awareness of alternative ways of negotiating problems or difficulties experienced in life.

Supervision and consultation are two methods of support. Supervision is usually offered by line managers and should be distinctive from case management. Case management focuses on the practical tasks, supervision deals with the details of the work, feelings and issues arising from this.

Supervision can be formal and/or informal. Each worker will have their own preferred method of supervision and it is helpful to ensure that these needs are discussed with the supervisor or consultant and recorded at the outset of work.

Consultation does not necessarily have to be provided by line managers. It may be that there is a more experienced colleague who could consult as to the planning, debrief and evaluation of the work. Again, think creatively and construct a support network that works for you.

References

Bolton, F., Morris, L., and MacEachron, A. (1989). *Males at Risk: The Other Side of Sexual Abuse*. California: Sage.

Briggs, F. (1995). *Developing Personal Safety Skills in Children with Disabilities*. London: Jessica Kingsley.

Burgess, A., Groth, N., Holmstrom, L., and Sgroi, S. (1978). *Sexual Assault of Children and Adolescents*. Lexington, MA: Lexington Books.

Carroll, J. (1998). *Introduction to Therapeutic Play*. London. Blackwell Science Ltd.

Cupoli, J., and Sewell, P. (1988). One Thousand and Fifty Nine Children with a Chief Complaint of Sexual Abuse. *Child Abuse and Neglect*, 17.

Eckenrode, J., Munsch, J., Powers, J., and Doris, J. (1988). The Nature and Substantiation of Official Sexual Abuse Reports. *Child Abuse and Neglect*, 12.

Ennew, J. (1986). *The Sexual Exploitation of Children*. Oxford: Basil Blackwell.

Fahlberg, V. (1991). *A Child's Journey Through Placement*. London: BAAF.

Finkelhor, D. (1986). *A Sourcebook on Child Sexual Abuse*. California: Sage.

Haugaard, J., and Reppucci, N. (1988). *The Sexual Abuse of Children*. Jossey-Bass Ltd.

Jewett, C. (1984). *Helping Children Cope with Separation and Loss*. London: B.T. Batsford Ltd.

Laing, B., Bogat, G., and McGrath, M. (1993). Differential Understanding of Sexual Abuse Prevention Concepts Among Pre-schoolers. *Child Abuse and Neglect*, 17.

Nemerofsky, A., Carran, D., and Rosenburg, L. (1994). Age Variation in Performance Among Pre-school Children in a Sexual Abuse Prevention Program. *Journal of Child Sexual Abuse*, 31.

Repucci, N., and Haugaard, J. (1989). Prevention of Child Sexual Abuse: Myth or Reality? *American Psychologist*, 44: pp1266–75.

Reppucci, N., and Haugaard, J. (1993). Problems with Child Sexual Abuse Programs. In Gelles, R.J., and Loseke, D.R. (Eds.). *Current Controversies on Family Violence*. Newbury Park, CA: Sage.

Porter, Blick, and Sgroi (1982). Treatment of the Sexually Abused Child. In Sgroi, S. *Handbook of Clinical Intevention in Child Sexual Abuse*. Lexington, MA: Lexington Books.

Rose, K., and Savage, A. (1999). Safe Caring. In Wheal, A. (Ed.). *The RHP Companion to Foster Care*. Lyme Regis: Russell House Publishing.

Saslawsky, D., and Wurtele, S. (1986). Educating Children About Sexual Abuse: Implications for Paediatric Intervention and Possible Prevention. *Journal of Paediatric Psychology*, 11.

Senn, C. (1988). *Vulnerable: Sexual Abuse and People with an Intellectual Handicap*.

Webster, R. (1991). Issues in School-based Child Sexual Abuse Prevention. *Children and Society*, 5: pp146–64.

Wong, D. (1987). Preventing Child Sexual Assault

Among South-east Asian Refugee Families. *Children Today*, Nov/Dec 1987.

Wurtele, S., and Owens, J. (1997). Teaching Personal Safety Skills to Young Children: An Investigation of Age and Gender across Five Studies. *Child Abuse and Neglect*, 21(8).

Some useful resources: therapeutic workbooks

Blank, J. (1982). *The Playbook for Kids About Sex.* London: Sheba.

Briggs, F. (1995). *Developing Personal Safety Skills in Children with Disabilities.* London: Jessica Kingsley.

Dayee, F. (1982). *The Private Zone.* NY: Warner Books.

Elliott, M. (1991). *Feeling Happy, Keeping Safe.* Sevenoaks, Kent: Hodder and Stoughton. Inc.

Ironside, V. (1984). *The Huge Bag of Worries.* Edinburgh: Children First.

Johnson, K. (1986). *The Trouble with Secrets.* Seattle: The Parenting Press.

Johnson, T.C. (1998). *Sexuality Curriculum for Abused Children, Young Adults and their Parents.* Self-published.

Palmer, P. (1977). *The Mouse, the Monster and Me.* California: IMPACT.

Peake, A. (1989). *My Body, My Book.* London: Children's Society.

Pithers, and Greene (1986). *We Can Say No!* London: Arrow Books Limited.

Rayner, C. (1978). *The Body Book.* London: Pan Books.

Rouf, K. (1989). *Mousie.* London: Children's Society.

Rouf, K. (1989). *Secrets.* London: Children's Society.

Shore, H. (1995). *Angry Monster Workbook.* US: The Centre for Applied Psychology Society Press.

Striker, and Kimmel (1978). *The Anti-colouring Book.* London: Scholastic Publications.

Wright, and Loiselle (1992). *Shining Through (for Girls).* Brandon, VT: Safer.

Wright, and Loiselle (1997). *Back on Track (for Boys).* Brandon, VT: Safer.

You're in Charge (1988). Alton, Hampshire: Scriptographic Publications.

Use of 'ordinary' books.

Ordinary story books can also be used to reinforce certain messages. The following are some examples of short books with a particular theme:

Joe Useless
A book about a different kind of dog who seems to be useless until something happens and people recognise his worth. Written by D. Reader (1999) and available from Diamond Books in London.

Piper
Piper is a kind, good dog whose owner is cruel. One night he escapes and his life changes. Written by E. Clark (1995) and available from Random House Children's Books in London.

Someone, Somewhere
A story about a young girl who never knew her mother. She escapes from an unhappy situation and finds adventure and courage. Written by H. Braanford (1995) and available from Random House Children's books in London.

My Best Friend
About valuing friendship, giving and taking in relationships. Written by P. Hutchins (1993) and available from Random House Children's books in London.

Nobody Likes Me
A young boy tries to cope with angry feelings that burst out affecting friendship and relationships. Written by F. Weldon (1997) and available from Random House Children's books in London.

Grandpa Bodley and the Photographs
The value of memories. Written by Castle and Bowman (1993) and available from Random House Children's books in London.

A Framework for Identifying the Focus of Work with a Child and the Most Appropriate Method for Undertaking This

Finkelhor's four preconditions

1. *The presence of someone with a predisposition to sexually abuse a child (completed from known information in retrospect).*

   Who was the perpetrator?

   Relationship to the child?

   Same household?

2. *Their ability to overcome their own internal inhibitors (completed from information in retrospect).*

   What is known?

   How did this impact on the family?

   What could the safe carer learn from this?

   What might the safe carer need to know?

3. *Creating opportunity (manipulating child and safe carer— completed retrospectively).*

   What were the specific circumstances, if known?

   What does the safe carer know about sexual abuse, cycles of abuse, reasons why children find it difficult to tell?

   What are the strengths of the child/safe carers relationship?

   What difficulties did the safe carer experience at disclosure? (How did they respond?) What conflicts did they experience in believing? How did they perceive the child's disclosure?

4. *Overcoming child's own resistance.*

What was the grooming process, if known?

Did the perpetrator use threats, bribes, tricks, coercion?

Where did the abuse take place?

Was the child protecting anyone else?

Impact Issues (Porter *et al.*, 1982)

Damaged goods syndrome

Behaviour?

Frequency?

Whose concern?

Guilt

Behaviour?

Frequency?

Whose concern?

Fear

Behaviour?

Frequency?

Whose concern?

Depression (sadness and loss)

Behaviour?

Frequency?

Whose concern?

Low self-esteem (and social skills)

Behaviour?

Frequency?

Whose concern?

Anger/hostility

Behaviour?

Frequency?

Whose concern?

Trust

Behaviour?

Frequency?

Whose concern?

Confusion

Behaviour?

Frequency?

Whose concern?

Pseudo-maturity

Behaviour?

Frequency?

Whose concern?

Self-mastery

Behaviour?

Frequency?

Whose concern?

Appendix Three

Impact Issues for Males

Guilt

Behaviour?

Frequency?

Who identified the problem?

Sexuality

Behaviour?

Frequency?

Who identified the problem?

Anger

Behaviour?

Frequency?

Who identified the problem?

Low self-esteem

Behaviour?

Frequency?

Who identified the problem?

Sexual language and behaviour

Behaviour?

Frequency?

Who identified the problem?

Depression

Behaviour?

Frequency?

Who identified the problem?

Self-harm/suicidality

Behaviour?

Frequency?

Who identified the problem?

Anxiety

Behaviour?

Frequency?

Who identified the problem?

Fear

Behaviour?

Frequency?

Who identified the problem?

Inability to trust

Behaviour?

Frequency?

Who identified the problem?

Recapitulating his victim experience

Behaviour?

Frequency?

Who identified the problem?

Why All Children Need Personal Safety Skills (Briggs , 1995)

- All children are vulnerable to sexual abuse.
- All children are powerless.
- Uninformed children trust all adults.
- Young children are incapable of assessing adult's motives.
- Children are taught that goodness equates with obedience to adults.
- Children are curious about their own bodies.
- Children are deprived of information about their own sexuality.
- Uninformed children do not realise that abusive behaviour is wrong.
- Sexual abuse is often presented as evidence of affection.
- Children are even at risk in their peer groups.
- Children are confused by sexual misbehaviour.
- Children are seldom encouraged to express their anxieties and fears.

The Child's Current Eco-map

Who is involved with the child?

Main carers (known information).

Who believes the child (known information)?

Best friends (child's view)?

Safe family members (child's view)?

Who can the child talk to if they are upset/have a problem? (child's view).

Who would help the child? (Child's view).

Who does the child go to at school if they have a problem? (child's view).

Who is good at listening? (child's view).

What adults or grown-ups does the child go to if they need any help or need to talk about a problem or how they feel?

Any other significant person?

What relationships may need promoting: Why?
How?

Chapter Ten

Contact, the Perpetrator and the Child

Kate Rose

Alice! A childish story take,
And with a gentle hand,
Lay it where Childhood's dreams are twined
In Memory's mystic band,
Like pilgrim's withered wreath of flowers
Plucked in a far-off land

Verse and all quotes taken from
Alice's Adventures in Wonderland by Lewis Carroll.

I want to try and explain why I think that a sexually abused child should not, in the first instance anyway, have contact with the perpetrator. I want to do this not just so that I can understand it for myself, but also so that all of the children and young people who have for years tried patiently to explain it to me, will not have tried in vain.

'You see, Cake' (Vickie, who is five, cannot, or chooses not to, pronounce my name properly) 'Uncle Bob has a gun and kills girls who tell lies as his job'. It has finally dawned on me why Vickie's contact with her dad is psychologically controlled by him, when he tells Vickie that he'll be telling Uncle Bob he's seen her. Vickie was sexually abused by her dad. Vickie wasn't able to tell us that directly, she's not ready to, but her behaviour at home and school while he still lived with her, her drawings and her nightmares and bedwetting, and her masturbating until she was sore helped the professionals in her life and her mum put the pieces of the jigsaw together.

The aim of this chapter is to consider the differences between the legal and judicial process for considering contact between a parent who has allegedly sexually abused a child and that child (and their siblings); and the process for statutory agencies in making recommendations to the court and parents. The result, I hope, is a broad framework that will facilitate professionals in making an assessment that is child-centred, whilst also providing information to assist the court in its judgement.

Given that the issue of contact normally only arises in situations where the perpetrator is the victim's parent or step-parent, this chapter chiefly addresses intra-familial abuse, although I would suggest that the issues raised are equally applicable where the perpetrator is a partner, cohabitee, family friend or relative.

'Consider your verdict' the king said to the jury.
'Not yet, not yet!' the rabbit hastily interrupted.
'There's a great deal to come before that!'

Contact, and the decisions around it, are often viewed from the perspective of the rights of parents, with the inherent assumption that this will simultaneously be in the best interests of the child. The 1989 Children Act makes the assumption that contact between a parent and their child is therefore to be promoted, i.e. 'requiring reasonable contact to be allowed' (Children Act 1989).

In many situations it is right and appropriate that local authorities pursue maintaining relationships where children are not living with their birth parents. However, a tension exists if the 'rights' of the parent are not assumed to be in accordance with the rights of the child. Where contact is contentious and subject to legal proceedings the reality is that children do not do the deciding, and it would be inappropriate therefore to suggest that the issue of contact is the right of the child, but more honestly, a right *for* the child. It is this right for the child both to embrace and reject the need for contact, which must be protected and promoted by the adults who are asked to act in *loco parentis*. Our responsibility to make effective assessment and representation to the courts is crucial in a climate where delays can mean frustration and irrelevant waiting for the child. Research reported in *Unreasonable Fears, Child Contact in the Context of Domestic Violence* suggested that evidence of harm to children was not always presented in court by professionals and that risk assessments were not always adequate to protect them (Radford, Sayer and AMICA, 1999). The role of the professional in these circumstances is two-fold; they must represent the wishes and feelings of the child (Section 1(3)(a) Children Act 1989), and place these, and other relevant views within the context of their assessment of the *welfare* of the child. This inevitably leads to some consideration of the effects or consequences of contact for the child. How a worker approaches this will depend on whether their starting point about contact is that it should promote the welfare of the child, and thereby be of positive benefit, or whether the issue is that welfare is assured as long as contact is not detrimental to the child. The issue I wish to address is that for children who have experienced sexual abuse, the approach of the worker, including their starting point, has to begin with the assumption that until there has been fundamental change, contact for the child with their perpetrator will be detrimental.

I will start by considering what I feel the approach of the courts is; then consider how the effects of sexual abuse on family members renders this approach inappropriate. I will then provide a framework to assist workers in their assessment and thereby facilitate the courts in making decisions, which more accurately reflect the needs of the child. In considering the term contact, I will be making the assumption that this can include direct and indirect communication between a child and an adult who has sexually abused them. There are different but equally important issues for siblings of victims, which will also be considered. There are also some different issues about contact following sibling abuse, but this chapter will not address these directly. Crucially, I will be viewing contact not only as a noun, but also as a verb, or 'doing word'.

> *'That's the most important piece of evidence we've heard yet', said the King, rubbing his hands.*
> *'If any one of them can explain it', said Alice.*

Jones and Parkinson (1995) argued that:

> *English courts have made extensive use of the option of supervised access as a means of keeping alive the parent-child relationship with the expressed hope that at a later time perhaps when the child is older and better able to protect themselves, or when the parents propensity to sexually abuse has diminished, unsupervised access will be possible.*
>
> (Jones and Parkinson, 1995)

In Re: W in 1998 on appeal, Judges Pill and Ward held that a child having made allegations of sexual abuse against her father, who lived separately, should not continue to have staying contact with him during the period of assessment. However, they did state that contact should continue and should not be required to be supervised. The assumption here would appear to be that the child was possibly only at risk of abuse during the night. The Judicial process operates on the need to make definite findings of fact. The application of Section 1(3)(e) of the Children Act 1989, which directs the court to have regard for any harm which a child has suffered or is at risk of suffering, appears to be crudely applied in contact following sexual abuse. In C v C (1988), direction given was that where a child has suffered abuse, including sexual abuse, the court may still grant contact so long as the child is not disturbed by it and the contact order provides for the safety of the child. The risk here is that the courts view child sexual abuse as an event, or series of events, rather than an abusive process. It is inevitable that at the forefront of the courts' minds will be the knowledge that stopping contact may damage a relationship between a parent and child and contravene the rights of the parent. When considering 'harm', the long and short-term consequences are distinguished (re. O (1995) 2 FLR 124) and these are weighted against the harm caused to the child in losing their father; 'the fundamental emotional need of every child to have an enduring relationship with both his parents…(would be)…outweighed by the depth of harm which, in light, inter alia of his wishes and feelings…this child would be at risk of suffering…by virtue of a contact order' (re. M (1995) 1 FLR 274). I will seek to re-examine the validity of this view on the basis that the risk of long-term harm to a child in promoting contact where there may have been sexual abuse is far greater than any interruption to a relationship which is based on abusive distortions. The interpretation of the welfare principle should reflect the needs for contact to have positive benefit for the child. In other words is the contact desirable if it is free of abuse?

The research by Jones and Parkinson identified four factors, which most influence courts in making decisions about contact where sexual abuse is a concern. These are:

1. The strength of the relationship between the father and the child prior to the discovery.

2. The need to have the same contact arrangements for all the children.

3. The child desires the contact.

4. The view taken by the parent with whom the children are living.

Importantly, Jones and Parkinson also highlighted that courts are reluctant to pursue contact against the recommendation of the local authority. This again raises the value for workers in making clear recommendations to court, which reflect their broader understanding of how the process of sexual abuse impacts on the relationships within a family.

It has been suggested that courts use the option of supervised contact as an interim measure or compromise to the difficult dilemmas they are faced with. In the following section, I will briefly consider the impact of sexual abuse on family relationships and the physical, psychological and emotional processes perpetrators use both for themselves and their child victims to distort that relationship. The suggestion I will make is that 'supervision' of contact by a trained professional or a close relative or anyone else, cannot ensure safety for the child. As Vicky pointed out to me, I will probably never understand the psychological threats and distortions used by her abuser, and cannot understand the significance of words, phrases or gestures for Vicky unless she tells me, and she may not, or it may be too late.

> *'Who are you?' said the Caterpillar. This was not an encouraging opening for a conversation. Alice replied, rather shyly, 'I—I hardly know, Sir, just at present—at least I know who I was when I got up this morning, but I think I must have been changed several times since then.'*

No individual can be understood apart from the relationships within which they live. The kind of person we are forms and arises in our social relationships. The type of self we are depends upon the quality of those relationships; and the way we manage new and present relationships, depends upon those we have experienced in the past (Howe, 1995). Children's healthy development is dependent upon stable and nurturing relationships with their parents or carers. Where a child's experience of these relationships is abusive, it must follow that any contact intended to

maintain them must be unpacked and evaluated before promoting them. We cannot therefore make the assumption that for the child who has been abused the relationship with their abuser is beneficial to them.

The Child

In applying the welfare principle to contact issues, workers are evaluating the consequences of contact for that child. To do this specifically the worker requires a general conceptual framework on the effects of sexual abuse on child victims in order to make sense of the behaviour and needs of the child before them. There are many extensive and involved pieces of research which consider both the longer and shorter term effects of sexual abuse on the child victim, (Finkelhor, 1986). We also know that the process through which an allegation or suspicion arises, i.e. accidental or purposeful disclosure, together with the responses of family members and the way in which an investigation is conducted and it's outcome will all have a bearing on the responses for the victim. The impact for the child may also be directed by the duration and frequency of the abuse; their relationship with the perpetrator; the use of force, aggression, weapons; the age of the victim; the nature of the sexual abuse; and the use of threats, intimidation and inducements. Children who have a disability or are from minority ethnic or cultural groups or refugees will have additional obstacles to overcome. It is, of course, possible that there are children who may not be affected by the abuse they have experienced. However, sexual abuse is, at it's most fundamental level, a betrayal of trust and a distortion of relationships and involves a degree of stimulation that is far beyond the child's capacity to encompass and assimilate.

> *Consequently, there is interference with the accomplishment of normal developmental tasks. The progression of mastery of one's self, environment, and relationship with others is significantly disrupted by the child's permanently altered awareness and new role vis-à-vis the perpetrator. Their very identities are at issue as they ask 'Who am I, that I am both a child and a sexual partner of someone who is supposed to be parenting and nurturing or protecting me?'*
> (Sgroi, 1982)

Porter *et al.*, (1982) identified ten impact (and consequently treatment) issues for child victims (outlined in detail in Chapters Seven and Nine):

1. 'damaged goods' syndrome

2. guilt

3. fear

4. depression

5. low self-esteem and poor social skills

6. repressed anger and hostility

7. impaired ability to trust

8. blurred role boundaries and role confusion

9. pseudo-maturity coupled with failure to accomplish developmental tasks

10. self-mastery and control

They argue that the first five of these impact issues are likely to affect all children who have been sexually abused, regardless of their prior relationship with the perpetrator. Whereas the last five are most likely where the abuse was intra-familial or by a perpetrator with a significant relationship with the child.

It is vital that in conjunction with the conceptual framework, a knowledge of the child's learning ability and intellectual functioning is ascertained. Similarly, child sexual abuse rarely occurs in isolation from other problems, which may also have an impact on the welfare of the child. These difficulties can be multiple, and they include domestic violence, environmental and financial stresses, as well as other forms of abuse. This may have created other areas of un-met need for the child. The assessment of the child in relation to contact will also need to encompass these wider issues that may significantly influence their emotional and physical safety and well being.

The Non-abusing Parent or Carer

For the purposes of this chapter, I will refer to the non-abusing parent or carer as the mother, although I am aware that this is not always the case. The advance in our understanding of child sexual abuse has for the most part developed in relation to victims and perpetrators. There is significantly less information available on the impact for the mother, although this is being redressed by

Calder in Chapter Seven and Calder, Peake and Rose (forthcoming). However, it is most likely that both child victims and professionals will expect the mother to take the immediate protective action deemed necessary, and then to continue to support the child and any siblings and aid their recovery. This then fulfils both societal and statutory agency expectations on the role of the mother. There is the risk that the needs of the mother and the context of those needs is missed or not given enough significance by professionals (Jones and Ramchandani, 1999). An understanding of how perpetrators shape and control the relationships they have both with adults and children in order to abuse, raises the importance of examining the distortions which may exist for the non-abusing carer. At the point of disclosure, mothers experience major cognitive and emotional dissonance (Timmons-Mitchell, Chandler-Holtz and Semple, 1997, Salter 1988). The impact reduces the likelihood that they will seek support or be able to unpack what sort of help they need. If contact is to be of positive benefit to the child it will be within the context of their relationships at home and with their main carer. The worker must, therefore evaluate the nature of those relationships and ensure that they do not perpetuate any of the distortions established in the process of the abuse. For many, this will require some fundamental changes. It is likely that many of the practical, physical functions of parenting will have been achieved by the non-abusing carer, but the psychological functions are likely to have been undermined. For example, boundary setting, role modelling, psychological nurture. It would not be unexpected for competition, rivalry and jealousy to exist within the child-mother relationship, and for the child to perceive the mother as impotent. This can, on occasion, result in a reversal of roles (Sgroi, 1982). In a more generalised sense, the dysfunctional patterns in the family means that the systems of communication between the non-abusing carer and the child are impaired, and this is perpetuated with the keeping of the 'secret' of the abuse. The distorted patterns of dependency established within the family are thereby reinforced.

As well as the direct impact on the relationship between the mother and child, it is likely that the mother's relationships outside the family and with their partner are also distorted. Their own needs or the need to develop strategies to survive may have resulted in the woman's own mental ill health, alcohol or drug misuse. They may also be victims of violence and abuse themselves.

The issues for assessment and change for the non-abusing carer may be seen as:

- impaired trust
- poor self-image, including past history
- difficult adult relationships including those that have been abusive
- distorted body awareness
- sense of failure
- limited belief in self
- depression
- diminished parenting skills
- denial
- distorted expectations of partner and children
- victim empathy
- poor or distorted boundary setting
- anger
- ability to communicate
- assertiveness
- impaired socialisation/social skills
- poor concrete environmental support

In order for a non-abusing carer to understand and make changes to the distortions and then participate in planning for any future contact between the perpetrator and their children that will be safe, they need time, information and more time. The mothers need to know that they are not being judged for the actions of their partners, nor are they helpless victims in the solution (Rose and Savage, 1999).

The Siblings

As with the mother, it is inevitable that the sexual abuse of one child within a family will have an impact on siblings who have not been direct victims. Rather like the ripples in a pond after a stone has been thrown in, the effects spread out of control far beyond the point of contact. Siblings will have the same confused range of emotions as the victim and the

mother, particularly if the allegation has led to the perpetrator leaving the family home. The impact and areas of work when considering contact with the siblings may include:

- understanding of events
- anger
- disbelief
- rejection
- jealousy or rivalry
- isolation
- fear, uncertainty or anxiety
- betrayal or mistrust
- poor boundaries
- limited self-mastery
- communication

Younger siblings will also not have the knowledge to aid their understanding of what has happened. This will affect the context within which their wishes and feelings towards the perpetrator and future contact must be evaluated.

The Perpetrator

There are many lengthy publications which address the processes through which male perpetrators abuse, (Finklehor 1986; Wolf, 1984; Wyre, 1987). I will not attempt to represent or evaluate these models here as this has been achieved by Calder and Skinner in Chapter Six. However, the research and frameworks for understanding and treating these men indicate that the abusive act is the culmination of a series of psychological distortions or thinking errors that the perpetrator has had to achieve. The sexual abuse of a child is not an event, but a planned process that can take a long time to progress. The perpetrator develops the capacity to deny and reframe his thoughts, feelings and actions to himself and others. Significantly less information is available about female perpetrators. The work of Jackie Saradjin provides some insight for those who are facing the dilemmas of contact where the perpetrator is the female carer. Not surprisingly, there appear at this early stage to be some important similarities, and some significant differences. Knowledge of the process of abuse for the perpetrator must be applied by the worker when assessing the child's needs in relation to contact.

At the initial stage, the worker can make the following assumptions:

- The development of the relationship between the perpetrator and the child is based on a distortion of thinking and action.
- Within the relationship there will be blurred role boundaries.
- There will be long-standing cognitive manipulation of the child.
- The child will lack conviction that what happened was wrong and was not their fault.
- The relationship between the child and their mother is also likely to have been distorted by the perpetrator.
- The child will believe in the domination and power of the perpetrator.
- The non-abusing carer will not have had time to unpack the overwhelming and conflicting range of emotions for herself, let alone those of her children.
- Siblings will have experienced distortions in their relationships with other family members.

(Jones and Parkinson, 1995)

Any consideration of the child's own wishes and feelings in relation to contact, including ambivalence, needs to be viewed not only in the context of their age and understanding, but all of the above.

> 'You're thinking about something, my dear, and that makes you forget to talk. I can't tell you just now what the moral of that is, but I shall remember it in a bit.' 'Perhaps it hasn't one', Alice ventured to remark.

It is now accepted good practice that following allegations of child sexual abuse, the primary action should be in seeking to remove the alleged perpetrator from the family home, rather than the child. Where an alleged perpetrator remains at home, it stands to reason that the ability of the worker to carry out an effective assessment that facilitates the fundamental changes outlined previously, is undermined. The nature of the abuse indicates that change will be an involved and gradual process. Physical separation from the perpetrator does not in itself change distorted

thinking or emotional damage. The implications of all this are that in families where a child has alleged sexual abuse, contact with the perpetrator needs to be suspended. A failure to do this leaves the opportunity for the controls exerted on the child to be further exploited. The risk of any temporary damage to the adult-child relationship is far less significant than the risk of ongoing damage for an abused child. If the allegation or concerns are unfounded and there are positives for the child in maintaining a non-abusive relationship, then it should be equally possible to repair any distance engendered by the separation.

Once contact is stopped the assessment will fall into five possible areas of work:

- Individual work with the child (as outlined previously). This work should address both the effects of the abuse for the child; validate their feelings, and counteract the distortions.
- Individual work with the non-abusing carer. This needs to occur at their pace and ensure they have time and opportunity to assimilate the information. It should include supporting the carer in managing the impact on them (as described previously), as well as the issues identified in Appendix One.
- Work with the siblings (non-abused) as outlined previously.
- Work with the child and the non-abusing carer together. This work should promote the strengthening of their relationship and systems of communication. (See Appendix Two.)
- Individual risk assessment and treatment of the perpetrator.

Where there is not a clear allegation or the perpetrator denies any cause for concern, it is important that the assessment explores the functioning and relationships within the family as well as the original reasons for concern. At the very least, the child needs to have increased self-esteem and an understanding of where the responsibility for any abusive behaviour lies. Without the necessary changes, the physical, emotional and psychological risk to the child is unacceptable. The task, therefore, in any consideration for the renewal of contact is to provide evidence that this risk is no longer significant, rather than the assumption that parent-child interaction can continue whilst an abusive 'act' does not occur.

The primary onus to provide this evidence must be in the risk assessment of the perpetrator. That is, there should be acknowledgement of the risk without minimisation, and acknowledgement of the harm caused to the child. The task in presenting the information to the courts to aid them in their judgement should reflect:

- The nature of the allegation, abuse or concerns.
- The impact on the child in relation to their psychological, physical and emotional functioning and vulnerability.
- The distortions in the relationships between the child and the perpetrator together with the assessment for change, time-scales and preconditions.
- The assessment and responsiveness of the non-abusing carer.
- The issues for siblings.
- The wishes and feelings of the child within the context of their age, understanding and experiences.
- The risk assessment of the perpetrator and prognosis for change.
- The consideration of the likely impact of contact for the child and family given all of the above.

When Contact is Supervised

Alice did not quite like the look of the creature, but on the whole she thought it would be quite as safe to stay with it as go after that savage Queen: so she waited.

As stated previously, promoting contact where it is supervised does not in itself safeguard the child from harm, nor promote their well being, if the areas of change have not been identified and actioned. If contact is supervised, a tremendous responsibility lies with the supervisee. There are some fundamental ground-rules that need to be established and agreed with the child, the perpetrator and non-abusing carer. This may fall into a number of areas:

- The purpose of contact; is this an assessment session, is it to facilitate the

child therapeutically, is it taking place because of direction from the court etc.?

- Venue; ensuring visibility and safety.
- Time and duration; is it sensitive to the needs of the child, including school commitments, tiredness, times of abuse etc.?
- Role of the supervisor; there must be a shared understanding as to whether the supervisor is there to observe and intervene if concerns are raised or has a more proactive role in facilitating the contact. It will also be important to establish for the child whether the supervisor is neutral and therefore does not have a relationship with the child, or is their ally and clearly present to empower the child.
- Child's arrival and departure from contact; who brings and takes the child, who leaves first, and are greetings and goodbyes allowed particularly in relation to physical contact?
- Agreed activities during contact; contact needs to be carefully planned and should reflect the interests of the child. It should also maximise the positive aspects of the adult's parenting skills. This should be based on the acquired knowledge of what, if anything, positively binds the child and adult together.
- Agreements about talking and touching; it is important to clarify whether kissing, hugging, sitting on knees etc. is alright, or not. It is also helpful if the worker establishes with the child anything that they do not wish or is inappropriate to talk or be asked about by the adult i.e. the abuse, passing messages home, providing information.
- Time alone with the child; it is crucial that everyone knows whether the child and parent are allowed to be alone together unsupervised at *anytime*. This may involve making plans if the child needs taking to the toilet or for a drink or snack making etc.
- Presents; It is not unusual for estranged parents to want to bring gifts for the child. The meaning of this for the abused child must inform any decision about it.

- Intervention; The supervisor must be clear with the child and the adult how they will intervene if they are concerned during contact and what response they expect from the parent.

- Recording; if the contact is part of an ongoing assessment, agreement must be reached about what will be recorded, how it will be recorded and where the information may be shared.

- Worries and safety plans; It is important that the child identifies to whom and how they can communicate any worries they may have during contact. In my experience it can be useful to agree an 'emergency code word' that the child chooses and can use during contact if they become anxious or need the contact to stop. It is also useful if the child has access and permission to speak with an adult not involved in supervising the contact with whom they can express any feelings they may have.

- The non-abusing carer; It is likely that the non-abusing carer will have their own feelings about the contact, and it will be important to ensure that the child understands what is to be fed back and by whom. It may also be necessary to identify what part the child wants the non-abusing carer to play after contact i.e. don't ask me any questions about it, I need time on my own, I need you to hug me etc.

- There should also be an agreement about immediate action the perpetrator should take to stop contact if they are aroused, and the process of debriefing within the context of any treatment they receive.

These and any other issues relevant for the individual situation must form the basis of a written agreement both with the child and the adult. The agreement with the child must reflect their age and understanding and can make use of pictures or diagrams where words are not understood. The starting point should be that the perpetrator has apologised to the child and that they alone are responsible for the abuse. The supervisor should feel confident that they are in control of the contact. The impact for the child needs to be evaluated and should take into account not only what happens during contact but what is said and how the child behaves and presents following contact.

Conclusion

The right to contact with their child is an important presumption built into the Children Act 1989. It is vital that adults who act on behalf of children bring to the courts the strengths that a broad perspective on the nature and impact of sexual abuse gives them. If we are to be child-centred in our practice, decisions about contact must be based on it being of positive benefit for the child. The nature of sexual abuse and its impact on the child victim prevents any contact between the perpetrator and the child being safe for the child, and should not in the first instance take place. Any risk of damage to the parent-child relationship by stopping contact must be seen within the context of that relationship being based on distortions and, as such, an unacceptable risk of harm to the child. Decisions about the longer term needs for contact must be informed by careful work and assessment with all family members. The long-term welfare of the child is dependent upon the recognition that in contact for a child who has been sexually abused the inherent risks to them must no longer be significant, and their relationship with the perpetrator has been assessed to be of positive benefit to the child if it is free of abuse.

> *Thus grew the tale of Wonderland:*
> *Thus slowly, one by one,*
> *It's quaint events were hammered out-*
> *And now the tale is done,*
> *And home we steer, a merry crew*
> *Beneath the setting sun.*

References

Calder, M.C., with Rose, K. (forthcoming). *Mothers of Sexually Abused Children: A Framework for Assessment, Understanding and Support.* Lyme Regis: Russell House Publishing.

Carroll, L. (1989). *Alice's Adventures in Wonderland.* Century Hutchinson Ltd.

Finkelhor, D. (1986). *A Sourcebook on Child Sexual Abuse.* Sage Publications.

Howe, D. (1995). *Attachment Theory for Social Work Practice.* MacMillan Press Ltd.

Jones, D., and Ramchandani, P. (1999). *Child Sexual Abuse, Informing Practice from Research.* Radcliffe Medical Press.

Jones, E., and Parkinson, P. (1995). Child Sexual Abuse, Access and the Wishes of Children. *International Journal of Law and the Family,* 9: pp54–85.

Kroll, B. (1999). *Practitioners' Child Law Bulletin,* p104. Sweet and Maxwell.

Radford, L., Sayer, S., and AMICA (1999). *Unreasonable Fears? Child Contact in the Context of Domestic Violence: A Survey of Mother's Perceptions of Harm.* Women's Aid Federation of England.

Rose, K., and Savage, A. (1999). Safe Caring. In Wheal, A. (Ed.). *The RHP Companion to Foster Care.* Lyme Regis: Russell House Publishing.

Rose, K., and Savage, A. (2000). Living with Risk. In Wheal, A. (Ed.). *Working with Parents: Learning from Other People's Experience.* Lyme Regis: Russell House Publishing.

Salter, A.C. (1988). *Treating Child Sex Offenders and Victims? Assessment and Treatment of Child Sex Offenders: A Practice Guide.* Beverley Hills, CA: Sage.

Saradjian, J., with Hanks, H. (1996). *Women who Sexually Abuse: from Research to Practice.* John Wiley.

Sgroi, S. (Ed.) (1982). *Handbook of Clinical Intervention in Child Sexual Abuse.* D.C. Lexington Books Heath and Co.

Timmons-Mitchell, J., Chandler-Holtz, D., and Semple, W.E. (1997). Post-traumatic Stress Disorder Symptoms in Child Sexual Abuse Victims and their Mothers. *Journal of Child Sexual Abuse,* 6(4): pp1–16.

Wolf, S. (1984). *A Multi-factor Model of Deviant Sexuality.* Paper at 3rd International conference on victimology. Lisbon, Portugal, November, 1984.

Wyre, R. (1987). *Working with Sex Offenders.* Oxford: Perry Publications.

C v C (1988). *Child Abuse: Access* 1 FLR 462

Re: W (a minor) (staying contact) (1998). A minor: Staying contact 2FCR p453.

Work Plan with the Non-abusing Carer

1. What is sexual abuse? Definitions, understanding, range of 'acts'.
2. Information about the cycle of offending—process.
3. Effects of sexual abuse on the child victim.
4. Why children don't tell.
5. Issues for siblings; short and longer term.
6. Impact for the non-abusing carer.
7. Responsibility for the abuse—treatment issues.
8. Parenting issues—practical and emotional.
9. Future adult relationships.
10. Safe caring.
11. Future contact—safety planning.
12. Support.

Work with the Non-abusing Carer and Children Together

1. Busting the secrets—shared understanding of who is responsible for what has happened, promoting shared understanding of what happened, breaking down isolation, diminishing the perpetrator's power base and control.
2. Acknowledgement of the feelings of the child by the non-abusing carer.
3. Empathy work   • re-nurturing the child:
     • building trust
     • changing the mothers position in the family
4. Developing positive communication systems—this may also need to include identifying safe adults for the child outside of the family, and ensuring the parent facilitates contact for the child.
5. Agreeing boundaries and limit setting—safe care in the house, and in relationships.
6. Future systems for resolving difficulties and confusion, particularly in situations where the child may feel dis-empowered.
7. Help and support that builds and develops the skills the non-abusing carer needs in order to parent their child safely and well (Rose and Savage, 2000).

Chapter Eleven

Outcome Indicators

Martin C. Calder

Introduction

It is impossible for me to try and cover all the individual outcome indicators for the assessments required when a case of intra-familial child sexual abuse comes to the attention of the professional agencies. There are, however, some frameworks that are overarching and are to be used when trying to consider the way forward from several separate assessments. These are presented in this chapter.

A Model of Change (Prochaska and DiClemente, 1982; 1986)

This model offers an overview, which allows for a range of change methods and skills to be delivered by different professionals according to the needs of individual offenders and their families. It is a very useful model for setting out realistic plans of work at the outset, for setting attainable targets, and for reviewing what progress, if any, has been made. Tony Morrison (1991) originally applied the model to the broader child protection arena, and it is very appropriate to the child sexual abuse field as it originated from work with addicts. The model is set out visually below:

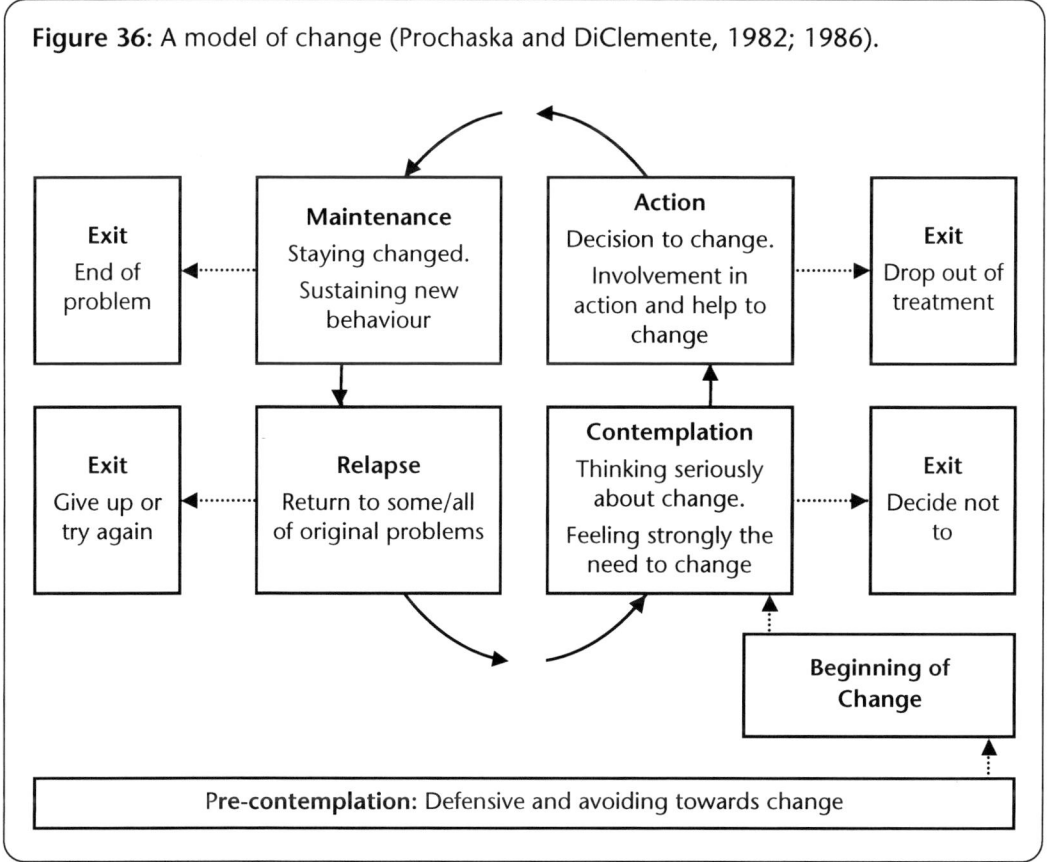

Figure 36: A model of change (Prochaska and DiClemente, 1982; 1986).

Pre-contemplation

This is where the individual is considering change far less than the professionals, who are often reacting to the presenting situation. Morrison (1995) pointed out that this phase is characterised by blaming others, denying responsibility, or simply being unaware of the need to change, e.g. depression. Whilst in this stage no change is possible. Individuals thus require information and feedback in order that they can raise their awareness of the problem and the possibility of change (Miller and Rollnick, 1991: p16). Pre-contemplation is the point at which the initial assessment takes place in order to ascertain, and hopefully enhance motivation, to at least consider and contemplate the need for change. Whilst the professionals enter the work at the action stage, the perpetrator is probably only in the pre-contemplation change. Such a combination cannot succeed as the two groups are at incongruent stages of change. There may also be a very different definition of the problem between the two groups. For the perpetrator, they are unlikely to be in a position to meaningfully engage in the proposed assessment work and a legal mandate often has to be sought. Perpetrators are the prime candidates to be resistant to any change efforts.

DiClemente (1991) identified four categories of pre-contemplation. Reluctant pre-contemplators are those who through lack of knowledge or inertia do not want to consider change. Rebellious pre-contemplators have a heavy investment in the problem behaviour and in making their own decisions. The resigned pre-contemplator has given up on the possibility of change and seems overwhelmed by the problem. The rationalising pre-contemplator has all the answers but have discounted change as they have figured out the odds of personal risk, or they have plenty of reasons why the problem is not a problem or is a problem for others but not for them (pp192–3).

Contemplation

Perpetrators in this stage are most open to consciousness-raising interventions, such as observations, confrontations, and interpretations (Prochaska and DiClemente,

1986: p9). Through this process, their awareness of the problem increases, and they are then free to reject or adapt to change. The worker's aim is to tip the balance in favour of change (Miller and Rollnick, 1991: pp16–7). Contemplation is often a very paradoxical stage of change. The fact that the client is willing to consider the problem and the possibility of change offers hope for change. However, the fact that ambivalence can make it a chronic condition can be very frustrating. It is the stage where many of the offenders will be waiting for the one final piece of information that will compel them to change. The hope is that the information makes the decision for them. Failing this, we need to offer them incentives to change by looking at past changes and by accentuating the positives (DiClemente, 1991: pp194–6). It is only after such contemplation that a viable contract for work can be made. There are six steps to the contemplation stage before we can move into the action stage and attempt change. They are:

1. I accept that there is a problem.
2. I have some responsibility for the problem.
3. I have some discomfort about the problem and my part in it.
4. I believe that things must change.
5. I can see that I can be part of the solution.
6. I can see the first steps towards change.

In the determination stage, the offender may now accept that something has to change although they may be unsure how it can be achieved. The task for workers is to remove any barriers to change, and create an environment where change is a realistic possibility. Change remains a very painful process.

Action

Is the stage where the perpetrator engages in structured work to bring about a change, in a way that they believe they have determined. Such a tactic avoids dependency on the workers. Yet action is a potentially stressful stage of change as they can fail and feel that they have failed or been rejected. We need to plan for relapse and involve the wider family and the community networks, for it is they who are most likely both to spot the early signs of lapse, and who will provide the most day-to-day support (Morrison, 1995). This stage is where the individual is seen 'in action', implementing the plan. It is where they feel able to make a public commitment to action; to get some external confirmation of the plan; to seek support; to gain greater self-efficacy; and finally to create artificial, external monitors of their activity (DiClemente, 1991: pp198–9). For the worker, they should focus on successful activity and reaffirm the client's decisions. They should point out that change is predictable where a person adheres to advice and the plan. The focus should be on learning, exploring and rehearsing ways of relating, thinking, behaving and feeling. All change is essentially a combination of these four basic human processes. This stage may take several months as new behaviour takes time to become established. At the end of the initial planning stage, the aim is to produce a longer term plan of work.

Maintenance

Is about sustaining and consolidating change and preventing relapse. This is the real test. It occurs when the new ways of relating and behaving become internalised and generalised across different situations. They do not now depend on the presence of the workers, but become consolidated and owned by the individual or family as part of themselves. It is through this process that the client's sense of self-efficacy has been increased (Morrison, 1995). Successful maintenance builds on each of the processes that has come before, as well as an open assessment of the conditions under which a person is likely to relapse (Prochaska and DiClemente, 1986: p10). Stability and support will be essential to sustaining change, especially with the many families who have such poor experience of problem-solving (Morrison, 1991: p96).

Relapse

The cyclical model of change allows for the reality that few people succeed first time round. Change comes from repeated efforts, re-evaluation, renewing of commitment, and incremental success. Relapse is thus part of,

rather than necessarily hostile to, change. Change is a battle between the powerful forces that want us to stay the same, and our wish to be different (Morrison, 1991: p96). It usually occurs gradually after an initial slip (often due to unexpected stress), rather than occurring spontaneously (DiClemente, 1991: p200). It can lead to a loss of all or most of the gains, resulting in a giving up and a return to pre-contemplation. This can be counteracted by the worker, giving feedback, on how long it takes to accomplish sustained change. They should aim to keep the change effort going rather than becoming disengaged and stuck. Morrison (1995) noted that where it is noted quickly enough, and help is urgently sought and available from friends, family or professionals, all is by no means lost. This may lead to further work through the contemplation stage.

The assessment of change is a very uncertain process, and is often very fragile where it is achieved. Attitudinal changes are often the most noticeable to the workers, although we should also look for evidence of a willingness to engage and struggle with painful issues; a clearer understanding of their own continued potential for abusiveness; a willingness to share new information; and a clearer grasp of the victims experiences of the abuse (Willis, 1993).

It is important that we acknowledge that change is very slow and it is often clearer to trust the lack of change as being an indicator of treatment failure than trusting change in a target area as evidence that the treatment is working.

A Continuum of Motivation

Morrison (1991) offered us a very useful continuum of motivation (Figure 37), which can help us assess the level of motivation to change within the perpetrator:

Figure 37: A continuum of motivation (adapted from Morrison, 1991: p34).

Internal motivators

I want to change.
I don't like things as they are.
I am asking for your help.
I have resources to help solve this.
I think you can help me.
I think things can get better.
I have other support, which I will use to encourage me.
I accept that I am doing something wrong.
I accept what you say needs to change.
I accept that others are right (family, friends, community, agencies).
You defining the problem clearly helps.
I understand what change will involve.
I accept that if I do not change, you will take my children away.
I can change if you do this for me.
I'll do whatever you say.
I agree to do this so the family can be reconstituted.
It's your job to solve my problem.
You are my problem.
I am right and you are wrong.
I don't have any problems.

External motivators

Within this framework, any parent who argues that they do not have any problems is unlikely to agree to any of the necessary work on a voluntary basis, and some legal mandate is usually needed to ensure their compliance. Those who argue that they want to change need similar careful assessment to determine their motivation for this stance. Whilst many are genuine and do want to undertake the work necessary to effect change, we need to identify and manage those who adopt this stance in the hope that they can circumvent the necessary work.

Resistance Behaviour

Resistance can take a variety of forms, and there are a number of different categorisations to draw from.

Four categories of client resistance behaviour (Miller and Rollnick, 1991: p103) are:

1. *Arguing*. The client contests the accuracy, expertise, or integrity of the therapist.

- Challenging: they directly challenge the accuracy of what the therapist has said.

- Discounting: they question the therapist's personal authority and expertise.

- Hostility: they express direct hostility towards the therapist.

2. *Interrupting.* The client breaks in and interrupts the therapist in a defensive manner.

- Talking over: they speak while the therapist is still talking, without waiting for an appropriate pause or silence.
- Cutting off: they break in with words obviously intended to cut the therapist off.

3. *Denying.* The client expresses an unwillingness to recognise problems, co-operate, accept responsibility, or take advice.

- Blaming: they blame other people for problems.
- Disagreeing: with what is said without offering any constructive alternative.
- Excusing: their own behaviour.
- Claiming impunity: from any danger caused by the presenting behaviours of concern.
- Minimising: the risks and dangers by claiming they are exaggerated, and that things aren't really that bad.
- Pessimism: where they make general statements about self or others that are pessimistic, defeatist, or negativistic in tone.
- Reluctance: they express reservations and reluctance about information or advice given.
- Unwillingness to change: they express a lack of desire or an unwillingness to change, or an intention not to change.

4. *Ignoring.* The client shows evidence of not following or ignoring the therapist.

- Inattention: where the client's response indicates that they have not been following or attending to the therapist.
- No answer: where they respond to a query in a way that does not answer the question.
- No response: the client gives no audible or a non-verbal reply to a therapist's query.
- Side-tracking: the client changes the direction of the conversation that the therapist has been pursuing.

It is important that workers try to understand the source of client resistance and what part, if any, the worker's approach may be playing in the parental response. This is essential when trying to look at the way forward and the engagement of the client remains one of the most under-rated tasks of the professional. For a detailed discussion around this point, the reader is referred to Calder (forthcoming a and b).

Eligibility for Treatment

Juveniles

McGrath (1991) cited three factors as being crucial in determining suitability for treatment:

1. The perpetrator must acknowledge that he committed the sexual abuse and take responsibility for his behaviour.
2. He must consider his abusive behaviour a problem that he wants to stop.
3. He must be willing to enter into and participate in treatment.

One of the aims of the assessment is to gate keep treatment, which is lengthy (12–24 months) and should arguably be reserved for cases where some success is anticipated. Yet we need to target the high risk groups where the cost of not intervening substantially is ongoing, arguably escalating patterns of offending as they get older. This may not do wonders for the success rates for treatment, but it has to be cost effective (Breiling, 1994).

My view is that every juvenile has to be considered eligible for treatment as the costs of not offering it to them are evident in the longer term. If choices have to be made on the basis of resources, we should opt to treat the high risk groups, whilst using a legal mandate to determine a safe and appropriate placement, and supervised contact with other children. It is futile to make a treatment recommendation when we are not in a position to offer any input, or where the quality of the treatment programme is questionable.

We should not duck the need to make a 'no-treatment' recommendation where necessary, as inappropriate treatment recommendations are harmful to both the perpetrator and to society. Frances, Clarkin, and Perry (1984) suggested the following benefits that may follow from a no-treatment decision:

- Avoiding a semblance of treatment when no effective treatment exists.

- Delaying treatment until a more appropriate time.

- Protecting the juvenile and the workers from wasting time, effort and money.

The National Task Force (1988) dispute this stance, arguing that 'at this time, we do not know for sure that any offender is 'untreatable', although some may not appear treatable in our present systems' (p26). McConaghy *et al.*, (1989) reported that young sexual perpetrators may be more resistant to treatment because their sexual urges are in part under the control of behaviour completion mechanisms. As such, a more intensive follow-up treatment appears to be indicated in their management (p97). Their research found that juveniles treated for a sexual offence were significantly more likely to relapse and to require additional treatment than those treated in adulthood.

Adult male perpetrators

A number of factors are key in determining perpetrator suitability for treatment.

Most treatment programmes require that the perpetrator must acknowledge that he committed the sexual abuse and take responsibility for his behaviour. Realistically, many still have a long way to go at the end of the assessment, but they must have shown some commitment and movement in the right direction if they are to benefit further from treatment. We also need to note that some dimensions of denial, such as admission with justification, are less responsive to intervention, often entrenching the denial further. In order to benefit from treatment, the perpetrator must acknowledge that their behaviour has been harmful to the victims; they must consider their offending behaviour a problem that they want to stop, and that they have expressed a desire to change; they must be willing to enter into and participate in treatment, and they must be prepared to comply with any conditions relating to the management of the risks they pose. Simply being in treatment should help reduce the risks.

There will be some who meet the above eligibility criteria, but whose offences are so serious that they need to be incarcerated. In general terms, the offender eligible for community treatment is the individual who has an overall pro-social lifestyle; one who has demonstrated the capacity to follow through on tasks; who has relationships in the community; and who has no history of pronounced physical violence (Wolf *et al.*, 1988).

Mayer (1988) argued that some perpetrators do have a very poor prognosis and remain a high risk, regardless of what the workers might like to try to achieve. She set out numerous factors which contribute to poor-risk candidates for treatment. They included: the use of force or violence during the offences; they have a prior criminal record; they present with bizarre rituals associated with the offences; they chronically use alcohol or drugs; they sexually abused very young children; there is evidence of severe mental health problems; a history of severe childhood abuse; low IQ/capacity for insights; and chronic stressors in the environment.

The issue of whether to allow perpetrators in denial into treatment is a crucial and contentious issue. Ethically, there is an argument against allowing them access whilst in denial, particularly as this can be misleading to the courts and others. It also appears unfair to allocate some of the precious places in treatment to those who claim they are innocent. If the denier is to remain in the community, we have to consider whether they will be accepted by the community and, if rejected, how this will affect their chances of relapse. The alternative view is that there is such a broad range of denial, with a clear starting point, that we should allow them access to treatment in order to facilitate some positive movement. This group does pose such a high risk for re-offending that they should be offered priority treatment places so they do not cause continued harm to others and themselves. Unfortunately, even where treatment is mandated, there is no guarantee that the perpetrator will be engaged in the process of change.

Given that denial is central to most cases of sexual abuse, we have learned to develop some strategies for confronting these defences and assisting the perpetrator to participate fully in any treatment programme. There needs to be time-limited focus on challenging denial in the first stages of treatment, and the perpetrator can be very responsive to the recognition that they are viewed as a 'whole' person and the focus is not simply on their sexual offences in isolation. The reader is referred to Schlank and Shaw (1995, 1997) for discussions of how to treat those in denial. Brake and Shannon (1997) explored the concept of using a pre-treatment phase to increase admission in sexual perpetrators. They argue that a programme for 'deniers' offers the advantage of being able to evaluate the perpetrator over time and deal with the range of their oppositional behaviour as it arises. Such a programme acknowledges that treatment requires a gradual, incremental approach, allowing for a systematic approach from the workers. Their pre-treatment programme aims to lessen denial so the perpetrator can become eligible for the broader treatment regime. The programme consists of six stages:

- containment: to de-escalate and contain power struggles
- symptom relief: which allows the perpetrator to shift from their defence mechanisms which entrench rather than resolve their despair
- reframe denial: by exploring with them the protective function served by denial
- reframe accountability: so they may become ready to risk abandoning old defensive manoeuvres and accept increasing accountability and pro-social behaviour
- enhance empathy: as the perpetrator begins to accept increasing personal responsibility for his behaviour, he can begin to recognise the pain of others and identify it as his own
- successive approximation of confrontation: where they may now be ready to accept gradual confrontation of his behaviour.

Using this approach, the authors have found a significant reduction in denial in 58 per cent of perpetrators.

They argue that an accurate assessment of denial should take into account the full range of perpetrator resistance and defensiveness, both conscious and unconscious. Those who deny some aspect of the offence or who

minimise and justify their behaviour are less amenable to change than other groups of deniers, as they become more entrenched in their resistance.

Treatment Goals and Planning

Children

The aim of working with children who sexually abuse is to understand the underlying causes of their behaviour and to decrease their problematic sexual behaviours by getting the child to develop better self-control.

The components of this work will include:

- Admitting they have a problem with their sexual behaviour.
- Sexuality: challenging any distorted thinking around sex and teaching them appropriate ways of dealing with their sexuality.
- Sex education: providing factual information about sex and placing it in the context of 'natural' sexual development.
- Personal and social skills: to build their self esteem and help them handle problems in a more appropriate way.
- Victim empathy.
- Creating a healthier family environment.
- Resolving any abuse in their history.
- Identifying their sexual abuse cycle.
- Identifying high risk situations.
- Developing a relapse prevention plan and finding ways for them to interrupt any dangerous situations (adapted from O'Hara, 1995; and Pithers *et al.*, 1993).

Juveniles

The aims of treatment work with juveniles who sexually abuse include:

- To help them control their actions in a way that avoids, or lessens, the risk of further abuse.
- To lengthen the time between the abusive incidents.
- To reduce the seriousness of the abusive incidents.

- To encourage pro-social interactions by the young person.
- To strengthen the family unit by focusing on healthier interaction and communication patterns.
- To decrease the pathology by creating healthier family dynamics (adapted from Griggs and Bold, 1995).

Whilst each treatment package should be tailored to meet the needs of each individual, the components of a treatment package could include:

- Acceptance of responsibility.
- Victim awareness.
- Full understanding of their abusive cycle.
- Full understanding of their targeting and grooming behaviours.
- Fantasy work: fully exploring their distorted thought processes.
- Sexuality and perception.
- Sex and relationship education.
- Communications skills.
- Personal and social skills.
- Anger management.
- Assertiveness training.
- Reinforcement of internal and external inhibitors.
- Addressing family dynamics.
- Work with the family or primary care givers, and the
- Identification of a relapse prevention programme.

The treatment principles should be that the individual must:

- Learn to take responsibility for the sexual offence.
- Develop an understanding of the thoughts, feelings and behaviour that lead toward an offence event and that for each step in the path toward an offence, he must develop an intervention, that stops the process at that point.
- Become aware of the victim's position and express empathy for the victim's position. (Bremer, 1993)

Adult males

If the assessment is aimed at risk management, then the goal of assessment is to identify the factors related to the risk for sexual offending, and the goal of treatment is to change these risk factors amenable to change (Hanson, Cox and Woszcsyna, 1991). Other aims may include:

- To help them control their actions in a way that avoids, or lessens, the risk of further abuse.
- Developing relapse prevention skills and establishing supervision conditions.
- Accepting responsibility and modifying cognitive distortions.
- Developing victim empathy.
- Controlling sexual arousal.
- To lengthen the time between the abusive incidents.
- To reduce the seriousness of the abusive incidents.
- To encourage pro-social interactions by the offender improving social competence.
- To strengthen the family unit by focusing on healthier, interactional communication patterns.
- To decrease the pathology by creating healthier family dynamics (adapted from Griggs and Bold, 1995).

Whilst each treatment package should be tailored to meet the needs of each individual, the components of a treatment package could include:

- Acceptance of responsibility.
- Confronting denial.
- Victim awareness and increased victim empathy.
- Full understanding of their abusive cycle.
- Full understanding of their targeting and grooming behaviours.
- Fantasy work: fully exploring their distorted thought processes.
- Decreasing cognitive distortions.
- Decreasing deviant arousal.
- Sexuality and perception.

- Sex and relationship education.
- Communications skills.
- Personal and social skills and increased social competency.
- Anger management.
- Assertiveness training.
- Reinforcement of internal and external inhibitors.
- Addressing family dynamics.
- Identifying risk factors.
- Where appropriate, addressing their experiences of being abused.
- Work with the family.
- Identifying a relapse prevention programme.

Any treatment programme, regardless of its theoretical base, can only stand a chance of being successful if it is both flexible as well as being rigorously and properly implemented. Treatment programmes should be individualised, planned, implemented and fully evaluated by fully trained staff, under supervision.

Treatment outcome and treatment planning are linked: poor and unclear planning and goals correlate with poor and unsafe outcomes. The workers need to translate the aims of treatment into measurable goals and an explicit plan. They must be specific to the individual case, and must include dates for review and revision as new information or changing circumstances present themselves. Carich and Adkerson (1995) set out twelve common sexual perpetrator treatment goals:

- Acknowledge and accept personal responsibility for complete sexual assault history.
- Improve understanding of human sexuality, including normal sexual development and functioning, reproduction, and sexual health.
- Develop an understanding of how sexual assault negatively impacts the victim (short and long-term harm and risks) and develop empathy for own victim(s).
- Develop social and relationship skills to improve ability to meet social and sexual needs through appropriate relationships with age-mates.

- Separate anger, power, and other motivational issues from sexual behaviour. Improve anger management skills and re-mediate other motivations as needed.
- Clarify sexual arousal patterns and utilise modification techniques as appropriate.
- Clarify personal sexual offence cycle, include thoughts, feelings, behaviours and situations preceding offence. Demonstrate ability to recognise recurring aspects of the cycle.
- Actively change the distorted thinking and lifestyle supports of the sexual offence behaviour.
- Develop realistic, achievable intervention plans for each step in the sexual assault cycle. Demonstrate ability to intervene in cycle.
- Develop motivation and commitment to recovery and to remaining offence-free.
- Inform significant others completely and honestly about offending problem and seek support in offence abstinence from appropriate sources.
- Explore unresolved issues from personal victimisation, sexual or other, and work toward healing (p57).

Mothers

The treatment needs of mothers are often very similar to those of the child. Impaired self-image can be repaired through teaching them to recognise and respond to their own needs. Denial can be confronted as they learn to ventilate conflicting motivations and loyalties. Focus on universal aspects that can help shape reasonable expectations of their husbands and children. Practice in limit setting is required to overcome failures in establishing and enforcing limits. Anger needs to be recognised and validated, with appropriate outlets found (Bagley and King, 1990).

Mothers are the key factor in the reconstructing work of sexually abusive families, although they have often been overlooked. Bagley and King (1990) set out the following issues that they cover in any counselling with mothers:

- Providing a clear outline of the treatment process and approximate time frame.
- Allowing the ventilation and validation of feelings. Normalisation of ambivalent feelings the mother may feel towards both her husband and her daughter. The mother is placed in the unfortunate position of having to support one of the people she loves while at the same time withdrawing that support from another. She typically vacillates back and forth and requires encouragement to realise that only through the initial support of her daughter can they hope to regain any semblance of a happy family life.
- Alleviation of guilt feelings.
- Reassurance that the child will not necessarily be irreparably harmed for life as a result of the experience.
- Reinforcement of the perpetrator's responsibility for the abuse.
- Exploration of the mother's own childhood experience.
- Provision of emotional support and guidance in coping with the numerous new life tasks she finds herself suddenly facing. We must remember that the mother is suddenly faced with many new responsibilities, which she may or may not be equipped to handle at the time. For example, financially supporting her children and maintaining the household, seeking legal advice, etc.

Guidelines when Considering the Reconstitution of Families

Bentovim *et al.*, (1987) set out a useful framework for considering the prognosis of a successful reconstitution of the family.

Hopeful:

- The perpetrator accepts responsibility for the abuse, and informs all family members of this. He needs to accept punishment or treatment, as well as accepting the primary responsibility for monitoring and managing his future behaviour.

- The child is not blamed, and is not scapegoated by any family member.
- The child needs to be heard in the family and allowed to speak for themselves.
- The marital relationship is improved.
- The mother accepts some future responsibility for protecting the child, and is caring and supportive.
- The seriousness for the child has been recognised and accepted.

Doubtful:

- Multi-generational culture of abuse is evident.
- There is evidence of a collusive coping pattern.
- There is uncertainty about what ought to happen to the perpetrator or the marital relationship.
- There is conflict between adult and children's needs and they remain unresolved.
- There is a likelihood of the child being scapegoated.
- The child is unsure of themselves and remains tentative, silent, and half-frozen.
- Siblings old enough to distance themselves from any risks.
- The perpetrator does not accept any responsibility for the abuse.
- The mother is a 'victim'.
- The relationship between mother and victim is very poor.

Hopeless:

- The responsibility is denied by all the adults.
- The child is blamed and rejected outright.
- The mother is unable to protect the child.
- The perpetrator shows no guilt and remains powerful in the family.
- Generational evidence of abuse.
- Parents put their own needs first, above the child.

- Child seen as the initiator.
- Unable or unwilling to accept help.
- Career paedophile.
- Long-standing problems with alcohol, patterns of promiscuity, psychiatric illness etc.

(adapted from Bentovim *et al.*, 1987).

Powell and Ilett (1992) provided us with the following criteria (Figure 38) that try to separate out poor from good prognosis factors for intra-familial child sexual abuse:

Figure 38: Prognosis factors for intra-familial child sexual abuse (from Powell and Ilett, 1992: p420).

Good prognosis	Poor prognosis
• Perpetrator attends treatment sessions.	• Perpetrator wishes to leave treatment.
• Perpetrator does not prefer children as sexual partners.	• Perpetrator prefers children as sexual partners and/or same-sex victims.
• Abuse was situational (when partner away).	• Abuse was not limited to specific situations.
• Abuse was limited to touching.	• Severe forms of abuse were inflicted.
• Perpetrator is self-referred and not mandated.	• Perpetrator was involuntary mandated to attend treatment, or he persistently denies the abuse and refuses help.
• Abuse was minimal and/or began recently.	
• Perpetrator displays many areas of appropriate parental functioning.	• Abuse was over a long period and with frequent encounters, or involved children outside the family as well.
• Abuser experiences guilt regarding the abuse and displays genuine empathy for the child.	• Perpetrator has a long history of extensive antisocial behaviour, alcohol or drug addiction, or many areas of problem behaviour.
• Perpetrator accepts full responsibility for the abusive behaviours.	• Perpetrator's guilt relates to their apprehension rather than concern for the damage caused.
• Abuse involved the use of verbal persuasion only.	
• There is no history of abuse in the perpetrator's family.	• Blame for the abuse is directed at the non-abusing family members or external stressors.
	• Abuse involves physical force.
	• Perpetrator was sexually abused as a child.

Criteria for the reconstitution of the family:

- The father acknowledges responsibility for the sexual (and other) abuse and does not project blame onto the daughter. They must also accept that 'old rules' no longer operate.

- All family members appreciate the seriousness of what has occurred and the need for change.

- The workers and all family members express reasonable assurance that the child is safe from repeated abuse.

- The daughter expresses and demonstrates the ability to seek professional help in the event that she is again approached. The workers must be confident that the child victim is not pressured by other family members, to request, or agree to, the perpetrator's return home. They may be aware of the effects on the family of their disclosure and self-blame, or be scapegoated by the family.

- The mother has demonstrated an ongoing ability to prioritise the protection of the children and herself from abuse. Where the perpetrator continues to pose a high risk, then he clearly should not be at home, as it is unfair and unrealistic to expect the mother to assume the primary responsibility for his behaviour.

- The worker and family members are confident that sufficient progress has been made towards the resolution of short and long-term treatment goals. This should include all identified problems, particularly where different forms of abuse co-exist.

- Communication between family members has improved and there is evidence of setting appropriate boundaries and listening/talking to each other.

- The mother-daughter relationship has improved and the mother does not hold the victim accountable for the abuse.

- The relationship boundaries have been strengthened resulting in more appropriate family roles and improved marital relationship.

(adapted from Server and Janzen, 1982)

Matthews *et al.*, (1991) explored the effects of reunification on sexually abusive families in order to isolate factors that could give professionals early warning that reunification would either be detrimental or constructive for individual family members or for the family as a whole. They set out the following desirable preconditions for family reunification:

Figure 39: Desirable preconditions for family reunification (Matthews *et al.*, 1991: p149).

Victim
- Able to acknowledge and discuss the sexual abuse.
- Does not blame self for the abuse.
- Willing to be reunited with entire family.
- Confident about ability to report any further abuse.
- Feels safe and protected in the home if the perpetrator is to be returned.

Perpetrator
- Accepts full responsibility for the sexual abuse.
- Shows empathy for the victim.
- Shows remorse for the offence.
- Willing to talk with the victim about the abuse, making appropriate apologies.
- Demonstrates understanding about the motivation for the abuse.
- Resolves family-of-origin issues.

Spouse
- Able to put victim's need for protection first.
- Able to confront the offender and express anger.
- Able to discuss the abuse openly.
- Holds offender responsible for the abuse.
- Does not blame the victim.

The family
- Desire to reunify.
- Completed treatment.
- Openly discussed the sexual abuse together.
- Potentially risky situations identified and a protection plan formulated.
- Involved in a family support system; not isolated.
- Demonstrates healthy ways of interacting.
- Makes concrete changes in the home.

Criteria for reunification of families where sibling incest has occurred (Hackett et al., 1998)

Victim

- Able to acknowledge and discuss the sexual abuse.
- Does not blame self for the abuse.
- Willing for the sibling who abused to be united with the whole family.
- Confident about own ability to report any further abuse.
- Feels safe and protected in the home if the sibling who abused is to be returned.

Young man who sexually abused

- Accepts full responsibility for the sexual abuse.
- Has been able to demonstrate empathy for the victim and awareness of the impact of his behaviour on other family members.
- Shows remorse for the abuse.
- Is willing to talk with the victim, and other family members, at their request about the abuse, making appropriate apologies, but does not overwhelm (flood) the victim or family members with unrequested and self-serving apologies.
- Demonstrates understanding about his motivation for the abuse.
- Is able to acknowledge ongoing risk factors and can communicate these to those inside and outside of the family, as appropriate, in order to seek help to prevent relapse.

Parents

- Are able to put the victim's needs for protection first.
- Have been able to confront the young person who abused and express feelings about the abuse.
- Are able to discuss the impact of the abuse upon themselves as carers.
- Hold the young person who has abused as responsible and do not blame the victim.
- Can accept the differing needs of the victim and the brother who abused and yet can accommodate these within their schema of the family.
- Can make any necessary changes in parenting style and skills, in order to manage risk and facilitate openness.

The family

- All family members have made an informed choice for re-unification.
- Therapeutic intervention has been offered and has been successful.

- Potential risk situations are shared and the family has a holistic protection plan, involving external supports or checks, as appropriate, which are agreed and in operation.
- Family dynamics are open, whilst boundaries sufficiently protected.
- Evidence exists of healthy family interactions.
- Physical issues in the home requiring attention has been addressed (e.g. location of bedrooms, etc.).

Risk Measurement

Risk factors for children

Toni Cavanagh Johnson (1993) has offered a very useful risk index framework which considers various risk factors related to the child, the problematic sexual behaviours, the family and the home environment, and can be used to estimate the seriousness of the child's problematic sexual behaviours:

Risk factors related to the child

- Displays oppositional behaviour.
- Has poor peer relations/coping skills/ self-concept/academic record/few, if any, friends.
- Disregards rules and regulations at school, at home, in the community.
- Is aggressive at school, home, or neighbourhood towards adults and/or children.
- Destroys own property and/or the property of others.
- Threatens others with harm.
- Behaviour is beyond parental control.
- Has no (apparent) positive affective connections with adults or children.
- Extremes of affect, poor modulation of affective responses.
- Is cruel to animals/sets fires.
- Displays volatile temper, or rage reactions/manipulative behaviour.
- Has witnessed physical aggression directed at his or her primary caretaker.

- Is a victim of physical, sexual, or emotional abuse, abandonment or neglect.
- Has low cognitive ability (in conjunction with aggressive physical and sexual behaviours).

Risk factors related to problematic sexual behaviours

- Denies the sexual behaviour, although there is good evidence that it occurred.
- Dislikes or has a highly ambivalent relationship to the other child.
- Has no sexual relationship to the child with whom he or she engaged in the sexual behaviour.
- Planned the sexual behaviour without the knowledge of the other child.
- Doesn't seem to care that the other child might be hurt physically or emotionally.
- Other child is highly vulnerable.
- Blames other people or circumstances, and takes no responsibility for the sexual behaviour.
- Has a history of sexual behaviours apart from this incident.
- Caught multiple times for coercive sexual behaviours.
- Hurt the other child while engaging in the sexual behaviour.
- Has very intrusive sexual behaviour.
- Recruited other children to engage in the sexual behaviour with them.
- Doesn't think it was serious to engage in coercive sexual behaviour.
- Used physical strength to gain compliance of other child.
- Bribed, teased, coerced, or threatened other child.
- Used threats or other leverage to reinforce secrecy.

Risk factors related to the family

- Parents-caretakers with very confused sexual boundaries and confused notions about sexuality; poor physical and emotional boundaries in the family.
- Parent-caretaker uses child to meet his or her own dependency and sexual needs.
- Spousal battering.
- Mother with a personality disorder with dependent, narcissistic, and borderline characteristics, and depressive features.
- Psychiatric diagnoses in parents.
- History of prostitution; history of living in motels, the street, or cars.
- History of violence and impulsivity in the family to which the child has been privy.
- History of emotional, physical, or sexual abuse to parents themselves; history of emotional, physical or sexual abuse to other family members.
- History of child protective agencies or police involvement with the family.
- History of perpetration in the family.
- History of family disruptions including divorce, out-of-home placements.
- History of drug and/or alcohol abuse; history of inadequate parenting to the child (i.e. inconsistently meeting the child's needs).
- Parents know little about the offence or deny the child committed the offence or do not see the offence as a real problem.
- Parents dislike the child or project negative attributes onto the child.
- Victim was a favourite child in the family.
- Father is incarcerated or otherwise involved with the law.
- Absent father who was authoritarian and distant from family members and emotionally/physically abusive to mother.
- Multi-generational sexually abusive family.
- Role reversals in which the child feels the intense need to care for the parent who cannot care for himself or herself without the child's assistance.
- Single parent with other children in the home.

Risk factors related to the environment

- Child who molests has access to vulnerable children.
- Economic stresses.
- Poor supervision.
- No sense or orderliness or predictability in the child's life (Johnson, 1993: pp169–71. Reproduced with the kind permission of the author).

The greater the number of factors present, the more serious the behaviour, and the higher the risk of further abuse. In young children, a number of factors may indicate a high risk for re-offending. These factors include the following:

- The use of force, threat or violence.
- A history of impulsive aggressive behaviour.
- A history of victimisation, which has remained untreated.
- Predatory, compulsive, and repetitive behaviour.
- An unresponsive family in denial.
- Selection of multiple victims
- Pervasive sexual behaviours across settings.
- Lack of remorse and refusal to stop the behaviours (Gil, 1993: p196).

Risk factors for juveniles who sexually abuse

Wenet and Clark (1986) produced the following framework for anticipating future risks from juveniles who sexually abuse:

Low risk

- First documented offence, without evidence of a developing pattern.
- Offender willing to explore offence in a non-defensive manner.
- Offender acknowledges and understands the negative impact of the offence on the victim.
- Offender willing to accept responsibility for committing the offence without blaming others or circumstances.

- Offender is guilty and remorseful because of the negative impact of the offence on victim.
- Offender understands the exploitative nature of the offence and reasons for its wrongfulness.
- Offender admits to committing the entire offence for which they were charged.
- Parents/carers acknowledge and understand the negative impact of the offence upon the victim.
- Parents/carers hold the juvenile responsible for the offence without externalising blame onto others or circumstances.
- Parents/carers acknowledge the entire offence for which their son was charged.
- Offender has healthy attitudes about sexuality.
- Offender has no history of behaviour disorder involving physical aggression.
- Offender's family unit is functional.
- The family is supportive of treatment and willing to be involved in it.
- Family identifies problems within their unit and among members other than the deviant sexual behaviour of the offender.
- The offender has adequate social adjustment, including presence of a peer support group and participation in peer group activities.
- Offender has no history of behavioural and/or academic school problems.

Moderate risk

- Offender has committed two or more documented offences.
- Discontinuation of offence behaviour if/when victim showed distress.
- Offender resists describing and exploring offence in a non-defensive manner.
- Offender does not understand the exploitative nature of the offence.
- Offender minimises the negative impact of the offence on the victim (little empathy).
- Offender has little or no guilt or remorse

because of the impact of the offence on victim.

- Offender externalises blame for offence onto others or extraneous circumstances.
- Offender minimises their extent of involvement in the offence, admitting to only part of it.
- Offender resists participation in the evaluation without refusing.
- Parents/guardians minimise the negative impact of the offence on the victim.
- Parents/guardians externalise blame for the offence onto others or extraneous circumstances.
- Parents/guardians minimise the extent of the offender's involvement in the offence, holding him only partially responsible.
- Parents/guardians resist participation in the evaluation without refusing altogether.
- The offender has negative self-esteem.
- The offender has depressive symptomology.
- They have unhealthy attitudes about sexuality.
- They are the victims of sexual or physical abuse, though this has not been a chronic or repetitive pattern.
- Mother or father is a sexual offender.
- Mother or father is a victim of sexual or physical abuse.
- The family is unable to identify problems within the family unit or among members other than the deviant sexual behaviour of the juvenile.
- The family is dysfunctional in response to transient situational factors, such as life cycle changes or other crisis.
- Offender has a history of behavioural disorder involving physical aggression.
- They show poor social adjustment, including isolation from peers and they have few peer group activities.
- The offender has a history of behavioural and/or academic school problems.

High risk

- They have been already treated for a previous sexual offence.
- The offence was predatory.
- The offence was ritualistic.
- The offence was sophisticated, involving precocious knowledge of sexual behaviour; and resulted in a physical injury to the victim.
- And was associated with the use of drugs and/or alcohol.
- And involved violence, physical force.
- Which continued despite the victim's expression of distress.
- And there is evidence of a progressive increase in the use of force used to commit repeated crimes.
- They completely refuse to participate in the evaluation.
- They completely deny the referral offence.
- Parents/guardians refuse to participate in the evaluation.
- And deny their son committed the offence.
- And deny their son has any psychosocial problems.
- The offender engages in compulsive masturbation fantasies involving deviant sexuality or offensive behaviour.
- There is evidence of thought disorder.
- There is a history of fire setting.
- There is a history of torturing animals.
- There is a history of chronic substance abuse.
- They have been the victim of chronic and repetitive sexual and/or physical abuse.
- Their family unit is chronically dysfunctional.

A broader framework was developed by Gray and Pithers (1993) and which can be useful in organising the information for any direct work with the juvenile. They organise risk factors into three different categories:

- **Predisposing risk factors:** are those that occur during early development or that fall very early in the abuser's sequence of precursors. They include sexual victimisation, physical abuse, family chaos, absence of empathic skill, insufficient skills, and low self-esteem.

- **Precipitating risk factors:** generally occur shortly before the sexually abusive behaviour and tend to determine what type of abuse performed will involve coercive sexuality. They include emotional mismanagement, thinking errors, opportunity, low control of impulses and urges, absence of conflict resolution skills, and fantasies about sexual abuse.

- **Perpetuating risk factors:** which increase the likelihood that sexually abusive behaviours will continue in the future. They include lack of supervision by caregivers, gratification from emotional or sexual release, lack of information about the sexuality, displacement of responsibility and gender shame. Considerable progress is required to move us from general categorisations of risk with this group (see Calder, forthcoming d for a detailed exploration on this point).

Risk issues for adult males

There are no 'low risk' offenders and, without treatment, recidivism is almost inevitable.

(Giarretto, 1982)

Risk factors place the individual at risk to re-offend. They are guidelines only and not absolute predictors. A risk factor is defined as:

...any experience, event, environmental influences/ parameters, internal/external behaviour, historical factor, situations, that presents or enhances the offender's chances of re-offence. These may or may not be cycle behaviours and triggering events.

(Carich, 1994)

In determining the risk a perpetrator presents we need to consider the types of offences committed, sexual history, treatment history, and amenability to treatment. McGrath (1992) suggests that we focus on a further five factors, in order to look at perpetrator risk: probability of re-offence; degree of harm most likely to result from a re-offence; conditions under which re-offence is most likely to occur;

likely victims of a re-offence; and the time-scale within which a re-offence is most likely to occur. These are dealt with below.

Perpetrator risk: cannot be exclusively defined by the nature of the problem for which the perpetrator has been referred, when we are aware of potential cross over of acts, the genders and ages of the victims, and the context of the offence, e.g. inside or outside the family. For example, Abel *et al.*, (1985) also found that 75 per cent of recidivists crossed both age and sex in their choice of victims. The incest perpetrator has the lowest recidivism rates (although they are known to offend against more than one child), whilst untreated exhibitionists have the highest recidivism rates. The younger the incest victim, the higher the risk of re-offence (Williams and Finkelhor, 1992). Perpetrators who abuse unrelated boys have higher recidivism rates than those who abused unrelated girls (McGrath, 1991), whilst the probability of recidivism rises with each offence. The degrees of force is associated with an increased risk to re-offend, especially those who are sexually aroused by aggression. Deviant sexual arousal is also associated to recidivism. Repeated sexual crimes remain an important predictor of future behaviour. The sexual abuse may well not be the only concern that needs to be resolved before rehabilitation can be effected. Stermac *et al.*, (1995) found that 55 per cent of incest perpetrators demonstrated non-sexual forms of violence and abuse within their homes. As such, issues of anger, power, and control need to be addressed. An offender's specific beliefs about his own behaviour is likely to be predictive of future behaviour (Marshall and Eccles, 1991), as is their general attitude to sexual aggression (Segal and Stermac, 1990). Serin *et al.*, (1994) found that psychopaths are at higher risk of re-offending than non-psychopaths, they re-offend sooner, and they are likely to become increasingly violent.

Harm from the offence: is again correlated with the use of weapons or force, and any escalation in the patterns of offending is significant.

Conditions associated with re-offending: embraces their response to the assessment, degree of co-operation or compliance with any requests or conditions set down; the opportunity to access victims, either through family, friends or leisure interests, e.g. football coaching; the use of substances; availability of sexually stimulating material; level of mobility, e.g. through work, leisure outlets such as train-spotting; and any anger related to job loss or restricted contact with their birth children.

Likely victims: through preference in previous offences, or as admitted by the offender in the work to date.

When?: many perpetrators act when they have opportunity, or they actively create them. The degree of supervision the perpetrator receives from professionals and others, such as the family, will have a bearing on this point. In broader terms, research does suggest that the risks from sexual perpetrators against children is over a significant length of time and it is a myth that the risk reduces over time (particularly in the absence of treatment).

Assessing risk accurately is difficult when we know that this group lacks any distinct profile, and there is an absence of longitudinal studies post-offence to accurately predict recidivism. The task is compounded further if the perpetrator is selective in the provision of information, or where the information derives solely from a single source.

There are as many different sets of risk factors from different instruments, authors and lists, that workers do not know where to begin. Some argue that there has been too great an emphasis on risk at the expense of rehabilitation, although there is a continuing difficulty in allowing rehabilitation in the absence of acknowledgement (Lusk, 1996).

Conclusions

This chapter has attempted to pull together some of the accessible frameworks to guide workers in the post-assessment arena. The reader will find far more substantial information in other books in relation to juveniles and children (Calder, 1997, 1999 and forthcoming c), mothers (Calder, forthcoming a), adult males (Calder, 1999b) and adult females (Saradjian and Hanks, 1996). Treatment issues for mothers are addressed in more detail in Calder with Rose (forthcoming); treatment issues for adult males are covered in Carich and Calder (forthcoming); and treatment issues for young people are covered in Calder (forthcoming d).

References

Abel, G.G., Mittleman, M.S., and Becker, J.V. (1985). Sex Offenders: Results of Assessment and Recommendations for Treatment. In Ben-Aron, M.H., Hucker, S.J., and Webster, C.D. (Eds.). *Clinical Criminology: The Assessment and Treatment of Criminal Behaviour*, pp191–205. Toronto: M&M Graphics.

Bagley, C., and King, K. (1990). *Child Sexual Abuse: The Search for Healing*. London: Routledge.

Bentovim, A., Elton, A., and Tranter, M. (1987). Prognosis for Rehabilitation After Abuse. *Adoption and Fostering*, 11(1): pp26–31.

Brake, S.C., and Shannon, D. (1997). Using Pre-treatment to Increase Admission in Sex Offenders. In Schwartz, B.K., and Cellini, H.R. (Eds.). *The Sex Offender: New Insights, Treatment Innovations and Legal Developments*. Kingston, NJ: Civic Research Institute.

Breiling, J. (1994). Paper presented at the 10th national training conference of the National Adolescent Perpetrator Network. Denver, Colorado, February, 1994.

Bremer, J.F. (1993). The Treatment of Children and Adolescents with Aberrant Sexual Behaviours. In Hobbs, C.J., and Wynne, J.M. (Eds.). *Baillieres Clinical Pediatrics: International Practice and Research*, 1: pp269–82.

Calder, M.C. (1997). *Juveniles and Children who Sexually Abuse: A Guide to Risk Assessment*. Lyme Regis: Russell House Publishing.

Calder, M.C. (Ed.) (1999). *Working with Young People who Sexually Abuse: New Pieces of the Jigsaw Puzzle*. Lyme Regis: Russell House Publishing.

Calder, M.C. (1999b). *Assessing Risk in Adult Males who Sexually Abuse Children: A Practitioners Guide*. Lyme Regis: Russell House Publishing.

Calder, M.C., with Rose, K. (forthcoming a). *Mothers in Sexually Abusing Families: A Framework for Assessment, Understanding and Support*. Lyme Regis: Russell House Publishing.

Calder, M.C. (forthcoming b). The New Assessment Framework (NAF): A Critique and Reformulation. To appear in Calder, M.C., and Hackett, S. (Eds.). *The RHP Child Care Assessment Manual*. Lyme Regis: Russell House Publishing.

Calder, M.C. (Ed.) (forthcoming c). *Work with Young Sexual Abusers 2001*. Lyme Regis: Russell House Publishing.

Calder, M.C. (forthcoming d). *Juveniles and Children who Sexually Abuse: A Guide to Risk Assessment* (2nd edition). Lyme Regis: Russell House Publishing.

Carich, M.S. (1994). A Review of Different Risk Factors. *INMAS Newsletter*, 7(4): pp3–10.

Carich, M.S., and Adkerson, D.L. (1995). *Adult Sexual Offender Assessment Packet*. Brandon, VT: Safer Society Press.

Carich, M.S., and Calder, M.C. (forthcoming). *A Handbook of Contemporary Sex Offender Treatment*. Lyme Regis: Russell House Publishing.

DiClemente, C. (1991). Motivational Interviewing and the Stages of Change. In Miller, W., and Rollnick, S. (Eds.). *Motivational Interviewing*. London: Guilford Press.

Frances, A., Clarkin, J., and Perry, S. (1984). *Differential Therapeutics in Psychiatry*. NY: Brunner/Mazel.

Giarretto, H. (1982). *Integrated Treatment of Child Sexual Abuse*. Palo Alto: CA, Science and Behaviour.

Gil, E. (1993). Individual Therapy. In Gil, E. and Johnson, T.C. (Eds.). *Sexualised Children: Assessment and Treatment of Sexualised Children and Children who Molest*, pp179–210. Rockville, MD: Launch Press.

Gray, A.S., and Pithers, W.D. (1993). Relapse Prevention with Sexually Aggressive Adolescents and Children: Expanding Treatment and Supervision. In Barbaree, H.E., Marshall, W.L., and Hudson, S.M. (Eds.). *The Juvenile Sex Offender*, pp289–319. NY: Guilford Press.

Griggs, D.R., and Bold, A. (1995). Parallel Treatment of Parents of Abuse-reactive Children. In Hunter, M. (Ed.). *Child Survivors and Perpetrators of Sexual Abuse: Treatment Innovations*, pp147–65. Thousand Oaks, CA: Sage.

Hackett, S., Print, B., and Dey, C. (1998). Brother Nature? Therapeutic Intervention with Young Men who Sexually Abuse their Siblings. In Bannister, A. (Ed.). *From Hearing to Healing: Working with the Aftermath of Child Sexual Abuse*, pp152–79. London: John Wiley.

Hanson, R.K., Cox, B., and Woszcsyna, C. (1991). *Sexuality, Personality and Attitude Questionnaires for Sex Offenders: A Review*. Cat no JS4-1/1991-13. Ottawa: Supply and Services, Canada.

Johnson, T.C. (1993). Clinical Evaluation. In Gil, E., and Johnson, T.C. (Eds.). *Sexualised Children: Assessment and Treatment of Sexualised Children and Children who Molest*, pp137–78. Rockville, MD: Launch Press.

Lusk, A. (1996). Rehabilitation without Acknowledgement. *Family Law*, 26: pp742–5.

Marshall, W.L., and Eccles, A. (1991). Issues in Clinical Practice with Sex Offenders. *Journal of Interpersonal Violence*, 6: pp68–93.

Matthews, S.K., Raymaker, J., and Speltz, K. (1991). Effects of Family Reunification on Sexually Abusive Families. In Patton, M.Q. (Ed.). *Family Sexual Abuse: Frontline Research and Evaluation*, pp147–61. Newbury Park, CA: Sage.

Mayer, A. (1988). *Sex Offenders: Approaches to Understanding and Management*. Holmes Beach, FL: Learning Publications, Inc.

McConaghy, N., Blaszczynski, A., Armstrong, M.S., and Kidson, W. (1989). Resistance to Treatment of Adolescent Sex Offenders. *Archives of Sexual Behaviour*, 18(2): pp97–107.

McGrath, R.J. (1991). Sex Offender Risk Assessment and Disposition of Planning: A Review of Empirical and Clinical Findings. *Interpersonal Journal of Offender Therapy and Comparative Criminology*, 35(4): pp328–50.

McGrath, R.J. (1992). Assessing Sex Offender Risk. *American Probation and Parole Association Perspectives*, 16(3): pp6–9.

Miller, W., and Rollnick, S. (1991). *Motivational Interviewing: Preparing People to Change Addictive Behaviour*. NY: Guilford Press.

Morrison, T. (1991). Change, Control and the Legal Framework. In Adcock, M., White, R., and Hollows, A. (Eds.). *Significant Harm: Its Management and Outcome*, pp85–100. Croydon: Significant Publications.

Morrison, T. (1995). *Core Groups: A Catalyst for Change?* Presentation to the National conference on core groups. Manchester Town Hall, 14th July, 1995.

National Adolescent Perpetrator Network (1988). Preliminary Report from the National Task Force on Juvenile Sexual Offending. *Juvenile and Family Court Journal*, 39(2): pp1–67.

O'Hara, S. (1995). Work with Adolescents who Abuse and Sexualised Children. *Child Care in Practice*, 1(4): pp14–21.

Pithers, W.D., Gray, A.S., Cunningham, C., and Lane, S. (1993). *From Trauma to Understanding: A Guide for Parents of Children with Sexual Behaviour Problems*. Brandon, VT: Safer Society Program and Press.

Powell, M.B., and Ilett, M.J. (1992). Assessing the Incestuous Family's Readiness for Reconstitution. *Family in Society*, 73(7): pp417–23.

Prochaska, J.O., and DiClemente, C.C. (1982). Transtheoretical Therapy: Toward a More Integrative Model of Change. *Psychotherapy, Theory, Research and Practice*, 19: pp276–88.

Prochaska, J.O., and DiClemente, C.C. (1986). Towards a Comprehensive Model of Change. In Miller, W.N., and Heather, N. (Eds.). *Treating Addictive Behaviours: Processes of Change*, pp3–27. NY: Plenum Press.

Saradjian, J., and Hanks, H. (1996). *Women who Sexually Abuse: From Research to Clinical Practice*. Chichester: John Wiley and Sons.

Schlank, A.M., and Shaw, T. (1995). Treating Sexual Offenders who Deny their Guilt: A Pilot Study. *Sexual Abuse: A Journal of Research and Treatment*, 8(1): pp17–23.

Schlank, A.M., and Shaw, T. (1997). Treating Sexual Offenders who Deny: A Review. In Schwartz, B.K., and Cellini, H.R. (Eds.). *The Sex Offender: New Insights, Treatment Innovations and Legal Developments*. Kingston, NJ: Civic Research Institute.

Segal, L.E., and Stermac, L. (1990). The Role of Cognition in Sexual Assault. In Marshall, W.L., Laws, D.R., and Barbaree, H.E. (Eds.). *Handbook of Sexual Assault*, pp161–76. NY: Plenum.

Serin, R.C., Malcolm, P.B., Khanna, A., and Barbaree, H.E. (1994). Psychopathy and Deviant Sexual Arousal in Incarcerated Sex Offenders. *Journal of Interpersonal Violence*, 9(1): pp3–11.

Server, J.C., and Janzen, C. (1982). Contradictions to the Reconstitution of Sexually Abusive Families. *Child Welfare*, 61: pp279–88.

Stermac, L., Davidson, A., and Sheridan, M. (1995). Incidence of Non-sexual Violence in Incest Offenders. *International Journal of Offender Therapy and Comparative Criminology*, 39(2).

Wenet, G., and Clark, T. (1986). *Juvenile Sex Offender Decision Criteria, The Oregon Report on Juvenile Sex Offenders*. Children Services Division, Department of Human Resources, State of Oregon.

Williams, L., and Finkelhor, D. (1992). *The Characteristics of Incestuous Fathers*. Unpublished manuscript: University of New Hampshire Research Laboratory.

Willis, G.C. (1993). *Unspeakable Crimes: Prevention Work with Perpetrators of Child Sexual Abuse*. London: Children's Society.

Wolf, S.C., Conte, J.R., and Engel-Meinig, M. (1988). Assessment and Treatment of Sex Offenders in a Community Setting. In Walker, I.E.A. (Ed.). *Handbook of Sexual Abuse of Children*, pp365–83. NY: Springer.